Andrea H. Schneider-Braunberger (Ed.)

BIRKENSTOCK

Andrea H. Schneider-Braunberger (Ed.)

BIRKENSTOCK

THE EVOLUTION OF A UNIVERSAL PURPOSE AND ZEITGEIST BRAND

PRESTEL

MUNICH • LONDON • NEW YORK

The publisher expressly reserves the right to exploit the copyrighted content of this work for the purposes of text and data mining in accordance with Section 44b of the German Copyright Act (UrhG), based on the European Digital Single Market Directive. Any unauthorized use is an infringement of copyright and is hereby prohibited.

Penguin Random House Verlagsgruppe FSC® N001967

In cooperation with the Gesellschaft für Unternehmensgeschichte
www.unternehmensgeschichte.de

First published in 2024
Copyright © 2024 by Prestel Verlag, Munich · London · New York, a member of Penguin Random House Verlagsgruppe GmbH, Neumarkter Strasse 28, 81673 Munich
Translation:
Richard Pettit: Introduction (p. 18–33), Chapters 1774–1895 (p. 36–58), 1896–1945 (p. 62–117), 1945–1963 (p. 120–171) and 1963–2024 (p. 174–301); apart from the essays by Mary A. Yeager, Alice Janssens and Emily Brayshaw
Wiebke Vogt: Preface (p. 8–9), Foreword (p. 12–16)
Editing: Andrea H. Schneider-Braunberger
Proofreading: Simon Cowper
Layout: Büro Jorge Schmidt, Munich
Typesetting: Markus Miller, Munich
Design Cover: BUREAU BORSCHE
Picture editing: Regg Media GmbH, Munich
Printing and binding: GGP Media GmbH, Pößneck
Printed in Germany 2024
ISBN 978-3-7913-9332-2

www.prestel.de

CONTENTS

Preface
Oliver Reichert 8

1774 – 2024
Foreword and INTRODUCTION

Foreword
Jochen Gutzy 12

Introduction
Andrea H. Schneider-Braunberger 18

1774 – 1895   The Beginnings: The Birth of a Shoemaking Dynasty

The Shoemaker Family Birkenstock –
Kai Balazs-Bartesch and Andrea H. Schneider-Braunberger 36

- Shoemakers around 1774 – *Johanna Steinfeld* 42

- From the Traditional Craft of Shoemaking to the
Modern Shoe Factory – *Johanna Steinfeld* 55

1896 – 1945   From a Shoemaker's Workshop to a Manufacturing Company

Misjudged Innovations: The Struggle for Foot Orthopedics,
1896–1945 – *Roman Köster* 62

- "The Truly Ethical Man Does Not Cripple Himself": Shoe
Designs by the *Lebensreform* Movement – *Johanna Steinfeld* 76

- Fish Leather and Wooden Sandals: Leather Shortage during
World War II – *Johanna Steinfeld* 99

The *System Birkenstock*: The Footprint for Walking as Nature
Intended – *Andrea H. Schneider-Braunberger* 104

1945–1963 Beginning of the Industrial Era

On the Path to "Walking as Nature Intended":
From the *Footbed* to a Shoe – *Jörg Lesczenski* **120**

■ The Desire for Fashion: From the Jedermann Program to
Mass Consumption – *Johanna Steinfeld* **141**

■ From a Silver Leg to Healthy Shoes: The History of Podiatry
and Orthopedic Footwear Technology – *Johanna Steinfeld* **149**

■ The Names of the *Original Birkenstock-Footbed Sandals* –
Andrea H. Schneider-Braunberger **169**

1963–2024 Rise to a Global Brand

From Family Business to Global Corporation –
Alexander von den Benken **174**

■ Outsourcing and the Division of Labor: The Global Shoe –
Johanna Steinfeld **182**

■ Health Loafers and Eco-footwear: The Sandals of the
Protest Movements – *Johanna Steinfeld* **205**

BIRKENSTOCK: A Purpose Brand –
Christian Kleinschmidt and Andrea H. Schneider-Braunberger **218**

■ "If the Shoe Fits ...": Comfortable Shoes on the Rise –
Johanna Steinfeld **227**

Birkenstock Identities – *Mary A. Yeager* **233**

■ Different Sides to Shoes: Protection, Status Symbol,
Emblem – *Johanna Steinfeld* **243**

International Fashion and Luxury in Birkenstocks –
Alice Janssens **246**

■ Bare Toes under Straps: The History of the Sandal –
Johanna Steinfeld **252**

Brands without Borders: Collaborations in the
Fashion Segment – *Johanna Steinfeld* 262

From Hilarious Hippies to Hair-Raising Horror and
High Fashion: 30 Years of Birkenstocks in Film –
Emily Brayshaw 286

1963 – 2024   The Development of Birkenstock in the Early Key Markets

From Hippie to High Fashion: The Evolution of Birkenstock
in **North America** – *Taylor Brydges* 304

Birkenstock in **Italy**: A Creative Adventure –
Emanuela Scarpellini 315

Birkenstock in **Britain** – *Liz Tregenza* 325

Birkenstock in **France**: Uber Fashionable? –
Hayley Edwards-Dujardin 335

Birkenstock in **Japan** – *Pierre-Yves Donzé* 345

Birkenstock in **Australia** 1992–2022: A Stable Shoe for
Shifting Terrains – *Emily Brayshaw* 355

Birkenstock Models since 1963 368

Appendices
Notes 379
Literature and Archives 443
The Authors 453
Index of Persons and Companies 456
Picture Credits 463

PREFACE

BY OLIVER REICHERT, CHIEF EXECUTIVE OFFICER
BIRKENSTOCK GROUP

It was a long and rather improbable transition from the poor shoemakers' workshops of the brothers Johannes and Johann Adam Birkenstock in the 18th century to the present day. Nobody in the family ever entertained the idea that their name would one day adorn the façade of the New York Stock Exchange. Least of all Karl Birkenstock, who became a laughing stock when he first presented the sandals he had invented to the public at the 1963 GDS international shoe fair in Düsseldorf. The Birkenstock family story is also a story of getting knocked down and getting back up again, of rebelling against the societal mainstream, and of tirelessly championing a greater cause, coupled with being really tough on oneself.

We now know that the family's main place of residence in the vicinity of the Via Regia, one of the key east-west axes of the early modern period, offered shoemakers good conditions—there was a great need for shoes and shoemakers where there were a lot of people covering long distances on foot. This may explain why generations of this shoemaking dynasty focused on functional footwear and why the family had an unquenchable interest in foot health. They couldn't make money with brocade stiletto shoes in provincial Hesse. Fashion has never been our thing—neither then, nor now. Birkenstock is a purpose brand that's rooted in orthopedics. And this has since been proven by historical research.

This research project was and still is a huge task. It was a chance find in 2016 which prompted Birkenstock to establish a company archive and subsequently have the company history academically evaluated. While tidying our warehouse, we came across handwritten notes made by Carl Birkenstock, book manuscripts, business documents, family photos, and advertising materials. We instantly realized we knew surprisingly little about our past—even though we were all constantly talking about "Tradition since 1774."

And this realization prompted me to have Birkenstock's company and brand history academically evaluated—by independent historians with undisputed reputations, in an open and unbiased process in which we consciously accepted we would have to question the brand's existing historical image, which was primarily passed down orally, and possibly also correct this. Our upcoming 250th anniversary obviously had a part to play in the decision, too. As a company with German roots, you cannot celebrate a moment like this without first having fully established what your company's own role was during the time of National Socialism.

It was clear to me from the outset that this couldn't end up being a flat marketing project. In this project, the historians' expertise and independence ranked above everything else. We therefore opened all of our archives up to the historians and afforded them full access to all sources. A global and all-encompassing perspective was also important to me. From many discussions with our partners all over the world, I know that the brand is perceived very differently abroad to how it is perceived in Germany. For German consumers, we're a shoe brand, whereas the rest of the world sees us as a lifestyle and zeitgeist brand. I'm therefore delighted that we were able to get historians from the USA, France, the UK, Italy, Australia, and Japan interested in our project and that we take a look at the societal context as well as the historical and cultural significance of our brand.

History is written where the present and the past meet. It is in the nature of things that historical research into a company like ours can barely keep pace with the actual developments. We are therefore already considering further questions. My hope is that this book will present us with further research focal areas and that we can tap additional sources.

I would like to thank everyone who has contributed to this project—in particular, Dr. Andrea Schneider-Braunberger and Jochen Gutzy. It can certainly not be taken for granted that a project lasting seven years will be concluded by the same individuals who were involved in initiating it in the first place. But this does explain the consistency and quality of this book. I hope the book is given the recognition it deserves and I hope to see the research findings being evaluated openly, critically, and constructively.

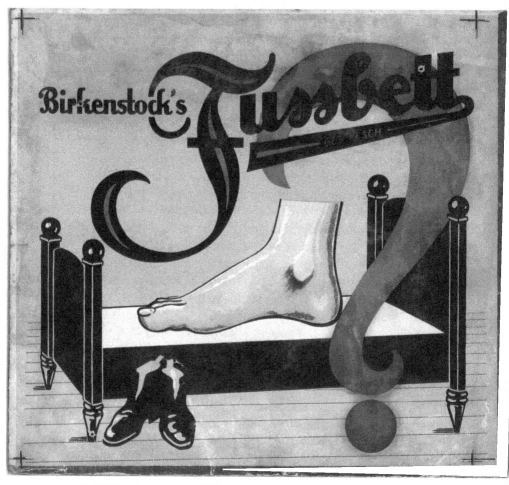

Fig. 1: Advertisement for the *Birkenstock-Footbed*, 1920s.

1774 – 2024
FOREWORD AND INTRODUCTION

FOREWORD

BY JOCHEN GUTZY, CHIEF COMMUNICATION OFFICER
BIRKENSTOCK GROUP

There is a huge number of quotes and bon mots in circulation on the subject of history—some of them inspirational, others rather melodramatic, like mottos on calendars. Sometimes they are extremely powerful, like the insight of the German natural scientist and scholar Wilhelm von Humboldt (1767–1835): "Only those who know the past have a future."

Inspired by the fortuitous discovery of handwritten manuscripts by Carl Birkenstock and the upcoming 250th anniversary in tradition of shoemaking, we set out in 2016 to research the brand and history of Birkenstock—and thus, to some extent, the history of the Birkenstock family, a dynasty of shoemakers—and to give it a firm foundation in fact. It was the first attempt at a scientific reappraisal of our history, which until then had been passed down mainly orally and recorded only in fragments. Not an easy exercise, as no archive existed when we kicked off the project. We have thus embarked on a journey into the past with an unknown destination that took us back to the time of Wilhelm von Humboldt—to the second half of the 18th century—a historically turbulent era.

The historical reference point of the BIRKENSTOCK brand, the year 1774, the big bang of this global zeitgeist brand, is framed by key historical moments such as the Boston Tea Party in 1773, a rebellious act of resistance by outraged settlers in the US colonies against the policies of the British Empire, and the execution in 1793 of Louis XVI, the last French king of the Ancien Régime, during the French Revolution.

We must assume, though, that the members of the family were largely unaware of the historical upheavals of their time. As evidenced by the findings of our research, they struggled to make a living under

Fig. 2: The human foot carries us; it masters all surfaces and connects us with the earth.

somewhat precarious circumstances in the rural province of Frankfurt am Main in the shadow of these historical events. It's hard to imagine that they dreamed that the family itself would one day make history, with four groundbreaking inventions—which we refer to as the *System Birkenstock*—that have fundamentally changed our understanding of the modern shoe to this day and laid the foundations for a global "Super Brand" that is more relevant today than ever before.

While historiography has its roots in antiquity, business history is a comparatively young field of research. Interest in it has been growing internationally since the 70s, as can be seen, for example, in the opening of the Business History Conference for international research, the creation of the European Business History Association (EBHA), and the establishment of the World Congress of Business History in 2014. In Germany, this discipline gained momentum when a critically minded public sought answers to questions about the role of German corporations during the dark years of the Nazi era. Besides that, among German SMEs there are a large number of family-owned businesses spanning multiple generations that have a long history behind them. It's no surprise, then, that business history has a particularly long tradition in Germany.

The increasing interest in business history that has been evident in recent years may be prompted in part by the growing pressure that large companies are under to legitimize corporate action. Understanding one's past is a moral obligation, especially for family businesses that operate across generations in different economic, societal, and political contexts. Beyond that, cultural aspects are gaining in importance in an increasingly globalized world. More and more companies are also recognizing the potential of history as a means to set themselves apart from the competition. This may explain why corporate history is increasingly finding its way into communications departments.

There are many reasons why a company might examine its own history. Our primary concern was to tap into our corporate history to better understand our roots and to be able to share our history both with our employees and with the outside world. In addition, right from the start it was our aim to build up an archive that might also serve as a source of inspiration for our product development and brand communications.

As a science-based brand, informed by a deep understanding of foot orthopedics, it was clear to us from the beginning that our global history project must meet the highest scientific standards, regardless of the findings. Over a period of seven years, a team of 15 renowned historians, under the scientific guidance of Dr. Andrea H. Schneider-Braunberger, researched the company, the brand, and the family's history and created, on the basis of over 10,000 hours of research, a highly condensed and granular picture, which, in some cases, brought surprising insights to light. Given our current modes of communication, which are becoming more and more real-time with hardly any room left for reflection, seven years weigh like half an eternity. Now that the results are available, we can clearly say that the investment was worthwhile.

While we have had to correct or expand our view of history to include a host of details, many aspects of it have been confirmed. First, Birkenstock is a multigenerational business with a family tradition in shoemaking dating back to the year 1774. This heritage alone is an asset that comes with a great responsibility and a major obligation. Second, Birkenstock is a brand with a clear purpose deeply rooted in orthopedics—our purpose is to empower all people to walk as nature intended. It is based on an insight that is both simple and convincing: humans are made to walk on natural and yielding ground. This awareness, which draws on observations of the biomechanics of the feet and has been comprehensively explained in books by Konrad and Carl Birkenstock and his son Karl, materializes in a groundbreaking invention: the *Footbed*, which inspired Carl to his vision of the "ideal shoe" and Karl to his invention of the *Original Birkenstock-Footbed Sandal*. And third, this is about the projection of history into the future: the foundation on which this brand stands is solid and its potential enormous, almost

Fig. 3: With the increasing sealing of surfaces, the natural motor function of the foot is being restricted. The flexible *Birkenstock-Footbed* compensates for this development and enables "walking as nature intended."

unlimited. The history of the brand has only just begun—and there is no end in sight. The most exciting chapters are probably still ahead of us.

What makes me so confident? The observation that the family has never given up despite all the setbacks it has faced. That is typical of the brand and all those who have dedicated themselves to it: a certain tenacity that sometimes even resembles stubbornness and a rebellious element that challenges established conventions and is never satisfied with what has been achieved—qualities that go into creating a fertile ground for innovation.

Just as many people have contributed to the rise of Birkenstock as a global brand, so too is this book the fruit of a communal effort. My greatest thanks go to Dr. Andrea H. Schneider-Braunberger. Without her, this book would not exist—it's as simple as that. She opened up many private and public archives, especially in the initial phase, gave the project a sound direction, and mobilized a team of renowned and experienced historians all around the globe for this project. The archive situation presented us with some major challenges at the beginning, so I am all the more excited about the results of this research project.

My heartfelt thanks also go to all the researchers and authors—as well as to the team at the Business History Society (GUG). Moreover, I would like to sincerely thank our long-standing wholesale and retail partners all over the world and our long-serving employees, who have supported us in building up the archive and reappraising the past from a scientific perspective.

I would like to especially thank the CEO of the BIRKENSTOCK Group, Oliver Reichert, who made this project possible and supported it with great foresight. I would also like to thank all the people who witnessed events at the time and have shared their memories with us. My special thanks go to the family of Margot Fraser, founder, former CEO, president, and majority shareholder of Birkenstock USA, who gave us her private archive after her beloved husband passed away. Last but not least, I would like to thank the Birkenstock Communications team, who contributed to the creation of this book in manifold ways—in particular, Simon Kahles, Nolan Giles, Christian Meister, Armin Block, and Wiebke Vogt—as well as Christian Heesch, Steffen Schäffner, Anja Hofmann, and Moritz Schumacher from our legal team.

I invite you, the reader, to immerse yourself in this fascinating history of Birkenstock. I wish you an exciting journey through two and a half centuries of medicine, culture, fashion, and industrial history.

INTRODUCTION

BY ANDREA H. SCHNEIDER-BRAUNBERGER

> Tradition is not the keeping of ashes, but rather
> Keeping a flame alive—
> That is, the conviction and idea,
> Progress, responsibility, justice, and purity in thinking,
> And keeping action as a constant flame.[1]
> *Carl Birkenstock*

This passion of the Birkenstock family paved the way for the emergence of a global brand. Their uncompromising commitment to foot health was central. For a long time, Birkenstock was not in step with the zeitgeist: its innovations were ahead of their time. In the recent past, however, the fashionable zeitgeist and the brand have been closely linked. In FAZ magazine's ten trends of the last ten years, BIRKENSTOCK dominated the "shoe" segment for six years straight.[2] The Mainstream has moved towards BIRKENSTOCK. The explanation for this is that a natural lifestyle, comfort, and healthy eating are on the rise worldwide.[3]

But how did BIRKENSTOCK become a global brand? How did the creation of the *Original Birkenstock-Footbed Sandal* come about, prior to its launch in 1963? How does today's mainstream footwear jibe with its historical connection to the hippie movement? And wasn't there a particular turning point with the orthopedic shoe? To what tradition do (and did) the people at Birkenstock who took this path belong? How did the brand find its way from being a health shoe into the world of fashion? And did it really start with a sandal? An international research team of 15 historians investigates these and other questions in this study. In the book, we write BIRKENSTOCK in capitals only when we speak about the brand; Birkenstock refers to the company or the family.

Fig. 4: Karl Birkenstock created the *Original Birkenstock-Footbed Sandal* in 1963 – an avant-garde design icon.

State of Research and Sources

Scientifically researched company histories are common today, but by no means standard, even if large and small companies—some well-known, some less so—in a variety of industries have already had studies written about them by scientists and scholars. Surprisingly, though, there are only a few studies in the area of shoes, health, and fashion. General descriptions of the shoe industry in the 20th century, particularly for the decades after 1945, hardly take the business sectors served by Birkenstock into account at all.[4] Adidas is a pioneer in the shoe industry.[5] A comprehensive work is available for the "Shoe in the Third Reich" in which Birkenstock is not mentioned, although it covers numerous actors with whom Birkenstock was in contact.[6] The studies on the family companies Seidensticker and C&A touch on the textile fashion sector,[7] while health issues are dealt with in studies on various pharmaceutical companies.[8] There are no historical studies available on Birkenstock's competitors from the orthopedic industry. The state of research in the history of medicine looks somewhat better. There is also an overall description of orthopedics under the Nazis.[9] Books on the world of fashion may have intriguing layouts and contain fascinating photographs and essays, but they are rarely scientifically based.[10] The biographies or autobiographies of well-known designers seldom take a look at the companies behind the fashion labels.[11] Only the recently published "Oxford Handbook of Luxury Business" offers a scientific approach to the luxury goods segment.[12] Thus, for the wealth of aspects presented here, in addition to the thin state of research on business history in the narrower sense, a range of literature can be found, which has been brought together in the appendix.

Owing to the at best rudimentary state of research on business history, the presentation here is mainly based on unpublished sources from the Birkenstock company archive, which was newly established in preparation for this study, drawing on material from various public archives and, for the more recent past, on articles from newspapers and magazines. The main inventory is the estate of Carl Birkenstock, which, in addition to business and advertising material, also includes a great deal of theoretical material that became the basis for his own publications. For the postwar period, in addition to material in the Carl Birkenstock inventory, there is an inventory of catalogs and information material that can be regarded as almost complete. This material in particular—in keeping with the way the company saw itself—was not only designed for advertising purposes but was also linked to the idea of providing information about foot health. The estate of Margot Fraser, who built up Birkenstock in the USA and, alongside Karl Birkenstock, is therefore a formative figure for the company, from which the development of Birkenstock USA, Inc. can be reconstructed, is also to be found here. In addition, there is a small collection on the early history of Konrad Birkenstock GmbH (Frankfurt). Business records are available, at least to some extent, for the period focused on by our study here: 1945 to 2023. The historical footprints of Carl Birkenstock and Margot Fraser can be described more impressively through the dense historical transmission, while Karl Birkenstock, who is probably even more important for the Birkenstock company, remains a more shadowy figure, insufficiently illuminated owing to a lack of source material. Karl's development of the *Original Birkenstock-Footbed Sandal* laid the foundation for the company's success, so it is all the more regrettable that there is hardly any extant knowledge about him.

For many decades, there was no single history of Birkenstock. There was not one company that developed continuously, but there were workshops, factories and small businesses that emerged, closed again and also existed in parallel. While the years of conflict between Carl and his two brothers are visible in the sources, other important questions, such as the concrete repercussions of the entrepreneurial family's interactions on corporate policy, cannot be reconstructed. Important questions, which are fundamental for the history of an owner-managed company, can at best be answered only partially, so it is all but impossible to infer how the next generation was prepared for their tasks at the top of the company, what course the generational transitions in management took, and whether, for example, there was friction in the process.

As material on Birkenstock's employees and human resource issues is also almost completely lacking, nothing coherent can be said about training, recruitment, or the company's internal culture. However, the dispute between Karl Birkenstock and the trade unions, which shaped Birkenstock's public image for a long time, is covered.[13] Owing to a lack of sources, this study is sadly unable to present an inside view of the company and its structures over the last 70 years, and how it developed into a decentralized company with a more or less amorphous structure.

Since Konrad Birkenstock GmbH and the various Birkenstock companies that came into being from 1929 onwards were small businesses with fewer than 20 employees, only a few traces of them can be found in the official files. Nevertheless, it was possible to obtain relevant information about the history of Birkenstock from the holdings of the Institute for the History of Frankfurt (ISG), the city archive Friedberg, the state archive Bückeburg, and other state archives. Numerous newspapers and magazines were evaluated for questions about recent history and the world of fashion. In addition, a large number of eyewitness interviews were conducted in order to close gaps in the history of the Birkenstock tradition. We would like to take this opportunity to thank the many archivists for their support, as well as the GUG staff, above all Michael Bermejo-Wenzel, who researched and unearthed sources, and Simon Kahles, who made the files of the Birkenstock Corporate Archive available to all authors. Finally, our thanks go to the in-house employees, who supported the aim of this study in many ways through interviews and their search for relevant material.

Key Questions Addressed by the Study and Main Findings

The study presented here is one of the few scientifically developed company histories to touch on the areas of orthopedics, shoes, and fashion. Four essential characteristics of the Birkenstock firm stand out: first, a tradition in shoemaking that can be traced back to 1774; second, the company's establishment as a family company; third, its anchoring in the orthopedic industry with groundbreaking innovations over three generations; and fourth, its emergence from this tradition with the manufacture of sandals as it embarked on the path to becoming a global brand. Ever since Konrad Birkenstock invented the fully anatomically shaped last in 1897, the family had had a vision of shoes that would be healthy for the foot, which Konrad's son Carl further developed into the handmade *Ideal-Schuh* (ideal shoe). His son Karl then designed the *Original Birkenstock-Footbed Sandal* in 1963, which made a shoe that preserved foot health suitable for mass production.[14] Thanks to cultural circumstances, the powers of persuasion, and passionate associates, this brand found its way around the globe into all social classes, became a symbol of various subcultures, and even reached out to the luxury fashion segment.

The diversity of perspectives and the questions derived from them divide the concept of this volume into four epochs with different focal points: the emergence of a shoemaker dynasty; the development from a workshop to a manufacturing company; the beginning of industrialization at Birkenstock; and the rise of the global brand. The company's history is presented in a historical context, with its watershed moments, stages of development, and important players.[15] Additional materials relating to the topics of shoes, health, and culture are integrated into the narrative.[16] In light of the key importance of Carl's empirical observations and the conclusions he came to about "walking as nature intended," a separate short chapter is dedicated to his "foot orthopedics."[17] A very particular perspective opens up with the world of film: here the symbolic power of the *Original Birkenstock-Footbed Sandal* becomes particularly obvious.[18] Lastly, the reader is sent on a journey around the world, affording a view of the company from a variety of shifting perspectives and showing how Birkenstock interacted with the local culture in different regions.[19]

In order to allow the reader to read the chapters one at a time while having a context of the story, the following section presents the central aspects of the book in a longitudinal view in order to make long-term developments visible and to establish links between single chapters of the book.

The shoemaker dynasty and the Birkenstock family business

Birkenstock is based on a 250-year tradition of shoemaking, beginning in 1774, when Johannes Birkenstock, who was already working as a shoemaker, is mentioned in a document. However, he was not alone in this profession: his younger brother Johann Adam was also a shoemaker, and his nephew Johannes Jr. became one, as did his descendants. A collateral family line (Valentin) also practiced this profession, and Birkenstock daughters married into other traditional shoemaking families. This makes the Birkenstock family a shoemaker dynasty. Unlike other dynasties,[20] the Birkenstock family remained within the confines of the craft, poor, and marked by severe blows of fate.[21]

Konrad Birkenstock opened his shoemaker's workshop in Frankfurt am Main in 1896, moved to Friedberg in 1915, and ten years later took on his sons Carl and Heinrich as partners in the company, which was now producing the *Birkenstock-Footbed* on an industrial scale. The second generation only managed to be harmoniously integrated for a short time: new companies were founded, reorganized, and transformed up until the 50s. During this phase, the three brothers, their brother-in-law, and also their sister acted in various constellations with one another or against one another, with or without their father.[22] This period is characterized by quarrels and distrust, as well as by repeated attempts to work together in spite of everything.[23]

The company of greatest relevance was Gebr. Birkenstock GmbH für orthopädische Spezialitäten in Steinhude, which Carl Birkenstock continued to run alone after his brothers left. Despite the fragmentation that took place from 1929 onwards, the Birkenstock siblings still marketed the same product—flexible insoles. They also tried to work together again after the end of World War II; they even wanted to found a joint company for shoe production. In the end, however, this proved impossible, and Carl went his own way. He founded a new company in Bad Honnef under the name C. B.-Orthopädie GmbH—the nucleus of today's Birkenstock group.

Having a 250-year tradition also means having been active during the Nazi period. Therefore, this study also asks about the role of the acting persons and the companies during this time and comes to the conclusion that neither the companies nor the members of the Birkenstock family participated in aryanizations, i. e., the acquisition of assets from Jewish property; nor were any forced labor employed in the companies; Birkenstock did not produce armaments or deliver insoles to the Nazi regime and thus did not profit from National Socialism; and no ideological proximity to the National Socialists can be found.[24] Nevertheless, Carl Birkenstock also tried to secure government support for his footbed during the Third Reich. He carried out a large-scale experiment with 170 soldiers from Adolf Hitler's personal bodyguard unit in 1934, whose feet he cataloged according to his foot disease categories. There was no further cooperation with the Nazi regime, and he did not receive any product orders. While many family entrepreneurs joined the NSDAP, in some cases even at an early stage, not necessarily out of ideological conviction, but in order to profit economically[25]—we find a clearly different behavior in the Birkenstock family: Konrad Birkenstock and his three children—Catharina, Heinrich, and Konrad Jr.—did not join the NSDAP and other Nazi organizations; also the very late entry of Carl Birkenstock into the NSDAP in April 1940 was not ideologically motivated, but took place because of ongoing local attacks on him. This, too, is a more frequently observed reaction of entrepreneurs.[26]

The Birkenstock business family therefore stayed apart from the Nazi regime. As an entrepreneurial family construct, it behaved very typically from the 20s until the end of the 20th century. Thus, we find repetitive patterns as well as the risk posed by the family itself, which can threaten the survival of the business in many different ways, through internal family disputes, for example.[27] The conflicts between Konrad's four children led to the division of the small business; the splitting up of the company in the 90s under Karl Birkenstock led to similar conflicts between his three sons and resulted in the establishment of a large number of companies with different brands.[28] The multi-brand strategy and the challenges posed by the expanded company now made the limits of the family-run firm visible.[29]

The realignment in 2013 was key to getting the company back on track. With an external manager and the introduction of a new global orientation in group structures and a global brand strategy, a quick turnaround was realized with Oliver Reichert. The entry of L Catterton in 2021 represented the logical next step as the company progressed from its small-scale origins (first half of the 20th century) to become a medium-sized family business (second half of the 20th century) and then a global corporation (21st century), followed by the IPO on 20 October 2023.

Consequently—and also because it contributes to the company's overall strategy—Birkenstock recalls its traditions as a shoemaker dynasty and family business. Its historical core is the family, which spawned a series of scions who liked to tinker, innovate, and create. At the same time, the family had difficulties in thinking through and planning both the entrepreneurial side—there were complaints about a lack of business management skills right from the start[30]—and the organizational side, the inner framework of an entrepreneurial family. It was not the destruction of the company by the family that served in the Schumpeterian sense to unleash the creative power in product design but rather it was the radical nature of the innovations, which survived these very processes of disintegration. All of the creations (fully anatomically shaped lasts, flexible *Footbeds*, the *Ideal-Schuh*, and the *Original Birkenstock-Footbed Sandal*) were ahead of their time—they were not signs of the zeitgeist but rather of the avant-garde. And they always fulfilled a higher purpose, an orientation, to a certain extent, toward the common good: the desire to improve foot health.

The avant-garde: The *Health Footwear*, the *Ideal-Schuh*, and the *Original Birkenstock-Footbed Sandal*

Three generations played a special role in the company's success: Konrad (1873–1950), Carl (1900–1982), and Karl Birkenstock (born 1936). Their importance lies, on the one hand, in their innovative strength and, on the other, in their perseverance, passion, and uncompromising approach to foot health.

After completing his apprenticeship, 23-year-old Konrad moved to Frankfurt, and thanks to a groundbreaking innovation, he escaped the impending fate of ending up as a cobbler because of industrialization. Influenced by the theories of shoe reform, Konrad invented a fully anatomically shaped shoe last. Until then, the foot had been forced into the shoe; shoe lasts were straight and often did not distinguish between the left and the right foot. Konrad's shoe last was anatomically shaped, also on the underside of the foot—and this distinguished his last from that of other reform-oriented shoemakers.

His idea of *Health Footwear* at Birkenstock was born early: in 1902, an anatomically shaped insole sole was introduced—a *Footbed*, as Konrad would soon call it, which he had registered as a utility model. Konrad was a typical inventor. It wasn't money that drove him, but an idea. He encountered fierce resistance from shoemakers, since his shoe last was difficult to produce and made shoe production more demanding. As one of the first orthopedic shoemakers, he sought in vain for support from doctors to corroborate his belief in the effectiveness of his metal-free insoles. He didn't give up, however, but set out on a mission to convince everyone that his *Health Footwear* was helpful for people with healthy feet as well as for people with foot problems.

This idea of foot health, and the passion to fight for it, was inherited by Konrad's eldest son, Carl, who at the age of 15 followed in his father's footsteps and spread his teachings. He perfected the *System Birkenstock*, which consistently focused on the foot. According to Carl, the insoles—his *Footbed*—had to be adapted to the foot and not the other way around. He opposed the metal insoles that were dominant at the time and were preferred by doctors, orthopedic surgeons, and truss makers. To prevent his insole from being misused, Carl preferred to forgo sales and demanded that his clients attend his training courses. Only the shoe salespeople, shoemakers, and orthopedists whom he taught to use his system correctly were allowed to sell his insoles.

But Carl wasn't satisfied with theories alone. He developed his father's idea of *Health Footwear* and in 1936 invented the *Ideal-Schuh*, which over time he patented in several countries. This shoe was anatomically conceived, was designed to be made in different widths and lengths for every shoe size, and had a flexible insole that could be adapted to the foot of the wearer, thus supporting the highest goal in Birkenstock's thinking, "walking as nature intended." This orientation toward nature, the idea of an anatomically healthy shoe, made it possible for Carl to attract the interest of doctors for the first time. The fact that he also attracted the interest of a Nazi ideologue led him to hope that he would now also be successful with doctors. However, Carl did not allow himself to be infected by racist ideas.[31] He managed to handcraft several hundred copies of his *Ideal-Schuh* during World War II and received positive feedback for his efforts from many people.[32] However, the mass production he was now striving for was a challenge that could not be overcome. In cooperation with various shoe manufacturers, he tried his hand at this complex task in cooperation with various shoe manufacturers until finally giving up in 1961 and devoting himself to his publications on foot health.[33]

Karl Birkenstock joined the company in 1954. He had inherited his ancestors' innovative genes and focused his attention on developments in materials and on the product itself. His interest in design and architecture was deeply rooted in him—his father, Carl, had actually wanted to study architecture.[34] When Carl's uncompromising nature led him to cease work on his *Ideal-Schuh* after almost 20 years of searching, his son Karl decided on a new approach. Inspired by the architectural trend of the time (Brutalism), he chose the most minimalist variant of a shoe (a sandal) and coupled it with a minimalist solution for fastening the sandal to the foot (a strap).[35] The built-in footbed—in contrast to the individually adjustable insole of the *Ideal-Schuh*—was developed by Karl from the size of the average human foot. The result was the *Original Birkenstock-Footbed Sandal*, which Karl created with inspiration from the lessons he had learned from Konrad and Carl Birkenstock: it is still available today in an almost unchanged form. It is now considered a perfect, minimalist sandal in design terms,[36] clearly showing the material used, forgoing a heel or wedge shape, and informed by a gender-neutral appearance that is nothing less than radically modern.

The purpose: Foot health

Karl Birkenstock continued to persuade and educate people about the importance of foot health in the two magazines "Birkenstock-Post" and "Informationen" that the company sent to specialist dealers, doctors, orthopedists, and customers. Does this make Birkenstock one of the oldest companies to pursue a "purpose," to contribute, that is, to the common good? According to Colin Mayer,[37] such companies are characterized by the fact that they strive for a higher purpose and do not work for profit. This was demonstrably the case for the three generations in question. Konrad invented lasts and insoles, forgot about sales, and devoted himself to lobbying. The same was true for Carl, who placed the goal of foot health so high that he tied the sale of his products to his training courses, which he also offered mostly free of charge. He thus limited his market to serve the cause of foot health. The additional lectures, trips, essays, writings, etc., realized by father and son also served to advance this cause and were not directed toward generating a profit.

The Birkenstocks enjoyed success during and after the two world wars because of the goal targeted by their product, which was to bring relief to damaged feet. Because of this, they were able to sell insoles in larger quantities to address the foot problems of soldiers. Their second aim, the prevention of foot damage caused by the wrong footwear, remained unchanged.[38]

Karl also remained true to this family tradition. He developed the *Original Birkenstock-Footbed Sandal,* which was intended to cater to foot health. Functionality and quality, which were known from the *Footbed,* were employed in conjunction with a unique design. Nor did this design take into account the trends in fashion—the pointed Italian stiletto with heels, for instance. In pursuing his aim to create a shoe that was healthy for the foot, Karl accepted that he would be unable to sell it. And this is what indeed happened, as he was unwilling to submit to the demands of shoe stores and fashion retailers. They refused to order the shoe, which was dubbed the "tree trunk" based on the family name (Birkenstock = "birch branch"). The uncompromising nature of the Birkenstock leadership and the fact the company was once again ahead of its time (in terms not just of design but also of its gender-neutral concept) almost led to corporate catastrophe. Paradoxically, its salvation lay in pursuing its original purpose: remembering the example set by his ancestors—Konrad and Carl had tried to convince doctors and orthopedists of the efficacy of their products since the 1910s—Karl turned directly to the medical profession, sent those who were interested his *Original Birkenstock-Footbed Sandal,* and explained its particular qualities in the accompanying letter. And this time, the strategy met with success!

The power of disputability

What is striking in the Birkenstock family of entrepreneurs is their disputatiousness over the centuries. This not only applies to the conflicts between family members but also to the willingness and will to implement and, above all, push through their own ideas with conviction and against a great deal of resistance. Possibly shaped by the harsh living conditions of the first generations, Johannes Jr. and his son Johann Conrad Birkenstock signed a petition as part of the 1848 revolution—the first glimpse of an attitude that could be characterized as standing up for one's convictions.[39] Konrad had spent years dealing with shoemakers, orthopedists, and doctors in discussions, lectures, and articles. He accepted humiliation, and stuck to his guns undeterred. He also fought for the rights for the trademark "footbed," which he had been using since 1909, and which was registered in 1925 as a trademark.[40] The same applied to Carl, who also pursued disputes in court proceedings and vociferously opposed the trends in his trade. The Birkenstocks made no friends with their behavior. In attributions, in their comments and correspondence, an abrasive tone can repeatedly be heard.

This intransigence, this willingness to fight for foot health—because that's what it was all about—persisted for over a century. Karl Birkenstock took just as much action against the shoe industry and his competitors as his father and grandfather had done. Then in the 90s, this inbred attitude also led to Karl's conflict with the domestic trade unions, which colored the corporate image of Birkenstock in Germany for many years and blotted Karl's copybook with the unions. Here, too, he fought for his convictions without thinking about his image.[41]

All this reinforces the idea that the patriarchs of the family were a group of strong personalities who were by no means everybody's darling. Hugo Stortz from the truss makers' association blamed Konrad and Carl Birkenstock for getting in their own way with their "uncompromising and demanding manner, which was often perceived as arrogant."[42] Nevertheless, the wide range of different publications produced by Birkenstock forced its opponents and competitors to engage with the metal-free insole: this had a lasting impact on the field of orthopedics. Georg Hohmann, one of the most important orthopedic surgeons and university lecturers of his day, also became one of the foremost advocates of metal-free insoles in the 30s.[43] However, bucking trends and swimming against mainstream opinion in the industry (for over a century) probably required exactly this kind of strong, dogged, almost stubborn character. As a result, the members of the Birkenstock family repeatedly made themselves outsiders.

Images of Birkenstock: The Birkenstock imprint

Birkenstock has left a footprint in history. The flexible insole as a groundbreaking invention in the orthopedic field, combined with the perseverance and the strong will to persuade, led several manufacturers in the late 20s to turn away from metal to produce flexible insoles. This process culminated in the 50s, when the majority of manufacturers, doctors, and orthopedic specialists began to follow many of the Birkenstock ideas on foot health, such as the flexible insole.

When Birkenstock brought the *Original Birkenstock-Footbed Sandal* onto the market in 1963, two things happened. First, Birkenstock remained wedded to specialist shops and the field of orthopedics, using the same sales channels as it had for its insoles and footbeds. This image soon caught on in Germany, California, and Italy, where the sandals

Introduction 29

were sold in orthopedic shops and organic and natural food markets.[44] The primary target group there was an older audience and customers with foot health problems. This is how the sandals conquered Europe in the 60s and 70s, as is documented in this volume with examples from Italy, France, and the United Kingdom.[45] In the 80s, Birkenstock sandals were introduced in Japan specifically as health shoes for the over-40s.[46]

Second, Birkenstock itself aimed at society as a whole.[47] The various sandal models developed from 1963 onwards, with their unique designs, offered particular advantages for certain activities or professional groups—from the secure support of the boot (the *Athen* model) to the toe-protecting clog (the *Boston* model) of 1976.[48] Especially in this first phase, the idea behind the sandals becomes clear—namely, to offer a shoe with a minimalistic design that would be healthy for the foot and cater to all people, regardless of age, gender, or nationality. These goals were not always explicitly communicated but were nevertheless made implicitly visible. While the catalogs spoke of "for young and old" or "for work and at home," the "unisex" topic was not addressed verbally, only shown (see fig. 4).[49] This was the result of the product's historical development, since Birkenstock did not come out of the world of shoes but rather of footbeds. The *Footbed* did not distinguish between men and women; following this logic, Karl Birkenstock designed the *Original Birkenstock-Footbed Sandal* to be gender-neutral.[50] This concept was also avant-garde for the fashion industry: Pierre Cardin first introduced the unisex style concept "Space Age" to the fashion world in Paris in 1968—five years after the launch of the unisex sandal by Birkenstock.[51]

Was this a mark of confidence with regard to the fashion world or merely the ignorance of the outsider? Whatever the case, the *Original Birkenstock-Footbed Sandal* was ahead of their time and broke with established conventions. This facilitated an unplanned but decisive breakthrough for the German shoe manufacturer. *Original Birkenstock-Footbed Sandals* were discovered by the hippies themselves when Margot Fraser, who learned to love the shoe because of feet health problems, came to the USA. Why were American hippies attracted to these sandals? Because the sandals' obvious break with all conventions gave visibility to the countercultures' own protests.[52] In addition to Woodstock and flower power, another well-known name—from the emerging computer industry—was associated with the sandals of Birkenstock in the USA: Steve Jobs. Meanwhile, the androgynous character of the sandals created, for example, a connection to the LGBTQIA+ movement in Australia.[53]

While the effect of the sandals became visible on the outside in subcultures, the voice of Margot Fraser ensured a separate identity on the inside.[54] The interplay between Karl and her brought out a feminine side in the company that had a lasting influence on the names and colors it used and on its sales. The liberation of women from the compulsion to wear shoes with heels, which was implicit but never explicit at Birkenstock, was lived out with entrepreneurial self-determination by Margot Fraser as "Miss Birkenstock" in the USA, where she founded her own company to sell the sandals.

The example of Italy, where subcultures hardly existed, shows how closely existing subcultures and the spread of Birkenstock sandals were related. In Italy, whose fashion trend for stilettos was diametrically opposed to the *Original Birkenstock-Footbed Sandal*, sandals were seen as

Fig. 5: One of the early brand supporters, Steve Jobs, appreciated the functionality and clear design of the Karl Birkenstock sandals.

an expression of the simple life of monks or as colorful beach accoutrements for women.[55] The Birkenstock sandals that appeared with German tourists in Italy, which were primarily worn with white socks, were an outrageous breach of fashion taboo from the point of view of Italians, creating an image that has persisted in the memory there to this day. It was only after the fashion world became more closely associated with Birkenstock sandals that they were accepted as fashionable and penetrated further groups of buyers. Similarly, in the UK, where the decision to go for more color resulted in a fashion breakthrough that—enhanced most notably by Kate Moss starring in a photo campaign in *Palermo* and *Rio* sandals[56]—catapulted the Birkenstock niche product into the mainstream.[57] Something similar happened in Japan when young designers and musicians discovered BIRKENSTOCK and the brand became "cool."

Fig. 6: The *Arizona*—worn by hippies in the USA in 1973 and environmentalists in Germany in the 80s. This pair was designed by VALENTINO in 2019.

While in Germany and the USA, the *Original Birkenstock-Footbed Sandals* were part of the ecological movements early on, nature lovers in Japan joined them in the late 90s when a camping and outdoor boom in the country made sandals and simple shoes a trend. The nature-conscious lifestyle of many young people in Japan is catching on, and health shoes have enjoyed a new popularity.[58]

The *Original Birkenstock-Footbed Sandals* have not followed any fashion trends over the decades but have instead remained uncompromisingly true to their minimalist design functionality[59]—this is how cooperation partnerships are now allowed to change the colors, material, and accessories of the upper sandal, but under no circumstances can they touch the footbed or the silhouette. Penetrating the world of luxury fashion was never a strategic goal for Birkenstock. However, connections with the fashion world began early in the 80s when the first fashion designers sent their models down the catwalk in Birkenstock sandals. These were, however, not collaborations as yet. Fashion designers used the existing models and adapted them. From 2012 at the latest, the fashion world, as represented by Phoebe Philo, looked closer to Birkenstock.[60] Through the collaborations with Valentino, Dior, or Manolo Blahnik, Karl Birkenstock's *Original Birkenstock-Footbed Sandals*—and implicitly Konrad Birkenstock's *Health Footwear*—then reached also the luxury segment of the market.

But Birkenstock did not just move into the luxury goods category. The shoes also found their way to Hollywood. The *Original Birkenstock-Footbed*

Sandal became iconic soon after its invention in 1963. From hippies in the USA to staid, white-socked German tourists in southern Europe, the sandals' appeal was both conservative and revolutionary. This symbolic power was also incorporated into the world of movies. In comics, the sandals were synonymous with hippies, and over time these hippies also aged in the films. New cinematic categories of sandal-wearing outsiders followed: the lazybones, the stoner, the backpacker, the eco-terrorist, and the humorless lesbian or feminist all appeared in Birkenstocks.[61] Today, it is no longer outsiders who wear Birkenstocks—and not just in the movies. In 2019, Frances McDormand appeared in neon-yellow *Arizonas* at the Academy Awards, plunging the rainbow press into trauma (see fig. 56).[62] Basically, McDormand was repeating Karl Birkenstock's basic idea from 1963, which involved not sticking to the fashion of the time but deliberately ignoring it. The headline in Vogue ran "Why stick to the dress code?"[63] The hippie shoe of the 60s entered the world of the movies via comics and left it again, stepping into reality on the biggest Hollywood stage of all.

After seven decades, the *Original Birkenstock-Footbed Sandals* have left their niche as a comfort shoe for the elderly, a subcultural symbol, or a piece of functional footwear and have reached the general public, who wear them today for reasons of fashion, function, health, or comfort. From teenagers to retirees, the *Original Birkenstock-Footbed Sandal* has found the balance between health and fashion. At the same time, the androgynous *Original Birkenstock-Footbed Sandal* remains grounded in its minimalistic design and in its goal of walking as nature intended.

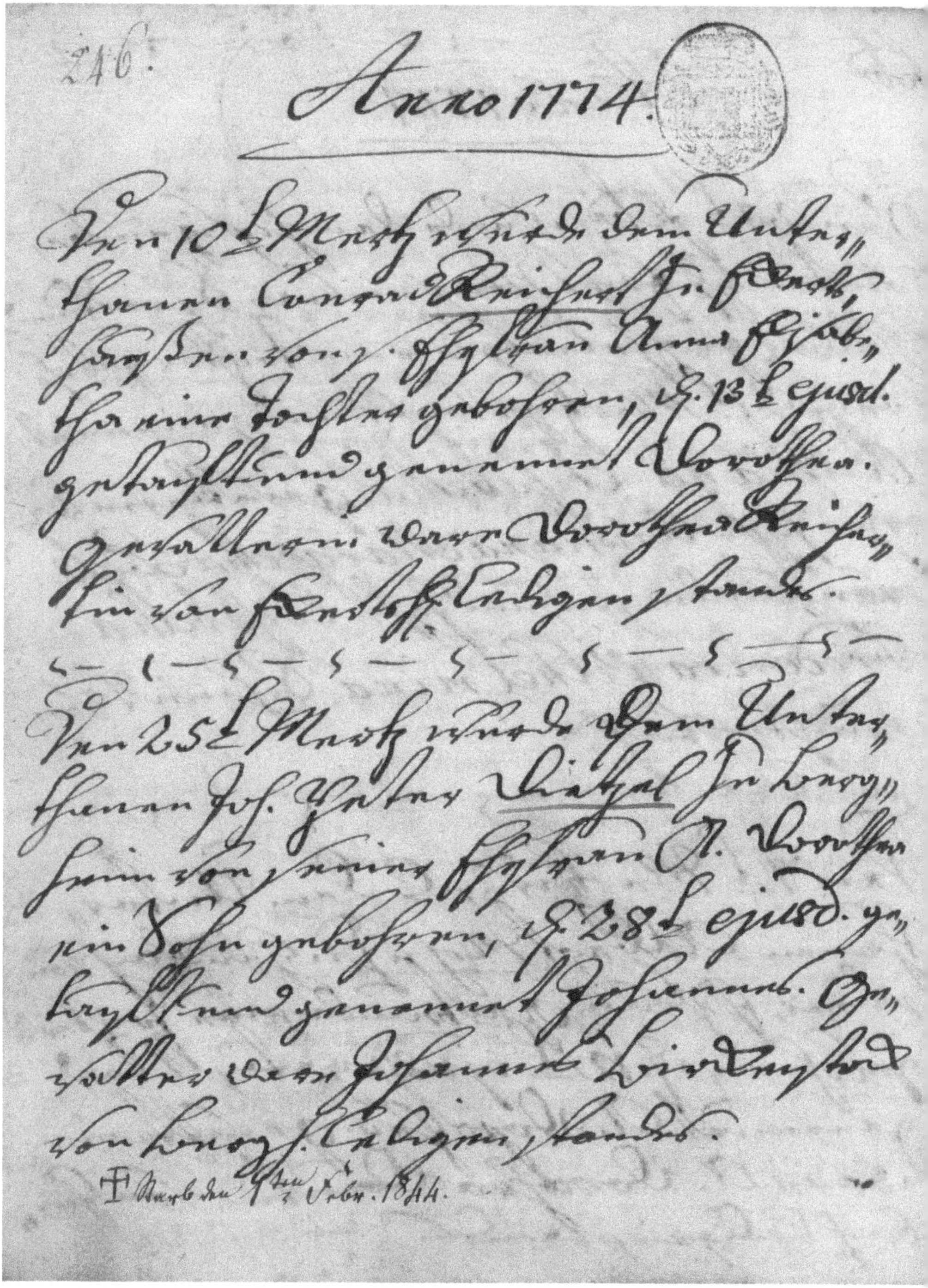

Anno 1774.

Fig. 7: A document tucked away in the Langen-Bergheim church register reveals the line of tradition beginning in 1774, when Johannes Birkenstock was a shoemaker.

1774 – 1895
THE BEGINNINGS: THE BIRTH OF A SHOEMAKING DYNASTY

THE SHOEMAKER FAMILY BIRKENSTOCK

BY KAI BALAZS-BARTESCH AND
ANDREA H. SCHNEIDER-BRAUNBERGER

We first encounter the Birkenstock shoemaker family in 1774 as rural craftsmen in the Wetterau region in the western German state of Hesse. The following chapter traces the path they took, a journey that begins with Johannes Birkenstock and his younger brother Johann Adam, and leads to Frankfurt am Main at the end of the 19th century and to the founding of a shoemaker's business by Konrad Birkenstock.

What destiny awaited the shoemaking family and the home they came from? How did the shoemaking trade develop during these almost one and a half centuries? And what impact did the changes in this trade have on the family's biography?[1]

It has been established that the Birkenstock family lived in the municipality of Langenbergheim for a long time. However, the sources provide little information about daily life, the family's status in society, or their economic situation. In the 1780s, the family moved to Mittel-Gründau, not far from Langenbergheim, where two more generations spent their lives before Konrad, the great-grandson of Johann Adam Birkenstock, moved to Frankfurt to lay the foundations for a global brand with his inventions.

The History of the Wetterau Region

The home of the Birkenstock family at the end of the 18th century was the Wetterau, and more precisely the small town of Büdingen, whose medieval facades towered over the area, which at that time was characterized primarily by rural agriculture and village crafts. The Birkenstock family comes from the village of Langenbergheim,[2] located very close to the manorial seat of the noble family von Ysenburg. Why was the shoemaking trade so important in this region, which is still rural today? And what caused the members of the Birkenstock family to move to Mittel-Gründau, a few kilometers away, in the late 18th century, and to Frankfurt a century later?

Langenbergheim was first mentioned in a document in 1057 under the name of Bercheim. Situated near the villages of Bergheim, Marköbel, and Himbach, it was a gift from King Heinrich IV to the Lord of Münzenberg. The area occupied by the town was probably still uninhabited at the time when the Roman *limes* ran through this area; the oldest remains can be traced back to the early Middle Ages.[3] At that time, the history of the town was shaped primarily by two parties: the princes of Isenburg/Ysenburg and the bishops of Würzburg. The exact circumstances of the political developments are complex and varied and will not be pursued in detail here, but one factor that was of great importance for the shoemakers in the region stands out: not far from the village ran the medieval Via Regia, one of the most important east-west axes in Europe. And where there is a road, shoes are needed.

Before the invention of the railway and in areas far from large rivers, the movement of goods and people was limited largely to transport on foot, on horseback, or in carts or carriages. As a result, walking was the most important means of transportation for most people. Furthermore, since the roads were not all paved, and often uneven and overgrown, people needed solid shoes to walk securely and safely over this demanding terrain.[4] Running through the Wetterau, the Via Regia—which connected the Rhineland with Silesia, and western Europe with the east, stretching from Santiago de Compostela via France, Germany, and Poland all the way to Moscow—constituted one of the most important roads for trade and long-distance traffic. On a more regional level, it connected Frankfurt am Main with Leipzig.

It can be assumed that owing to the large number of people passing through this region, there was a considerable need for shoes to be repaired and purchased. Other professions such as innkeepers, farriers, and related tradespeople are likely to have benefited from the heavy traffic on this route. After all, both Frankfurt and Leipzig were important trading and trade fair cities, so not only did large numbers of people pass through the region but also large quantities of goods. Furthermore, pilgrims who made the long and arduous journey to Santiago de Compostela from Silesia or Saxony crossed through the area to reach this pilgrimage destination on the Atlantic.[5]

It was not until the construction of the first railways in the second half of the 19th century that the mode of traffic changed permanently and resulted in a significantly reduced volume of pedestrian travelers. Up until the 1840s, the movement of goods and people offered many craftsmen a stable reservoir of customers and thus a reasonable livelihood. As the biography of the Birkenstocks shows, this changed radically later on, and it became increasingly difficult to make a living from the manufacture or repair of shoes.[6] Especially in the region east of Frankfurt, the construction of the railway altered the road network permanently. With the founding of the German Customs Union (Deutscher Zollverein) and the accession of the smaller Hessian states to it, the road from Frankfurt to Leipzig experienced a boost in importance and became even more significant again in the 1840s as a connecting axis in Central Germany. Owing to the construction of the railway, however, it lost this position within a very short time, since the train as a means of transport surpassed road travel in terms of both speed and comfort. The change in the region affected all the occupational groups that were dependent on road traffic, such as innkeepers, coachmen, and shoemakers too, since they were able to generate less income and were often forced to relocate or discontinue their activities.[7] As early as the late 17th century, several Birkenstocks are recorded in the Wetterau, probably belonging to two local lines of the family.[8] These two lineages are not demonstrably related.[9] Starting at the latest with Johannes Georg Birckenstock, who was born in 1688 and died in 1748 in the village then still called Bergheim, the first ancestor of the later Birkenstock line can be documented. However, his profession was not given in the church registry, so the beginning of the shoemaking tradition can only be traced back to his grandchildren. Johannes Georg also appears to have been one of seven children of Hans Bürckenstock. Nothing more is known about him other than his name.[10]

At this time, the House of Ysenburg still played an important role as rulers of the region; the small principality was subject to a feudal system of rule and the craftsmen were mainly organized in guilds. The guilds determined how many craftsmen were allowed to work in a region and kept prices stable so that overproduction was avoided.[11] The area was mediatized in the course of the Napoleonic Wars at the beginning of the 19th century and was ruled by the Grand Duchy of Hesse (often referred to as Hesse-Darmstadt) already before the Congress of Vienna. This political change was not to remain without consequences for the shoemakers in the region, since the grand dukes ruling in Darmstadt were striving for a liberalization of the guild system, as had already become reality west of the Rhine.[12]

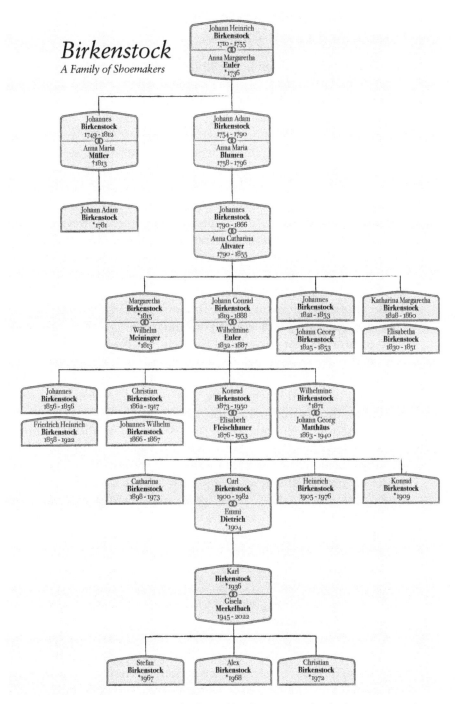

Fig. 8: Birkenstock stands for heritage: the shoemaking dynasty stretches back seven generations.

The Shoemaker Family Birkenstock

The First Shoemakers in the Family: Establishing a Craft Tradition

The shoemaking tradition in the Birkenstock family can be traced back in Langenbergheim to 1774. The first representative of the family who demonstrably pursued the shoemaking trade was Johannes Birkenstock (1749–1812), a great-grand-uncle of Konrad Birkenstock, the owner of the shoemaker workshop in Frankfurt. Johannes Birkenstock is mentioned in a document in 1774,[13] when he was 25 years old[14] and had already completed his apprenticeship as a shoemaker, since it was customary to start an apprenticeship between the ages of 14 and 16 and this training usually lasted three years.[15] Seven years later, in 1781, he had already received the title of master.[16] Johannes, however, was not the only representative of this generation who pursued the shoemaking trade. His younger brother Johann Adam Birkenstock was also a master shoemaker.[17] It is not known what profession the father of the two brothers, Johann Heinrich Birkenstock, pursued.[18]

The shoemaker, Johann Adam, who was born in Langenbergheim in 1754, married Anna Maria Blumen on January 16, 1783.[19] In view of the guild constraints that prevailed at the time, it is likely that both brothers pursued their craft in their own workshops. It is no longer possible to determine why they chose the profession, where they completed their apprenticeships, and when exactly they received their master's titles, or whether they spent their journeyman years on the move or made a good living from their trade. The relationship between the two brothers appears to have been close. Shortly after the baptism of little Johannes, a family tragedy occurred, because the "subject Johann Adam Birkenstock zu Langenbergheim" died only a few months after the birth of his son on September 14, 1790, at the age of only 36.[20] This must have been a difficult ordeal for the family and especially for his wife Anna Maria, who now had to survive alone with a newborn. It seems probable that Johannes Birkenstock adopted the child as godfather and next of kin and later trained his nephew in the shoemaking trade. This is supported by the fact that in the 19th century the young Johannes lived, like his uncle, not in Langenbergheim but in Mittel-Gründau, where he pursued the shoemaking trade.

Although little Johannes grew up in a time of war and poverty, the family community of solidarity was still a central social institution at this time. Since the 1790s, the French Revolution and the Coalition Wars had increasingly affected the area of what is today's Germany, and thus also the Wetterau. The late 18th and early 19th centuries were characterized by great economic hardship that affected large parts of the population, and challenges arose over the course of the century, contributing to the impoverishment of master craftsmen and the transformation of traditional professions. Economic hardship was to accompany the Birkenstock family throughout the course of the 19th century and was an abiding feature of their early history. Several members of the Birkenstock family were in debt in the late 18th century and were not always able to settle their debts on time.[21] This applies not only to the part of the family that is the focus of this family history; other branches of the Birkenstock family were also affected by similar hardships, such as the shoemaker Valentin Birkenstock (1747–1819), a relative who may have come from the second Birkenstock line in Langenbergheim.[22] His son Jakob, who died in 1853, was the last Birkenstock in Langenbergheim, and with his death the name died out there permanently.

Johann Adam Birkenstock[23] and Valentin Birkenstock owed money to various members of the Schatz family; numerous other entries about debts and payment defaults document the plight of the shoemakers. Johann Adam Birkenstock's death left his wife and newborn son in debt. Presumably the debts were paid off from the inheritance and left the young mother and her child destitute, so that, as already mentioned, she moved in with the brother of her deceased husband, who also took over the education of his nephew.

As early as in 1719, a shoemaker by the name of Heinrich Birkenstock from Himbach, the village neighboring Langenbergheim, is mentioned. He had drowned in the Linderheimer Bach across the border from his home in the domain of the Princes of Büdingen. Heinrich's relatives from Himbach then came to Langenbergheim to reclaim his body for burial. However, this met with resistance from the local authorities, who did not want to release the body, whereupon Heinrich's relatives took it by force. This offense was eventually settled by the imposition of a fine. Whether Heinrich is a relative of the Birkenstocks considered in this family history cannot be conclusively proven, since the church registries of Langenbergheim and the neighboring towns contain no reference to him. In any case, the incident shows that the shoemaker's trade and the name Birkenstock were also connected in this region beyond the family in question.[24]

Shoemakers around 1774

BY JOHANNA STEINFELD

Being a shoemaker around 1774 could mean many things. Some master shoemakers were well-paid craftsmen with one or more apprentices and a large workshop. They were to be found less in the countryside and more in the city, where demand was higher and the supply of shoes more extensive, covering various types of women's and men's shoes, not to mention slippers.[1] Owing to the economic conditions of the day, not only were new shoes produced but shoemakers often improved old shoes they had bought up. A tally for the north German city of Bremen dating from 1799 shows how much the guild of so-called "old shoemakers" produced per year for about 35,000 inhabitants: 180,000 shoes, 20,000 pairs of boots, and 20,000 pairs of slippers. If only in light of the sheer volume of "old" shoes produced, it is not surprising that the profession of shoemaker was the most common commercial vocation around 1800:[2] in Frankfurt, where Konrad Birkenstock was later to open his shoemaker stores, there were an average of 196 master craftsmen during the 18th century.[3] Since Frankfurt had an average population of around 35,000 at the time, this meant there were about 175 people for every shoemaker.[4]

In the countryside, things could be quite different. The demand from farmers was steady but not as high as in the city, so it was not uncommon for shoemakers to practice the trade as a sideline. It was also more common here for them to work as cobblers, that is, to focus on mending and repairing shoes. Reusing old leather to make shoes was common, as new leather was expensive and customers often had to provide the leather for the shoemaker themselves.[5]

Anyone who wanted to become a shoemaker was apprenticed to a master craftsman as an adolescent. Unlike today, the apprentice was not paid; in fact, he or his family had to raise the so-called apprentice's dues themselves. The apprenticeship lasted three to four years and was followed by an equally long period as a journeyman. Completing the *Meisterstück*, or "masterpiece," we're still familiar with today marked the end of the apprenticeship.[6] The regulations for the shoemaker's trade were laid down in the rules of the guilds, which were associations of craftsmen. Originally, the guilds were to be found only in cities, but they later spread to the countryside, especially in the 17th century.[7]

The production of a shoe began with the measurement of the foot.

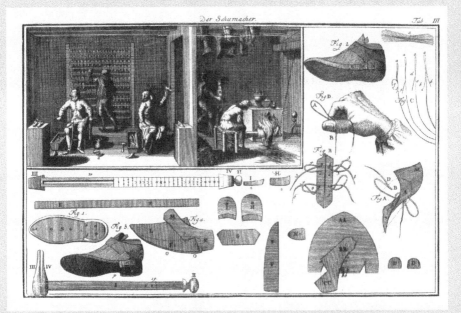

Fig. 9: Although the manufacture of the shoes was already sophisticated in terms of craftsmanship, the anatomy of the foot was hardly taken into account.

The measuring device used for this purpose, a kind of sliding sizer, was already quite similar to today's aids for foot measurement and functioned according to the same method. With this device, the length of the foot was measured from the heel to the tip of the big toe. With the help of paper strips, the width and height of the foot were also determined.[8]

Based on these measurements, the last—i. e., the replica of the foot in wood—was made, or old lasts were adapted. Back in the 18th century, the now entirely self-evident idea that a left and a right shoe should be made for the left and the right foot respectively did not exist. Hence, only one last was made, which served as a model for two completely identical shoes, which together formed a pair.

A few more steps followed before the pair of shoes was finished. First, individual parts had to be cut out of the leather and sewn together (see fig. 9). The resulting top of the shoe, the so-called "upper," was stretched onto the last and sewn to the insole, the inner sole of the shoe, and the outsole. A heel completed the shoe, which was removed from the last once the process was completed.

The consequences of unsuitable footwear for the body were first addressed by anatomist and physician Peter Camper in 1781. Camper taught as a professor at the universities of Amsterdam and Gronin-

Shoemakers around 1774   43

gen and wanted to show that even the supposedly "most trivial object" could become interesting if a knowledgeable person dealt with it. The paper that resulted from this preoccupation, "On the Best Form of Shoe," produced interesting results. Camper highlighted the strange discrepancy between, on the one hand, the detailed preoccupation with the peculiarities and condition of horses, donkeys, and oxen as livestock on the farm and, on the other, the virtual absence of any examination of human feet. He criticized the fact that in the manufacture of shoes, mere empirical knowledge ("practice") was repeatedly adopted without it being questioned in any way. As Camper saw it, the knowledge of shoemakers was insufficient to meet the anatomical needs of feet with regard to their footwear. By contrast, Camper devoted himself to the process of shoemaking on the back of a scientific approach. He drew here on the findings of the physicist Alfonso Borelli, who had studied the movement of muscles and the anatomy of the rigid and the moving foot.

Shoemakers' ignorance of the anatomy of the foot had consequences. The shape of the shoe did not match the foot, making it less comfortable to wear and leading not infrequently to injuries and physical impairment. Camper's criticism was unambiguous: "Thus, from our earliest infancy, shoes, as at present worn, serve but to deform the toes and cover the feet with corns, which not only render walking painful, but, in some cases, absolutely impossible."[9] Walking was also made impossible by bent toes, ingrown nails, ulcers, and inflammation of the main joint of the big toe and foot. In addition, toe deformations and even stretching of the ligaments could damage the foot.

The bottom line for Camper was that shoe manufacturing needed to change. Hence, among other things, he called for improvements in measuring, the abandonment of harmful shoe fashions, such as the heel, and for a separate last to be used for each foot. Yet there must have already been attempts in Camper's time to manufacture shoes according to the asymmetrical form of the feet, as shown by another treatise dating from the 18th century. In the encyclopedia of techniques known as "Descriptions of the Arts and Trades," published by the French Academy of Sciences at the end of the 17th century, there is an article by François Alexandre Pierre de Garsault about the shoemaker, his work, his tools, and the shoe itself. Here, Garsault reported on an attempt to make two individual shoes to form a pair, but the result did not arouse enthusiasm in the wearer, namely because the soles of the shoes apparently did not adjust well to the foot if the same shoe was worn every day. On the contrary, it was more comfortable, the user reported, to wear two shoes of the same shape that one had to change every few days so that the shoes would not wear out on one side and the shoe would not adapt too much to the foot. Thus, not even the empirical attempt to make shoes according to the natural shape of the feet helped to dislodge old beliefs about the comfortable shape of shoes. These, therefore, prevailed for a long time, while Camper's powerful critique of shoe manufacturing continued to be welcomed by podiatrists and those who worked to improve shoes. It is not surprising, then, that Carl Birkenstock was also aware of Camper's writing, which came out in a new edition in 1939. In his 1961 manuscript "Fuß und Spur in Trittspur" (Foot and Track in the Footprint) he quoted a few passages from Camper's work and called for his writing to be "made more available to the professional world."[10]

Relocation to Mittel-Gründau and Early 19th-Century History

The family's meager income and mounting debts in Langenbergheim endangered its survival in the late 18th century. Presumably these circumstances contributed to the decision to leave Langenbergheim. The family of Johannes Birkenstock, the brother of Johann Adam Birkenstock, moved to Mittel-Gründau in 1781 or 1782.[25] Johann Adam's son Johannes probably moved to his uncle in Mittel-Gründau after the death of his father in 1790. The fact that he later took over the shoemaking trade from his father and uncle is probably due to training he received from his uncle. Since his uncle Johannes Birkenstock had seven children himself, with only one, however, reaching adulthood, the close connection between uncle and nephew is understandable. The children of Johannes Birkenstock (*1790) were all born between 1815 and 1830 in Mittel-Gründau; most of them also died there.

The reasons why the family moved to Mittel-Gründau of all places can be surmised on the basis of a few clues. At the time, Mittel-Gründau, which belonged to the Ysenburg domain, bordered on the Electorate of Hesse.[26] The towns of Gründau and Lieblos (with which Mittel-Gründau has formed a municipality since the 1970s) and the town of Gelnhausen were already on the Hessian side. The thriving city of Mittel-Gründau with its numerous trades and crafts formed an important junction on the east-west axis from Frankfurt to Leipzig.[27] Prosperity in this area increased, while Langenbergheim, one can assume, lost its attraction at this time for the Birkenstock family as well as for many other people. Emigration bans, which were issued for numerous Hessian regions at the end of the 18th century, support this view, since they were intended to prevent the decline of the less sustainable regions, which at that time also included the Wetterau. Thus, the Birkenstocks did not relocate to a more distant region but only to the closer, more prosperous surroundings of their own homeland. At that time, the district of Büdingen and the Wetterau in general were among the economically more backward areas of Hesse. In a parallel relocation, a new family of shoemakers named Matthäus moved to Langenbergheim, replacing the Birkenstocks.[28] Even moving to a region that was probably better off than Langenbergheim was, however, not able to protect the Birkenstock family from poverty. Far-reaching economic changes took hold of the profession of shoemaker and aggravated the economic situation of the already precarious handicraft in the countryside. Furthermore, the Napoleonic Wars also impacted the early part of the 19th century, making survival in the field of rural handicrafts difficult owing to the recruitment of numerous men as soldiers, the movement of armies through the region, and starvation due to crop failures.[29]

These social problems were also reflected in the Hessian district of Gelnhausen, where the shoemakers had started petitions in 1823 to limit the number of master shoemakers, since there were at least 64 of them in the city at that time.[30] One of the aims of these petitions was to ensure that the master craftsmen "were not left completely without a job" due to excessive competition.[31] Similar complaints from shoemakers and other craft groups can also be found in the Grand Ducal Landgraviate of Hesse as early as in the late 18th century. Even if "complaining" was part of doing business back then and served to assert one's own interest, the rural handicrafts were still clearly suffering economic hardship. In addition to the shoemakers, weavers and tailors in Hesse-Darmstadt all lived in poor conditions at the beginning of the 19th century and could barely make a living from their work.[32] But it was also a time of technical advancement that put great pressure on the master craftsmen in the countryside, who traditionally worked alone. Therefore, the craftsmen in many places resisted the introduction of freedom of trade, an innovation that had already spread through Napoleon's conquests in the French-occupied areas on the left bank of the Rhine. They demanded a return to the guild system with its firmly regulated markets and restricted numbers of master craftsmen. In Gelnhausen, this movement was successful; the Electorate of Hesse held on to the old handicraft regulations for a long time.[33]

However, the masters often had no journeymen or apprentices in their workshops—a sign that they lived for the most part below the subsistence level. In the words of the national economist Bruno Hildebrand in 1848: "[A foreman] who works without any assistants is actually just a special kind of day laborer."[34] This was the situation of Johannes Birkenstock the younger. His uncle Johannes had died in 1812 at the age of 61 in nearby Lieblos, while he, in the meantime a master shoemaker in Mittel-Gründau, found himself in precisely that group of master craftsmen working alone who were just able to make a living from their daily work and had to struggle to feed their families.[35] This poor standard of living exacerbated the already high mortality rate of the time; only two of his six children ever reached middle adulthood. It must therefore have been difficult for his only surviving son, Johann Conrad Birkenstock, born in 1819, to undergo official training as an apprentice, a journeyman, or a master shoemaker in his youthful years.[36] However, it can be assumed that he was trained as a shoemaker by his father. In the 1820s and

1830s—shortly before Johann Conrad would have started his apprenticeship—the number of journeymen and apprentices in the Grand Duchy of Hesse had fallen to its lowest level (from 17,102 in 1815 to a low of 11,626 in 1821). It was not until the late 1840s that the craft began to recover and grow again. Johann Conrad Birkenstock presumably had to support the family in earning a living by working in his father's shoemakers workshop as well as in the farming that went on alongside it.[37]

Two other factors suggest that the family did not lead a prosperous life: four of Johannes Jr.'s six children died in early adulthood, between the ages of 20 and their early 30s. These were the sons Johannes (1821–1853) and Johann Georg (1825–1853) and two daughters, Katharina Margaretha (1828–1860) and Elisabetha (1830–1851). The eldest surviving daughter, Margaretha Birkenstock, married Wilhelm Meininger, who was born in 1813.[38] Her trail is lost later on, which suggests that she emigrated to the USA with her husband and daughter, a common trend at the time. In any case, after 1840 she is no longer mentioned in the local church records. The next generation of Birkenstocks would not fare much better either. Johann Conrad Birkenstock, who lived a long life in Mittel-Gründau, had six children like his father, two of whom died in infancy. It is also striking that the marriage age in the Birkenstock family in this era is generally quite high. Male descendants often did not marry until they were well over 30 and thus started a family quite late. This, too, can be interpreted as an effect of the family's modest financial situation. The young men first had to earn enough money to support a family before they could even think about marriage.

As a result of the Napoleonic conquest, the mediatization of smaller territories, and the Congress of Vienna, at which the new order of Europe after the wars against France was decided in 1815, the Ysenburg dominions became part of the Grand Duchy of Hesse. The Grand Duchy had its seat of government in Darmstadt, but at the same time united widely distributed and unconnected areas lying left of the Rhine, south of the Main, and in Upper and Middle Hesse. Initially, there was no uniform law within this area.[39] It is more difficult to determine to what extent the guilds had a serious impact on the practice of crafts in the part of the Grand Duchy examined here. In the areas on the left bank of the Rhine in the state governed from Darmstadt, there had been no craft guilds since 1815; French administrative reforms had already allowed extensive freedom of trade to prevail here. In the other areas of Hesse-Darmstadt, there were also the beginnings of a liberal, trade-oriented economic policy, but the guilds remained in existence at the same time and the traditional, long-established handicrafts in the cities were promoted by trade associations. There were, however, some changes: 1821 saw the lifting of the ban on guild districts, which prevented master craftsmen from moving to other cities or regions and practicing their trade there. The number of assistants was also no longer restricted, although master craftsmen working alone, such as Johannes Birkenstock, were in no way able to benefit from this. As a master craftsman, he was probably not even subject to tax, since the tax laws were also adjusted, and master craftsmen without journeymen usually did not have to pay taxes on their trade earnings.[40]

The Shoemaking Trade in the 19th Century and the Economic Situation of the Birkenstocks

In the course of the 19th century, the economic environment and the profession of the shoemaker changed fundamentally.[41] As early as in the middle of the century, the economic situation of many shoemakers in rural areas was precarious and many lived just above the poverty line.[42] The demand for shoes was simply not great enough to provide shoemakers who were no longer protected by the guild system with enough income to survive, since now all the restrictions and price-fixing that existed earlier had finally been removed.[43] Furthermore, there were technical innovations such as the sewing machine or the McKay machine,[44] which intensified competition, especially within the city trades. Increasing competition from machine-made shoes also caused rural handicraft sales to drop. While larger markets gradually opened up in the cities, which were shaped more by fashionable tastes than by work-related necessities, in the countryside competition with large shoe factories increased toward the end of the century. These factories had the advantage of significantly more efficient production methods and correspondingly lower prices for mass-produced goods. As a result, the production of shoes by rural craftsmen continued to decline and services such as repairs or alterations to the shoe came to the fore as a business model. In the second half of the century, many shoemakers kept their heads above water by supplementing their craft businesses with the sale of shoes from industrial sources.[45] Others were forced to stop making shoes and to refocus their business model entirely on shoe repairs. Repairs had also previously been part of the trade but were only carried out full-time by so-called cobblers, who were mostly outside the guilds. The change in the shoemaking trade in the 19th century ultimately caused a shift in the job description away from the production of shoes toward service-oriented activity consisting mainly in the repair and sale of shoes. Getting into the shoemaking trade was still relatively easy at the beginning of the 19th century, since the abolition of the old guild regulations in some regions meant that neither extensive qualifications nor start-up capital were required to set up and run a workshop. Consequently, the demands on shoemakers entering the profession also expanded throughout the second half of the century as machines and specialized skills played an increasingly important role in the production of shoes. This development significantly favored the emergence of shoe factories over master craftsmen who produced by themselves, since capital and know-how were bundled in factory production and technical innovations could be implemented more quickly.

Until well into the 18th century, technological advances in the shoemaker's trade had been slow. Mechanization of production did not take place until the middle of the 19th century, which had lasting effects on the economic situation and the tasks of the craftsman. New production methods, such as the use of the sewing machine and the shoe peg machine, which made it much easier to sole with wooden pegs, accelerated the production process considerably and reduced the man-hours required, and thus the costs for a single pair of shoes were also reduced. The uppers were now often no longer made by the shoemakers themselves, but rather manufactured in factories, purchased, and only fastened to the shoe soles by the shoemakers.[46] The extension of the freedom of trade laws had an effect on the shoemakers, but in the region around Büdingen it was only fully implemented in the course of the general dissolution of the guilds in 1868, which suggests that traditional rural handicrafts had a longer lifespan here than elsewhere.

In addition to the forms of production, the demands on the shoes themselves also changed. In the early 19th century, durable boots or work shoes for field and harvest work were still the norm, but with the rise of the bourgeoisie and industrial workers in the late 19th century, fashion shoes were increasingly preferred, and the demand for long-lasting footwear declined.[47] At the same time, rural populations stagnated or even declined slightly, while towns grew into cities and industrial centers, leveling off and in some cases reducing the local clientele and the needs of the rural population. The new urban working class no longer had much interest in robust, long-lasting footwear that could be worn for decades and be repaired again and again. Moreover, the increase in general purchasing power over the course of the century also meant that even ordinary people could afford more than one pair of shoes and chose their shoes according to the trends of fashion. This development

Fig. 10: The workshops of shoemakers were mostly modest. In many cases the profession was carried out as a sideline.

led, in turn, to an expansion of customers' demands for quality in the shoes produced, which many rural craftsmen simply could not meet. The rural handicraft businesses were therefore no longer competitive and, with their outdated production methods, could not keep up with the newly emerging factories. The long-term effects of this shift meant that although shoemakers were one of the largest occupational groups among tradespeople up until the 1920s, many shoemakers ultimately became cobblers who repaired industrially manufactured shoes.[48]

In view of this development, the fate of Konrad Birkenstock's grandfather, Johannes Birkenstock Jr., can be surmised. In rural areas, it was customary anyway at this time to work two or more jobs—for example, agriculture in addition to handicrafts—in order to secure one's own livelihood. Johannes Birkenstock Jr. was a "local citizen, farmer, and master shoemaker."[49] In the summer, he and his son Johann Conrad probably farmed a small plot in the village that belonged to the family. In winter, when the fields lay fallow, he no doubt devoted himself more to making and repairing shoes in the workshop in his own home. Unlike his father, Johann Conrad was not successful in becoming a member of the shoemakers' guild. To regulate the number of masters and journeymen, the guilds set very high apprenticeship fees, which Johann Conrad might not have been able to afford.[50] Practicing any craft without the sponsorship of the appropriate guild was forbidden in the 18th century. Johann Conrad, however, would have been able to repair shoes within the rules of the guild. He was officially listed as a farmer, while his father was recorded as a master shoemaker and farmer.[51]

Johann Conrad's life and that of his father were shaped by poverty. His youth and early adulthood came at a time of crisis. The revolution of 1848, hunger caused by failed harvests, and economic change produced a population decline in the rural regions of Hesse-Darmstadt.[52] Whether the great economic pressure of the 1840s contributed to the decision by Johannes Jr. and Johann Conrad Birkenstock to take part in the 1848 revolution together cannot be clearly ascertained. The 1848 revolutionary movement campaigned against the rule of the princes and called for a united, democratic Germany. In any case, father and son seem to have been caught up in the spirit of optimism of that time, and they both signed the resolution of April 19, 1849, in support of the Mittel-Gründau Democratic Association's campaign for an imperial constitution. In doing so, they made clear their progressive political attitude and protested against traditional rule, which did not seem to be to their advantage.[53]

From the Village to the Big City: Hopes for a Better Life

In Mittel-Gründau, too, the Birkenstock family was not one of the wealthier families in the town, which can be seen from the horse census of 1872, in which a total of 23 horse owners in the town were recorded, none of whom were Birkenstocks. At that time, a horse was a sign of prosperity and extremely advantageous for use in agriculture and as a means of transport.[54] Nevertheless, Johann Conrad Birkenstock did not have a serviceable horse.[55]

The continuing misery of the family is also reflected in the fact that two of Johann Conrad's six children did not survive infancy. In 1856, Johann Conrad and his wife Wilhelmine, née Euler, had a son named Johannes, who died at the age of three months. Tragedy struck again in 1867 when little Johannes Wilhelm Birkenstock died at the age of just over one year.[56] Like his father, Johann Conrad had a total of six chil-

52   **1774–1895** The Beginnings: The Birth of a Shoemaking Dynasty

dren. The four other siblings included Friedrich Heinrich, born in 1858, Christian, born in 1862, Konrad, born in 1873, and the only sister, Wilhelmine Birkenstock, born in 1871.[57] After graduating from school and without having served in the military, Konrad began an apprenticeship at a shoemaker's company named Philipp Ditschler in Büdingen.[58]

At the same time, in 1894, before Konrad moved to Frankfurt, his sister, Wilhelmine, married a master shoemaker named Johann Georg Matthäus, who lived in Büdingen.[59] The name may seem familiar, since it was the Matthäus family who settled down as shoemakers in Langenbergheim after the Birkenstocks moved away, and they stayed there much longer than the Birkenstocks.[60] As a result, Wilhelmine married into a shoemaking family that came from the same place as her own ancestors, which meant that the shoemaking tradition was also continued directly on the female side of the family. Whether the brother's education and the sister's marriage into the same trade in the same town were related is uncertain. It is possible that Konrad knew his sister's groom through his trade activities, and the couple got to know each other that way. In any case, the family was firmly integrated in the shoemaking trade and was part of a thriving network involving other shoemakers in the region. Both lived in Büdingen until the 1940s: at any rate, their marriage certificate contains subsequently added references to the death of husband Johann Georg on December 20, 1940.[61]

After completing his apprenticeship in 1896, Konrad moved to Frankfurt am Main, where he opened a shoemaker's workshop. He had probably acquired the necessary capital by selling his parents' agricultural property in Mittel-Gründau. This first workshop was initially located in his own apartment at Oppenheimerstraße 51. In the years that followed, he moved several times within Frankfurt, which was typical for practitioners of the small trades. In 1899, he moved to Schweizerstraße 36, then in 1904 to Oderweg 15.[62] Even after that, Konrad Birkenstock, who had married Elisabeth Fleischhauer in September 1897 and had four children with her in Frankfurt, often changed his residence. His last stay as a master shoemaker in Frankfurt was at Töngesgasse 34. He moved to this address in 1912, and in 1915 he finally left Frankfurt to move to Friedberg with his wife and four children and not only continued his business there but expanded it into a factory.[63]

The Shoemaker Family Birkenstock   53

Summary

Over three generations—Johann Adam, Johannes, and Johann Conrad Birkenstock—a shoemaking dynasty developed through sidelines and marriages. However, this was not characterized by dynastic wealth but by poverty, hard work, and multiple strokes of fate. Despite all the adverse circumstances, the family remained true to its tradition as shoemakers, developed a high degree of resilience, perseverance, and down-to-earthness, and thus laid the foundation for the next three generations.

Roman Köster and Jörg Lesczenski trace the paths taken by these generations in the 20th century.

From the Traditional Craft of Shoe-making to the Modern Shoe Factory

BY JOHANNA STEINFELD

Industrialization in the 19th century fundamentally changed the means of production. At the heart of these changes was the introduction of machines powered by steam and later by gas engines, which revolutionized the world of work. Machines were able to carry out tasks previously done by humans much faster and more accurately while, at the same time, the standardized work processes of these machines reduced material wastage. Both of these factors led to a significant reduction in the production costs incurred. Owing to the large quantity of products manufactured in factories, raw materials and supplies could also be purchased more cheaply. This had a significant influence on the prices of the products, which in turn affected the structure and organization of the world of work.

The shoe trade was also affected by these profound changes. From the middle of the 19th century onwards, the centuries-old method of making shoes by hand found itself facing time-, energy-, and cost-saving alternatives. The first change in the traditional process of manufacturing shoes came in the 1830s with the adoption of a technique developed in North America for joining the sole and the upper, the top part of the shoe sewn together from several individual leather parts. Instead of the continued use of so-called pitched thread for sewing, which consisted of several individual threads coated with a mixture of wax and pitch as well as other ingredients, the sole and the upper were now hammered together with small wooden nails.[1]

Finally, the sewing machine, which was also introduced into Germany from North America and quickly adapted to the requirements of shoe processing, significantly accelerated and facilitated production. It could be used for sewing the upper parts of shoes, which was an exacting job: "Since the upper work, with its seams requiring a great deal of care in execution (which do not escape the scrutinizing eye of the observer as is usually the case with work on the base), was often the most laborious part of the whole enterprise. The workers who stitched a beautifully even seam were in much demand. Yet the machine did this in a surprisingly safe and fast way."[2] In quick succession, additional machines were developed to carry out other steps in the shoemaking process, which made it worthwhile to set up companies that produced merely one part of the shoe at a time, such as heels, decorative elements, etc.[3] At the same time, machines that could assemble the individual parts of the shoe were developed, and thus more and more steps of shoe manufacturing became mechanized. The results of such mechanical production, which became increasingly widespread from 1870 onwards, were remarkable: at the beginning of the 20th century, for example, the working time for a shoe made by hand totaled 13 hours, whereas the factory could turn out the same shoe in 2 hours and 18 minutes.[4] This provided incentives for the establishment of shoe factories that could produce an ever-increasing number of shoes: in Pirmasens—in southwest Germany—the center of the country's shoe industry at the end of the 19th century, this trend set in as early as in 1857. The first larger manufactory in the country was founded here, initially relying on manually operated machines. From there, exports were already being sent to neighboring European countries, but the new means of transport available (the railway and steamships) made it possible for deliveries from Pirmasens to be sent as far afield as North Africa, the USA, and the Ottoman Empire. Just seven years later, in 1864, a total of 76 firms employing more than 1,600 workers made use of over 66 stitching machines, a sole-cutting machine, and a smoothing machine.[5] Around the same time, in 1865, 1.8 million pairs of shoes were produced in Pirmasens; by 1877, production numbers already exceeded 4 million pairs of slippers and ankle boots, ultimately climbing to some 14 million pairs of shoes in 1892.[6]

At the same time, the origins of the shoe industry rarely lay in the workshops of shoemakers, as the smaller craftsmen, in particular, had little equity capital at hand. More often, it was leather merchants who became the shoe industrialists—in other words, traders who had sold the shoemakers ready-cut pieces of leather and given them credit. These leather merchants acquired sewing machines and sold the shoemakers finished uppers, which they then processed into shoes.[7] As the number of shoemaking steps now performed by machines increased, shoe factories became larger and eventually produced whole shoes. This changed the entire structure of the shoemaking trade, and between 1882 and 1907 the number of businesses shrank from around 248,000 to around 200,000, a decline that mainly affected shoemakers who worked alone or had few assistants. Nevertheless, even in 1907, the vast majority of production facilities (140,000) were still in the hands of shoemakers working alone.[8] Of the total of about 369,000 people working in the shoe trade and shoe industry in 1907, 37.9 percent were shoemakers working on their own.

In Germany, then, this industry was strongly characterized by small businesses; companies with more than 1,000 employees tended

Fig. 11: Modern factories turned shoes into mass-produced goods and devalued the shoemaker's profession. While some were forced into the role of cobbler, others sought their future in the manufacture of orthopedic shoes.

to be the exception. The largest German shoe factory was the Salamander company in Kornwestheim near Stuttgart, which employed around 3,500 people in 1913.[9] Apart from Pirmasens (1907: 14,730 people employed in the shoe industry), Erfurt (3,600) and Weissenfels (4,000) also became centers of the shoe industry, as did Offenbach (1,760) and Frankfurt (1,300).[10] In addition, there were laborers from the factories in the surrounding areas who worked for the companies from home. This kind of cottage industry meant companies did not have to pay for factory premises, social insurance, etc., and could therefore rely on more flexible working hours.[11] After the growth of the cottage industry up to the 1890s, its share consistently fell until 1914, partly because the use of machines became even more intensive during this period.[12]

The prerequisite for the development of shoe factories was the dissolution of the guilds, into which craftsmen were organized during the Middle Ages and the Early Modern period: in the various territories of the German Confederation, the regulations for practicing a trade were gradually abolished in the first two-thirds of the 19th century and the special status of guilds thus terminated. Significant in this regard were the political unifications brought about by the founding of the North German Confederation in 1866 and the German Reich in 1871, which ultimately brought nationwide laws on freedom of trade.

The craftsmen not only found themselves deprived of their traditional form of organization, given the abolition of the guilds, but also complained about the competition from machines as a threat to their professional existence. Admittedly, the machines could not be considered the only culprits responsible for the shoemakers' ills, since the number of people occupied in the sector had risen sharply due to the freedom of trade and the low barriers to market entry for the profession. Yet this did little to change the economic reality for shoemakers: although the shoe industry was one that paid relatively low wages, shoe factory workers still earned more than journeymen shoemakers and sometimes even more than master craftsmen working alone.[13] Renowned economist Gustav Schmoller therefore wrote about the situation of shoemakers in 1870, which did not change significantly until World War I: "The mass of master craftsmen is in a wretched, miserable situation. Anyone who has paid attention to the poor in our large cities will be familiar with the starving, impoverished shoemaker with his numerous children as a typical phenomenon. And a new shock is preparing itself as the machines advance victoriously."[14]

OHNE METALL
OHNE METALL
Ges. Gesch.
Birkenstock's
Fussbett
heilt
alle Fussleiden
Birkenstock's
Fussbett
GES. GESCH.
heilt alle Fussleiden
J. Mauch, Schuhwaren, Heidenheim,
Jäckleplatz 27
Spezialgeschäft für empfindliche Füsse. Kostenlose Beratung und Anprobe für diese Einlage. Eigene Mass- und Reparaturwerkstatt.

1896 – 1945
FROM A SHOEMAKER'S WORKSHOP TO A MANUFACTURING COMPANY

Fig. 12: Advertisement for
Birkenstock's *Footbed*, 20s.

MISJUDGED INNOVATIONS: THE STRUGGLE FOR FOOT ORTHOPEDICS, 1896–1945

BY ROMAN KÖSTER

The Beginnings of the Birkenstock Company

Konrad Birkenstock was born on June 4, 1873, to Johann Conrad and Wilhelmine Birkenstock in the village of Mittel-Gründau in the Büdingen district, northeast of Frankfurt. Growing up in this rural milieu, Konrad Birkenstock attended elementary school—as was the well-established family tradition—and began at an early age with the manual production of shoes. At the age of 14, he undertook an apprenticeship as a shoemaker at the Ditschler company in Büdingen, where the shoemaker Philipp Ditschler had set up his own shoe manufactory in 1876. By this time, however, both of Konrad's parents had already died, and according to his children, this greatly affected his childhood (and arguably his character), which was "tough, sober, and solitary."[1]

After successfully completing his apprenticeship, Konrad set up his own business in 1896 in the nearby Hessian city of Frankfurt am Main and ran a workshop together with a shoe shop, which somewhat later was expanded to include an additional shop.[2] To finance the workshop and shoe business, he sold parts of the family farm.[3] During this time, Konrad lived on Oppenheimerplatz in the middle-class district of Sachsenhausen.[4] He soon met Elisabeth Fleischhauer, who was three years younger, from Schwalheim near Friedberg, and—like himself—a Protestant. Unfortunately, nothing more is known about her family history. They married in 1897 and had four children: Catharina (born 1898), Carl (born 1900), Heinrich (born 1905), and Konrad Jr. (born 1909).[5]

Fig. 13: The zeitgeist and the shoe reformers in Frankfurt turned Konrad Birkenstock into an orthopedic shoemaker. The Birkenstock shoemaking workshop, Oppenheimer Platz (cornerhouse, right).

Konrad was soon confronted with complaints from customers who found it difficult to adapt to factory shoes, especially to the metal insoles that were common at the time for impaired and aching feet. Above all, however, he was influenced by the scientific reorientation of the shoe reform movement, which reflected on how shoes were worn and offered theoretical solutions for producing shoes that did not damage healthy feet.[6] This led him to work intensively on shoes that were more orthopedic in nature and on the development of insoles that were better adapted to the foot.

In 1897, one year after setting up his workshop in Frankfurt am Main and in the year of his marriage, Konrad founded Birkenstock as a limited liability company (Konrad Birkenstock GmbH) with a share capital of 500 marks.[7] The founding of such a company was made possible by the GmbH law passed in 1892, which established this legal business category in the German Reich. Prior to that, the norm had been to set up general commercial partnerships, which generally did not limit the liability of the owner. In that year—and this was probably the reason for founding the company—the young master shoemaker introduced the first orthopedic shoe lasts, which were anatomically shaped and thus distinguished between the right and left feet.[8] This invention made Konrad part of a group of young shoemakers who turned the theoretical considerations of the shoe reform movement into practical applications. In doing so, they revolutionized the world of shoes and foot health, since these lasts, which were initially handmade, were later also used in the industrial sector, making shoes more comfortable and healthier for everyone.

The more important innovation, however—one that was to determine the history of the Birkenstock company up to the present day—was his development of a metal-free and therefore flexible insole, which was brought to market in 1902.

At the turn of the century, foot health had become a topical issue. Back in the 1880s, a doctor by the name of Groß von Ellwangen had published a (little-noticed) work on the "natural shoe."[9] Consumers became increasingly aware of foot diseases, with the fashionable penchant among the bourgeoisie for pointed shoes foreshadowing the orthopedic challenges that would accompany the then modern footwear.[10] Nevertheless, Konrad was an unlikely candidate to meet such a challenge. With the fin-de-siècle mood around 1900, expressed in the bourgeoisie through social movements such as *Lebensreform* or the *Naturkult,* there was a general striving, in the face of an "alienated" modernity, to return to a natural way of life.[11] Konrad had little to do with these movements. His son Carl was the first to speak of "walking as nature intended," an expression that later became a watchword for the functionality of the *System Birkenstock.*

In order to solve his customers' problems, Konrad experimented almost nonstop in his workshop and developed new lasts, from which he first made shoes for his own use before selling them to his customers. His son Carl later said that these shoes were exemplary in terms of form, function, and performance. "His shoes, which are perfectly sculpted in every respect, showed amazing differences from all other made-to-measure and factory shoes."[12] Konrad was not primarily interested in earning money from his inventions but rather focused his efforts on developing anatomically shaped shoes that would maintain foot health. He devoted nearly all of the time he could spare from managing his shoe business to experimenting in his workshop.

One of the first results of these efforts was the development in 1897 of the new type of shoe last mentioned above—i. e., a template for the manufacture of shoes. This last was characterized by a "spherical heel" and a plastic longitudinal curve. Konrad's son Carl later saw the "anatomically formed sole track," the shape of the shoe adapted to the foot,

Fig. 14: Konrad Birkenstock (1873–1950) revolutionized shoemaking with his invention of *Health Footwear* Picture from 1924.

Fig. 15: The fully anatomically shaped last invented by Konrad Birkenstock in 1897 mimics the foot anatomically. Unlike in other modern lasts, also on the lower side towards the sole of the foot. A perfection with manufacturing challenges.

as a groundbreaking innovation in the orthopedic shoemaking trade, even comparing his work to that of "Hans Sachs," the famous Nuremberg folk poet and shoemaker from the 16th century.[13] Furthermore, contrary to what was customary at the time, his father's lasts clearly differentiated between the right and the left foot:[14] "Such a revolutionary finding could only come from someone schooled in the shoemaker's trade, because the improved last had to pass its test as a shoe with every patient."[15] This required numerous tests and adjustments for each pair of lasts, taking into account the health of the feet in question and the sensitivity and age of the patient. In this way, Konrad acquired growing expertise, on the basis of which he attempted to give his ideas a broader appeal.

As soon as he had concluded his experiments with the new shoe last, Konrad began work, in 1900, on the invention that was to be of decisive importance for the further development of the young company: a metal-free shoe insole. Insoles are placed inside the shoes and are intended to enable a more comfortable and healthier fit. In contrast to the rigid metal insoles that were common at the time, the metal-free insole was designed to adapt to the moving foot so that it would carry the body weight properly, and existing foot damage would not progress any further. It would, however, be some time before this idea had fully matured. Numerous, sometimes very expensive attempts had to be made to find the right shape and the right material for the insole. In 1909, before they finally came up with a (then very modern) rubber mixture that could offer the necessary material properties, Birkenstock was still making its insoles from cardboard reinforced with leather scraps,[16] and by 1912 from a cork-rubber mixture.[17] A sales brochure from 1920 stated that the insole was made of "rubber mixed with cork or sawdust."[18] Even if cork was already being used in some cases, this material—contrary to what may be claimed elsewhere—was only used to a limited extent in the *System Birkenstock*[19] in the early days of foot orthopedics. In the 30s, Birkenstock still rejected insoles made primarily of cork.[20]

At the beginning of the 20th century, Konrad's customers—shoe shops and private individuals—came from the surrounding area. An accounting book from 1906 lists customers from Marburg to Mannheim.[21] For example, an exchange of letters from 1908 with the shoe store Carl Stiller, which operated a total of four branches in Berlin, has been preserved in the Birkenstock archive. Birkenstock's intention to establish a shoe last storehouse in Berlin was discussed in these letters but probably never realized, even though the company had a sales office in Berlin in the 30s.[22] In any case, winning customers for the modern insoles was a tedious business that required a great deal of time and perseverance.

Konrad referred to some of his insoles as *Footbed*. The company had been using this term in advertising since 1909 in connection with the registered utility model of *Gesundheits-Schuhwerk* (*Health Footwear*) and applied for the term *Footbed* as a trademark on August 5, 1925; it was registered on November 11, 1925.[23] Until the trademark, which had already been registered by a Leipzig shoemaker since December 5, 1913, was cancelled in 1924, Konrad Birkenstock used the trademark *Footbed* with the latter's consent. In the late 20s, this led to lengthy legal disputes with other shoe manufacturers, which requested the cancellation of the trademark.[24]

Konrad Birkenstock was quite confident that he had made a decisive breakthrough in foot orthopedics with the invention of the anatomically shaped last and later the metal-free insole. This motivated him to proclaim his invention in countless specialist lectures starting in 1899. "The older generation of the shoemaking trade will still remember the passionate lectures which were intended to awaken the tradesmen and inspire them to progress."[25] The resounding success he anticipated, however, did not materialize: most of the experts to whom Konrad presented his ideas remained apathetic or were even opposed to these ideas. "But the creative fighter who is convinced of his cause only becomes tougher and more determined when faced with hostility," as his son Carl put it when commenting on this rejection.[26]

Fig. 16: From his insole invented in 1902, Konrad Birkenstock developed several insoles, two of which he sold under the name *Footbed*. It became a bestseller decades later as the *Blue Footbed*.

But perhaps it was precisely this persistent, almost stubborn attitude that after a few years led to the depletion of the family assets and to a loss of Konrad's stamina.[27] In 1910, owing to his financial difficulties, he felt compelled to grant a general license to sell his insoles and lasts to Patent-Centrale GmbH Frankfurt am Main, a private-sector sales company.[28] Now he acted as a "representative" and sold his own lasts and insoles as a licensee of Patent-Centrale. Two contracts have survived, from July 4 and 8, 1910, for 120 and 180 marks.[29] Consequently, the insoles and lasts were officially available only through this office. In a letter to customers, Patent-Centrale then spoke of Konrad Birkenstock's "poor, uncommercial" management and now assured "service that was prompt, sound, and the quickest possible," which makes it clear that this had hitherto not been the case.[30]

Nevertheless, Carl Birkenstock said the arrangement with Patent-Centrale would have startled his actual competitors, who would have seen it as a kind of unfair competition. All things considered, Patent-Centrale did a good job of advertising the *Birkenstock-Footbed*. In any case, this is how Carl explained that his "deeply religious" father had become the target of unjust accusations from his competitors, with allegations ranging from perjury to falsification of documents.[31]

But Carl also remembered that his father had repeatedly advised him not to follow in his footsteps professionally. He should rather do something else:[32] "In families of inventors, life is restless due to the economic ups and downs; every family member lives, whether they like it or not, with constant experimentation and moods, which are prone to sudden changes. Even as a schoolboy, I took a keen interest in my father's orthopedic ideas and incomplete experiments, and the experiences he had in life. In particular, what I observed at a young age left a deep impression on me; the insights only gained deeper value after years of personal practice because they had to be experienced."[33] This quote also makes clear how focused Konrad was in pursuing his goals.

Carl's observations were relevant to his further development because he was the eldest son and joined his father's business in 1915 at the young age of just 15. Shortly before this happened and just after the outbreak of World War I, the business had been relocated, just north of Frankfurt am Main to the small town of Friedberg, the hometown of Konrad's wife. He bought a house there on Fauerbacher Straße, where he also installed the production facilities.[34] The company now operated under the name "Fabrik für Platt- und Hohlfuss-Einlagen, K. Birkenstock" (Factory for Flat and Hollow Foot Insoles, K. Birkenstock).[35] Sales success, especially relating to the insoles—i.e., the *Footbed*—had probably provided the basis for this step. A little later, World War I also reached the Wetterau, and Konrad was drafted into the army. He had already completed his military training and was waiting on the train platform in Frankfurt to be transported to the western front when something quite astonishing happened to him. Having gained a reputation on the basis of his lectures, he was recognized there and conveyed to Karl Ludloff, the director of the Friedrichsheim Clinic in Frankfurt. Ludloff saw an opportunity in this recruit to improve the foot orthopedic expertise of his clinic and managed to have Konrad's marching orders revoked. Konrad spent the remaining years of World War I in the orthopedic workshop of the Friedrichsheim clinic, caring for soldiers' feet and making shoes and insoles for the war-disabled.[36]

The experience was fortunate for him in more ways than one. He not only managed to escape the inferno on the western front, but he was also able to further improve his orthopedic expertise. The war put an enormous strain on the feet of the soldiers, some of whom could not get out of their heavy boots for weeks on end. "The soldiers' deficient footwear under harsh marching conditions also generated symptoms of sagging and stasis in their sore feet."[37] This situation resulted in a great demand for foot orthopedics and for Konrad it presented an excellent opportunity to expand his knowledge in this field. Furthermore, the contacts he made in the clinic later proved to be important not only for him but also for his son Carl. In 1930, the orthopedist Georg Hohmann, who was one of the most important podiatrists of the interwar period,

Fig. 17: The orthopedic shoemaker's shop of Konrad Birkenstock on Bleichstraße in Frankfurt am Main (1907).

became head of the Friedrichsheim clinic.[38] The orthopedist Wilhelm Thomsen also worked at this clinic and was the senior physician there in the 30s. He was one of the most important advocates for metal-free insoles. Carl was still corresponding with him in the 40s and was repeatedly assured of his professional support.[39]

The Friedrichsheim clinic was founded in Wiesbaden in 1896 with a subsidy from the state government of Hesse-Nassau, which enabled the creation of a provisional facility for "care for the crippled."[40] It quickly became one of the 20 most famous orthopedic specialist clinics in Germany.[41] It was then, in 1906, that the first "counting of the crippled" in Germany acted as a wake-up call. Instigated by Konrad Biesalski, the Berlin pioneer of social work and care for the disabled, this initiative made it clear how many people—a number that included more than 100,000 children—were struggling with a permanent physical impairment.[42] The construction of the clinic, which was explicitly intended to treat cripples, was first attempted in Wiesbaden, where it failed on account of protests from residents in this exclusive residential area.[43] An alternative location was found relatively quickly in Frankfurt's Niederrad district, facilitated by Frankfurt's Lord Mayor Franz Adickes, who was committed to the project and promised a connection to the newly founded Frankfurt Foundation University. The construction of the clinic was completed in the fall of 1914, when the war was already in full swing. Initially the Friedrichsheim clinic served primarily as a reserve hospital for the wounded in battle, although orthopedic issues played a major role.[44]

Because of his work at the clinic, Konrad had to severely limit his commitment to his business, although it was located in relatively close proximity to the clinic. The young Carl Birkenstock, who had just finished school, had to take on responsibility in the family business at an early age. His actual career aspirations of "working as a designer and becoming an architect" were off the table.[45] Evidently, he was quite adept at running the business, and demand for the *Footbed* flourished. However, the rubber had to be temporarily replaced with other materials owing to restrictions imposed by the war. After countless attempts, Carl found a substitute material—which is not described in any detail in the sources used for this work—that had the special property of remaining elastic in the shoe through the warmth of the foot. This was ultimately the starting point for another important product in Birkenstock's interwar portfolio, namely the *Elastigang* (elastic stride) insoles.[46]

Remarkably, Carl also took over his father's lecturing and advertising activities for insoles and *Footbeds* during the war. Later, he was himself surprised by the fact that, following an "inner impulse," he had acted as the representative of his father's controversial ideas, especially since he described himself as extremely shy at that time.[47] This lecturing activity, as he later recalled, was a tough school, in particular since he was often not taken seriously by his audience owing to his youth.[48] At the same time, during these early lecture tours, he got the impression that some people had no wish to be convinced, and rejected the metal-free insole on principle because it represented an innovation and would have forced them to rethink their position. Nevertheless, Carl learned in this way to refine his arguments and justifications and to adapt them to different audiences. He did not simply adopt his father's ideas but developed them further and later even expanded them into a "system." This progression was probably due not least to the fact that he had to deal with these ideas intensively from an early age on.[49]

After the end of World War I, a wide range of possibilities opened up in the field of foot orthopedics, and Konrad and Carl attempted to make their insoles better known. Nevertheless, their experiences were rather sobering: it was not long before Carl, like his father, developed an image of himself as an outsider and lone warrior for the right kind of podiatry.

There were, however, also exceptions to these disappointing experiences. Carl reported how, in 1920, he and his father had a public debate in the shop of one of the best-known representatives of metal insoles for shoes. This shop owner was open enough to let the Birkenstocks hold their first foot consultation days in his store. Afterwards, there was an intensive discussion about when metal insoles and when non-metal insoles would be more favorable for patients with foot problems. In the course of these discussions, the Birkenstocks then developed the idea that would later become the basis of foot orthopedics according to the *System Birkenstock*: namely, that the vast majority of foot diseases ultimately represented just one problem in a six-phase series of consequences resulting from culturally induced stress on the feet.[50]

Not yet even 50, Konrad withdrew for the most part from the sales activities of his business in the early 20s. His appearance at a trade fair in Hanover, where he was supposed to present his podiatry, but which ended in dire humiliation, is probably the reason for this withdrawal.[51] Placed on the stage in the largest lecture hall at the fair, he watched as a large number of listeners left the hall early. The condescending attitude of the "leaders of the shoemaker's trade" demoralized the innovative shoemaker. His son, however, was undeterred and continued doing the rounds of the shoe shops. People with foot problems often came to the foot consultation days, bringing bagfuls of insoles with them, with which they were mostly dissatisfied. To ensure better advice, the Birkenstocks began to keep foot control books in which the "patients" could log their experiences with different insoles. Of course, this approach required that the foot consultation days be repeated and held regularly so that the effect of wearing insoles could be properly recorded.[52] In a way, the immediate postwar period represented a formative phase in the development of Birkenstock orthopedics: their *System Birkenstock* would be expanded and refined in the years that followed, without undergoing any fundamental changes.

The admiration that Carl felt for his father's innovations and the obvious inner harmony associated with these foot orthopedic ideas did not, however, prevent serious personal conflicts from arising on a regular basis between father and son. At the beginning of the 20s, their relationship proved to be so complicated that Carl moved to the Austrian capital of Vienna for a year and a half and started Kabi (evidently an abbreviation for Carl Birkenstock, who in those years wrote his name with a "K"), a sales company not only for lasts and insoles but also for an insole with heel support, the so-called *Blue Ring*,[53] which he developed himself. Nonetheless, by his own assessment, Carl's experiences in Vienna were mixed. In 1924, he worked briefly in Basel, while his two younger brothers, Heinrich and Konrad Jr., were gaining their first business experience in Vienna at the Kabi sales company.[54] However, Carl's brothers' management practices were not entirely above board: Heinrich had to leave Vienna in the summer of 1924 because the Kabi company had accused him of forgery and embezzlement. He was entrusted to the guiding hand of his father, Konrad. The youngest son, Konrad Jr., remained temporarily in Vienna.[55]

In 1925, Carl also returned to Hesse, as the sale of Birkenstock insoles increased significantly in the first half of the 20s, and the company had space problems. The firm was able to resolve this issue in July of 1925 by acquiring the former Derfeltsche soap factory in Friedberg.[56] Carl became a partner in the parent company, which was re-established on May 2, 1925, as a limited liability company K. Birkenstock GmbH with a share capital of 5,000 Reichsmarks (which was rather low). The partnership was apparently the main reason for Carl's reconciliation with his father.[57] Konrad's two youngest sons were also introduced to the business and worked at the K. Birkenstock GmbH. Konrad Birkenstock Jr. officially entered the business in 1925, his brother Heinrich (possibly as a result of the problems that had arisen in Vienna) a little later.

Shortly thereafter, however, tensions between Carl and his father flared up again, prompting Carl to move to a large northern German city that he referred to only as "H."[58] In 1929, Carl set up his own business in Steinhude am Meer, west of Hanover, when he and his younger brother Heinrich founded the Gebr. Birkenstock GmbH für orthopädische Spezialitäten in October 1929 in Steinhude with a share capital of 20,000 Reichsmarks.[59]

The founding of the firm in Steinhude can definitely be interpreted as a "flight" by the Birkenstock sons from their authoritarian father, with whom they lived in a state of constant dispute. Heinrich worked as managing director of Gebr. Birkenstock GmbH in Steinhude until 1931, when he lost this position due to a preliminary injunction by the district court of Stadthagen, apparently ordered by Carl.[60] After leaving that firm, he and his brother-in-law, Alfred Weber, entered the limited liability company under the name of K. Birkenstock GmbH in Friedberg with a share capital of 20,000 Reichsmarks.[61] Their father, Konrad, had previously been asked several times to register his company in the commercial register, which he delayed in doing, and announced in November 1931 that it was now a GmbH (limited liability company), which was set up on September 2, 1931—the same company that his son Heinrich and son-in-law, Alfred, joined as managing directors.

Konrad Birkenstock Jr. was also employed by the Gebr. Birkenstock GmbH in Steinhude starting in 1937, before relocating to Berlin in 1939 after conflicts with his brother Carl. The relationship between the siblings thus proved early on to be complicated and strife-ridden.[62] While Gebr. Birkenstock GmbH in Steinhude applied for liquidation in 1939—a process that was not completed until the late 40s—the Friedbergers converted the company into an OHG (Offene Handelsgesellschaft, general commercial partnership). Carl's sister, Catharina Weber, joined as a partner, and the company operated as Gebr. Birkenstock OHG. Carl in turn traded, after 1939, as Carl Birkenstock, Steinhude.

Apart from these family disputes, there were also many conflicts involving the business management of Gebr. Birkenstock GmbH in Steinhude. These conflicts centered on authorities in the field of "orthodox" orthopedics, whom the Birkenstocks accused of refusing, out of habit or malice, to recognize the benefits of metal-free insoles. After World War I, there were millions of disabled people who had to be cared for, at least to some extent, by the state. In this regard, the delivery of medical products to state hospitals was highly controversial. In 1929, the Hesse Main Supply Office, which was responsible for supplying the medical and sanitary needs of war invalids, explained in a letter to the Wiesbaden Chamber of Crafts why the number of approved suppliers was so small: the necessary relationship of trust with the supplying companies was difficult to establish, the need for these medical supplies was declining as the war receded in time, and the deliveries could be accepted only on certain days when medical examinations were taking place. For these reasons, it was actually very difficult for many companies to break into the system of government procurement.[63]

On the other hand, there was the suspicion that only members of certain professional associations would benefit from these orders. There was also speculation that the partially state-owned Deutsche Orthopädie-Werke would be given preference in the awarding of contracts. The chambers of commerce tried to persuade the pension offices to adopt a more open procurement policy, but they were only partially successful.

Another very controversial aspect in this regard was which insoles were recommended and paid for by the health insurance companies. Birkenstock insoles were not approved for coverage by health insurance companies for a long time. As late as in the 30s, the company was still vehemently complaining in advertisements that health insurance companies should not fight for or against a system of insoles but work to ensure "that the patient is helped and the health insurance companies spend their funds carefully."[64] That the health insurance companies had a fixed circle of suppliers that outsiders could only penetrate with great difficulty remained, in particular, a thorn in Birkenstock's side.

In the face of these institutional obstacles, the Birkenstock family continued to rely on its lecturing engagements and word of mouth as marketing vehicles. Its hopes rested on the shoemakers and shoe dealers, since government agencies and health insurance companies were still not ready to endorse metal-free insoles. With the establishment in 1922 of the "Association of Orthopedic Master Shoemakers," the orthopedic practitioners had for the first time their own organization to represent their interests.[65] But Carl's problem was actually quite different: "I soon realized that my opponents' knowledge was surprisingly poor, and their lack of interest in orthopedic problems was all the greater."[66] For him, the barriers mentioned above were ultimately just an expression of ignorance of the ideas that he and his father had developed.

In the 20s, Birkenstock began selling its insoles in other European countries. At the same time, and until the outbreak of World War II, a foreign competitor appeared on the European market in the field of metal-free insoles: the American Dr. Scholl company, which was founded in 1906 and specialized in orthopedic foot-care products.[67] None of this mattered to Carl. Undeterred, he continued to pursue his own path in the field of podiatry.[68]

Overall, during the 20s Birkenstock was able to increase its insole sales continuously.[69] Nevertheless, the K. Birkenstock GmbH in Friedberg and the Gebr. Birkenstock GmbH founded in Steinhude in 1929 remained small companies, each with fewer than 15 employees. Birkenstock had established a niche for itself as a supplier of orthopedic specialties—primarily insoles, as well as shoe lasts, foot powder, and other items. The numerous positive customer testimonials that Konrad had collected since the turn of the century make it clear that the company had a relatively small but enthusiastic following early on. The world economic crisis of 1929, which shook the German economy severely, led to a significant drop in sales, but the company's existence does not appear to have been seriously threatened.[70]

"The Truly Ethical Man Does Not Cripple Himself":[1] Shoe Designs by the *Lebensreform* Movement

BY JOHANNA STEINFELD

Naked men and women dancing (see fig. 18): the photograph is reminiscent of the hippie scene of the 60s, but it actually originates from the days of the German Empire and shows a group from the so-called *Lebensreform* movement. This movement included various groupings of primarily middle-class people in Germany and other countries in Europe who aspired to a natural life away from the "mainstream." This natural life was intended to be the opposite of the perceived alienation of living in the rapidly growing, cramped, and polluted big cities as well as the capitalist-cum-materialist way of life. The focus was also on the body, which had to be respected, liberated, cared for, and strengthened.[2] In this context, clothing and especially footwear were granted a new status: the latter was likewise now to take its cue from the natural state of things, an idea that seemed almost revolutionary in relation to the footwear that had previously been symmetrical and poorly adapted to the foot.

In this regard, members of the movement were able to draw on ideas that had been developed and discussed decades earlier by sci-entists: in the mid-19th century, Hermann Georg Meyer (1815–1892), an anatomy professor at the Swiss Federal Institute of Technology in Zurich, created shoe designs based on the line of the inside of the foot between the big toe and the center of the heel—the Meyerian line, as it was later called in his honor.[3] In practice, his concept was initially applied where suitable footwear was particularly important owing to the long distances to be covered, namely in the Swiss and Prussian military.[4] Meyer's findings, which he published in his 1858 paper "Die richtige Gestalt der Schuhe" (The Correct Shape of Shoes), were adopted by other medical doctors, who addressed the topic in lectures and publications. Among them were Albert Hoffa, professor at the University of Würzburg and one of the founders of German orthopedics, who in his 1899 booklet "Der menschliche Fuss und seine Bekleidung" (The Human Foot and Its Clothing) contrasted the "unspoiled" state of the foot with the state in which it would be placed by wearing shoes that were not appropriate for the respective foot.[5] When advocating the use of "proper shoes," Hoffa field-

Fig. 18: A return to nature—an early 20th century trend.

ed arguments that corresponded to the social Darwinist ideas of the time: "Not only is the soldier unfit for battle if he cannot march, but also in the struggle for existence every man needs his feet for his 'advancement.'"[6] To demonstrate his remarks, Hoffa used X-ray images of feet. After the discovery of X-rays in 1895, these pictures were, as Hoffa himself wrote, "a very nice means" to prove scientific hypotheses.[7]

The scientific findings on the "reform shoe" also reached the shoemakers and were partially taken up by them. Some shoemakers even interpreted them according to their own lights or developed them further in the belief that they understood more about their craft than the "learned gentlemen." Konrad Birkenstock also dealt with the flaws of conventional shoe models, which he contrasted with the *Ideal-Schuh*.[8]

Alongside the reform-minded shoemakers, however, there were also those who wanted to stick to conventional designs and came out in fierce opposition to the so-called rational shoe.[9]

The *Lebensreform* members took up the ideas for the new shoes (the "reform shoes") and developed various shoe models, often without consulting the scientific findings. One popular choice were the sandals by the Wörishofen priest Sebastian Kneipp (1821 – 1897), who became known for his water treatments, as well as advice on nutrition, education, and clothing, and advised his patients to wear airy shoes in a shape suitable for their feet. The company August Wessels in Augsburg adopted this model and began producing Kneipp sandals around the turn of the century.[10] In addition, however, closed "reform shoes" were also produced, initially in smaller workshops and later also in factories.[11] Some particularly far-fetched models provided individual chambers for the big toe or for all the toes, although the toe-chamber shoe model, for which Max Mannesmann applied for a patent in 1906, failed to catch on—only followers of the *Wandervogel* movement wore the unusual shoes.[12]

This movement, which emerged in Berlin at the turn of the century and quickly found followers throughout the country, brought together young women and men who developed their own, youthful interpretation of the *Lebensreform* ideas. The young people focused primarily on a natural way of life, renouncing alcohol and tobacco and immersing themselves in nature. For parts of the *Wandervogel* movement, the choice of rational footwear was not only motivated by hygiene or orthopedics but was also associated with higher values. This was matched by the exaltation of clothing appropriate to the body and foot by Paul Schultze-Naumburg (1869–1949), who described it in his writing on fe-

male clothing as an "expression of higher humanity."[13] It was no surprise that Schultze-Naumburg's linking of footwear with ethical issues struck a chord with the youthful *Wandervogel* adherents, who also expressed their attitude by wearing "System Schultze-Naumburg" boots.[14] The new "essence" of the youth movement was also to be expressed in a new form of clothing, as Christian Schneehagen, a student and member of the *Wandervogel* movement, wrote in "Unsere Kleidung" (Our Clothing).[15]

This booklet was published on the occasion of the *Freideutscher Jugendtag*, a meeting of the emergent youth in 1913 on the Hoher Meissner mountain in Hessen with participants numbering between 2,000 and 3,000. Several short chapters in "Unsere Kleidung" were intended to inspire the design of a "new men's and women's folk-wear." A separate section, written by the artist Hermann Pfeiffer, was devoted to shoes and exposed the chauvinism of the Germans: for while they made fun of Chinese women's bound feet, offenses against their own feet went unremarked. Pfeiffer tied in here with Paul Schultze-Naumburg and brought together the striving for a higher humanity with blood-and-soil arguments: "The crippling of the body, be it out of vanity or indifference, is a barbarity, especially unworthy of a people that is proud of having shaken off foreign rule, while being all the more unconditionally obedient to another, that of foreign fashion."[16]

World War I abruptly ended the imperial era with its favorable climate for experimentation, in which doctors, scientists, shoemakers, and *Lebensreform* advocates had tried their hand at new designs and models of the "reform shoe." Yet some of the ideas about reform clothing and "reform shoes" that were linked to higher ethical or political issues survived and later combined with the Nazis' racist-ethnic outlook. However, to what extent did the new insights and ideas prevail in shoe manufacturing all the same? Although the shoe designs of the *Lebensreform* members were often not suitable for everyday use, the ideas of the "reform shoe" became known to a broad public through the rapid translation of the rational shoe into production. The military also acted as a driving force for progress: as early as World War I, soldiers of all nations were fighting while wearing foot-friendly shoes. Even though it was still a long way from there to the "comfortable shoe," at least the production of shoes in a pair—i. e., "the minimal objective of all shoe-reforming movements and schools"—had largely become established after the war.[17]

Between a Sense of Purpose and Generating Sales: The Question of Finding the Right Partner for Foot Orthopedics

Konrad Birkenstock gave numerous lectures in a bid to market the shoe last and insoles he had developed. In addition, he was able to record successes at various trade fairs. He received an honorary diploma at an orthopedic trade fair in Augsburg in 1914; silver medals followed in Darmstadt and Frankfurt in 1921 and 1924, respectively, before the company was awarded a gold medal at a trade exhibition in Darmstadt in 1924 for its achievements in the field of foot orthopedics.[71]

Although three of Konrad's children showed far less missionary zeal, Carl continued to develop his father's innovations, systematizing them into an independent "system" of foot orthopedics, and writing books about them: "I can certainly claim to have studied everything that was for or against our science with open eyes and fanatical zeal,"[72] he stated. This led to numerous conflicts with other players in the field of foot orthopedics, especially in the 30s, and Carl was vehement in dealing with these conflicts. However, it is doubtful whether this helped his business. The fundamental importance that his ideas had for foot health was not reflected in the sales figures for the insoles. But that didn't matter to Carl; like his father, he was concerned with the core idea, the purpose of what they were doing—namely, helping people to choose shoes that would keep their feet healthy.

Podiatry was still a relatively young field in the 20s and 30s. Little was known for sure about the foot and the causes of foot problems, which Georg Hohmann—the well-known expert on foot orthopedics and "orthopedic teacher of a whole generation"[73] (as well as head of the Friedrichsheimer Klinik since 1930[74])—more or less openly admitted in his textbook "Fuss und Bein." However, the general consensus was that insoles had to be fitted to each foot individually, and that this should be the task of a doctor. Here, however, the accusation arose that there was also an economic interest behind this practice, because doctors were able to secure a lucrative business in their medical practice with a simple insole compactor. At the same time, the physicians actually favored metal insoles that were individually fitted using a plaster cast and were designed to correct foot deformities.[75]

In practice, there were a large number of insoles, some of which actually had little to do with today's ideas of effective foot treatment and comfort. There were insoles with metal springs, made of aluminum or other metals, which were at most covered with a thin layer of celluloid. Carl was polemical in his rejection of these insoles, but he was certainly not entirely wrong in his criticism. In 1934, the Reich Ministry of the Interior even said it had to warn against some shoe inserts in the Reichsärzteblatt, because in many cases they could aggravate foot problems.[76] However, Birkenstock was by no means the only supplier of metal-free insoles: for example, the "Pneumette" insoles, which worked with air cushions, were made by the Klotz company in Munich and were still on the market; the Lettermann insoles were also still available, as was an insole brought out by the Gustav Krause company in Berlin, which advertised their products with the catchy slogan: "Ich laufe wie eine Biene" (lit.: I walk like a bee).[77]

From the early 20s, Carl worked to organize his father's ideas and shape them into a "system."[78] Everything was subordinated to the struggle against the metal inserts, which he described as "instruments of torture."[79] He introduced a number of innovations to justify the superiority of nonmetallic shoe inserts: more clearly than his father, he explained that a large proportion—according to him up to 90 percent!—of the population suffered from foot diseases in one way or another. These foot disorders, in turn, were not due to special circumstances but rather to the effects of civilization: "unnatural" walking on stone and asphalt stressed feet in ways not intended by nature. According to Carl, the human foot evolved to walk on natural ground: "The foot is designed by nature to walk barefoot on soft, uneven natural ground. [...] Natural soil means earth, sand, grass, fields, pebbles, rocks, and other uneven terrain. The ground in its natural state provides a diverse and varied surface for the foot; this interaction with ordinary soil is of great importance for the natural functioning of the foot."[80]

In walking "as nature intended," the different arches of the foot were evenly burdened, creating what is known as a *Trittspur* or footprint. The toes were intended to act as grippers, guaranteeing a safe forward push-off and also serving as anti-slip protection. However, under the conditions of modern civilization, this natural way of walking on uneven ground was no longer easily possible. On hard stone floors, the feet were constantly under the wrong pressure because the shoe was only designed for three points of contact. The feet would therefore almost inevitably become impaired. Having determined this, Carl focused on the fact that the large number of foot diseases diagnosed by contemporary orthopedics could basically be systematized with comparative ease. Contrary to what many orthopedists claimed, in his opinion not all feet are different; rather, there were essentially feet with weak tendons and ligaments (the majority) and feet with strong tendons and ligaments (the minority). Feet with weak tendons and ligaments developed six stages of foot disease; those with strong tendons and ligaments would develop only two stages of disease. According to Birkenstock, these were not different clinical cases, but rather stages of increasing foot damage caused by the effects of civilization.

With weak tendons and ligaments, these stages of foot disease were "soft splayfoot" (1), the mildest form, in which the transverse arch of the foot was slightly deformed. This was followed by "skew foot up to the five metatarsals" (2), in which the metatarsals had begun to deform and loosen from the arch formation. The third and fourth stages were "skew foot up to the three cuneiform bones" (3) and "skew foot up to the navicular bone" (4), which in turn were defined by the extent of the deformation of the foot bones. This was followed by "fallen arches" (5), in which the navicular bone had loosened from its structure, and the ankle bone (talus) had started to give way. While the typical symptoms of the first four stages of the disease, such as gout or hammer toes, often disappeared, pain in the foot and leg and rapid fatigue when walking began to occur. The last stage of the disease was the notorious "flat foot" (6), for many people the epitome of a foot disease, which, contrary to general opinion, was comparatively rare according to Birkenstock.[81]

Feet with extremely strong tendons and ligaments only developed two types of disease, but both were extremely painful. On the one hand, there was the "cartilaginous splayfoot" (1) and the *pes cavus* or hollow foot (2), both of which were, according to Birkenstock, the result of permanent improper burdening of the feet.[82]

The therapy for these foot diseases of all eight types (feet with weak and strong tendons and ligaments) consisted in wearing the insoles developed by Birkenstock, which were intended to replicate the natural footprint. In doing so, he developed a differentiated scheme for their use: unlike many standard insoles prescribed by health insurance companies, the Birkenstock insole was to be adapted to the individual foot and not to the shoe.[83] In addition, there were insoles with different degrees of hardness, which were to be selected according to the degree of damage to the specific foot.[84] A characteristic feature was the "ring," which was patented in the 30s and allowed for the foot support to be individually adjusted. With this insole ring, the heel bone was softly bedded and the foot was laterally supported by the raised edge of the insole. The toes had enough space for free movement and the instep was relieved of pressure. An important keyword here was "walking mobility"—i. e., the feet were not "locked in" by the insoles but were able to move relatively freely.[85]

Carl Birkenstock was well aware that his superior insole would not prevail in the market by itself, which is why "phlegmatic" waiting was out of the question for him. Later he would continue to emphasize the importance of advertising in conveying the right idea of foot health and to quote the motto: "He who doesn't advertise, dies."[86] One way to convey his system was to write books and articles in the specialist journals. In 1930, the publication of "Der Fuß und seine Behandlung" (The Foot and Its Treatment) marked the beginning of this advertising campaign. In 1935, the more extensive text "Mit dem Arzt gegen Fußkrankheiten und Irrlehren" (With the Doctor Against Foot Diseases and Heresies) followed. Both books were self-published and only handed out to selected customers. The reason given was that there would otherwise be a risk that reading one of these books might replace attendance on his training course. Because he was not a doctor, Carl had failed in his attempt to place the manuscripts with a medical publisher.[87] This meant that only the self-publishing route remained.

In 1941, Carl then wrote a partially autobiographical text entitled "40 Jahre Einsatz für vernünftige Fußbekleidung" (40 Years of Commitment to Reasonable Footwear), which he revised 20 years later and then wanted to give the title "60 Jahre Einsatz für vernünftige Fußbekleidung." However, the manuscript remained unpublished, even though Carl occasionally referred to it in other works. By his own account, the print runs for his works were quite impressive: 35,000 copies for "Der Fuß und seine Behandlung"; 24,000 copies for "Mit dem Arzt gegen Fußkrankheiten und Irrlehren"; and 19,000 copies for "Fußorthopädie: Das System Carl Birkenstock". Nevertheless, the fact that these editions, as Carl claimed after World War II, were "completely out of print," and he had to buy antiquarian copies at high prices, would seem rather to indicate a more generous distribution.[88]

In addition to his book publications, Carl repeatedly published articles and "letters to the editor" in the relevant specialist publications such as Schuh und Leder or Schuhmarkt, in which he tried to give his ideas a broader impact. In so doing, however, he regularly wavered between wild insinuations about the various groups that were supposedly preventing the implementation of his concepts, and appeals for reconciliation, combined with the demand that conflicting interests be put aside in favor of the joint effort to improve foot health.[89] This was, of course, always to be done under the banner of the podiatry he had developed. The sometimes offensive tone of his writing led to many conflicts in the 30s, whereby he was obliged to withdraw some statements. For example, the book "Mit dem Arzt gegen Fußkrankheiten und Irrlehren" was prefaced with the text of a court settlement from 1935, in which Birkenstock undertook to no longer speak of "so-called specialist shops" and also to refrain from other insults.[90] In addition, the settlement text also found fault with the title of the book, in particular its handling of the term "doctor," when not a single licensed physician was cited.[91]

To better understand these conflicts, one must take a closer look at the field of orthopedics during the 20s and 30s. During the interwar period, there were three main interest groups in the field of foot orthopedics: First, there were the physicians, who in principle had the greatest professional authority owing to their academic background. Secondly, the truss makers played a crucial role. These were practical orthopedic specialists who fitted and adjusted orthopedic aids (particularly prostheses) and sometimes even constructed these devices themselves.[92] Today this profession is no longer common but was important after the two world wars because of the high number of war invalids. Thirdly, the shoemakers played a role as they often also acted as specialist dealers for shoes. The Birkenstocks felt the strongest connection to this group because they themselves came from their ranks. Furthermore, Carl also argued that the shoemakers had the most frequent, often everyday, contact with their customers and were also the first to hear about their experiences. What they might lack in academic knowledge, they made up for in practical experience. Carl therefore harbored the hope for a long time that his insoles would gain acceptance through specialist shoe retailers, which would have forced other interest groups to pay more attention to his system.[93]

The Birkenstock training courses were an important means of publicizing the metal-free insole. These had their origins in the previously mentioned foot consultation days which the company had organized and conducted since World War I. Beginning in the early 30s, Birkenstock had been holding week-long seminars designed to teach shoe salespeople the basics of how the *Footbed* worked. An important reason for this was that by the end of the 20s, the Birkenstock company was already supplying about 6,000 specialist shoe shops, although this was by no means considered sufficient: "In practice, it often had to be established that people with foot problems could only be completely satisfied when all facets of customer service were working in harmony."[94] According to Carl, the sales staff's lack of understanding of how the insoles worked prevented the correct application of the *System Birkenstock*, and it was therefore not possible for it to achieve its full healing effect.[95]

The conclusion that Carl drew from this observation was both radical and self-assured: in 1933, he decided to supply his products only

Fig. 19: Driven by his uncompromising demand for quality, Carl Birkenstock (2nd f. l.) supplied his *System Birkenstock* from the early 30s only to successful graduates of his training courses. Picture from 1935.

to specialist shops whose representatives had attended a one-week training course with him. At the same time, there was a wide range of training courses offered by all kinds of providers at the time, most of which were commercially oriented and for this reason did not have a good reputation. The first training course that Carl organized only had seven participants, two of whom were from the Netherlands and Romania.[96] In the years that followed, however, his training courses, which had the great advantage of being tuition-free, became quite popular. At the end of the 30s, around 9,500 specialist shoe shops were still selling Birkenstock insoles.[97] Nevertheless, in the mid-30s the state education authorities made efforts to ban the courses, because the diplomas issued after course completion stated that the graduates of the courses were "foot orthopedists."[98] Carl was able to successfully defend himself against this ban, however.[99]

In addition to the training courses, Carl's extensive correspondence was also very effective in conveying his system. As he had done since his father initiated this practice, he devotedly collected testimonials that reported positively on their patients' experiences with Birkenstock insoles. Gustav Steinrück assured him in a letter from 1941 that he had already prepared himself to walk on crutches, and that he had sacrificed the six marks for Birkenstock insoles only with great skepticism. These insoles had actually helped him a great deal, and now he could walk longer distances again largely without pain.[100] Another reason Carl collected such reports was because the positive practical experiences with his insoles seemed to prove the extent to which doctors and truss makers ignored the actual problems.

Nonetheless, Carl also used these letters as "evidence" in legal disputes, some of which he conducted in the 20s and 30s. As already mentioned, in 1935 he had to conclude a court settlement with the Reich Association of Truss Makers and Orthopedic Technicians, in which he retracted individual formulations of his book "Mit dem Arzt gegen Fußkrankheiten und Irrlehren." In the years 1937 and 1938, he dealt with the "Reich Working Group to Combat Crippling Illness" which also accused him of denigrating the truss makers in various advertising brochures.[101] Again and again, he became embroiled in legal disputes owing to polemical statements he had made about metal inserts and the work of the truss makers.[102]

From Carl's point of view, the biggest opponents to his concepts and practices were actually the truss makers. He also sometimes found the medical profession to be aloof and arrogant in the language they used. Furthermore, it annoyed him that they claimed sole authority over the correct treatment of the foot and thus also over the use of insoles.[103] The problem with the truss makers, however, was that they—like the shoe-makers—worked practically with people's feet every day and yet could not decide to abandon the metal inlay. As "craftspeople," they were in direct competition with the shoemakers for a collaborative exchange with the medical profession.[104] Carl had his most serious arguments with the professional associations of these competitors under the Third Reich, although the podiatrists were also by no means always well disposed toward him. For example, in 1937 the well-known Leipzig podiatrist and co-founder of the Testing and Research Center for Shoe and Shoe Last Construction, Franz Schede, wrote a partially sympathetic but ultimately negative account of Birkenstock's orthopedics. In particular, he became irritated over the fact that Birkenstock's training courses were supposed to enable shoe retailers (i. e., lay people!) to acquire enough knowledge in just one week to be able to provide specialist orthopedic advice to customers. In Schede's opinion, that was simply not possible.[105] Back in 1934, the prominent podiatrist Eckhardt had admitted that Birkenstock's products, in particular the ready-made insoles, were better than most of the others on the market. At the same time, however, he stated that Birkenstock would harm public health by claiming that it could in general cure foot diseases.[106]

However, there were also doctors who supported Birkenstock's ideas: one doctor from Steinhude (Carl's place of residence) named Alfred Bredthauer published an article in the Schuhhändler-Zeitung in 1935, which was more or less a summary of "Mit dem Arzt gegen Fußkrankheiten und Irrlehren."[107] The most important proponent of Birkenstock's approach, however, was the podiatrist Wilhelm Thomsen, who in 1941 published the widely acclaimed work "Kampf wider die Fußschwäche" and made intensive efforts during the Third Reich to motivate shoe manufacturers to produce shoes that were more suitable for the foot.[108] Thomsen already knew Konrad Birkenstock from their time together at the Friedrichsheim clinic in Frankfurt am Main. Although he himself considered foot massage and gymnastics to be the most effective healing methods, Thomsen was an advocate of Birkenstock insoles. Carl Birkenstock emphasized this enthusiastically and often. Thomsen once wrote to him, "Your cause is so good that you no longer need to fight for it."[109] In his publications from the early 40s, Thomsen saw the military fitness of the German people endangered by the incorrect treatment of feet and insoles.[110] Carl met Thomsen in the mid-30s and had several very open discussions with him. They then carried out walking exercises together with soldiers. It was, however, not possible to convince the military doctors—who in turn could have influenced the procurement system—of the serviceability of Birkenstock's insoles.[111] Another "ally" of Birkenstock was the well-known shoemaker Max Sahm, whose father had known Konrad Birkenstock during his time in Frankfurt.[112]

All in all, it does seem remarkable that despite the relatively small economic "footprint" of the Birkenstock companies, Carl, in particular, succeeded in making the metal-free insoles widely known and winning new customers through his publications, training courses, and advertising brochures. It was precisely through his sometimes provocative rhetoric and over-the-top formulations that he forced his opponents to confront his theses and to justify the metal insert. On the other hand, this also had the negative effect that Birkenstock increasingly began to portray himself as an outsider who had found the "truth," but whose findings were not recognized because of tradition, laziness, or simple ignorance. This form of self-portrayal was by no means atypical for the interwar period,[113] but it did little in real terms to increase the prospects for success of Birkenstock foot orthopedics.

Birkenstock in the Third Reich

During the 20s, Carl Birkenstock made a self-sacrificing effort to popularize Birkenstock insoles. His younger siblings, however, only slowly began to take on more responsibility in the company. In 1929, the establishment of the Gebr. Birkenstock GmbH, Steinhude was a step toward dividing up the territory between Konrad Birkenstock and his three sons and resolving internal family conflicts. There are some indications that Carl was not alone in making the move to set up his own business in Steinhude, and that his brothers went along with him. Nevertheless, there were repeated shifts during the 30s before the situation of the company stabilized to some extent in the second half of the decade.

For the Gebr. Birkenstock GmbH in Steinhude, the Nazi period began with a real "bang," in the shape of Carl's decision to only supply specialist shops that had attended a training course based on his system. He himself described the economic consequences of this measure as drastic: the company had more than 6,000 customers and had made great efforts to retain them in the past.[114] For the most part, these customers were all dropped, "since my remedies were, for prestige and scientific reasons, only sold to specialist companies with trained staff. Hence the strong reputation of our restorative correctives."[115] The background to this decision was Birkenstock's assumption that metal-free insoles would not catch on if they were not used and fitted properly by shoe retailers. This decision shows that for Carl the "ideal" factors in foot orthopedics had priority over business considerations. On occasion, he also railed against excessive prices for insoles and spoke contemptuously of "commercial foot aids."[116]

At the same time, however, Carl saw the Nazi takeover of power as an opportunity to interest the state authorities in his insoles. He later wrote that in 1933 podiatry was also changing. "Professional groups and organizations now saw the unique opportunity to use power to achieve their goals, when confusion did not allow for a peaceful settlement."[117] In plain language, this meant that the state institutions should now enforce the right podiatry from above, so to speak, after this goal had not been achieved under democratic conditions. Accordingly, under the new circumstances, Carl did everything in his power to make his insoles known to government agencies and organizations: "In the years 1933/34, I applied to the military authorities, health insurance associations, ministries, labor services, H.J. [Hitler Jugend = Hitler Youth], BDM [Bund Deutscher Mädel = League of German Girls], etc. etc. and tried for months at my own expense and under medical supervision to prove in terms of practice that my system was correct."[118]

These efforts, nevertheless, do not seem to have been particularly successful, but they did probably lead to a series of test cases he was permitted to conduct. In 1934, Carl visited "the highest health authorities" in Berlin, which enabled him to carry out "practical experiments on a broad basis." These were intended for Adolf Hitler's Leibstandarte SS (Personal Bodyguard Regiment). "The author and Walter Cohen (at his request, of course) appear, and the following information is announced to the Team outside Basic 8, as it came to be known: the test trial in Lichterfelde must be postponed. It was suggested to the regiment doctor to gather all those left behind at the infirmary in 2 hours. Result: 170 men, who had not been selected."[119]

In 1934, Carl was given the opportunity to demonstrate the military suitability of his insoles in this "large-scale test." He fitted his insoles to 170 members of this SS company in Berlin-Lichterfelde, whose feet he meticulously cataloged and whose suffering he classified into his 6/2-phase scheme of foot weakness caused by the effects of civilization. He himself described the result as clearly disastrous and blamed the poor condition of the SS men's feet on the riding shoes used by the formation. These shoes had a longitudinal shaft which was said to cause massive damage to the feet (see table 1).

Despite all this, these efforts did not lead to any government contracts. Subsequently, Carl tried again and again to advertise his products to government agencies. His most important goal was the state Research Center for Shoe and Shoe Last Construction founded in 1938, in which Georg Hohmann and Wilhelm Thomsen played an important role. In this instance, Birkenstock even suspected that the researchers at these institutions had some type of foot injury that his insoles could help to alleviate.[121] In any case, cooperation with the research center was a goal that he was striving for and which he came comparatively close to achieving, in that he was actually (probably in 1938) invited to a meeting at the center. Birkenstock complained, nevertheless, that the promised

0: Normal feet	1
1: Splay feet	10
2: Skew foot (talipes valgus) metatarsal bones	29
3: Skew foot (talipes valgus) cuneiform bone	78
4: Skew foot (talipes valgus) navicular bone	48
5: Flat feet (fallen arches)	3
6: Flat feet (talipes planus)	0
7: Cartilaginous splay feet	1
8: Hollow feet (talipes cavus)	0
Sweaty feet	28

Table 1: Results of the foot examination of the Leibstandarte SS Adolf Hitler, Berlin-Lichterfelde 1934.[120]

tests with his insoles were not due to be carried out in his presence. In addition, he later regarded it as a proven fact that one of the examining doctors himself was contractually bound to a health insurance company and was therefore "biased."[122]

There was another aspect of the new Nazi regime that was a thorn in Carl Birkenstock's side: in 1935, orthopedic shoemakers were assigned to the specialist subgroup "Precision Mechanics and Optics" which at first glance did not seem to fit. The economic groups of the Third Reich (which were each divided into specialist groups and specialist subgroups) were the state-organized successor to the professional interest groups of the Weimar Republic.[123] They were supposed to represent the interests of the different sectors in relation to the state and at the same time organize an exchange of knowledge. The main problem here was that orthopedic shoemakers were now organized together with truss makers in a specialist group and at the same time were separated from the shoemakers and shoe dealers. In Carl's opinion, this constellation diminished the shoemakers' unity and political power in the arguments about insoles and the right footwear.[124] It also brought restrictions with it because many shoemakers were forbidden by the specialist subgroup from fitting orthopedic objects (including insoles) on their own.[125]

From Carl's point of view, the reorganization of the professional representation of interest groups was also a problem, not least because he was involved in various legal disputes in the second half of the 30s, which involved "denigrating" statements he had made. He later attributed these disputes to his courage in aggressively defending his own point of view on foot orthopedics under the political conditions of the 30s.[126] All in all, however, they can partly be understood—and his later statements support this view—as an unmistakable expression of bitter resentment, because he was not granted any real opportunity to promote his insoles and his foot orthopedics. This bitterness was not always understandable, because at least during World War II, his sale of insoles increased significantly, and the health insurance companies now also often assumed the costs for Birkenstock insoles.[127]

During the 30s, there were also several changes in the company structure. In any case, Konrad Birkenstock Jr. seems to have had problems with his brother Carl early on, and registered a shoe factory in Bad Nauheim in June 1934, which subsequently no longer appears in the company records.[128] And in 1937 there was a change in the Gebr. Birkenstock GmbH in Steinhude: Heinrich and Konrad Jr., who had previously been listed there together with their brother Carl as shareholders and managing directors, now left the company. Konrad Jr. moved to Berlin in the

Fig. 20: Although the family dynamics were complex, despite all the differences in interests, the family pulled together when it came to foot health. Front (left to right): Konrad, Elisabeth, Konrad Jr.'s wife, and Konrad Jr. Birkenstock. Back (from right to left): Carl and Emmi Birkenstock, Alfred and Catharina Weber, Heinrich's wife, and Heinrich Birkenstock.

same year and managed his own sales area there.[129] At the same time, the "Birkenstock Community" was founded, which, among other changes, undertook a division of sales areas to correspond to the production sites in Steinhude, Friedberg, and Berlin (Büdingen was later added).[130] This arrangement was obviously an attempt to ease the conflicts between the five interest groups (Konrad, Catharina, née Birkenstock, with her husband Alfred Weber, and the three brothers Heinrich, Konrad Jr., and Carl) after Konrad Jr. exited the Gebr. Birkenstock GmbH in Steinhude "without any reason," according to his brother Carl.[131] Another change came in the form of the uniform design and addition of the phrase "in the Birkenstock community" used on the letterheads in the correspondence of the Friedberg, Berlin, and Steinhude companies.[132]

Nonetheless, this arrangement only lasted until 1939, when Carl left the association and no longer felt bound by the division of sales areas. The liquidation of the old Gebr. Birkenstock GmbH, Steinhude took an unreasonably long time. Carl considered his insoles to be orthopedically superior to those produced in Friedberg or Berlin.[133] In the same year, K. Birkenstock GmbH in Friedberg was converted into an open trading company, owned by Alfred Weber and his wife Catharina and Heinrich and Konrad Birkenstock.[134] Converting to a partnership was a common choice in the late 30s, because in 1934 the Nazis had introduced better tax conditions for partnerships.[135] Heinrich soon set up his own business in Büdingen, the family's old hometown.[136] The division into sales areas was subsequently maintained, and the Birkenstock community continued to exist without Carl.[137] However, the sales areas were evidently violated again and again by all parties, which led to continuing arguments between the siblings.[138]

Why was the market divided up in this way? Personal incompatibilities between the siblings certainly played an important role. While dealings within the Birkenstock family were generally characterized by an abrasive tone,[139] tensions arose again and again, especially in the collaboration between Carl and his siblings. Against this background, the division of business made sense after Konrad Birkenstock gradually withdrew from day-to-day business in the period up to 1939. In the following years, however, various "nasty little things" still occurred and even after the war ended, they tried to poach customers from each other—for instance, at trade fairs.[140] In particular, Konrad Birkenstock Jr., whom his nephew Erich Weber would later describe as a winning "gentleman," excelled in this unpleasant competition between the Birkenstock brothers.

In the second half of the 30s there were repeated conflicts between Carl and Konrad Jr. Immediately after Gebr. Birkenstock GmbH in Steinhude was reassigned in 1937, they fought a protracted legal dispute that revolved around the problem of who owned the machines in the Steinhude plant and, above all, who was entitled to the allocation of the state-regulated quota of rubber. Here, Konrad Jr. probably made misleading statements in the court proceedings.[141] Furthermore, in the protracted and tedious disputes in 1937/38 with the Reich Working Group to Combat Crippling Illness, Carl and Konrad Jr. again clashed about who was responsible for certain prospectuses that the association objected to. Their correspondence reveals a deep distrust, which helps to make the separation of the companies in the years 1937 to 1939 plausible.[142]

Since the end of the 20s the K. Birkenstock GmbH in Friedberg was managed first by his son-in-law, Alfred Weber, and then, from 1931 on, by Heinrich Birkenstock. In 1936, the company had eight employees, and during World War II the number of employees fluctuated between six and nine.[143] Konrad Jr. opened his own company in Berlin in 1937, at Wilhelmstraße 30–31; "dazzling" character that he was, he remained more or less unaffected by his older brother's brooding tendencies. His nephew Erich Weber remembered him as a talented salesman: "When he stepped in with his stately, highly elegant appearance and his irresistible charm, he could sell anything to any man or, in particular, to any woman." The fact that in the 30s he married a Berlin cabaret dancer seems to fit the picture drawn here.[144]

After the watershed year of 1933, Carl Birkenstock was able to gradually expand the customer base of the Gebr. Birkenstock GmbH in Steinhude again. He also expanded his activities to include the European markets and traveled frequently to his foreign sales offices. In the 40s, he was able to list an impressive number of foreign sales and distribution offices on his company's letterhead, covering Sweden, Norway, Finland, Austria, the Netherlands, Switzerland, and Hungary. At the same time, he continued to experiment with insoles and tried to gradually improve them. This had a knock-on effect, however, inasmuch as his experimentation used up his scarce raw materials to such an extent that he was sometimes no longer able to meet customer demands.

Shortly before the outbreak of World War II, Carl also decided to no longer limit himself to the manufacture of insoles but rather thought of manufacturing shoes. After countless attempts, he believed that he had developed a suitable orthopedic shoe.[145] In 1936, he tried to get his *Ideal-Schuh* patented for the first time. A number of other patent applications followed later, mainly in other European countries. The *Ideal-Schuh* was consistent with the logical further development of the innovations and ideas of his father, Konrad. Taking into consideration the observations of foot diseases caused by the wrong shoes, Carl took on this topic, and made it his own. Hitherto, all attempts to keep modern people's feet healthy in their shoes had failed because shoemakers and shoe factories were now producing shoes on anatomically formed lasts. However, these still did not follow the idea of walking like nature intended. Shoes were subject to fashion trends, and thus Carl had no choice but to adapt the flexible insole, his *Footbed*, to the conditions of the shoe. As a result, the insole was designed without a toe section, since this was the area in which the incongruence between fashionable shoes and the requirements of "natural" walking was most evident.

Thus, it was a logical consequence to take the next step: to design a complete shoe that satisfied the foot's own health requirements. It was one thing that these shoes, now handmade, catered to the foot's own needs—as set out not only by Carl Birkenstock but also, at long last, by the medical profession—and quite another that they could not be mass-produced at the time and up-to-date. It was not until almost three decades later that the long and intensive attempt to mass-produce this shoe was stopped. The production of the *Original Birkenstock-Footbed Sandal* in 1963 based on an own creation, with a new theoretical approach and a complete new design of Karl Birkenstock.[146]

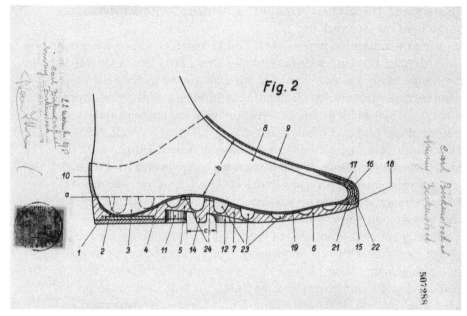

Fig. 21: Building on the insights of his father Konrad, Carl Birkenstock created the vision of a perfect shoe (drawing of the *Ideal-Schuh* from a patent application).

As had been the case in World War I, the demand for insoles increased noticeably during World War II. At the same time, however, Carl Birkenstock had to cope with the fact that six of the 13 company staff members were drafted into the army. As was often the case with smaller companies, he tried to replace the draftees temporarily with female workers. But the raw materials for production were also scarce: natural rubber for his insoles was no longer available, which is why he used the plastic material Weschulin. Despite these war-related restrictions, sales of his insoles increased substantially. Exports were subject to quotas and only made a minor contribution to the company's total turnover. Domestic demand, nonetheless, more than made up for the lack of foreign export opportunities. According to Wilhelm Thomsen, there was an increased demand for insoles, especially in the Wehrmacht. This was because custom-made products were not available owing to the lack of raw materials or the fact that available resources were used primarily for the production of artificial limbs. Therefore, many soldiers supplied themselves with ready-made insoles, which opened up a potentially lucrative market for Birkenstock products. Carl Birkenstock, however, remained disappointed that once again official Wehrmacht orders never materialized.[147]

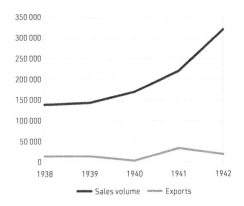
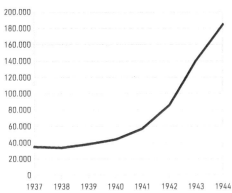

Chart 1: Sales volume and exports of the Gebr. Birkenstock GmbH (later Carl Birkenstock) in Steinhude (Reichsmark).[148]

Chart 2: Annual income of Carl Birkenstock, 1937–1944 (Reichsmark).[149]

This increase in turnover looks quite remarkable when one considers that it was achieved with less than 20 employees; in 1938, the company had 8 employees, which increased to twelve to 13 during the war.[150] By way of comparison, a clothing company like Hugo Boss from Metzingen generated sales of a little over one million Reichsmarks in 1944 with more than 300 employees.[151] Accordingly, Carl Birkenstock's production and income also increased significantly during World War II, especially in light of the company's minimal staffing.

This increase in sales is all the more astonishing because Carl Birkenstock was not able to secure any large military orders. Overall, as Carl Birkenstock later complained in his writings, there was hardly any demand for his insoles on the part of the Wehrmacht and the SS.[152] Along with the small number of people employed by the company, the hours worked during the war show that large government contracts were out of the question. Nevertheless, the company was quite successful during World War II, judging at least from the sales figures available for the period up to 1942.

How close was Carl's ideological affinity with the National Socialists? He joined the Nazi Party on April 1, 1940, quite some time after it had lifted its long-standing membership ban, and millions of Germans had already joined the party. In this regard, he was comparatively late to join. In 1944, Carl noted in a letter that he enlisted to the SA a year earlier "under the impact of

1938	1939	1940	1941	1942
48,000	50,000	55,000	75,000	106,000

Table 2: Annual insole production of Gebr. Birkenstock GmbH (later Carl Birkenstock) in Steinhude (pairs of insoles).[153]

events in Stalingrad," but was not admitted. This attempt was also made under the impression that the local National Socialist Dröge continued to harass Carl Birkenstock. His calculation to be protected from attacks by joining the party had finally not worked out.[154]

During World War II, Carl Birkenstock wondered whether his manuscript "40 Jahre Einsatz für vernünftige Fußbekleidung" would attract more attention if he introduced it with quotes from the cult figure Leo Schlageter or with a foreword by the physician Heinz Neu. Both remained ideas that he did not implement.[155] This is evident when Carl perceived the need for a philosophical "aggrandizement" of the metal-free foot insole.[156] Back in 1939, he had come into contact with the Düsseldorf doctor Heinz Neu, who in 1938 had written an "open letter" to the Reich Guild Association of Shoemakers in Berlin, demanding, among other things, that the "German shoe be worthy of the new German people."[157] Neu's main concern was that natural footwear should be worn in the interest of the "people's health" (*Volksgesundheit*).

Carl became aware of Neu via an old Birkenstock customer in Düsseldorf, and in the early 40s they considered producing a joint publication. This came about because they had a common vision, a shoe for healthy feet. However, they were clearly driven by very different motives. While Konrad and Carl Birkenstock had been working on improving foot health for everyone for 40 years without any racist agenda manifesting in their efforts, Neu was one of the proponents of the Nazis' racial theory with a penchant for naturism and esotericism. In 1933, Neu had published a small pamphlet entitled "Biologische Politik: Deutschland, das künftige Reich gesunder Wohlfahrt, sozialer Gerechtigkeit und pflichtbewusster Freiheit," in which he advocated an aggressive racial and health doctrine. In the period that followed, he authored other rather obscure writings, such as a work on Paracelsus, whom he described as a fighter against his time and the emissary of a cultural revolution.[158] When Neu turned against the medical profession and the incomprehensible language behind which many doctors hid, he was grappling with the same fundamental experience that Carl had had in his years of struggling against the attitudes of the medical profession, which he perceived as arrogant.

Carl hoped to be able to publish his manuscript "40 Jahre Einsatz für vernünftige Fußbekleidung" together with a text by Neu. In August 1941, he completed a roughly 150-page draft with this title. Neu was to write a supplementary article in which he explained the ideological and philosophical basis of Birkenstock's foot orthopedics. For reasons that are unclear, however, there was no further cooperation between the two. Overall it is evident, though, that because of the lack of recognition he felt from the orthopedic establishment, Carl was always on the lookout for others with more "exposure"—as he put it in a letter to Wilhelm Thomsen.[159] But then he was obviously willing to join forces with a radical blood-and-soil ideologue like Heinz Neu, even if there are no racist statements or ideas of the blood-and-soil ideology in Birkenstock's writings.

During the war, Carl stayed in Steinhude and, unlike his younger brother Konrad, who became a soldier in the Afrika Korps, did not have to fight. At the same time, he became involved in numerous controversies in this period. Later, as part of his denazification process, he said he had been the victim of repression because his name sounded "Jewish." This was an argument frequently used in such proceedings and is difficult to verify.[160] Even so, he did procure genealogical data and officially submitted his "Aryan proof," which suggests that this was demanded of him. Consequently, for the first time it seemed appropriate to refer to the long shoemaking tradition of the family. Thus, the addition "Tradition since 1774" was added to the company name.[161]

In fact, in December 1943, at a Nazi Party Christmas celebration, Carl was also beaten by members of the party.[162] There are contradictory statements about what exactly happened there. Apparently, a long-standing animosity between Carl and the party's head of propaganda in Steinhude led to the "accusation" that Carl's hooked nose gave him the look of a "Jewish half-breed." Birkenstock said that if the speaker weren't in uniform, "he'd smack him." The altercation did in fact end in physical violence, which also had legal consequences. Because of his outsider status in Steinhude, Birkenstock probably had no real chance of success with his libel suit.[163]

All in all, the war years were not particularly good to Carl Birkenstock on a personal level. He had health problems and in the spring of 1944 was instructed to take a cure in Baden-Baden owing to "heart failure, poor circulation, and nervous exhaustion" (probably related in part to the events at the Nazi Christmas party). A year earlier, he had had to interrupt a similar cure because of bombing raids on Hanover.[164] In 1943, he took in his wife's sister Emmi with her husband and three children.[165] But this soon led to conflict. According to his later testimony, his sister-in-law tried to denounce him to the authorities, while she claimed after the war that Carl had reported her for listening to "enemy radio stations" (which he—with good reason—vehemently denied).[166]

Summary

The turbulent times of the fading German Empire, World Wars I and II, the drama of the Weimar Republic, and the horrors of National Socialism had little effect on the entrepreneurial family Birkenstock. However, there was a notable increase in sales of insoles to alleviate foot pain, catering, during and after the war, to the many soldiers with bad feet. For Birkenstock, the first half of the 20th century was characterized instead by the groundbreaking inventions of the fourth and fifth generations of the shoemaking dynasty. With the construction of the fully anatomically shaped last in 1897, the development of the flexible, anatomically shaped insole, later called *Footbed* in 1902 and the *Ideal-Schuh* in 1936, Konrad and his son Carl changed the idea of walking "as nature intended" to promote the health of the foot. Strengthened by the resilience of the family tradition, they pushed through their innovations in a spirit of perseverance and refusal to compromise, flying in the face of the trends of the time—and even the quarrels within their own family. At the threshold of industrial production of an ideal shoe, however, their ideas initially came to a halt after 1945.

Later in this chapter, Andrea H. Schneider-Braunberger delves into Carl Birkenstock's thoughts on podiatry, while in chapter 3 Jörg Lesczenski traces the failure of attempts to mass-produce the *Ideal-Schuh*, as well as Karl Birkenstock's subsequent new idea of a mass-produced foot-healthy sandal.

Fish Leather and Wooden Sandals: Leather Shortage during World War II

BY JOHANNA STEINFELD

"We must likewise put our standards aside, simplify our collections, and always remain ready to draw the conclusions from any situation. Let's never forget that we are at war, and that in any war the impossible can become possible. Pride of place must once again go to frugality across the board."[1] This was the appeal with which M. W. Wittstock, director of Arola Schuh AG (the sales organization of the Bally holding company), responded to the outbreak of World War II. After all, the war spelled the end of the imported leather on which Swiss shoe company Bally depended—it required two million hides a year.[2] Wittstock therefore called for far-reaching changes in design: the simplification of shoe collections signified a profound change in the differentiated shoe market of the 30s. After all, during the 20s not only had the shortening of skirt lengths brought increased attention to (women's) shoes per se, but the boot—the common standard footwear until the end of World War I—was also replaced by the low shoe during this period. The low shoe offered completely new design opportunities and therefore a variety of shoe types emerged, for which, in turn, numerous models were developed: before World War II, Bally produced various men's shoes, sandals, pumps, work and sports shoes, and slippers and, on top of these, made school and golf shoes, all of which were manufactured for the domestic market and for export.[3] At the same time, the differentiation evident in all the various types of shoes reflected how shoes had changed from being a commodity to being a fashion accessory. From the 30s onwards, this change was expressed in the use of extravagant and luxurious materials such as reptile leather.[4]

While Bally was forced to respond to changing supply conditions with the start of the war in September 1939, German shoe manufacturers had already been facing leather shortages for years. This shortage had in a sense been politically decided at this point anyway, as the political agenda from the 30s had focused on prioritizing the armaments industry and creating an economy that was as independent as possible of foreign countries. As a result, from 1933 onwards, companies had had to produce under anticipated wartime conditions, and shoe manufacturers had to deal with difficulties such as quotas placed on rawhide. Various plans by the Nazi government stipulated that the economy and the army had to be ready for war quickly—within four years in the case of the Four-Year Plan of 1936.[5]

Since shoe production was dependent on foreign imports such as rawhide and tanning materials for its most important raw material, leather, the Four-Year Plan of October 1936 stipulated that shoes for civilian customers should be produced without leather wherever possible. The available leather, meanwhile, was to be used mainly for military purposes. There were two ways to reduce leather consumption. The first option was to replace it with either natural or synthetically produced materials. The development and production of such materials fell to the chemical industry, which quickly notched up successes. As early as in 1936, the first synthetic materials were used in shoes, above all the synthetic rubber Buna manufactured by the I. G. Farbenindustrie consortium, which replaced leather and natural rubber in shoe soles.[6] For rubber soles, such as those used by the Dassler company, synthetic rubber and regenerated Buna (recycled synthetic rubber) were used from 1939 at the latest.[7] Buna was initially produced in three plants, and work on a fourth plant in Auschwitz, to be built by concentration camp prisoners, began in 1941—a project that cost the lives of more than 20,000 prisoners.[8]

The second option for substituting cowhide was to make use of other types of leather for civilian production. Hence, leather from pigs and the skins of fish were used for shoe production, with the latter used primarily for women's work shoes and leisure footwear.[9] However, these types of leather were not of as high a quality as the leather that was still so popular with consumers and were used mainly for women's shoes and later for shoes for slave laborers.[10] Recycling already worn leather also played a major role, as did the general reuse of any material that women at that time knew how to skillfully put together. In December 1943, the predecessor of the fashion and women's magazine "Brigitte"—namely, "Blatt der Hausfrau"—presented some "useful" gifts for Christmas, including "a particularly pretty shoe pattern to make yourself." This model was to be made from purchased reed soles, a small leather belt, a few silk scraps and small fur scraps, for which the Blatt der Hausfrau also supplied the cutting sheet.[11]

In addition, the leather shoe was also to be replaced by wooden shoes, which Nazi propaganda therefore tried to promote as everyday shoes for women. Although wooden shoes were still widespread among the lower classes anyway, now they were no longer to be reduced to being mainly used just as

Fig. 22: Necessity is the mother of invention! During the Second World War, straw was discovered as a shoemaking material (1944).

1896–1945 From a Shoemaker's Workshop to a Manufacturing Company

work shoes.[12] European designers, whose companies also suffered from a shortage of leather, likewise turned to wood: After Italy went to war with Abyssinia in 1935, designer Salvatore Ferragamo started producing shoes with wooden as well as cork soles. André Perugia in France worked in a similar way, patenting a textured wooden sole in 1942.[13] The shoe models developed by designers out of necessity and materials newly utilized for shoe manufacturing in some cases continued to be used well after the war.

Synthetic materials also survived beyond the end of World War II. Rubber soles, largely made of synthetic rubber, and other synthetic soles accounted for more than half (63 percent) of all soles in 1954.[14] These innovations, which were developed in response to the Nazi regime's policies on an autonomous economy and on armaments therefore created a launchpad for further advances in the consumer goods industry in the postwar period. The dissemination of technologies that were already known but little used was also significant. By 1945, for example, the "glued shoe" had established itself, the design of which had actually been developed before World War I.[15] It was not until adhesives were developed in the 30s, however, that city shoes could be produced in this way—namely, starting at the beginning of the 40s.[16] For shoe manufacturing, this signified a major step toward lighter shoes and cheaper production, on the basis of which sneakers were later able to become widespread.[17]

THE *SYSTEM BIRKENSTOCK*: THE FOOTPRINT FOR WALKING AS NATURE INTENDED

BY ANDREA H. SCHNEIDER-BRAUNBERGER

The Beginnings: Konrad's Inventions

At the turn of the 20th century, Konrad Birkenstock took a step away from the path trodden by his shoemaker ancestors and designed completely new shoes—*Health Footwear*,[1] a combination of the fully anatomically shaped shoe last (1897) developed by him, together with a flexible insole (1902).[2] He soon described his small business as "orthopedic and fashionable shoemaking."[3] He was also one of the group of early orthopedic shoemakers who finally came together in 1917—in the middle of World War I—to form the Association of German Orthopedic Shoemakers. In 1920, Konrad moved from Frankfurt am Main to Friedberg with his "K. Birkenstock factory for flat and hollow foot insoles."[4] His insoles were first recognized as an orthopedic remedy at a trade fair in 1914; additional awards followed, including a gold medal in 1924.[5]

Nevertheless, a quarter of a century had passed before this success was achieved. During this period Konrad had continued to develop the material of the flexible insoles, two of which he called *Footbed*.[6] Although some orthopedists appreciated his inventions, Konrad did not win the approval of the medical community. When he worked in the orthopedic department of the Friedrichsheimer Klinik during World War I, he made contact with the leading figures in the orthopedics field and thus managed to secure their support in the medium term.[7] His attempts to obtain government support to supply the *Footbed* or his other insoles to the invalids of the war were, nevertheless, unsuccessful. And the health insurance companies still did not recognize the insole *Footbed* as an orthopedic remedy.

Working at the clinic nevertheless gave Konrad the opportunity to study foot diseases intensively for several years. His son Carl, who followed in his father's enlightened footsteps, continued these empirical studies. At foot consultation days, which were conducted in specialist shoe shops in the 20s, he recorded the customers' foot problems systematically and repeatedly in order to be able to categorize their characteristics, healing processes, and development, and to be able to use them for the further improvement of his anatomically shaped, flexible insoles.

Carl also developed his own products in the 20s: the Carl Birkenstock heel pad, which he produced in his own company KABI (Karl Birkenstock) in Vienna during this episode. The insole part that he developed, which could be flexibly installed between heel and sole, was named *Blue Ring* and later marketed as a standout product for the insole *Footbed with the ring D. R. P.* and sold as *Blue Plastic Without Metal*.[8] Birkenstock developed various *insoles*, including insoles called *Footbed*, which were made in different materials. The best-seller later became the *Footbed,* which was described as a blue insole without metal from the 20s onwards.[9]

The *System Birkenstock*

The combination of the fully anatomically shaped shoe last developed by Konrad Birkenstock with the flexible insoles manufactured in different sizes and thicknesses was offered as the *System Birkenstock*. From their knowledge of the variety of feet and foot diseases, Konrad and Carl Birkenstock concluded that the insoles must be individualized if they were to have a positive effect. Although preform insoles could be produced according to foot types, these still had to be adapted to the customer's foot and shoe by hand. In order to meet the exacting demands of foot health, Carl Birkenstock therefore decided to sell the *System Birkenstock* only to those shoe salesmen and shoemakers who had undergone professional training with him. These training courses covered the anatomy and diseases of the foot, as well as selection criteria relating to the insoles that were required in each case. The linking of the sale of Birkenstock plastics (insoles) to the acquisition of the course diploma was an unusual step, which also immediately provoked criticism from contemporary orthopedists, who argued that the shoemaker or shoe salesman could not be trained to become an "expert" in a mere week (Franz Schede).[10]

The positive reception of the specialist lectures that Konrad and Carl Birkenstock gave early on throughout Europe encouraged them to write books as well as articles in specialist journals, such as the paper "Fußbett: Ein Wunder im Schuh" (Footbed: A Miracle in the Shoe) by Konrad Birkenstock, which was published in the 30s. Most importantly, Carl Birkenstock—inspired by the graduates of his training courses—authored several works of his own: beginning with the book "Der Fuß und seine Behandlung" (The Foot and Its Treatment), which was published in 1930 with a circulation of 35,000 copies, followed by "Mit dem Arzt gegen Fußkrankheiten und Irrlehren" (With the Doctor Against Foot Diseases and Heresies) from 1935 (with a print run of over 24,000 copies),[11] which Carl Birkenstock himself described as "a pamphlet for shoe professionals, an orthopedic training course." Since Carl Birkenstock insinuated in the title that his remarks were based on medical findings, the Reich Association of Bandagists and Orthopedic Mechanics went so far as to file a suit to suppress this publication.[12]

Carl Birkenstock's Pioneering Observations on Foot Orthopedics

The publication that decisively founded Birkenstock's thinking about healthy footwear and still shapes the company's core values today is "Fußorthopädie: Das System Carl Birkenstock." Carl Birkenstock had worked for five years on the manuscript, which was published in Düsseldorf in 1948/49 with a circulation of 19,000 copies.[13] Another of his manuscripts, "40 Jahre für die vernünftige Fußbekleidung" (40 Years of Sensible Footwear, 1941), and its sequel 20 years later, "60 Jahre für die vernünftige Fußbekleidung" (60 Years of Sensible Footwear, 1961), remained unpublished.

The empirical basis of the study "Fußorthopädie: System Carl Birkenstock" were the observations of Konrad Birkenstock, the surveys and evaluations of the customers during the shoe consultation days conducted by Carl Birkenstock, and a 1934 study of 170 soldiers of the Leibstandarte SS (Personal Bodyguard Regiment of) Adolf Hitler,[14] which helped Carl understand which foot diseases were most prevalent and how they were distributed in the population.

After more than 20 years of collecting empirical data, the experiences in the training courses, and information from the first publications, Carl completed his findings in 1948. His study of diseased feet focused on two aspects: on the one hand, the question of healing and, on the

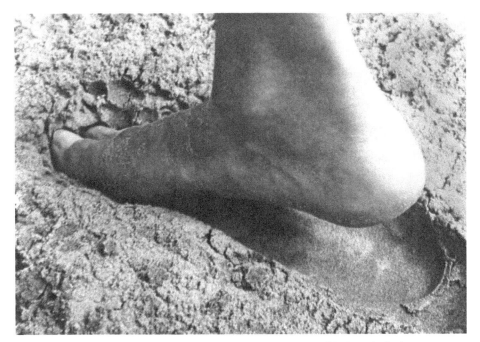

Fig. 23: Model for the idea of the Birkenstock footprint and the *Footbed*. The footprint in the sand is a symbol of the foot's groundedness.

other, that of prevention. For—according to his sobering conclusions—between 80 and 90 percent of the test subjects examined had foot problems, caused primarily by stressful pressure on the foot in the shoe. Through implementation of the "health shoes" in the *System Birkenstock*, Carl hoped to prevent foot diseases caused by civilization from developing in the first place.

Walking as Nature Intended

In his book, Carl described in detail the anatomy and functioning of the foot and the consequences that living in an urbanized world has for the feet. The core statement is as simple as it is convincing: the human foot is made for walking in nature. It is able to move exceptionally well on uneven, natural ground. In observing this natural movement, Carl came up with the concept of walking as nature intended, leaving a footprint on soft ground. The foot creates a footprint on natural, uneven, and flexible ground by sinking into it with the sole of the foot. The gripping motion of the toes is an essential part of the movement, as it activates the muscles along the sole of the foot.[15] Walking barefoot is a natural type of foot gymnastics, which was no longer part of everyday life even in Carl's time. His vision was therefore to create a footprint that underpins the foot so that it receives support from all sides: "The foot is grounded, secure, and firm,"[16] as he himself put it.

His further thoughts, that one can "maintain a healthy body [...] in the long term only through a natural way of life,"[17] read today in 2023 as visionary and show that relevant knowledge sometimes takes a very long time until it prevails. In principle, his ideas were in tune with the modern zeitgeist, as the natural reform movement or biodynamic agriculture were in the making at the time. The reconnection of the human foot in the shoe to nature, nevertheless, is probably Carl Birkenstock's pioneering achievement.

From an orthopedic point of view and in order to counteract the consequences of the fact that since the 19th century people have been walking more and more on paved streets, that uneven clay floors in the house were no longer common, and that many activities were carried out standing up, rather than walking or running, shoe inserts with a footbed could be used to supplement modern shoe production. Based on the general physiognomy of the foot, Carl confronted the foot diseases caused by civilization with podiatry-based remedies, producing anatomical, orthopedic shoes with a focus on quality.

Orthopedic Shoes

As far as curing foot ailments was concerned, according to Carl Birkenstock, success depended not only on the type of ailment but also on the individual adaptation of the remedy. According to his observations, most foot diseases develop in a six-phase sequence of civilization-related improper loading.[18]

The prerequisite for making any kind of orthopedic shoe was the anatomically shaped inner sole developed by Konrad Birkenstock. It was developed by shoe specialists for shoe specialists and orthopedists and was intended as an aid for people with foot problems.[19] It was immediately clear that the greatest challenge lay in the variety of foot shapes in terms of length, width, and curvature. It was necessary, therefore, to find a means of systematizing people's foot shapes according to different types.

Concentrating his attention on the shoe, Carl called for a "revolutionary footwear reform"[20] in order to promote foot health. In doing so, he focused on and called into question the function of the heel of the shoe, which puts the foot in a permanent situation of going downhill, forcing the toes to constantly act as brakes and thus compressing the transverse and longitudinal arches of the foot. This one-sided stress leads, he reasoned, to the deterioration of the foot apparatus over time. The shoe of that time—and today's shoes too—often offered too little space for the toes, had too little upper leather on the ball of the foot, or was too wide. In addition, it stressed the ankle joint because of the heel and was also insufficiently adapted to the foot at the heel, shoe last, and shaft. Pumps, the favorite shoe style of women in those days, were considered to be particularly harmful to foot health.[21]

Carl's holistic perspective was particularly evident in his advice to parents regarding the rearing of their young children. Very young children should not, he claimed, be encouraged to stand and walk too early—which was fashionable at the time—since the crawling phase is important for the development of the back and feet.[22] In general, Carl was not a fan of fashion shoes, which for him were characterized by too much commercial competition, too many models, and too much concentration on speedy turnover at any price.[23] "The shapes are created from the liveliest imagination," he stated, "just not based on the naturally healthy shape of the normal foot." This combination, the inventive power and lively imagination to create a shoe based on the shape of the foot, was only achieved by his son Karl in 1963. If the core purpose of this "reasonable shoe shape" was to achieve "as straight a position as possible for the big toe," then there were no creative limits on the shape of the rest of the shoe.

The prerequisites for walking as nature intended were, among other things, flexible soles, low heels (maximum 2 cm for men and 3–5 cm for women), loose lacing on the instep, and a shaft that was not too low. Carl Birkenstock's ideas were central to the development of this shoe: "But even such a well-conceived shoe, which should be short on the outside and quite long on the inside, can only serve foot health fully if it is completed by an individually adapted anatomically shaped shoe last—i. e., an orthopedic design in the truest sense applied to the stepping surface."[24] A flexible anatomically shaped shoe last based on his model was therefore required.

Konrad Birkenstock had already made the problems of the foot visible in two drawings from 1901 (see fig. 24). In the kind of movement referred to as civilization-conditioned walking, the flat insole causes the foot to stand on three bones, the heel bone and the first and the fifth metatarsal bone. This three-point system (see fig. 24)—as Carl explains in detail—is permanently harmful to healthy feet. The *System Birken-*

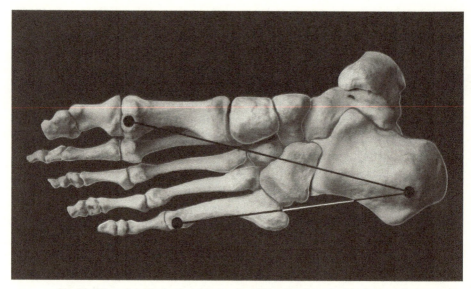

Fig. 24: Although not trained as a doctor, Carl Birkenstock used evidence-based methods and developed theories from his observations of the biodynamics of the foot, many of which are still valid today (here the foot's three-point load).

stock replaced this three-point system with the natural footprint and thus distributed the weight evenly. The cavity between the foot and the insole, which would allow the foot to drop, is filled, so the heel and ball of the foot are relieved.

The *System Birkenstock* supplied a shoe manufactured according to the above specifications on a fully anatomically shaped last, equipped with an anatomically shaped insole. Carl was adamantly against the manufacturer installing the insoles permanently. Ideally, the stepping surface should be available in several "shapes, widths, and arch lengths," because feet are particularly individual. "The ideal situation arises when the walkable anatomically shaped insole, the substitute for natural soil, is firmly connected to the shoe after a trial period."[25] Thus, his idea was to deliver the shoes without an insole under the conditions described above, have the insoles individually adapted to the customer's foot by the shoemaker, shoe retailer, or orthopedic surgeon, and then nail the insoles into the shoe after a trial period.

It is obvious that the complexity of this process did not facilitate its mass implementation. Setting aside foot problems, the advice given when buying shoes was and still is challenging, and not only in a professional sense. But that was the first step on the way to the well-fitting, foot-healthy shoe. Even then there were "fluoroscopy devices" that were supposed to check the fit of the foot in the shoe—but in terms of the required differentiation of the arches, lengths, and heights, they were often inadequate.

Carl Birkenstock distinguished between three types of shoes with differing levels of quality: 1) sensible shoes, 2) health shoes, and 3) orthopedic shoes. He branded the orthopedic shoe with an adjustable insole as "incomplete" because it did not have an anatomically shaped insole.[26] Producing these in series was not easy, even with healthy feet, and depended on the following factors:

- the correct length of the foot
- an individually designed anatomically shaped insole suited to the length of the arch of the foot
- at least three different arch lengths for each shoe type (shape and width) and each shoe size
- with fully anatomically shaped shoes, adjustment of the length, shape, instep, ball area, heel closure, and shaft height—which is even more difficult than with more rigid shoes

In addition to these foot-related sizing challenges, Carl also anticipated the problems that would occur in sales and production: because much larger stocks would be required in the shoe stores, thorough orthopedic training for the staff would be a prerequisite, as would educating the customers. In addition, for the standardized production of orthopedic shoes, shoe last material worth several million Deutschmarks would have to be installed at shoe factories and by master shoemakers.

These almost irreconcilable problems, Carl concluded, would be insoluble in view of the 80 to 90 percent of all people with diseased feet, because the insoles would have to be much more differentiated to fit each customer. This is how he came to a momentous realization: "Is one to accept the diverse and almost insurmountable difficulties involved in just producing a shoe with permanently installed anatomically shaped insoles if it is not only better—i.e., more exact—but also simpler and less expensive to achieve the best possible condition with loose anatomically shaped insoles?"[27]

He went one step further with this idea in the *System Birkenstock*. Up to now, it had only been possible for him to adjust the models he described as less suitable with the help of his flexible insoles. However, it was clear to him that good insoles in the wrong shoe would not help. He therefore declared that his goal would have been achieved "when enough trained shoe specialists have mastered my system to produce an *Ideal-Schuh* that meets the requirements. Because only with an orthopedically trained sales organization is it possible to completely customize the shoe using

Fig. 25: Carl Birkenstock portrayed by a contemporary caricaturist (50s).

anatomically shaped insoles to eliminate all difficulties and to take all technical issues into account."[28]

Carl developed a shoe that met his expectations in all respects and applied for the first patent for this *Ideal-Schuh* in 1936. The insoles were not permanently installed in the shoe—this is shown by later production tests.[29] According to Carl's ideas, the insoles were to be individually adapted to the customer's feet by the shoe dealers or shoemakers and then installed.

In 1948/49, when Carl published the book on foot orthopedics, he confidently announced: "The 'shoe that the future belongs to' should be brought out as soon as possible on our own initiative and in cooperation with shoe factories. Patent claims are pending."[30] Nevertheless, the problems that arose when looking for a production partner in the industrial sector were immense. The need to use masses of new shoe lasts, which he himself indicated, soon became a problem when shoe manufacturers repeatedly complained during the test series that Birkenstock was not supplying sufficient quantities of shoe lasts. The same applied to the acceptance of direct delivery of insoles to shoe retailers. The latter were unwilling to purchase a shoe without an insole from a shoe manufacturer and then order and customize the insole from Birkenstock.[31]

C.-B. Orthopedics GmbH (Bad Honnef) nonetheless successfully brought out the specially developed *Fußfriede* (foot peace) insole, which was to be installed in the *Ideal-Schuh*:[32] such a shoe, however, had not yet been mass-produced.

The Flexible Insoles: The *Footbed*

Since the 20s, Birkenstock's success has been rooted in the manufacture and distribution of various flexible insoles. Konrad and Carl Birkenstock were "uncompromising champions of nonmetallic foot aids," which they initially saw as a shoe equalizer and also as a foot healer.[33] While the footbed for healthy feet can be easily customized and worn according to its width, length, and strength, foot deformities, malalignment, or foot diseases require adjustment.

Konrad rejected metal insoles because an elastic, flexible insole, by contrast, provided a "flexing, massaging effect" that initiated the gripping effect of the toes described above and thus imitated walking as nature intended. Furthermore, the material had to be "firmly elastic"—i. e., return consistently to its original shape—in order to fulfill its function, and finally the thickness of the packing should never change.

The mix of materials changed frequently in the first few years: Konrad started with a cardboard and leather mix, followed by either rubber or Goudron (tar) combined with a cork or sawdust mixture. Then, in the 30s, a "thermoplastic material" came into use.[34]

The *Carl Birkenstock Regular Plastic*, an insole, had a round heel and was as thin as possible in the middle, with a bulge-like edge that grew thicker around it; the inner arch was elongated, the outer arch was shorter, and the outer longitudinal arch was supported on the sides with a transverse arch. The *Carl Birkenstock Regular Plastic* was meant to help the foot by making the heel cushion round again, making the hard skin disappear, bedding the heel bone, and giving it support. The foot could not slip forward, the shoe closed better in the heel area, and the toes had more space. The insole itself is secured by the heel bed of the shoe, so the arches of the foot are precisely underpinned, and the muscular power of the foot is not used for support, but for locomotion. In this way the foot muscles are activated, and the soles of the feet are stimulated.

Carl Birkenstock was not targeting those with foot problems with his publications and insoles but rather wanted to see his foot orthopedics primarily as a preventive measure. The foot plastics are a "benefit and preventive measure" for healthy feet,[35] he stated. "In addition, they greatly improve the shoe from an orthopedic point of view. It is idle to argue about this; every doubter is free to convince himself by making trial of the facts that are now available."[36] This conviction, often misunderstood as arrogance, was the result of his observations over many years. Birkenstock also emphasized that in contrast to a metal insole, the elastic footbed is not harmful to the feet.[37] In his eyes, metal was a "rigid makeshift" that always "remains a foreign body on the foot and shoe." To keep the foot healthy, Birkenstock not only recommended healthy shoes, ideally through an orthopedic anatomically shaped design of the sensible shoe, but also foot care through foot baths, nail care, removal of calluses and corns, or foot massages.

The flexible insoles developed by Konrad Birkenstock in 1902 and called *Footbed* since 1909 at the latest, were already being produced in various designs from 1910 onwards. In the 20s, new plastics (insoles) were developed—*Naturette, Naturaform,* and *Elastigang*; the latter was made from material that Carl Birkenstock had developed from substitute materials during World War I. In 1949, Carl Birkenstock and his company C. B. Orthopädie GmbH in Bad Honnef also offered the models *Fußfriede* and *Completta,* which, like *Naturaform* and *Naturette,* had the D. R. P. ring and were all made of artificial leather/moleskin.[38] *Elastigang* was no longer produced in the 50s.

114   **1896–1945** From a Shoemaker's Workshop to a Manufacturing Company

Foot Diseases

Carl followed the presentation of his new footbed with a detailed description of the existing foot diseases he had observed and systematized over the years.[39] In it, he went into detail about foot ailments, how to recognize them, the pain associated with them, what effect they have on the shoe, and how they could be cured. He basically grouped these ailments into two areas: 1) weak tendons and ligaments: the soft splayfoot, valgus foot, in various forms, fallen arches, flat feet, and 2) in the case of strong tendons and ligaments (not so common): cartilaginous splayfoot, *pes cavus*, and heel spurs.

Carl repeatedly stated that healing was only possible to a limited extent and produced quite varying results: "Normal anatomically shaped insoles exert a different bedding and pressure effect at every stage of the disease."[40] The standardization of insoles introduced by Birkenstock into hard, soft, wide, and narrow sizes made it easier to customize the shoe. Carl saw an improvement in foot problems as a result of the footprint system. Consequently, he recommended his patent no. 768843—*Footbed, Naturaform, Naturette with the ring*—and explained its exact application and the special effect of the "thermoplastic material." He further described to his readers in detail how the anatomically shaped insoles were to be adjusted by a specialist, as well as the consequences of incorrect use.

Metal Inlays and Other Competing Foot Supports

Carl Birkenstock also dealt intensively with competing solutions in the field of foot supports, explaining their effectiveness, application, and disadvantages. He had hardly anything positive to say about the classic metal insole: "Metal is too hard for healthy feet, so it must be even less suitable for people with ill, sensitive feet" because the muscles would be weakened further, since they are not in line with the natural walking movement. According to the three-point system explained earlier, metal inserts promote an unnatural loading of the foot and strengthen the foot cavities. Their cheap metal springs were almost impossible to adjust; newer metal insoles lacked, among other things, the round heel and upper flexibility; Carl Birkenstock also took a critical look at custom-made metal inserts. The argument against these was that the feet "are fixed in their existing condition," whereas the aim is "to improve the suffering foot."[41]

He judged the adjustable, metal-free insoles more positively: "It can be conceded that the well-trained specialist with effort and care is able to achieve a 'normal shape' from adjustable leather insoles through the conscientious, time-consuming gluing of pieces of leather, with which satisfying results can be gained with foot patients." He was critical, however, of the insole material made of pure leather and cork, since the thermoplastic effect was missing. Finally, he took a critical look at self-shaping insoles, rubber bandages, insoles with 27-fold adjustments, insoles made of wood, corn plasters, toe clips, X-ray machines, and orthopedic shoes.

The main proponent of Birkenstock's approach was the podiatrist Wilhelm Thomsen.[42] Although he himself considered foot massage and gymnastics to be the most effective healing methods, Thomsen was a frequent advocate of Birkenstock insoles. But even after the invention of the *Footbed*, Birkenstock published "acknowledgments" in the 90s when customers such as doctors had boots made on Konrad Birkenstock's shoe last and with the "patented" insoles.[43]

Summary

While Konrad Birkenstock revolutionized the manufacture of shoes with his two groundbreaking inventions of the fully anatomically shaped shoe last and insole and was already beginning to spread his knowledge about health shoes to convince shoemakers, orthopedic surgeons, and customers of their effectiveness, Carl Birkenstock was involved not only in the further development of flexible insoles but also in the innovative design of *Health Footwear* into the *Ideal-Schuh*. In addition, however, he laid the foundation for the success of his company by writing down the knowledge he had gained in the training courses and collected in his "Fußorthopädie: System Carl Birkenstock" which is still valid to this day.

With the invention of the *Original Birkenstock-Footbed Sandal* by Karl Birkenstock in 1963, a footbed developed by Karl Birkenstock was firmly anchored in the shoe. Contrary to Carl Birkenstock's idea that the footbed should only be built into shoes afterwards, it has been permanently installed ever since. Why is this? Because what Carl had strived for and requested was finally realized—namely, to make all shoes available in different widths and lengths. And thus there were two, and soon three, different widths when the sandals of Karl were offered as unisex models. The built-in footbed that Karl Birkenstock had created preserves the natural anatomy and shape of the foot and thus acts as a preventive measure before foot problems occur.

To this day, however, the *Ideal-Schuh* of Carl Birkenstock—i. e., the anatomically correct shoe with a footbed that is individually adapted to the wearer—has, for reasons relating to production technology, logistics, and application, not yet been realized.

1945 – 1963
BEGINNING OF THE INDUSTRIAL ERA

Fig. 26: Birkenstock models in front of the 1972
shoe fair wearing the *Zürich*, *Madrid*, and *Athen*
sandal models (from left to right).

ON THE PATH TO "WALKING AS NATURE INTENDED": FROM THE *FOOTBED* TO A SHOE

BY JÖRG LESCZENSKI

New Beginning and Continuation: A New Start in Bad Honnef. In Search of the *Ideal-Schuh*

World War II and its aftermath hit the suppliers of orthopedic services hard. In the wake of Allied bombing raids, countless workshops had to temporarily cease production; those outfits that had been spared destruction in the closing months of the war concentrated on manufacturing prosthetics for the war injured and were soon no longer able to meet the demand for orthopedic aids. Moreover, the Allies had divided Germany into four zones of occupation, and this made it harder to supply materials and finished goods across the zonal border lines.[1]

The British Army's advance from the West led in early April 1945 to the de facto collapse of the Nazi regime in the Lower Saxony region. On April 7, 1945, the Wunstorf fighter airfield was taken, and two days later US troops were at the gates of Hanover. The final desperate engagements, such as the deployment of "ramming fighters" against a US squadron over Steinhuder Meer lake in Lower Saxony, did nothing to stop Germany's defeat. While the war and the heavy bombing raids had severely damaged industrial outfits and countless residential districts in the nearby metropolis of Hanover, in Steinhude Carl Birkenstock's factory and home were almost unscathed. The immediate war damage primarily involved invoices no longer paid by customers for goods deliveries that failed to reach their destinations during the closing months of the war.[2]

The further impact of World War II swiftly caught up with Carl Birkenstock. As of April 1945, he worked together with the military administration (his residence was at first placed under special protection), and initially things went well. However, in the summer of 1945 his private life changed dramatically. During Whitsun 1945, the United Nations Relief and Rehabilitation Administration (UNRRA, founded on November 9, 1943, by the United States, the Soviet Union, Great Britain, and China) appropriated his house, and Carl was only allowed to use one room in the basement. As the UN's relief and reconstruction agency, the UNRRA was responsible, after the end of the war in Europe, for supporting the military authorities in getting displaced persons (survivors of the concentration camps, POWs, and slave laborers) back to their home countries.[3] Carl was now prevented for months from returning to his private residence with his family. From mid-November 1945, following the UNRRA's appropriation of the house, three British Army officers were quartered there, while Carl himself lived together with his family in the office premises attached to the factory. There were no wardrobes for clothes, and they spent the nights on beds he had borrowed. According to his memory, in the factory "private and family life [...] simply ceased completely."[4]

In the immediate postwar period, not everything went smoothly in factory operations either. On the night of July 8, 1945, the works was plundered, ostensibly by looters of Polish origin (possibly slave laborers). Alongside all the food, among other things, 750 pairs of insoles, 2,500 cans of foot powder, 108 kilograms of calf leather, one bicycle, and a typewriter were stolen.[5] Despite these interferences, operations slowly returned to normal. In August 1945, Carl Birkenstock was allowed to make business trips to the US occupation zone, and one month later he received permission to hold orthopedics courses and to use an automobile for business purposes. On November 12, 1945, the Chamber of Commerce and Industry for the states of Lippe and Schaumburg-Lippe finally issued a provisional operating permit.[6] Prior to it being granted, long-standing customers had stood by him, requesting the military authorities to approve the permit as a matter of urgency. Frankfurt-based Hako Hammer KG, for example, which ran a total of 40 shoe stores in the US and British occupation zones in September 1945, pointed out that without the "products so very necessary for those with foot injuries" there was no guarantee that such injuries could be cared for. The company stated that the goods in question were "top-notch items" that had hitherto been available in all Hako branches.[7]

In Steinhude, as of late summer 1945, a total of 14 employees (up from ten before the war broke out) used three presses to turn out 10,000 pairs of orthopedic insoles a month (1944: 18,000 pairs). Domestic demand was certainly higher in 1945 and stood, by Carl's estimate, at around 500,000 pairs a year; such a production volume would have required five presses and generated sales of 1.5–2 million Reichsmarks. As for the policy on unit sales, the regional organization system dating from the 30s was initially maintained, with the plant in Steinhude serving customers in the provinces of Westphalia, Hanover, Holstein, Hamburg, and Schleswig. Moreover, Birkenstock succeeded in swiftly re-establishing its business relationships with clients outside Germany. The regional agreement between the brothers also specified their respective export quotas, with Steinhude contributing 25 percent of total exports by all Birkenstock factories to other countries in Europe.[8]

Often it was long-standing partners who initiated contact, pointing to the high demand for *Footbed* insoles. For example, Belgian maker of specialist articles, Maison Resimont, emphasized the strong interest among certified orthopedics experts—for example, in Antwerp, Arlon, Brussels, Charleroi, Ghent, and Namur—all of whom spoke of hordes of customers who, thanks to their Birkenstock insoles, had experienced a clear improvement in the foot ailments from which they suffered. The Belgian company applied to the German Amt für Wirtschaftswiederaufbau (Office of Economic Reconstruction) to be permitted to import 5,000 pairs.[9]

Carl rated the economic prospects on the domestic and foreign markets as being especially promising. The company, he said, was the "leading manufacturer for nonmetallic insoles" and enjoyed "the best of reputations [...] in trade circles." If the bottlenecks in supplies of raw materials were overcome and the production plant and machinery were quickly modernized, then, he opined, there were truly "superb opportunities" for the company to swiftly make hay. Without the regional agreement, "there will be no constraints on the possibility of free operations inside and outside of Germany." And it was not as though Carl lacked an entrepreneurial vision. In the future, Birkenstock should not limit itself, he said, to only manufacturing metal-free orthopedic insoles. Rather, he set out as a long-term strategic goal "the initiation of shoe manufacture in line with his own findings and ideas"—which amounted to a "jewel in the crown of scientific work"—and thus returned to the idea of the *Ideal-Schuh*, which had preoccupied him since 1936 and resulted in the production of several hundred handmade pairs in 1942–43.[10]

His future career and the fate of his company now crucially depended on how the relevant British (and later German) authorities judged his behavior during the Third Reich. The four victorious Allies had agreed at their conferences prior to the end of the war that Germany would

122   **1945–1963** Beginning of the Industrial Era

be comprehensively liberated from the Nazis and that German society would be educated to be democratic. A key element of the occupying forces' policies was denazification, the political "purging" of the public service and corporate Germany alike. On the basis of an extensive questionnaire, the authorities also shed light on the biographies and political pasts of those who had run medium-sized businesses.

Next to nothing is known about the actual course that Carl Birkenstock's denazification proceedings took. At the end of November 1945, he submitted his completed questionnaire on his political past to the military government and stated that he had been a member of the NSDAP (Nazi Party), the Deutsche Arbeitsfront (German Labor Front, Nazi replacement for trade unions), the Nationalsozialistische Volkswohlfahrt (Nazi People's Welfare Association), and the Reichkolonialbund (Reich Colonial League). Moreover, for two four-week stints he had been a member of the Volkssturm Steinhude, the local "People's Militia." The British denazification effort found the rigorous moral thrust of the US occupying forces somewhat foreign. Decisions about people were often based on pragmatic considerations, and in cases of doubt the British tended to try to preserve administrative and business efficiency and prioritized this over hasty punishment of those investigated. At present, it is not known just how long Carl had to wait for a decision by the British authorities and what the result was. We can effectively rule out his having ever been a member of the circle of "major offenders" or "offenders." The severe punishments and sanctions (several years' incarceration in labor camps, confiscation of assets, etc.) would have prevented him from continuing his career.[11] A brief note penned in summer 1949, by which time Carl had long since moved to Bad Honnef, would, however, suggest that the denazification process was more protracted than he had hoped. He was advised to appear in person before the Main and Appeals Committee for Denazification in the Administrative District of Cologne in order to "have his case concluded quickly."[12]

In August 1949, the Allies and the West German investigation committees had already bid farewell to the idea of thorough denazification. The overall political climate as of 1947–48, the beginnings of the Cold War, and the harbingers of Western integration, not to mention the fact that the West German population largely considered the unwieldly process to be disreputable, prompted the occupying powers to abandon their policy of purges and to consider business and administrative functionaries to be partners and allies in the competition between East and West.

In the summer of 1945, the factories run by Carl's two brothers in Büdingen and Friedberg recommenced operations (the Berlin branch

Fig. 27: Success with anatomically shaped insoles likewise came with tenacity, passion, and resilience. Gebr. Birkenstock GmbH building in Steinhude.

had been completely destroyed; Konrad Jr. returned to Friedberg, severely wounded). After US troops had pulled up outside the gates of both communities at the end of March 1945, it was only a matter of days before, in early April, it was the military authorities who were making the decisions.[13] The Büdingen plant, Fabrik für Orthopädie, Heinrich Birkenstock, resumed manufacture of orthopedic foot supports and foot-care products on May 25, 1945—a little less than two weeks, that is, after the German capitulation—with the Büdingen district administration having approved production output at 30 percent of the prewar volume. The very small outfit, with its four trained staff members, was turning out 1,500 foot supports and 500 kilograms of foot-care products in March 1946. The production approval by the chamber of commerce and industry responsible was finally issued on July 14, 1947.[14]

As the county seat, Friedberg, unlike Büdingen, suffered severe damage from aerial bombardment. By the end of the war, of the roughly 500 buildings hit during the raids, about half were completely destroyed or badly damaged. The scale of destruction was most pronounced in the district of Feuerbach, which was more or less razed to the ground.[15] Of all the hubs, the plant in Friedberg was thus the worst affected. The residence in Feuerbachstrasse had been left more or less in ruins, and the "last remnant of the house" looked set to collapse. Since the plant had likewise sustained damage, Konrad Jr. and Alfred Weber had to inject considerable sums, albeit on an unknown scale, "to preserve the factory and the house in the inner courtyard [...] as assets."[16]

In Friedberg, the Gebr. Birkenstock OHG company, for which Konrad Jr. and Heinrich were personally liable as partners, was granted permission on August 1, 1945, to manufacture up to 15 percent of the peacetime output of orthopedic foot supports for drug stores and the shoe industry. In its monthly reports, the plant stated that in October 1945 it produced 1,234 pairs and in November 1945, 653 pairs. The company expected that production figures would rise swiftly going forward and went on record saying that the output target for the next three months was 2,500 pairs a month. As in Büdingen, the plant in Friedberg, which received definitive permission to resume production on July 14, 1947, was essentially a small workshop in terms of size; in March 1946, the payroll consisted of two skilled staff members, two semi-trained workers, and two untrained pairs of hands.[17] Permission to resume production was issued for both Friedberg and Büdingen, subject to the proviso that the owners had an unblemished political record.[18]

Konrad Jr. opened his orthopedic factory on January 1, 1945, at Gebrüder Lang-Straße 13 in Friedberg, having left Berlin after his factory there had been bombed out. On February 1, 1947, he also registered a wholesale business for medical and nursing supplies, and in the same year his sister, Catharina Weber, registered a wholesale business for shoe insoles.[19]

Even if business with domestic and foreign clients had already started up again, in the winter of 1945–46 Carl resolved to leave Steinhude for personal reasons. As had been the case during the Third Reich, he felt threatened and bullied by prominent representatives of the local elite. However, he now found himself in the sights of the local political decision-makers for different reasons: before the end of the war, Birkenstock had faced down the allegations made by the local Nazi Party that he was of (half-)Jewish origin; he was now faced with accusations that he had actively supported the regime. His hope of "finally finding peace of mind" after Germany's military capitulation was not fulfilled.[20] These allegations by the mayor's office and the district administrator of Stadthagen, which Carl was baffled by for a long time, can be traced back to his sister-in-law, who had denounced Carl after World War II for allegedly reporting her to the police for "listening to foreign enemy radio stations." In fact, no complaint by Carl could be found.[21] In December 1945, the former police officer called as a witness admitted that Carl had not filed a complaint against his sister-in-law. Her affidavit turned out to be false.

In any case, these unsubstantiated allegations led to increasing hostility between Mayor Hobein and Carl Birkenstock, who noticed a "powerful sense of general repudiation" in the second longer conversation in the mayor's office. According to Hobein, there was no point in him starting up and expanding his company, since the looting was only the beginning of further hardships that awaited him in Steinhude. A typewriter was confiscated, and the company could not expect any support from the mayor's office. A return to his house was also ruled out.[22]

At the end of July 1945, Carl first started thinking about leaving Steinhude. He wanted to return to Frankfurt am Main "in light of the unjust persecution and denunciations." However, the local British military authorities gave him support and, assuring him there would be no further attacks on his family, requested that he remain in the town, so he initially put his plans on ice.[23]

In October 1945, the dispute between Carl and the town hall escalated. Hobein had the last remaining company bicycle confiscated and a day later, at the instruction of the head of the prefecture in Münster, sought to have the company car sequestered. The prefecture intended the measure to affect those persons who were known to have been "active Nazis." Carl now felt "extremely threatened in continuing operations at the plant, which was key to reconstruction and considered crucial by the English Military Government" and again requested the military authorities to provide protection.[24]

At the same time, at the end of November, Carl again gave thought to leaving Steinhude. He now considered Baden-Baden as a possible destination, as he felt that "he could acclimatize to life in the north of the Reich only with difficulty or not at all."[25] He intended to set up a warehouse supplying his foot-care products in Baden-Baden in order to make deliveries to customers in the French occupation zone. In a second step, he planned on establishing a subsidiary plant in Baden-Baden or in Baden-Oos. The idea of setting up a business in Baden-Baden was clearly not a hasty decision. In October 1943, he had already obtained right of first refusal to the purchase of a house that would be suitable as an administrative office. He also had the opportunity of acquiring land for the plant northwest of the Baden-Oos train station.

Birkenstock submitted a report on his company and a copy of his denazification questionnaire to the mayor's office in Baden-Baden—having only shortly beforehand filed the questionnaire with the British military authorities. However, the mayor declared that the documents as tabled were not sufficient to provide an adequate picture of Birkenstock and his operations and subsequently demanded further information about his person, the exact size of the proposed warehouse, and the equipment it required, as well as details of the products that were to be sold. He presumably feared that Birkenstock's relocation there would noticeably increase competition for the local providers of podiatry products.[26] It would appear that discussions on opening a subsidiary in Baden-Baden were discontinued in February 1946.

In the meantime, by the late fall of 1945 relations between Carl Birkenstock and Steinhude's mayor had reached an absolute low. Carl's hopes that he would be allowed to use at least part of his house were dashed. His request that he be permitted to move furniture from his house to his provisional accommodation was turned down by Hobein who, among other things, remarked that Birkenstock was constantly ignoring his instructions, and indeed was "treating me like dirt on his shoes."[27] For his part, Carl felt that in his professional world he was now surrounded completely by enemies and was the victim of a witch hunt, of a "systematic attempt to poison the well" that was being "conducted by all persons who interact with me either in an official or a semi-official capacity."[28]

Consequently, after December 1945, when it had been proven that Carl's sister-in-law's family (the Endres family) had done everything in the postwar period to blacken his name with the authorities in Steinhude and Stadthagen, and to paint him in the worst possible light, Carl's attorney appealed to Hobein, asking him to acknowledge the results of his investigation and "in future not to accept such talk as true."[29]

The Nazi period and World War II were a catalyst for existing family tensions, something that did not just apply to the Birkenstock family. Different experiences and different interpretations of individual behavior deepened the conflicts—especially in those family businesses that were run by brothers or members of different family lines—fueled distrust between family members, and put a strain on the joint management of companies, sometimes for years.[30]

By this time, the divide between Carl Birkenstock and the mayor's office had gone past the point of no return. At any rate, he continued to feel under pressure. Hobein had not altered his opinion and sought to "damage him and bring production to a halt," he believed. He felt that "countless small means" were used to "continue the pernicious campaign, although it seems obvious that there is absolutely no substantive material—aside from envy and resentment—that can be adduced."[31]

In their review of the allegations, the authorities came to conclusions that were similar to Carl's views on important points. Former employees had testified that Carl had "exploited his affiliation with the Party for business purposes." Since this claim was made by employees who had been fired by Birkenstock, its validity is at least questionable. A police officer called Niemeier retracted his statement that Carl had filed a complaint against his sister-in-law. However, according to Niemeier, Carl had suggested that his sister-in-law listened to "enemy radio stations," whereupon Niemeier warned Mrs. Endres about this. Therefore, or so the enquiry concluded, Carl Birkenstock should "not complain if he is regarded and treated locally as a convinced supporter of the Party."[32] Carl sought to defend himself against this insinuation by citing the arguments presented above.[33]

In the midst of all these family disputes, personal animosities, and local power struggles, given the heated relations between the various actors involved, possibly coupled with the propensity to want to settle "old scores," the question as to how Carl Birkenstock had behaved during the war years could obviously no longer be answered in any kind of level-headed manner. There are indications that he was in part himself responsible for his postwar difficulties, because "he missed no opportunity for self-aggrandizement, and in the event of even the most minor slight on his person immediately submitted voluminous reports and petitions to the various authorities and had made a huge fuss about a statement by Mrs. Endres that had not yet had any impact on him, and all of that contributed to things becoming as intractable as they have now become."[34] At times, Birkenstock also tended to drastically exaggerate. For example, in one postwar letter he even suggested that his name not only sounded Jewish, but that he had indeed been forced to suffer immensely as a "Jewish half-breed." In such a case, he was evidently prepared to bend the truth in order to defend himself.[35]

In the final analysis, Carl saw no other way out of his predicament than to leave Steinhude. Although the decision meant him "abandoning part of his life's work," having now had his "nerves injured by the most unbelievable methods" for what was now 16 years, he decided he did not want "to be tormented to death" and would look for a new base for his business and his private life that was close to his "old home."[36] By early May 1946, when Carl explained the reasons for his decision to the staff in Steinhude, he had already found a new location for his plant.

On March 29, 1946, Carl applied to the Chamber of Commerce and Industry in Bonn to found (the application also speaks of "re-opening") a plant for podiatry products in Bad Honnef. With a monthly output of 8,000 to 10,000 pairs of shoe insoles, so the application stated, miners, hospitals, former soldiers with amputated limbs, and other "persons with podiatric complaints" were to be supported.[37] One day later, he filed a request with the District Housing Authority in Stadthagen to be permitted to relocate to Bad Honnef. There, he wrote, he intended to live with his wife and three children in order to open a "branch factory for orthopedic products." At the same time, he asked the District Housing Authority in Siegburg to issue him with "permission to take up residence." With the agreement of the municipal authorities in Bad Honnef, he wrote, he rented an "empty log cabin" outside of the town in the Schmelztal valley. Thus, the conditions were in place for him to swiftly open a "factory for orthopedic foot-care products."[38]

A few days later, the Chamber of Commerce and Industry welcomed the foundation of the company "in the interests of the populace's health," and on April 23, 1946, the Military Government Headquarter in Siegburg approved the "re-opening" of the plant in Bad Honnef. Exactly when the company started manufacturing there and discontinued operations in Steinhude is unclear. Since the production facility in Lower Saxony has a permit dated November 21, 1946, for the continuation of production, it can be assumed that production continued in Steinhude for a transitional period.[39] It took at least five months before provisional permission to commence manufacturing was received by the company Carl Birkenstock, Fabrik für orthopädische Spezialitäten, in Bad Honnef.[40]

Alongside the difficult family and business conditions that Carl had to contend with after the end of the war, more than ever there was the issue to be resolved of the cooperation between the three locations (Steinhude, Friedberg, and Berlin). The focus here was on the fundamental product strategy, on possible collaboration between the different locations, a division of business on the basis of newly defined regions, the still incomplete liquidation of Gebr. Birkenstock GmbH in Steinhude (in liquidation since December 1939), and the future of the family property in Friedberg, which was by and large in ruins. All of this needed to be sorted out quickly if, or so Heinrich Birkenstock opined in September 1945, "the existing chaos is not to be crowned by something even worse."[41]

The different branches of the family were in agreement in principle that a debate on the overall strategy was needed if they were to constrain the brothers' self-centered approach to business and thus balance the entrepreneurial interests of all involved to a better degree than before. However, the discussion of strategy that ensued soon revealed different ideas about the future emphasis of company policy. Long before the market launch of the *Original Birkenstock-Footbed Sandal* in 1963, the idea of the company concentrating on the production of their own shoe had surfaced in the postwar period, as mentioned briefly above. The notion was first aired in October 1947 by Konrad Jr., who recommended "starting joint shoe production and initially focusing on making an orthop[edic] sandal." The item was "comparatively easy to make" and was "urgently needed on a large scale." The inception of the production branch "would no doubt achieve far greater successes with substantially less effort than was required for the 50-year development of the nonmetallic insole." In the period up to the next joint meeting of the brothers, in-depth conceptual proposals relating to the idea tabled by Konrad Jr. were to be submitted.[42]

Carl himself pursued a different strategic concept. He believed establishing an "Elastigang company" would be the proper way of better satisfying the interests of all the brothers. He rated the market opportunities for the insole he had developed in the early 30s to be extraordinarily good in Europe as a whole—in principle, according to Carl, this meant strong demand and the chance to supply the article to those specialist shoe retailers who would not qualify for the *Footbed* (this involved, by his estimate, some 8,000–10,000 stores) because they had not completed the training courses that Carl required to ensure the correct use and adjustment of the *Footbed*.

The product was very easy to make using existing materials, so, in his opinion, it was tantamount to gross negligence not to seize such an opportunity, especially as this "great and fine endeavor" would, he felt, bring the brothers closer together again. As soon as a consensus was reached, he continued, there could be discussion about involving or bringing on board his brother-in-law Alfred Weber to make him part of the new Elastigang company, which was to be managed by Konrad Jr. His plan was for the article to be manufactured in Friedberg.[43]

In the months that followed, there was no detailed discussion of Carl's suggestions. Heinrich would probably have been prepared to pursue the idea, but Konrad Jr., by contrast, did not respond to Carl's repeated request that he take a clearer position on the proposal. The criticism was leveled at Konrad Jr. that over the past two years any attempt to reach a common agreement had "not led to any sort of result or to practical work."[44]

With the Soviet occupation of East Germany, Heinrich, above all, saw that for obvious reasons there was an urgent need to take action with regard to how the brothers divided up the business regions between them. The growing political division of postwar Germany and the currency reform of 1949 were "not exactly pleasant" for him,[45] and the markets in the Soviet occupation zone were in danger of being irretrievably lost. Yet again, no swift solution was found. A firm proposal by Heinrich that he would swap a part of the region assigned to him for a region in the Soviet occupation zone came to nothing owing to opposition from Konrad Jr., who evidently wanted a completely new "division": the Birkenstock brothers (and presumably their brother-in-law Alfred Weber) should each be assigned a region in West Germany, he said.[46] An agreement on this seemed well-nigh impossible, especially as Konrad Jr. was now clearly intent on going his own way in his conduct of day-to-day business.

In October 1948, Heinrich made a detailed report to Carl: "At the Frankfurt Trade Fair, I had a small, modest exhibition booth, as I did not expect many guests from my region. Konrad Jr. together with Alfred had a large, well-designed booth, on the assumption that many interested parties would come from Alfred's old region. At the beginning of the trade fair, I naturally sent all the customers from the region that wasn't mine to Konrad Jr.'s booth in order to maintain the existing order."[47] His brother was not interested in fair business play, however, as Heinrich went on to say: "I have now studied the matter a little more closely and have sadly been forced to conclude that the two gentlemen set out to capture my customers and accept orders intended for me without informing anyone of the situation. [...] Moreover, I noticed [...] that business friends who specifically wanted to visit me and, without knowing better, ended up at the [...] Friedberg booth, were deceived by references to correspondence with me and the pretense that everything was as it should be." Heinrich also wrote that he had learned from his sister that Konrad Jr. was specifically assigning Carl's old sales reps to the others' individual business regions in order to acquire customers there.[48]

In Heinrich's opinion, there was no longer any common ground for a business relationship. Konrad Jr. had declared, he reported, that "he was now going out into the world, which was his oyster" and was "consistently rejecting any collaboration with his brothers, [...] allying himself instead with Alfred Weber." The two of them, Heinrich believed, "no doubt intend to use any means necessary to exploit the decades of work put in by others." "Under these circumstances, there is no expectation of" any cooperation between them, "which may never perhaps be possible."[49]

The discussions on a joint strategic focus for the Birkenstock companies were overshadowed by further disputes. The liquidation of Gebr. Birkenstock GmbH in Steinhude, which had still not been completed, emerged as a permanent bone of contention between Carl and Konrad Jr. At issue was the whereabouts of the gold-embossing press, the printing molds, the Geha duplicator, the plaster molds, and the cutting dies, and the final financial accounts. The brothers once again found it very hard to reach a consensus. Both sides accused the other of not adhering to the agreements that had been made and blamed each other for the long overdue settlement of the liquidation. The dispute did not involve any life-and-death business issues, and yet it escalated from month to month, fanning the flames of animosity between Carl and Konrad Jr. and preoccupying the family until the early 50s.[50]

Last but not least, the focus was also on material support for their parents, who were no longer in the best of health: they depended on cost-intensive medical support and, having lost some of their wealth owing to the currency reform, now led their lives with modest financial resources. This went hand in hand with the question of how, and with what capital, the destroyed property in Friedberg could swiftly be rebuilt. One of the ideas discussed was to have the profits from sales of the *Footbed* accrue to their father to help him pay the rent and to devote part of the earnings generated in Friedberg to reconstructing the home on Feuerbachstrasse.[51] There is no documentation to show what agreements were then reached.

Birkenstock in the Years of Economic Reconstruction

Although the brothers could not reach an agreement on any of the key issues, and the gap dividing them was clearly apparent, all the families persevered with the idea of the companies cooperating—or even merging. It was evidently Carl, who, in early 1951, sought to advance cooperation, eyeing a potential amalgamation of the different locations. The issues of joint procurement, price categories, etc., were discussed in several rounds of talks in which a representative of the Friedberg Chamber of Commerce and Industry participated.[52]

Not for the first time, there were differences of opinion as to the objective the talks were to achieve. Heinrich, for example, proposed founding three new companies and in that way expanding the range of orthopedic systems on offer: a "Schritthelf-GmbH" (the "Schritthelf System" was a version of the orthopedic support) to be based in Büdingen; a "Gebr. Birkenstock GmbH" in Bad Honnef, which would manufacture and distribute the "second orthopedic system"; and a "Birkenstock AG" in Friedberg, where a new shoe factory would be established. The proposal was poorly received, particularly by Carl, who wanted to focus energy on two limited liability companies (GmbH)—his exact ideas in

132   **1945–1963** Beginning of the Industrial Era

spring 1951 are not known.[53] Evidently, the brothers did not succeed in negotiating a mutually agreeable solution to founding a joint wholesale company for orthopedic footwear and other articles to be domiciled in Friedberg. The partnership agreement was more or less ready to be signed in April 1951 but was jettisoned for reasons unknown.[54]

The brothers were no longer able to agree on the smaller-ticket items, either. In spring 1951, Carl, Heinrich, and Konrad Jr. failed to reach agreement on joint advertising in the orthopedic specialist publication "Fuß und Schuh." A few weeks later, the idea of running a joint booth at a health trade fair in Cologne likewise proved impossible to realize. Carl believed that reaching consensus on what should be exhibited and who would man the booth at what times was an issue that could be swiftly resolved. However, Konrad Jr. ended up distancing himself from the plan, pointing out that there was too little time left to prepare.[55]

In July 1951, Carl drew his own conclusions from these aborted efforts to find a basis for cooperation acceptable to all the brothers and declared that the search for the lowest common denominator had failed once and for all. Since he had, for several years and "to the point of self-sacrificing" his own interests, put up proposals for discussion without any success, he was henceforth discontinuing any effort to find a compromise. He said that he regretted "most bitterly the relations between the Birkenstock brothers" but "the thirst for absolute independence seems in the course of the years to have become so pronounced that there is no clear way of sorting out what is needed." He, too, would therefore "have to go his own way" now.[56]

As the years went by, the significance of the plants in Büdingen and Friedberg gradually dwindled. In 1952, Heinrich relocated his company for producing and trading orthopedic articles and footwear as well as goods for the shoe and healthcare supply sectors from Büdingen to Bad Homburg. The limited liability company was only in business for another two years and was then deregistered on July 24, 1954. The Gebr. Birkenstock OHG as general partnership in Friedberg had a checkered history that amounted to a process of slow decline. After Catharina Weber died, the company's almost 65-year history in Friedberg came to an end in 1980, when Alfred Weber and their son Erich discontinued operations and sold the plant. The new owners tore down the factory buildings and built houses on the former company grounds.[57]

In Carl's opinion, in West Germany's early years the "way out of the orthopedic chaos" was still a long way from being found. "Things were especially complicated" in the field of "orthopedic chiropody products" because "alongside doctors, surgical truss makers, master shoemak-

On the Path to "Walking as Nature Intended": From the *Footbed* to a Shoe   133

Fig. 28: As trend-setting as the inventions and publications of Carl Birkenstock (1900–1982) were, the entrepreneurial balance of these ideas remained mixed. The concept of the *Ideal-Schuh* was too ambitious and not suitable for mass production.

ers, shoe manufacturers and retailers, as well as masseurs and chiropodists all felt themselves authorized and able to play a part in supporting many people with foot complaints." In what were at times "fierce debates," the emphasis was on economic self-interest, prestige, and competence. Frequently, the exchange of opinions was anything but "matter-of-fact." In such a situation, anyone wanting to push through ideas for reform needed to be "willing to put up a fight," to "go on the attack, be tenacious, and be able to field comprehensive arguments in debate and reasoned disputation."[58] Indeed, since the late 40s, Carl had been trying to convince doctors, health insurance companies, and professional associations of the effectiveness of his idea for a flexible, metal-free insole. In the tough and at times passionate discussions, he proved himself once again—just as in the 30s—to be an "uncomfortable idealist."[59]

In the postwar period, Carl continued undaunted in his attempt to establish a common basis of business with the truss and healthcare products specialists and soon expressed his interest in "pleasant collaboration with the leading surgical truss experts." He considered a fruitful specialist exchange of ideas "with a shot of the necessary serious idealism" to be one key precondition for the entire sector to make progress.[60] He was from the outset very confident in such discussions, and to his mind there could be no question that the exchange of ideas would serve, in the final instance, to inform members of the specialist associations "of the superb performance achieved by my system."[61] As of spring 1947, Carl exchanged frequent letters with Hugo Stortz, the chairman of the Consortium for the Orthopedics, Surgical, Technicians, and Surgical Truss Makers trades. Initially, Stortz could see no argument in favor of collaborating with Birkenstock. On the contrary, he concluded that Birkenstock's "entire propaganda" and the sale of its insoles were far too strongly geared to the shoe business, and for that reason alone cooperation was out of the question. In addition, the companies represented by the consortium championed the view "that the right insole can only be provided by the specialist and not by a saleswoman in a shoe store who had familiarized herself with foot anatomy for a day or two." Moreover, no proven expert would subscribe to the claim made in publications and circulars that the *Footbed* "moved with the foot," massaged the sole, stimulated circulation, and contributed "to a constant rejuvenation of one's powers." Opinions on the Birkenstock insoles diverged too greatly to allow for a more extensive exchange of ideas.[62]

In the weeks that followed, both sides nevertheless tried hard to overcome their prejudices, place the talks on a more sober footing, and find a viable basis for collaboration—successfully so, it would seem. After in-depth preliminary talks, Carl Birkenstock's Fabrik für orthopädische Spezialitäten in Bad Honnef concluded an agreement with the consortium led by Hugo Stortz and with the Professional Association of Surgical Instrument and Healthcare Product Retailers. The June 1, 1949, agreement envisaged, among other things, that Birkenstock provide any companies interested, for a trial period of three months on commission, with an assortment of products from the *Fußbett mit dem Ring DRP*, *Naturaform*, and *Naturette* lines, as well as foot powder, foot bathing salts, and *Flüssigol*, a preparation designed to combat sweaty feet, for the companies to assess more closely. After the end of the three months, all companies that were members of the professional associations would then be supplied with the *Naturaform* and *Naturette* products in a special edition.[63]

The first upset occurred only a few days later. The contractual partners had agreed that Carl would send the agreement to all members of the associations and the companies would then, of their own volition, decide whether they wished to receive the specimen delivery. Birkenstock, by contrast, felt it appropriate to send the member companies not only the agreement but the shoe insoles too, along with a specialist book on the *System Birkenstock*. This aggressive approach caused some irritation among several firms in the consortium, and they refused to accept the agreement with Birkenstock.[64]

The dispute is a prime example of how talks then proceeded for almost the next four years. Carl explored how far he could push the limits of collaboration and at times simply overstepped the mark. He tended to interpret agreements generously in his own favor, and now and again he lacked the necessary sensitivities in business dealings to do justice to the interests and needs of the consortium. In particular, his deliveries of insoles to chiropodists and almost any foot-care provider caused real annoyance.[65] Furthermore, in the talks he was often very confident and exaggerated the purported benefits of his products, which were, so he claimed, far superior in quality and in terms of how they fostered good health to the articles offered by surgical truss makers. Besides this, there were, on several occasions, discussions about whether the agreement reached between the parties in June 1949 was even legal in the first place.

In autumn 1953, Carl had forfeited any trust he had established with Hugo Stortz and the consortium. Birkenstock admittedly remarked that he was pursuing "truly idealistic intentions" and said he "would happily collaborate with the surgical truss makers for the benefit of those with foot complaints," and that he was not to blame for what were by then bad relations between the parties. In West Germany's early years, Carl noticed a strong aversion to his company on the part of the surgical truss makers that he found "more than puzzling."[66] By November 1953, the consortium and the central guild association had had enough and decided to pull the plug. Despite professing a continued interest in cooperation, Stortz could see no way around the fact that Birkenstock's "propaganda and methods had undermined any support" among the specialist surgical truss makers," noting that "none of us set any store by a collaboration."[67]

Aside from that, the agreement did nothing to improve the relationship between the three brothers. Heinrich raised objections to it early on. When visiting clients in Southern Germany, he wrote, it had come to his attention that member companies of the consortium had been recommended products from Bad Honnef, a business practice that violated his "sole supply rights" for the insole *Footbed* in Southern Germany.[68]

Carl also devoted a lot of energy to developing champions and allies among medical doctors. He continued to have great expectations of help from Wilhelm Thomsen, who in the postwar years was, as a professor of orthopedics, still one of the preeminent members of the profession and held high-profile positions on various committees of the German Orthopedics Association. Initially, Carl was not disappointed in his expectations. Thomsen had for many years been following Birkenstock's work and repeatedly confirmed the health-enhancing effect of the *Footbed* and *Fußfriede* products. Among the other express advocates of Birkenstock products was Dr. Erich Druschky, who in 1952 made a key contribution to the foundation of Kosmetikschule Neckarbischofsheim, a cosmetics school that functioned as an educational venue for the doctors' wives.[69]

Birkenstock felt a strong bond with Druschky for years, praising his articles and publications as "marvelous summaries of our system" that

136 **1945-1963** Beginning of the Industrial Era

Fig. 29: Carl Birkenstock offered a diverse range of insoles, which he distributed internationally. It was the basis of the company's economic success.

were highly scientific and "conclusive." As previously envisaged with Heinz Neu, it was now Druschky who provided the *System Birkenstock* with a quasi-philosophical superstructure. By contrast, relations with Thomsen clearly cooled over the years. At the latest in summer 1958, Thomsen forfeited any remaining sympathies Carl had for him when, in an essay for the Monatszeitschrift der Deutschen Angestellten-Kranken-kasse, he provided "concrete advertising" for a wooden sandal made by Hamburg-based firm Berkemann. Carl Birkenstock felt it was no longer possible to overlook the fact that Birkenstock insoles and their benefits were "consciously not being mentioned," while at the same time "he is increasingly using our ideas for his own purposes." Thomsen, Carl concluded, no longer had any ideas of his own.[70]

The efforts down through the years to woo support among medical doctors apparently bore little fruit. On the 60th anniversary of the foundation of the Konrad Birkenstock GmbH in Frankfurt, Birkenstock did not beat around the bush when complaining about the lack of backing from that quarter. He could not "understand why our courses and constructive advertising are being overlooked, done down, and frustrated." Every "insider" knew that there were "invisible" and apparently "inaccessible" forces that, for example, "by excluding any competition based on performance, grant small vocational groups with no knowledge of feet and shoes a certain persistent monopoly position," something that also harmed the medical profession, which should instead assume the role of "arbitrator," given the wide range of orthopedic auxiliaries.[71]

Carl found it just as difficult to persuade the health insurance companies to recognize his insoles as "standard items for reimbursement" and assume the costs for those they insured. In the early 50s, opinions among the health insurers were divided in this regard. In February 1950, the health insurers association for the Cologne district, for example, strictly rejected "the assumption of costs in any cases whatsoever."[72] At the same time, there were associations that included the Birkenstock insoles in the services they covered, only, however, to withdraw that approval a little later. The situation was simply unclear. The stance taken by the health insurance companies was a prime reflection of Birkenstock's position among the various providers of orthopedic auxiliaries in the period between the end of the war and economic reconstruction. Despite his enthusiastic statements in praise of his system, the benefits of his insoles remained controversial in specialist circles and in the final instance more or less a matter of faith.

The Birkenstock company's subordinate importance or outsider role in the industry is also highlighted by the relevant debates held by the Ger-

138 **1945–1963** Beginning of the Industrial Era

man orthopedic society (Deutsche Orthopädische Gesellschaft-DOG), the most important expert association for the orthopedic sciences. The *System Birkenstock* played no part in its discussions on the impact of personally made or factory-produced insoles. Associations such as the society for the promotion of foot health (Gesellschaft zur Förderung der Fußgesundheit—GFF), which strongly supported Carl Birkenstock, met with little backing at DOG level. The GFF's German Foot Health Conventions organized between 1951 and 1953, which were a forum especially well suited to Birkenstock's needs when it came to familiarizing a broader swathe of the public with his insights regarding podiatry, attracted a few expert speakers from DOG but were nevertheless regarded more as "an advertising activity by businesses engaging in foot care."[73] Likewise, the extensive memoirs of Franz Schede, a renowned German podiatric doctor during the first five decades of the 20th century, do not once mention the Birkenstock philosophy or the company's patents.[74]

From the early 50s onwards, business conditions improved for just about all industrial sectors. Throughout West Germany, swift progress was being made to rebuild "the society of ruins."[75] The modernization of the economy and society, the swift acceptance of the democratic constitutional order, and the dreams of "small-scale affluence"[76] can primarily be attributed to the spectacular economic development that, for many contemporary observers, amounted to a veritable miracle. There was an array of reasons why West Germany's economy boomed so swiftly. From 1948 onwards, the country benefited from American aid (loans, raw materials, etc.) designed to rebuild the European economy. In addition to the "Marshall Plan," as it was called, which closely integrated West Germany politically into the Western alliance, the transition to a social market economy, West Germany's return to the global markets, and a large pool of well-trained workers also helped power the boom. The sharp economic upturn was also facilitated by global politics. The Korean War (1950–1953) noticeably boosted demand for goods produced by the armaments industry (the "Korea Boom"), demand that West German corporations also sought to meet once the country's former enemies in the West had resolved to lift the production caps on iron and steel products. Moreover, mechanical engineering, the chemical industry, and carmakers were all among the main beneficiaries of the upturn: together, they ensured that for 15 years West Germany prospered economically.

Between 1950 and 1956, real social product per capita grew on average by 5.6 percent (France: 3.7 percent; Great Britain: 2.3 percent; USA: 2 percent). Labor productivity rose, corporations invested more than ever before, and unemployment remained triflingly low.[77] The economic upturn was also something that countless families started to notice in the form of increasing disposable income. Average monthly net income climbed between 1950 and 1955: in workers' households, from DM 283 to DM 474; in the households of white-collar workers and government employees, from DM 346 to DM 570; and in the families of the self-employed, from DM 437 to DM 754.[78]

Companies such as Birkenstock (in 1950, C. B. Orthopädie – Carl Birkenstock – Fabriken für orthopädische Spezialitäten was entered in the commercial register and in 1952 was transformed into C. B. Orthopädie GmbH) did not benefit as strongly from the economic upturn as did corporations in growth sectors such as mechanical engineering and the automobile industry. The boom was less frenetic for shoe manufacturers, who, between 1950 and 1964, only enjoyed about half the growth seen by the industrial sector as a whole.[79] There were various reasons for this. The service life of shoes was longer now than with previous models; large sections of the population were, moreover, not willing to simply throw away shoes that did not have substantial material damage. The growing degree of motorization also had a major impact on the distances being walked, and shoes were thus exposed to less wear and tear than in the past.[80] Nor did the structure of private consumer spending play into the hands of the shoe industry. Surveys conducted at the time show that in 1954, a four-person working-class family spent its monthly disposable income as follows: 22 percent on housing, heating, and lighting (DM 55), 49 percent on food, drink, and tobacco (DM 122.50), 14 percent on clothes (DM 35), and 15 percent on other needs (DM 37.50). Put differently, a total sum of about DM 420 was available each year for clothes. Estimates suggest that of this figure, about 20 percent (DM 85) was spent on shoes—a budget that at best allowed one pair of leather shoes to be purchased per family member.[81] From the point of view of a shoe manufacturer marketing orthopedic products such as Carl Birkenstock, there was another specific challenge to be overcome. In his opinion, the population did not yet have sufficient awareness of foot health. He considered it more or less a permanent task to bang the drum for foot care and stress the great importance of his own orthopedic articles for personal well-being.[82]

The Desire for Fashion: From the Jedermann Program to Mass Consumption

BY JOHANNA STEINFELD

The end of World War II on May 8, 1945, spelled poverty and existential hardship for the German population on a scale that was inconceivable in the years that immediately preceded it, when the exploitation of foreign slave laborers in farming and the looting of the occupied territories had kept the home front comparatively well supplied.[1] A full 2,700 calories per day per person had been the target set for the Germans at the beginning of the war by the Nazi leadership, and in the spring of 1945 the figure was still around 2,100 per day. In the first year after the war, public nutrition looked much more meager, as the Allies rationed the daily calorie count of the German population to 1,500 per capita.[2] Accordingly, one of the biggest concerns of West Germans immediately after the war was (or so surveys by the US military government revealed) the procurement of food. Other concerns cited by West Germans were fears that missing persons might not be found and that clothing and footwear would be difficult to obtain.[3] This highlighted the fact that people were existentially dependent on clothing to protect and warm their bodies and feet and to participate in public life.

A somewhat changed—but not necessarily improved—situation emerged after the currency reform in the three western occupation zones in June 1948. Goods were once again available in stores, but they became increasingly unaffordable. At the same time as the currency reform, most of the prices that had been fixed until then were also deregulated and rose to such an extent that the government of the time felt compelled to act. The situation was aggravated by protests and strikes that broke out because of the high prices and in support of fundamental political demands. The policy tool of choice here was not renewed regulatory intervention in the prices that had just been liberalized but rather a supply-side boost to trigger a reduction in prices.[4] This agenda found expression in the so-called Jedermann ("Everyman") Program, a short-term measure aimed at the mass production of plain consumer goods without any fashionable design.[5] Among these, textile goods and shoes were a particular focus, as they were considered an "especially sensitive sector in terms of economic and social policy" for the reasons explained above.[6] In August

1948, 700,000 Jedermann shoes had already been rolled out, a high proportion compared with a total of two million shoes that had been produced in the Bizone, the combined American and British zones of occupation, that month.[7] Production quotas for Jedermann shoes continued to rise through December 1948, with a major factor in this production expansion being that the companies involved in production were able to obtain scarce leather.[8]

As clothing prices fell from the beginning of 1949, the Jedermann program became less important but was nevertheless extended into the early 50s. Despite the large overall production volumes compared with the total supply, the main effect of the program was more of a psychological nature as it did not really bring about significant changes in the real economy.[9] These changes therefore took place independently of the Jedermann program and were also made possible in part by American support in the form of the Marshall Plan.

After the founding of the Federal Republic of Germany (West Germany) on May 23, 1949, the consolidation of the economy progressed. With respect to shoe consumption, this meant the level started to approximate that of prewar conditions; back then, for the majority of the population, their patterns of consumption might not have been particularly lavish, but they had been able to rely on a solid supply of shoes. A representative survey conducted by the Emnid polling institute in Bielefeld found that the volume of shoes purchased between the currency reform in August 1948 and the time of the survey in November 1949 was roughly equivalent to the amount purchased in the year before the outbreak of World War II. Indeed, almost half of the respondents (44.4 percent) had purchased a pair of shoes between August 1948 and November 1949, just as the bulk of respondents had also done before the war (46.6 percent). A total of 26.1 percent had purchased two pairs during this postwar period, while only a fraction had purchased three pairs (7 percent), and only a small minority had purchased four (1.6 percent) or five pairs (0.8 percent). Overall, a man in West Germany owned an average of 2.8 pairs of shoes in November 1949, while a woman possessed an average of 3.2 pairs.[10]

As the Jedermann shoe had already shown, the need for beauty and fashion was an essential criterion in decisions about consumption, despite daily shortages. For, as the Frankfurter Allgemeine Zeitung reported in December 1949, "even those with less purchasing power were not to be persuaded to buy the models labeled as Jedermann shoes." Shoe companies therefore had to adapt and change to more pleasing and fashionable designs, including for lower-income strata of the population.[11] As soon as people's

1945–1963 Beginning of the Industrial Era

Fig. 30: Three years after the end of the
Second World War, people's desire for
fashion had returned in Germany, too
(a shoe shop in Hamburg, 1948).

existential needs were satisfied, fashion criteria seemed to dominate purchasing decisions. As a result of the desire for fashionable shoes, the dichotomy that had emerged in the 20s between standard shoes (i. e., shoes with no focus on a particular design) and fashion shoes with designs oriented to international trends and seasonal developments thus became more prevalent again after World War II.[12]

These desires for fashionable shoes were thus driven by the requisite purchasing power, which rose to an unprecedentedly high level for large sections of the population during the years of the "economic miracle." The fact that real wages doubled between 1949 and 1963 during Konrad Adenauer's government spawned entirely new consumer opportunities.[13] By the end of the 50s, society was characterized by mass consumption—i. e., there was a supply of goods for the broad population thanks to mass production. However, while the purchasing power of consumers had risen sharply, making it more likely that consumers' needs could be met in the market, the desire for fashion posed major challenges for German shoe companies. As a result, these companies reacted somewhat cautiously to the production of fashionable, constantly changing collections.[14] This was because these also went hand in hand with a "fashion risk," as the designs had to prove themselves on the market.[15] Moreover, the labor-intensive shoe industry was dependent on mass production, which was difficult to combine with a focus on fashionable designs.[16] The German shoe industry was not up to dealing with these seemingly intractable problems of fashion footwear production. From the 60s on, it was increasingly confronted with a process of shrinkage that was unique within the West German economy.

The Third Generation of *Health Footwear*

Between the end of World War II and the period of economic reconstruction, at Bad Honnef the next generation of the family was prepared to assume greater entrepreneurial responsibility. Born in 1936 in Hannover, Carl's son Karl Birkenstock started his career in the family-owned business in 1954. In his early years, he evidently showed a strong interest in technology, work materials, and raw materials. His specialist knowledge was something he acquired at his father's side—when accompanying him on his training courses. Added to which, he gained some experience when visiting the Bad Honnef specialty store for shoe insoles. He familiarized himself with all the different foot complaints caused by people wearing unsuitable shoes. He also picked up on the fact that not all complaints and pains could be cured using the *Footbed*.

So how did Birkenstock succeed in holding its own in what is still a decidedly heterogeneous sector? What factors helped the company consolidate and enjoy a moderate upturn in its fortunes? In the 50s, the core of the C. B. Orthopädie GmbH product lines continued to be made up of the tried-and-true patented articles: the flexible insole *Footbed* which followed the footprint of a healthy foot; and the *Fußfriede* custom sole, which promised to alleviate more pronounced foot problems (hollow, skew, or splay feet, etc.) and required extensive orthopedic know-how for it to be adjusted correctly. A strong ring mounted on the lower side of the insole *(Birkenstock Ring)* also enabled foot complaints to be offset. Then there was the neutral insole, a blank with no trademarking (again featuring the *Birkenstock Ring*), from which a flexible, personalized insole could be made by hand. The insole *Naturette* was intended for lightweight shoes and was aimed more at lighter persons with less pronounced foot complaints, while the *Naturaform* devised on the basis of the *Footbed* was geared to fashion-conscious customers with clear cases of splay foot. The *Completta* was intended for contemporary fashion shoes, including open shoes, and as a blank could be easily glued into the shoe. Last but not least, the Birkenstock lines included a "second heel," a small "support element" that was glued to the insole plastic. This took the weight off the front of the foot and was used for more extreme cases of splay or hollow foot. The range was complemented by foot-care products such as a footbath for tired feet.[83]

In the mid-50s, Birkenstock managed to expand its range to include an innovative product that was soon in great demand. The new *Zehenfrei* insole required no toe section and for that reason offered various benefits. The toes could move more freely, blood circulation was improved, and muscles were strengthened. This special construction took the weight off the ball of the foot and preempted pain from squeezing. The foot bedding was raised and sculpted and in this way the entire weight of the body was evenly spread across the insole. The *Zehenfrei* took the strain off the heel and prevented foot splaying. Another substantial benefit was that the insole was suitable for a broad range of applications, as it fitted in all shoe types and could be used in any season.[84] Over the years that followed, this model became a bestseller, achieving popularity almost as soon as it was launched. In one "medium-sized town," whose name the company did not reveal, the number of pairs of *Zehenfrei* that were sold rose between 1954 and 1956 from 866 to 2,700.[85]

In the second half of the 50s, the product portfolio clearly reflected the fact that Birkenstock factored current fashion trends into the range offered. Specifically, the insoles *Naturaform, Naturette,* and *Completta* were distributed to shoe retailers who prioritized a fashionable program. It was by no means a matter of course for Carl Birkenstock to follow new shoe fashions. Seen from a strictly orthopedic point of view, fashion shoes and foot health were more or less natural opposites as far as he was concerned. He was not the only one to view women's shoes with high heels as a prime example of unsuccessful footwear. Concerned orthopedic doctors and shoemakers warned against the unnatural shortening of the calf muscles and pointed to the great pressure that the ball and arch of the foot came under by virtue of the body's weight being shifted forwards. Moreover, there were representatives of the profession who doubted the aesthetic appeal of high heels, which were truly not "beautiful." Women "wobbled from side to side with each step they took on the heel, [...] they had to walk with their knees bent [...] and their lower spines curved forwards."[86]

Carl was anything but a trendsetter in the shoe industry and at the end of the day treated the emerging world of shoe fashion with the pragmatism of a businessman. He paid tribute to the "outstanding cognoscenti and experts" whose "wealth of ideas, efforts, and dynamism" had provided regular stimulus to the "fashion sector" and consistently driven its expansion. He likewise acknowledged that this segment of the market offered the entire shoe trade new business opportunities. Nevertheless, he argued, the situation should not be misjudged: the upturn in fashion shoes would not by any means solve all the industry's problems. The dynamism of this area might not, he continued, prove advantageous for smaller and medium-sized specialist retailers but would primarily benefit the "self-service stores."[87]

At the latest by 1960–61, there could be no doubting that Birkenstock likewise needed to take the "dictates of fashion" seriously. Karl took a stance not unlike that of his father when considering how best to assess fashion trends. It was obvious to one and all, he suggested, that in the industry the debate was no longer about "shoes that are good for the feet" but had shifted its focus to fashion. No less than 90 percent of the articles the trade press published were on fashion themes, he noted, such as the most appealing shoe color or different types of toes. Retailers were now only offering products that took their cue from the current shoe fashions and no longer shied away from presenting shoe models in their adverts that "have very little in common with a natural foot." He claimed it was already becoming clear that "deformed feet would increase on a horrific and alarming scale." However, he continued, it was from the outset pointless "to say anything against fashion." Instead, the emphasis must now be on taking the different fashion trends into consideration, exploiting the new business opportunities, and "making a major play for a modern kind of foot service."[88]

Product policies and advertising now increasingly centered on current trends in the shoe industry. In 1961, Birkenstock identified a trend in men's shoes toward "torero heels" of at least four centimeters, with the height of the heels essentially "prescribed" by the fashion industry. The result of this, it was forecast, would be that "many gentlemen will have painful feet" requiring specialist treatment more than ever.[89] Birkenstock believed the set of men with painful feet would constitute a new, larger customer group and recommended to sales reps that they draw shoe retailers' attention to the fact that the *Zehenfrei* insole could be sold alongside the shoe. There was, the company felt, the justified prospect of *Zehenfrei* registering "huge sales."[90]

Birkenstock's sales policy hinged considerably on extensive product advertising. Carl considered advertising to be a "matter of life or death." Among the ad media used, the publications, essays, and shorter articles Carl himself authored played a major role. Back in the 30s, he had already been publishing at a brisk rate, and he continued to do so in the postwar period. Three larger specialist books, published between 1930 and 1948, were followed by countless articles in the relevant trade press. He tended to then have his own publications sent to prospective business partners, medical doctors, and health insurance companies.

In addition to this raft of publications, Birkenstock also relied on an extensive package of advertising measures. Classic brochure advertising was one instrument used, accompanied by others such as ads in newspapers, which were considered the "queen of advertising". Moreover,

Birkenstock also opted for advertising in movie theaters. With the help of "modern, attractive slides," no less than some 20,000 moviegoers—or so in-house calculations suggested in 1961—could be reached in a day in a district covered by a single sales rep. Moreover, the company provided its "external sales staff" and customers with extensive materials for decorating shop windows, with the intention of convincing specialist shoe retailers to set up "C. B. Corners" in their window displays. Carl expected that issuing vouchers to specialist medical doctors would have a real impact. Thus, for example, the "Ärztebriefe" newsletters for medical doctors were accompanied by vouchers for a pair of insoles with a value of up to DM 14. Birkenstock set great store by ensuring that the owners of shoe businesses and their staff were fully conversant with the ins and outs of their products. The foot consultation days that had been running since the 20s, organized by the external sales team in cooperation with a specialist store, were considered an especially important advertising medium and were quite a success, especially in small towns and rural regions. The nationwide training courses had a similar function (as of 1946 they only ran for two days) and were intended to introduce the participants to general issues of foot health and, above all, practical daily work with the products.[91]

Birkenstock's business success depended to a great degree on the performance of the external sales staff and sales reps, and Carl regularly reminded them of that duty in no uncertain terms. No "external sales staffer" should, he said, ever be content with what he had achieved but should always do everything he could to improve his "performance" and sales figures. Birkenstock provided the external sales team with innumerable hints on how to best meet individual targets. For example, he insisted that business trips be carefully planned in advance (the customer lists updated along with the portfolio of advertising materials, the schedule well organized, and with it the route for the trip, etc.), gave "small psychological sales tips," and offered advice on the best use of advertising materials when dealing with specialist retailers, department stores, and medical practitioners.[92]

From a Silver Leg to Healthy Shoes: The History of Podiatry and Orthopedic Footwear Technology

BY JOHANNA STEINFELD

The term "orthopedics" is composed of the Greek words *orthos* for "straight, upright" and *paideia* for "education" and/or *pais* for "child."[1] It dates back to French doctor Nicolas Andry, who coined it in a 1741 treatise on measures to preempt deformations in children. This narrowly defined concept of orthopedics came to be used for the entire specialist field of medicine that addressed congenital or acquired malformations of the human locomotor system.[2] The symbol for orthopedics and orthopedic technology also originated in Andry's treatise: a young tree that has grown crooked and is tied to a post, which is supposed to make it grow straight.

Andry's elaborations were based on far older ideas about orthopedic illnesses and malformations. The writing of Hippocrates (ca. 460 – ca. 370 BCE) is devoted to treating orthopedic complaints.[3] Moreover, back then medical aids were already being devised to compensate for deformations. Well-known later examples of advances in orthopedic technology include the iron hand said to have been worn by knight Gottfried "Götz" von Berlichingen, 16th-century hand prostheses, and the silver leg of Friedrich II, Landgrave of Hessen-Homburg (1633 – 1708). These prosthetic devices were developed by craftsmen, and the importance of their role in orthopedics becoming established as a discipline and in developing orthopedic footwear should not be underestimated.[4]

In the Age of Enlightenment, the ancient Greeks' insights into orthopedic complaints were resurrected and given greater depth, as in Andry's treatise. The notion that a deformed body was the result of divine will increasingly gave way to the view that the human body needed to be influenced while the person was still growing, and the ailment thus corrected. An important step toward establishing and disseminating forms of treatment was the foundation of the first orthopedic institute, set up in Orbe in Switzerland in 1770 by Jean André Venel (1740 – 1791).[5] One of the fundamental orthopedic insights was that deformations needed time to heal, and here it was applied in daily practice: the children being given treatment received school lessons for the duration of their stay. Venel's institute and his work became a role model for other orthopedic institutes and encouraged publications on orthopedic treatment.[6]

The orthopedic procedures were initially conservative, with surgical interventions as a way of correcting deformation being a later phenomenon. In the first half of the 19th century, surgical interventions started to be used to heal club feet, meaning feet that were misaligned such that the soles were turned inwards.[7] Progress in scientific medicine and technologies in the 19th century enabled orthopedic surgeons to rely on a range of treatments that went far beyond smaller interventions. The introduction of ether anesthesia in 1846 and subsequent findings on how to apply antiseptic measures to prevent germs and infections spreading made it possible to open up joints, cut through and straighten bones, and even heal lame limbs.[8] Furthermore, the discovery of X-rays by German physicist Wilhelm Conrad Röntgen in 1895 led to great improvements in diagnostics. Keeping pace with all the scientific advances being made, in the course of the 19th century medical doctors pressed ahead with defining orthopedics as a field in its own right and establishing its scientific foundations. This process was also driven by the foundation in 1901 of the Deutsche Gesellschaft für Orthopädische Chirurgie (German Association for Orthopedic Surgery; in 1913, it was renamed Deutsche Orthopädische Gesellschaft—German Association

of Orthopedics),[9] which had almost 600 members by the beginning of World War I.[10]

Anatomical-orthopedic research also focused on the feet. Medical practitioners such as Peter Camper in the 18th century and Hermann Meyer in the mid-19th century investigated the structure of the foot and how to treat ailments caused by shoes (see Shoe Designs by the *Lebensreform* Movement). Drawing on this body of knowledge, prior to World War I, adherents of the *Lebensreform* movement developed models for shoes that did justice to the shape of the feet. The same was true of shoemakers who, following in the footsteps of their predecessors in past centuries, tinkered about developing healthy shoes. Progress was also triggered by demand from the army for well-fitting boots that were made for long marches and for war, the consequences of which—and the related injuries—had to be mitigated by special forms of treatment.[11]

The demand among those injured in the war for orthopedic footwear eventually led in 1917 to the establishment in Leipzig of the Verband der Orthopädieschuhmachermeister (Association of Orthopedic Master Shoemakers), whose profession was not yet officially recognized by law.[12] However, at this point in time, there was not yet a particularly pronounced body of basic medical knowledge on the subject,[13] and only a few orthopedic experts assumed

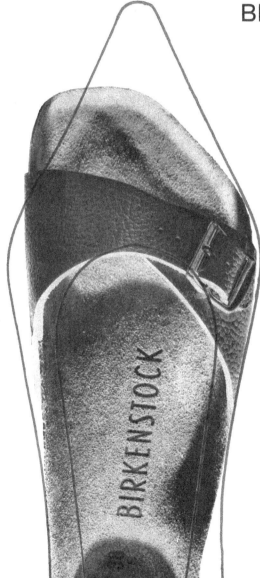

Fig. 31: Ahead of their time and bucking the trend back then: the *Original Birkenstock-Footbed Sandal* (Birkenstock Post 16, 1966).

that the wrong shoes could lead to deformation of the feet. Moreover, orthopedic insights were rarely taken into account in shoe manufacturing, and in any case it was only possible, in essence, for the larger shoe corporations to apply these insights to industrial shoemaking to a limited extent.[14] During the Third Reich, the leaders of the Nazi regime were interested in issues relating to improving the health of the populace, drawing on the understanding that good shoes were an important part of military equipment. The idea that orthopedics experts, medical practitioners, and the manufacturers of shoes and shoe lasts could jointly work to improve healthy shoes became reality in 1938 when the German Prüf- und Forschungsstelle für den Leisten- und Schuhbau (Testing and Research Agency for the Production of Lasts and Shoes) was set up. In principle, however, the isolation of German sciences and the large number of orthopedics experts who were persecuted or murdered weakened orthopedics in Germany.[15]

After the end of World War II, the agency was re-established in 1949 by Deutsche Orthopädische Gesellschaft under the proviso that its work was to promote the development of shoes and preserve the health of people's feet.[16] However, it was especially difficult to put this undertaking into practice owing to the fact that at this time, in the 50s, the trend of fashionable women's shoes started to boom, giving rise to

shoes that had heels and sharp tips. The resulting pains and ailments were not limited just to feet, as a psychiatrist emphasized in an article in a 1960 issue of *Constanze* magazine: "I see a third of my patients just once in my consulting room. After examining them, I send them straight to an orthopedics expert. Their physical and mental ailments come straight from their feet. In the case of women, I can diagnose 'foot disorders' from seeing how they sit in the waiting room."[17]

Although in the decades that followed fashions that were friendlier on the feet evolved, orthopedic and orthopedically inspired shoes still only occupied a niche market—despite the spread of some models such as Birkenstock sandals in the mass market. Today, we are still seeing innovations in this segment, and they can be expected to continue going forward.[18] Here, scientific-orthopedic research on feet plays a role, as does the development and improvement of materials and advances in shoe technology and the measuring of shoes to fit. This is also of significance as the demand for orthopedic shoes remains high, driven now by new factors, such as the increase in diabetes, the need to provide the right shoes for sportspeople, and longer life expectancy.[19]

Internationalization

When designing his product and sales strategies, Carl always also factored in demand and what was on offer on foreign markets.[93] In the mid-50s, Fritz Gygax, who distributed Birkenstock articles in Switzerland, was considered within the company to be the "best European partner" with the highest sales.[94] Birkenstock had a 20-years-plus business relationship with French companies Stock and Amos, while in Sweden Edwin Jönsson was reputed to know the *System Birkenstock* better than almost anyone else. There were also "agencies and distribution warehouses" in the Netherlands, Denmark, and Norway.[95] From 1958 onwards, Birkenstock articles were distributed in Italy, with Ewald Pitschl in charge of sales as of 1974. That same year, the first specialist retailer for orthopedic shoes opened in South Tyrol.[96]

In spring 1952, Carl's idea of setting up a distributor system outside Europe gradually started to take shape: there were concrete discussions on taking the step of launching in Canada. In May 1952, Carl reached an agreement with three Canadians—Vasilijs Kils, who had evidently been a distributor of Birkenstock insoles, Ray N. Bryson, and James C. Shorter—to establish a company that would then acquire the necessary rights to initiate the production, distribution, and retailing of Birkenstock insoles in Canada and later also in the United States.[97] Once agreement had been reached on how to handle and transfer the industrial copyrights and on the scale of license fees, the segmentation of the shares in the company, the partners' respective executive duties, and Carl's costs for traveling in Canada, a contract was ready to be signed in January 1954. C.B. Orthopädie GmbH joined with James C. Shorter, Vasilijs Kils, and Serge Knyshynski (in place of Ray N. Bryson, who for reasons unknown did not, as originally intended, form part of the group of founding members) in launching C.B. Orthopedics of Canada Ltd. The four partners each paid Canadian $12,500 into the new company. Carl Birkenstock assumed the role of president, with Shorter backing him up as vice-president.[98]

South America was also of interest to Carl. In Brazil, distribution of the insoles was managed from 1955 by L. Schmitt, C.B.-Orthopedics Rio de Janeiro. Carl felt that their distribution partner was ideally positioned to tap into additional markets on the continent.[99]

The level of sales revenues (revenues from Birkenstock products sold inside and outside of Germany) showed a process of consolidation for C.B. Birkenstock Orthopädie GmbH during the years of West Germanys' economic reconstruction. Sales fluctuated from one business year to the

On the Path to "Walking as Nature Intended": From the *Footbed* to a Shoe   153 next, but the overall trend was upward. Thus, between 1953 and 1960 sales rose from about DM 270,000 to around DM 480,000. Over the next three years, sales surged appreciably to reach some DM 713,000. Nevertheless, Birkenstock only benefited modestly from the overall economic upturn, as profits remained volatile, with one business year closing with an annual net profit, only to be followed the very next year by a net loss being posted. The annual return on sales in West Germany in the early years varied accordingly: outstanding performances in 1959 (4.82 percent) and 1960 (5.77 percent) were followed in 1961 by a negative return of –7.71 percent).

	Sales Revenues (in DM)	Net Income (in DM)	Return on Sales (in percent)
1949	285,913	27,587	9.65
1950	234,462	14,754	6.29
1951	242,810	2,926	1.21
1952	338,067	–14,343	0.00
1953	269,716	11,906	4.41
1954	297,696	4,661	1.57
1955	297,696	–3,593	–1.64
1956	233,771	–28,550	–12.21
1957	366,165	20,253	5.53
1958	319,294	–12,659	–3.95
1959	441,378	21,277	4.82
1960	427,938	24,692	5.77
1961	454,068	–35,013	–7.71
1962	506,394	19,273	3.91
1963	713,475	20,986	11.19
1964	n. s.	n. s.	n. s.
1965	1,086,713	–40,898	–3.76
1966	1,477,406	148,348	10.04
1967	2,020,723	263,937	13.06
1968	2,515,043	20,313	0.81
1969	3,287,499	220,064	6.69
1970	3,796,612	102,970	2.71

Table 3: Sales revenues, net income (net profit/loss for the year) and return on sales in percent, C. B. Birkenstock Orthopädie GmbH in Bad Honnef, 1949-1970.[100]

From the *Ideal-Schuh* to the
Original Birkenstock-Footbed Sandal

As previously explained, when he filed a patent for his *Ideal-Schuh*—a perfect shoe—in 1936, Carl had stated that his goal in life as an entrepreneur was to develop shoe manufacturing on the basis of his own knowledge and ideas and to advance the ideas of his father Konrad. The compromises proposed by Konrad Jr. in 1947 in the course of discussions about a renewed merger of the Birkenstock brothers were therefore not pursued further for the time being.[101]

In the 40s, Carl had already realized his dream of hand-producing the best possible shoe, bearing the unmistakable signature of his company and representing a combination of the fully anatomically shaped last with the anatomically shaped and flexible *Footbed*. From October 1954 on, he sought to proceed gradually toward mass production in cooperation with Emil Neuffer KG. Carl's advertising brochures had given him a foot in the door with Neuffer's company, which was based in Pirmasens, close to the border with France in Alsatia.[102]

The two sides reached an initial agreement over the next four weeks or so, and on November 13, 1954, they agreed that Neuffer would, in the course of the next fortnight, produce a specimen collection of orthopedic women's and men's shoes using Birkenstock's thermoplastic insoles as removable inserts. The requisite lasts would be developed in Bad Honnef. Subsequent industrial manufacture would be handled exclusively by Neuffer, and the future distribution run by Birkenstock's sales section.[103]

However, Carl changed the terms and conditions for the cooperation. He was insistent that it was also time to produce children's shoes and work boots with Birkenstock insoles and to establish a "German working and interest group" with German shoe manufacturers. The group would then also produce the *Ideal-Schuh* for men and women. The Neuffer company feared its exclusivity was under threat and rejected the idea as an overall package but was prepared to make children's shoes and work boots featuring Birkenstock insoles.[104] It proved possible to brush off the initial troubles and on January 18, 1955, the contract was duly signed.[105]

For Carl Birkenstock, nothing now stood in the way of the swift success of the partnership. In a specimen letter to long-standing business partners, which he wrote on the day of the provisional closing of the contract, he was already talking about the *Ideal-Schuh* being a "revolutionary creative/novel shoe structure" that after decades would at long last "be available" and its "details" would continue to be fine-tuned going forwards. What was primarily key now was to "give the new product the right launch." Birkenstock initially identified medical practitioners as the most important advertising multipliers.[106] However, his joy at the purported breakthrough thanks to the cooperation was premature, as of all things the services to be provided by Birkenstock as stated in the contract became a bone of contention between the two parties. The contract specified that Neuffer would manufacture women's and men's shoes using the lasts developed in Bad Honnef as well as the anatomically shaped insoles, which would be inserted into the shoes either permanently or as removable items. However, the contract was only to officially come into force under specific conditions. These include the proviso that "C. Birkenstock must make available to the Neuffer company perfectly modeled anatomically shaped insoles that fitted the developed lasts exactly [...] for a women's and a men's shape for all the sizes customary in the trade."[107]

In February 1955, Neuffer issued a very negative report on the "trial insoles," saying they were poorly worked especially at the edges and did not fit snugly or smoothly to the leather uppers. Moreover, they claimed that the colored design of the insoles did not correspond to the fashionable zeitgeist. Added to which, the insoles were, Neuffer complained, much too heavy and needed to shed a least a third in weight. In the versions hitherto sent to Neuffer, the soles were "too heavy and clumsy" and actually seemed "primitive and unprofessional."[108] Not only was the cooperation partner in Pirmasens incensed by the poor quality of the deliveries, but Carl seemed loth to accept the critical pointers and from Neuffer's point of view did not set the right priorities. Thus, we read in a letter of April 27, 1955:

> "It is not primarily of decisive importance that the key persons in our company and all Neuffer sales reps take part in a course. What is crucial in our opinion is that the trials be concluded that you are conducting with the goal of developing a far lighter and more elastic insole that at the same time superlatively matches the contours of the shoe. [...] You make all manner of suggestions for handouts, advertising, and training courses and present realization of these measures as especially important. We, however, are waiting for you to first and foremost supply us with perfectly fitting insoles."[109]

Neuffer repeatedly complained in spring 1955 that the insoles were, in part, of substandard quality and questioned in principle whether the collaboration could continue. Carl, by contrast, pointed out that the project managers had on several occasions visited Neuffer's factory and provided countless details on the unique properties of the insoles. However, the Birkenstock recommendations as regards the production technology had not been heeded.[110] For all the troubled mood, the two sides agreed that from June onwards several models of the *Ideal-Schuh* would be sent out to specialist retailers. The reality check turned out to be anything but favorable. Retailers and their customers complained about the uncomfortable fit of the shoes and reported that their feet hurt. If anything, the "C. B. Shoe" seemed only to be of interest to sales staff who for years had been used to insoles in their shoes. Essentially, the specialist reps were in agreement on what the shoes' weaknesses were: the Birkenstock insoles were too broad at the sides and had one fundamental structural error—there was no "support for splay feet," something that substantially improves user comfort.[111]

The problematic market launch placed an ever greater burden on business relations between Birkenstock and Neuffer. The tone struck in communications became harsher from one week to the next, and in what can be termed his characteristic modus operandi, Carl accused his cooperation partner of deliberate sabotage of the joint project. It was a grave accusation and one that Neuffer immediately rejected in no uncertain terms. He then attacked Carl for his unusual business behavior. His conduct did not "lay any productive basis on which a fruitful cooperation that would be mutually gratifying can arise," Neuffer argued.[112]

At this point, the two companies had not completely given up hope of finding a joint objective basis on which to collaborate, and they explored the options for cooperating without it being shored up by a contract. Neuffer, for example, was still willing to supply models of the "C. B.-Shoe" to Birkenstock subsidiary C. B. Orthopedics of Canada, which for its part believed the product definitely had market prospects. However, preliminary negotiations did not lead to specific agreements or contracts. Neuffer indicated that it was open for discussion but pointed out that recent experiences had caused ill feeling, and the tension between the two companies had by no means been dispelled. Added to which, there were no lasts on hand for a sandal. A joint venture did not come about, as in the final instance any reciprocal trust had been irredeemably damaged, and Neuffer regularly turned down further enquiries for projects in 1957–58.[113]

The failed cooperation with Emil Neuffer KG was not the only attempt Carl Birkenstock made in the 50s to team up with a shoe factory in order to advance his *Ideal-Schuh* such that it would be ready for market. In fall 1953, he contacted Schuhfabrik Georg Mayer in Götzis, in the Voralberg region of Austria, and in September 1953 and January 1954 concluded a similar agreement and a contract with clear preconditions. Birkenstock and Mayer intended to develop women's and men's shoes, not to mention children's shoes, work and ski boots, and open sandals with Birkenstock insoles that would be manufactured exclusively by Georg Mayer.[114] The collaboration followed almost down to the smallest detail the pattern and arguments that had defined the cooperation with Emil Neuffer. If we ignore the legal hurdles to importing the insoles, from an early date the Mayer company complained about the product quality. It said the insoles did not have the right fit and were too heavy and too coarsely finished. For his part, in September 1954 Carl Birkenstock felt the business relationship "was dead in the water" and pointed out that Mayer, contrary to his recommendations, had pursued its own solutions when manufacturing the shoes. He complained that he was often treated "like a little boy" during discussions.[115] In December 1954, Mayer declared the cooperation terminated, and it was now down to the lawyers representing the two firms to fight it out.[116]

The Breakthrough in 1963: Karl Birkenstock and the Creation of the Sandal

Alongside the growing demand for fashionably designed shoes as of the early 50s, there was another significant trend in the industry. In the "light street shoes, slippers, and support shoes" segment, it was sandals and non-lined high-heeled sandals with leather uppers that were making above-average inroads into the market. Unit sales rose from about 4.3 million pairs in 1952 to 10.9 million pairs eight years later. The share of the product segment they accounted for increased between 1952 and 1960 from 11.4 to 20.2 percent, whereby a considerable proportion of overall output can be attributed to girls' and women's sandals.[117]

One major reason for the extraordinary growth was without doubt the increase in leisure time enjoyed by the population.[118] In the second half of the 50s, the country adopted a five-day working week, and this trend culminated in "long weekends," something that gave employees an opportunity to pursue their personal leisure-time interests in a single block of time, as it were. Between 1956 and 1960, the hours worked per week by industrial blue-collar staff fell from 47.1 to 44.1 hours and that of white-collar workers from 47.5 to 44.5 hours.[119] The experiences of war and imprisonment, the fact that heavy labor was still required in some industrial sectors, and the wish for rest and recreation meant that leisure time was focused on the home and family. The consumption of media remained of special importance. People read newspapers, magazines, and literature and listened to music and the news on the radio.[120] The fact that ever fewer customers now wanted to buy themselves the camel-hair slippers that had been so popular for many years opened the gates to the manufacturers of mules.[121]

In this respect, the market for sandals was already very much in flux when Karl Birkenstock started seriously thinking about creating a sandal. There were already some suppliers who had previously put their money into mules and now held a comfortable share of the market. Founded in 1885 in Hamburg and having been in contact with Carl Birkenstock for some time, the Berkemann company, with the support of Wilhelm Thomsen, introduced his "Original Sandal" in 1956 with a wooden sole and an orthopedic insole that held the foot stable with a cross strap. The model was very popular, including among Olympic Games participants, and became a bestseller. In 1964, Berkemann followed up with the "Toeffler" model, a clog with a hefty wooden sole and a closed toe section.[122]

On his way to producing the *Ideal-Schuh*, Carl had had disappointing experiences with the shoe manufacturers, as described above, and in January 1961 he decided to withdraw increasingly from day-to-day business dealings in order to "devote himself to the large specialist book he had long been planning, which he now wrote in his private office."[123] Contacts had been made with Chasalla Schuhfabrik GmbH in July 1960. The joint work progressed rapidly: at the beginning of November, four sample shoes (women's and men's models) were available for the *Zehenfrei* insole, and the practical tests followed. In September 1961, however, the cooperation suddenly ended. The shoe factory no longer considered the production of an *Ideal-Schuh* to be what the market wanted: "Even purely orthopedic specialist shops are increasingly having to bow to the realization that more and more shoes are being purchased on the basis of fashion trends and the dictates of the head rather than the actual needs of the feet." The shoe industry must "adapt its production programs to market requirements if it wants to successfully maintain its market share in the face of increasing competition."[124]

After Carl had retired, his son Karl took over the development of a shoe. He broke away from his father's plans, which had failed because of the shoe manufacturers,[125] and now had the Birkenstock representative Helmut Wegerth search for suitable shoe companies in Southern Germany with his own designs and ideas.[126] The concrete idea of producing a sandal was new. However, even under Karl's leadership, no suitable partner was initially found who could produce the sandal he had designed.[127]

In the early 60s, Karl had nevertheless succeeded in producing the prototype of a footbed sandal. Neither his father nor his uncles, who all initially endeavored to produce a shoe according to the ideals of the Birkenstock family, were involved in this final step.[128] It was only after the creation of the *Original Birkenstock-Footbed Sandal* and the successful production of the first pieces that Karl Birkenstock informed his uncle that he too could now obtain the sandal for distribution, as he had succeeded in developing a "novel, promising sandal, [...] which is rationally produced in large quantities on modern machines."[129]

In the Birkenstock company—with its less than 50 employees—there was no design or development department. Karl was responsible for the design drafts and the material development. He succeeded in producing a light and flexible mixture of cork and latex. When designing the *Original Birkenstock-Footbed Sandal*, he was inspired by the trend in building design of the time: brutalism.[130] The extent to which his creation was to be anchored in design history was demonstrated decades later when the sandal became part of an exhibition on the theme of "German Design 1949–1989. Two Countries, One History."[131] Karl's extraordinary, minimalist design with its avant-garde components of unisex and iconic timelessness was style-defining.[132]

The *Original Birkenstock-Footbed Sandal* was then presented at the Düsseldorf Shoemakers' Trade Exhibition in spring 1963, prosaically labeled as article number "400" (the *Original Birkenstock-Footbed Sandal* was not given the name *Madrid* until 1979). According to press reports, the sandal was not manufactured by C. B. Birkenstock GmbH alone but by other companies as well, although there was only one other company involved, which produced 5,000 pairs. The cooperation partner was provided with templates and cutting dies from Bad Honnef for the production. The shoe company used the same materials, sourced the footbeds from Birkenstock, took over the color range and, according to the press, sold the sandals on their own account under the Birkenstock name in the usual packaging. In terms of pricing, Birkenstock gave the manufacturer the option of offering discounts for more extensive business with wholesalers or purchasing groups.[133]

The new Birkenstock sandal did not by any means become a sales hit overnight. Initially, the new product enjoyed a varied reception in the industry. The relevant trade press was rather taken with it, emphasizing its advantages and innovative performance: the sandal was "completely

160   **1945–1963** Beginning of the Industrial Era

new in terms of its type." In addition to the eye-catching design, the trade press also drew attention to the quality of the shoes: the cork footbed guaranteed a decidedly lightweight product, while its upward bulge ensured a "light, natural, and lively step," and the straight inside edges were "tailored entirely to a healthy foot." Moreover, qualities such as the non-slip suede leather that completely covered the *Original Birkenstock-Footbed Sandals* were praised, as were the "barrel-tanned high-grade leather uppers." Furthermore, there was a seamless transition from the footbed to the leather of the uppers.[134]

By contrast, during the launch at the Düsseldorf show, the trade visitors were far less enthusiastic in their response. Karl recalls that instead of giving their approval, some treated the sandals with scorn or ridiculed them: "The shoe manufacturers flocked to the stand and heaped us with insults. It was terrible. We were the troublemakers. We had undermined the fashion. [...] There were only shoes with pointed tips; no one was wearing anything else." The industry insiders viewed the "wide, beaklike" sandals as behind the times, not to say "indecent." Among shoe retailers, there were voices who disparaged the new product (playing on the name of the originators) as "idiotically hollowed-out tree trunks," and even vilified those prepared to sell them. Anyone wanting to market such a sandal must "have a screw or two loose."[135]

The shoe retailers' negative response may also have been due to the fact that Karl's innovative sandal went against the conventions of the time and, more importantly, flouted the fashion trends brokered by the shoe retailers. Once again, the Birkenstock family—this time represented by Karl as innovator—were outsiders and simultaneously ahead of their time.

The lack of sales revenues from the new sandals did not constitute serious economic jeopardy for Birkenstock. The idea was for the sandal to round out the product portfolio meaningfully. Earnings were mainly reaped from sales of the classic *Blue Footbed*. In the trade, however, Birkenstock in part forfeited its good name: in the weeks that followed, an ever greater number of companies withdrew their orders for the *Blue Footbed*, and the order book deteriorated appreciably.[136] Alongside the real difficulties of finding people interested in selling the new sandals, there was an additional concern: as of June 1963, the German Federal Monopolies Commission started examining the production and distribution of the *Original Birkenstock-Footbed Sandals*, since Birkenstock was suspected of breaking legal stipulations against restricting competition. The Monopolies Commission wanted to know more about Birkenstock's relationship to those companies that were expected to produce and distribute the *Original Birkenstock-Footbed Sandals*, and its interest focused specifically on contracts on pricing.

The executives in Bad Honnef initially showed little inclination to ensure the matter was swiftly cleared up and ignored the three requests received from the Monopolies Commission to submit the relevant documentation. The Bonn-based agency thereupon asked the North Rhine Westphalia State Monopolies Commission to pursue the matter on its behalf, suggesting it would help to have Karl Birkenstock appear before it in person. Although he was legally obliged to comply, his willingness to cooperate with the authorities remained limited over the next few months. Attempts by the state agency in Bonn to schedule a date for the hearing kept on being torpedoed by Karl, who did not regard it necessary to face questions in Düsseldorf in person. Instead, in October he went on record on the phone saying that "he still did not know what he was supposed to say."[137]

The civil servant handling the case felt that their interaction showed that Birkenstock "does not understand the significance under monopolies law of collaborating with other producers—i.e., several manufacturers cooperating in producing one and the same article and selling the article at a uniform price." Incidentally, his attorney had apparently instructed him that the market share of the *Original Birkenstock-Footbed Sandals* was minuscule, and the article therefore did not come under the stipulations of the laws on competition restriction.[138] According to Birkenstock, there was at that point only one company left in southern Germany (the exact name of which is unknown) that manufactured the footbed sandal under the Birkenstock name and used "modules" from Bad Honnef for the production process. The collaboration was evidently necessitated by Birkenstock's own production capacities being overextended. The shoe company followed C.B. Orthopädie GmbH's lead on prices but also offered the sandals at more favorable conditions if there was demand from a group or key accounts, an approach that Karl did not necessarily appreciate but ultimately tolerated. Should the collaboration contravene the monopolies laws, he said, he would discontinue it.[139]

While the investigations by the anti-trust agencies were still ongoing in the fall and winter of 1963–64, production was once again reorganized. In January 1964, Birkenstock informed the Federal German Monopolies Commission that the shoe company in question had only processed a "minimal trial series of 5,000 pairs." Since the challenges in terms of production technology were at the end of the day too great, and major difficulties arose during manufacturing, with unit sales

162 **1945–1963** Beginning of the Industrial Era

Fig. 32: The expansive design of the foot-healthy sandal did not fit the trend of the time's fashion, whose guiding principle was the perfectly coordinated appearance of clothing and shoes (Birkenstock Post 13, 1965).

down on expectations, both companies decided to discontinue their cooperation. C. B. Orthopädie GmbH was henceforth the sole producer and distributor of the *Original Birkenstock-Footbed Sandals*.[140] The Federal Monopolies Commission now concluded that "the cooperation with another company such as was communicated [...] was evidently a one-off episode, which has since been brought to an end," and in February 1964 closed its investigation.[141]

Birkenstock later worked together with Alsa Schuhbedarf GmbH in Steinau/Uerzell to produce the *Original Birkenstock-Footbed Sandal*. Alsa was founded in 1945 by Alfons Saum and sold in 1968 to Continental AG, which wanted to expand its product portfolio, contribute to the internationalization of the shoe industry, and gain "more proximity" to the shoe industry. In 1988, the company was finally taken over by Birkenstock.[142] Prior to that, the footbeds and soles were produced in the Hessian company according to Birkenstock's specifications and designs, while Birkenstock manufactured the straps with buckles in Bad Honnef.

Since he had not succeeded in 1963 in arousing extensive interest in the *Original Birkenstock-Footbed Sandal*, Karl now faced the task of at least generating a small demand segment for a product that had not exactly been greeted with enthusiasm. Once more he felt that medical practitioners, medical care staff, and nurses were suitable buyers of his new product. He had brochures sent to them (including via medical newspapers) and, if interest was shown, had the sandals sent straight to the prospective customer. And his plan came up trumps: in only a few weeks, orders rocketed. Many doctors praised the sandals and also acted as brand ambassadors, recommending the product to their colleagues, to family members, and to friends. Birkenstock now used the same advertising and sales strategy to target dentists—and was equally successful.[143] In this way, he established a stable demand base for the sandals business and at the same time the special customer group ensured that for many years members of the German public perceived the *Original Birkenstock-Footbed Sandal* as a product for the health sector.

The sandal presented in 1963 was supplemented with another creation in 1964. At that year's Federal Trade Show in Hamburg, the "Fuß und Schuh," Karl presented a new closed-top sandal he had designed. The *Closed Model*, as the product was branded in 1966 (from 1979 onwards *Zürich*), then went on offer two years later in different versions (in leather and in sturdy wool felt) and was specifically meant to target customers who wanted a more stable sandal model that offered better support.[144] In its advertising and PR work, from the late 60s onwards the company was visibly making an effort to tap into a broader clientele for

164 **1945–1963** Beginning of the Industrial Era

Fig. 33: Karl Birkenstock created a design icon in 1963 with the *Original Birkenstock-Footbed Sandal*, which is characterised by clear lines and, in keeping with the architectural style of Brutalism, leaves the materials used visible.

the sandals. The in-company brochures and the advertising in the relevant magazines continued to focus on the image of the Birkenstock sandals as a health-sustaining product that was highly popular among medical practitioners but now clearly combined that traditional image with the latest social trends and a "paradigm of modernity."

Since leading a modern life meant, not least, having an open mind when it came to the latest medical insights, the *Original Birkenstock Footbed-Sandal* were showcased as a crucial symbol of a modern lifestyle. The suggestion was that anyone wearing sandals bearing the Birkenstock logo was expressing their health-conscious, contemporary, fashionable, and even sporting way of life.[145] The sandals were essentially showcased as a feel-good factor "at home and at work,"[146] making the difference between an intolerable and a tolerable day at work in the office or the store, and promising to provide leisure-time compensation for professional life. The message was that in a modern family no one could get by any longer without Birkenstock sandals. At the same time, a contemporary middle-class lifestyle depended on having the financial wherewithal. Depending on the shoe size and the specific model, in January 1968 a Birkenstock sandal cost between DM 24 and DM 59. Prices were thus on the high side compared with a mass supplier such as the

Deichmann company, in whose stores customers around 1965 usually paid between DM 19 and DM 29 for a pair of shoes.[147]

The surviving documents do not allow us to ascertain what product segment contributed what share to the company's overall growth. What can be said is that total sales in 1965 for the first time topped DM 1 million, truly surged in the following years, and in 1970 ran at about DM 3.8 million (see tab. 3).[148] Sales revenues inside and outside Germany can be more accurately specified for the second half of the 60s: sales booked in the domestic market rose from about DM 1.54 million (1967) to some DM 3 million (1970), while sales outside of the country grew over the same period from around DM 580,000 to about DM 790,000. Profits and the return on sales continued to fluctuate in the 60s; however, with the exception of the 1965 business year, the company now avoided posting a net loss for the year or a negative return on sales. It also succeeded in mastering the years of accelerating expansion without a huge payroll. In 1970, a total of 57 staff worked for Birkenstock Orthopädie GmbH: 37 were blue-collar workers, and there were twelve commercial and two technical salaried staff members as well as six apprentices.[149] The prime business performance from about the mid-60s onwards was reflected in the expansion of the production hall in Bad Honnef in 1967 and in a new production plant going into operation in 1974, this time in St. Katharinen, built specifically to cut leather to size.[150]

In the 70s and early 80s, the company's product policy essentially followed the principle of creating new sandal models with new functionalities for new customer groups. Following the prevailing trends, Birkenstock designed sandals with more appealing colors and also locked into current fashion trends to a greater extent than before. Introduced in the early 80s, the *Rio* and *Florida* models in blue, which likewise sold well over the long term, emphasized the new way the company saw itself, as did the five new thong sandals launched in 1983. The models bearing names like *Ramses, Gizeh, Kairo, Luxor,* and *Medina* consciously adopted the traditions of ancient Egypt and were perhaps the best expression to date of how the product designers sought to symbiotically link health and fashion. Birkenstock's advertising largely continued down the already well-trodden path. Direct communication with retailers, shoe stores, and orthopedic professionals, with offers of specialist courses and the like, continued to be crucial. The specialist orthopedic books authored by members of the family also retained their importance. In 1972, Karl Birkenstock brought out his "Buch der Fußgesundheit" (Manual of Foot Health), and in 1983 his advertising brochure, the "Fuß-Fibel" (Foot Handbook). Both publications summarized the insights afforded by the *System Birkenstock,* enhanced the company's reputation among medical practitioners, and became indispensable reference works for the staff.

It was also at this time that wearing *Original Birkenstock-Footbed Sandals* first became a political statement in West Germany, symbolically expressing an alternative way of life and an environmentally conscious, "leftist" protest stance. The "health sandals" became increasingly popular among the circles of the West German peace movement and the new ecological scene (backed, above all, by members of the churches and trade unions), partly driven by the Green party, newly founded in January 1980, and by some rank-and-file Social Democrats.[151] It was not entirely unexpected that the sandals met with remarkable interest among a specific political subculture, as this had been witnessed previously in the mid-60s in the establishment of the US arm of the business. In the first decade after the introduction of the *Original Birkenstock-Footbed Sandal,* Karl developed seven other models—the *Closed Model* was more protective and easier to wear, the *Strap Sandal* was more secure on the foot, the *Boot* supported climbing stairs or mountain hiking, the *Loafer* covered a large part of the foot, and the *Closed Model,* introduced in 1973 and later described as a two-strap model, was "opened" for the summer. At the beginning of the 70s, new approaches were tested with the *Noppy* massage sandal made of plastic (see model overview in the appendix). The lightweight *Cork Clog,* introduced in 1976, was aimed at professionals who needed toe protection from falling objects. Another model, *no. 024,* which was only made for a year, was a first attempt to introduce color. However, this model, which could be ordered in a variety of colors, was not satisfying in terms of comfort and appearance. In 1983, the thong models were introduced as a major innovation.

Summary

In the 50s, Carl Birkenstock's newly founded company was able to profit more than before from the general conditions of the so-called economic miracle. But while the flexible, anatomically shaped insoles finally became established after 50 years in terms of sales, he did not succeed in bringing the handmade *Ideal-Schuh* into serial production. The manufacturing requirements were too complex and the inventor too unwilling to compromise. Instead, Carl turned to publishing writings on foot health and left the further development of healthy footwear to his son Karl and thus to the next generation. Following his grandfather's core innovations, Karl had created the third innovation: the *Original Birken-stock-Footbed Sandal*. His avant-garde design allowed him to successfully cater to the demands of foot health. While his father, Carl, sought to create a largely individualized footbed for his *Ideal-Schuh*, a standardized footbed enabled Karl to create his *Original Birkenstock-Footbed Sandal*. Drawing on his family's own experience of having to persevere and assert their ideas, Karl was able to disregard the conventions of current shoe fashion. In doing so, he developed a distinct design that was not dependent on current trends and seemed to be far ahead of its time. The sandal's initial grand failure in the world of shoe fashion was followed by surprising success among doctors. From here began a journey that saw it adopted by subcultures before passing through mainstream society to become a luxury item.

Alexander von den Benken and Alice Janssens trace this journey in chapter 4.

The Names of the *Original Birkenstock-Footbed Sandals*

BY ANDREA H. SCHNEIDER-BRAUNBERGER

When Karl Birkenstock designed the *Original Birkenstock-Footbed Sandal* in 1963, it was simply advertised under that name and as item number "400". The creation that followed it, which was launched the following year, was called the *Closed Model*, followed by the *Strappy Sandal* (1965), the *Boot* (1969/70), the *Loafer* (1969/70) and the *Cork Clog* (1976). Even the *Arizona*, which has become an icon today, was launched in 1973 under the name *Closed Model* and then appeared in the catalogs in 1976 as the *Pater* model.

The impetus for naming the shoes came from US distributor Margot Fraser,[1] who was the first to start changing the descriptive German model names—which were unpronounceable for the US market—into catchy names. Thus, back in 1968, she introduced the names *Mayan* for the *Madrid*, which was also given a name in Germany in 1979, *Franciscan* (*Zürich* in Germany from 1979), and *Roman* (*Roma* in Germany from 1979) for the second and third Birkenstock models. The half-shoe that was still being manufactured in the 60s was named *Californian* by Margot Fraser (*Oslo* in Germany from 1979) and the 1973 *Arizona*, which was still marketed as the *Closed Model* in Germany, was called *London* for six months in

1979 and then sold in Germany too under the name *Arizona*.

From 1979 onwards, there were numerous changes in production: the buckles were given the company name, the footbeds were stamped—soon followed by the bone pattern as a new trademark on the sole—and the shoes were now given their names. While Fraser still used various models, such as the names of states, in Germany the company stuck with cities. Whether Karl Birkenstock was motivated by having worn the *Florence* and *Rome* models from the Neuffer company to try them out when he was young remains uncertain.

The open models—such as *Madrid*, *Milano*, and *Roma*—were given the names of Southern European cities, while the more closed models—such as *Zürich* and *Davos*—were given city names in cooler regions. Later names also followed the spirit of the times—such as *Tokio* in 1984, when Japan was considered innovative, progressive, and hip, and Birkenstock sold shoes through a retailer in the country for the first time—or a year earlier the thong sandals *Gizeh*, *Cairo*, and *Ramses*, an allusion to Egypt as a newly discovered travel destination that inspired people's wanderlust.

Fig. 34: The C. B. Birkenstock GmbH range at the end of the 60s: *Closed (Zürich), Strap Sandal (Roma), Massage Sandal (Noppy), Original Birkenstock-Footbed Sandal (Madrid) and Boot (Athen)* (from left to right), the various insoles.

Gymnastic sandals?

In the early 70s, when Birkenstock brought out a sandal made of plastic called *Noppy*, which massaged the foot, it was advertised as a "gymnastic sandal." The term gymnastic sandal had previously been used by Berkemann. In the early thinking of the 50s, the idea of a separate "gymnastic sandal" was also considered within the Birkenstock family and vis-à-vis the shoe manufacturers. Gymnastics, however, did not refer to the practice of sports, as the expression might suggest when used in relation to gym shoes. In the case of Karl Birkenstock's *Original Birkenstock-Footbed Sandals*, gymnastics referred to the possibility for the toes to use the free space in the shoe for toe gymnastics.

However, the sandals—apart from the *Noppy*—were not generally referred to or advertised as gymnastics sandals. It was not until 1985 that Birkenstock introduced the *Ibiza* model as a "gymnastic sandal." Here, it was made clear that the shoe was for toe gymnastics, insofar as it encouraged the toes to do more gripping movements. In the late 80s, the *Madrid* model was briefly billed as a "gymnastic sandal."

1963 – 2024
RISE TO A
GLOBAL BRAND

Fig. 35: On June 24, 2017, the traditional German brand presented its spring-summer 2018 collection in the temporary pavilion set up at the Orangerie Ephémère in the Jardin die Tuileries. With this side event, Birkenstock celebrated its premiere at Men's Fashion Week in Paris.

FROM FAMILY BUSINESS TO GLOBAL CORPORATION

BY ALEXANDER VON DEN BENKEN

"Hippie" Sandals: Birkenstock in the USA

At the beginning of the 70s, there was a growing feeling in the West German shoe and textile industry that the best times were long gone.[1] In what was once the showcase industry of the German economic reconstruction—104,000 people were employed in the industry nationwide—a significantly changed competitive environment was emerging.[2] Wage increases due to collective bargaining agreements, coupled with price increases in energy and raw materials, had made the manual production of shoes in West Germany increasingly difficult and, at the same time, had made foreign production in low-wage countries attractive. As Germans' prosperity increased, so their consumer behavior toward distinctive fashionable purchases had also changed. This forced West German shoe manufacturers not only to follow a rapidly changing series of international fashion trends but also to shift to cheaper and more flexible mass production methods. New competition arose in low-wage countries such as Italy, Portugal, and Spain when the European Economic Community (EEC) gradually reduced import and export duties on shoes and leather goods in the mid-60s. The German shoe manufacturers became more and more caught up in a price war that has not changed to this day.

For smaller producers such as Birkenstock, the situation in the early 70s did not seem very promising, with 30 companies having to close their factories in 1972 alone.[3] In desperation, Walter Joneck, spokesman for the board of the Association of the German Shoe Industry, announced to the Frankfurter Allgemeine Zeitung (FAZ) newspaper in the spring of 1972 that "all attempts to stop the decline through rationalization measures have failed."[4] Furthermore, owing to the competition between strong wholesale associations, retailers, department store chains, and shoe companies, conflicts about pricing repeatedly erupted, especially in periods when there was great fluctuation in demand. In 1973, the year of the oil crisis, a veritable mood of crisis spread through the trade fair for the shoe industry, the Düsseldorf Schuhmusterschau. Major daily newspapers such as FAZ reported that "never [...] at the trade fair have there been so many rumors about drastic production cutbacks or imminent bankruptcies as there are now." According to voices from within the industry, this was due to declining production figures, rising costs, and the appreciation of the Deutsche Mark. In such times of crisis, the significantly more price-conscious behavior of consumers also played an important role.[5] Between the oil crises of 1973 and 1979, severe processes of concentration shaped trends in the shoe industry. Long-established quality suppliers who could not make their production flexible enough were forced to close down.[6] And thus the foreign competition from Asia, Southwest Europe, and the Soviet Union was able to conquer a market share of over 55 percent in Germany within a few years and hence secured a permanent place among shoe retailers across all market segments.[7] Last but not least, the two oil price crises meant that the supply of raw materials for the entire shoe industry became considerably more expensive and forced manufacturers to switch to cheap, inferior-quality materials such as synthetics.[8]

Bad Honnef-based insole and shoe manufacturer Birkenstock seemed to be relatively unaffected by this mood of crisis and the general downward trend in the shoe industry. Since the market launch of *Original Birkenstock-Footbed Sandal* in 1963, the firm had slowly but surely developed into the "hidden champion" of comfort footwear. The Bad Honnef family business, which Karl Birkenstock took over as sole owner from his father Carl in the mid-60s and managed together with his wife Gisela from 1968 onwards, managed to steadily increase its sales year after year.[9] As early as the mid-60s, Birkenstock Orthopädie GmbH (the former C. B. Orthopädie GmbH) reported constant growth, with sales exceeding DM 1 million for the first time in 1965.[10] Although Karl's sandals were still being reviled by the trade at the beginning of the 70s and the "shoe crises" did not offer good conditions for the small family business anyway, already in 1972 the company achieved sales of DM 7.7 million, doubling the turnover from 1970.[11] The product policy, which was focused primarily on the health-promoting features of the footwear, ensured the development of a loyal customer base in Germany during the "economic boom years" and appealed principally to health-conscious customers. The significantly faster growth of the brand at the beginning of the 70s cannot, however, be solely attributed to the purchasing behavior of the German customer base, which consisted mostly of doctors. With the emergence of the "hippie movement" in the United States in the late 60s, younger customers suddenly started wearing Birkenstock sandals in greater numbers, not for professional or health reasons but as an expression of a new "lifestyle."

From the late 60s, in California in particular, open-toe shoes made of cork developed into a symbol of a non-conformist, anti-bourgeois lifestyle, which the student generation propagated more and more. At music festivals such as the famous Woodstock Music & Art Fair, which took place in August 1969 in the state of New York, the German sandal embedded itself most effectively and visibly in the consumer world of the "alternative" scene. A trend toward homemade, open-toe shoes and sandals had been evident in this community for a long time, and the Birkenstock sandal seemed to fit in perfectly.[12] As Karl later recalled, "very, very many people wore our sandals" on the mud-covered festival meadows, so that the product became known in the United States by word of mouth.[13] The fact that the first Birkenstock sandals were available on the other side of the Atlantic in the first place was due less to the Bad Honnef company itself than to a passionate sandal wearer who gradually introduced to the United States the sandal that had been developed and produced by Karl Birkenstock, and promulgated it there in the late 60s.

Margot Fraser, a German American living in California, discovered Birkenstock sandals in 1966 during a stay at a health resort in her former homeland and brought them back with her to her adopted country, where she immediately started selling them on a small scale to family and friends.[14] Although the established shoe trade in the United States initially showed little interest in the sandals, Fraser firmly believed that there were potential buyers for the orthopedic cork sandals over and above her immediate circle of friends.[15] After her business on this small scale continued to blossom, she began importing, at her own expense, larger quantities to the United States beginning in the late 60s. Without a doubt, this was only possible because of the so-called Kennedy Round, which ushered in the decision in 1967 to relax customs policy on foreign shoe articles and thus facilitated the cost-effective import of several hundred different orthopedic insoles and sandals.[16]

With the popularization of a "hippie lifestyle" in the early 70s, Fraser's sandal importation activities developed into a more lucrative business that required professional management.[17] Although Fraser sold the sandals at health fairs and in health-food stores with great success, Karl remained reluctant to become more involved in the US market. As a result, Fraser, encouraged by the initial successes, sought to set up professional distribution and sales in the United States on her own. As a divorced woman, it was not easy for her to take out a business loan, and so she needed financial support. With the consent of the husband-and-wife team of Howard and June Embury, who ran a health-food store in San Rafael, a suburb of the "hippie capital" San Francisco, Fraser installed a small Birkenstock outlet in their shop.

Just one year later, this modest operation developed into an independent company, Birkenstock Footprint Sandals, Inc., which Fraser entered in the local commercial register on September 28, 1972. Although the establishment of this trading and import company took place with Karl's approval, it did not initially result in an official distributorship in the United States. Because apart from verbal agreements between Karl Birkenstock and Margot Fraser, there were no contractual regulations as to how Birkenstock sandals were to be imported and sold in the United States. Consequently, over the next two years Fraser continued to order Birkenstock insoles, sandals, and other accessories in Bad Honnef, and sell these products in the Emburys' store, at health fairs, and in other health-food stores. Over time, the sandals also made their way into the professional shoe trade so that Fraser was able to sell 10,000 pairs in her first business year and generate sales of US$ 116,700, which she managed to more than double the following year.[18]

Even while the first oil crisis was paralyzing entire branches of industry in the winter months of 1973–74, the US Birkenstock business

Fig. 36: The idea behind the sandals was catchy. Margot Fraser built Birkenstock up in the USA with the same passion and tenacity that inspired Konrad, Carl, and Karl Birkenstock. Karl Birkenstock with Margot Fraser (70s).

performed superbly and soon became the central pillar of Karl's company. In the meantime, not only had sales quadrupled but Fraser was even able to set up the first two "concept stores" in Carmel and San Rafael, California, in order to be able to offer customers the entire Birkenstock product line. This development did not go unnoticed far away in Bad Honnef. Impressed by the growing sales, Karl signed an official import agreement with Fraser's Birkenstock Footprint Sandals, Inc. on October 1, 1974, making Fraser the sole US importer of Birkenstock products and replacing earlier verbal agreements.[19] Fraser's company was contractually assured of comprehensive and exclusive branding and distribution rights for Birkenstock products on the US continent, something Fraser would retain until she exited the business in the 2000s.[20]

However, since Fraser did not have the capacity to cover the entire US continent, with Birkenstock's approval, she immediately negotiated a contract with the 3HO Foundation in Washington, DC, which then took over the task of supplying shoe retailers on the East Coast.[21] Founded by the Indian entrepreneur and spiritual master Yogi Bhajan, this tantra and yoga organization had not only operated various spiritual centers in the United States since its foundation in 1968 but also owned numerous natural food restaurants, potteries, horticultural businesses, and furniture stores in the DC area. The Khalsa International Industries and Trading group of companies founded by Yogi Bhajan also specialized in the sale of medicinal and natural food products such as the Ayurvedic "Yogi Teas" and the "Golden Temple Granola" muesli varieties.[22] Birkenstock sandals had long been an integral part of their range of organic/ecological yoga products, which they sold with great success in their cultural centers and stores on the East Coast. They were extremely interested in taking over the entire East Coast distribution of Birkenstock sandals.[23] Highly self-confident, they applied to Fraser in the fall of 1974 with an offer to carry out such sales in accordance with the latest marketing knowledge and thus achieve a significantly higher market penetration "than can be done with a California-based operation and with word-of-mouth advertising."[24] The Yogi representatives' suggestions to not only open a Birkenstock store in the US capital but also set up a large-scale East Coast sales organization were well received, especially in far-away Bad Honnef.[25] With great enthusiasm, Karl immediately invited the Yogi devotees to come to Bad Honnef and visit the production facilities.[26] Just a few weeks later, Fraser and Yogi Bhajan's representatives signed a contract—mainly covering the formation of a new trading company, Birkenstock East Inc.—which reserved the right to supply the entire US region east of the Mississippi.[27]

Overall, Fraser's activities in the United States in the mid-70s heralded a cautious process of internationalization at Birkenstock. Thanks to this expansion strategy, which was not so much planned as driven, in large part, by enthusiastic Birkenstock supporters like Margot Fraser, the Birkenstock sandal was able to establish itself much more sustainably and credibly in the consumer world of the alternative "New Age" movement than other comparable consumer products. The unconventional "learning by doing" strategy of Karl Birkenstock and Margot Fraser, which relied from the start on alternative sales channels, seemed to be bearing more and more fruit. In 1975, Birkenstock Footprint Sandals, Inc. managed to break the sales barrier of US$ one million for the first time, only to double turnover two years later.[28]

The unconventional sales concept seemed to work well at first; but it soon became apparent that the relatively heterogeneous dealer network was causing steadily increasing organizational costs, which Fraser urgently needed administrative help to manage and coordinate.[29] At the end of the 70s, Karl—who had previously acted rather cautiously—was also under pressure to enhance the company's entrepreneurial image in the United States. In order to pool financial resources and better coordinate the marketing and sales activities between the parent company and Fraser's US company, Karl finally founded Birko Advertising, Inc. with Margot Fraser in the spring of 1977, in which Birkenstock personally held a 90 percent stake and the Fraser Company had a 10 percent interest.[30] The central organ of the company was the board of directors, to which both Karl Birkenstock and Fraser belonged: this was where future product and pricing policies, as well as distribution and advertising strategies, were discussed and developed.[31] However, the actual reason for founding Birko Advertising, Inc. was that Karl was now able to invest in expanding Fraser's storage and logistics capacities without major legal hurdles. For example, the new company bought real estate near the headquarters of Fraser's San Rafael site and leased it to Fraser's organization.[32] This ensured that Birkenstock Footprint Sandals, Inc. could expand its storage capacity under favorable conditions and thus supply more retailers with goods. By the late 70s, it was supplying over 700 boutiques, health-food stores, and shoe and orthopedic shops in the United States, which demonstrates how fast the Birkenstock sandals operation was able to expand in the United States in the 70s.[33]

There were, however, also competing products. For example, the orthopedic Earth Shoes of the Danish yoga teacher Anne Kalsø represented the main competitor since they had come onto the market in the United States in the early 70s through the efforts of the couple Raymond and Eleanor Jacobs.[34] The unusual footwear, which was supposed to improve the wearer's walking apparatus and posture through a lowered heel, initially experienced a boom in demand similar to that of Birkenstock sandals.[35] Nonetheless, their US business soon ran into difficulties when there were problems in licensed production and the company's own Earth Shoes dealer network.[36] By the end of the 70s, sales in the United States had to be discontinued, and in the mid-80s all production was abandoned.[37]

With the steady enlargement of the US market, the Birkenstock production volumes in Bad Honnef increased significantly. An expansion of the production capacities became all the more urgent when the facility in the spa town of Bad Honnef ceased to offer any further development opportunities, having finally reached its spatial capacity limit. In a first step, the family business moved to Rhineland-Palatinate and put the first branch in nearby St. Katharinen-Hargarten into operation in July 1974.[38] By 1980, two further similar site expansions in Rheinbreitbach and Linz am Rhein, which were also close to the main plant in Bad Honnef, had been completed.[39] In order to finance the expansion of the production works, Karl had to take out loans for the first time, starting in 1978, since his own financing capacities were exhausted.[40] Within a short time, Birkenstock therefore increased his credit reserves with the local financial institutions of the city of Bad Honnef and the Landesbank Rheinland Pfalz to a total of almost DM six million.[41] The brisk investment activity in equipping the new plants also led to an increase in the number of employees, which grew from 57 employees in 1970 to 147 in 1980.[42] As a result of the expansion, a significant increase in the number of units produced was also recorded, which resulted in sales of DM 20 million in 1980, doubling the turnover attained in 1975.[43] The return on sales also remained at a reasonable level of around eight percent at the end of the 70s, despite significantly increased investments and borrowing.[44] Thus Birkenstock was a solid, growing company that could service its loans on time and invest the profits it made in the company. This differentiated it from many other companies in the West German shoe industry, which found themselves in a downward spiral by the end of the 70s at the latest. Of the 759 shoe factories counted in 1961, only 439 were left in 1978, and it was only a matter of time before the next one would have to close down.[45] Birkenstock seemed completely immune to this negative development. Despite a structural shift in demand in favor of cheaper everyday shoes from the Far East, the Bad Honnef-based orthopedic and sandal specialist found itself in a largely secure niche position. This advantage was secured not only because of successful penetration of new overseas markets but also because the family business was conquering new market segments with new product lines. With the introduction of the children's shoe series "Birki's," the garden shoe "Clogs," and the semi-synthetic "Birko-flor" sandals in the mid-70s, the customer base was successfully expanded, and the brand core was further strengthened. Although other shoe manufacturers had also noticed that the children's, youth, and leisure shoe trend was definitely gaining momentum in the 70s, it was only at Birkenstock that the health aspect of the sandal footbed, which had been its focus for decades, was matched skillfully to the fashion trends of the children's shoe market in a credible and natural way.[46]

Outsourcing and the Division of Labor: The Global Shoe

BY JOHANNA STEINFELD

The term globalization was coined in the early 90s to describe the increasing interdependence of the world; an interdependence that fosters interaction between countries while at the same time making them dependent on one another.[1] With regard to the globalization of the economy, this trend primarily impacted on foreign trade, the financial and labor markets, and the organization of production. Since the 90s, technological developments have enabled companies to break value-added chains down into individual links on a large scale, and relocate specific elements to other countries where local conditions are more cost-favorable. Thanks to lower transport costs, this process of production fragmentation has evolved to such an extent that today's production chains may be spread across several countries on different continents.[2] In Germany, this so-called international division of labor has first and foremost affected the automotive, textile, and shoe industries.

The German shoe industry initially experienced strong business growth and a sharp rise in payroll in the 50s and 60s, albeit from a low baseline after World War II. In 1944, in the penultimate year of the war, the German leather shoe industry had a total payroll of about 68,000 workers, less than half the number employed in 1925 (128,000 workers) and about 40 percent less than in the first year of the war, 1939 (112,000 workers).[3] As early as the 60s, however, parts of the German shoe industry's production were relocated to nearby foreign countries, specifically to Italy and France.[4] The conditions for this were created by the establishment of the European Economic Community (EEC) in 1957, followed in 1968 by the abolition of customs duties on footwear within the EEC.[5] One reason for the internationalization of production was German consumers' increasingly strong demand for fashion items. This posed problems for the already labor-intensive industry, as automated mass production was hard to reconcile with a high degree of product differentiation and rapidly changing fashion designs.[6] This challenge was quickly outsourced to the foreign, mainly Italian, shoe industry as opposed to devising entrepreneurial solutions at home. In addition to the high labor costs in Germany, this rapid relocation of production can primarily be attributed to the special structure of the German shoe industry. The industry was characterized by smaller-sized companies that

Fig. 37: Bucking the trend again: ever larger parts of shoe production are being relocated to the Far East. Not so Birkenstock sandals, which remain "made in Germany".

Outsourcing and the Division of Labor: The Global Shoe

found it more difficult to shoulder the research and development costs required to improve industrial manufacturing processes—to the extent that they even wanted to do so in the first place.[7]

The momentum behind outsourcing production became more pronounced in the 70s and 80s, when it was possible to find ever newer, more favorable production locations. German companies were now also outsourcing manufacturing to Spain, Portugal, and Romania,[8] causing simultaneous shrinkage in the former or original countries of production. At the beginning of the 90s, following the collapse of the Soviet Union and the reorganization of Europe, production locations in Eastern Europe came into focus. Finally, Asian countries followed, with China in particular emerging as an important production hub following its accession to the World Trade Organization in 2001 and thanks to the liberalization of the world market for textiles and apparel.[9]

With regard to the effects of the international division of labor on the situation in the German shoe industry, the figures speak for themselves, although the consequences of rationalization and mechanization have also had an impact here.[10] While more than 1,000 manufacturing companies existed in Germany in the 60s, in 1994 there were only 228 and in 2014 there were just 66.[11] Today, footwear companies based in Germany often only con-

sist of a head office along with a design department, and the marketing and sales divisions. The associated reduction in personnel is unique in a comparison of German industries, with the number of employees plummeting by around 87 percent between the 1960s and 2015.[12] In 2021, 16,800 employees remained in German shoe manufacturing.[13] The town of Pirmasens, once the proud center of the German shoe industry and with close ties to shoemaking that date back as far as the 18th century, has been particularly hard hit. In the 20s, some 13,700 workers were employed there in 263 factories, and the city reached its highest level in 1969, with the total payroll exceeding 32,000 employees.[14] Shortly thereafter, the city started to go into decline as a shoemaking hub: in 2002, the Pirmasens shoe industry employed only 1,600 people.[15]

However, there were also exceptions: for example, German manufacturers of comfort and health shoes were much less likely to follow the lead of the rest of the German footwear industry because there was less foreign competition.[16] The same was and is still true for manufacturers of safety footwear, whose orientation to national standards, guidelines, and specifications has meant it has usually not been advantageous to relocate production abroad.[17]

The shoemaking countries that lost out in the international competition were not only Germany and oth-

1963–2024 Rise to a Global Brand

er European nations; the USA, too, has seen the outsourcing of production since as early as the 50s—especially to Asia, where the industry had enormous growth rates. Today, the world's largest shoe manufacturer and exporter is China, and most of Germany's footwear imports likewise come from Asia: in 2019, 736.1 million pairs of shoes were imported from there, contrasting with around 48.1 million pairs of shoes still manufactured in Germany that same year.[18]

The problems brought about by the outsourcing of manufacturing to Asia became more apparent in the 2010s. The precarious working conditions often lead to human rights violations that are hard to prevent due to the lack of, or failure to enforce, national labor laws and international agreements.[19] However, there are other reasons why German and European companies have been withdrawing from the Asian region in recent years:[20] these include a greater reliance on local production due to higher labor costs in China and the proximity to their own market.[21] Moreover, the COVID-19 epidemic revealed the structural weaknesses of global supply chains, which are also being impacted by extreme climatic events and the war of aggression against Ukraine. It remains to be seen how deglobalization strategies will change the world economic order, and what significance they will have for the footwear industry.[22]

Outsourcing and the Division of Labor: The Global Shoe   185

Birkenstock as a Symbol of the Environmental Movement in the 80s

In the early 80s, Birkenstock continued to grow unabated. Completely detached from the general economic decline in the textile and shoe industry, the Birkenstock family business seemed to be able to brace itself against the downward spiral. The mantra "structural change" had long been making the rounds in the German press and slowly made "traditional and long-familiar forms of business and employment" disappear.[47] Symptoms of the increasingly difficult situation in this industry were a nationwide wage strike at the end of 1980, during which the leather trade union demanded a 10.5 percent increase in wages for the 55,000 employees in the shoe industry.[48] While the aftermath of the second oil price crisis in 1979–80 dampened the consumer climate, in 1981, Birkenstock was actually able to record the largest increase in sales in the company's history.[49] With the cost of living soaring in the Western hemisphere, it was remarkable that the Bad Honnef-based company's sales were up nearly 40 percent from the year before, and its return on sales increased from eight to an impressive 18 percent.[50] Expressed in figures, the turnover had increased to just over DM 35 million by 1982, which meant that Birkenstock had almost doubled the sales yield of 1978.[51] One of the main reasons for the improvement in yields in the early 80s was reflected in the increases in productivity made possible by the plant expansions in the mid-70s. Significant savings were made in the use of materials alone compared with previous years, and some synergy effects in the production chain were leveraged.[52] Birkenstock stood out, especially when compared with the competition: at the end of the 70s, the company's market share in the health and leisure footwear sector in Germany was around five percent and increased to twelve to 15 percent within a few years.[53]

The tripling of Birkenstock's market share in the German health and leisure shoe sector was also reflected in the distribution of Birkenstock's sales markets and demonstrated that it was not just with its products that Birkenstock was swimming against the tide. Instead of being highly dependent on export markets to a large extent—like most German quality manufacturers—the company achieved almost two-thirds of its main sales in Germany, and this with an upward trend.[54] While Birkenstock's home market remained the main sales driver despite the energy and economic crisis, Fraser's Birkenstock sales in the United States suddenly stagnated.[55] This development was caused not only by major price increases, which were a response to the second oil price crisis, but also by a change in image that emerged in the clothing and consumer culture of the United States at the beginning of the 80s. In an internal memorandum, Fraser made the observation that with the election of Ronald Reagan as the 40th US President in the spring of 1981, "a definite shift to more traditional values" had taken place and the "New Age" movements had come to an end. Instead of "hippie," the "preppy" style was now in.[56] She feared that, 20 years after the market launch of the first Birkenstock sandals, Karl's predominantly constant product policy would soon no longer suit the wishes of US customers and suggested trying new ideas and concepts to follow the market. In 1982, Fraser and Birkenstock agreed that the joint company Birko Advertising, Inc. should intensify its marketing efforts, "to develop advertising and promotional campaigns suited to the US markets." The entire Birkenstock product development program should also be geared more toward the US market, "to help expand the lines and make them more appealing to the consumers."[57] In order to investigate changing customer demand, Fraser commissioned professional market research institutes for the first time in Birkenstock's history to give the Bad Honnef center a better understanding of the US market. The aim was to advise Karl on product development for the US market in order to do justice to the changed customer behavior in the 80s.[58] Nevertheless, knowing that the headstrong, product- and technology-focused Karl would not blindly listen to marketing agency suggestions, Fraser tried to persuade him to travel to California more frequently and familiarize himself with US customers, in order to be "better able to design for the US market."[59] Although Karl was seldom in California in the 80s, he was certainly aware of the interests of the US market and accommodated Fraser's wish for a wider range of colors, as he was now increasingly buying leather goods from US tanneries that were better at satisfying the color tastes of the local customers.[60]

Since the coordination effort between Bad Honnef and California had increased significantly, Karl Birkenstock and Margot Fraser also considered the idea of setting up a highly automated production facility for Birkenstock sandals in the United States in the early 80s. Fraser, who was always characterized by great drive and inventiveness, suggested that the United States should be considered for the production of the *Blue Footbed* since, as sports insoles, these already had a large market potential in the emerging "fitness wave" of the 80s.[61] It became clear that both sides were serious about the idea of setting up a US plant when Fraser and Birkenstock realigned Birko Advertising, Inc.'s activities in February 1984. In the spring of 1984, the German American duo renamed the company Birko Orthopedic, Inc., and decided "that the corporation shall withdraw from the advertising business and concentrate on analyzing the possibility of manufacturing Birkenstock sandal products in the United States."[62]

Nonetheless, before US production was set up in the years that followed, Karl's attention was drawn back to the home market. Because here, after years of niche existence, the health-conscious sandal suddenly seemed to be the trend among more and more Germans. In the spring of 1982, the FAZ newspaper stated that a "growing health awareness among the population" was noticeable and that manufacturers such as Birkenstock would benefit from this.[63] Here, too, the growth was grounded in the alternative movements, which experienced their first widely visible heyday in the Federal Republic at the beginning of the 80s. Public and private life in Germany "turned green" in the mid-80s with the strong media presence of the anti-nuclear movement, peace activists, and the environmental movement. "Environmentally friendly behavior became a widely accepted [...] norm of everyday action," which was also expressed in health and environmentally conscious forms of diet and clothing.[64] The Birkenstock sandal became socially acceptable in the political context. When the green party Die Grünen entered the Bundestag in 1983, media attention shifted to the sandal-wearing type of alternative politician. On German streets, orthopedic sandals became the means of choice for making a political statement. For example, protesters wearing Birkenstocks could be seen at the peace demonstrations on the Bonn Hofgartenwiese in autumn 1983, raising the public visibility of sandal wearing.[65]

The exponentially increasing demand, especially domestically, prompted Karl to carry out major structural changes in the family business and to prepare it for further growth. At the shareholders' meeting on November 12, 1985, he increased the company's share capital from DM 30,000 to 50,000 as sole shareholder or owner and had the articles of association of Birkenstock Orthopädie GmbH changed in order to be able to make company acquisitions more easily in the future.[66] The intention was to convert Birkenstock Orthopädie GmbH into a head or holding company, in order to include further production companies and branches in the Birkenstock production chain and at the same time reduce liability risk.[67] From the mid-80s on, an extensive group developed according to this model, which connected and secured a number of companies with the main company through mutual sub-participations.

For example, Karl founded a limited partnership—Birko Schuhtechnik GmbH & Co. KG—which initially had the stamping plant in

St. Katharinen overwritten by Birkenstock Orthopädie GmbH in April 1986. The new structure was also reflected in the new, more flexible status of the employees. As a result of this measure alone, 130 staff members switched from one company to another without having to leave their Birkenstock jobs.[68] Bit by bit, the main plant in Bad Honnef was outsourced and converted into the headquarters for administration and management. When the plant in St. Katharinen was added to the Honnef production area covering the "manufacture of bedding and orthopedic products" in mid-1988, large parts of the Birkenstock production had already been removed from the spa town and relocated to Rhineland-Palatinate. The procurement of raw materials and primary products, which was previously organized under one roof together with sandal production, had also been reorganized. Karl founded his own company here in mid-1986—Karl Birkenstock, Import and Export of Shoe Industry Supplies, St. Katharinen—which was to ensure a steady stream of supplies to the factory.[69] Over the next few years, every division, no matter how small, was spun off from the parent company, so that even the family-owned retail shop in Bad Honnef was converted into a "profit center" with the founding of „Birkenstock Fachgeschäft GmbH & Co KG" (specialist shop) in June 1989. This action removed it from Karl's personal liability.[70] Birkenstock had thus already spun off three key elements of its production and value-added chain (raw materials, manufacturing, and local sales) from the original company and initiated the establishment of a group of companies.

While Karl was preparing his company structure for further growth, a fortunate circumstance helped him to integrate Birkenstock's most important supplier, Alsa Schuhbedarf GmbH—founded by Alfons Saum in 1945—into the company. A favorable opportunity arose when the tire corporation Continental, which had acquired Alsa in 1968, decided in the late 80s to concentrate its "core business on automotive parts production and [...] to detach from areas that had nothing to do with automotive production," as a result of which the Continental subsidiary Alsa was put up for sale at the end of the 80s, according to the company's then managing director Karl-Heinrich Herber.[71] In the early 70s, the Alsa Group, in association with its subsidiaries in France, Italy, and Spain, manufactured cork-latex footbeds for Birkenstock at its headquarters in Steinau-Uerzell in Eastern Hesse and made its mark with several product innovations in the field of shoe beddings.[72] During this time, for example, Alsa developed the prototypes of the Adilette rubber-and-plastic sandal, which were later launched on the market by the sports shoe company Adidas.[73]

The takeover of the former supplier in January 1989 was another milestone for Birkenstock.[74] With it, one of the most important footbed suppliers could be integrated into the production chain of the company. At the end of the 80s, the steadily growing Karl Birkenstock group of companies had an almost completely integrated production chain. In addition, the takeover of Alsa allowed Birkenstock to benefit from the high level of research and development expertise of this specialist company. With the help of Alsa's so-called "model department," it was now possible to develop new products with significantly more resources and personnel than before. For example, the Steinau product developers had been researching new manufacturing processes for several years to produce high-quality and environmentally friendly soles from the new plastic polyurethane, which could be used in work and functional shoes or in shoes designed for wet areas.[75]

The spacious and modern production facilities in Steinau-Ürzell, which fully complemented the plants in St. Katharinen, Linz, and Rheinbreitbach, were also very advantageous for Birkenstock's expansion process. Over the next few years, Birkenstock Orthopädie GmbH mobilized considerable financial resources at the East Hessian location in order to purchase additional, modern production facilities.[76] This was also urgently needed, as not only did increased demand have to be met but stricter environmental regulations from the mid-80s onward also kept the shoe industry on its toes. Beginning in the early 80s, media reports such as the Spiegel cover story "Der Wald stirbt" (The Forest Is Dying) created political pressure to act and sparked a broad public debate about industrial emissions. When the liberal-conservative Kohl government took office in October 1982, it was confronted with the environmental concerns of the population and could not avoid passing laws to make industrial plants more environmentally friendly.[77] When "acid rain" was diagnosed as an acute danger to flora and fauna in Germany's forests, and US researchers simultaneously discovered a huge hole in the ozone layer above the Arctic Circle, industrial plastic production in the Western Hemisphere was subject to considerable restrictions.[78] In the spring of 1985, 197 countries signed the Vienna Convention for the Protection of the Ozone Layer and defined concrete measures to protect the ozone layer. These aimed to ban the use of solvents such as chlorofluorocarbons (CFCs) in the manufacture and processing of plastics.[79] With the founding of the Federal Ministry for the Environment in 1986, environmental protection in the Federal Republic also became a fixed institutional factor when it came to approval procedures for industrial and commercial plants. For the shoe companies, which now relied

Fig. 38: Due to rapidly growing space and personnel requirements, Birkenstock relocated a large part of its corporate functions from the provinces to the media and creative metropolis of Cologne in 2019.

heavily on plastics, modernization of their industrial plants was essential if they wanted to continue producing in the Federal Republic. For example, the revised Federal Immission Control Act of 1990 presented companies with the challenge of filtering their exhaust air even more than had been done previously and establishing a closed processing cycle for recyclable material.[80]

This posed a problem for many shoe manufacturers, since the PVC plastics, which were increasingly used in everyday, leisure, and sports shoes in the 80s, could not yet be produced without the CFC propellant.[81] While other manufacturers in the clothing and shoe industry reacted to the tightened production conditions and steadily increasing price pressure by relocating their production to Asia, the GDR (German Democratic Republic), or Southeast Europe, Birkenstock increasingly advertised its environmentally friendly sandal production.[82] In 1990, Birkenstock published the brochure "Respect nature – Understand nature – Protect nature" and added the phrase "Birkenstock – For the environment's sake" to their brand lettering. The 14-page information paper, which was intended as a communication guide for the specialist trade, emphasized the company's long-standing tradition of manufacturing sandals and orthopedic products in an energy-conscious and environmentally friendly manner. As early as in the 60s, according to the brochure, Karl began "with determination and sometimes obstinately to develop energy-saving technologies and machines," which alone saved 70 to 80 percent of heating energy and reduced the power consumption in the stamping plant from 25 to 1.8 kWh.[83] With the installation of the latest exhaust gas cleaning systems and the industry's first use of water-soluble adhesives, Birkenstock counted itself among the "most active and progressive companies" in the field of sustainability and environmental protection in the 80s.[84]

The environmentally conscious company not only made key advances in these areas of sustainability and environmental protection in the processing of natural products such as jute, cork, latex, and leather. Birkenstock also set new standards in the German shoe industry when it came to plastics. For example, conventional PVC was no longer used in the manufacture of the plastic-coated sandal treads or the purely synthetic garden clogs.[85] Thanks to the long-standing cooperation with Alsa, Birkenstock was able to benefit at exactly the right time from the fact that Alsa was already known throughout the industry for being the first shoe parts manufacturer "to process polyurethane, which was no longer CFC-dependent," said former Alsa managing director Herber.[86] As a result, Birkenstock's new synthetic sandals not only complied with the latest environmental legislation but also helped to maintain credibility with the predominantly environmentally oriented customer base, despite the increased use of plastics. With Alsa's modern production facilities and methods, Birkenstock had created a good starting position for maintaining the German production site in the 90s and ensured that the core product range of cork-latex footbeds could be expanded to include other synthetic products. The fact that Birkenstock also systematically relied on synthetic materials was also mentioned in the aforementioned nature conservation brochure. There, Birkenstock addressed the topic of longevity and sustainability and explained to the reader that, compared with purely natural products, the use of plastics makes an "immense difference [in] the wearing time" and thus conserves resources.[87] In addition, at the end of the 80s it became obvious that a large part of the Birkenstock product range now came from the "world of plastics" and that the further development of the production processes would play an increasingly important role in maintaining Birkenstock's promise of quality and environmental awareness.[88]

As important as Alsa was for Birkenstock's product development, little changed within the family business when Alsa was acquired. For the Alsa employees, everything remained the same in relation to Birkenstock, since Karl made no effort to integrate Alsa into the structures of the expanding company. Only at the highest level were there working groups in which Birkenstock executives met with Alsa executives, so that ultimately only in the Bad Honnef headquarters did all the threads come together.[89] Beyond that, however, no attempts were made to create an integrated company with a common corporate culture. This was evident from the fact that no structural or organizational reforms were carried out at Alsa after the takeover, and both firms remained relatively autonomous for a long time in the decentralized Birkenstock group of companies. Consequently, for many years it was common for Alsa to retain its own management and business customer division, which even included Birkenstock's competitors. In fact, Karl himself instructed the Alsa management during the takeover that "the customers that Alsa has supplied in the past [...] should, if possible, continue to be supplied" and that there was no intention of Alsa working exclusively for Birkenstock.[90] Birkenstock thus made it clear that he did not want to jeopardize the solid growth of his family company by hastily setting up a centrally controlled group of firms. Instead, he preferred the form of a low-risk group of companies whose management and control functioned primarily through personal relationships between himself and the other executives. As Alsa's technical director at the time, Klaus Noll, remembered, "[There was] not this cut that is usual with everything being made anew, but he [Karl Birkenstock] tried to incorporate the existing structures and to develop them further."[91]

By the end of the 80s, with the acquisition of Alsa and the changes in the corporate structure, Karl Birkenstock gave his family company an entirely new look. He had relocated the former Bad Honnef manufacturing business mainly to Rhineland-Palatinate and Hesse in order to serve the increased demand, and had transformed his small family business into a complex group of companies through various spin-offs and acquisitions. In the 80s, Karl, who was the sole representative of the company with his wife, Gisela, set himself the goal of securing the recent positive development of the company and closing the gaps in the in-house production chain. Shy in public, as the "sandal king" always had been, concrete reports or figures about Birkenstock's remarkable business success seldom leaked out in those years. In view of the dramatically negative development of the German shoe industry as a whole, Birkenstock's growth in the 80s represented an extraordinary success story. In figures, Birkenstock increased its sales during the 80s to over DM 226 million in the financial year 1990. Despite the massive growth in those years, the profitability of the company was also extremely good, with a return on sales of almost twelve percent.[92]

Works Council Dispute, Sub-brands, and the Fall of the Wall: Birkenstock Becomes a Multigenerational Company in the 90s

With the fall of the Berlin Wall on November 9, 1989, political events came to a head. German reunification a year later would not only turn the political map upside down but also dramatically change the domestic industry and business landscape. For handicraft companies like Birkenstock in particular, the possibility of using the former GDR industrial combines and state-owned enterprises (VEB) to rapidly increase their production capacities in Germany suddenly became apparent. In order to bring about the transformation of the East German planned economy into a market economy, the GDR Council of Ministers, led by Hans Modrow, had already decided before reunification to set up an Institute for the Fiduciary Administration of National Property and to initiate an unbundling of the East German combines through the so-called Treuhandgesetz (Trust Law). The aim was to convert the individual companies that had been detached from the combines, from which around 8,500 companies were created, into corporations. When reunification took place on October 3, 1990, the Federal Ministry of Finance took over supervision of the Treuhandanstalt (Trust Agency) and staffed it primarily with West German bureaucrats, managers, and politicians. So-called economic miracle doctors, spearheaded by the former CEO of Hoesch AG—Detlev Carsten Rohwedder—as Trust president, quickly took over in the summer of 1990 and occupied the management floors of the former VEB companies to facilitate their transition to a market economy.[93]

At the company headquarters in Bad Honnef, Karl also noticed that the market transformation of East Germany offered enormous opportunities for his own company. Since the end of the 80s, Birkenstock had realized that owing to the high demand, the Alsa production capacities in Steinau/Ürzell were "running out" sooner than expected, as Alsa managing director Karl-Heinz Herber put it.[94] In addition, in the western metropolitan areas of the Rhine-Main area, where Birkenstock's main plants were located, there was strong competition in the labor market, which made it increasingly difficult for Birkenstock to retain or recruit qualified workers. The fact that German reunification made available not only large-scale factories but also a workforce of over 40,000 skilled

194   **1963–2024** Rise to a Global Brand

workers from the East German shoe industry was a stroke of luck for Birkenstock.[95]

The idea of setting up footbed production in the United States, which had been discussed only a few years previously with Margot Fraser, was now finally passé after reunification. Although Karl, who always wore sandals, didn't really seem to fit in with the "predominantly double-breasted" guild of "western managers," he too had followed "the insistent calls and appeals of the Treuhandanstalt" and from October 1990 on, armed with a travel guide, he undertook exploration trips to the former GDR.[96] In fact, he and other shoe and textile entrepreneurs had always had close ties with shoe and textile factories in the GDR. Quite a few East German companies, for example, had produced for large West German shoe manufacturers such as Salamander AG and, with their low production costs, represented a welcome alternative to Asian production facilities.[97] For Birkenstock, for example, the VEB Trumpf Schuhfabrik Seifhennersdorf located in Saxony, which had grown into one of the most modern shoe factories in the GDR after its foundation in 1973, had already been active as a supplier for some time.[98] After months spent traveling in the years around reunification, during which Karl obtained detailed information about the local shoe industry and its operations, he gave an enthusiastic report to the Alsa managing directors about "fabulous factories in the furthest corners" and waxed lyrical about the large-scale manufacturing and production facilities that he had found, especially in Saxony.[99]

As with the takeover of Alsa in the 80s, Karl wanted to facilitate the expansion of his production capacities. But this intention was successful only on the second attempt. Although there had been an intensive business relationship with the Seifhennersdorfer Kombinatsbetriebe for many years, Karl was not able to close a deal favorably in the takeover negotiations with the Trust administration, meaning that VEB Trumpf remained a supplier for clog production.[100]

Karl did not, however, give up on his quest for suitable factories in East Germany that would support his plans for further growth. Just a few kilometers from Seifhennersdorf he finally identified two factories in Bernstadt and Schönbach that corresponded to his ideas of expansion.[101] The weaving mills located in the Görlitz-Zittau-Löbau triangle belonged to the former VEB Oberlausitzer Textilbetriebe Lautex, which had been operated at times by the textile combine Zittau and formed the largest textile complex in the GDR.[102] Although these were not classic shoe factories, Birkenstock and the executives who had traveled with him were overwhelmed by the sheer size of the facilities when they inspected the huge factory halls, which housed up to 260 looms. "[Deeply] impressed by the area [and] the mass" of the industrial plants that the Birkenstock tour group found in the textile cities of the former GDR, the family patriarch decided to invest in the two factories.[103]

After the purchase of the buildings and land, Bernstadt and Schönbach were quickly equipped with over 500 punches, presses, and embossing machines, and a large part of the cork/latex and PU (polyurethane) footbed production was relocated from West Germany to the East German factory facilities. Since Birkenstock knew that the East German weaving mill complexes had to contend with serious efficiency and productivity problems due to the previous GDR planned economy, while at the same time offering huge industrial workspaces, he relocated only those production sections that required the most space and had reached their capacity limits in the main plants in West Germany.[104] Nonetheless, the expansion and conversion of the two plants in Bernstadt and Schönbach were carried out surprisingly fast. Within a few months, the experienced Alsa technicians set up a completely new system periphery, including new heating and hydraulic systems in the former combine factory halls and started manufacturing footbeds, leather parts, outsoles, and buckles.[105] Years later, the Schönbach plant moved to Görlitz, when production capacity had again reached its limit.[106]

While Birkenstock took an important step toward maintaining Germany as a production location by taking over the former GDR textile companies, the next generation of Birkenstock entrepreneurs came knocking on the door at the company's headquarters in Bad Honnef. Karl Birkenstock's sons, Stephan, Alex, and Christian, pushed their way into the company and were officially accepted into the management of their father's company in 1992 and 1996.[107] This significant decision was preceded by their gradual introduction into the company over the preceding few years. The three brothers had already taken on their first tasks in the company in the mid-80s and were later granted banking powers or powers of attorney, so that they shared responsibility for the company's development from early on.[108] After Karl Birkenstock took over the company from his father Carl in 1965, the family business returned to the status of a "multigenerational project" in the mid-90s.[109]

However, the change of generations at Birkenstock had serious repercussions, with the entry of the junior members of the Birkenstock family inevitably leading to a reorientation of the company's strategy, which was to keep it in suspense for the next 20 years. Instead of the hitherto much-vaunted one-brand strategy, which included various product lines, a whole series of legally independent sub-brands were to

196   **1963-2024** Rise to a Global Brand

Fig. 39: Global brand made in Germany. Birkenstock *Footbed* production at the Birkenstock plant in Görlitz (2022).

be created at the beginning of the 90s. These were intended to address new customer groups, close price and product gaps, and enable the Birkenstock sons to gain experience in active company management.[110] An initial step in this direction was the foundation of the new sub-brand Tatami Schuh GmbH in July 1990. The task of this premium Birkenstock brand, managed by Alex Birkenstock, was to establish much more of an emphasis on fashion and open up new markets through cooperation. The family council followed the same pattern in the early 90s with the founding of the feminine sub-brand Papillio Schuh GmbH and the children's shoe brand Birki Schuh GmbH, which had emerged from the existing product line for children's shoes.[111]

At almost the same time as these events in Bad Honnef, on the other side of the Atlantic, Margot Fraser announced that she too wanted to introduce a generational change at the top management position of Birkenstock Footprint Sandals, Inc. Because Fraser's distribution company was run like a family business—and was also set up like one—her closest associates feared that the company was not yet ready for a change in leadership. Against the backdrop of a noticeably changed relationship with the parent company, a strategy paper from 1992 stated:

> "The relationship with Birkenstock USA's supplier in Germany is rapidly changing, as the Birkenstock operation in Germany has greatly expanded its operation and production capacity over the past 2 years. Both companies are having to respond to each other's changes in growth, personnel, structure, operations, and MIS [management information systems] systems."[112]

At the Birkenstock Footprint Sandals, Inc. headquarters in California, the executives of the US organization were deeply concerned about the rumors surrounding Fraser's retirement and the now stagnating or falling sales figures in the United States. The company had come to the conclusion that Birkenstock's product policy in the US market was no longer working and that a realignment of the management structures was urgently needed in order to establish "really close cooperation and coordination" between Bad Honnef and California.[113]

However, the fact that the exchange between California and Bad Honnef was not intensified in the years that followed was due to a corporate crisis that hit the Birkenstock group of companies from 1993 to 1997. The exorbitant growth that the company experienced in the years after German reunification had consequences. From 1990 to 1993 alone, the family business had seen an increase in sales of almost 40 percent, which was also reflected in a massive increase in personnel, causing unprecedented problems. For example, the main plant in St. Katharinen grew into a company that now employed 700 people.[114] Although Birkenstock had always been publicly praised for the fact that its employees were allowed to work independently in small, flexible teams, and even received performance bonuses, the rapid growth in the preceding years and the progressive integration of the group of new companies threw up new challenges that were quite unknown to the management.[115] Despite the massive expansion in the 80s and early 90s, there had been no attempt on the part of management to adapt the work and corporate culture or establish it anew. When the Birkenstock sons came along with their new subsidiaries, the concept of the family factory practiced by Karl and his employees threatened to falter.[116] In 1990, the year of reunification, the ever-growing family business was already being targeted by the trade unions. The trade unions for the leather industry (GL) and for the timber and plastics industry (GHK), organized in the German Trade Union Confederation (DGB), became interested in Birkenstock because they had noticed that there was still no trade union organization for the workforce at Birkenstock.[117] The timber union, which in the years around reunification had lost around 30 percent of its members owing to the increasing number of company bankruptcies in the timber industry, seemed in the case of Birkenstock to be significantly more active than the leather union.[118] Internally, the ailing union therefore threatened the leather union with the notion that a works council would be set up at Birkenstock without consideration for the colleagues of the leather union if the latter did not intensify its activities at Birkenstock.[119]

At the company headquarters in Bad Honnef, the efforts of the timber and plastics union were followed with suspicion, since there had never been a union at Birkenstock up to that point. In general, concerns about outside interference were not uncommon in family businesses. They often feared that the continued existence of the officially sworn-in company or works family would be endangered as soon as union-affiliated works councils were formed in their companies. However, the "democratization of the economy" with the introduction of the Works Constitution Act of 1952 and the Codetermination Act of 1976 was clearly being promoted by politicians.[120] More often than politicians and unions had hoped, however, there was no reason at all for the workforces in family businesses to form works councils, with or without unions. Instead, well-functioning informal information, communication, and participation systems had developed over decades, especially in family businesses, which made an organization of workers' rights appear unnecessary.[121] Since the initiative to form a works council according to the Works Constitution Act did not have to come from the employer but from the employees and was associated with a great deal of bureaucracy, there was simply no need for it in many small and medium-sized companies.[122] Statistically speaking, in the early 90s, for example, only around ten percent of all West German companies had an elected works council.[123]

Although Birkenstock had the largest sales growth in the company's history in the fiscal years 1990 to 1992 and had, in turn, hired a large number of new staff, the efforts of the leather union to unionize the staff were apparently not particularly fruitful.[124] Since the leather union had not even bothered to take care of the "mother company Birkenstock Orthopädie GmbH near Bonn," they had completely failed to notice "that the other company, Birkenstock Schuhtechnik, had opened two new plants in Sankt Katharinen and Asbach in Rhineland-Palatinate. To this day, they don't seem to have noticed that they are legally independent companies," the Andernach office of the timber union complained to the Düsseldorf headquarters. In the years that followed, the timber union looked for a suitable pretext to finally gain a foothold in St. Katharinen and to outsmart the leather union. When one of the employees working there protested against a personnel measure in the spring of 1993 and asked the union for legal support, the timber union immediately recognized an opportunity and took advantage of it. The Düsseldorf headquarters quickly assured the responsible regional office in Andernach that they wanted to grant the employee "legal advice and legal protection because the dispute is important to us in terms of organizational policy, and also in connection with the question of the responsibility of the DGB trade unions."[125] Through this individual case, the timber union slowly but surely began to gain a foothold in the Birko factory in St. Katharinen and asserted itself against the leather union, which was actually authorized to represent the plant.[126] As a countermeasure, management even tried to hold talks with other unions to get involved at Birkenstock, but the company's efforts to acquire a labor-friendly union were ultimately in vain.[127]

In the meantime, however, the timber union had long since established its position and, in April 1993, held the first works council election in St. Kathrinen.[128] How closely the works council in St. Katharinen was now connected with the timber union became apparent when the chairman of the works council of Birko Schuhtechnik GmbH invited people to the first works meeting, which was to take place in St. Katharinen shortly before Christmas 1993.[129]

200   **1963–2024** Rise to a Global Brand

When the works meeting started on December 21, 1993, in the canteen of Plant 4, it quickly became apparent that the event was a turning point in the company's history. The chairman of the works council—seconded by the timber union leader—criticized the company management in strong language and decried alleged shortcomings in the areas of work organization, wage and personnel policy, and the material quality of the cork bedding and leather goods. At the center of the criticism was Karl Birkenstock, who had devised a system dividing the workforce into teams of ten to 15 employees, with the production of shoes and sandals supervised by the team leaders. If a team managed to produce more pairs of shoes than planned, they were rewarded with the help of a finely devised bonus system in addition to their base salary.[130] When Karl finally stepped up to the lectern to give a report on the company's situation, he seemed visibly surprised and personally offended. His worldview as an entrepreneur had faltered. He struggled for words and composure because of the sudden and massive criticism voiced by the works council. He was hit particularly hard by the common trade union demand that "equal pay for equal work" must be adhered to—i. e., the bonus system should be abolished, and numerous new occupational safety requirements had to be met.[131]

The disaster in communication, nevertheless, had already become apparent beforehand. Since the summer of 1993, the freshly elected works council had bombarded Birkenstock almost weekly with dozens of demands and suggestions for improvement, calling on the company patriarch to take action.[132] Karl considered this behavior to be intrusive but did not take it as an opportunity to seek direct dialogue with the works council.[133] He had also previously ignored the works council's requests to convene a joint economic committee meeting, thereby making it clear that he rejected active interference in company management by employee representatives.[134]

At the end of the works council's meeting, Karl was deeply shaken, but, still willing to compromise, he promised "that he had recognized that there was a lot wrong with the team leaders and that he would call them together for a meeting so that some changes could be made."[135] However, when he met with the team leaders for a discussion, they were extremely critical of the newly formed works council and gave written support to his negative stance.[136] This letter confirmed a hardening of the fronts between company management, executive employees, and the works council.[137] Over the Christmas period of 1993–94, Karl, who could not countenance the idea that "the working atmosphere was so bad," developed a deep-seated indignation and defensiveness toward the works council.[138] An emphatically explosive atmosphere prevailed when operations in St. Katharinen started up again after the Christmas holidays, and there were wild protest actions and office raids within the factory walls. A battery of written rebuttal from Karl accompanied the acts of the heated crowd and were intended to refute the allegations made by the works council.[139]

After the works meeting in December 1993 got out of hand, a drama unfolded in several acts. Within a few days, the internal dispute between Birkenstock and the members of the works council at the St. Katharinen plant escalated into a public conflict. When violent arguments occurred between employees and the works council in the first days of January 1994, the timber and plastics union made sure that the conflict quickly became public. Within a few days, this press coverage intensified the highly emotional dispute between the company founder and the works council.[140] Fuel was added to the public debate a little later when Birkenstock announced that it would have to cut up to 200 jobs in St. Katharinen in order to make better use of the newly renovated Saxon companies with their modern facilities.[141]

Beginning in February 1993, the general public was able to follow the internal conflict at Birkenstock's main plant almost daily in the regional daily media. This coverage also prompted local politicians to enter the scene, and they began to intervene in the disputes in St. Katharinen. In January 1994, Ulrich Schmalz, a member of the Bundestag for the CDU from Rhineland-Palatinate, was chosen to initiate arbitration between the two hostile and socially conflicted partners. In Schmalz, the right man seemed to have been found, and a solution appeared to be in sight. After all, the former local politician not only had experience of dealing with such conflicts in his constituency in neighboring Westerwald but also had himself previously been an entrepreneur. Initially, Schmalz went into the talks with the motto that the Birkenstock conflict was "purely a communication problem" and that the company patriarch urgently needed to find a new basis for discussion with the works council.[142] When everything seemed to be going well, the talks suddenly broke off at the end of January 1994.[143] The trigger was a letter of solidarity from the Neuwied IG Metall (industrial union of metalworkers) office, which fiercely attacked Karl Birkenstock and described him as an entrepreneur of the 19th century who "fomented a pogrom mood against the works council."[144] Karl suspected that the works council and the timber and plastics union had been the instigators of this and there was thus now no longer any basis for discussions.

202　**1963–2024** Rise to a Global Brand

With one emotional injury following another, the situation became all but impenetrable, and the role of the trade unions could hardly be separated from that of the works council.[145] The leather union, which had earlier been expelled from the negotiations, also got involved again for a short time and politicized the internal dispute.[146] Numerous legal proceedings between Birkenstock, the works council, and the timber and plastics union had meanwhile influenced the public image of the sandal manufacturer as a peace-loving and environmentally conscious family business. By mid-1994, there were signs of tangible damage to the company's prestige, which also endangered Birkenstock's economic foundations. During the high season of sandal sales in the summer of 1994, there was a backlog of orders for over 926,531 pairs of shoes, which had not been manufactured owing to the constant disputes in the St. Katharinen factory.[147] The key economic figures also painted a grim picture. In the 1994 fiscal year, sales fell by more than six percent compared with the previous year, only to collapse later by a whole 20 percent.[148] Karl, who no longer knew what else to do from an entrepreneurial point of view, began to split up the company in St. Katharinen in order to resolve the conflict. He founded numerous new production companies, which were to replace the functions and output of what had once been the largest Birkenstock shoe production company.[149] The companies Betula Schuh GmbH, Fußbett Schuhproduktion GmbH, Happy Schuh GmbH, and Albero Schuh GmbH were entered in the commercial register in the summer of 1994 and took on almost all of the previous Birko factory facilities and employees. According to the breakup plan, these new companies were later to be developed into independent sub-brands by Karl Birkenstock's sons.[150] The production plants in Bernstadt and Schönbach as well as those in Asbach and Bad Honnef, which formally belonged to Birko Schuhtechnik, were converted into new companies. Birkenstock founded the new company Birkenstock Schuhproduktion GmbH Sachsen for the East German plants and Birko Orthopädie GmbH and Footprints Schuh GmbH for the production companies based in the Rhineland. Within a few weeks, what was once the largest Birkenstock factory was broken down into legally independent production companies, and a network of companies was created at the St. Katharinen site that was now almost impossible to ignore.[151]

Although the original works council left the company in the summer of 1994 and a new council was elected at the Birko plant in St. Katharinen, which now had only 158 employees, the conflict dragged on into 1997.[152] Despite changing works councils and further attempts at conciliation, for years no agreement could be reached between Karl

Birkenstock and the respective employee representatives. Even when a federal minister, Norbert Blüm, got involved in the case in mid-1995, there was no end in sight to the conflict.[153] The reason for this was the same tension that had led to the escalation in the previous year. The works council dispute at Birkenstock had long since taken on a life of its own over the years and triggered a veritable media phenomenon.[154] Articles with bellicose titles like "Karl's War," "The Empire Strikes Back," "War in the Works," and "Psycho Terror at Birkenstock" had a damaging effect not only on the company's image in Germany but also in other important Birkenstock markets, such as the United States.[155] In the meantime, wealthy US customers on the other side of the Atlantic were also able to glean from the press that Birkenstock was in the midst of a deep corporate crisis.[156] The public dispute between Karl Birkenstock and the Neuwied district association of the Bündnis 90/Die Grünen party, for example, was not a particularly good advertisement for the ecologically oriented customer base.[157] Even the head of US sales, Margot Fraser, felt compelled to intervene and write a clarification to Die Zeit. In this, she pointed out that "in the heat of the moment the management had certainly made some mistakes," but that the "power struggle of the trade unions" raging in the background was completely ignored in the media reports.[158]

From the outset, it was a matter not only of a dispute between the management and the works council but also of a conflict in which the timber and plastics union played a central role. Consequently, the works council dispute could only be ended when the company management not only came to terms with the works council but also was able to agree on a social compensation plan with the trade union official Conrad in the spring of 1997. This was only possible because a promise had been made to the timber and plastics union that a works council would be formed in other Birkenstock companies as well. Another reason for the resolution of the conflict was that Karl, who was most affected emotionally, had meanwhile left the conflict resolution to his son Alex.[159] From an economic point of view, the works council dispute from 1993 to 1997 left behind a catastrophic balance sheet and brought the company to the brink of bankruptcy. At the end of the 1997 fiscal year, the books showed a 25.3 percent drop in sales and a return on sales that had shrunk to one percent.[160] Now it became clear that the company was in a situation that threatened its existence if a turnaround was not initiated soon. However, mastering this predicament was no longer the task of the family and company patriarch, Karl, but that of the next generation.

Health Loafers and Eco-footwear: The Sandals of the Protest Movements

BY JOHANNA STEINFELD

The 60s were years of social upheaval in West Germany: the young generation rebelled against the "establishment" and protested against staid sexual morality, the fact that their parents had buried their heads in the sand over the Third Reich, and the Vietnam War. In 1968, the events culminated in strikes and demonstrations that were not limited to Germany but spread to many countries around the world.[1] Part of the protest culture was a specific style of dress, which sought to stand out from prevailing fashion habits and to be provocative. Women, in particular, no longer wanted to live according to predefined "dress codes," but rather to determine for themselves what and how much of their bodies they showed. This turned the relationship between fashion and consumers upside down: now fashion picked up on social trends, as in the case of Yves Saint Laurent, whose pantsuits for women brought clothing that had previously had a clearly male connotation into women's fashion.[2]

In terms of footwear, all eyes turned to sandals: in 1967, Rainer Langhans, Dieter Kunzelmann, and Ulrich Enzensberger, all members of Kommune 1, were photographed wearing sandals when they were summoned to appear before a committee of inquiry at the Berlin House of Representatives in July 1967 to clarify the events surrounding the Shah's visit on June 2, 1967.[3]

The choice of this inappropriate footwear seemed to make a mockery of the occasion and the officials involved. The sandal's provocative potential was one reason for its popularity in the protest movement, and over and above that it offered even more compatibility with their values and goals. At first, owing to its unisex character, the sandal resisted the dichotomous classification of shoe fashion: then as now, there was a face-off between the flat black leather shoe and the stiletto, which were assigned to the different sexes with an unambiguity that has scarcely been questioned outside of the realm of queer fashion.[4] The "shoe for all" allowed men and women to move away from heteronormative concepts of dress; the design was simple, and the materials used for the sandals included neither the ornaments and textile fabrics used for women nor the smooth, black leather traditionally used for men's shoes.[5]

For women in particular, sandals increased their scope of expression, for after gender roles had become confused during World War II, when women had taken over the duties of men conscripted into the armed forces, the 50s had seen a return to conventional female and male roles. This was also reflected in high-heeled women's shoes, which clearly corresponded in appearance to notions of the feminine but also strongly influenced women's gait and restricted their freedom of movement.[6] Here, the flat sandal brought real and symbolic freedom in equal measure. Moreover, it had an egalitarian effect as it served to blur socioeconomic differences, something also expressed in the clothing worn by students in particular, who sported working-class clothes. In this context, the sandal was not worn to underscore the status of the wearer but to express a certain way of life and worldview.

How quickly the sandal was identified, even from the outside, as part of the various social movements of the 60s can be seen from a cartoon that appeared in the Berliner Zeitung in 1967. Here it also becomes clear how older generations perceived the youth and young people: among those waiting at the veterinarian's office sits a long-haired man who has brought no animal with him but, in a sense, himself. The unkempt patient wears sandals on his feet.

Members of the protest, freedom, and peace movements now discovered Birkenstock sandals, whose first model, *Madrid*, had come onto the market in 1963. It was, in particular, hippies in the USA who bought Birkenstocks, and they were likewise worn by people attending the Woodstock Festival in 1969.[7]

In Germany, members of the environmental movement of the 70s and 80s increasingly turned to Birkenstocks. For them, sandals as footwear may have been attractive in themselves for the reasons outlined above, while another factor may have been a greater health awareness among the movement's followers, who found footwear that felt right to them in the form of Birkenstock's healthy and comfortable footbed with its natural materials of leather and cork. Added to this was a certain aesthetic of poverty that, in the face of the crises and misery of the world, refused to "take fashion as such seriously at all."[8]

Through the spread of the Birkenstock sandal among environmentalists, it took on green connotations and became the "toddler's shoe(s)" for the young Green movement, as Green politician Werner Schulz recalls "when describing the early history of his party."[9] This connection gave the sandal a clear image for the first time, which eventually took on a life of its own and had an effect on its wearers. Those who wore Birkenstocks belonged to a separate breed of people, who seemed more niche than mainstream, and unattractive and uncool.

Remarkably, this process eventually led to such a negative image

206 **1963–2024** Rise to a Global Brand

Fig. 40: The sandal was the footwear of the protest movement.

that the Green Party, which had diffused into the mainstream, publicly distanced itself from the Birkenstock brand. In 1994, Norbert Franck of the Green Party's public relations department said that a narrow image was being painted that no longer corresponded to the party: "Bündnis 90/Die Grünen no longer fit the picture of 'Birkenstock-wearing' women and sweater-knitting men that the media like to paint of it. Jacket and tie are no longer frowned upon."[10] During the 90s, in particular, when companies were trying to make the themes of "environment," "nature," "organic," and "eco" attractive to a broader public and to market them as something enjoyable and wholesome, they were hampered by the image of "Birkenstock wearers," which rubbed off on the brand.[11] The message then was "lifestyle and enjoyment rather than Birkenstocks."[12] Despite this, or perhaps because of it, this was precisely the time that the Birkenstock brand was discovered by designers for the catwalks.

Betula, Papillio, and Tatami: Building Up the Multi-brand System among Karl Birkenstock's Sons and Taking Over US Sales in the 2000s

In the transition to the 2000s, the new generation began to initiate a change in strategy toward a multi-brand system, the realization of which had initially been hindered by the long-standing works council dispute. BIRKENSTOCK's reorganization away from a core brand with different product lines to different, equally positioned brands was to fundamentally change the family business and would powerfully reshape the entire sales periphery of the sandal and shoe manufacturer. Since Birkenstock did not have its own import and sales company in its largest export market—the United States—the Birkenstock sons' plan to bring the new brand companies Tatami, Betula, Birki's, and Footprints onto the US market inevitably steered into the next conflict.

With Margot Fraser, the Birkenstock sons were dealing with a staunch opponent of the multi-brand system, who would not be easily persuaded to change her entire distribution system to suit their wishes. And she was by no means an inexperienced opponent. Not only had she been awarded the German Order of Merit in 1986, and other prizes for her entrepreneurial accomplishments, she had also been dealing with the topic of *brand management* for a long time, when this was still a foreign concept in the German company headquarters of Birkenstock.[161] Shortly before the turn of the millennium, she explained during a lecture she gave to Birkenstock dealers in Germany that it was important to retain the core components of Birkenstock's brand values in the future in order not to lose customers and dilute the brand essence:

> "Today's consumer has changed, or rather, the hippie generation of yesteryear has come of age. In the meantime, they have earned money and had professional success, but are now returning to their old values. Health, convenience, and naturalness are in great demand again. Brands are important, the ideas behind them, the feelings, and memories a brand triggers, all of that stimulates sales."[162]

With her corporate philosophy of "serving the customer better," Fraser had in mind primarily her regular customers and was therefore on a collision course with the new approaches of the new generation.[163] Specifically, she feared that the newly established brands could lead to mutual cannibalization of the core and subsidiary brands, since "Tatami, Papillio, Birki's, and Footprints would [ultimately] all be considered Birkenstock brands [sic]." An even bigger problem, however, was that the new subsidiaries began to establish their own sales channels in the United States, reaping the fruits of Fraser's groundwork in the process.[164] For this reason alone, she repeatedly admonished Karl Birkenstock and his sons to give greater consideration to the needs and interests of the US market in their plans and to seek close coordination with her company.[165]

She was visibly surprised that the Birkenstocks had stuck to their plans even during the difficult years of the works council dispute, without ever having made any concrete agreements with her. In the 90s, the uncoordinated shift in strategy promptly resulted in a jumble of the various BIRKENSTOCK brands in the US market. For example, Fraser's Birkenstock Footprint Sandals, Inc. advertised the products of the new brand with the well-known BIRKENSTOCK lettering and reduced the new brand name to such an extent that the Birkenstock core brand identity was undoubtedly in the foreground. On the other hand, in the United States new dealers suddenly came on the scene who sold the new brands like Betula or Tatami with self-created "corporate identities" and used the lettering in a completely different design. The result was that there was more and more competition not only in-house but also for Fraser's company. In the deadlock, both sides, Fraser and the Birkenstocks, blamed each other for not understanding the new concept. Shortly before the turn of the millennium, Stephan Birkenstock told her that she finally had to switch completely to the new multi-brand system in order not to jeopardize the generational change:

> "Carrying along the old brand to all other brands has long since become a massive self-inflicted handicap. With consistent separate brands, we would build a lot more business, which was the main purpose of separate brands. [...] On the other hand, we didn't really want to switch the old customers over to all the new brands, but to set up the second and third stores in the small town or in the mall with the new brands [...]. We also want to open up other sales channels such as TV sales, the internet, discounts, etc., with new brands. [... But] there is another absolutely compelling reason for an absolutely consistent separation. The brands belong to different people. These independent companies are managed by owners who have their own ideas and go their own very different ways."[166]

After several years of uncertainty as to the status of the various ancillary brands in the US market, Fraser finally gave up her fundamental opposition in the early 2000s. Instead, she now tried to persuade the

Birkenstock family in her own interest to share the US market fairly. With urgent appeals, she repeatedly turned to the headquarters in Bad Honnef, claiming that "the other brands [admittedly] have their own right to life" and "need to be geared toward different buyer segments." Nonetheless, one should under no circumstances jeopardize "the umbrella brand with its reputation for quality, function, and comfort." Fraser said the "cheap deal" approach for the new Betula brand, which was being marketed in the United States by Christian Birkenstock himself, had to be ended. In fact, tangible economic problems had meanwhile arisen for Fraser's organization, which was contending with severe sales losses with wholesalers.[167] At the same time, her warnings that such a low-price policy would be bad for business, "where no one wins in the end," went increasingly unheeded.[168]

Until the mid-2000s, no solution emerged as to how the US market should be structured in the future. Over the years, a veritable generational and cultural conflict had broken out between Fraser and the sons of Karl Birkenstock. Although Karl Birkenstock, who had largely withdrawn from the operational business of the firm, occupied an intermediary position for a long time, he increasingly felt that he was no longer able to play this role. He let Fraser know that he was "completely pessimistic regarding my qualifications to untie the knot, because I have not been able to do that in all these years." But for the first time he also explained to her that the general conditions in Germany simply "wouldn't give him the slightest chance of handing over the Birkenstock brand to the next generation" if he did not break it down into several independent sub-brands. He attributed this to the impending inheritance tax, which—according to Birkenstock in the original wording—was a "socialist-communist arbitrary system." Although the legislature had already tried, with the inheritance tax reform of 1996, to reduce the tax burden on business assets through deferral models, they were unable to prevent the effective tax burden for family businesses from remaining comparatively high.[169] He emphatically explained the consequences for his family business: "Stephan, Alex, and Christian cannot take over the Birkenstock brand, it is completely impossible. And it's of little use if you don't like it, because that doesn't change anything. That's why the only way to proceed for Stephan, Alex, and Christian is to build up their own independent brands."[170] Maintaining the dynastic principle had top priority for the family entrepreneurs. One thing became increasingly clear to the Birkenstocks: if Fraser did not recognize the multi-brand strategy, further cooperation with the US dealer would no longer be possible.

After the Birkenstock Footprint Sandals, Inc. got into troubled waters in the early 2000s, Fraser saw—also from an economic point of view—that the time had come in 2002 for her to step down as president and CEO and hand the management of the company over to Matt Endriss and Eugene Kunde.[171] With this change, new managers came to the helm, who harbored far fewer reservations about the new sub-brands than Fraser did. This was all too understandable, since her life's work had involved convincing US customers of the advantages of the original Birkenstock sandal in the first few years and literally "proselytizing" them.

At the end of 2002, the new Birkenstock Footprint Sandals, Inc. Chief Officer of Organization (COO) traveled to Bad Honnef for an inaugural visit to get a personal impression of the problems in cooperation with the parent company and to venture to propose a fresh start in the working relationship. He noted that the declining sales figures of Birkenstock Footprint Sandals, Inc. should be attributed not only to the oft-criticized new brands but also, in part, to their own mistakes. A trip report stated that "Birkenstock Germany seems to be much more future-oriented than us. They are responding to changes by their customers, and looking further down the road than we are."[172] He also saw Birkenstock's change of strategy toward a multi-brand portfolio as going well and concluded with the remark "that the brands are becoming more comfortable in their move from product to a marketing focus, although they are each at different stages in evolution."[173]

Although the new management of the world's largest Birkenstock dealer was beginning to understand the problems in the business relationship, the economic development of the US sales company did not promise a bright future. More and more frequently, the US import partner had to be granted new commercial credit, or pre-produced items had to be stored. In 2005, Alex and Stephan even accused the US sales of Birkenstock Footprint Sandals, Inc. of "serious management errors" that would jeopardize the importer's solvency.[174] One of these management mistakes, according to the three Birkenstock managing directors, was that the importer had for years failed to expand the dealer network and align it with fashion or lifestyle trends. Specifically, they complained that the existing network of 2,000 to 3,000 dealers was not sufficient and called for "a significantly more intensive processing of the market." And finally, they determined that there were in fact up to 30,000 shoe retailers in the United States who could sell Birkenstock products.[175]

It seemed as if the new US Birkenstock Footprint Sandals, Inc. management was no longer able to turn things around, and in the spring of 2005 the situation was all but hopeless. Matt Endriss resigned as presi-

Fig. 41: After decades of restraint, Birkenstock first made a global brand statement with the global retail box concept (Birkenstock x 10 Corso Como, Birkenstock Box, Milan, 2017).

dent and CEO in December 2004, and Margot Fraser stepped in on an interim basis. Financially, however, things continued to look bleak. If no new investor were to step in to pay off the liabilities to the banks, it would no longer be possible to avert bankruptcy.

In this dire situation, Christian Birkenstock entered the picture. He had been active in the US market for some time with his Betula brand and in April 2005 made an offer to Fraser to take over 75 percent of Birkenstock Footprint Sandals, Inc.[176] Since the German Birkenstock manufacturers were no longer willing to deliver new goods owing to payment arrears, the Americans gratefully accepted the offer.[177] After the youngest Birkenstock son joined the company, however, one thing led to another and the US sales partner was swiftly integrated into the Birkenstock group of companies. In a first step, the dealer agreement between C. B. Orthopädie GmbH and Birkenstock Footprint Sandals, Inc., which had existed since 1974, was terminated on December 31, 2005, and replaced by a new dealer agreement.[178] In the new contract, a joint subsidiary, "Birkenstock Distribution USA Inc.," was founded, which was now controlled from Bad Honnef through the mirrored transfer of Christian's majority shares. At the same time, in a further step, Birkenstock Footprint Sandals, Inc. was prohibited from acting as an importer or retailer. This move effectively sealed the fate of the long-standing sales partner, whose logo, for example, was no longer displayed on the shoeboxes. The preamble to the contract stated that the Bad Honnef parties were compelled to undertake these steps because of "tens of millions of dollars of debt to the manufacturer [and] fundamental disagreements over the representation and use of the BIRKENSTOCK® brand in the American market." In addition, they had now decided to undertake "the establishment of a new business relationship on a new business basis to save the dealer and the market, and to protect the interests of the manufacturer."[179]

The new import and trade agreement with the new sales company created the basis, in essence, for the US sales organization to become an integral part of the parent company and for the formerly contentious marketing issues to be settled. It was precisely in these areas that there had been repeated conflicts with Fraser's sales company, which became the main point of contention between the Birkenstock companies in Germany and the United States.[180] With the establishment of their own US import company, the next Birkenstock generation were successful in continuing the efforts of their father, Karl, who had endeavored, to manage the integration of all upstream and downstream processes in the company.

How successfully the US business would be managed by the three brothers in the future, however, remained an open question. This was because the family business, which was divided into brands and divisions, harbored enough potential for conflict in this constellation. It had still not been definitively clarified how the new sub-brands would be placed on the market independently of one another, and who was ultimately in charge. For years, there had been serious friction in the brothers' differing views regarding the future direction of the company.[181] These disputes within the family, some of which were based on personal animosities, were not yet known to the general public, however. Instead, a sideshow of the complicated situation in the family business became public in the press. From 2004 to 2006, whenever the public's attention was drawn to Birkenstock, the dispute between Christian and his former wife, Susanne, known as the "sandal war," dominated the headlines.[182]

This dispute was mainly about a court battle over the commercial use of the brand name BIRKENSTOCK, which Susanne Birkenstock wanted to use to market her own "Beautystep" fitness sandal. After several court cases in 2005 and 2006, each of which was eagerly commented on and followed by the daily press, Susanne finally agreed to dispense with advertising using the brand name and, for example, to change and shorten the company name to "SB International."[183] In 2006, however, her company began to falter when less than a third of the publicly communicated sales figures actually corresponded to reality, and the product innovations that had been announced failed to materialize.[184]

In the late 2000s, things became relatively quiet around the family-run company. Smaller stories, such as the relocation of the Saxon plant facilities from Bernstadt and Schönbach to Görlitz, which took place in 2008 and 2009, only made it into the regional press in Saxony.[185] Public interest in the company only began to grow once more when the family managing directors started to grate on each other again. The multi-brand system had ultimately

Fig. 42: Success demands change. It took a strong personality like that of Oliver Reichert to take the Birkenstocks' vision into the 21st century.

created the chaos that Margot Fraser saw brewing in the 90s. The Birkenstock brothers had finally fallen out over the new corporate strategy at the end of the 2000s and needed outside help. They found this in 2009 in the former managing director of the sports channel "DSF," Oliver Reichert, whom they initially brought on board as a consultant.[186] He recommended not only the establishment of a family constitution, which was to settle internal family conflicts via a mediation office, but also the dissolution of the independent sub-brands and a return to the core brand. After Stephan left the company as a shareholder, the transformation into a manager-controlled family company followed step by step. In 2013, Alex and Christian, who had continued to run the family business as managing directors and partners, also decided to place the management of the company's business in the hands of Reichert and co-managing director Markus Bensberg, who were to put the company back on the path to success after years of internal family friction.[187] Within a very short time, Reichert and Bensberg succeeded in dissolving the opaque shareholding structures of the Birkenstock Group and establishing a modern corporate structure, streamlining the chaotic brand portfolio, increasing efficiency in the manufacturing plants, and consistently aligning the company with a uniform, modernized marketing concept. As if the international clientele had simply been waiting for these long overdue steps, the external managers succeeded in coaxing unimagined growth potential out of the company. Judging by the bare figures, a veritable "turnaround" began to happen in the mid-2010s, leading Birkenstock back toward success.[188] Just one year after the appointment of the non-family management, Birkenstock's sales results, which had been stagnating at the € 100 million sales mark for several years, had jumped. A doubling of turnover to € 272 million was recorded for the first regular financial year after the restructuring of the corporate group in 2013–14, and a clearly rising growth curve could be observed until the end of the decade. It became increasingly apparent that the brand and product cannibalization of the various Birkenstock sub-brands feared by Margot Fraser in the 90s had considerably slowed down the company. It was only with the careful consolidation and rationalization strategy of the new managing directors that Birkenstock was able to embark on a phase of scintillating growth in the 2010s, the provisional peak of which was reached in the 2020 financial year.[189]

When the US investment firm L Catterton became involved in Birkenstock in the spring of 2021, the outside managers began writing a completely new chapter in the company's history, which ushered in a second phase of internationalization focused on opening up the Asian markets.[190]

Summary

When Karl Birkenstock, as a member of the sixth generation of the shoemaking family, continued its traditions with the invention of the *Original Birkenstock-Footbed Sandal* in the 60s, sales success came slowly, steadily, and then rapidly. With the expansion into other markets, first in the USA, Canada, and Europe, then Asia, the company enjoyed strong growth until the 90s. The various development paths in these regions are described in the following essays.

For the parent company, the transition to the seventh generation proved to be a repetition of the experiences of the fifth generation: the division of the parent company, emerging conflicts, and strategic differences. The challenges of a company that was still growing strongly in the

21st century could no longer be tackled using internal family resources, so an external solution was found for the management of the company. The restructuring of what had become a global group was key to its continuing success. Despite all the quarrels, problems, and challenges of the last 30 years, the core innovations have remained unchanged. The *Footbed* and the *Birkenstock-Footbed Sandal* continue to form the bedrock of the company's philosophy, its unapologetically sacrosanct foundation. In the fast-moving fashion business in which Birkenstock finds itself today, this makes it a true outlier.

BIRKENSTOCK: A PURPOSE BRAND

BY CHRISTIAN KLEINSCHMIDT AND
ANDREA H. SCHNEIDER-BRAUNBERGER

Conviction as Strategy

Since the 60s, consumer goods companies have usually acted in accordance with their brand orientation to develop a brand strategy. This has not been the case at Birkenstock, and yet BIRKENSTOCK is a global brand. If there is no strategy behind it, how did the brand get there? The driving force was more conviction than strategy, and it began in the early 20th century with the invention of Konrad Birkenstock's *Health Footwear*.

It continued to develop over the first half of the 20th century and is thus deeply anchored in the entrepreneurial family and the company. It is the persistent will to convince people that keeping your feet healthy is worthwhile and that it is possible.[1] Today, one would speak of a purpose-driven approach or an orientation toward the common good, which has been evident at Birkenstock from the very beginning. Konrad, Carl or Carl Birkenstock: all of them have lived their convictions, accepted the economic disadvantages, and, despite all resistance, not given up.[2]

Advertising in Service of Foot Health

With his inventions of the fully anatomically shaped shoe last and insole, Konrad had no less a goal than to keep people's feet healthy. In determining his target market, he had everyone in mind. Consequently, from the company's earliest beginnings, he took a very revealing path in the realm of advertising, reprinting statements from his customers and doctors in specialist journals as early as in the first decade of the 1900s.[3]

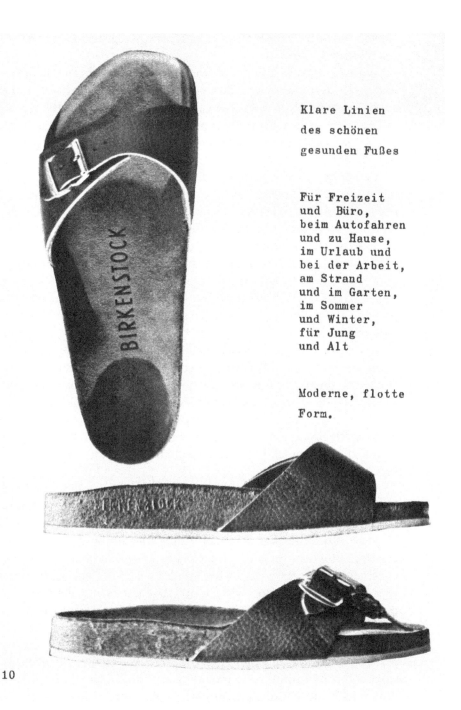

Fig. 43: Inspired by brutalist architecture, the clear design of the *Original Birkenstock-Footbed Sandal* remains unchanged to this day (Birkenstock Post 8, 1964).

He had the utility model of his *Health Footwear* registered, and the *Footbed* trademark followed.[4]

With the spread of industrial production and the introduction of various footbeds in the 20s and 30s, Birkenstock developed advertising for specialty stores. The Birkenstock companies delivered advertising material to these stores in the form of posters, displays, and advertisements. The focus was always on foot health and the relevant information surrounding it.

Carl Birkenstock broke new ground with his training courses, which in retrospect can be classified as an early form of business-to-business marketing. At the time there was no planning for the linked establishment of a selective distribution system, which creates artificial shortages. Carl's background reasoning had to do with the idea of purposeful sales service: the specialist dealers had to be trained in the correct application of the *Footbed*. Otherwise, its health-promoting effect would be negated. Access to the product was only granted to those shoemakers who had previously completed one of Carl's courses, training them in the *System Birkenstock*.

In this way, the product had scarcity value in marketing terms, and at the same time specialist dealers were trained, and long-term relationships with them were formed early on. Birkenstock felt it was necessary to explain the correct application of the flexible insole which was understandable given the complexity of the product's correct usage. In essence, the Birkenstock company has remained true to this approach. Although the form and toolkit have changed, the focus is still on the function of the product.

With the development and creation of the *Original Birkenstock-Footbed Sandal* in 1963, Karl Birkenstock initially wanted to contact potential customers via the professional fashion realm: the Düsseldorf shoe fair. However, since this path to undermining the fashion world remained closed to him because of the negative attitude of the shoe dealers, Karl continued down the path of his father and grandfather and turned to the medical profession with informative letters and the first product brochures. In the years that followed, material was distributed to retailers in the form of the Birkenstock Post and information newsletters, which also explained the functionality of the shoes in detail and praised the idiosyncratic design of the sandals as modern.[5] The Birkenstock company continued to provide advertising material for specialist dealers with advertising signs, displays, and posters, as well as with educational books such as the "Buch der Fußgesundheit" (Manual of Foot Health) and the "Fuß-Fibel" (Foot Handbook).[6]

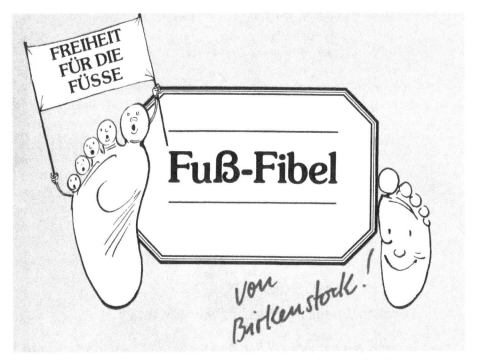

Fig. 44: Educational information serving foot health for consumers rather than advertising claims ("Fuß-Fibel", 1983).

Birkenstock advertising and products were not aimed at a specific population group but rather at all generations and all professions.[7] The firm saw itself as a unisex brand right from the start, without making this explicit, and long before the unisex concept was introduced into the fashion world by designers such as Pierre Cardin at the end of the 60s. Deeply rooted in the concept of "walking as nature intended," which was aimed at a universal human need, BIRKENSTOCK naturally positioned itself as a universal brand that broke through the limitations of current target group definitions. Thus, it is no wonder that the company did not have a marketing department until the early 2000s.

Marketing has been primarily derived from the product. In the beginning, there was a product that had a clear product promise—a "purpose," as we would say today: to enable everyone to walk, according to the anatomy of the foot. Communication was (and still is) not designed to aggressively advertise the products. Rather, it has been about informing consumers and pointing out the advantages of the firm's products in an objective form. It is a counterintuitive form of marketing that seems to work very well for BIRKENSTOCK. In any case, the many millions of satisfied customers have taken over the advertising for the brand—initially through personal recommendations from family and friends, and now, millions of times each day, through product discussions ("reviews"), photos, videos, comments, and likes in social media. It is this intimate connection between the fans and "their" brand that makes BIRKENSTOCK what can rightly be called a "love brand."

Initially, the sandals were only advertised in the catalogs of specialist retailers. As in the past, the entrepreneurial family relied on convincing these specialists of the quality of their products so that they could reach out to the customers. Birkenstock did not advertise in the true sense of the word—i.e., through direct customer acquisition—and was therefore very much in line with the trend of the time. Volkswagen, for example, also refrained from extensive advertising measures in the 50s. While marketing departments were established in other companies based on the American model in the 60s and 70s,[8] this never happened at Birkenstock.

Success Comes by a Roundabout Route

In terms of shoe fashions, Karl did not allow himself to be influenced by the fashion trends of his time when it came to the innovative creation of the *Original Birkenstock-Footbed Sandal*. He did, however, adopt the zeitgeist of the "transformation society" in West Germany in his Birkenstock Post editions and in the advertising material made available to retailers. And he was also happy to be inspired by the America-oriented youth movement,[9] which exerted its influence directly on the German company through Margot Fraser.[10] In the USA, Fraser placed her own advertisements in newspapers early on and also developed her own posters,[11] while the dealer catalogs remained the same for all countries, combining health, modernity, and fashion in one publication. Fraser's desire for more color[12] was met in Bad Honnef with model no. 024 from 1977, which was released in a number of different colors. However, the dealers did not order it, with the result that it was no longer offered in the following year. The color scheme for sandals at Birkenstock did not actually change fundamentally until the late 80s.

Birkenstock was therefore less about "going with fashion," since fashion trends in their view sometimes had unreasonable traits. Rather, it was about offering a modern alternative that maintained foot health.[13] After footwear fashion had given Birkenstock the cold shoulder in 1963, and direct advertising with doctors had proved successful, Karl developed and designed further models in the 60s (*Closed Model*, *Strap sandal*, *Loafer*,

Boot). In 1970, he introduced the massage sandal, the *Noppy*, which for the first time was a product made entirely of plastic.[14] This "infidelity" was followed in 1983 by some models made of polyurethane (PU), and was permanently integrated into the sandal production program with the introduction of EVA shoes in 2014. Through its own catalogs, the specialist shoe trade seized on the expanded Birkenstock range, which was also aimed at professional groups such as doctors, waiters, construction workers, etc.[15] In addition to the professions,[16] the entrepreneurial family took aim at the entire population, following trends such as the "fitness movement"[17] and the German desire for vacation and travel.[18]

After two decades of upheaval, social modernization, and reforms, the 80s and 90s are associated in Germany with a change that was billed as a "spiritual and moral turning point," coupled with a transition to conservative-liberal politics. An economic trend reversal in the direction of "neoliberalism," economization, and globalization was also heralded internationally.[19] If the success of the Birkenstock sandals had been furthered by countercultures in the USA, they had now attained a level of comfort that anchored them in the mainstream.[20] In Germany, meanwhile, sandals enjoyed an apogee as a niche product with the founding of the Green Party (Die Grünen), as well as numerous social movements committed to civil society, and a more intense ecological awareness in large parts of the population.[21]

Birkenstock Establishes Itself as a Global Brand

While the Birkenstock family was always part of the avant-garde when it came to foot health or fashion—Konrad with shoe lasts and his insoles *Footbed*, Carl with the *Ideal-Schuh*, and Karl with the creation of the *Birkenstock-Footbed Sandal*—it was not until the 90s that the first attempt was made to keep up with the times and seek a systematic approach to the world of fashion, without, of course, compromising on the functionality or the design of the sandals. Here, the focus was on the colors that were offered in the boutique program.[22] These small steps ventured by the company in the direction of shoe fashion were matched by the first approaches made by fashion designers in the 80s.[23] While there were now reports about shoes in fashion magazines, and a felt *Boston* sandal was depicted in the magazine Elle and called the trendsetter of the season,[24] Birkenstock advertising was and is until this day still rarely found in newspapers and magazines. Nevertheless, the new millennium started with the largest retail advertising campaign in the company's history, including a nationwide insert campaign. The company reached 25 million readers in more than 80 journals and magazines. At the same time, Birkenstock was present at numerous shoe, orthopedic and office trade fairs and also addressed the international specialist trade via the GDS Düsseldorf.[25] After Adidas, Salamander, and Puma, BIRKENSTOCK was one of the best-known shoe brands on the German market and ranked third in terms of popularity.[26] The British fashion magazine Drapers Record even named BIRKENSTOCK "Best Shoe Brand of the Year" in 2004.[27] This reconciliation of fashion and health—which Birkenstock itself had not thought possible for a long time because the company refused to submit to the fast-moving trends of the fashion—was now successful. This was also because in the meantime an ecologically oriented way of life, healthy nutrition, and a new body awareness had become widespread, and this made fashion, lifestyle, coolness, and health awareness appear compatible. David Kahan, President of Birkenstock Americas, summed it up in a recent quote: "We are cool because we don't try to be cool."[28]

While the Birkenstock specialist shops had been supplied with advertising material since Konrad began distributing it, the firm found a new orientation with the "shop concept 2000," which involved using only high-quality materials for the interior fittings in accordance with the requirements of the sandals.[29] From 2015 on, Birkenstock offered retailers a new "shop-in-shop" option, and finally their own concept stores were created in major cities around the world.[30] In doing so, Birkenstock remained true to the motivation behind the training courses introduced back in the 30s with the goal of selling perfectly fitting shoes to their customers. As part of the new concept, retailers could also continue to receive promotional material from Birkenstock. At the same time, BIRKENSTOCK finally presented itself as a global premium fashion brand during the Paris Fashion Week and at other international trade fairs and special events.

The quality of the Birkenstock products attracted imitators early on. However, the discussions about brand and product piracy reached a new peak after the turn of the millennium, extending far beyond the companies themselves into the media and even academic disciplines.[31] According to an article in the Birkenstock Post, the company warned specialist retailers as early as 1966 against "questionable imitations," although at that time it was still primarily focused on national competitors, who were making life difficult for Birkenstock with their cheap wooden sandals made "by taking over and copying the finished results of other people's work at their expense."[32]

Fig. 45: The company's hunger for innovation remained unbroken: the *Noppy* massaging sole used plastics for the first time (advertising photo, 70s).

While at that time it was more a question of isolated cases, brand and product piracy has grown into a global mass phenomenon since the advent of globalization in the 90s.[33] Product and brand piracy in China has been particularly widespread.[34] Such piracy—with all the associated problems for the company concerned—is nonetheless an expression of the special importance and appreciation of a brand and its products and an indicator of its recognition value among competitors.

Summary

Looking at the *Original Birkenstock-Footbed Sandals*, Birkenstock has succeeded over the course of 60 years to move from an outsider position, as disruptive footwear that broke all conventions and was therefore taken up by subcultures, to spreading their product to all sections of the world's population and finally arriving in the realm of high fashion. The company's current strategy remains firmly anchored in its roots—namely, to produce footbeds, sandals, and shoes that allow people to walk as nature intended. Birkenstock remains sustainable (because it is durable), resource-friendly (because it uses renewable raw materials such as cork), and quality-oriented (because it is made in Germany).

Did Birkenstock have a brand strategy? No. It seems that from the outset given the usefulness of the products, Birkenstock's underlying strategy was to convince customers—and then doctors, orthopedists, and shoe retailers—of the benefits of their products. The global success of the brand is due not so much to the fact that it strategically serves specific customer groups—the exception being the function-related targeting of certain professions—but rather that certain groups use the brand. Right from the start, Birkenstock had no less a strategy than serving the common good by preventing foot defects.

When BIRKENSTOCK tried at one point to introduce an actual strategy in the 90s—namely, a multi-brand strategy—the company almost failed.[35] As a global purpose brand—which is how the company sees itself today—the new management then reverted to the original path of catering to foot health.

"If the Shoe Fits ...":
Comfortable Shoes on the Rise

BY JOHANNA STEINFELD

The anatomist and medical doctor Peter Camper was already associating shoes with the adjective "comfortable" in the last third of the 18th century, when he penned a treatise addressing the issue of suitable footwear. For him, "well-made and easy shoes" were the means of choice to prevent diseases and ailments of the foot.[1] Even in the terminology of the 18th century, "comfortable" meant the "pleasant, snug" shoe, which, at that time, was still wishful thinking,[2] if only because back then, when producing shoes, shoemakers did not take into account the shape and characteristics of the foot. Added to which, there is, of course, the problem of combining beauty and comfort in a shoe, which was tantamount to squaring the circle—something that was already evident in the middle of the 19th century. Hermann Meyer, a medical doctor, wrote, for example, that in the case of foot ailments and deformities, all one could do was decide "with a degree of resignation to wear unattractively designed shoes in order simply to have comfort."[3] By the end of the 19th century, shoes were designed to fit the shape of the foot, but this did not mean that they necessarily also had to be comfortable, let alone correspond in any

way to fashionable ideas. Such ideas were, in fact, contrary to the principle of naturalness that characterized many of the designs of that period that sought to do justice to feet.

After World War I, a small market segment emerged for health shoes and orthopedic shoes, which was often (mis)understood as consisting of products for deformed feet and those that had been shaped by injury; it existed in parallel to the market for fashion shoes that emerged in the 20s.[4] The contrast between beautiful or fashionable as opposed to comfortable or healthy shoes was reinforced in the 50s—especially in the women's shoe segment, because the prevailing role models dictated that the woman was responsible for looking after the household, the family, and her husband, and was expected to look feminine and appealing, in fashionable shoes with high heels and narrow toes.[5]

Warnings that specific shoes might damage the foot and posture had no influence on purchases of fashion shoes, regardless of whether they were issued by doctors and orthopedists, publicized at the German Foot Health Weeks in 1953 and 1954, or voiced during public debates.[6] The only remedy could be the emergence of an entirely new

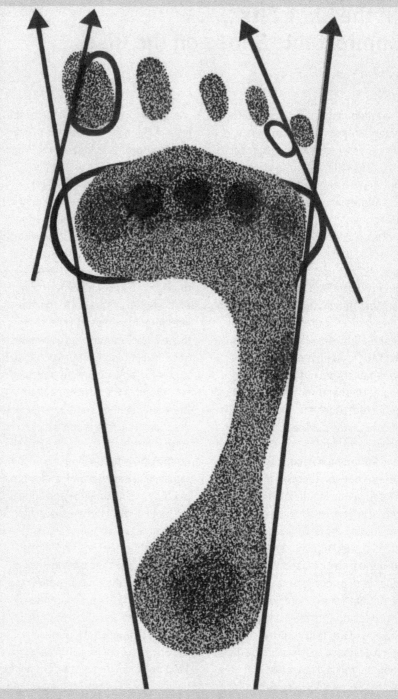

Fig. 46: Sights set on healthy feet at all times (sketch).

market segment, as suggested by Karl Sigg, director of the Polyclinic for Venous Diseases at the Basel University Women's Clinic, and Felix Oesch, a medical doctor from Bern, in their 1958 book "Schuhmode und Gesundheit" (Shoe Fashion and Health): a "new branch of shoe manufacturing, which follows the fluctuations of fashion only as far as they are compatible with a healthy foot," had to be created.[7] However, the technical challenges of production, shoe design, and the poor reputation that health shoes had as footwear for the old and sick were major obstacles.[8] Instead, in 1964, the cosmetics industry developed a women's foot spray that was intended to alleviate the pain caused by wearing the shoes.[9]

Ultimately, the connection between comfortable shoes and the mass market for fashion emerged from a very different quarter. Sports shoes have been produced since the end of the 19th century and were first worn by young people in everyday life in the USA after World War I. The discovery of the vulcanization process by US chemist Charles Goodyear in 1839 made it possible to convert natural rubber into elastic rubber, which was used for the soles of leather or canvas shoes.[10] In 1917, the Converse Rubber Shoe Company in Massachusetts launched the "Converse All Star" basketball shoe, whose popularity grew simultaneously with the popularity of basketball. Away from professional and amateur sports, this shoe was increasingly worn in everyday life, where the achievements of sports shoe technology led to increased comfort.[11] When sports shoe manufacturers such as the German company founded in 1926 that later became Adidas, and Reebok, which was founded in the United States at the end of the 19th century, stepped up marketing for the sports shoe from the 70s onwards,[12] the sneaker became a lifestyle product, especially for men.[13]

In the 90s, the sneaker reached the adult market for everyday fashion, catering as much to the newly emerging awareness of comfort as to the need for a casual, youthful lifestyle. When designer brands such as Jil Sander and Prada included sneakers in their ranges in the 90s, they also moved up into the luxury segment.[14] Other factors favoring the triumph of sneakers in almost all areas of life were leisure patterns influenced by sports and travel, as well as the loosening of clothing conventions.

It was therefore precisely the combination of high-performance technology, fashion consciousness, and the promise of fitness that was responsible for the success of the sneaker, which bridged the gap between comfortable and fashionable footwear without this having been an explicit goal. For Birkenstock sandals at least, it is clear that the path to fashion was something the company was striving for,[15] but, un-

"If the Shoe Fits ...": Comfortable Shoes on the Rise

like the sneaker, the combination of comfort and fashion in Birkenstock sandals was only made possible by a complete reversal of its eco-image by the fashion scene. After the turn of the millennium, other comfort shoes became popular, such as the comfortable Crocs—shoes made of expansive foam that were originally developed as boating and outdoor footwear—which were launched in 2002. Finally, in the 2010s, the "Ugly Fashion" trend, which favored aesthetically questionable fashion and accessories, as well as the "Athleisure" trend, which made athletic fashion suitable for everyday wear, favored the development of shoes that were both fashionable and comfortable. At the same time, there were repeated attempts to make even classic shoe shapes more comfortable or to launch them on the market directly as comfort shoes. Examples of this are the "Weber shoe"—produced by a company in Bavaria—which was designed as a business shoe with a cork footbed, as well as the 18-hour shoe, which was created by shoe designer Shaherazad Umbreen as a high heel intended to guarantee its wearers 18 hours of comfort.[16]

Fig. 47: Birkenstock advertises to the female public (Birkenstock Post 2, 1959).

BIRKENSTOCK IDENTITIES

BY MARY A. YEAGER

"Healthy footwear" throws off a wide range of emotions associated with wearing comfortable shoes. For Konrad Birkenstock, the combination of a fully anatomic last and flexible insole provided an innovative platform for the family's subsequent moves into podiatry, orthopedics, and the manufacture of sandals, clogs, and boots. Neither the Birkenstock family nor the brand that they created took healthy or problematic feet for granted. The "foot" and its care have remained central to Birkenstock's core identity over time.

Identity, however, is not a simple singular concept, even when applied to a human appendage like the "foot."[1] Linked to a 200-year-old tradition in shoemaking bound up with foot beds, foot care, foot comfort, and footprints, identity hangs like a fog over Birkenstock's history.[2] Identities are multiple, changing over time and ranging across extended families and generations, geographical divides, economic crises, and world wars. They are personal, linked to self-discovery and self-making: "Who am I? Am I the same person I was 20 years ago?"[3] They are social, focused on affinities and interactions with other individuals and groups, including family members, politicians, shopkeepers, wholesalers, retailers, and customers. Most importantly for this essay, identities are also distinctly business-oriented and organizational, bound up with a firm's purpose, values, and culture, embedded in brands, practices, and processes. Shaped by human agency, context, and time, they provide an indispensable guide to the history of Birkenstock, nurturing an appreciation for the familial, interpersonal, and transactional relationships in business over time.

Karl, and other Birkenstock family members have offered only scant information about their private lives. The only mention of children comes from Margot Fraser, a family outsider and native-born German and American émigré who established the only US distributorship.[4]

Margot mentions a stepson who worked in her US company, and the Birkenstock boys who accompanied their father Karl, on trips to visit her in America. Children matter to how gender identities are perceived and performed. They too had Birkenstocks that were made especially for their feet. Children remember and forget. Their perceptions of parents, of fathers and mothers change as their own lives, inside and outside business families, evolve.

Historical narratives about identities matter.[5] They shape how the Birkenstock firm, its footwear, and its various family members have come to be remembered, celebrated, or forgotten. "History itself," claims Jeffrey Fear, is "a representation of an organization's identity or self-understanding that shapes its sensemaking process."[6] It was in the fourth generation of shoemakers that Konrad Birkenstock showed himself from a young age to be more entrepreneurial and ambitious. In 1897, he married 21-year-old Elisabeth Fleischhauer, who produced a daughter, Catharina, in 1898, followed by sons Carl in 1900, Heinrich in 1905, and Konrad Jr. in 1909.

Konrad acted as footwear missionary, self-publishing information and lecturing about footwear and foot comfort. By 1925, he had built his first factory in Friedberg to produce a curved insole using proprietary technology. His sons paid attention, especially the eldest, Carl. Carl's only sister, Catharina, and his two younger brothers, Heinrich and Konrad Jr., played a variety of roles in the Birkenstock enterprises.[7]

The footprints and voices of women are faint and few, if they are noticed at all. Konrad, the family patriarch, granted his wife Elisabeth power of attorney in 1920, long before he exited the business, and not long after the Weimar Constitution granted women and men the same fundamental rights and duties as citizens, including the right to vote and hold office. Emmi Birkenstock co-signed a 1951 patent application with her husband Carl, the elder son of Konrad, but implications about agency remain unexamined. Scant information renders most female family members invisible.[8]

The one woman to make her voice heard was Margot Fraser.[9] Having secured sole US distribution rights in the 60s over a handshake with Karl, son of Carl Birkenstock, she went on to create Birkenstock Footprint Sandals, Inc., in 1972.[10] In 2009, several years after she exited the business, Margot went public in print.[11] In so doing, she added a woman's voice to the male choir most recently heard in interviews with several Birkenstock heirs.[12]

In the larger world of global footwear, she was one of the few women—if not the only woman at the time—to own a US distribution company tied

234   **1963–2024** Rise to a Global Brand

to a foreign supplier, who owned the brand and produced the footwear that stood out from the usual uncomfortable, pointy-toed, fashion shoes. Timing, place, and gender were key. In the 60s, Birkenstocks proved to be in tune with the changing American zeitgeist, nowhere more so than in Northern California. American anti-war, anti-establishment protestors and other disgruntled people were in search of a new and better world, where gender, sex, and racial identities did not matter. They demanded a takedown of bad institutions and immoral decision-makers.

The personal became the political. The pill, which became available in the 60s, liberated women to be who they wanted to be and do what they wanted with their own bodies, and by extension, their feet. Simone de Beauvoir's *The Second Sex* and Betty Friedan's *The Feminine Mystique* showed upper-middle-class educated women that biology and high-heeled shoes and fancy dress were no longer their destiny. Footwear and identities merged. Worn by lesbians and hippies, Birkenstocks became freighted with new and controversial meanings about sex and gender. The implications for business were as yet unexplored.

A full-scale cultural revolution with global reach was underway. If the gender identities of revolutionaries varied across nations, so did the targets of their protests and the impact on societies. The income effects of the "German economic miracle" were distributed unevenly, directing attention to social inequalities and identities, especially in West Germany, where mass student protests against the political establishment intersected with growing anti-war and anti-American sentiment. "It was a revolutionary period that aimed to create a better world," said one German student activist years later. "We students felt the leaden weight of antiquated bourgeois German society—the complacency of it."[13]

American political leaders responded with new agencies and new laws. John F. Kennedy established the Commission on the Status of Women in 1963. The Equal Pay Act followed in 1964, the same year that Betty Friedan launched NOW, which promoted childcare, abortion rights, equal rights, and the "full participation [of women] in the mainstream of American society now." In 1972, the Civil Rights Act Title IX banned sex discrimination in employment and education, and a year later came Roe v. Wade, promising women control over their own bodies and the right to have an abortion.

Margot Fraser did not claim identity as a feminist. She hailed from a conservative country, where the rights of women took a back seat to manly war and postwar reconstruction efforts. Even the occupying Americans ignored gender. Their own male-dominated military and

und vernünftig

und zu Hause

Fig. 48: Gender-neutral or unisex? *Original Birkenstock-Footbed Sandals* are made for everyone (Birkenstock Post 13, 1965).

civilian reconstruction corps were slow to address the concerns of German women, despite the fact that they vastly outnumbered the men.[14]

Without taking gender seriously, the fog of identity surrounding Birkenstocks is likely to thicken. The Birkenstock insole and shoe were initially designed and marketed "to do justice" to the human foot.[15] The identity of Birkenstock footwear was bound up with foot anatomy. There was a left and a right foot, which proved useful when politics intruded. Pins sporting the words "I support Arches," "I like Cork," "I support the Left," "I support the Right" injected humor and protective cover into a 2008 American advertising campaign.[16] Birkenstocks could be sold to anyone. In modern parlance, Birkenstocks were "gender neutral." By the late 20th century, however, Birkenstock footwear had been genderized and differentiated. There were different sizes, widths, styles, colors, and prices for "women" and "men."[17]

Marketing data showed that men's feet tended to be larger and wider than women's, necessitating more leather and other materials. Birkenstock gave women a price break. Men paid more for the same sandal style, a pricing strategy that made sense at the time, given the market, even if it went against standard practice. Birkenstocks had become more or less feminine and masculine, depending on the identity of the wearer. Gender fluidity paid. Gender inequalities linked to pricing strategies made business sense. Male Birkenstock wearers, like many of the female sex, proved subject to cost and profit calculations that led to unequal outcomes too.[18]

First Konrad, then his son Carl, and by the 50s, Carl's son Karl Birkenstock, de-genderized footwear. They initially paid more attention to the foot and to insoles than to shoes. Feet could be disassociated from bodies. Sexual differences didn't matter if feet were sore or uncomfortable. Feet needed tending to and caring for, regardless of sex or gender. Foot problems needed to be addressed before shoes could be made comfortable. Even as shoes began to be mass-produced at the turn of the century, Konrad clung to the idea of comfortable footwear; flexible, anatomically shaped insoles could be inserted into shoes. Carl followed Konrad's lead and continued to prioritize feet rather than shoes.

Birkenstocks were designed with human feet in mind. Does the absence of sex-typing a product help to explain Birkenstock's emergence as a global cultural icon?[19] After all, there are few private family firms, brands, or products that can lay claim to so many contested and varied descriptors, so many markets, so many trademarks, and so many identities. Birkenstocks have been called ugly,[20] even "indecent," and likened to "idiotically hollowed out tree trunks."[21] Phoebe Philo introduced

Birkenstock Identities   237

Birkenstock-like shoes to the fashion world, which were called "Furkenstocks." They have been associated with a variety of social movements, including public health, women's and LBGTQ rights, animal rights (PETA), multiculturalism, liberalism, egalitarianism, feminism, masculinism, counterculturalism, environmentalism, globalism, and more recently with both the barbarizing and civilizing of German foreign policy and policymakers.[22] They have been worn by the military, workers, farmers, businesspeople, models, celebrities, teachers, and athletes.

A focus on "feet" and footbeds rather than shoes kept Birkenstocks closer to the healthcare than the fashion industry, which proved to be an advantage in the footwear market, or as some would argue, "an unfair advantage."[23] "Not all feet are different," insisted Carl Birkenstock. "But rather there were feet with weak tendons and ligaments (the majority) and feet with strong tendons and ligaments."[24] The emphasis on foot anatomy had consequences: (1) it facilitated business entry into a continuously growing footcare market across a wide range of suppliers and consumers in rural, urban, and global markets; (2) it plunged Birkenstocks into the competitive business of professionalizing podiatry, an occupation that proved difficult to define, legitimize, or regulate;[25] (3) it assured consumers both voice and exit, given that insoles and Birkenstocks were designed to be adapted to the individual foot and not to the shoe; and finally, (4) it both incentivized and ultimately doomed the efforts of both Carl Birkenstock and Margot Fraser to create the "ideal shoe" and "an ideal company."

When the sprawling German family of Birkenstocks joined forces with a lone female distributor in the United States, its leaders were not thinking about sex or gender. Nor was Margot Fraser. They were envisioning footwear to make feet more comfortable. Personalities, familial affinities, and a common national origin cemented business bonds.[26] Margot was closest in age to Karl Birkenstock. They spent their childhoods experiencing the horrors of war from inside different family cocoons. Each was part of a family whose members' lives were upended in different ways by World War II.

The Nazi state had not liberated women. They worked more outside the home as industries shed male employees, but their wages continued to be far below those of men. "Women became the providers. Black marketing became their method of survival for themselves and their families," reports one historian.[27] The struggle for women's rights slid backwards, replaced with cultural slogans emphasizing *Kirche, Küche und Kinder* (church, kitchen, and children). Whereas Carl kept pushing to create "the ideal shoe."[28] Margot kept her eyes out for exit ramps, hoping one day to follow those good German merchants into a more commercial business.[29]

Born in Berlin in 1930, Margot grew up reading and dreaming about German merchants overseas. When her father pointed out that all these German merchants were men and that she "could never do that as a woman," she insisted that she was going to be an international merchant. Urged by a female anti-Nazi Prussian elementary school principal to attend a dressmaking school, she dutifully complied and, in hindsight, considered it to be a great choice. It taught her to innovate not copy, to create her own designs, and to earn currency.[30] After the first clothes she made during the war, she set up her own business in US-occupied Bremen,[31] before emigrating alone to Canada at age 21, then to Northern California, where she set up her own dressmaking firm.

Dressmaking was a business historically dominated by women.[32] Margot interacted with as many if not more women than men. By the 60s, she was living in Santa Cruz. The region's economy was notable for its historically female-friendly small business environment and its laid-back lifestyle. After a handshake with Karl Birkenstock that secured her the US distribution rights, Margot began to distribute Birkenstock sandals in 1968 on a tiny scale in private circles, especially to independent, female-owned health-food stores, which, at the time, were novel. Their owners and patrons became her best customers, associating the business with a countercultural flavor from the outset.[33] Her infant enterprise grew at a snail's pace but proved encouraging enough for her to launch Birkenstock Footprint Sandals, Inc., in 1972.

Margot paid attention to gender. If she had not, there were plenty of men around to remind her. Her husband initially derided the sandals as "ugly." Male shoe suppliers in the US and in Germany often balked, insisting that women would not wear such unfashionable shoes. Margot's entrance into the Birkenstock-world left some notable footprints. Her US marketing campaigns imprinted the US perception of BIRKENSTOCK. The first impact was on the names of the sandals. When she brought the *Original Birkenstock-Footbed Sandal* to the US it was difficult to sell under the long and complex German name. She began to name the sandals: *Mayan, Franciscan, Roman, California,* and *Arizona.* In 1979 the German firm introduced names for the sandals as well, bringing in the *Madrid, Zürich, Milano, Oslo, Arizona,* which initially was called *London* for six months, and *Boston.*

The second impact she had was in the area of color. Eager to attract newer and younger countercultural customers, Margot urged Birkenstock Orthopädie GmbH to embrace colors that popped. Margot's pitch to include a greater variety of colors and styles took time to get used to. In 1977, Karl Birkenstock produced a new model no. 024 in eleven colors—a novelty in the product program. One male Swiss distributor exploded when he learned that Margot had urged Birkenstock to introduce more colors: "This *woman* [my emphasis] is going to ruin us. We are orthopedic—we don't need color."[34] This and other like-minded distributors did not order the model no. 024 in sufficient numbers. It was discontinued the following year.

For Fraser, those structural constraints would remain. The Birkenstocks owned the brand and produced the footwear. Margot imported the sandals and used the left arm of her American distribution company to twist the right arm of German production. There was little strategy or planning but a great deal of mutual learning about how to genderize the Birkenstock brand. Birkenstock men listened. Margot was persuasive, and with the fashion world getting in touch with the BIRKENSTOCK brand, things changed. In the 90s, bright-blue, green, and yellow Birkenstocks began to appear, adding rainbow colors and new styles to what had been a very limited line of classic styles in muted earth tones of grey, brown, and sand. Race and gender injected new energy into advertisements that capitalized on the sexual revolution.[35] As the millennium approached, a wedge sandal named "Emmy" appeared. The Birkenstock men surely never imagined being partnered with a cofounding matriarch, but it is notable that Emmi was the name of Carl's wife (his son Karl's mother). Whether or not this maternal connection applies, Margot Fraser blithely dubbed herself "Mrs. Birkenstock," and believed that she would "probably always be remembered that way."[36] Without the Fraser nudge, Birkenstock executives would have presumably taken far longer to genderize and diversify footwear styles and colors.[37]

The Birkenstock founders and heirs may have been less forthcoming about their personal fears, but they too were passionate about running a value-driven business that did not fetishize money: "Maximizing our profits is not our chief goal," claimed a Birkenstock CEO in 2015. Past and present Birkenstock insiders have often touted their own "authenticity," which they, like Margot, associated with modest size and profits. But to run a values-based, socially responsible business, payrolls had to be met. Balance was not a matter of decision-making as much as a continuous negotiation with various stakeholders.[38]

Margot may well have had better knowledge than most entrepreneurs about the trustworthiness of a Birkenstock business partner and the Birkenstock heirs. Karl himself was said to have partnered with Margot, not because she was a professional but because she was a "trustful

240 **1963-2024** Rise to a Global Brand

Fig. 49: The *Original Birkenstock-Footbed Sandal* was designed as a unisex product from the very beginning (advertising shot around 1970).

person."[39] She has been described by those who knew and worked with her as "a loving person," "introverted and introspective," "unknowable," "a Birki Archetype: self-confident, function-oriented, not a fashionista, [...] the heart and sole" of Birkenstock, "full of kindness, integrity and respect for the earth," a "feel good person with a business vision and a people vision."[40] In *Dealing with the Tough Stuff*, Margot's self-description emerges from the contexts and challenges she had faced in business over time: "intuitive, resilient, flexible, creative, frugal, action-oriented, a good negotiator, a visionary who gave away her vision, truthful, joyful, a risk taker, veering between self-doubt and self-confidence."[41]

The entwined histories of Margot Fraser and Karl Birkenstock remind us that perceptions of gender may not account for business success or failure, but gender identities certainly have mattered. Margot's arrival in the Birkenstock world was like the abrupt twist of a kaleidoscope that had a perspective-shifting impact.

Birkenstock was onto something important. But, exactly what? As late as the 90s, one Dutch distributor "spoke about the almost mysterious way that Birkenstock sandals had spread out into the world. He attributed the footwear's success to an invisible spirit inside each box. Its magic unfolded once the box was opened [...] you had to believe in it before it could manifest itself."[42] Historical agency works in mysterious ways, none more beguiling than the agency associated with gender, which continues to confound even as it clarifies how, why, and when businesspeople do what they do. Margot spotted a new sales opportunity. She had a talented employee create the *Birki Boy*. He was the "spirit made visible."[43] *Birki Boy* proved to be a popular addition to trade association shows. He symbolized the "feeling" of Birkenstocks.

This essay suggests that Birkenstock-succeeded as business and brand by transforming the human foot into a flexible managerial tool. Feet may not be so different, as Carl Birkenstock maintained, but in order to survive and thrive, the all-male cast of decision-makers had to learn how to genderize and de-genderize business processes and practices at the right time, in the right way, at the right place.[44] Margot helped and sometimes led. Birkenstock men listened, as did she.

The use of gender as a verb helps to nudge debates about gender away from an emphasis on gender inequalities and the oppression of women toward business practices and processes. This shift both reflects and shapes gender identities in the context of industry dynamics, for better or worse. Such a focus does not rule out an evaluation of outcomes for different genders, but it does invite greater scrutiny of gendered interactions as they emerge in the context of doing business.

242 **1963–2024** Rise to a Global Brand

Different Sides to Shoes:
Protection, Status Symbol, Emblem

BY JOHANNA STEINFELD

It is hard to overestimate the importance shoes had in a world without cars and public transportation, without roads and paved sidewalks. Shoes protected the skin of the foot from cold and heat; they compensated for uneven surfaces, prevented contact with dirt, and reduced the risk of injury. As a result, the shoe has always been a crucial item in everyday life. Before there were shoes, people made use of leaves, leather, or skins: cave paintings dating back some 14,000 years show people wrapping skins around their feet with straps.[1] It therefore seems plausible that the word "shoe" might have originally derived from the Indo-European root "skeu", meaning "to cover, to envelop," although this is only one of several possible explanations found for the origin of the word.[2]

That said, down through human history the development of shoes has not meant the end of people walking barefoot, if only because shoes were not a given everywhere—and this is still the case to a certain extent—be it because walking barefoot is part of the culture, because the social order of the day does not allow shoes for everyone, or because shoes are simply not affordable. Until the 20s, it was common for people in Ger-

many to walk barefoot: among the lower classes in rural areas (due to poverty), and among children and young people in the city.[3] Hence, the very fact of whether or not someone wears shoes says something about the status of the wearer. The symbolism of poverty and humility associated with walking barefoot was elevated to an ideal by Franciscan monks, for example, who aligned their own way of life with these Christian values.[4]

The effect of the design of the shoe and the materials used for it on the rank of its wearer is by no means a modern phenomenon.[5] The more nuanced fashion and clothing became, the less the function of the shoe played a role and the more clearly it became a symbol of social standing.[6]

Heels, which had been fashionable in Europe since the 17th century, were also symbolic of higher status in a double sense—and were worn by both sexes. This did not change until the 19th century, when the dichotomy of men's flat shoes and women's higher shoes emerged, and this was reinforced in the following century by the development of high heels. The high heel emphasized the erotic-sexual symbolism of women's shoes, which had existed since classical antiquity. Thus, Venus removing her sandal became a popular motif in the visual arts of that period, because observing Venus at this intimate moment conveyed a sensual-erotic impression.[7]

The sexual connotations of shoes are likewise found in Grimm's fairy tales. The scene in which the prince tries the slipper on Cinderella's foot is interpreted as an image of sexual union.[8] The lady's foot paired with the lady's shoe are representative of the male and female genitals, a symbolism that is also contained in the ritual of putting on the bride's shoe.[9] Cinderella losing her beautifully designed shoe on the stairs is what prompts the prince to find out about her, with the shoe acting as a proxy for its owner.[10] This quality is also reflected in the neatly cleaned boots that children leave out in Germany on December 5 in anticipation of St. Nicholas, like Christmas stockings in the United States or Great Britain. The boots represent irreproachability and goodness, which are rewarded by St. Nicholas with gifts.

Other aspects of the symbolism of shoes have also been dealt with in fairy tales: in "Puss in Boots," we encounter shoes as a status symbol.[11] The cat demands that "a pair of boots be made for me, that I can go out and be seen among the people" and, with the help of the pair of boots and his cunning deeds, he successfully pretends that he is the servant of an earl. Moreover, the boots also seem to act here as a symbol of power, al-

though this is rather a modern interpretation, given that boots were the predominant footwear at the time of the Brothers Grimm.[12] Nevertheless, boots have a special connotation, partly due to their use in a military context and the fact that originally only men wore them. The powerful and domineering nature of boots has therefore also carried over into the fetish scene.

Through many other fairy tales such as "The Twelve Dancing Princesses" or "Thumbelina," shoes are deeply anchored in German folklore, as well as through numerous proverbs.[13] Many of them refer, in particular, to the correct fit of the shoe, such as the sayings *In engen Schuhen ist nicht gut tanzen* ("It's not good to dance in tight shoes") or *Wo drückt der Schuh?* ("Where does the shoe pinch?"). These refer to the importance of shoes as a "symbol of a lack of freedom to develop."[14] It is precisely for this reason that supporters of protest movements have been rediscovering sandals since the 60s. In this context, the shoe also became a symbol of worldviews, values, and lifestyles. Through more recent fashion developments, shoes have also gained a special significance for youth and street culture. Here, too, they act as a status symbol, albeit one that no longer refers to status bestowed at birth, yet still provides a classification within the social hierarchy. Today's demonstrative consumption of shoes points to individual characteristics: in the

Fig. 50: The wonderful world of shoes. The St. Nicholas boots are always a huge treat.

case of luxury shoes, to wealth; in the case of more outlandish models, to a particular sense of taste; and in the case of pairs typical of their day, to coolness and fashion consciousness. More than ever before, shoes have symbolic properties: the differentiation of models and design styles, the use of numerous materials, the fame of designers, the profile of brands, and the creativity of design can all combine in one a shoe. The result is a complex web of codes that make the shoe simultaneously an expression of socioeconomic status, a sign of individual characteristics and preferences, a token of belonging to a certain group or class, and a representative of worldviews and attitudes. It may well be true that this can apply to items of clothing in general. More than any other item of clothing, however, the shoe has an effect at a distance from the wearer: as clothing for the lowest part of the body, it tends to evade classification in an outfit, and because of its three-dimensionality—in contrast to most items of clothing—it always retains its shape when worn.

INTERNATIONAL FASHION AND LUXURY IN BIRKENSTOCKS

BY ALICE JANSSENS

It's 1990 at a concert at the Hollywood Palladium in Los Angeles, California. Alternative rock band Jane's Addiction are playing and just as they begin their song "Up the Beach," someone throws a Birkenstock sandal on the stage. Lead singer, Perry Farrell picks up the shoe, turns to the crowd, and says, "I thought it would never come to this, but the guy threw a Birkenstock. I mean, this guy's a real moron. He doesn't even understand fashion."[1] Farrell's voice, heard berating the thrower on the band's *Live & Insane* album, typifies the image of the Birkenstock and its American wearer during the second half of the 20th century as decidedly unfashionable. Skip to 30 years later and Birkenstock has collaborated with pinnacle luxury fashion brands Christian Dior and Manolo Blahnik, has its own luxury line, and is in partnership with investor L Catterton and Financière Agache, a holding company specialized in luxury. So, how did Birkenstock get there?

This contribution traces the company's relationship with fashion and luxury. It explores how, since the late 80s, Birkenstock has developed a profile as a fashion brand while maintaining its position as a producer of democratic goods. Addressing how Birkenstocks have been picked up by the fashion industry since the 80s, it details the company's attempts to respond to these trends. It highlights the fashion successes of international distributors in targeting their products to regional markets and explores how changes in company structure and strategy from the mid-2010s onward have enabled the company to position itself within the fashion sector amidst growing popularity and lookalike designs.[2]

The Fashion Industry

To assess Birkenstock's role as a fashion brand, we must first consider what fashion is. The Oxford English Dictionary defines fashion as "a popular or the latest style of clothing, hair, decoration, or behaviour" or "a manner of doing something."[3] The academic journal "Fashion Theory" identifies fashion as "the cultural construction of the embodied identity" encompassing clothing and beyond.[4] Fashion historian and theorist Christopher Breward describes it as "a bounded thing, fixed and experienced in space—an amalgamation of seams and textiles, an interface between the body and its environment. It is a practice, a display of taste and status, a site for the production and consumption of objects and beliefs; it is an event, both spectacular and routine, cyclical in its adherence to the natural and commercial season, innovatory in its bursts of avant-gardism, and sequential in its guise as a palimpsest of memories and traditions."[5] These open-ended definitions allow for choices dictated both by the gatekeeper and the individual and engage carefully with the key points of materiality, meaning, and social connection. However, a significant role is also played by the massive industrial complex of fashion that creates, publicizes, and disseminates what is culturally popular. In this conception, employed in this chapter, fashion functions as a "system of institutions, organizations, groups, producers, events, and practices."[6]

What we consider to be the modern global fashion industry developed during the 19th century in Europe, born out of key geographic centers of making and wearing and the legacy of sumptuary laws mixed with the birth of print media, technological developments, and changing patterns of consumption. Within these locations, clusters of makers and the associations they founded fostered the birth of industries focused on high-quality manufacturing. This, in turn, led to the development of spaces not only for production but also for communication, distribution, and consumption.[7] Formed around a series of recognized designers of elite goods, who presented at events to an established group of tastemakers, the Western fashion industry blossomed throughout the 19th and 20th centuries. It grew with the help of standardization, trade organizations, and educational institutions and, significantly, through the gatekeeping of information by intermediaries involved in retailing, promotion, marketing, and reporting.[8] These intermediaries take the form of nodal events such as trade fairs and runway shows, and the individuals involved include models, stylists, photographers, PR agents, retail buyers, and media.[9] While many authors emphasize that fashion is too often directly linked to historical and modern Europe, pointing out that its relationship with other cultures and geographic regions is not recognized (which is still largely true), the construction of the global fashion system from an industrial and economic perspective rests predominantly on this base.[10]

This system has adapted in response to technological and media growth, changes in consumer demand, and the solidification of the designer as a public figure.[11] From the second half of the 20th century onward, fashion production has moved from a predominantly elite phenomenon from which trends and styles disseminate downward, to a system characterized by mass consumption, short product lifecycles, and constantly changing trends.[12] This is driven by increased production, distribution, and retailing capacities and is influenced not only by top-down communication but also by the global reach of media and "trickle-up" trends from the street.[13] The increasing speed of trend cycles and the lead times of production have impacted the traditional fashion calendar and also led to a break between items that are easily accessible and trend-related and those elite products that are crafted in a more traditional way.[14] Meanwhile, those involved in fashion structures have reached out and relied on the power of celebrity and collaborations to reinforce their positioning, employing the fame, skills, innovation, and influence of societal figures and other makers. This helps to bolster or increase the symbolic positioning of fashion items, acting as a key marketing tool for both parties, providing new points of market entry, increasing reputations, and driving global visibility.[15]

Taking a chronological perspective, this contribution places the development of Birkenstocks as fashion items into this system. It considers Birkenstock's positioning in relation to key fashion intermediaries and actors and explores how the brand's engagement with these has developed. It grounds these changes in the context of the company's global markets.

A Sandal Made to Fit

By the mid-20th century, the fashion industry was extending its hold on consumer markets with the development of the ready-to-wear segment, tapping into growing consumer spending power. Ordinary items increasingly developed a fashionable aspect.[16] In the shoe sector, advances took place in design, and the industry moved away from the remit of the cordwainer.[17] At the same time, an alternative market that had begun in the late 19th century, was growing, focused on comfort, mobility, and foot health. Following the orthopedic shoes Wörishofer and the Flexiclog, the 50s saw the launch of the Hush Puppy, followed by Scholl's Pescura sandal with an anatomically crafted wooden sole, the Earth Shoe, and negative-heeled footwear.[18] While these shoes remained niche, except for the Scholl sandal, which was worn by models Twiggy and Jean Shrimpton, their appearance coincided with the rise of the hippie movement in the United States and later Europe. This was typified by a bohemian look paired with "Jesus sandals" and a focused critique of traditional markets, economic systems, and fashion, along with a leaning toward naturalism.[19]

At the turn of the 20th century, the Birkenstock family was creating orthopedic shoe lasts and metal-free insoles, two of them named *Footbed*.[20] The goal of their products was to maintain and support feet, which often suffered in the mass-produced and symmetrically shaped footwear of the period.[21] In the 1930s, 40s, and 50s, Carl Birkenstock extended the company offerings, writing publications, holding training seminars and attempting to license designs and mass-produce his own footwear employing the footbed technology.[22] By the mid-20th century, Karl Birkenstock had joined the firm and was following his father Carl's footwear ambitions.[23] In 1963, Karl Birkenstock created the *Original Birkenstock-Footbed Sandal*—now called the *Madrid*—and presented it at a trade fair in Düsseldorf. However, according to Karl, the shoe was considered problematic. Fair participants ridiculed the footwear as it was felt that Birkenstock and his sandal were undermining fashion.[24] Although this period proved a struggle for the company, by the early 70s they had launched a range of models including those now called the *Zürich*, *Roma*, and *Arizona*.[25]

Throughout their first few decades, Birkenstock sandals, though pitched at a broad range of consumers and branded "chic" in early advertising catalogs, were associated with foot health and anti-fashion countercultures.[26] The firm's promotional marketing from the 60s and 70s pitched the shoes as a healthy footwear. Advertisements bearing titles like "Why Birkenstock Footprints Feel So Good (and why they are so good for you)" extolled the impact of the sandals on foot placement and gait, appealing to those with foot concerns, as well as those looking for footwear that was not subject to the dictates of fashion.[27]

During these decades, Birkenstock developed a presence in Europe and further afield thanks to a number of local distributors. Italian distribution began in the 50s with Carolina and Karl Fill, who sold the *Madrid* with little success. Sales picked up when Ewald Pitschl and his family opened the first comfort shoe store in South Tyrol.[28] But, as Ewald's brother Gerhard Pitschl remembers, in the 80s "people would frequently smile at our healthy shoes, as these didn't have the appearance that fashion dictated—which in Italy was then the be-all and end-all."[29]

Margot Fraser, a German-born, US-based dressmaker, discovered the footwear while on holiday in Germany in 1966. Finding them to be an effective solution to her foot concerns, she decided the products should be available in the United States and formed an agreement with the Birkenstock family, initially selling the shoes from her house. In 1972, Fraser set up Birkenstock Footprints Sandals, Inc. to expand retailing, which was focused on a number of health stores and "mom and pop shops."[30] In developing relationships with retailers across the USA, Fraser emphasized the role of foot health, attending conferences, holding seminars, and training colleagues in the anatomical benefits of Birkenstock sandals.[31] She developed a key consumer market and grew the company, moving to an extensive campus in Novato, California, in 1982.[32] As Fraser indicated, the 70s through to the early 80s was a successful period, with Birkenstock sales doubling annually. However, the rise of Ronald Reagan and "dress-for-success" resulted in the company having a "year or two of no growth."[33] It was able to bounce back from this, as Fraser stated, "Birkenstock turned out not to be a fad."[34]

Across the Atlantic, the introduction of the brand BIRKENSTOCK to the UK in the 70s was aided by the efforts of entrepreneur Robert Lusk. Having contacted a man who brought the sandals over from Germany every few months in the boot of his car, Lusk saw the potential to create a business. He envisaged a shoe shop that offered "different ways of walking and different ways of being" and opened a location in West London retailing alternative footwear.[35] He did so, despite admitting that "the German sandal absolutely did not fit into [...] UK fashion in any way whatsoever," making it difficult to sell.[36] Building the business and advertising in magazines did not prove challenging, but there was little interest in wholesale as the British shoe sector was dominated by large corporations.[37] His business gained momentum and in 1976 Lusk opened a store in Covent Garden in London and later a second location on the King's Road.[38]

In Japan, the distribution of Birkenstock's main product line began in the mid-80s through a trading company under the Sanyei Corporation. The company found Birkenstock products at the Global Destination for Shoes and Accessories trade fair in Düsseldorf in 1983. Initially retailing in the Japanese market was challenging because, in the absence of a slipper culture akin to that in Northern Europe, the shoes were only seen as holiday footwear.[39]

Birkenstock's alternative footwear positioning was clear in their international retailers' marketing materials throughout the 70s and 80s.[40] Retailer Bed 'n Back etc. ran a campaign in The New York Times in October 1985 with a picture of a dumpster full of shoes. It suggested that its readers should "Trash the shoes that hurt you" during their "Dumpster Days," where said painful shoes would be donated to charity and participants would receive eight US dollars toward the purchase of a pair of "comfortable" Birkenstock sandals.[41]

This approach continued with a Natural Shoe Store advert in the "Irish Independent" from January 1986 which named fashionable shoes as culprits of foot pain. Entitled "Shoo away all those fashion-mad footwreckers," it highlighted the fashion industry's view of shoes as "accessories" and "feature[s] that must blend with an overall look [...] assessed in terms of [...] visual impact rather than [...] comfort or appropriateness to the human foot."[42] The advert recommended the Dublin Natural Shoe Store's range of products as a contrast to the pain-inducing footwear, describing the heritage and range of Birkenstock models that could be purchased instead.[43] These marketing approaches, developed from the company's health-focused values, were common among Birkenstock retailers globally, fostering a consumer group who prioritized comfort over style.

Bare Toes under Straps: The History of the Sandal

BY JOHANNA STEINFELD

The sandal is probably one of the simplest basic forms of footwear to manufacture. It consists only of a sole and straps, for which relatively little leather, cork, or other materials are needed, and yet it provides reliable protection against hot, cold, and dirty surfaces. This explains why sandals have been worn since early human history. The oldest shoe finds are the "Fort Rock sandals," named after their place of discovery, the Fort Rock Cave in Oregon, USA; they are made of the woven bark fibers of a sagebrush and are estimated to be over 9,000 years old.[1] Several millennia later, the sandal was held in high esteem in the Mediterranean cultures of classical antiquity, as demonstrated by wall paintings and archaeological finds: in addition to the discovery of simpler sandals made of reeds and raffia, sandals that were intricately painted and gilded were found in the tomb of Egyptian pharaoh Tutankhamun.

In ancient Greece, sandals were likewise part of the clothing of the upper class, and—in contrast to shoes manufactured in the early modern period—were designed with a different fit for the left and right foot. Roman shoemakers also designed and made shoes based on the shape of the foot.[2] It is hardly surprising that, as befit the Mediterranean climate, sandals were worn there, although they were intended mainly for women, while male members of the nobility wore closed or half-open shoes (*calceus*).[3] In the first century BCE, when poet and philosopher Cicero wanted to disparage his opponent, Roman statesman Verres, he referred to him in a speech as *soleatus praetor*, a praetor who wears sandals. His choice of words implied the accusation that Verres the statesman was behaving in an un-Roman manner because sandals were associated with an unwanted influence from Greek culture.[4] It was not until the end of the Roman Republic in the last third of the first century BCE that this view changed. From then on, sandals also served men as shoes for use outside the home.[5] Besides the term *soleatus* used by Cicero, which is derived from *solea*, sandal, other Latin words denoted different types of sandals. The modern English word "sandal" derives from one of them, *sandalium*, whose linguistic roots lie in the Greek "sándalon" (σάνδαλον), meaning "strapped shoe."[6]

It is true that sandals or sandal-like shoes continued to be worn in Europe during the Middle Ages, as shown by depictions across the cen-

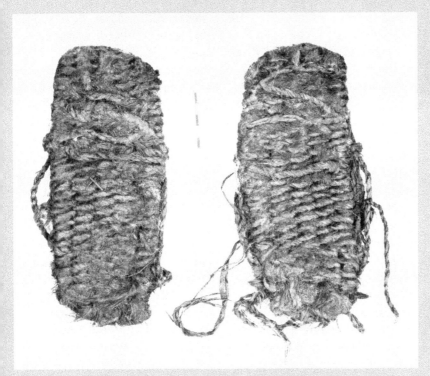

Fig. 51: Foot protection is a human need: sandals in the Neolithic period (Fort Rock Cave).

turies of monks[7] and people from rural areas, especially in southern Europe.[8] At the royal courts, however, closed-toe shoes were fashionable, especially since it was not possible for women to wear sandals if only on the basis of Christian morality, which required that all parts of the body be covered.[9] Prior to their widespread use in Germany after World War II, there were several more times when sandals made an appearance. For example, as the bourgeoisie started to evolve around 1800, middle-class women wore sandals, reflecting the fact that in the so-called neoclassical period ancient Greece and Rome were embraced not only intellectually but also as a lifestyle influence.[10] However, this only involved a very small section of society, since the exposed lady's foot was generally still considered immoral. This was still the case[11] when the Lebensreform movements were founded at the end of the 19th century; their followers and adherents strove to lead lives that took their cue from naturalness, distancing themselves from the densely populated and unhygienic big cities. This led to clothing and shoe designs that were intended to bring the body into as much contact as possible with light, air, and sun. Those who did not simply walk barefoot chose sandals, which were also produced and sold by representatives of the *Lebensreform* movement. During the Third Reich, the sandal finally came into focus for both economic and orthopedic reasons. Against the backdrop of efforts to create an economy impervious to outside influence and restrictions on raw and other materials, the sandal, which had hitherto been worn only rarely, was championed by the Nazi leadership. While in 1924 sandals still accounted for only slightly over three percent of the total production of shoes manufactured in Germany, this ratio changed in the sandal's favor from the early 30s onward.[12] For the Nazi regime, the sandal offered two advantages: it made it possible to save not only on leather but also on scarce cotton, since the wearers did not need socks.[13] Moreover, during the Third Reich further advances were made in the field of orthopedics. The orthopedist Wilhelm Thomsen, for example, who combined existing ideas and concepts on foot health with Nazi ideas, worked on a "gymnastic sandal."[14] This was to provide support when you stood and help to train you when you walked.

The modern age of the sandal was finally ushered in with the gradual emergence of the market for fashionable sandals and health sandals in the 50s. Examples are the fashion sandal "Rapallo," first manufactured in 1953 by Frankfurt's Angulus-Patos shoe factory, and in the orthopedic field the "orig-inal sandal" produced, from 1956 on, by Hamburg's Berkemann company.[15] Berkemann developed its claim to producing well-fitting shoes early on and had already started to mass-produce orthopedic insoles at the turn of the 20th century.[16] In 1958, the patent for the sandal was registered with the addition "according to Prof. Thomsen."[17] In 1961, around five percent of all shoes produced in Germany were sandals. Only a decade later, this proportion had already more than doubled (to around 12 percent), which can also be explained by the role sandals played in the protest movements from the late 60s onwards as well as by the further development of fashionable designs for flat sandals. This ensured the sandal's permanent place in the shoe market, in the women's shoe segment especially,[18] whereby this latter emphasis changed in the 90s, when men's sandals were included in the Gucci, Ralph Lauren, and DKNY collections and thus also became "presentable" for fashion-conscious men.[19]

At the same time, health sandals like Birkenstocks were discovered by designers. The further triumph of the sandal was supported by the softening of conventional ideas about fashion, with ever fewer people taking offense at feet being bare, and the gradual acceptance of comfortable sandals as permissible footwear not only for leisure but also for school, university, and even the workplace. The fact that show-

254   **1963–2024** Rise to a Global Brand

er sandals such as the "Adilette" also entered the market gave these trends additional momentum, most recently spawning the latest fashion of "ugly sandals," which are based on a mixture of a health shoe and a trekking sandal and thus combine two types of footwear that had long been ridiculed in the fashion scene.

First Steps into Fashion

Meanwhile, in the broader fashion sector the 80s saw the introduction of sharp suits, glitz, glamor, and traditionalism with the likes of designers Gianni Versace, Ralph Lauren, and Giorgio Armani.[44] Toward the end of the decade, a contrasting response to structured dressing arrived. As economic and material culture historian Giorgio Riello relates, postmodernist and minimalist ideas moved into the fashion field "based on the 'disintegration' of dress [and] unusual and clashing combinations."[45] Such abstract fashions had already appeared in the 70s and 80s in the work of Japanese designers such as Yohji Yamamoto, Issey Miyaki and Rei Kawakubo who brought their inventive designs to the Parisian runways.[46] This was a space in which Birkenstock could have a role.

One of the first appearances of Birkenstocks in an editorial was in British Elle magazine from November 1985 in a spread insensitively titled "Jap." Taking notes from the Japanese designers, the editorial featured outfits created out of high street items. Styled by Senior Fashion Editor Lucinda Chambers, it featured suede *Boston* clogs, cited as shoes from Robert Lusk's Natural Shoe Store, not Birkenstock products.[47] Paired with rather eccentric looks for the period, the shoes were chosen to reference footwear popular in Japan.[48] This was followed by a February 1989 feature in the American teen magazine Sassy. The article highlighted "earth mother-type shoes that everyone wore to Woodstock" as the next big thing.[49] It even suggested that its readers should "snag a vintage pair [of Birkenstocks] from your mom."[50] It's fascinating to note that featuring clogs and Birkenstocks in the up-and-coming footwear section of the magazine caused contention. Editor Jane Pratt wrote, "It provoked some interesting commentary around the office ('yuck' was one reaction)." [51]

The budding association between Birkenstock and fashion remained controversial. And yet a file from the Birkenstock Archive from 1985 entitled "Famous, Well-Known Persons & Celebrities Who Wear Birkenstock Footwear" not only cites popular actors, one of the Beach Boys, and Steve Jobs as Birkenstock wearers but also refers to American fashion designer Andre Walker using Birkenstock sandals on the runway.[52] Photographer Amy Arbus captured an image of young Walker in New York in 1983 (see fig. 52) wearing a waistcoat and shorts of his design accompanied by socks, sock garters, and a pair of Birkenstocks.[53] However, little other information about his fashion show is available. Even so, it's clear not only that fashion was connecting with the footwear but also that American distributors of Birkenstock were aware of this.

Fig. 52: The *Athen* hits New York — Andre Walker discovered the Birkenstock model *Athen* in 1983 (Suspenders & Socks, photographed by Amy Arbus).

International Fashion and Luxury in Birkenstocks

By 1988, the US-based Birkenstock Footprint Sandals, Inc. even had three full-time customer service representatives focusing on high-end and luxury department store accounts including R. H. Macy & Co. (now Macy's) and Nordstrom.[54] This period also brought about a shift in positioning. The distributor brought in a sales and marketing director to target the brand, introducing "a less funky logo, point-of-sales materials, a public-relations department, and most noticeably, a brighter, upscale catalog" featuring "ordinary, good-looking people wearing Birkenstock shoes."[55]

The Footwear of Grunge

"If a Ferragamo pump is a sonnet, then the Birkenstock, the humble sandal that has found a new following lately, is a haiku: simple, spare, unadorned," wrote Richard Stengel in The New York Times in August 1992.[56] This comparison between footwear from the Italian luxury accessories and ready-to-wear label Salvatore Ferragamo and BIRKENSTOCK seems in stark contrast with the reactions of only a few years earlier. In the 90s, Birkenstock sandals entered the fashion world, brought up from the streets by not just one but a number of fashion designers, celebrities, and periodicals. The shoes appeared at the New York, Milan, and Paris Fashion Weeks and became more visible to global consumers.

Their first clearly documented appearance on the catwalk was not the famous show that had designer Marc Jacobs fired from American brand Perry Ellis. It was two years earlier at the Spring/Summer (S/S) 1991 fashion show of Ronaldus Shamask at New York Fashion Week. Shamask's male models wore boxy suits with light-colored socks and Arizonas.[57] While the American press asked if the outfits could be fashion, shocked by Shamask's stubbled models and relaxed looks, the German newspaper Die Zeit described the ensembles, Birkenstocks and all, as "pathetic" and "second-hand."[58] The second appearance created far more of a furor. For his S/S 1993 "Grunge" collection for Perry Ellis, designer Marc Jacobs sent supermodels including Kate Moss, Naomi Campbell, and Christy Turlington down the runway in Doc Martens boots, Birkenstocks, and Converse.[59] The collection featured unpolished, casual clothing that took from the grunge and punk music scenes, a far cry from previous Perry Ellis aesthetics.[60]

In conversation with fashion trade periodical Women's Wear Daily about the fashion show, Jacobs said that the shoes "needed to be the real thing. [He] didn't want to put a marcasite buckle on a two-strap sandal.

Birkenstock Featured In Perry Ellis Show

Almost two years after Birkenstock was included in a show by the late designer Renaldus Shamask, super-label Perry Ellis Menswear has followed suit.

In a July 27 Central Park fashion event, Birkenstock footwear was featured with Perry Ellis Menswear's Spring '93 collection by designer Andrew Corrigan. The line integrated natural fibers and earth tones for an "environmental" feel, and Birkenstock made a perfect choice for footwear.

The show received great reviews, and it spawned feature stories about Birkenstock in the **New York Times** (see insert), and **New York Newsday**.

Seen in Comfort

If you read supermarket tabloids (of course you don't — nobody does, right?) you've seen the photograph of **Woody Harrelson** (Cheers) playing a guitar and wearing Birkenstock shoes. The photograph appeared in the August 4th issue of the National Enquirer.

Olympic swimmer Anita Nall, world record holder in the 200m breaststroke, has been spotted in Birkenstock footwear. "I love them," she says, "they're comfortable on my feet and really nice to wear."

New Shopping Bags

New shopping bags are now in stock. Printed in three-colors on white recycled paper, these new shopping bags feature the Birkenstock logo in blue and maroon, with an illustration of the classic Arizona style on one side and the Granada on the other.

We streamlined this shopping bag to be a little easier to handle. Birkenstock features and benefits are appear prominently in large, easy-to-read type, and convenient handles make it easy to carry up to three shoe boxes.

These updated new shopping bags are available at $25/unit of 100, item #80521. To order these new shopping bags, call the order department at 1-800-487-2475.

Promo Item of the Month

Back-to-school business is well under way, and the demand for Birkenstock is still high. School related gift-with-purchase items are an effective tool to stimulate this business.

Canvas totes and nylon duffel bags are great for carrying books and make ideal GWP's. Birkenstock coffee mugs work well for late night studying.

To order special promotional items, call Courtney Hill at 1-800-487-2475, ext. 217.

Fig. 53: Birkenstocks (*Arizonas*) at New York Fashion Week in 1992.

It had to be on a Birkenstock."[61] According to Danny Wasserman of Tip Top Shoes in New York, Jacobs bought the shoes before decorating them and placing them on the runway.[62] Jacob's collection created a wave of media attention, but he was not the only one to use Birkenstocks. Perry Ellis menswear designer, Andrew Corrigan, also sent his models down the runway in the sandals that season.[63] Still, it was Jacob's collection that brought about the first Birkenstock feature in the key fashion periodical Vogue USA, when in November 1992 the magazine published a column drawing parallels between Marc Jacobs, Fred Flintstone, Harrison Ford, Keanu Reeves, and "that true pioneer of the bohemian look, Jesus Christ."[64]

What we see here is the designer's wish to reach for something un-fashionable, something real, something authentic. This almost seems to prefigure Birkenstock's path into fashion—an item off the streets that was picked up by fashion's greats and turned into a success in its own right. The same year, according to media reports, Birkenstock sandals also appeared on the New York and Milan runways of designers Calvin Klein, Joseph Aboud, Randolph Duke, and Giorgio Armani.[65] In 1993, they featured in the Parisian fashion shows of Koji Tatsuno and Martine Sitbon.[66]

The next decisive media appearance for Birkenstock was in British magazine The Face. Less known as a purveyor of fashion brands but recognized for its role in changing culture, it was credited with the launch of Kate Moss's career. The 1990 editorial responsible, "The Third Summer of Love," shot by Corinne Day, featured the 16-year-old Moss, running around a beach in East Sussex, wearing Birkenstocks *Rio* and *Palermo* from Robert Lusk's Natural Shoe Store.[67] The editorial wasn't just a happy coincidence for Birkenstock. Robert Lusk and his colleagues were working with Modus, a PR agency in London, who were responsible for placing the sandals in the photo shoot, linking Birkenstocks to street fashion.[68]

The popularity of BIRKENSTOCK within the fashion community was growing, with industry gatekeepers sharing the footwear with their audiences. As Women's Wear Daily reported in September 1990, students at the Fashion Institute of Technology and Parson's School of Design in New York were bringing Birkenstocks and the "Earth Girl" style into street fashion.[69] American celebrity advocates of the sandals included André Leon Talley of Vogue USA, actors Whoopi Goldberg and Cybill Shepherd, and even pop icon Madonna, who wore the sandals for magazines and in their daily lives.[70] By 1993, even Vogue USA included Birkenstocks in two editorials, though both pitched the sandals as holiday footwear.[71]

Away from the world of celebrity and runway fashion, Birkenstock, who, according to a Sales Manager, "didn't want to have anything to do with fashion," were developing their offering.[72] Karl Birkenstock's sons, Alex, Stephan, and Christian, took on a bigger role in the business and in the 90s they launched a number of sub-brands.[73] Tatami was set up in 1990, followed by Papillio, a trend-focused sandal line in 1991, and Betula in 1994.[74]

With the launch of Tatami came the extension of the Japanese market and the birth of a new distributor, Seed Corporation. Set up in 1997 by Koji Tanemoto, the company took over the distribution of Tatami products as the sandals, featuring a higher arch than other Birkenstocks, were unusual. The sandals became popular thanks to celebrity endorsement, and to capitalize on this, Seed Corporation began offering their products in a range of colorways, reaching a new market of younger consumers.[75] The Sanyei Corporation was taking a similar approach to marketing Birkenstocks, targeting the shoes to 20- and 30-year-olds, and by 1997 they took over wholesale and retail. As the Japanese yen rose in value and the public's capacity to purchase imported goods increased, the popularity of Birkenstocks products grew.[76] This, along with the development of relationships with a number of independent fashion "select shops," drove the success of the brand in Japan.[77]

As BIRKENSTOCK became more popular in the UK, Robert Lusk decided that rather than trying to control their distribution, the best approach would be to offer the sandals to all those interested. The strategy worked, as each retailer had a different customer base.[78] In 1996, Lusk opened the first Birkenstock store at 37 Neal Street and while the company's popularity rose, it was a slow process. Meanwhile, Birkenstock's reach had extended to Australia, where they quickly landed in the fashion world. Marcel Goerke set up his business distributing the sandals, and he remembers a woman who came into the store exclaiming "You're here, you're finally here!" [79] The woman in question worked for Australian Elle magazine and requested to borrow a pair of sandals for a shoot to showcase the arrival of the footwear in Australia.[80]

While Birkenstocks had become more prevalent, by January 1996, columnists in Vogue USA were criticizing Marc Jacob's grunge collection as one of the worst looks of the decade.[81] And yet the sandals appeared in editorials by acclaimed photographers Steven Meisel and Mario Testino and in an interview with Gwyneth Paltrow, where the actress effused that her idea of cool was pairing "Birkenstocks with Gucci."[82] They reappeared on the fashion runway in November 1997 at Stephen DiGeronimo and, only a few months later in 1998, Narciso Rodriguez brought out Birkenstocks in Milan, customizing the *Boston* with cashmere and styling them with thick socks.[83] The style was so popular that Birkenstock was "deluged with enquiries" to which it was unable to respond.[84] An unfortunate position for those wishing for the cashmere covered clogs, but excellent marketing for the *Boston*. The same season, American designer John Scher showed Birkenstocks, while for the S/S runways, Paco Rabanne, Eddie Rodriguez for Wilke-Rodriguez, Gene Meyer, and Jerry Kwiatkowski for Perry Ellis all featured the footwear.[85] Despite the designers' use of the sandal, none of these different models were what can be termed "true" collaborations, created with Birkenstock for retail purposes.[86] Rather, designers were given, borrowed, or purchased the pieces, and customized them.[87] It seems that both the German producer and its distributors missed the market opportunities provided by Jacobs, Rodriguez, and many others.

Brands without Borders: Collaborations in the Fashion Segment

BY JOHANNA STEINFELD

So the label Karl Lagerfeld and H&M, the Swedish clothing manufacturer for the masses, are launching a collection together? What came as such a surprise for the fashion world of 2004 is now a common model: collaborations between luxury designers or brands and major clothing retailers or streetwear and sports brands. Thanks to the hype triggered by "Lagerfeld X H&M," the collection designed for the European and North American markets—a total of 30 different pieces priced between 14.90 and 149 euros—was completely sold out almost within a day.[1] In the years that followed, H&M continued along the special path of product development it had begun in 2004 with collections by other luxury designers and brands. After all, it was a win-win for everyone involved: buyers were able to afford "real" Lagerfelds, luxury products accessible to broad groups of buyers that were otherwise to be found in a completely different market segment. And for Lagerfeld, too, the collaboration is said to have been a profitable business.[2] H&M saw numerous people streaming through its doors who were potential buyers of other products in addition to the Lagerfeld collection. Furthermore, the joint collaboration enabled both partners to enter new markets and garnered particular attention from the press and fashion world, creating favorable marketing opportunities. More generally, collaborations between luxury brands or designers and major retailers enable the "democratization of luxury," whereby their luxury products can be brought to the people.[3] This lays the ground for a demand for further products, which can then be marketed as more easily accessible in a lower price segment.[4]

The "Lagerfeld x H&M" campaign plays a special role in the history of collaborations because of the extraordinary press campaign and the public attention it generated. The fact that Lagerfeld's image was not tarnished in any way was by no means a given: only 20 years earlier, there had been collaboration between the luxury designer Halston and the retailer JCPenney, as a result of which the designer was reviled by the fashion world.[5] The situation was different, however, for collaborations between fashion and art, which since their beginnings have not only been tolerated but have also been able to give luxury brands a higher profile, partly because fashion itself can be and has been interpreted as a form of art. Similarities

Fig. 54: Supermodel Heidi Klum introduced new colors and materials to the Birkenstock sandals (2003).

between fashion and art lend themselves to an alliance: the importance of quality, of skill and design—not to mention the exclusive nature of both fields.[6] Collaborations between fashion and art can, in some cases, even produce new art.

One of the first significant examples in the history of the connection between designers and artists is the collaboration between Elsa Schiaparelli, the Italian-born star of the fashion world during the 20s and 30s, who worked in Paris, and Salvador Dalí. The two surrealists shared a close friendship that then laid the foundations for a 1936 collaboration which resulted in the famous Lobster Dress and Shoe Hat.[7] Andy Warhol's collaboration with Yves Saint Laurent likewise attracted a great deal of attention: Saint Laurent integrated the designs of the pop art movement into his 1966 fall/winter collection, and Warhol painted portraits of the designer. To this day, Warhol's work has been cited again and again in haute couture items by Gianni Versace and Jean-Charles de Castelbajac, among others. Eventually, the kind of partnerships we now call collaborations emerged: not only does the fashion cite art and artists, in a collaboration based on non-material values, but at the end of a partnership (also) aimed at commercial success, there is a product which unites the essence of the brands of both partners.

The significance of such collaborations as a marketing tool can be seen in the 13-year partnership between Louis Vuitton and Japanese artist Takashi Murakami, who introduced the "Multicolore" monogram bag, which sparked great demand over the years, its colorful and garish versions shaping, for a time at least, the design of the bag.[8] Evidence of the various forms of collaboration becoming more and more creative can be seen in the Japanese brand Uniqlo Today, which releases about 20 art-related projects every year, including collaborative collections with established art institutions such as the Louvre.[9]

In addition to the partnerships between the luxury and low-end segments and the links between art and fashion, the trend over the last decade has shown an increasing desire in the fashion industry for collaboration, which has seen all kinds of links between designers, artists, and brands going beyond these two spheres and now also increasingly extending beyond the boundaries of the fashion industry. The same applies, incidentally, to other consumer goods sectors. There are various gradations in the degree of collaboration, ranging from celebrity endorsements of a fashion company to collaborations in which both partners contribute their brand identity and product development. In the 2010s, collaborations were boosted by social media, as attention itself became currency, and competition for publicity increased. Here, collaborations with surprising combi-

264   **1963–2024** Rise to a Global Brand

nations or exciting product developments promise to kindle public interest, such as the shoe launched by Adidas together with the Berlin public transport company (BVG), whose pattern imitated the fabric of the subway seats and was also incorporated into BVG's annual passes.[10] The press and PR work accompanying collaborations was further intensified by the involvement of influencers.[11] It naturally followed that influencers themselves became collaborative partners, something that is rewarded by high sales figures, as shown, for example, by the collections of several members of the Kardashian family.[12]

Shoe manufacturers such as Adidas, Nike, and Birkenstock entered into various forms of cooperation early on, and collaborations are now an integral part of their product development. A few examples from the Nike Air Force 1 sneaker series—which mostly appeared in strictly limited editions too—reveal the wide variety of collaborations and quasi-collaborations: for example, Nike released the Nike Air Force x PlayStation with electronics company Sony (2006), the High Supreme World Famous Red with streetwear brand Supreme (2014), and the VLONE x Nike Air Force 1 Low together with the Vlone brand, which is associated with hip-hop artist collective A$AP Mob (2017). In 2018, Nike and the label Off-White, founded by star designer Virgil Abloh, jointly released the Off-White™ x

Nike Air Force 1 "MoMA" shoe to coincide with an exhibition at the Museum of Modern Art in New York. In the process of all this, hierarchies between "low fashion" and "high fashion," which previously seemed clear-cut, have been turned upside down: luxury brands are increasingly benefiting from the sporty chic of streetwear and sports brands, which see collaborations as part of their branding. The Nike Air Force 1 "Craig Sager" in 2016 also showed that collaborations can be linked to messages.[13] Nike developed this model in honor of US sports presenter Craig Sager in order to raise funds for his "SagerStrong Leukemia" foundation using the income generated from sales. The fact that other socially relevant topics such as ecology and sustainability are also included comes as no surprise: Spanish fashion chain Bershka and National Geographic, for example, dedicated themselves to the topic of sustainability in 2019 and brought out a collection made of environmentally friendly materials,[14] while Tommy Hilfiger and Timberland likewise relied on sustainable materials and processes in a joint collaboration in 2021.[15]

Making Fashionable Footwear

In the 2000s, Birkenstock's place in fashion was solidifying. Magazines such as Vogue USA featured the sandals on a regular basis, and by 2004 they were receiving clear product references in editorials and articles.[88] Even general media outlets cited the rise of Birkenstocks as a fashion item, with The Evening Herald referring to the "Birkenstock effect"—the effect by which the shoes "were so uncool as to be ultimately cool."[89] The footwear made national headlines in Britain in summer 2003 as queues formed on Neal Street.[90] Lusk's Birkenstock-focused location was proving a great success, causing "mass hysteria" as he called it in The Guardian.[91] He reported that the popularity "just ballooned into this, as far as I was concerned as a retailer, quite a sad situation, because there was far more demand than we could satisfy."[92] Lusk approached this from a democratic perspective wanting to provide for the needs of potential clients, while the scarcity and demand he was struggling with were increasing the shoe's acclaim, driving it toward fashion item status.[93]

Meanwhile, Birkenstock and its competitors were shifting their design focus.[94] In fall 2001, the Birkenstock collection included dark denim tones, picking up on the trend for Western-inspired styles.[95] They also expanded their offerings through the introduction of more masculine designs. Shelly Glasgow, then Birkenstock USA's Director of Product Development, stated in a New York Times article that "it was never a goal of ours at Birkenstock to be fashionable with a capital F, [...] but when we saw pictures of male celebrities like Leonardo DiCaprio and Usher wearing Birkenstock products that we hadn't in any way placed with them, we didn't want to let that go."[96] This drove a move toward more fashionable styles. Conversely, the whole thing led to high fashion designers being inspired by elements of Birkenstock sandals. One of the most fascinating versions of this appeared in Vogue in May 2003. The editorial features the "Birkenstass," a glittering sandal by Christian Louboutin retailing for a hefty 935 US dollars.[97] Perched on a stiletto heel, this bejeweled sandal makes a clear reference to the strap of the *Gizeh* model. Little information is available about the shoe or its market, but it is a clear indication that Birkenstock styles were making waves, and those who saw this would have understood the playful reference.

Beyond the realms of high fashion, Alex, Christian, and Stephan Birkenstock brought a breath of fresh air to the company which included a move toward the creation of Special Make-Up (SMU) products. These were planned to develop Birkenstock's position, lending the cultural cachet of celebrity collaborators to the shoe and increasing its market.[98] The first move taken by the German producer with its American distributor was an ambitious one, an agreement with German model, lifelong Birkenstock wearer, and toast of the American fashion media, Heidi Klum.[99] This exclusive contract, spanning the years 2003 to 2008, involved the model designing Birkenstocks under the name "Birkenstock styled by Heidi Klum."[100] Her first collection included a studded white *Arizona*, a bejeweled cow-skin *Amsterdam*, and a distressed denim *Madrid*, each retailed for a price point higher than the average Birkenstock, at about 250 euros.[101] The collection was launched internationally as a move to bring Birkenstock shoes into the fashion sector.[102] Later collections included a range of animal prints, sandals bearing writing, boots and sneakers with fur and patches, and flip-flop styles with sub-brand Betula.[103]

Despite media popularity, the collaboration brought about multiple challenges. In the American market, the majority of retailers remained the usual Birkenstock outlets and comfort footwear shops, with only Saks Fifth Avenue, Parisian Inc., and online shoe retailer Zappos as more fashion-focused outliers.[104] Birkenstock made an effort to enter the fashion market, but in doing so did not have access to fashionable retail locations and underestimated the importance of product scarcity, which is what makes a fashion item valuable.

A second collaboration was undertaken with Swiss designer Yves Béhar for Footprints, the Birkenstock sub-brand of closed shoes. Footprints was developed during the early 2000s, with the aim of attracting a broader, urban audience through the introduction of shoes and boots suiting that lifestyle.[105] The goal was to help them reach out to the "one market the $100 million-a-year company definitely hadn't conquered: the fashion-conscious."[106] While the company probably received some press coverage, one Birkenstock employee recalls that the line didn't have a significant impact.[107]

With the turn of the millennium, the Japanese fashion for Birkenstocks faded and both Birkenstock and Tatami distributors suffered. For Seed, the situation was the fact that Birkenstock Germany discontinued the special footbed for Tatami, which caused a great deal of unrest as it was the most important quality feature of this sub-brand. Then the Tanemoto brothers also asked to engage in collaborations.[108] The first of these, in partnership with Disney, used high-quality Japanese denim for the upper of the sandal. From then on, the company created SMUs with a range of international and Japanese brands including Levi's, A Bathing Ape, and Philip Lim.[109] Birkenstock's European bosses also gave the Sanyei Corporation the opportunity to develop SMUs.[110] The first of these was with Takahiro Miyashita's Americana-inspired Number (N) ine, resulting in the production of collaborative models of the *Zürich* and *Boston*.[111] A Louis Vuitton collaboration, organized in 2009 through a contact from one of the select shops, had to be undertaken with sub-brand Papillio, as their request to make sandals from crocodile leather went against Birkenstock policy. While this unusual partnership only resulted in about ten pairs of sandals, it increased proximity between Birkenstock Japan and the fashion world.[112]

Changes in Japanese marketing content also helped to redevelop the footwear's hold. While Birkenstock Japan catalogs had previously depicted idyllic images of Germany, from 2005 onward, they took on a more fashionable focus.[113] Exemplifying this is the "Birkenstock Style Book" released in collaboration with the Japanese version of fashion and lifestyle magazine Dazed & Confused. Showcasing the Spring and Summer 2005 models and further collaborative designs, this 100-page volume was almost indistinguishable from an issue of the magazine. It included one-off customizations by popular artists, a cover story with actor Hiroki Narimiya, and a feature on the Covent Garden Birkenstock shop in London.[114]

The Birth of the "Furkenstock"

Driven by the reappearance of the footwear, and its lookalikes, on the runway and in fashion magazines, the early-2010s were a period of growth for Birkenstock. While the Japanese distributors continued their SMU operations, the American wing of Birkenstock developed a new marketing strategy using advertising campaigns. Sarah Ruston, the fashion director of luxury department store Lane Crawford indicated that at Milan Fashion Week in June 2010 "the shoe for the season is certainly going to be a new reworked version of the Birkenstock."[115]

By the beginning of the decade, relaxed shoes from espadrilles to Birkenstocks and the orthopedic Wörishofer sandal heralded the rise of the ugly shoe trend.[116] The increase in copies and the proliferation of the iconic Birkenstock style snowballed.[117] While Bottega Veneta had already made reference to the sandals, the driver of the trend was Phoebe Philo, Creative Director of Céline, who sent *Arizona*-esque mink-lined sandals down the runway in Paris in October 2012 accompanied by lean, slouchy silhouettes.[118] Dubbed "Furkenstocks," the shoes became a hot item in magazines and with celebrities like Miley Cyrus.[119] Philo was not the only designer inspired by Birkenstock, with the Burberry Prorsum Men's

Spring 2013 collection showcasing foil-wrapped sandals on the feet of its suavely suited models, and Italian designer Giambattista Valli featuring metallic, studded versions soon after.[120] In Women's Wear Daily, shop owners Claire Distenfeld and Beth Buccini effused over the Céline Furkenstocks, attributing their rise in popularity to public discussions encouraged by Instagram. Both placed orders that season—Distenfeld for Giambattista Valli's subtler sandals, and Buccini for Celine's slides.[121] In February 2013, the British newspaper The Guardian published an article entitled "It's the year of the Birkenstock!" focusing not only on the eponymous shoe but also on a number of Birkenstock inspired footwear, specifically Philo's, which retailed at about 700 euros.[122]

Genuine Birkenstocks also reappeared in the fashion sections of magazines. Vogue USA published an article in July 2013 summing up the popularity of the footwear with the fashion crowd entitled "Pretty Ugly: Why Vogue Girls Have Fallen for the Birkenstock." Inside, editor Chioma Nnadi shared stories of her Vogue colleagues bringing their indoor love of Birkenstocks onto the streets and laid down the rules for wearing the footwear stylishly.[123]

It seemed that for Birkenstock, the rise of the Furkenstock was not something that the company was able to take advantage of. As Cathy Horyn noted in The Cut, "Philo's twist brought favorable publicity, but at the time, Birkenstock didn't even have a sales force, let alone a real marketing and PR operation. People had always discovered Birkenstocks on their own."[124] This wasn't true everywhere. Birkenstock's importers in Japan were already engaging with fashion, and Birkenstock USA, Inc. had just stepped in with marketing campaigns targeted toward American magazines. While still uncoordinated, both distributors and their offices were moving in a direction to benefit from fashion trends.

In the early 2010s, Birkenstock USA, Inc. didn't have any strategic account distribution but started to think that a new approach was needed, signing onto a national advertising campaign. As a result of the ongoing impact of the recession, the campaign rates were cheap and Birkenstock USA, Inc. selected a package which not only gave them advertising but also brought added value opportunities in the form of events. The adverts were simple, featuring top-down pictures of the sandals, but the events allowed the brand to get into contact with the media gatekeepers of fashion. Senior colleagues would staff these, using the opportunity to introduce themselves and arrange appointments with employees of publications including Vogue, Harper's Bazaar, Elle, and GQ.[125] One internal source remembers visiting the offices of Condé Nast and meeting personally with the then marketing editor for Vogue and Vogue.com, to whom she gave a pair of Birkenstocks. This was an approach used with other magazines that "started the buzz" around the company, creating consumer demand and requests for Birkenstocks in department stores and retailers beyond the "mom-and-pop stores" in which they were available at the time.[126] However, as the source indicates, until a new CEO came on board in 2013, the company wasn't quite able to capitalize on this buzz because they "didn't have that level of sophistication to open those doors of distribution."[127]

While the American firm was developing greater press and strategic relationships with fashion, Japanese capsule collaborations continued.[128] In 2012, the German headquarter of Birkenstock integrated its sub-brands, including Tatami, into the BIRKENSTOCK brand, causing a shock at Seed.[129] Seed Corporation distributed Tatami, Betula and Birki's but not BIRKENSTOCK so they had to find a way to build the value of the main brand in the market by transferring the awareness and loyalty of the Tatami brand to Birkenstock.[130] During this multi-year process, Seed continued their collaborations with Japanese department stores and designers, including one celebrating Birkenstock's 240th anniversary. This collaboration, for sale at the flagship luxury Isetan department store in Shinjuku, Tokyo, featured five styles of men's sandals with only 100 models of each released.[131] Continuing their partnerships in 2013 and 2014, Tatami launched SMU models under the Tatami label with Chitose Abe of Sacai, People Tree and Pendleton. They also began a second collaboration with A Bathing Ape, this time with Birkenstock.[132]

A Change of Course in Germany and Beyond

By the mid-2010s, BIRKENSTOCK's positioning began to shift. As Chief Sales Officer Klaus Baumann states, until this period the company "did something unexpected without any strategy. They just tried to bring their product out of the factory very fast to many feet."[133] He explains that there was little coordination or consideration of their market. In 2012, Stephan Birkenstock left the firm, handing his ownership to his brothers Alex and Christian.[134] They brought in new management, introducing Oliver Reichert and Markus Bensberg as co-chief executives.[135] Their radical new approach, steering the company away from rigid traditionalism toward a simplified group structure, proved the beginning of a renaissance.[136]

With these changes came an increased focus on the core of the brand—the *Footbed*, as well as an emphasis on flexibility and change.[137]

As Reichert emphasized, "We don't want to move Birkenstock into being a fashion brand, but we also don't want to be a museum for the traditional Birkenstock wearers, the old hippies [...]. It's a 360-degree approach to brand awareness, and for this you need people."[138] Under Reichert's leadership, the firm was restructured and streamlined, and new staff members were brought in.[139] They focused on modernization, facilitating connections with the fashion industry and introducing more fashionable designs into the general Birkenstock collections.[140] As Baumann states, "This was the moment when Birkenstock took the position to move from a production-driven company to a market-, or even [...] a customer-oriented company," shifting its focus to demand. Baumann recalls that when he first joined Birkenstock, there was "this start-up feeling [...] we felt like there's a new chapter coming."[141] Focus also shifted to solidifying and strengthening trust with partners to ensure that supply would meet the demand of retailers. Baumann is hesitant to label the changes in the company since he joined as a move toward fashion; he relies more on the concept of authenticity.[142] Externally, the change was also noticeable, with the former Berlin correspondent of Women's Wear Daily, Melissa Drier, recognizing the move toward an updated image. "They started trying to figure out what fashion meant for them in about 2013," she recalls, though she notes their initial approach did not quite hit the mark.[143]

Along with the introduction of new management staff in Europe, in 2013 David Kahan was brought in as president of Birkenstock America. Fostering greater connections with Germany and the footwear and fashion industries, Kahan had, according to a Birkenstock USA, Inc. employee, "the key to the door" that they had created through their early 2010s' marketing push. She explains, "then the wheel starts to move, much faster, and this is where we really start to build the company globally and locally [...] for the future."[144] She goes on to say that the changes during the early 2010s shifted the brand from just being a shoe producer to a lifestyle or fashion brand.[145]

Whether Birkenstock was developing into a fashion or lifestyle brand or not, it began to strengthen its positioning, recognize and leverage its heritage and DNA, and move toward the new luxury sector. As brand researcher Jean-Noël Kapferer explains, "in the luxury market, clients not only buy an exceptional product—partly handmade, with the savoir faire of artisans—but also a legend: a great tradition made modern to fit one's present life, a culture anchored in a country. In addition, they also buy exclusivity," created through the limiting of supply.[146]

International Fashion and Luxury in Birkenstocks

In the 80s, the luxury market expanded with consumers extending throughout society and the sector opening up a space between high-end, elite goods and upmarket mass consumer products. This led to the development of "accessible luxury," "new luxury," or "masstige" goods.[147] These goods and their brands "enjoy a reasonable level of perceived prestige, which differentiates them from middle-range products, but at the same time, they are sold at prices that are only slightly above those of comparable middle-range products in order to reach a broader target than the niches of traditional luxury brands."[148] However, the development of the luxury business since the 80s has not just been based on the pillars of heritage and authenticity. Along with image, brand, and communication, the industry has also involved the "restructuring of production systems" adapted from the smaller, often family-run businesses of traditional luxury of decades past.[149] This double-edged approach is visible in Birkenstock's development.

Birkenstock USA, Inc. heralded this change with an increased focus on SMU partnerships. The first true American collaboration, the co-creation of a product for retail, was undertaken in 2013 with American mass-market men's and women's wear retailer J.Crew, recognized for its preppy styles and capsule collections.[150] An internal Birkenstock source explains, "we were really still at the stage where all we could do was say what color upper, what color sole, what color buckle," but the J.Crew team were happy, as they were interested in exclusivity.[151] The brands came together to design two Birkenstocks in a range of colors with the name of both brands stamped in silver on the footbed.[152]

The next year's release of a number of exclusive colors, most importantly the *Arizona* in metallic silver and gold, drove a significant trend. This partnership proved successful and was a key brand-building tool for Birkenstock, helping to develop relationships with high-profile brands and accounts, and with future collaborators.[153] But as the Birkenstock USA, Inc. Director of Product Development Shelly Glasgow explained in a 2012 Daily Beast article, brand regulations limited the collaborations that could be undertaken: "It's why Birkenstock has been so successful, because we really have held tight by holding really true to our values."[154] This care in the consideration of collaboration partners and products has become typical of luxury and new luxury brands since the 2000s.[155]

Inundated with requests for collaboration, in the mid-2010s, Birkenstock USA, Inc. also partnered with a number of emerging designers.[156] One of these was Jérôme LaMaar and his 5:31 line. After receiving approval from the American distributor, LaMaar's Birkenstocks appeared at New York Fashion Week covered in sand and Swarovski crystals. The collaboration continued with fur-covered sandals customized by a cobbler, and *Boston, Madrid,* and *Arizona* models covered in Swarovski crystals, ocean coral, feathers, seashells, and pearls. LaMaar even attached a wedge heel to the back of a *Madrid*.[157] Speaking about the partnership, he believes that Birkenstock agreed to collaborate because he was receiving attention in the press and that the collaboration was beneficial for both parties.[158]

BIRKENSTOCK's popularity and the ugly shoe trend were growing beyond these collaborations. In September 2013, the New York catwalks featured Shades of Grey models in classic Birkenstocks, while Edun and Trina Turk showed sandals that were easily recognizable as a reference.[159] Fashion was lauding the ugly shoe, with Birkenstocks and Tevas as coveted products.[160] Similar sandals, dubbed "Norm-Kors" by The New York Times, picking up on the understated "normcore" trend, appeared in the resort collection of Michael Kors in 2014, while Calvin Klein's pre-fall 2014 show exhibited shoes that were probably inspired by the model *Amsterdam*. By October 2015, Birkenstock-esque strapped sandals featuring strips of miniature LED landing lights arrived at the Chanel airport terminal set up in the Grand Palais in Paris. It seemed that chunky heeled sandals had truly found their footing in the fashion world.[161]

Amidst this, Birkenstock USA, Inc. continued developing SMUs for retail with a range of brands. Their first collaboration with Opening Ceremony in 2014 formed part of the brand's collection with the Foundation of René Magritte. The footwear bore the paintings "The Lovers," "Sheherazade," and "Double Reality", each printed on the upper of a *Boston*.[162] Co-founder Humberto Leon explains that Opening Ceremony aimed to reinterpret "original brands"—"people and companies who were the masters of what they did," a category within which they placed Birkenstock.[163] Further collaborations were released in 2018, 2019, and 2021. Debuted at the brand's Spring 2018 fashion show at Disneyland, the first of these featured glittery pink and silver *Arizona* and *Boston* models. Despite difficulties in construction, the glitter styles were very successful.[164] Opening Ceremony's website crashed due to high traffic on the release of the collection. The part of the collection that Birkenstock wanted to sell through its own web store was then redirected to Opening Ceremony for sale.[165]

Meanwhile, in Germany feelers were being extended back toward SMU models. An example of this was a 2014 collaboration between Birkenstock, 55DSL, artist Aaron De La Cruz, and art magazine Arkitip. For this, De La Cruz painted a mural on the wall of 55DSL's headquarters, lining up 700 pairs of black *Monterrey* sandals underneath before beginning to paint. The result was a collection bearing unique white splatters.[166] This collaboration was one of the first of its kind for the global production team, but it resulted in stock issues as Birkenstock USA, Inc. couldn't get the classic sandal into its inventory, because the models had been used.[167] While this was one of the first steps of Birkenstock Germany into PR-related events (the whole process was filmed), the coordination required for this sort of project was not, as yet, standardized.

The Consolidation of the BIRKENSTOCK Brand

From 2017, Birkenstock's projects shifted from the schemes of international branches to carefully planned programs overseen by a centralized global management team, though space was still allotted for international diversity. As Melissa Drier of Women's Wear Daily described in an interview with CEO, Oliver Reichert,

> "Reichert didn't only rouse the giant to its feet. [He was] preparing it for a sprint, powered by a new global marketing director and international P.R. team, a growing network of worldwide offices and showrooms, unexpected line extensions, ads by Dan Tobin Smith that are both high-profile and low-key and a slew of innovative projects."[168]

The company undertook a multi-prong approach including extensive marketing campaigns, engagement with fashion gatekeeping structures, and collaboration on luxury SMU models. They consolidated their position by opening a creative space in Paris, developing an accessible luxury product line, expanding production capacities, and opening own-brand retail locations.

Birkenstock and its distributors had occasionally used PR firms, but it was at this point that the company began developing international campaigns with renowned art directors, creatives, and agencies. One of the first of these was a campaign shot by Dan Tobin Smith, a photographer known for his work with Apple, Louis Vuitton, Alexander McQueen, and Nike. Under the creative direction of studio Delerue Roppel, Smith developed campaigns for Spring/Summer (S/S) 2017, Fall/Winter (F/W) 2017, and Spring/Summer (S/S) 2018. The images depicted cropped details of classic Birkenstock footwear, showcasing their craftsmanship and presenting them as iconic.[169]

Another clever piece of marketing was launched in September 2018. The "Personality Campaign" monopolizes on the endorsement of key

274   **1963–2024** Rise to a Global Brand

cultural figures. Shot by photographer Jack Davidson, it features the diversity and lives of real Birkenstock wearers highlighting the age, patina, and usage of their footwear. The first portraits included actress Luna Picoli-Truffaut, ballet dancer Romany Pajdak, filmmaker Sean Frank, and Thomas Südhof, Nobel Laureate in the Physiology of Medicine at Stanford University, all wearing their beloved Birkenstocks. Later images from the campaign star faces from the fashion world including Grace Coddington, former creative-director-at-large of Vogue USA, iconic shoe designer Manolo Blahnik and his niece Kristina Blahnik, the CEO of the Manolo Blahnik brand.[170] Speaking about the campaign, a Birkenstock employee noted, "It was good to see people that resonate, that are culturally relevant [...]. It's more about selling an idea of who are Birkenstock wearers. Everyone. It's a democratic brand, and it's shoes that you wear for a long, long time."[171] The campaign addressed the difficulty of marketing to the diverse groups of Birkenstock wearers while acknowledging the growing importance of sustainability.[172]

Beyond the brand's own advertisements, sandals by Birkenstock were often featured in fashion magazine editorials and style suggestion pages. Industry publications such as Footwear News and Women's Wear Daily reported on company changes, advertising campaigns, and new product releases.[173] Birkenstock were also cleverly engaging with the media. In 2018, the company staged a "Global Press Factory Event," during which international fashion journalists visited the Bernstadt, Görlitz, and Dresden factories, learning about the brand, its history, production process, quality control, and products. Explaining the event, a Birkenstock News Magazine article reads, "Positive and expertly correct reports in the regions concerned are essential for the further development of international markets. Nowadays, contact between the manufacturer and the press is most often done digitally, via e-mail, or at best, by phone. Personal contacts are rare."[174] To resolve this, the company invited 30 international journalists, editors, bloggers, and influencers to travel to the Birkenstock production sites for three days.[175]

The result was a slew of articles in both fashion and general press focused on the company's heritage and production process. One of these from The Cut, written by fashion critic Cathy Horyn and accompanied with images by German fine-art and fashion photographer, Juergen Teller, details BIRKENSTOCK's rise and success from 2013 onward. Teller's photographs focus on the making of a pair of Birkenstocks in the Görlitz factory. He captures the bark employed to create the cork bases of the sandals and shoes, the glue used to attach soles, and the final products on display, detailing to the reader the hard work involved in the production process.[176] Such an emphasis on German-based, man-made production provided great support for BIRKENSTOCK's new positioning as brand of the *zeitgeist*, as did the association with Teller himself.

Birkenstock further broadened its horizons by attending key fashion weeks and fashion-focused trade fairs. These spaces allowed them to bring their new products to a broader group of customers, partners, and suppliers according to a Birkenstock trade fair magazine in 2018.[177] What Birkenstock was doing was integrating itself into a network of global fashion intermediaries who could share details about their products, values, and context with different clientele and markets. As economic geographer Mariangela Lavanga indicates in her study of fashion trade fairs, the temporary proximity provided to the fashion world by these events allows for knowledge and information sharing and the reduction of quality uncertainty. But the reputational role of the trade fairs plays even more of a role, acting as a validator for brands and producers allowed to participate and associate themselves with the events, especially those most established, such as the fashion weeks in the major global fashion capitals of Paris, New York, London, and Milan.[178]

A pivotal change for Birkenstock, a "BirkenShock," according to one Vogue.com commentator, took place on June 24, 2017 with the brand showing its first collection at Paris Men's Fashion Week.[179] Labeled by Birkenstock as a Collection Launch and Global Sales Conference, the event included a showcase and party in the Tuileries Garden within a purpose-built pavilion called The Birkenstock Greenhouse. The greenhouse featured elevated meandering pine catwalks providing guests with a view onto models' feet. The show was a massive endeavor for the company with the majority of the company's board and senior staff as well as key press representatives invited to attend.[180] And yet, CEO Oliver Reichert stated almost paradoxically in a Women's Wear Daily interview that Birkenstock was "not willing to say we're part of Paris Fashion Week, but somehow we are. We're on the schedule [...]. It's another first step for the company, to bring these guys out and say let's talk about these shoes."[181] This indicates the company's acknowledgement of the importance of the fashion industry and its product differentiation toward that market, as well as a clever approach ensuring that they did not ostracize any of their other consumers.

Pitti Uomo, an internationally renowned bi-annual menswear trade show based in Florence, provided the next opportunity for Birkenstock to "unveil its newly developed trade fair concept."[182] The Birkenstock exhibition for the 93rd fair took place in both indoor and outdoor spaces decorated with trees, shrubs, and grass at the Fortezza Basso in Florence from January 9 to 12, 2018. It included a workshop space for Munich-based collaborator, Patrik Muff, and a private breakfast for approximately 700 retail partners, editors, journalists, and influencer guests. They also premiered a short film by photographer Dan Tobin Smith. As a follow up to the launch of this collection, the brand planned pop-up windows in department stores in Italy, Japan, and Germany.[183]

Birkenstock launched their Sport Tech line at their second Pitti Uomo fair in June 2018.[184] Their attendance included a runway show featuring the mainline sandal and looks from their collaboration with American fashion designer Rick Owens.[185] The event facilitated a key press moment, and it was from here that visiting journalists and editors traveled to the Global Press Factory Event in Germany. As one internal source says, Birkenstock "used the time the press was in Florence to do a little factory on top, right after the presentation. The outcome was always press. It was event coverage. It was runway pictures—what other fashion brands are doing as well. It's just creating a magic moment."[186] While it may seem that attendance at these fairs was little more than an expense, their role as intermediaries and temporary clusters for the international decision-makers, media, producers, and buyers cannot be discounted. Birkenstock's use of these platforms placed them in a space to take advantage of media and partnership opportunities.

Along with sophisticated marketing campaigns and participation at fashion events, Birkenstock strengthened its focus on SMU collaborations. The majority of these took place with higher-level, specialized makers, craftsmen, and designers with global reputations. These linked the brand increasingly with the luxury market or popular and elite segments of the fashion industry. With the growing use of SMUs came an awareness of their benefits and of how the process ought to be standardized.[187] This resulted in regulations about what styles and materials could be used, the format of briefs, deadlines for design proposals, and the financial, marketing, and retailing relationships with collaborators.[188] This shows a move toward new luxury positioning due to the clear need to maintain control of the brand identity, while enacting a growth strategy often employed by luxury brands, co-branding.[189] The collaborations and surrounding marketing from 2017 onward were developed with partners who were completely committed to the project. As one internal source explains, "This was [the] key to success, having the partner involved saying yes to interviews, giving us, for example, [...] rooms for free for press [...] because from the beginning it was like one plus one has to equal three."[190] Both partners had to be financially committed and provide the manpower to support the collaboration and make it a success.[191] As Chief Sales Officer Klaus Baumann highlights, an important role is played by strategy: "Before doing a collaboration, maybe you should think if it makes sense for us to do a new *Arizona*."[192] He explains, "We are matching two worlds because our entrance to the market is different than others. [At] the end of the day, both sides are gaining something," but this, in turn, "opened the credibility for those clients also to buy into the main line."[193]

In 2017, German-led collaborations accelerated with a traveling retail experiment.[194] It was, in essence, a Birkenstock pop-up shop in a shipping container that traveled the globe, linking into SMU projects with designers and fashion retail locations. Dubbed the "Birkenstock Box," this marketing concept was designed by Berlin architecture and design firm Gonzalez Haase AAS and traveled within Berlin and then to Milan, New York, and Los Angeles.[195] According to an internal source, "The Birkenstock Box concept was really a starting point also when Birkenstock hired PR agencies, were investing more in teams and [...] realized that you can create nice stories by collaborating together with creatives and designers that are themselves wearing the Birkenstock."[196] The Box's first stop was outside the renowned Berlin concept store of Andreas Murkudis. Murkudis and the architects had previously worked together to design his retail locations, so when he and his brother, Kostas Murkudis, began collaborating with Birkenstock on an SMU, they made the connection with the Gonzalez Haase founders to create the space that would exhibit their sandals.[197]

The Box was designed to mirror the Murkudis shop aesthetics while introducing cork materials that would relay the DNA of the Birkenstock brand.[198] It opened for Berlin Fashion Week, exhibiting not only a hand-picked selection of Murkudis's favorite Birkenstocks but also his limited-edition line of *Arizonas*. The Box, and its linking to Murkudis's shop, allowed customers to pair sandals with fashionable clothing items. What was valuable was that it acted as Birkenstock's own space, providing an advertising and marketing opportunity that would not have been possible with a pop-up inside the store. To celebrate the collaboration, Birkenstock and Murkudis arranged events for fashion figures, guests, and press. Birkenstock also created a microsite with information and interviews with the collaborators which was extended at each new Box location.[199]

The Box then traveled to New York for a project with department store Barneys. The initial plan was to place it on Fifth Avenue, outside of Barneys flagship store. This proved impossible, so Birkenstock rented a space in Manhattan's Meatpacking district, opening a pop-up store and placing The Box outside.[200] Situated across from the Whitney Museum of American Art, The Box featured pieces co-developed with Barneys New York creative director Matthew Mazzucca who designed its interior. The pop-up, Birkenstock's first own-brand store in the United States, included cork, oak, and leather elements and design pieces by Hella Jongherius Polder, Jasper Morrison, and Alvar Aalto, drawing parallels between revered designers and the products on display. To continue to create traffic in the area, Birkenstock partnered with the Whitney to sponsor their Whitney Art Party event, which brought together New York's cultural elite.[201]

The third location was Piazza XXV Aprile in Milan during Milan Fashion Week in September 2017 for a collaboration with 10 Corso Como, the concept store of ex-Vogue and Elle Italia editor-in-chief, Carla Sozzani. The Box, along with six pairs of SMU *Arizona* sandals, was designed to match the aesthetic of the Milanese shop by American artist and partner of Sozzani, Kris Ruhs. Along with the pop-up, an event—the "10 Corso Como x Birkenstock" evening—was held, bringing together Oliver Reichert with Milan's fashion elite.[202] In response to a query about the collaboration in which Fashion Network described BIRKENSTOCK as the "least 'fashion' of all the brands," Sozzani justified the collaboration by saying, "It is fashion that was inspired by Birkenstock and not the other way around. Like Hermès, it is a brand that has always shown unerring, foolproof stability."[203]

Landing next outside of Rick Owen's Los Angeles boutique in April 2018, The Box showcased 13 footwear and three legwear pieces within an interior designed by Owens himself.[204] This partnership, facilitated by the family-owned nature of both companies and their strong fan bases, was a starting point for bigger collaborations. One Birkenstock employee described the whole Box campaign, and specifically the Rick Owens aspect of it, as "a totally new level for Birkenstock," with the shoes priced in a higher range for the company as well.[205] The SMU Birkenstocks were also featured in Owens's Spring/Summer (S/S) 2019 Ready to Wear and Menswear fashion shows in Paris, a pop-up was organized at Parisian department store Le Bon Marché, and some of the Birkenstock team traveled to China with Owens's partner Michele Lamy for pop-up events in collaboration with multi-brand retailer I. T.[206] What we can clearly see here is a well-constructed PR campaign linking not only luxury retail locations with BIRKENSTOCK but also cultural institutions and figures of the cultural elite. It allowed for the sharing of cultural capital, creating a buzz around Birkenstock's collaborative and more general products.

Beyond The Box, a wealth of SMU projects were organized, including a partnership with Marie-Louise Sciò, CEO and creative director of Pellicano Group and Hotel Il Pellicano. The sandals, with uppers of silk and raffia as well as suede, leather, and EVA, responded to her desire to create an elevated Birkenstock that could transition from day to night wear.[207] The collection was entitled "Il Dolce Far Niente," a phrase meaning "the art of doing nothing" in Italian, evoking the feel of the hotel.[208] Three events were linked to its release; a private breakfast preview, a press trip with fashion editors to Il Pellicano in April 2019 in collaboration with retailer Matchesfashion.com, and a pop-up at the newly opened Galeries Lafayette luxury department store on the Champs-Elysées.[209]

A different relationship was created with British Art School, Central Saint Martins (CSM) of the University of the Arts London, and its BA Fashion Communication, Fashion History and Theory, and MA Fashion Design students. Initially intended to last six months, the two-year project was not just based around the development of new footwear, but also around the recognition of the company's heritage as a fashion-proximate brand. It included research into the brand's history across its international locations and the creation of a database of fashion editorials to be included in the brand's archive. This information was used to brief the design students who proposed new Birkenstock styles.[210] Of the 30 original designs, four by students Alex Wolfe, Saskia Lenaerts, Alecsander Rothschild, and Ding Yun Zhang (the *Bukarest*, the *Cosy*, the *Terra*, and the *Rotterdam Moto Boot*) were selected for production along with a redeveloped version of the *Tallahassee* sandal.[211] The resulting collection was released online and in select retail locations in March 2021.[212] CSM Professor Alistair O'Neill calls this project brave of Birkenstock as "they just had no idea what they were going to get when they were going to work with us. That's to their great credit, I think."[213]

Cementing their foothold in fashion and its international capital in early 2019, Birkenstock opened a Global Paris Office on the Rue Saint-Honoré. The space was conceived as an innovation incubator and the home of their new luxury collection Birkenstock 1774. The intent was not to turn BIRKENSTOCK purely into a fashion brand but rather to capture "the city's 'global creative energy,'" according to Reichert, while also offering the brand a showroom.[214] Paris, Birkenstock staff realized, was the location of "basically all our partners, the brands we're working with, press, buyers, even creatives [...] photographers, stylists."[215] The higher-end diffusion line, 1774, was launched in 2020, "marking its evolution from a practical shoe brand into one offering luxury status

Fig. 55: Birkenstock's new creativity in the 21st century — "1774" developed its own creations.

symbols," according to The Financial Times.[216] Their first collection was made in-house while the second was created in collaboration with Austrian stylist Suzanne Koller.[217] To Birkenstock's Chief Sales Officer, 1774 is a collection that reinterprets Birkenstock's iconic products, but only accounts for a tiny part of the brand's total business, "say it's 1% of the business max."[218] CEO Reichert says that the range is a tool to stop Birkenstock from becoming insular as a heritage firm and to imbue it with new energy by inviting "influential and creative people" to engage with the products, bringing "their view and interpretation of the brand."[219] It's interesting that some Birkenstock retailers may not even know what 1774 is, and are not offered the products, as they are reserved for specific locations.[220] This shows that while BIRKENSTOCK places itself in the field of fashion and luxury, the mainstay of its business remain its more traditional models.

Beyond marketing, PR, and design moves that brought the brand toward the fashion and luxury sectors, Birkenstock streamlined its production capacities and expanded its businesses. In addition to the production processes, international distribution and retail sales were now integrated. Birkenstock entered new markets and strengthened its position in the markets in which it was already active. While the relationship continued with the Sanyei Corporation, now called Benexy, in 2016, a Japanese subsidiary of the German company was set up to manage and market the brand. The now director of Benexy, Yasuyuki Umino, was sent to Germany for two and a half years with the aim of stabilizing operational problems. A shift was also made from whole-sale to retail, with the firm opening further stores including one in the Tokyu Plaza vertical mall in Tokyo's luxury focused Ginza District.[221] In 2017, Birkenstock also established direct sales, opening an office in Tokyo to account for the importance and needs of its Japanese market.[222] This included the refocusing, strengthening and supporting of relation-ships with both Seed Corporation and Benexy, along with the hunt for new partners as Birkenstock "aspire[d] to stronger product and market segmentation at the point of sale."[223]

Changes were also made in the British market, with Birkenstock launching their online retail site in April 2017, opening their own London sales office and showroom, and taking over distribution later in the year. In November, the first company-owned store was opened at 48 Neal Street.[224] Explaining the choice, the UK country manager wrote that the company "has recognized that connecting with the end consumer is essential to tell the Birkenstock story and that the direct connection with retailers in the UK was key to be able to meet consumer demand." He stated that the UK distributor, Central Trade, had taken a traditional approach, leading the BIRKENSTOCK brand to have "no major segmentation in the market."[225] At this point, the brand also took over direct distribution in Denmark and opened their online store to 19 countries beyond the already accessible European and US markets. This complemented the range of in-store products offered, "taking a consist-ent step towards being closer to its customers."[226]

In the United States, own-brand stores were opened in New York and Venice Beach, California, and in 2019 the company took over sales of their products in Switzerland and expanded into the Mexican market.[227] By this point, according to Fashion Network, Birkenstock was retailing its products in 90 countries, across five continents with eight shops in Germany alone. It had sales offices in the United States, Brazil, China, Hong Kong, Japan, Denmark, Slovakia, Spain, the UK, and the UAE.[228] As journalist Jonathan Heaf explained in the Financial Times, increased control of production, distribution, and retailing allowed the company to "react to growing or shrinking markets, control and trademark each part of the shoe-making process, and protect its heritage as a German company."[229]

A New Era for a World Brand

With the COVID-19 pandemic and global lockdowns, Birkenstock's popularity exploded. Even before, in the financial year finishing in September 2019, the Financial Times reported that Birkenstock retailed 23.8 million pairs of shoes and "saw an 11 per cent increase in sales to €721.5 mn."[230] The growth of work-from-home culture and the movement of consumers to the great outdoors brought about increased searches for Birkenstocks online.[231] According to British shopping platform Lyst, the shearling-lined *Boston* was the "second hottest women's product of 2020 with searches for the style jumping 367 per cent, compared with the same period in 2019."[232] One member of the Paris office staff cites the pandemic as a key driver of Birkenstock's recent popularity, describing the footwear as not only stylish and comfortable but also suited to home and outdoor wear.[233] Footwear News lauded Birkenstock as the "Brand of the Year" in December 2020 at their first virtual achievement awards, while Tacey Powers of American department store Nordstrom described Birkenstock's success as resulting from it being "a brand consumers can trust in what otherwise has been a really hard year."[234] The migration of office workers into the home brought about a significant casualization of the working wardrobe, at least for employees not in managing positions.[235] It was almost a return to Birkenstock's era as *Hausschuhe*—house shoes or slippers—but, this time, fashionable ones.

Part of Birkenstock's success during the pandemic period was undoubtedly their control over their own production. As Oliver Reichert told the Financial Times, "We don't need to source anything, and we didn't have worries about the impact on the global supply chain—everything we own can be moved around using trucks."[236] While the effects of COVID-19 regulations on production capacities and delivery dates as well as concern about the leather tanneries in Italy played a role, and the company did close down its production sites, it still had a very successful year.[237]

In 2021, the formation of a strategic partnership catalyzed Birkenstock's expansion strategy and touched the luxury sector. Alex and Christian Birkenstock sold a majority stake of the firm to L Catterton, a leading consumer-goods-focused growth investor, and the affiliated Financière Agache, the family holding company of Bernard Arnault, CEO of luxury goods conglomerate LVMH Moët Hennessy Louis Vuitton.[238] Rumors of a partnership and the final amount of the sale had been the subject of much speculation, with Women's Wear Daily predicting in February 2021 that the talks might drive the brand toward the center of luxury.[239] The purpose of this move? According to Birkenstock, it was considered the "next logical step" to expand markets into India and China, while allowing the firm to bolster its positioning in Europe, the United States, and online. It took place at the time of a "comprehensive investment offensive," aimed to better support the company's growth through the construction of a new production site and the strengthening of others across Germany.[240] Oliver Reichert stated that the partnership would allow the brand to achieve its growth ambitions through knowledge sharing and excellent international market access. Yet Reichert was clear that the change would not shake the brand's core, emphasizing that "as long as I'm here, we will never dilute the brand equity. We will never dilute quality nor functionality. No way. And the conversation about continuing our manufacturing in Germany was an easy one to have with the investors because I chose them."[241] Publicly, Bernard Arnault commented on the long heritage of the BIRKENSTOCK brand and its iconic nature as a driver for the agreement.[242]

The years 2020 and 2021 also brought about a broad range of collaborations with luxury fashion, ready-to-wear, and streetwear brands, each of which have a strong reputation and following. These included partnerships with Rick Owens, Proenza Schouler, Kith, and Stüssy as well as new partnerships with German fashion designer Jil Sander and British brand Toogood.[243] The formation of the strategic partnership may have supported two collaborations with pinnacle luxury brands. The first of these was with LVMH-owned Christian Dior and its Dior Homme creative director, Kim Jones, who adapted the historical *Milano* and *Tokio* styles, debuting them on the catwalk at Paris Fashion Week in January 2022.[244] The second, including velvet-and-leather *Arizona* and *Boston* models with crystal buckles, was with previous partner from the Personality Campaign, shoe designer Manolo Blahnik.[245]

Where Next for Birkenstock?

The history of Birkenstock's relationship with the fashion and luxury industries is most definitely a convoluted one. The company has shifted from being an outsider of fashion appropriated by designers in the 80s and 90s to become a broad-based brand that reaches into the luxury end of the fashion world. Its fashion forays were brought about by international distributors in their attempts to find new markets and fostered by co-branding exercises which lacked a true understanding of the nature of fashion products and the strategies required to retail them. While attempts by Birkenstock's international distributors found success in regional markets, Birkenstock's move into fashion and luxury began later, in the 2010s, facilitated by changes in structure and strategy. These approaches, introduced by the firm's new management, enabled the company to shift its positioning and brought greater control into its production, distribution, and retailing. The creation of relationships with intermediaries and gatekeepers in the fashion and luxury segments supported such moves. While waves of BIRKENSTOCK popularity have ebbed and flowed, the sandals have grown to become not only democratic products recognized for their orthopedic benefits but also fashionable goods. Where the company—Oliver Reichert's awakened giant, led by its strategic partnerships, iconic products, production developments, and retail changes—will head in the coming years is unclear. Nonetheless, it seems to have successfully maintained its positioning as a globally recognized firm focused on foot health, while growing into a fashionable brand.

FROM HILARIOUS HIPPIES TO HAIR-RAISING HORROR AND HIGH FASHION: 30 YEARS OF BIRKENSTOCKS IN FILM

BY EMILY BRAYSHAW

In 2022, video-on-demand streaming company Netflix released the dark teen comedy *Do Revenge*, in which the protagonist, Drea, calls Carissa Jones, the keeper of the school garden and leader of the farm kids' clique, a "human Birkenstock."[1] The film centers on the friendship forged between teen queen Drea and new girl Eleanor, when they team up to bring down each other's tormentors: Drea wants to punish her ex, Max, for publishing her sex tape and ruining her; Eleanor wants to take down Carissa for allegedly spreading rumors at camp when she was 13 that she was a lesbian predator. Carissa, as it turns out, is actually the lesbian. The film's director Jennifer Kaytin Robinson, producer Peter Cron, and costume designer Alana Morshead deliberately sought to blend the visual campness, satire, and soundtrack nostalgia of predecessor teen movies—such as *Clueless* (1995) and the dark comedy *Heathers* (1989)[2]—with "wholly contemporary tastes and issues" in music and fashion to reflect the diversity of today's youth.[3]

Stutesman notes that costume in film "is constructed to make the viewer feel a targeted emotion. Costume reveals meaning by riffing on meaning that culture assigns to clothes."[4] By using the line "human Birkenstock," as well as two subtle instances of Birkenstocks in the costuming of *Do Revenge*, Kaytin Robinson and Morshead expanded this nostalgic mood by referencing the tropes of Birkenstock imagery in film over the last 30 years, including teen comedies, romcoms, political satires, and horror.

These film tropes themselves build upon a longer lineage of the Birkenstock dating back to 60s American hippie counterculture, when Birkenstocks emerged as a popular shoe. They have since become a comedic visual shorthand for a hippie in popular culture, which is reflected in the Birkenstock-wearing characters that emerged in film in the 90s, such as the aging hippie, the slacker, grunge kid, stoner, backpacker, eco-terrorist, lesbian, and feminist. While Birkenstocks are often used in caricature, their countercultural meaning can also work to position film characters sympathetically as courageous social outsiders. This chapter considers the meanings that the English-speaking world has ascribed to Birkenstocks over the last 50 years—from their establishment in America as a countercultural symbol to their transformation into a contemporary icon of fashion—and looks at how these meanings have been used in film to amuse and terrify audiences since the mid-90s.

The Birth of the Birkenstock Hippie

The hippie movement emerged in the mid-60s in America, in the Haight-Ashbury district of San Francisco, as a generational youth counterculture responding to the country's massive social and political upheavals. Counterculture is a "sociopolitical term indicating a point of dissent between dominant or mainstream ideologies and alternative value systems, so creating a collective voice that can be considered a significant minority."[5] This dissent is voiced through music, art, protest, lifestyles, and dress practices. In 1966, hippies "became national figures [...] when they were beaten during protests they held against the curfews on Hollywood's Sunset Strip."[6] Clothing was integral to hippie counterculture from the start as a material expression of protest, signaling a direct opposition to mainstream American values in a mixture of Hindu patterns, psychedelic references, and tie-dye with cowboy boots, leather-fringed vests, long strings of beads and long hair, sunglasses and bell-bottomed jeans, and loose, flowing garments.[7]

The capricious, ludic nature, scruffy appearance, transient lifestyle, and vivid, kaleidoscopic clothing of the hippie recalled the carnivalesque costumes of the early 20th century deployed in the "advancement of radical agendas by ground-breaking visual artists who used it to embody their rebellion against the status quo."[8] This hippie clothing also included Birkenstocks, which first went on sale in health-food stores in California, at the end of the 60s.

American 70s hippie culture embraced BIRKENSTOCK's casual unisex appeal and the shoe brand's "core values of quality and comfort over fashion, high-quality craftsmanship, environmentally friendly materials, and long-lasting products."[9] Birkenstocks were also quickly adopted by readers of the Whole Earth Catalog, the product catalog and American counterculture magazine published by Stewart Brand several times a year between 1968 and 1972 and occasionally thereafter until 1998. Birkenstocks have been "a favorite with Whole Earth customers and staff for most of our 51 years. [...] The first Birkenstock style to make it big in the US was the Arizona. Once considered an essential identifying mark for an entire generation."[10]

The use of Birkenstocks as a visual shorthand for a hippie in comedy is deeply rooted in American counterculture. The shoe regularly appeared in the underground comix movement that ran concurrently with the publication of the Whole Earth Catalog between 1968 and 1975. These underground comic books focused on subjects central to the hippie movement—namely, politics, and sex, drugs, and rock 'n' roll—and were distributed mainly through "head shops" (shops selling cannabis-related paraphernalia). In May 1968, Gilbert Shelton, who just one year later cofounded Rip Off Press, created the Fabulous Furry Freak Brothers. The story of a trio of stoner losers whose lives—which revolved around scoring and enjoying drugs—presented a critique of the American establishment while satirizing the hippie counterculture itself. By recording, analyzing, and interpreting clothing, cartoonists provide invaluable testimony to the culture, manners, and vision of the times in which they live.[11] Shelton's character Phineas T. Phreak is the smartest of the three, a stereotypical, hairy, left-wing radical who is often illustrated wearing overalls and *Arizona* Birkenstock-style shoes. The stereotype continued in American popular culture with the cartoonist and founder of countercultural publication "Zap Comix," Robert Crumb, who contributed to the satirical stereotype of the Birkenstock hippie. Although the United States "counterculture movement came to an end when the [Vietnam] war did in 1975, the media kept the hippie image alive, albeit with shallow depictions."[12] In the early 80s, Crumb joined the local environmental newspaper Winds of Change in Davis, Northern California, as art director, and during his tenure he created a Birkenstock-hippie comic figure as an advertisement for the town's shop, Birkenstock Plus.

Crumb's cartoons also appeared in a later magazine of the Whole Earth Company, Co-Evolution Quarterly, inviting controversy in 1982 when reader Susie Pierce wrote in to protest Crumb's sexism and cynical critiques of the utopianism of the magazine's "eco-freak" readership, who, she felt, labored harder than Crumb to protect the environment:

> "People who read *CQ* are types who hop out of bed an hour early in the morning so that we can shoulder our Smith and Hawken pitchforks and rush out to our organic gardens to get in some double digging before breakfast. Or we slip into our bandanas and Birkenstocks and trudge 3 miles to the nearest co-op to bring back our bulk soybeans in a canvas shopping bag. [...] I picture all of us eco-freaks patiently pulling the world wagon, moving pretty well considering the steepness of the uphill slope, and there's Crumb, sitting up on the wagon, cracking the whip and hollering 'Faster! Faster!' Now if Crumb really wants action, why doesn't he get his ass going and help pull?"[13]

Crumb responded in early 1983 by sending Pierce a cartoon of a sturdy, hairy-legged woman in Birkenstocks and bib overalls pulling a wagon that carried the world uphill to "Ecotopia" while being poked in the backside by Crumb with a Smith and Hawken pitchfork.

As with Crumb's portrayal of Pierce, Birkenstocks are "stereotypically representative of a granola-crunchy, bohemian individual, if not optimistic naivete," which is still commonly used as a stock character to represent hippies in film.[14] Birkenstock's historical reputation as an ugly shoe in America has further contributed to the construction of the hippie stock character in film as a figure of ridicule set against the mainstream. It is through this ludic costuming that, as Barbieri writes, "the audience meets its own 'Other', the outsider, in a revelatory moment of recognition and laughter in the face of the solitary performer."[15] From the 90s, Crumb's style of Birkenstock hippie migrated to film in teen comedies as designers tapped into the Generation X grunge aesthetic that included Birkenstocks and ironically drew on elements of their parents' 70s countercultural dress.

From Woodstock to Laughing Stocks

The Stoned Age (1994) follows the adventures of two young stoners, Hubbs and Joe, who cruise around Los Angeles on a Saturday night in 1978 looking for fun.[16] They locate a house where it is said there are young women who are keen to party. There they meet the beautiful Lanie, who sends them to buy alcohol with the promise of sex when they return, but when they get back, the front door is opened by Lanie's jaded hippie friend, Jill, and Lanie is nowhere in sight. The comic contrast between Jill and Lanie is emphasized by how the women are initially presented.

Upon Lanie's opening the door, the camera moves up her body, first showing her cowboy boots, her bare legs and Daisy Duke cut-off denim shorts, then showing her bare mid-riff with cropped shirt and finally beautiful face and long blonde hair. Hubbs and Joe, it appears, are about to get lucky with a woman who looks like the perfect rock-and-roll groupie. In contrast, the tilt shot up Jill's body when she answers the door starts with her feet in *Arizona* Birkenstocks and socks and shows her modestly dressed in long flared jeans, a Mexican surfer Baja-style hoodie, and a sour expression. In this instance, Birkenstocks are a key costuming component within a binary opposition "between the deviant feminist and the ideal woman" in popular film.[17] This includes Crumb's problematic cartoon depictions of sexualized hippie feminists who are reduced to a laughing stock.

The dialogue of *The Stoned Age* also reveals the highly sexist and homophobic mores at play in 90s American society. It is evident from the presentation of Jill as a hippie feminist stereotype that the audience is supposed to laugh at, while commiserating with Hubbs and Joe: the sexy groupie has been replaced by an uptight, and possibly lesbian hippie, and they won't be getting laid.

The low budget of *The Stoned Age* meant that the costuming was at times anachronistic and based on Californian elements of 90s surfer and grunge dress that were popular and easily available for purchase. This dress shared many material and semiotic characteristics with 70s hippie clothing, including tie-dye and Birkenstocks and a "combination of modesty and androgyny" in dress, situating Jill in both eras. The comedy of the scene relies on the temporal disjunction of an outdated and outmoded style of dress that jars with contemporary mainstream femininity, but which nonetheless existed as a signifier of contemporary grunge style.

This simultaneous location of character in the 90s and the 70s is also evident in the character of Travis Birkenstock, a kind but clumsy stoner, skater, and slacker in the teen comedy, *Clueless* (1995). Written and directed by Amy Heckerling, *Clueless* is set in a wealthy Beverly Hills high school and is a loosely postmodern interpretation of Jane Austen's novel *Emma* (1815). Cher is the clueless, kind-hearted heroine who decides to give back to the community by taking the "clueless" new girl at school, Tai Frasier, under her wing. Cher and her best friend Dionne give Tai a makeover to quash the attraction between Tai and Travis, improve Tai's social currency, and set her up with popular Elton.[18] The trope of the

Birkenstock hippie and slacker was so prevalent in mid-90s America that Travis, despite being the heir to the Birkenstock fortune, does not wear Birkenstocks, and neither are they shown in the film; rather, the joke is as good-natured as Travis himself. Travis, like Birkenstocks, is ultimately reliable, comfortable, solid, and comforting, while the handsome Elton is a cad.

The comedy effect of Birkenstocks and the dual location of character in the past and present is expanded in the mockumentary comedy *A Mighty Wind* (2003) about a concert in 2003 in which three fabricated folk-music bands from the 60s reunite for the first time in decades for a television performance to honor the fictional folk-music producer Irving Steinbloom.[19] The film parodies the American folk music of the 60s, which was tied to the hippie movement, and features the character of Mark Shubb, an aging hippie who plays bass in the trio The Folksmen. Shubb's trio first met at the University of Vermont in the early 60s, a region in the United States that by the late-70s had developed a reputation for its "hippie enclaves [...], 'artsy' towns and organic farms."[20] The first time the audience sees Shubb, he is wearing khaki shorts, a collarless shirt with a geometric Native American–style motif, a blue cap hiding his bald spot, and *Arizona* Birkenstocks with white socks. The key to this Birkenstock joke is that Shubb is an old hippie who never moved on; his style, like his Birkenstocks, has fossilized. One of the features of the hippie movement was its youthfulness, with philosophies such as "Never Trust a Person over 30," and its distrust of the "adults" who were running the country. The Birkenstock joke is continued throughout the film, and even though The Folksmen are dressed in black tie at the reunion concert, Shubb wears his with *Arizonas* and socks.

Another aging Birkenstock hippie in film played for laughs is the character of Senator Ortolan Finistirre in the satire *Thank You for Smoking* (2006).[21] Finistirre is an anti-smoking, environmentalist Democrat senator from Vermont, who is now part of the establishment that the hippies mistrusted, and his dress is used to emphasize how his liberal earnestness and lack of empathy for his employees position him as a hypocrite and a laughing stock. Finistirre's first costume comprises a tweed suit in green tones, a pale-green check shirt with button-down collar and a tie in blues, forest greens, and russet browns with pictures of pheasants on it, the semiotics of which point to the so-called New England "Trad" style, which attempts to maintain a conservative look without appearing dated. A cutaway shot to Finistirre's *Arizona* Birkenstocks with white socks, however, transforms Trad style into a kind of clown outfit, transmitting messages about his hypocrisy and "abuse of power."[22] The film's director, Jason Reitman, told the press in 2006, "Nothing says, 'I want to tell you how to live your life' more than Birkenstocks. [...] The visual registers immediately. There's something about the shoe that is universally understood that makes it so funny."[23] The sandals, he noted, were "emblems of liberal do-gooderness [...] and the senator [...] wants to 'regulate the world.'"[24] The association of Vermont with Birkenstock-wearing hippies was so firmly established in American popular culture by 2006 that a senior executive at Birkenstock at the time, said of Finistirre, "He's wearing the Vermont costume."[25] Indeed, by 2011, Vermont was also home to 17 Birkenstock dealers, or one per 36,650 residents.[26] Finistirre's Birkenstocks locate him within America's countercultural past and within a present in which he upholds the status quo and has become a joke in the process.

A similar comedic device is employed in the costuming of the lead character, Lucy Kelson, in the romantic comedy *Two Weeks Notice* (2002).[27] Kelson is an earnest environmental activist and graduate from Harvard Law School who specializes in historic preservation, environmental law, and pro bono causes in New York City. Her costume in the opening scenes includes a hippie-style long cotton skirt with an Indian block print and *Milano* Birkenstocks, establishing her as a person with countercultural roots who seeks to do good and to hold those who seek to abuse power to account. In the opening scene, Kelson is placed in a comic situation that echoes the slapstick of early modernist silent cinema; she is wearing Birkenstocks and doggedly clinging to a gigantic wrecking ball in a bid to save a historic building that is scheduled for demolition by the Wade Corporation. Kelson's Birkenstocks continue to be the butt of jokes throughout the film to the extent that the handsome billionaire property developer and her love interest, Wade Corporation's CEO George Wade, accuses her of being so earnest and morally upright that "other guys bolted as fast as their Birkenstocks could carry them."[28] By the end of the film, however, Kelson has swapped her Birkenstocks and radical activism for high heels, transforming herself into an ideal woman whose reward is to live happily ever after with Wade.

Breaking Away

Birkenstocks in comedies in the late 90s and into the 2000s also began to signal a character's desire to break away from the pressures of everyday life. In *Notting Hill* (1999), for example, the American movie star Anna Scott wears *Boston* Birkenstocks and a long paisley skirt at the end of the film while relaxing in a London park with love interest William Thacker, signaling that she has left the high-pressure, glamorous world of Hollywood to live a more simple life.[29] In *Couples Retreat* (2009), Jason Bateman and Kristen Bell play Jason and Cynthia Smith, a troubled couple who to go to a couples retreat at a tropical resort to repair their marriage.[30] Bateman noted:

> "Jason and Cynthia are two people thoroughly convinced that the best way they can get through life is with deep analysis, pragmatic responsible decisions, and by staying within the lines marked by rules. Ultimately, I think it has all contributed to a very stagnant relationship that has lost a lot of its spontaneity, so they need to loosen up before they decide to do anything about it."[31]

The tropical retreat offers alternative, spiritual marriage therapies and Jason Smith's wearing Birkenstocks at the resort, including in the sauna, is both practical and signals that he is willing to try anything, including stripping therapy and yoga, to save his marriage.

The stock character of the Birkenstock hippie in comedies continued into the 2010s, and their presence signaled a break for the protagonists in *Wanderlust* (2012), in which George and his wife, Linda, leave their over-stressed life in Manhattan and join the commune they find themselves in when their car breaks down.[32] The aging hippie trope is also used in the costuming for the character Rob Hilliard in *Grown Ups* (2010).[33] Hilliard's break comes because he realizes, after three failed marriages, that he needs to change his behavior. One of Hilliard's key comedic moments that leads to his emotional breakthrough is a slapstick scene in which he wears *Milano* Birkenstocks, a green-striped, smock-style shirt, a long string of wooden beads, and beige cargo shorts. During the scene, Hilliard's friends accidentally shoot him in the foot with an arrow and the camera moves to a close-up of the arrow piercing his Birkenstock-clad foot, providing the laughs.

Yet Birkenstocks were also used in the cinema of the 2010s to emphasize the power and influence that American counterculture has had on the world since the mid-60s. Nowhere in film is this clearer than in the biopic *Jobs* (2013) about the pioneer of the personal computer revolution and the founder of Apple, Steve Jobs (1955–2011).[34] It has been said that no one was more influenced or inspired by Stewart Brand than Jobs, who credited Brand with being one of the most creative agents of change in the late 20th century. *Jobs* tells the story of Steve Jobs's life and career, from his early days in the mid-70s, when he dropped out of college and established Apple, to the launch of the iPod in 2001. *Arizonas* were a foundational part of Jobs's daily wardrobe throughout his life, and he wore them at many pivotal moments in Apple's history. Jobs's former girlfriend, Chrisann Brennan said that he even wore them in winter: "The sandals were part of his simple side. They were his uniform."[35] As Drake Stutesman has written in the context of stage and film, costuming allows the character "to be distinctive."[36] In the film, Birkenstocks marked Jobs as a distinctive "other" from the American mainstream, contributing to the mythos of Jobs as a genius who broke the rules and changed the world.

Birkenstocks and Horror

The use of Birkenstocks in costuming in horror and thriller films since 2000 to situate a character as "other" can also signal a more sinister break from the mainstream. Horror and thriller genres often employ a seductive mixture of attraction, desire, nostalgia, and comedy to break the anxiety created by fear and repulsion. Birkenstocks' association with counterculture, nostalgia, and comedy in the history of film mean they can act as a tool to break tensions and to "other" a character, as in the example of Clare Spencer in *What Lies Beneath* (2000), an American supernatural horror film set in a lake house in Vermont.[37] The protagonists, Norman and Clare Spencer, are a seemingly happily married couple until Clare uncovers a terrible secret: a young woman Norman had an affair with and murdered in their house, has returned as a vengeful ghost who seeks retribution. Clare is portrayed as a beautiful yet nervous, irrational, nostalgic, and lonely trophy wife who suffered a violent accident. Early in the film, she wears comfortable clothes and Birkenstocks while looking at old photographs and memorabilia from her youth and her time studying cello at Juilliard. Clare also has a hippie friend who believes in "psychic wellness" and brings her mushroom tea. Norman, conversely, is a prominent scientist and academic who was born into wealthy, elite Vermont society. He kills the young woman to preserve his prestigious social and academic positions and uses a complex, twisted logic to rationalize and justify his actions. As Stutesman has observed, food or clothing can recall the past in an instant, through their materiality, as "a sudden physical presence, representing another elusive presence [...] that transforms 'everything else.'"[38] Here, mushroom tea and Birkenstocks are used to cement Clare as an outsider from Vermont's elites, despite her marriage to Norman, and to align her with

Vermont's hippie counterculture, indicating that, perhaps, the elusive presence of the ghost is real and that she is not crazy. Psychological issues attached to breaking from mainstream society are also examined in *The East* (2013), in which a young, conservative Christian woman called Jane Owen is assigned by her boss, Sharon, at the private security consulting firm Hiller Brood to go undercover.[39] Jane's assignment is to infiltrate an eco-terrorist organization called The East because the group has been responsible for violent attacks against corporate leaders and is threatening two more in acts of retribution for ecological crimes. Upon telling Jane that she has the job, Sharon hands her a bright-blue, gift-wrapped box, which contains a pair of brand-new Birkenstocks. The shoes are used here as an anti-establishment symbol that contrasts with Jane's corporate outfit of a gray suit and high heels and indicates her new role as an anti-capitalist freegan and environmental activist.[40]

My own work in film saw me costume a character in Birkenstock-style shoes to draw on the comedic and nostalgic conventions at work within the postmodern gothic horror *Oil on Canvas* (2024).[41] The film is set in a high school and features the character Verena, an art teacher for whom everything is copacetic until she breaks down following her exposure to an unseen evil that lurks beneath the surface of a student's painting. The postmodern gothic genre ransacks "an imaginary museum of the past to create a visual mirage of stereotypes that abandon any thinking of future change" in order to create an indeterminate terror.[42] Comedy is also a feature of the postmodern gothic genre as it offers a break from tension. I wanted Verena to be a comic figure because there "is doubt, unease and horror codified in bathos—in staggeringly banal mechanisms of exaggerations."[43] I deliberately exaggerated the proportions and colors of Verena's costume, including the use of many necklaces and bangles and white 'Fakenstocks', to make her appear almost clown-like and to draw on the nostalgia of hippie counterculture and the history of misrepresentation and jokes about hippies. This visual joke of the stereotypical hippie art teacher offered the audience a moment of comic relief that was quickly snatched away as Verena's dark, troubled side is revealed.

Birkenstocks in *The Beach* (2000) and *Wolf Creek* (2005) are used in the costuming of young backpacker support characters and protagonists alike, simultaneously "othering" them and associating them with the comfort, freedom, and traveling lifestyle of the shoe.[44] In *The Beach* (2000), Richard, a young American seeking adventure, stays in a cheap, dirty backpacker hostel in Bangkok, where he meets a young French couple, Françoise and Étienne. Richard then meets the disturbed Daffy, who tells him of a pristine, uninhabited island with a beautiful hidden beach. Daffy explains that he settled there in secret several years earlier, but difficulties arose and he left. Daffy kills himself, leaving Richard a map to the island. Richard convinces Françoise and Étienne to accompany him there. Étienne is the Birkenstock-wearing traveler, the young European hippie wanting more from life than an office job and a mortgage. The trio make it to the idyllic beach and discover a commune there, which, although initially seemingly utopian, soon reveals its darker side as the sick and the weak are denied treatment and an uneasy alliance with the island's Thai drug farmers is maintained so that the beach, and the commune, can remain a secret. *Wolf Creek* (2005) is a text-book slasher film in which three backpackers find themselves taken captive and subsequently hunted in the Australian outback by Mick Taylor, a sadistic, psychopathic, xenophobic serial killer. The film, which is loosely based on true events, is set in remote Western Australia in 1999 and centers on two British tourists, Liz Hunter and Kristy Earl, who are backpacking across Australia with Ben Mitchell, their Australian friend. The early scenes of *Wolf Creek* show Liz and Kristy at a pool party in their backpacker hostel in Broome, with close up shots of their Birkenstocks illustrating their identities as travelers looking for freedom and adventure. The Birkenstocks also underscore Taylor's xenophobia, "othering" Liz and Kristy as outsiders because at the time the film was made, rural Australians did not generally wear Birkenstocks. In both films, Birkenstocks in the costuming allude to the presence of evil that will ultimately transform the young travelers' dream holidays into a nightmare.

The Revenge of the Birkenstock

Not every Birkenstock-costumed character, however, has been the subject of ridicule or horror in film; Birkenstocks have also been used to point respectfully to a character's sexuality. In *Something's Gotta Give* (2003), for example, Birkenstocks are worn by Dr. Zoe Barry, a lesbian feminist professor of Women's Studies at Columbia University and sister to the protagonist, Erica Barry.[45] The plot charts the growing relationship between Erica and Harry Sanborn, a wealthy, 60-something, self-satisfied playboy who only dates women under 30 and whose latest girlfriend is Marin, Erica's daughter. Marin and Harry drive to Erica's Hamptons beach house expecting to be alone for the weekend, but Erica and Zoe unexpectedly arrive. Zoe eloquently critiques Sanborn's obnoxious, entitled sexism at an awkward family dinner; her character's position as a wealthy, well-educated, lesbian feminist is reinforced via her costume of Birkenstocks, jeans, a soft, baggy, gray, long-sleeved sweater and minimal makeup and jewelry that signal a tasteful, refined version of the "lesbian clone style."[46] In this film, however, Zoe is not the object of ridicule like Jill, Carissa, Shubb, or Finistirre; rather, the joke is on selfish Harry. A similar use of Birkenstocks appears in *Tammy* (2014), in which the shoe is part of the refined lesbian clone style of the successful and wealthy Lenore.[47] The titular protagonist, Tammy, is a mess whose life lurches from bad to worse when she damages her car, is fired from her job, and discovers her husband is cheating. After going on a road trip and robbing a fast-food store to help bail her drunken grandmother, Pearl, out of jail, the two contact Pearl's cousin Lenore to help hide the evidence from the robbery. Pearl and Tammy then stay at the home of Lenore and her wife, where Pearl gets drunk and humiliates Tammy at a party in front of all the guests. Tammy, feeling sorry for herself, retreats to the boat dock and Lenore comes to talk to her. The Birkenstocks in Lenore's costume in the boat-dock scene point to the destabilization of Birkenstocks as a comedic device in film in line with the mainstreaming of lesbian and countercultural dress codes in the 2010s.[48] This mainstreaming is underscored by Lenore's tough love for Tammy in the scene, telling her, "Gay hasn't always been in fashion, my friend." In contrast to the well-dressed Lenore, the film's tragicomic figure is Tammy, who has big, frizzy hair that echoes a clown's wig and wears ill-fitting clothes with Crocs for comic effect. Similarly, the Birkenstock wearer, Liz, in the comedy-drama *Our Idiot Brother* (2011) is not the butt of the joke; instead, it is her brother, Ned, a biodynamic agriculture farmer, who is arrested for selling marijuana to a uniformed police officer and who wears bright-orange Crocs.[49]

The rise of Birkenstocks as a fashionable shoe means that they now regularly appear in film costuming as a component of mainstream, modish attire. For example, Rachel Mutombo wears a tie-dyed jumpsuit and Birkenstocks in *Single All the Way* (2021) to portray not a hippie or comic "other" but a casually dressed suburban housewife.[50] Margot Robbie as Barbie in *Barbie* (2023) similarly sports Birkenstocks to signal a fashionable, casual look.[51] The comic use of Birkenstocks in film, however, has not completely disappeared. In 2022, the character and audience alike now share the joke, as evinced in the "human Birkenstock" slur in *Do Revenge*, a gag that originated in *Clueless* and which is reinforced in costuming references to that film. For example, Drea's lilac-and-mint school uniform resembles Cher's yellow plaid Dolce & Gabbana school outfit. The "human Birkenstock" joke also directs itself to the uniform worn by the farm kids' group to which Carissa belongs, which consists of mustard overalls and a sage-green T-shirt underneath embroidered with two pink roses. This is an outfit that carries the decades-old association, in the popular imagination, with the agricultural feminist hippies captured in Crumb's countercultural comix. One scene shows Drea relaxing on the beach, close to Carissa, and when Russ Dara, the farm kids' "alt-boy" comes to talk to Drea, we see a pair of white, big-buckle *Arizona* Birkenstocks next to her, ostensibly signaling her alignment with the farm kids. Drea and Eleanor eventually enact their revenge by spiking the seniors' Ring Ceremony meal—cooked by Carissa with vegetables from the school garden—with the magic mushrooms Carissa has been growing in her locked greenhouse and alerting the police to Carissa's hydroponic marijuana crop. Carissa's punishment is to go to rehab for treatment, and when Drea visits her to gloat, a stylishly dressed Carissa is wearing Birkenstocks while playing croquet (a visual reference to the croquet scenes in the 1989 film *Heathers*). The use of Birkenstocks in *Do Revenge* alludes to the Birkenstock's multivalent visual functions in film—nostalgic countercultural symbol, laughing stock, high-fashion item, and historical lesbian clone style—indicating that the costume designer, Alana Morshead, was consciously aware of both the history and contemporary fashionability of Birkenstocks.[52]

Film director Greta Gerwig also used Birkenstocks in *Barbie* (2023) in a similar way. In one scene, the queer-coded character of 'Weird Barbie' holds a brown *Arizona* to symbolize the real world next to a satin, pink high heeled shoe, which represents Barbie Land. Weird Barbie tells 'Stereotypical Barbie' that she must choose the Birkenstock to enter the real world and save herself from becoming weird. At the end of the film, Stereotypical Barbie chooses to return to the real world and become human. In her last costume, Barbie sports jeans, a blazer, a white top and a soft, pink pastel pair of big buckle *Arizonas* that signals both her commitment to fashion and her transformation.[53]

In addition, Birkenstock does not engage in paid product placement and actively rejects such collaboration requests as in the case of *Barbie* (2023).[54] The result of filmmakers' still choosing to use Birkenstocks in the film underscores the shoe's far-reaching symbolic power and allows film makers to communicate these symbolisms with audiences in an authentic manner.

Morshead's and Gerwig's costuming shows how Birkenstocks in film now act like a physical presence that simultaneously represents fashion, counterculture, comedy, satire, and queer culture, transforming comedy into an experience knowingly shared by the character, the actor, and the audience.

Fig. 56: The real star of the Oscars: Frances McDormand wearing neon yellow *Arizonas* to the Academy Awards in 2019.

Conclusions and Considerations

This history of Birkenstocks in Anglophone film over the last 30 years has focused on how designers have used them in costuming to draw on the aesthetics of 70s American counterculture and 90s grunge to signal a character who wants to break away from the everyday, albeit sometimes with disastrous results; to point to a character's sexuality; and as a comedic device. The use of Birkenstocks in film costuming has also shifted over the last 30 years, and while the shoe still retains its comic role in film, Birkenstocks can also be used to convey a greater acceptance of the nuances of sexuality and gender representations beyond heteronormativity and to signal a wearer's fashionability. Yet the story of Birkenstocks in film will continue into the 21st century, and there is still much more research to be done on this topic. For example, there is scope to consider "invisible Birkenstocks"—that is, those worn by actors like Guy Pearce and Jason Momoa for comfort and mobility. Pearce, for example, has noted that he wore Birkenstocks for comfort in *Iron Man 3* (2013) that were not shown on-screen during fight scenes.[55] Momoa, meanwhile, works with his costume department to create boots that are appropriate to his character but are based on a *Birkenstock-Footbed*.[56]

It is also possible to consider the personal relationships that actors have with their Birkenstocks. Frances McDormand, for example, who starred as the Birkenstock-wearing Dr. Zoe Barry in *Something's Gotta Give* has since appeared onstage at major international film industry events wearing Birkenstocks, including custom yellow, Valentino x Birkenstock *Arizonas* at the 91st Annual Academy Awards on February 24, 2019, and red patent leather *Arizonas* at the 14th Rome Film Festival on October 19, 2019.[57] McDormand herself was responsible for the collaboration between Valentino and Birkenstock that resulted in her Oscars shoes. A study could be conducted into Birkenstocks in non-English speaking films, such as the Swedish horror film *Let the Right One In* (2008), in which Birkenstocks are a symbol of comfort and domesticity.[58]

There is also scope to consider Birkenstocks in television series, from their comedic use to represent hippie types, such as the horrible woman running a silent retreat in Phoebe Waller-Bridge's British comedy-drama *Fleabag* (2016–2019), to the American urban fantasy series *Lucifer* (2016–2021), where the immaculately dressed Lucifer wears a white tuxedo and white socks with white Birkenstocks when sitting on the Throne of Heaven in season six.[59] Additional research could also be conducted into the convergence of fashion and costume through the use of Birkenstocks in TV series, such as comedy-drama *The Bear*

(2022)—in which the protagonist, a chef called Carmy, has been lauded as a male style icon[60]—and in the *Sex and the City* (1998-2004) spin-off, *And Just Like That* (2021-), where ultimate pop-culture shoe fashionista Carrie Bradshaw says she looks "like a Vermont art teacher" when forced to wear Birkenstocks ahead of her hip surgery because high heels are too painful.[61]

This contribution has argued that the endurance of Birkenstocks in film costuming over 30 years and over a wide range of genres is tied to the powerful legacy and influence that the American counterculture movement of the 60s and 70s had on the world, and while Birkenstock hippies might have been the butt of jokes, perhaps they have had the last laugh.

La douleur

disparaît par le support breveté

Foot-bed

C'est la semelle de soutien la plus scientifique (**sans
métal**). Incassable, inoxydable, se porte sans douleur.

RENSEIGNEMENTS ET EXAMEN DES PIEDS GRATUITS ET SANS ENGAGEMENT

Adressez-vous en toute confiance à:

1963 – 2024
THE DEVELOPMENT OF BIRKENSTOCK IN THE EARLY KEY MARKETS

Fig. 57: International advertisement for the metal-free insole *Footbed*, 50s.

From Hippie to High Fashion: The Evolution of Birkenstock in North America

BY TAYLOR BRYDGES

Introduction

Developing this contribution provided the opportunity to investigate the presence of Birkenstocks not only in my life but in the North American market. Over the last 50 years, Birkenstock has evolved from its hippie roots to not only embrace fashion but dominate the sandal market, refashioning North American footwear culture. From Birkenstock's entry into North America, nestled alongside granola in health-food and wellness stores, to its prominence in the orthopedics business, to its recent stardom on the runway as an "It" shoe, the brand has undergone a fascinating evolution.

In doing so, Birkenstock has firmly established itself in North American fashion, footwear, and popular culture. For many, Birkenstocks have long held a revered place in the shoe closet as a utilitarian stalwart, comfortable and reliable (worn with or without socks) season after season. For others, Birkenstocks have become the cool sandal of choice, worn with everything from denim to dresses. Throughout, it becomes clear how the four pillars of the Birkenstock brand—*Footbed*-related tradition, quality, design, and value-based visions[1]—have remained at the core of the business and supported its success in this competitive marketplace.

But how did this transformation happen? This chapter explores the factors that enabled the Birkenstock sandal to not only take hold and succeed in North America but also become part of the local culture. In doing so, this chapter traces the history of Birkenstock from the shoe's introduction to this market in the 60s up to the present day. A key factor emerges: at each stage in its evolution, the brand has stayed true to its core values of quality, design, and function. This consistency has allowed Birkenstock not only to endure but to thrive, despite competition from luxury and mass-market rivals. Birkenstock continues to leave a lasting impression on North American foot fashion.

You're Wearing Birkenstocks?

My own experience wearing Birkenstocks over the past two decades mirrors this evolution. As young soccer (football) players in Canada, my sister and I spent our summers in cleats and sandals from Birkenstock, with the latter supporting our recovery from damage caused in the former. The options, as I remember, were the *Arizona* or the *Milano* in leather (black or navy) or suede (black, brown, or beige). Against the glittery fashions of the early 2000s, these options felt limiting and frankly uncool. Compared with anything else I had worn, I remember the leather straps being very hard, requiring time (and Band-Aids!) to break in, so I preferred the suede, which was immediately comfortable, albeit often dusty from a day of walking.

At the time, everyone thought of Birkenstocks as the shoe an older person would wear, sensible and good for the feet but not for the look. Rather, on more than one occasion, a friend asked, "You're wearing Birkenstocks?" with a raised eyebrow whenever I wore the sandal beyond the soccer pitch. It's worth noting this was also around the time when flimsy, brightly colored $3 foam flip-flops from Old Navy were very popular. While cheap enough to own one in every color and always match your outfit, they offered the least amount of comfort and support possible. Nevertheless, my sister and I continued to spend our summers in Birkenstocks because wearing any other shoes guaranteed a sore back the next day. Few would have known that Carl Birkenstock actually had a Canadian patent for "Orthopaedic Foot Support for Shoes" (dated August 11, 1950) for "improvements in foot supports."[2] This referred to Carl Birkenstock's *Ideal-Schuh*, which was never industrially produced. It was not until Karl Birkenstock successfully made his way to Canada with the *Original Birkenstock-Footbed Sandal*, which he designed in 1963.[3]

I can't remember the exact moment in the mid-2010s when the comments changed from questioning to approving. Friends began to say, "I love your Birkenstocks!" and then enthusiastically describe their own pair. It took that long for the rise of street-style blogs documenting celebrities and cool girl influencers wearing the sandals with countless outfits. Today, no matter where you're going, it seems like you can't leave the house without seeing someone in their Birks. At the same time, you can't scroll Instagram without seeing influencers from London to Stockholm to Sydney in their Birkenstocks, particularly the *Arizona* and the *Boston*. Here in summertime Toronto, I have my black leather *Arizonas* at the front door ready to slip on whether I'm going to lecture or heading to the park, and I have my eyes on a pair of *Bostons* for the fall.

Bringing Birkenstock to North America

For a brand as large as BIRKENSTOCK to enter a market as large as North America, it would need a carefully orchestrated business plan. Wouldn't it? Surprisingly, no. Instead, the North American chapter of the Birkenstock story begins with a German-American named Margot Fraser, who discovered the sandals in 1966 while in Germany. As the story goes, "Her feet hurt, the sandals helped, and she asked Karl [Birkenstock] if she might try selling some back home."[4] Birkenstock agreed, and as they say, the rest is history.

Fraser singlehandedly brought the brand to the North American market, launching the business from her home.[5] After having trouble getting Birkenstocks into traditional shoe retailers—over fears the shoes were too ugly[6]—she started selling them in health-food and wellness stores.[7] As legend has it, it was in these stores where "hippies discovered them next to vitamins and dried lentils, and as the Summer of Love unfolded, Birkenstocks became the shoe of choice for beatniks from San Francisco to Vermont."[8] Indeed, it is truly difficult to overstate the importance of Margo Fraser in the North American market, for which she won multiple industry and entrepreneurial awards and forever altered the trajectory of footwear culture and consumption.[9]

Birkenstocks were associated with a range of counterculture movements of the 60s and 70s in the United States. Visually, they feature in the works of countercultural cartoonists Robert Crumb[10] and Gilbert Shelton.[11] Crumb and Shelton contributed significantly to the visual language of the countercultural movement of the 60s and 70s via their work with Underground Comix and their album covers, and characters such Shelton's Fabulous Furry Freak Brothers and Crumb's Fritz the Cat.[12] Birkenstock are also visible in archival footage of the 1969 Woodstock Festival, and were sold by the store set up to sell goods featured in the Whole Earth Catalog.[13]

This counterculture movement had two strands—the "back to the earth" hippies and the "back to the Earth" utopians who placed technology at the center of society.[14] Birkenstocks were uniquely placed to become central to both movements, an association that permeated through the rest of the century and into the 2000s with hippies and techno types alike embracing the comfort and practicality of Birkenstocks. Perhaps no one better exemplified the marriage of these strands than Steve Jobs, who famously wore the same pair of tan suede *Arizona* Birkenstocks in the 70s and 80s as he built Apple Computers from his family garage in California.[15] According to reporting from Women's Wear Daily, Margot Fraser said that when Steve Jobs first discovered Birkenstocks, he wanted "to know everything about where it came from and the technical aspects of it."[16] The sandals became part of his uniform, even during the winter.[17] Those same sandals, with his feet firmly imprinted in the

Fig. 58: German-American Margot Fraser laid the foundation for the introduction of Birkenstock sandals in the USA. Fraser in her shop, 70s.

footbed, were recently sold at auction, along with an NFT, for $218,750, surpassing the expected sale price of between $60,000 and $80,000. The auction house reported it was the highest price ever paid for a pair of sandals.[18]

As such, the reputation—or indeed, stereotype—of Birkenstocks as "emblems of liberal do-gooderness" is longstanding.[19] Mention Birkenstock to a North American consumer, and to this day, tropes of "earth mother" or "flower child" probably come to mind. Association with environmentalism and counterculture continue to be among the brand's key selling points: the made-in-Germany credentials, the use of natural materials such as cork, and the ability to replace worn-out soles.[20]

Equally, the brand continues to emphasize comfort, with the custom, orthopedic market still one of the main ways for consumers, including me, to discover the shoe. Birkenstock advertisements from the late 90s and early 2000s reinforce this image by encouraging North American consumers to "walk the Birkenstock highway" and embrace having "comfort underfoot" by choosing Birkenstock.[21] My favorite ad, with the tagline "Let your feet make a place for themselves" is focused on the clog, described as "The Formal Birkenstock."[22] Evidently, influencers of the 2020s have taken note and just like the ad suggests, agree that their clogs are "perfect for all occasions."[23]

A recent cameo by Birkenstocks in the *Sex and the City* reboot, *And Just Like That ...*, reinforced Birkenstock's reputation as a comfortable shoe in the present day. In episode 4, Carrie Bradshaw, the show's shoe-loving protagonist, is having hip surgery and reaches for a pair of flat shoes—perhaps for the first time in the history of the show—and what does she put on? A pair of olive-green Birkenstock *Madrid* slides, worn with pom-pom socks. Gesturing to the lower part of what is still a very stylish outfit, she says, "From here down I look like a Vermont art teacher."[24] Carrie's choice of Birkenstocks not only nods to the brand's foothealthy reputation and comfort but also salutes the shoe's fashion-forward status.

Function Meets Fashion

Even though some people may still conjure up the stereotypical image of a person wearing socks with Birkenstocks as a classic fashion faux pas, the brand has gained a fashion-forward reputation. As Helen Jennings wrote for CNN Style, "Birkenstock makes an anti-fashion statement that transcends trends—yet somehow keeps managing to set them."[25]

Beginning in the 90s and 2000s, the brand experienced a period of transition. While BIRKENSTOCK continued to maintain its health and wellness associations, it began to evolve into a fashion shoe as well.[26] After an influential UK editorial spread for *The Face* magazine, which featured Kate Moss wearing Birkenstocks on the beach, American fashion designer Marc Jacobs put Birkenstocks on the runway as part of his Perry Ellis S/S 1993 grunge collection.[27] By challenging dominant conceptualizations of luxury, this runway show—one of the most famous of all time—captured the zeitgeist of the moment. In its wake, Birkenstocks evolved once again, this time moving from the runway to the wardrobe of the urban grunge movement.[28]

As the new millennium began, Birkenstock retained its reputation of offering "ugly" but functional footwear. As one reporter put it, this was a time when "the pejorative term 'Birkenstock liberal' was used by conservatives to invoke the stereotype of a granola-eating, Volvo-driver do-gooder."[29] This example and countless others like it illustrate how the early reputation of Birkenstocks as the "hippie" shoe of a largely older demographic continued to dominate.

Then, after 2010, something changed for Birkenstock. During this decade, as a combination of factors reshaped the brand's reputation, the sandal be-

Fig. 59: Fraser compensated for the lack of specialist shops in distribution with attention to detail. An innovative advertising campaign in the USA for the *Arizona*, 70s.

came an increasingly fashionable item. The Birkenstock organization itself led some of this transformation. When the company experienced changes in corporate management, the brand took on a new strategic direction in the North American market, including the creation of new sales targets for the brand and plotted a plan for expansion.[30] This included careful consideration of ways of introducing new designer collaborations and styles while continuing to deliver the core products and quality that loyal customers have come to expect. During this time, as a business, Birkenstock became a "well-oiled machine," connecting with retailers and expanding its retail footprint (pardon the pun).[31]

Notably, Birkenstock's rise to high fashion took place against the backdrop of a trend-driven aesthetic in North America (think low-rise jeans, Uggs. and Juicy Couture tracksuits). The more bling and bedazzle a garment had, the better.[32] In this context, Birkenstocks became one of the defining styles of the "normcore" trend, an aesthetic described as "about looking 'normal' but in a faintly stylized, self-aware kind of way."[33] Normcore was in direct opposition to the overtly and overly trendy styles that had come to define the look of the time.

While the fashion industry attached this label to Birkenstock, the brand itself disliked the term. As David Kahan put it in *Esquire*, "The term 'normcore' seems to have been invented by the fashion media. Within Birkenstock, we have never used the term, not even once. What does 'normcore' mean? I guess if it means consumers want to be comfortable in what they wear, or want their wardrobe to be built around core items that may remain in their wardrobe more than one season, then sure, that speaks to what Birkenstock is all about."[34] While the "normcore trend" may well be an oxymoron, there was widespread agreement that Birkenstock found new cultural relevance in the North American market during this time.[35]

Within this changing perception, a pivotal moment stood out. At the Céline October 2012 Paris runway show, Phoebe Philo presented a pair of sandals that resembled a black *Arizona*, but they were not original Birkenstock sandals.[36] Later they were described as "Furkenstocks." Seemingly overnight, the fashion crowd fell in love with the sandal, elevating it to the height of new minimalist chic.[37] A number of high-fashion collaborations have taken place in the decade that has followed, including with Rick Owens, Proenza Schouler, Dior, and Manolo Blahnik.[38]

The Real Deal

Yet BIRKENSTOCK's fashion influence in North America extends beyond the luxury market, with mid-market and mass-market retailers also popularizing the style. The North American customer base is typically value conscious, usually preferring the lower price, especially in apparel. This cultural and consumer emphasis on finding a good deal means that buyers are susceptible to lower-priced options.[39]

Thus, the company added ethylene vinyl acetate (EVA) Birkenstocks in 2015. The EVA collection was an immediate hit on the North American market, providing cost-conscious consumers with the chance to buy Birkenstocks at a lower price. In one glowing review of the *Arizona* made of EVA in a New York Times Wirecutter column, the writer described his anxiety purchasing expensive seasonal footwear and celebrated the EVA *Arizona* for being not only "affordable, durable and comfortable" but also "as presentable as the more-expensive Arizonas" and "easier to care for."[40]

This successful launch of EVA products epitomizes the company's approach to the North American market. Instead of engaging in a race to the bottom and cutting quality in order to compete on cost to appeal to bargain-hunting consumers, Birkenstock developed an effective way to appeal to a price-conscious consumer without compromising its core brand values. Birkenstock has stayed true to the production processes and materials that deliver the quality and comfort that customers expect. And in return, the brand has been rewarded with incredibly loyal customers, who share their love of the sandal through both word of mouth and countless positive reviews online.[41]

Fig. 60: The essence remains unchanged—walking as nature intended (Birkenstock catalog, 1977).

The Official Home Office Shoe

Over the past two years, Birkenstocks have taken on new relevance and prominence in the North American wardrobe. As Jake Silbert wrote in High Snobiety, "Whether it was for emotional or physical comfort, shoppers flocked to Birkenstock during and after quarantines."[42] With comfort fashions more important than ever, many of us have reached for Birkenstocks to accompany our Zoom-ready attire.[43]

Indeed, with 2020 one of the strongest years on record for the brand, BIRKENSTOCK Group CEO Oliver Reichert proclaimed that Birkenstock had become the "official home office shoe."[44] This new status was so much the case that the popular online shopping platform Lyst declared the *Arizona* the world's most popular shoe. As a result, product searches increased over 200 percent, and Birkenstocks sold out at many retailers.[45]

The company was well-positioned to capitalize on a growing consumer appetite for products offering not just comfort but sustainability and quality. Photographs of American celebrities and models, such as Gigi Hadid and

Kendall Jenner, wearing their Birkenstocks at home during the pandemic only reinforced the sandal's popularity.[46] The recent rise in demand has led industry commentators to place BIRKENSTOCK alongside other iconic shoes such as Vans, Dr. Martens, and Nike. As one observer put it, these are brands that "have cemented themselves" in such a singular market position that they are "kind of operating in their own orbit," almost beyond competition.[47]

Conclusion: Often Copied, Never Equaled

In its evolution from hippie to high fashion, Birkenstock has faced competition from both the luxury and mass-market segments of the market. But through its steadfast commitment to quality and comfort, the brand has retained a fiercely loyal customer base. In the end, Birkenstock remains in a category all its own, often copied but never equaled. Few brands have its longevity in the North American and indeed global marketplaces. As an article in High Snobiety put it, "Birkenstock will keep plugging away at its perfectly minimalist sandals. When all's said and done, the Birkenstock *Arizona* will be the last sandal standing."[48]

Fig. 61: Convincing—Birkenstock used the same messages in Italy, too (Birkenstock catalog, Italy, 1970).

Birkenstock in Italy: A Creative Adventure

BY EMANUELA SCARPELLINI

Birkenstock's Arrival in Italy

The landing of Birkenstock in Italy took place sooner than in many other European markets; it started, to be precise, in 1958 in the shoe shops of the spouses Karl and Carolina Fill in Bolzano and Merano. These stores specialized in comfortable orthopedic footwear, and the owners immediately appreciated the anatomical *Blaues Fußbett* (*Blue Footbed*), as well as the first Birkenstock sandals. In fact, sales of Birkenstock products had already begun earlier, as evidenced, for example, by a letter kept in the Birkenstock archive dated December 1957, in which the parent company asked Karl Fill to publish an advertisement in the Bolzano daily newspaper at least once a month, however in agreement with another reseller, the Bosin company of Merano.[1]

Even if the beginnings were not easy, the sales of these products established themselves locally, so much so that in 1973, when one of the salesmen, Ewald Pitschl, took over the business, together with the grandson of the Fills, Werner Steinhauser, he took steps to obtain the representation of the products exclusively for Italy. Thus began a path that was in many ways unexpected, which saw a gradual spread first in the region of the Alto Adige, and then gradually in other regions of the north and center of the country—through the NaturalLook company, managed by his brother Gerhard Pitschl, and later followed by his son Frowin.[2] But what were the problems they faced trying to popularize and distribute this particular shoe?

Italy has very specific characteristics with regard to the shoe market and clothing in general. It is in fact one of the main markets and places of production of fashion. As early as the end of the 50s and in the 60s, the country was distinguished by the presence of a large number of shoe artisans and small or medium workshops dedicated to the manufacture of shoes, especially of medium-high quality. There were numerous areas where high quality footwear was produced, sometimes following a centuries-old tradition, in particular in seven specialized districts in the regions of Tuscany, the Marches, Campania, Veneto, Lombardy, Emilia-Romagna, and Puglia. In some areas, there was a gradual shift from artisanal to industrial production, such as in the Vigevano district, near Milan, which had seen its footwear production grow strongly since the 19th century thanks to a galaxy of workshops and small or medium-sized industries.[3] In 1960, 870 companies were active just in this small territory with a production of about 21 million shoes, dedicated to all types of models, open and closed, for men and women.[4] For these reasons, in the early 70s, when the marketing of Birkenstock began, Italy had already established itself as one of the leading global producers, and in particular as the main manufacturer of quality leather shoes.

Furthermore, in the same period, the country quickly established itself as one of the most prominent showcases in ready-to-wear clothing, with the Milan stage internationally launching names such as Giorgio Armani, Valentino Garavani, Gianfranco Ferré, and Gianni Versace. It is interesting to observe how Italian fashion had asserted itself with a connotation of style that concerned the entire outfit, thus affecting not only the dress but also the shoes and accessories: the famous *total look*. It was a style designed for young people who wanted to innovate fashion both by modifying traditional garments (for example by making the men's jacket less formal and creating a specific version for women), and by inserting non-conformist garments such as blue jeans and T-shirts into the collections, and also by innovating fabrics and colors. Shoes were affected by the same influence of renewal, and so the traditional models for men and women were reconsidered, boots of all types, proposed with new shapes and materials, were offered, and sandals also found ample space. All under the banner of immediately recognizable brands thanks to a communication that bounced from specialized fashion magazines to the mass media.[5] How to situate the Birkenstock sandal in this context? As has been pointed out above, at first the spread was slow and not without problems, as the Pitschl brothers recall in their interviews.[6] For many Italians, the first visual "contact" with consumers who wore Birkenstocks were German tourists who came to Italy for their holidays, by the lake or by the sea, wearing T-shirts, shorts, and these comfortable sandals with white socks—a combination considered taboo from the point of view of fashion, which wanted sandals always worn strictly without socks. The cultural imagery of the sandal in Italy in fact referred to the figure of the monk, who wore basic dark sandals without socks, as a symbol of a simple and sober life. Or it referred to a fashionable figure, above all female, who used, in summer and in tourist places, open footwear of various types, colorful and often very sophisticated, also in this case strictly barefoot: the bare foot was part of the attraction exercised by these shoes.[7] In both cases, sandals and socks were an antithetical combination, and there seemed to be little space for comfortable slippers that were not aesthetically graceful.

It should also be remembered that, at the same time, the diffusion of Birkenstock in the counterculture era, starting from the 60s to the 70s, was quite limited in Italy compared with other countries. Partly because commercial distribution was still underdeveloped, based moreover on a network of small, specialized shops, which was not easy to serve adequately through commercial representatives. Partly because other "counter-current" shoes were more widespread, starting with the clogs, which were frequently seen in demonstrations of the time and in the feminist movement. Only relatively small and socially elevated groups of the counterculture adopted the Birkenstock, joining the customers who already knew them because they were oriented towards comfortable and orthopedic footwear. It was a limited phenomenon, but the history of Birkenstock in Italy had definitely begun.

The Development of the Company

After the acquisition of the Fill shop in 1973, Ewald Pitschl and Werner Steinhauser decided to open a shop specializing in orthopedic shoes in Bolzano, "Pediform", with Birkenstocks as the spearhead of the selection on offer. From 1974 to 1983, the spread of the shoes continued thanks to a double action: direct sales in shops and the distribution of illustrated catalogs, published twice a year and sent to already acquired customers, which allowed for sales by mail.

The next step in conquering a wider market came with a corporate transformation: partner Werner Steinhauser left to devote himself to the original shop of the Fill family, while Ewald Pitschl created a new business together with his wife Maria Thurner, which included both running the shop "Pediform" and the wholesaling business of the BIRKENSTOCK brand. To open up to further growth, the decision was to participate in the main specialized trade fairs of the sector: it began with Intersan in Milan (1983), followed by Fiercato in Bologna (1984), and Micam once again in Milan (1985), with good results in terms of visibility and new contacts.[8]

There was a parallel physical expansion in the territory. Starting from 1986, four new stores were opened, always in the Trentino Alto-Adige region, including an "Ewald" sales point in Bolzano, with a wide selection of orthopedic and non-orthopedic shoes (1986), one "Pediform" branch in Riva del Garda (1988), and one in the center of Trento (1994). These stores were joined by a new storage warehouse to cope with the growing sales, thanks also to the work of numerous sales agents operating in Italy. In 1992, for the wholesale trade, the old "Pediform snc" was transformed into "Passform Ltd."[9]

At the beginning of the 90s, everything seemed well on its way towards sustained expansion, when an unexpected external factor took over, which was linked to the general Italian financial situation. Until 1992, the country had enjoyed relative financial stability and was part of the European Monetary System (EMS), which guaranteed stable monetary exchange rates or, in any case, limited fluctuations (the Deutsche Mark/Lira exchange rate was around 750). In 1992, there was a serious crisis in the financial markets, the "Black Wednesday" of 16 September, which involved, in particular, the British pound and the Italian lira, causing their exit from the EMS and a sharp devaluation of both. In the case of the lira, further strong international speculation caused a period of instability, which culminated in the further devaluations of 1994 and 1995, when the Mark/Lira exchange rate reached an average of 1200. Only later did the crisis subside and the exchange rate return to below 1000, to then stabilize definitively in view of the adoption of the Euro.[10]

The Pitschl business was heavily affected by this currency trend, which suddenly made German products much more expensive for the Italian market, and significantly inflated the level of debts owed to the manufacturer. The situation became very difficult, to the point that the continuity of the exclusive relationship seemed in doubt, as Alessandra Albertoni and Susanne Pitro recount; only the close personal relationship between Ewald Pitschl and Karl Birkenstock made it possible to overcome the impasse, confirming the relationship of trust that had been going on for some time.[11]

The following five years were characterized by slow growth and the search for a new equilibrium. The central point of the new corporate structure was the gradual strengthening of the "NaturalLook" company, operational since 1993 and included in the Business Register of Bolzano in 1996, which centralized the management of sales, both retail and wholesale, and for which a new modern headquarters, with offices and warehouses, was created in south Bolzano in 2004. Having sold the "Pediform" sales points, but not the "Ewald" store in Bolzano, the new company subsequently opened five new shops in the area. Since 2001, when Frowin Pitschl, son of Ewald, joined the management of the company, he has been helping to push a product that had now established itself on the Italian market.[12]

The sources preserved in the Birkenstock Archives document the continuity and close relationship maintained between the Pitschl family and the Birkenstock company over time. Apart from letters concerning representation in Italy and administrative matters, there is no shortage of curiosities and aspects of entertainment. Like when Ewald Pitschl jokingly wrote to Birkenstock that archaeologists had found proof of "plagiarism" with the famous sandals: the South Tyrolean newspaper Dolomiten had in fact published an article on the discovery of a wooden shoe, which perhaps belonged to the famous "iceman" Ötzi, found the year before in South Tyrol, or perhaps to a local inhabitant in the Middle Ages.[13]

On the other hand, with regard to the sales trend in Italy, we can see a progressive, albeit non-linear, growth over time. Still in 1984, for example, only about 2,000 pairs of Birkenstock were sold in a year.[14] However, from the mid-80s, a rapid growth trend began that reached over 26,000 pairs after five years, in 1989, and paved the way for a real sales boom starting in the 90s (137,000 in 1992, 189,000 in 2001), followed by a further strong surge in the following decade (366,000 pairs sold in 2007). The Italian market had therefore become an important reference for the product, not only for the sales numbers, but also because it often anticipated fashion trends.[15] In an interview, Gerhard Pitschl recalled, for example, the role played by the Italian market in the decision to introduce additional colors alongside the traditional ones, and also to its general role as a source of inspiration in the development of new models.[16]

Birkenstock and Fashionable Consumers

How can one explain the particular trend of the spread of Birkenstock shoes in the Italian market? To understand this point, we need to change our perspective and analyze the consumer's point of view. With this goal in mind, I carried out several interviews, discovering a truly multifaceted world.[17]

To begin with, let us consider Angelo's experience: a 33-year-old journalist, he has been a Birkenstock enthusiast for at least ten years.[18] He owns several pairs in different colors, and is a keen observer of the world of customs and fashion. With him we talked about this rapid success. In his opinion, the "political" and well-being implications had a limited weight in the spread of the brand, which in fact only exploded on the Italian market when it acquired a different meaning: that of a fashionable shoe. A fundamental element was the fashion collaborations with big names in Italian fashion, which brought Birkenstock on the catwalks of the fashion shows, and "vetted" their presence among the trendsetters (actors, top models, fashion icons). In a world increasingly influenced by mass media images and later by social media, this has had a very strong impact especially on the young audience, which has therefore accepted this "new" fashion product, almost unaware of its previous history. The last few years in particular have witnessed prestigious collaborations such as those with Valentino, resulting in an alignment not only of image but also of prices with typical high fashion products.

The question that arises spontaneously concerns aesthetics: they have always been considered less graceful shoes, compared to many competing models, so how did they become accepted in the Italian fashion world anyway? The answer is that it is enough to look at how the youth today wear them: we may see a boy (or a girl, the genderfluidity here was a forerunner) walking around wearing a T-shirt and a pair of trendy shorts, accompanied by white sponge socks and a pair of Birkenstocks. This look immediately transmits a strong fashion message: it is street style, the bottom-up fashion that denotes a person who is attentive to a sophisticated and urban style, with strong allusions to grunge fashion. In today's complex cultural symbolism, this clothing style therefore accurately situates the person who wears it within the panorama of contemporary transnational subcultures. The combination of sandals and socks is therefore deliberately sought after. Alternatively, the Birkenstocks are worn in summer (without socks) combined with elegant clothing, even for the evening, both in the total black version and in the color variants, to create a highly refined, almost snobbish ensemble. Among other things, many like to wear Birkenstocks in this way to show off the tattoos they have on their feet and legs, which thus take on considerable visibility. Still others, and this is typical of the youth sensitivity towards sustainability, choose vegan Birkenstocks.

From Angelo's observations, we can therefore advance the hypothesis that we should not evaluate the sandal itself but the meaning it assumes in the overall ensemble or style, thanks to its combination with other garments. The fashion significance of the sandal, within a market that is sensitive to style and fashion like the Italian one, has been central to its success. Here a reversal of the typical symbolism linked to the Birkenstock (suitable for rest, for the elderly, for the maintenance of foot health) occurred in advance, and transformed them into a "cool" product for young people. It is also significant that the German origin of the shoes is not a strong cultural marker, due in part to the widespread lack of knowledge of the history of footwear, but is a neutral element. Basically, the brand and brand awareness are central to the product, especially for young people, as Angelo remembers: "It's a question of marketing: one follows the brand and then follows the wearer." This also has the consequence of a rapid rotation of the shoes: they are bought because they last many years, because they are "timeless," and because they represent a safe investment in clothing. They are more recently also purchased because they are fashionable, and therefore must be changed quickly, just like the rest of the clothing, with obvious commercial implications (purchase of several pairs of different colors and models at the same time, quick replacement at the first signs of wear). This analysis is confirmed by the accounts of Elena and Angela, university students from Milan, who have recently discovered Birkenstock, looking at the example of friends and trendsetters who show them off on social media, in particular on Instagram.[19] Unlike the other interviewees, the two girls were familiar with the names of the various models available, as well as the range of colors, after having seen them on websites (where they bought them). For them, they are simply fashionable shoes.

Birkenstock, Consumers, and Creativity

Someone who has a very different experience is Mauro, a sixty-year-old industrial manager, passionate about the mountains, who is instead a "historical" connoisseur of the brand.[20] As a boy, in the mid-80s, he remembers having been curious about the Birkenstock sandals worn by German tourists who arrived on the lakes in Lecco and Como. What struck Mauro and his group of friends was the anatomical footbed, not widespread in Italy at the time, which proved to be of great interest to young people who were passionate about long walks in the mountains on Saturdays and Sundays. Having bought the shoes, which was not without difficulty, given the few sales outlets (one of his friends specially organized a weekend in Merano and Bolzano to buy them), everyone found them comfortable. Mauro and his friends certainly did not have foot problems and did not need relaxing shoes: their use of Birkenstocks was above all for walks in the summer. The common passion for hiking and mountaineering in the Lecco area therefore suggested a very particular use of sandals, which were worn for the more undemanding walks or for the phase of approaching a difficult path, at which there was a change of shoes: the Birkenstocks ended up in the backpack, and mountain boots were worn in their place—and the opposite change was made for the descent. Mauro explains that those sandals were particularly suitable for long comfortable walks.

For this reason, the group of friends continued to use these sandals, especially appreciating their quality and durability. The history of the manufacturer was not known to them; they connotated the brand name with a lifestyle that loves the outdoors. To the point that the youth began wearing them also in the city, but with a trick: they always bought the same model, brown and with the double strap (the only one available for a long time), using the new pair in the city, and the more worn one for mountain walks. The sandals were never thrown away.

Later Mauro also tried the Birkenstock with closed uppers, to be used in the mountains when it was colder, in spring and autumn, sometimes with socks. He always continued to buy the traditional model, imitated in this by his family. The Birkenstock remained in place as comfortable summer footwear, even if now for the mountains they use other specialized sports shoes to complement the Meindl boots: according to him, both Birkenstock and Meindl are synonymous with quality, sports, and comfort that last over time. It is certainly no coincidence that, unlike various foot fashions that were very successful but fleeting, such as the British Clarks and the boat shoes produced in Tuscany by Sax, the Birkenstocks have remained and are still in use today. Finally, he remembers a nice anecdote, namely the quarrels with his parents who saw him go out into town for the first times in Birkenstocks as a boy, and scolded him because they were not adequate shoes; they were just slippers, and he would make a bad impression walking around without "real" shoes.

Elena tells us yet a different story. [21] A 40-year-old teacher, she remembers seeing Birkenstocks at a very early age because her father used them on vacation or as slippers at home (the classic model with double band). Partly the example of her father, and partly a little that of friends, led her to take an interest in the BIRKENSTOCK brand, but choosing a model with the cross over the big toe and the comfortable and secure ankle strap: "That for me has become my summer travel shoe." Elena has traveled extensively around the world, especially in hot and tropical territories. This shoe turned out to be practical, comfortable for walking a lot until the evening, and open to let the foot breathe in very hot countries. She always uses the same brown model: when the shoe sole in the heel area wears out, she buys an identical pair. Currently she also uses them to go to the beach, during her holidays, and when she has wet feet, avoiding using rubber slippers.

For her next purchase, she always goes to the same city shop, where she has always felt at ease; recently, she also tried the Birkenstock closed in front. For Elena, "her" model combines aesthetic pleasure and comfort; for a certain price, she has the security of a shoe that does not hold any surprises in store: it happens to everyone that they buy a nice shoe and then do not wear it because it is uncomfortable or hurts. Furthermore, Elena is careful to choose natural and quality materials: not only for ecological reasons but also for her own health, considering the frequency of coming into direct skin contact with products whose origins and characteristics are often unknown. Speaking of her Birkenstocks, Elena remembers that once in Thailand, she found herself having to constantly take off her shoes to visit the temples, not always in optimal hygienic conditions. She therefore found a way to use special toe socks, which could be worn with her thong sandals; in this way, she could quickly take off and put on her favorite shoes during these visits. In short, for her the Birkenstocks evoke beautiful memories of travels and adventures.

These and other interviews highlight a very varied world of consumers, who with difficulty fit into many stereotypes about the brand. Consumer studies, and cultural studies more generally, have, after all, taught us how important the agency of consumers is, and therefore how actively they choose and create new ways of using and consuming the products they buy, bending and transforming them for their personal and cultural needs. In Italy, more than the models the health-conscious person, the politically committed one, or simply the one looking for a comfortable slipper at home would choose but instead, the choice among young people seems to be oriented primarily to sports and travel, attentive to the "fashion" content of the brand. Attention to comfort is never separated from an aesthetic concern, which translates to the choice of specific models or a careful combination with accessories and clothing. In this way, the Birkenstocks fit perfectly into the cultural and stylistic canons that are the characteristic feature of Italian fashion.

1963–2024 The Development of Birkenstock in the Early Key Markets

Birkenstock in Britain

BY LIZ TREGENZA

In 1991 Francesca Luard, a journalist for the Daily Mail, wrote of Birkenstocks that it was "extraordinary but true, these clumpy but comfortable shoes are all the rage. Previously only seen on the feet of long-haired vegetarians, they are now essential footwear for well-heeled groovers around Soho."[1] This comment is indicative of the change that took place during the 90s in Britain, taking Birkenstocks from a niche shoe popular with alternative groups to a mainstay on fashionable feet everywhere.

The 90s were, in Britain, a key decade for the re-imagining of Birkenstocks, not just as an orthopedic comfort shoe but one that was also highly fashionable. This chapter considers how a number of cultural events during the 90s repositioned BIRKENSTOCK as a "fashionable" shoe brand, and how they have retained popularity since. Firstly, the chapter considers Robert Lusk, a pioneering shoe distributor and managing director of Central Trade Ltd, and how he brought Birkenstocks to Britain. It will then turn to question how various fashion trends of the 90s helped to ensure that Birkenstocks became part of the fashion conversation in Britain, before finally turning to consider why two pairs of Birkenstocks featured in the Victoria and Albert Museum's (V&A) 1994 exhibition *Street Style: From Sidewalk to Catwalk, 1940 to Tomorrow*, and what this suggests about the continued legacy of Birkenstock shoes in Britain.

Robert Lusk and BIRKENSTOCK

Robert Lusk's relationship with Birkenstock began in the 70s when he recognized that there was potentially a market for these alternative shoes in Britain.

Fig. 62: Even mass-produced shoes should fit accurately: Birkenstock therefore also introduced an uncomplicated measuring system directly with the *Original Birkenstock-Footbed Sandal*, which was available to all specialist retailers.

Lusk is an American-born entrepreneur and, prior to selling Birkenstocks, had sold his own handmade bags and sandals at both Kensington Market and Portobello Road market in London, and also imported handmade Afghan goods. In the 70s, Lusk expanded his business and began to look for other footwear to sell, which would potentially appeal to people engaged with the hippy or alternative lifestyle. He started selling Frye Boots from America and Danish clogs, and soon acknowledged that BIRKENSTOCK would complement these brands, offering high quality, comfortable footwear. Lusk's relationship with Birkenstock would endure, and he sold Birkenstocks in Britain for more than forty years.

Lusk opened his first Natural Shoe Store at 22 North End Road, W14, London, but by 1976, had relocated to 21 Neal Street, Covent Garden, purportedly the first footwear store in the area.[2] When Lusk relocated his business there, the area was just starting to become an exciting new location for independent shops and restaurants, with many stores catering to alternative lifestyles, including the pioneering vegetarian restaurant „Food for Thought" at 31 Neal Street. In 1979, Ann Galloway wrote of the area:

> "The new Covent Garden is the most vital thing to have hit London since the Chelsea of the early Sixties. It is also contagiously friendly, perhaps because the resettlement of the old market is still patchy. The character that is beginning to emerge is, above all, one of originality and personal involvement."[3]

Retailing in Covent Garden in the 70s was, as Lusk suggested, a "different proposition" to what it became. Property was available, and rents and business rates were "not crushing." He suggested that "it was possible to find a small shop, open up without great problems and present yourself to the public." Furthermore, he found that it was easy to advertise in magazines, and it "didn't cost a fortune to get your message across."[4] It is symptomatic of Lusk's success that by 1981 he was able to open a second store at 325 Kings Road.

Certainly, in the 70s and 80s, it was primarily an alternative market that Lusk targeted. It should be noted that at this time, in Britain, the most popular shoe styles were platforms and sky-high heels for both men and women. Birkenstocks became popular with those looking for comfortable shoes which could also be seen as healthy for the feet. Although the customer demographic was quite broad, as Lusk suggested, older consumers found a "great deal of relief" with Birkenstocks, and these were seen as shoes that were "approachable" and practical. However, as he went on to indicate, Birkenstocks were also appealing to a younger consumer too who was "willing to take a chance on something different."[5]

Kate Moss, Birkenstock, and Mainstream Fashion Acceptance

Beyond Lusk's sale of Birkenstocks, one editorial feature was to catapult the brand into the mainstream in Britain. In July 1990, Kate Moss, then a 16-year-old, unknown model, appeared in an 8-page editorial feature in the British music, fashion, and culture magazine *The Face*. Moss was casually, and even minimally dressed in each image, although significantly, the only shoes seen throughout the editorial were Birkenstocks. This helped to introduce Birkenstock sandals to a wider audience, and ultimately ensured that they became one of the most fashionable footwear brands in Britain during the 90s. The shoot was styled by Melanie Ward, and her description of working on it clearly portrays the relaxed, causal attitude surrounding it:

> "We went out to the beach at Camber Sands a few times. It was all very instinctual. It felt totally organic: friends hanging out, dressing up and taking photos. There was no grand plan to start a whole new Cool Britannia moment, we were just having fun. I always wanted the clothes to look effortless, real, character-driven like the subject was wearing their own clothes and we were documenting them. I collected up a mix of clothes I liked—some mine, some vintage, customised, even some designer—and put them on Kate."[6]

Ultimately, all of the clothes Moss wears in the shoot look relaxed, or as Ward put it, "effortless" and "real."[7] The editorial portrays Birkenstocks as comfortable shoes, part of a new, very different way of dressing than had been seen in the 80s. The images in *The Face* quickly became iconic, they helped to launch Moss's career, but also unquestionably led fashion journalists widely to pick up on Birkenstocks.

The appearance of Birkenstocks in this editorial was largely thanks to Julian Vogel, founder of PR Agency ModusBCPM, who worked closely with Birkenstock and the Natural Shoe Store for fifteen years. He stated:

> "Melanie Ward and Corinne Day (Photographer) used to come into the office all the time and hang out, and then they came in one day and said, "We just want the ugliest shoes you've got." And then they found these Birkenstocks, and they put them on Kate Moss."[8]

This idea of the shoes as "ugly" was in many ways central to their appeal as a cool, "new" shoe in the 90s. Indeed, many of the key cultural movements in Britain during the 90s, from Cool Britannia to Britpop to grunge (an American import, but still important in Britain), rejected the idea of beauty and aesthetics in the traditional sense. Previous decades had seen an increasing interest in clothing and footwear which was comfortable, certainly the 70s, for example. There was a plurality to the acceptability of comfort in fashion in the 90s. Moreover, one of the key appeals of Birkenstocks was that they transcended fashion trends, working well with a broad range of outfits and styles. As Claudia Levy suggested in 1994, "the sports sandal is set to become something of a fashion perennial. Comfortable yet trendy, Birkenstocks look right with almost anything, from slip dresses and drawstring trousers to jeans and trouser suits."[9] This can also be understood as part of broader change in fashion, with casual clothes increasingly coming to dominate the fashion scene. By 2003 Libby Brooks suggested that "comfort has now become an acceptable part of the package for many forms of footwear [...] there has been a marked decline in the purchase of formal shoes over the past decade."[10]

Whilst by the 90s, casual, comfortable shoes were more widely accepted by consumers in Britain, there was a need for some diversification by Birkenstock in order to appeal more broadly to fashion consumers. Until 1994, Birkenstock sandals were produced in a relatively limited color palette. However, Lusk persuaded Birkenstock to diversify the color palette. Initially, Birkenstock were resistant to making the shoes in a broader color range. Lusk stated, "we had to guarantee that we would pay for the materials if we were going to make them in color and they did not sell." The gamble was however a success. The increased range of colors Lusk suggested "woke the customer up [...] that this was not just black and brown, you know, this came in colors, and this was fun [...] fun for your feet."[11]

It is striking that in the mid-90s, coverage of Birkenstocks by the fashion press in Britain increased dramatically, thanks to the more diverse range of colors that Birkenstocks were available in, and the work of Vogel to ensure that they were seen on the feet of celebrities. It is clear that the demand for Birkenstocks consequently increased considerably: a stand-alone Birkenstock store was opened by Lusk at 37 Neal Street in the spring of 1996, and Birkenstocks were, by then, stocked by almost 100 retail outlets across the UK.

Birkenstocks and the Victoria and Albert Museum (V&A)

In November 1994, a new exhibition opened at the V&A, called *Street Style: From Sidewalk to Catwalk, 1940 to Tomorrow*, which set the tone for diversifying the types of fashion or dress that might be seen in a museum exhibition. On display as part of *Street Style* were two pairs of Birkenstock sandals. Whilst *Street Style* did not open until winter 1994, as early as in 1989, anthropologist Ted Polhemus was already lobbying various V&A staff to put on the exhibition. In a letter proposing potential exhibition ideas he suggested:

"It is appropriate that a British institution like the V&A should mount an exhibition celebrating street style as it is Britain which has always, and to mind, will always, lead the world in this field [...] Tourists more and more come to Britain as much to photograph the punks as to see the Crown Jewels. Yet Britain rarely, at least officially, celebrates its leadership in this area. A major exhibition at the V&A could go a long way towards correcting this situation."[12]

The exhibition was eventually curated by Polhemus and internal V&A curators Amy de la Haye and Cathie Dingwall. The Street the exhibition argued, was "a state of mind rather than a place—embracing not only pavement promenading but club culture, style magazines and the visual component of popular music."[13] Through the clothing of 45 different style groups, from homemade to haute couture, *Street Style* celebrated the fact that in Britain since the late 40s, sub-cultural and countercultural clothing had become an influential cultural phenomenon.[14] Focusing primarily on youth fashion, the exhibition illustrated how, between the 40s and the 90s, the parameters of fashion had changed. As a 1992 document relating to the exhibition suggested:

"It has traditionally been accepted that new, interesting fashion ideas invariably start at the top end of the market and "trickle down" to the high street. This may once have been the case but today, if anything, the reverse is more typical with new styles bubbling up from street level to influence even high fashion."[15]

Prior to *Street Style*, the museum's collecting policy, as Lou Taylor has suggested, was still oriented to acquiring "a comprehensive and international collection of objects of the highest artistic merit and quality." [16] However, for *Street Style*, the policy was radically widened. Some garments were lent for the exhibition, but most were added to the V&A's permanent collection. A real plethora of different garments and accessories were collected, in order to recognize and celebrate the importance of street style to British culture. By collecting these garments, the V&A aimed to create a legacy beyond the exhibition, and to form a vital street style archive, accessible to future dress, fashion, and social historians for display and research.

The early 90s were a prescient moment for this type of exhibition, as an information sheet connected to the exhibition suggested: "In the 90s, there has been an extraordinary explosion of choice as dozens of different 'looks' rub shoulders in a sort of hypermarket of style."[17] No longer did one fashionable "look" dominate for a season, or perhaps more, but rather there was a plethora of different looks which were broadly accessible to consumers. Birkenstock sandals fitted seamlessly within the broader narrative of *Street Style*: They were unquestionably an example of a trend which had "bubbled up," starting as a countercultural trend, yet by the 90s appealing to diverse markets. Furthermore, the aesthetics of Birkenstock sandals, as has previously been suggested in this chapter, ensured they worked with a variety of different garment types.

The exhibition was a huge popular success, with 108,950 visitors (70,000 had been expected). The exhibition was also successful in appealing to a broader demographic, particularly younger visitors. 75 percent of visitors were under 34, compared to a normal museum average of 35 percent (not including school groups), and over 40 percent of visitors were students.[18]

Two pairs of Birkenstock sandals appeared in *Street Style*; firstly, a pair of classic, light brown nubuck *Arizona* (T.726:1,2-1994), which Lusk indicated were amongst the bestselling Birkenstock designs in Britain,[19] and secondly, a pair of *Milano* in dark brown leather (T.657:1,2-1995). The *Milano* features a trio of adjustable straps. Like the *Arizona*, two straps span across the top of the foot while an added third strap wraps around the area above the heel. Both pairs of shoes were new and unworn, rather than being part of a "street style" outfit someone had actually worn. Furthermore, both pairs of shoes were displayed with contemporary outfits, pointing to the increasing fashionability of Birkenstock in the 90s. Indeed, the justification for the eventual acquisition of the *Milanos* states that "they were one of the most fashionable designs in shoes for 1994."[20] Both shoes came, albeit indirectly in the case of the *Milanos*, from Lusk; the *Arizonas* were donated directly by Lusk/the Natural Shoe Store, whilst the *Milanos* were given by Vogel. One story the exhibition explored was the increasing fluidity of gendered fashion garments. Particularly through the more contemporary garments on display, it showed the possible experimentation that fashion offered in terms of gender expression.[21] Whilst one pair of Birkenstocks accompanied a menswear ensemble and the other a womenswear one, Birkenstocks were certainly part of "gender-neutral" fashion trends of the 90s, worn by all.

The two ensembles the Birkenstock sandals were shown alongside were both representative of a turn in the 90s towards more sustainable thinking, which, at the time, was generally branded as "eco". It was appropriate that Birkenstocks were selected to be shown with such outfits because environmental concerns have long since been important to Birkenstock. They were one of the first brands to offer a vegan range.[22] Furthermore, BIRKENSTOCK sandals are designed for longevity, they are durable, and the different components of Birkenstocks—including the shoe's uppers, footbeds, and treads—can easily be replaced.[23]

Fashion Casual

The Birkenstock *Arizonas* were displayed as part of a menswear outfit designed by Katharine Hamnett called "Fashion Casual–Spring/Summer 1994". This outfit consisted of "trousers" (T.168-1994), sweatshirt (T.169-1994), hat (T.170-1994), and scarf (T.171-1994). The Birkenstocks were selected by Hamnett herself to complete the outfit, although documentation from the exhibition suggests that originally a pair of black, rather than brown, sandals was requested.[24] It is unsurprising that Hamnett selected a pair of Birkenstocks to accompany her outfit when one considers that Hamnett was an early pioneer of sustainable fashion. Hamnett established her business in 1979, and by 1989 had begun assessing how sustainable the brand's practices were. That year, Hamnett commissioned a study into the social and environmental impact of fashion, expecting not to find anything wrong. However, the report indicated that the fashion industry was causing serious problems. Hamnett stated, "thousands of deaths from accidental poisoning in the cotton industry; people working in conditions worse than slavery; every single fibre and process was having a negative impact–of course the carbon emissions are colossal." As a result of the report's findings, Hamnett switched to organic cotton, avoided using materials which were made with potentially toxic chemicals like PVC and polyester, and also moved production back to Europe to ensure that workers were being treated fairly.[25] Since then, she has been, as Alison Gwilt has suggested, "a vocal fashion activist," encouraging consumers to take note of the critical issues affecting people and the environment, and continually campaigning to improve ethical and environmental production practices.[26]

Eco UK 1993

The Birkenstock *Milano* were displayed as part of a womenswear ensemble designed by Sarah Ratty under her label "conscious earthwear." The V&A called this outfit "Eco UK 1993." The outfit consisted of a skirt (T.670-1993), jacket (T.671-1993), top (T.672-1993), necklace (T.494-1993), and hat (T.207-1994). Ratty was an early pioneer of sustainable fashion in Britain in the 90s and early 2000s, launching her "conscious earthwear" label in 1990. Ratty's designs focused on environmentally responsible production and materials such as organic cotton, recycled fibers, and certified eco-conscious textiles.

Overall, the inclusion of two pairs of Birkenstocks in this exhibition points to the plurality of the brand; indicative of the various ways in which they were seen as fashionable by the mid-90s, suitable to be worn with a range of outfits. It also demonstrates that, in the eyes of fashion designers and exhibition curators alike, Birkenstocks were a trend from the street up, effectively a countercultural trend that by the 90s had infiltrated the mainstream. Finally, it must be seen that these shoes were part of the increasing development of an ecologically concerned consumer in Britain.[27] It is clear from other garments shown in "Street Style", representing the "future" of fashion, that this was expected to continue to be a major concern for fashion consumers. One outfit, "future streetstyle 2045", was described as follows: "All the garments and accessories in this outfit are recycled and biodegradable [...] because of their related chemical and biological constituents they can be recycled into an entirely new form."[28]

It is however interesting that two pairs of distinctly "German" shoes were chosen to appear in an exhibition on British street style. This indicates in many ways how Birkenstocks have been "adopted" as a British shoe despite their origins. Whilst not all garments in "Street Style" were British, both of the outfits the Birkenstocks were shown with were. It can be argued that the popularity of Birkenstocks in London specifically is heavily representative of the melting pot nature of London fashion—a German shoe, brought to London by an American entrepreneur.

This chapter has demonstrated that the 90s were a pivotal decade for Birkenstocks in Britain. It should however be noted that London was at the center of this change. Whilst consumers outside of London purchased and wore Birkenstocks, buying their shoes from approved sellers or via mail order, much of Birkenstock's popularity was thanks to London associations. One only has to look at Luard's suggestion, cited at the beginning of the chapter, that they were worn by "Soho groovers." Indeed, even more specifically, Covent Garden was at the heart of this shift, bringing Birkenstocks into the fashion mainstream. This endured beyond the 90s, and until 2019, Covent Garden was still the location of the only BIRKENSTOCK mono-brand store in Britain. Birkenstocks were part of many of the key 90s trends, from Cool Britannia to eco-fashion, Britpop to grunge. Their appeal in the 90s was largely related to their versatility and comfort, and indeed this has secured their enduring appeal with fashion consumers until today.

Birkenstock in France: Uber Fashionable?

BY HAYLEY EDWARDS-DUJARDIN

Conversations sparked around Birkenstock shoes and sandals often center around their dual identity: utilitarian and fashionable. Manifold are the examples of countries that have seen different individuals adopt the Birkenstocks, often from the very opposite faces of the fashion spectrum, the anti-consumerist hippies to an uber trendy clique. Yet, this evolution doesn't seem to be as fluctuating in France, nor does it seem to happen in a similar order, specifically in Paris, on which this chapter concentrates. Has the city that has mythicized its own nature as the capital of fashion challenged the prevailing Birkenstock narrative?

Fashionable Comfort?

When temperatures rise in France, Birkenstocks seem to be everywhere. Obviously, while researching for this chapter, I could not help but become utterly attentive to (if not obsessed with) the shoes worn by the people I would come across or meet, and once the sun came out in the late days of spring, Birkenstocks were popular again.

Comfort has now become an obvious component of the contemporary fashion mindset, there's nothing surprising in seeing sneakers, sandals, or sweatshirts on a runway. With the 2020 pandemic, clothing items mostly dedicated to the intimacy of the home, or the practice of sports have become distinct elements of everyday silhouettes. Yet, comfort, in France, often comes with an air of style, a well-meant alternative to trends, a certain casualness that needn't neglect elegance. Birkenstocks settle themselves within this scope. Marianne Deparis, the director of La Botte Chantilly, a retail shoe

Fig. 63: Catwalk with the new collection
BIRKENSTOCK # Dior (2022).

company that owns four stores in the north of France, believes that wearing comfortable shoes in which we feel good is indispensable to a healthy lifestyle.[1] The brand's popular attractiveness these past ten years has been fueled by a quest for comfort. Jean-Michel Gross, the founder of the Parisian retail shoe stores Sagone, evokes how, when trying on their first pair of Birkenstocks, his customers exhale a sigh of relief, even pleasure. To him, the brand is linked to a "feel-good" aspiration, associated with relaxation, the weekend, the holidays (he acknowledges how much his boutiques only sell the brand during the warm season). He admits putting his Birkenstocks on when he comes home after work, thus symbolically leaving the stress of the day by the door.[2]

Presumably, in France, Birkenstocks originally belonged mostly to a fashionable elite. Unlike in other countries, there has been no obvious transition from utilitarian standard to modish object. In France, the story seems more straightforward, even reversed: Birkenstocks promptly carried a noticeable air of exclusivity. Jean-Michel Gross attests that his decision to sell Birkenstock models from around 2000 was influenced by the hipsters he observed in the popular Marais and République areas of the French capital.[3]

Those who choose to wear Birkenstocks not only emphasize their fashion sense but also assert an impulse to remove themselves from the authority of trends. A legacy from counterculture?

As in many countries, the spread of Birkenstock sandals is linked to postwar youth culture. Although unattested, it is possible that Birkenstocks became an alternative accessory among some of the insurgents of the May '68 events, who adopted garments that contradicted the conventional staples of Parisian elegance, so as to better oppose both tradition and modernity. Small groups of the revolutionary students adopted Birkenstocks, thus imitating their American hippie counterparts—but also the possibly few people who had bought the sandals because they were comfortable. In 1961, Birkenstock had already distributed a catalog with an orthopedic approach written in French.[4] Although it seems to be mainly addressed to a Belgian audience, it still attests to the brand's aim to open its market to the French-speaking customer. Interestingly, a 1971 French catalog edited by a shoemaker and distributor of the BIRKENSTOCK brand, Hoki, based in Ingwiller in Alsace, on the German border, already emphasized a more trivial and less "medical" strategy. The catalog's headline stipulates "Birkenstock for leisure and work," and as the brands' various models and colors are described, stylistic prescriptions are delivered. For example, the green 422 model is "young and seductive," and thus perfect for a "fashionable outfit"; the red 421 model is "fun" and suits "sporty outfits, pants, and socks"; and a "pleasant" cognac 412 model can be worn on "any occasion and matches all outfits."[5] When addressing a French market, the Birkenstock shoe appeared to already accommodate its fashion sensibility. Our young 1968 dissidents were thus not only subscribing to an anti-fashion ideology by rejecting the established authority of Parisian style; they were also outlining an alternative sartorial expression, as countercultural movements often do. By refusing what was the aesthetic norm, they were turning Birkenstocks into a radical and modern choice.

Deconstructing Fashion

Beyond its authority as the capital of haute couture, the Parisian fashion landscape was rapidly evolving in the 60s and 70s, as young designers and stylists were challenging the aesthetics of traditional couturiers. As fashionable silhouettes were simplified, as were accessories, "foot-revealing sandals were becoming a part of everyday women's dress."[6] Although Birkenstocks were not yet visible in fashion editorials, clogs and platform sandals were all the rage. The delicacy of stilettos or ballet flats popularized by the 50s, was now being contested. In France, comfort in fashion, which had previously been seen as a loosening of morals, had now become a feature you could advertise.[7]

Fashion evolved towards a more radical expression following the impactful transcriptions of the punk taste by Vivienne Westwood in the mid-70s, followed by the Japanese designers Rei Kawakubo or Yohji Yamamoto, who presented their work on Parisian catwalks in the early 80s, and introduced a new fashion manifesto, later described as deconstructivism. With silhouettes that didn't shy away from asymmetry, androgyny, and imperfection, these designers offered an unconventional proposition that contradicted the predominant 80s aesthetic made of high glamour, theatricality, luxury, and materialism. These new designs were paving the way for progressive inclinations. The stage was set for the 90s, and Birkenstock had a role to play in these new narratives. The decade that was emerging towards an economic recession embraced deconstructivism as a fashion staple, assisted by a minimalist aesthetic and the grunge postures delivered by teenagers. Designers such as Martin Margiela were then chiefly challenging Parisian fashion's standards, from presenting fashion shows in an abandoned metro station to turning plastic bags into garments. Following the highly documented Marc Jacobs for Perry Ellis Spring/Summer 1993 show in New York, which had sent the 90s' most coveted supermodels of the 90s' down the runway wearing Birkenstocks, it was the French designer Martine Sitbon who featured *Gizeh* Birkenstock sandals in her Spring/Summer 1994 show in Paris.[8] For their first appearance on a French catwalk, the sandals accompanied deconstructed historicist ensembles evocative of the 19th century that questioned masculine and feminine stereotypes and shapes. Metallic embroidered see-through dresses stood out; their romantic aesthetic alleviated by the utilitarian sandals.

It is in this context that the key Parisian fashion temple of the 80s and early 90s, Hémisphères, led by Pierre Fournier, among others, began selling its first Birkenstock models in around 1992–93.[9] The two Hémisphères boutiques located in posh districts were the only fashion retailers to market the brand outside of the orthopedic scope. The identity of these stores was established around rarity and exclusive foreign products hardly ever seen before in France. Pierre Fournier had witnessed the success of the Birkenstock shoes in the United States, where he purchased many of his boutiques' products. Motivated by an Americana style taste he shared with his customers, he installed the Birkenstock brand in Paris. Grunge and minimalism were then all the rage. He recalls the first clients of the brand: fashion editors, celebrities, people with an affirmed fashion taste and knowledge. Those who then bought the brand had also come across the shoes in the United States. During our interview, Pierre Fournier discloses a 1993 postcard issued by Hémisphères and adorned, on the front, with a black-and-white photograph of his left foot, while the back reveals the drawing of a Birkenstock *Boston* clog with the accompanying text: Birkenstock. Marchez mieux ("Birkenstock. Walk better"). The retailer already had a fixed idea in mind: to help customers dress well. Not only in a fashionable way but in a concrete, well-fitted sense, respecting the body and its contours. In 1994, he thus opened Anatomica, a boutique still located in the Marais, for which Pierre Fournier selects brands that have an eye for the human anatomy. BIRKENSTOCK was an obvious choice. So much, in fact, that he designed a metal sign with the illustration of an *Arizona* sandal (his favorite model), which overlooks the store's entrance. He recognizes that Anatomica's customers are mostly connoisseurs—and mostly Japanese visitors.

It was only at the very end of the 90s that Birkenstock found a solid place in the Parisian fashion industry. The first fashion editorial featuring Birkenstock shoes I managed to locate was highlighted by the magazine Elle in March 1997: a dynamic-looking model wears a lurex tank top, metallic pants, and on her feet, silver *Gizeh* sandals. The shoes are credited as loafers (sic!) and are the result of a collaboration between French ready-to-wear high street brand Claudie Pierlot and BIRKENSTOCK.[10] Following Narciso Rodriguez's much remarked cashmere clad *Boston* clogs presented during his Fall/Winter 1998–99 show, whose silhouettes French fashion journalist Laurence Benaim compared to those of "luxury farmers in a limousine"[11] in March 1998, Birkenstocks were more and more present on the French fashion scene. A few months later, an article in the newspaper Le Monde attested to the trend of orthopedic sandals, citing the popularity of Scholl, Berkemann, or Sensi. When evoking the Birkenstock sandal, the journalist reminds us how, although it still "repels" French customers, "it is becoming a trendy accessory" that individuals could wear to create a "nun-like style."[12]

Outside of runway reports, Birkenstock editorials remained rare, and when the brand did appear in the pages of fashion magazines, it was rarely, if not never credited. This is the case in Elle in July 1998, in which an editorial highlighting silhouettes borrowing from orientalist aesthetics features a pair of *Arizona* worn by a local Moroccan extra.[13] Neither his traditional outfit, a striped djellaba, nor his shoes are credited. His Birkenstock shoes seem to enhance an exotic narrative, bringing us back to the hippies wearing their sandals while travelling the world in the 70s. The same year, still in Elle, in November, an editorial promotes warm, layered silhouettes, one of them featuring uncredited *Boston*.[14] The shoe is however described when it appears in the "shopping page" of a previous October Elle issue featuring leather *Boston* Birkenstocks in a selection of clogs,[15] while Vogue Paris, in September 1998, promotes Narciso Rodriguez's Birkenstock cashmere clogs.[16] In June 1998, Vogue Paris had already featured Birkenstock felt clogs when portraying the essentials of a young fashion model.[17] Finally, in a November 1998 issue, Elle gives us a glimpse of the dark *Boston* worn on the Paco Rabanne catwalk,[18] whose models are described by Le Monde as the "urban icons of a revisited punk era."[19]

As the new millennium was nearing, Birkenstock shoes were being more and more trivialized in the fashion discourse, and they strongly belonged to the latest trends. So much that when the French newspaper Libération describes what the word "hype" means to its readers in September 1999, it insists on how some individuals can be part of a hype without knowing it, taking the example of the "last hippies in Birkenstock sandals [who] have been joined, two years ago, by the first visionaries turned fanatics of this German brand."[20] These editorials and articles are indicative of the forcefulness of BIRKENSTOCK as a fashionable brand in the 90s in Paris.

"Birkenbeaufs"[21] and Ugly Chic

A year later, in June 2000, the journalist Marie-Hélène Martin analyzes a new trend: men wearing sandals. She quotes outraged commentators: "It's ugly," some claim, another affirms: "French aesthetics are threatened because some find them [...] comfortable. Who? 'The Birkenbeaufs'" The journalist however concludes: "The sandal awaits men at Colette," and insists that "it's a trend that touches a young, fashionable, and sensitive man."[22] Ugly maybe, but certainly trendy. Did the ugly shoe craze appear in menswear long before its praise in the 2010s?

Marianne Deparis remembers that while she had begun selling the brand from the late 90s, it was then indeed unthinkable for male customers to buy the sandals. Even most women were not at ease with the shoes' design: too "hippie," especially for a provincial town bourgeoisie. Thus, her initial customers were mostly the "happy few" that had discovered the brand while traveling on the American West Coast, those who had fashionable or cool, artistic jobs, or those who had an inclination towards a functional, Nordic aesthetic.[23] Jean-Michel Gross attests the same phenomenon; his early Birkenstock customers were sophisticated clients.[24]

With its low-rise jeans, pink velvet sweatpants, and diamanté G-strings, the new millennium was glamorizing trends that could be qualified as tacky. Yet the Birkenstock, although sharing similar attributes in the eyes of its detractors, lost its appeal in a decade that favored bling statements. However, in the 2010s, a new trend appeared: that of normcore, seen as a celebration of normality in 2014 by Libération.[25] Of course, the Birkenstock became an indispensable component of the new look. It was elevated to its peak when, in 2012, Phoebe Philo, then creative director of French luxury brand Celine, created "black, fur-lined sandals in a Birkenstock vein. [...] The shoes were key to this collection: furry, witty, unhinged."[26] The ugly shoe trend was unlocked. The Birkenstocks now confirmed that the way one looks at an object considered ugly can change its meaning. The brand was "used to create highly legible punctuations to sartorial statements and in turn became part of consumers' constructions of their own 'personal brands'."[27] By usurping the codes of utilitarian "ugly shoes," Céline, as a luxury brand, transformed their primary codes and turned them into a postmodern language of luxury.[28] In 2014, a fashion article states how summer trends are all about ugly yet chic shoes.[29] Boundaries between good and bad taste have thus become more and more blurry. Even more surprising, bad taste seems to have become the privilege of an elite, as Alice Pfeiffer theorizes.[30] Wearing "ugly fashion" is subversive when one deviates from the primary disposition of the object. When Birkenstocks, considered unaesthetic and tacky, are worn by individuals who are neither, their bad taste becomes the norm of fashionable insiders,[31] thus excluding those that are not in the know; those, for example, who originally wore Birkenstock for health reasons, without any aesthetic consideration. Marianne Deparis, Pierre Fournier, and Jean-Michel Gross, all three playfully recall how the *Madrid* were then very fashionable in the South of France with men, and how that contributed to a forceful emulation of the brand.[32] Around that time, Pierre Fournier and his brand Anatomica launched an exclusive collaboration with Birkenstock Japan, of models made from *inden*, an ancient Japanese craft of lacquer applied on deerskin. The models were sold in Japan, where they met huge success, and in his Parisian boutique. French customers were more reticent: the models being too expensive, according to Pierre Fournier.[33]

In July 2017, as an ultimate symbol of its fashion appeal, the Birkenstock *Arizona* was revisited in an exclusive black and blue model for the iconic Parisian concept-store Colette, which had just announced it would permanently close its doors six months later. For the occasion, the boutique had launched a series of collaborations with brands such as Hermès, Balenciaga, or Repetto. Adding BIRKENSTOCK to the list symbolically consecrated the brand as an iconic staple. Marianne Deparis believes these various collaborations and ersatz—with a trajectory close to that of sneakers before—opened up the brand to younger customers especially attracted to the *Boston* model because of its high presence on social media.[34] Jean-Michel Gross approves, he sees more "fashion victims" entering his boutiques, especially the store located in the Les Halles area, where the customers are younger and more influenced by trends. They both identify two typical groups of clients: a cultivated bohemian clientele faithful to the brand, and a fashionable youth with a more passing taste dictated by trends and influencers.

Symbolically strengthening its stylish presence, Birkenstock made an emblematic move in 2017, by proposing its first fashion show in Paris during Men's Fashion Week: an occasion for the brand to, as the newspaper Le Parisien claimed, "take revenge after years of living as an outcast."[35]

The following year, Birkenstock worked with photographer Dan Tobin Smith for its "Personality Campaign" that, amongst various celebrities, featured young French actress Luna Picoli-Truffaut, granddaughter of iconic film director, François Truffaut.[36] By associating its name with that of a patrimonial figure of French cinema, Birkenstock suggested it was not only fashionable, but also chic and classic. Maintaining its representative presence in the French capital, and more importantly, fashion's capital, in 2019, a result of Birkenstock's collaborations with designers, more specifically with Rick Owens the same year, that also led to Owens's Spring/Summer 2019 Ready to Wear and Menswear fashion shows in Paris. The Parisian team not only produces the luxury line, but is responsible for all collaborations that started with the Hotel Il Pellicano and brought the Il Dolce Far Niente-collection in 2019.[37] Whereas the first "1774 collection", the own creation of the team, was launched in 2020 during the Frieze Show in Los Angeles.

The design of the office was then highly documented by niche decoration magazines such as Milk Decoration,[38] adding to the magnetism of the German brand. That year, the French economic magazine Capital dedicated an article to Birkenstock, saluting how ugly yet successful it is.[39] The article goes on to explain how the brand benefits from eco-oriented discourses and commercial strategies. As ethical and environmental approaches are more and more scrutinized in fashion, Birkenstocks stand out with their natural materials. Jean-Michel Gross corroborates how many clients tend to have an eco-friendly motivation, purchasing mostly the brand's natural tones.[40] Moreover, the brand has, in general, remained faithful to its 60s production methods, making it a perennial fashion proposition that reassures both the customer and a broader fashion system. This enduring identity is also what adds to the appeal of BIRKENSTOCK, for, as author Marnie Fogg discusses, "old objects carry a superior value to what is beautiful and flawless."[41] Marianne Deparis recognizes her own inclinations in these values: La Botte Chantilly is a historically family-owned business with a predilection for ethical brands and the preservation of craftsmanship. By bringing Birkenstock's purpose and her own together, she addresses a sensible customer.[42]

When, in 2021, Alex and Christian Birenstock sold a majority stake of the firm to L Catterton and to Financière Agache, the family holding company of Bernard Arnault, CEO of LVMH, what seemed an unexpected move merely illustrated the stability of the German brand.[43] What does a luxury group like LVMH and Birkenstock have in common? A marketing strategy based on timelessness, patrimony, and craftsmanship. While the company explained its plan with reference to their aim to expand their markets to Asia, the partnership also solidified Birkenstock's lasting iconic identity, as a model "that decade after decade, sometimes century after century, is still conceived the same way, not because of a fetishist taste for tradition, by the way, but because of humility. Indeed, what would a human being invent better than clothing born from experience, that has proven its efficiency."[44] LVMH and Birkenstock soon demonstrated their association when Kim Jones, the creative director of Dior Homme, owned by the French group, presented its Fall/Winter 2022–2023 collection in Paris. Celebrating the historical couture house's 75th anniversary, the designer revisited Christian Dior's iconic New Look silhouettes,[45] and paired them with Birkenstock's *Tokio*, as a tribute to the original couturier's passion for gardening, reinterpreted in gray, black, or cream, with rubber details, some of them embroidered with pastel flowers evocative of a Dior 1957 dress. Not presented on the catwalk but commercialized by the collaboration, there were also designed exclusive *Milano* felt sandals in Dior's emblematic gray tone.[46]

By associating its name with that of France's largest luxury group, Birkenstock crystalized its inevitable fashion appeal, yet without succumbing to outright trends but as a key player in what permanence evokes: elegance. How ironic for a brand described as "ugly" or "tacky."

Conclusion

As in many other countries, Birkenstock shoes and sandals were at first associated with German backpackers and tourists, who were mocked on French beaches or countryside roads for their limited sense of style or elegance. However, when distributed in France, the brand promptly embraced a stylistic strategy very much aware of the country's historical heritage in fashion taste. From alternative yet distinctive accessory or exclusive prestige to luxury brand, BIRKENSTOCK has addressed a fashionable authority that turned the brand into a staple. From the 90s onwards, commentators have observed the enduring appeal of Birkenstock sandals and clogs and, although they at first served very established trends, they have since managed to overcome the turnover of fashion fads. By remaining true to their primary form and concept, Birkenstocks have now become classic essentials of contemporary wardrobes, the kinds praised by luxury brands in France; the kinds that serve personal style and elegance.

Fig. 64: Birkenstock is impressed by Japanese culture (2006 catalog).

Birkenstock in Japan

BY PIERRE-YVES DONZÉ

The Beginnings

There are two ways to look at Birkenstock's entry into the Japanese market: First, I am therefore examining how the firm organized its presence in this country. Like many Western fashion and accessory goods, Birkenstock appeared on the Japanese market during the mid-80s through a trading company.[1] The increasing value of the yen that followed the end of Bretton Woods (1971) and the Plaza Agreement (1985) made Japan an attractive country for foreign brands, and the first non-Western country to become a major consumer of European and American luxury goods. However, accessing the market was difficult because investment in retail was still regulated, and Japan's complex distribution system made it hard for foreign companies to reach final consumers by themselves. Hence, trading companies were the common intermediaries. They had a deep knowledge of the Japanese market and knew where and how to sell foreign goods.

Sanyei Corporation, a medium-sized trading company that was founded in Osaka in 1946 as an exporter of personal accessories and ceramics, became Birkenstock's partner.[2] This company had a broad network of foreign subsidiaries, one of which opened in Düsseldorf, Germany, in 1967. It cooperated notably with the department store Horten. In the 80s, Sanyei diversified its business towards importing and selling European goods in Japan, taking the opportunity of the growing purchasing power of Japanese people. In 1983, BIRKENSTOCK was one of the first brands with which Sanyei signed a contract for the sole agency, through its subsidiary Samco Sanyei.[3]

The penetration of the Japanese market was not easy during the first years. Birkenstock was not sold as a fashion item but as a high-quality product; namely, a comfort, healthy sandal.[4] A Japanese journalist explained in 2003 that "when the brand first arrived in Japan, it was mainly the over-40s who were more likely to associate the concept with health and comfort."[5]

The market for German comfort shoes developed in Japan as a consequence of the emergence of large discount shoe stores in the late 70s. Due to this competition, several independent shoe retailers refocused on niche products to survive, introducing the idea of shoe comfort and functionality. They were encouraged by the activities of the Japan Institute of Footwear (JIT), an organization founded by a journalist in 1965 to promote health instead of fashion. JIT introduced the idea of measuring customers' feet and distributed fitters among small shoe retailers in the early 80s. The increasing demand for comfort shoes led some retailers to start importing orthopedic and comfort shoes from Germany and other European countries during these years. One promoter was a German woman established in Kobe, Alice Christians.[6] She was followed by several Japanese small retailers.

The company consequently introduced sandals by Birkenstock in the emerging market to answer consumers' demand for high-quality comfort shoes, different from the mass-produced footwear sold by discount stores. However, the number of consumers was rather limited—since these products were comfortable, but expensive and not fashionable.[7] The tradition of leather sandals in Germany viewed by a Japanese journalist:

> "These health shoes were first popularized by doctors and nurses. They then became popular with restaurant chefs, waitresses, and department store clerks who were on their feet all day. Now even university professors, monks, and nuns wear leather sandals. Politicians from the health-conscious Green Party even wear them on official occasions. In Bonn, barefoot political dialogue is spreading."[8]

Niche Brand for Highly Fashionable Young People

The second way to look at Birkenstock's entry into the Japanese market is to focus on its early adopters. This provides an alternate story, and the German sandal was used in a very different context. Another agent, without any link to German headquarters, played a determinant role: specialized stores providing American casual fashion to young Japanese consumers. The outlet owners, particularly Ships and Beams, directly imported clothing and shoes from the US. Birkenstock had become popular among American youth in the 70s in the context of the hippie movement and anti-Vietnam War demonstrations. While in the US purchasing clothing, the promoters of streetwear in Tokyo visited Birkenstock's store in California and brought back sandals to offer their customers in Tokyo. After 1983, they were supplied with sandals direct from Germany through the Japanese agent Sanyei.[9]

Hence, BIRKENSTOCK also started its expansion into the Japanese market as a niche brand for young people with a special interest in creating new fashion trends during the 80s and early 90s. There was a clear reaction against Italian luxury fashion brands, like Armani and Versace, which dominated the market during the 80s.[10] The new generation wanted clothing that was simpler and not created by renowned designers. In an atmosphere of counterculture, people in their 20s in Tokyo and Osaka developed a new style, using American casual clothes, outerwear, and military wear. Walking barefoot, and consequently shifting from traditional shoes to moccasins, sabots, and sandals, became popular.[11] Birkenstock's products were consumed in this context as unique products expressing a new form of fashion.[12]

While the first official store opened in 1986 in Ginza, Tokyo's luxury shopping district, it was the independent fashion stores offering niche brands from Europe and the United States that played a key role for BIRKENSTOCK during this phase. These "select shops," as Japanese people call them, were based in Harajuku, which became one of the main places where the new street fashion trends emerged.[13] Labrador Retriever, a store opened in 1988 by a fashion designer who had lived in New York City, was a popular supplier of German sandals at this time.[14] Fashion magazines for men, notably Boon, introduced the new trend to a larger readership and increased demand for Birkenstock sandals, leading other select shops to sell them. Popular artists active in the fashion district of Ura-Harajuku, such as fashion designer Jun Takahashi, contributed to the renown of Birkenstock during these years.[15] In 1997, Sanyei Corporation, which had taken over BIRKENSTOCK's sole agency four years earlier, followed and opened its first mono-brand store in Harajuku.[16]

In 1992, the Tanemoto brothers began a specific business to sell and distribute the Tatami brand, launched two years earlier by Alex Birkenstock in Germany. However, the unique design of these products made them difficult to sell to Japanese consumers. An adaptation was necessary. In 1997, the Tanemotos founded a new company, Seed Co., which would design, manufacture, and distribute new Tatami shoes for the Japanese market.[17]

Mass Market of Fashion

Harajuku's mono-brand store's opening and the development of new Tatami shoes gave rise to a period of fast expansion. BIRKENSTOCK became a cool brand on the fashion mass market, particularly among "people in their teens and 20s."[18] In October 1998, Japanese business newspaper Nihon keizai shimbun explained: "Shoes and sandals made by Birkenstock, a German brand of luxury health shoes, which used to sell only a few thousand pairs a year, sold about 200,000 pairs last year, mainly to young people, and this year's sales are almost double that pace."[19]

Japanese show-business stars had a major impact on this first consumption boom among young people. Takuya Kimura, an actor, singer, and member of the idol band SMAP, wore some Birkenstock thong sandals in a TV drama show at that time. He was at the peak of his popularity and deeply influenced booming sales.[20] Until then, except for a few niche customers, BIRKENSTOCK did not have a fashion brand image, but rather that of an expensive comfort product that distinctly lacked style. Kimura contributed to changing the product's image into something cool and fashionable. His thong sandals have remained a popular product until today. Some second-hand models are often offered on Japanese second-hand auction websites such as Mercari.[21] The Japanese business press offers excellent evidence of this popularity. In January 1999, Nihon keizai shimbun explained:

> "On weekends, the Birkenstock shoe shop on Meiji-dori in Harajuku, Tokyo, attracts between 300 and 400 young people from all over Japan [...] The shoes are expensive, but sales have almost doubled in the past two years as young people have gradually begun to buy them after celebrities started wearing them."[22]

Moreover, the second part of the 90s was characterized by a camping boom throughout Japan. Outdoor wear brands like Patagonia and Montbell, and Land Rover cars became very popular. Wearing sandals and simple shoes, like Adidas' Stan Smith and Converse, developed as a widespread trend among a broad range of people, which also contributed to Birkenstock's popularity.[23]

However, the transformation of BIRKENSTOCK into a fashion brand for the mass market was not the sole result of consumer behavior. The company developed various actions to improve its brand identity. First, it expanded its distribution network massively. New mono-brand stores were opened in 1998 in the Mitsukoshi department store in Shinjuku, Tokyo, and in Osaka, then elsewhere in the country.[24] Their total number amounted to seven in 2002 and ten in 2004.[25] In 2002, Sanyei founded a new subsidiary, Birkenstock Japan, to supervise the import of shoes and the management of boutiques in Japan.[26] Besides, the German shoes were offered in a growing number of the most famous and trendiest stores in Tokyo and Osaka, like Beams and United Arrows. Second, Birkenstock products started to appear in various fashion magazines popular among young people.

Still, to properly understand Birkenstock's success in Japan after 1998 means moving beyond the narrative of young people fascinated by Takuya Kimura. A general boom for healthy sandals occurred that year. Prada also experienced a fast increase in sales of its sandals at the same time.[27] A business newspaper specializing in marketing explained that "young people on the cutting edge of fashion have become obsessed with health shoes that are said to be uncool."[28] At the end of the 90s, there was a general reaction against the decade's dominant fashion trend, which had been obsessed with sexuality. Young people wanted to return to something more intimate, closer to nature, and following an organic lifestyle. This context promoted the popularity of Birkenstock. As the Asahi shimbun newspaper explained in 1999, "fashion-conscious young people are not shy about dressing up their feet. [...] Manufacturers such as Birkenstock and Trippen are very popular."[29]

Moreover, the success of Birkenstock in Japan after 1998 was not only related to sandals. The company Seed, which had a license to manufacture Tatami shoes, wanted to establish itself as a fashion brand for a broad range of footwear.[30] It chose the *Pasadena* model, and decided to change its color from black to white. Hiroshi Fujiwara, a musician, designer, and promoter of street fashion in Japan, picked up this model and promoted it in magazines, leading to a real boom for Birkenstock shoes.[31] For Seed's management, it was the opportunity to apply a variety of new colors to the *Pasadena* model. However, the core technology of shoes, namely the *Footbed*, was always made in Germany and imported from there. It represented the identity of the brand.

Yet the consumption boom did not last. Birkenstock and its Japanese partners caught the opportunity of young people's interest in 1998, but they made a mistake by oversupplying the market with novelties. They launched too many models and were not followed by consumers. The company made its first losses in Japan in 2001–02. Headquarters questioned the autonomy of Seed in developing Tatami shoes.[32] A new business model was needed.

Specific Position between Fashion and Health

A better balance between the two core aspects of the BIRKENSTOCK brand—health and fashion—was necessary to build a sustainable growth strategy. There had been too much emphasis on pure fashion in the late 90s. While Birkenstock shoes and sandals were cool, they were also functional. To increase the public's attention on the functional aspect as well, Birkenstock Japan used mono-brand stores as communication tools. It opened numerous new shops around the country, growing from ten in 2004 to 60 in 2016.[33]

Two important actions were implemented. First, the management decided to introduce small devices to offer fitting services to all consumers entering the store. Measuring the exact size of their feet and selecting the most suitable shoe strengthened the high value of the brand. Second, the company opened repair factories to stress that sandals by Birkenstock were high-quality goods that required long-term maintenance. It was far from the fast-fashion model.[34] In 2022, about 30,000 shoes were repaired, among total annual sales of about 600,000 pieces.[35]

Besides, the image of a fashionable comfort product was supported by magazines and books published in 2005–07. They featured celebrities from show business, fashion, sports, and design, showing how Birkenstock sandals and shoes could be combined with a range of clothes and accessories to create a unique style.[36] This contributed to raising the popularity of the brand among fashion-conscious consumers.[37]

The company Seed played an important role in developing this new market for Birkenstock. After headquarters decided to give up the Tatami model, the Tanemoto brothers negotiated to start manufacturing them for Japan (2003) and other Asian nations (2005). While all models were approved by Germany, they were designed and produced in Japan, contributing to the brand's localization. It developed several partnerships with global fashion brands, one of the first being Levi's. Collaborations followed with Tommy Hilfiger, Philip Lim and Disney, the latter giving birth to a Tatami shoe using high-end denim made in Japan. Collaborations were also undertaken with world-famous Japanese designers, particularly Yohji Yamamoto.[38] Cooperation with Louis Vuitton was even attempted in 2009, but the action was limited to a few unique models created for local celebrities.[39] Finally, in 2011, a collaboration started with the famous Japanese handmade sock brand Tabio to launch Birkenstock-Tabio socks.[40] However, such diversification towards fashion accessories was rare, and the German brand primarily remained focused on shoes and sandals.

In 2009, journalist Yukari Kawasaki explained:

> "[I]n 2003, the company began selling products designed and colored for the Japanese market. [...] Currently, half of the products are designed in Japan and the main advertisement is also made in Japan. The brand's competitiveness is the result of a combination of Europe's basic strength and Japan's ability to communicate trends, but as the population becomes more sensitive to physical sensations, the brand needs to be able to offer products that do not force people to choose between physicality and fashion."[41]

Moreover, this brand-image change dramatically increased Birkenstock's customer base. While young people in their 20s were the main consumers purchasing sandals purely as a fashion item, a broad enlargement of customers, from teenagers to retirees, followed the attraction of functional aspects.[42]

Finally, the image of BIRKENSTOCK during this period developed towards a third element: a brand whose products are durable and manufactured in compliance with strict EU regulations. It was in line with the healthy image and answered a growing interest from young consumers. Since 2008, Birkenstock Japan has stressed the limited impact of its goods on the environment, notably due to its maintenance services and the use of natural raw materials.[43] Six years later, in 2014, it opened a new flagship store in Harajuku, a boutique that expresses the quintessence of an eco-responsible brand. It merges traditional Japanese architecture based on simple lines and the use of wood with German eco-conscious high technology, embodied by solar power and titanium outers. Its ambition is to promote the brand's environmentally friendly concept and further raise its profile in Japan.[44]

Global Brand in the Japanese Market

The restructuring of the company in 2013 deeply impacted the brand image in Japan, as it had in many other countries. Birkenstock Japan, which had been actually wholly owned by Sanyei Corporation, changed its name in 2016 to Benexy. It retained sole distribution of the brand in Japan and also diversified to import and sell other brands. In 2016, a new Birkenstock Japan was opened as a subsidiary of German headquarters and placed, for the first time, under the direction of a European manager. Raoul Wortmann, who had been in charge of brand development in the Asia-Pacific region since 2014, was appointed as its new CEO.

A major objective was to understand who the final consumers of Birkenstock were. As the company had worked with local intermediaries until that time, it lacked direct knowledge of the Japanese market. The new global strategy aimed to increase the value of the brand. Hence a restructuring of distribution in Japan, based on the segmentation of stores, products, and consumers, was necessary. Another aim has been to be flexible and diversified in terms of stores and store concepts. Especially in Japan and Tokyo, there have been collaborations with local architects and designers. The objective has been to strengthen the position of BIRKENSTOCK as a premium brand and reconnect it with younger consumers and communities sensitive to fashion, an aspect that had declined with the large-scale distribution. Birkenstock Japan launched special make-up projects, designing specific shoes and sandals with influential and creative fashion retailers like Beams or United Arrows. Products they create with these partners bring new aspects to their designs and brand not only locally but globally, as well as connecting with new consumer segments. Always with the focus and the emphasis on the brand's core values. The abandonment of sub-brands and the refocus of Birkenstock Japan on retail was a major change that contributed to improving the brand's value and renewing its consumer base. The existence of a single BIRKENSTOCK brand positively affected sales because it gave a stronger image, particularly among new generations of consumers, who were an important target of the new management.

Finally, strengthening the BIRKENSTOCK brand in Japan led to a transformation of the distribution system, characterized by more consistent brand management from within the company. While Benexy had targeted the densification of mono-brand stores since the mid-2000s, reaching a total of 70 before the COVID-19 crisis,[45] Birkenstock Japan decided to refocus this network on a smaller number of stores that offered a higher value to the brand. Consequently, it ceased relations with large discount shoe retailers like ABC Mart. It also took over mono-brand store management from Benexy. At the same time, in 2018, Birkenstock opened its own online store in Japan and decided to withdraw gradually from other sales platforms like Amazon. Viewed from Japan, the implementation of a global brand strategy after 2013 saw brand management and retail being taken over by Birkenstock, but it also saw better localization with a few key independent retailers. These became close partners for the co-development of specific goods, with the final objective being to connect with customers more directly and more intensively.

Fig. 65: In 1992, Birkenstock sandals made it all the way to Australia. Catalog for the sales launch down under (1992).

Birkenstock in Australia 1992–2022: A Stable Shoe for Shifting Terrains

BY EMILY BRAYSHAW

The story of Birkenstock in Australia is a contradictory narrative that centers on an everyday object: a shoe. As a young Australian, my first widespread exposure to Birkenstocks and the seemingly "daggy" practice of wearing them with socks was at the age of 16 in 1989, when I commenced a nine-month stay in Germany as an exchange student. The term "daggy" in Australia has long been used as an affectionate insult that denotes a person, practice, or object that is lacking self-consciousness, unfashionable and/or ugly, but is nonetheless eccentric and loveable.[1] Prior to my time in Germany I had, like many other Australians, seen the dress practice of wearing Birkenstocks (with and without socks) by German tourists, especially backpackers, but I did not realize the popularity of the habit across Germany until I lived there. Giorgio Riello and Peter McNeil write: "Shoes indicate a great deal about a person's taste [...] and identity—national, regional, professional—class status, and gender. Shoes have, for centuries, given hints about a person's character, social and cultural place, even sexual preference."[2] Germans' earnest, unfashionable habit of wearing Birkenstocks with socks as appropriate footwear for the outdoors therefore contributed to a widespread Australian perception that Birkenstock shoes were themselves somewhat ugly and daggy.[3] Indeed, as Marcel Goerke, the Managing Director of Birkenstock Australia recollects, there were situations when curious shoppers visited the first Birkenstock store in Melbourne in 1992 and said, "That's a lot of money for very ugly shoes."[4] Even as late as 2015, Australian style journalist Rebecca Sullivan wrote on one of the country's leading news websites, "Birkenstocks are the daggy sandals usually worn by crusty-heeled blokes schlepping to the weekly farmers' markets [...] I thought they were ghastly and anyone who wore them displayed seriously poor judgement."[5]

However, in the 90s, in addition to being seen as a "daggy" German shoe in Australia, Birkenstocks were also an important marker of queer identity in

Fig. 66: In the early 90s, Marcel Goerke decided to leave his German home and family, who run one of the oldest Birkenstock specialist shops in Braunschweig. Goerke has sold Birkenstocks in Australia since 1992. This shows Goerke's grandparents touring Australia in their socks and Birkenstocks.

Australia, embraced in particular by lesbian communities, which championed the shoe for its dedication to comfort and practicality above fashion. This chapter explores how the "daggy" Birkenstock traveled from the establishment of Birkenstock in Australia in 1992 via the lesbian feminist community and grunge subculture of the 90s and adapted to Australia's social and environmental conditions over the next 30 years to become a popular, fashionable shoe celebrated for its style as much as for its comfort and history.

The Birkenstock Paradox: "Daggy", an Iconic Design, or Both?

Although Birkenstocks were widely considered "daggy" during their early years in Australia, a daggy object is not always an aberration of good quality, or good design; rather, since the establishment of the first Birkenstock store in Australia, the shoes have carried the mythic associations of German manufacture with notions of authenticity, practicality, high craftsmanship, and superior quality.[6] In Australia in the early 90s, these German manufacturing qualities were often associated with objects like the Staedler's writing and technical drawing implements and with automotive engineering, with brands such as BMW leading the luxury car market in 1991.[7] This emphasis on quality had been promoted by German industrial manufacturers since the foundation of the Deutsche Werkbund in 1907, an organization that aimed to "integrate traditional methods of craftsmanship into industrial mass-production techniques [...] [to] make Germany a leading global manufacturing center."[8] Birkenstock shoes, which are intended to be unisex, also carry these qualities and adhere to the principles of good design espoused by Swiss and German product design movements of the mid-20th century, including using the appropriate materials to create an object fit for purpose that also privileges pared-down, simple lines to achieve a "visual expression of unity of all functions."[9]

The first BIRKENSTOCK models sold in Australia in 1992 were the *Arizona*, the two-strap sandal designed by Karl Birkenstock in 1973, the *Florida*, the *Bali*, the *Milano*, and the children's *Birko-Flor* models. The concept of design, however, "extends to everything that is planned and/or made," and a designed object does not always adhere to conventional or even popular notions of fashion and style.[10] Goerke reveals that Karl Birkenstock was never interested in current fashion trends when he created the *Arizona* or one of the many other models. Instead, the basis for these designs was Karl Birkenstock's vision of healthy footwear. Alongside this, he strove to create "an absolutely functional shoe that mimicked natural walking."[11] In 1992, however, Birkenstocks did not look like other shoes that were widely worn in Australia.

The visual unity created by the unisex Birkenstock and its wearer was of a naturally aligned, healthy body created from the foot up, with the *Footbed* and straps privileging a minimalist design that supported the object's function of promoting good health over the communication of fashionability and gender which is typical of other fashion items. Birkenstocks were visibly different from the numerous fashionable and popular styles of footwear worn in late 20th-century Australia, including stilettos; sturdy, Australian-made work boots such as Blundstones and RM Williams; platformed shoes; men's dress shoes; sandals; and even sporting shoes and thongs (known outside Australia as "flip-flops"). These types of footwear worked with styles of body and dress to construct a visual unity based on an unnatural, distorted body and an understanding of gender which was cultural yet perceived as natural.[12] Dress conventions of high heels, skirts, and dresses combined to create what Australians culturally accepted as a "naturally" feminine silhouette, while the culturally accepted "naturally" masculine silhouette was created by the suit and shoes and/or boots, despite the suit's complexity of manufacture and its ability to hide and/or reshape the male body.[13] Although Australia experienced increasingly relaxed and unisex dress codes in the late 20th century due to the adoption of outdoor and athletic styles of casual dress to suit the warm, sunny climate, masculine and feminine styles of body and dress were nonetheless firmly entrenched. In the 90s, however, the androgynous Birkenstock contributed to an ambiguity of dress in Australia at a time when strictly defined cultural understandings of gender were being destabilized by third wave feminism, which built on women's freedom from compulsory heterosexuality, and argued for women's pleasure in expressing their sexuality. Masculinity was also forced "to take part" in the era's shifting gender debates, rather than to define them.[14] The androgyny of the Birkenstock and the desire of male wearers to experience the comfortable shoe also positioned it as antithetical to culturally constructed Australian masculinities associated with machismo and toughness. These notions, combined with the visual unity of an aligned, undistorted body that confused cultural understandings of gender also contributed to Australian social and cultural perceptions that the Birkenstock, and by extension its wearer, was daggy, unnatural, and ugly, despite the shoe's sophisticated design and high-quality manufacture.

Birkenstock: Queer Shoes and the Queer Community

The Australian lesbian-feminist community in the 90s appeared to embrace Birkenstocks as the sandals adapted to their new "physical terrain" and to Australia's changing "social one."[15] The 90s stereotype of the "Birkenstock lesbian" was grounded, in part, in the community's promotion of an androgynous style of dress known as "lesbian clone style," which was characterized as comfortable, and allowed lesbians nationally and globally to identify one another in solidarity.[16] The look was based on short hair and clothing such as "flannel shirts, loose jackets, and baggy pants," and comfortable, flat shoes including Birkenstocks and Blundstones.[17] Despite the preferred look, many Australians still clung to long-held stereotypes of "lesbians having poor fashion sense," which were based in "cultural prejudices about the mannish woman as unnatural and ugly" and the persistent idea in 90s popular culture that lesbians tended to "dress like men" because they were not dressing to attract the opposite sex.[18] Same-sex desire, however, "is not just a question of subcultural codes of mutual recognition and sexual attractiveness. It shapes 'ways of looking' beyond homosexual and homosocial contexts, thus making the study of Queer shoes central to understanding general shoe culture."[19] Even through its exotic model names, such as *Arizona*, *Bali*, *Rio*, and *Florida*, the Birkenstock expressed ideas of freedom via global travel, while it possessed the polarities of comfort and extreme stylization that characterized "media ideas and real-life experience for lesbians."[20] In particular, the ideas of freedom and authenticity expressed by Birkenstocks were at the center of one of the key changes to the social terrain in the 90s, the broadening of the gay rights movement that had been growing since Australia's first gay and lesbian activist group in 1970, Campaign Against Moral Persecution (CAMP), put gay liberation on the social agenda.

CAMP members were instrumental in the foundation of one of the leading events in the Australian LGBTQIA+ rights calendar in Sydney that continues to this day, the Sydney Gay and Lesbian Mardi Gras. On June 24, 1978, a small group of protestors in Sydney, who formed to contribute to the international gay celebrations, were met with police violence, arrests, and brutal beatings in custody.[21] In 1980, the Sydney Mardi Gras retained its focus as a protest parade and introduced a post-parade party. In 1981, the parade was moved to March, a warmer month in Australia, which encouraged more attendees. Protestors also set up an "Alternative Lifestyle Fair" in inner-city Sydney in 1979 as part of a week of activities around International Gay Solidarity Day. The annual event is now known as Mardi Gras Fair Day and is the kick-off event for the official Mardi Gras season for Sydney's wider LGBTQIA+ communities and allies. The event's name was changed in 1988 to the Sydney Gay and Lesbian Mardi Gras, and the event began to "enjoy extensive media coverage from the [mid-80s] onwards and the crowds continued to swell, from 200,000 in 1989 to more than 500,000 in 1993."[22] The dedication of gay and lesbian activism saw the Australian Commonwealth Government final legalize same-sex sexual activity between consenting adults (in private) throughout Australia in 1994.[23] Contemporary culture "provides evidence of a very specific relationship between sexual identity and shoes."[24] In Sydney, this evidence is in the form of photographs from the 1992 Sydney Gay and Lesbian Mardi Gras parade that show lesbians wearing Birkenstocks with socks. Additional photographs by C.Moore Hardy held in the City of Sydney Archives taken at the Mardi Gras Parade, Fair Day, and feminist and queer rights demonstrations throughout the 90s show the popularity of the lesbian clone style within the community, with numerous Birkenstock models, including the *Bali*, the *Arizona*, and the *Florida* proving to be comfortable and practical in the hot Sydney weather. An archival photograph taken in 1998 by C.Moore Hardy shows a pair of tan *Arizona* Birkenstocks being worn by a lesbian "78er" at the official pre-parade meeting of 78ers planning their commemoration of the 20th anniversary of the first Sydney Gay and Lesbian Mardi Gras parade in 1978.[25] The 78ers have led the parade since 1998.

Birkenstocks also became popular with Australian members of the 90s grunge youth subculture embracing the shoe's daggyness as well as its comfort and practicality.[26] This was due, in part, to a "blurring between lesbian dress styles [including Birkenstocks], popularized by the mainstream press as 'lesbian chic,' and the sexually ambivalent apparel worn by 'Riot Grrls,' which later crossed over into mainstream fashion."[27] This crossover occurred around 1994 in Australia, when the fashion magazine Elle ran an advertorial that promoted Birkenstocks as a core component of a comfortable, stylish, domestically worn wardrobe that was value for money.[28] The advertorial fea-

Fig. 67: Lesbian drumming band participating in the Sydney Gay & Lesbian Mardi Gras Parade, February 1992. One of the women is wearing yellow, striped socks with Birkenstocks.

tured a photograph of a straight, white, slim, attractive, blue-eyed brunette with subtle makeup and manicured nails wearing a soft blue top, white stretch jeans, and blue *Arizona* Birkenstocks relaxing seated in a closed pose on a white, cushioned chair. In contrast to the image of the domesticized woman in her Birkenstocks promoted in Elle magazine, a photograph taken at the 1995 Reclaim the Night march in Sydney shows a protester's Birkenstocks peeking from beneath the banner for the Women's Library. The march had its roots in the lesbian-feminist rallies of 1978, when Australia's first annual Reclaim the Night march was held by women and allies "demanding an acceptable response to violence against women in our community and worldwide."[29] Images such as the Reclaim the Night photograph ensured that Birkenstocks were still firmly associated in the Australian popular imagination with the lesbian-feminist community, Riot Grrls, and grunge kids in the '90s, despite its crossover into the mainstream press.

In addition to the comfort and practicality of Birkenstocks, Goerke posits that the popularity of Birkenstocks among the lesbian community and other subcultural groups is that in its first 30 years, Birkenstock never made an effort to push the shoe onto people:

"There was not visual [marketing] stimulation to anyone that could have said, 'This is not for me.' There wasn't a situation where people didn't understand the product or were pushed in a specific direction based on visuals they'd seen. Every single pair was sold by one individual selling the product to another. People made them their own and had their own relationship and experiences with the shoe."[30]

There was, therefore, a lack of heteronormative marketing materials around the Birkenstock that could have alienated any particular group from purchasing the shoes, and by the time fashion magazines like Elle started to feature the shoe, it had already been claimed by the queer community. The one-on-one sales approach around the Birkenstock also reinforced commonly held notions of authenticity associated with German products, further adding to its appeal as a queer shoe in Australia. Marcel Goerke explains:

"Authenticity comes through relationship building with the customer. Marketing isn't about authenticity. Marketing creates stories that are for specific groups of people. Historically, marketing is often artificial stories to entice people. It just wasn't in Birkenstock's history and the marketing now is authentic and actual Birkenstock wearers are telling their story and not getting paid. That's authentic. You can put a model in Birkenstocks, but if you make up a story that's not true, that wouldn't be Birkenstock. All the stories we have told have always been authentic. The people who work here now have always loved to engage with consumers and retailers and tell them where it's from, what it's about, how it works, and we encourage them to tell their own stories that they experience over a period of time."[31]

Adapting to Australia, Socially and Environmentally

Goerke notes that Birkenstock Australia experienced a growth spurt in sales between the mid-90s to the early 2000s in line with the rising popularity of the grunge and rave movements among Generation X. Many grunge and raver kids also hung out with the LGBTQIA+ scene in Sydney in the 90s, as it offered a safe alternative to the mainstream to young people who wanted to express their gender and identity in non-conforming ways. Yet in addition to his Melbourne store, Goerke says Birkenstocks were sold by smaller independent retailers during this time, including the Sydney-based Platypus Shoe Co. and Hype DC, which had not yet reached their mainstream status in malls across Australia. This, as Goerke states, "suited the grunge story" because "customers had to go hunting" to buy Birkenstocks.[32] Anecdotally, a friend told me he bought his first pair in 2002 when Birkenstock Soul, the first dedicated Birkenstock retailer in Sydney, opened its doors.[33] He also noted that Birkenstock Soul's location in

Petersham in the Inner West of Sydney—an area associated with punk, queer, grunge, rave, and alternative subcultures since the 80s—added to the thrill of the hunt. Birkenstocks also slowly found their way into Australian workplaces: chefs, for example, embraced the closed-toe *Boston* model in black for comfort and protection during long shifts on their feet in the kitchen. The increasingly casual nature of everyday dress and the global rise of so-called "athleisure" wear in the 2010s meant that more people than ever were seeking comfortable footwear. In 2012, for example, the designer Phoebe Philo at Céline sent models down the runway at Paris Fashion Week wearing shoes that resembled a fur-lined Birkenstock, while the Guardian declared in February 2013, "It's the Year of the Birkenstock!"[34] Australians were part of the international trend to embrace the Birkenstock, and by 2022, the fashions of the 90s were alive again,[35] embraced by Generation Z, who emerged from COVID lockdowns to discover the joys of ironic, ugly, daggy, yet comfortable style in their so-called "weird girl aesthetic," just as many of their grunge, queer, and raver elders still do.[36]

Australian Generation Z's embrace of Birkenstocks with socks, however, has not arisen in a vacuum. According to Alice Cicolini, "socio-political and cultural context is important in the selection of retro clothing." This, she argues, is

> "[...] particularly evident in high design. Walter Benjamin, in Theses on the Philosophy of History, speaks of the creative 'tiger's leap' into the past, the aggressive and specific selection of historical reference to serve contemporary comment. Historical revivalism is most often used as a tool to create a pervasive, and recognizable, environment for fashion that responds very pertinently to the times in which it is created."[37]

Since 2019, Generation Z Australians have carried the anxieties of spiraling economic inflation and job insecurity, surviving COVID-19, and coping with the vast environmental devastation of Australia through catastrophic bushfires and floods caused by climate change. In addition, they have grown up online, where their lives have been extensively documented. Embracing the bright, clashing colors, textures, and the Birkenstocks-with-socks look of the 90s' queer and women's rights movements and grunge and rave scenes allows Generation Z to tap into the ethos of these movements, which were as much about human rights and individual, authentic expressions of gender, sexuality, and self as they were about having amazing parties. Generation Z is now adapting these styles and using them to create their own ways of making sense of, and being in, the contemporary world, and to stand out in a sea of digital images.

Fig. 68: No distance too far for quality and service. Karl and Gisela Birkenstock visited Marcel Goerke at his Melbourne store in March 1996.

Birkenstock, conversely, has adapted its footwear to the Australian physical environment via a repair service. Birkenstocks last so long in Germany because the cooler climate and stark seasonal differences mean they are generally only worn outdoors for a few months each year. This is very different from how shoes are worn in Australia; the Sydney climate means Birkenstocks are seen on the streets and at the beach all year round, so they wear out quickly. Goerke explained that Australian consumers have the expectation that Birkenstocks last a long time, but that Sydney wearers find their Birkenstocks often need a replacement of the heel part of the shoe sole after three months of wear, and a sole replacement after six months.[38] From the early 90s, Goerke and his team quickly realized that Birkenstock also needed to offer a repair service. "For the last 30 years we've consistently operated a repair workshop so you can prolong the lifespan of your shoes and this is how we've adjusted to Australia," he said.[39] Birkenstock Soul in Petersham also started its life as a dedicated Birkenstock repair shop.

> "Birkenstock staff can readily tell from looking at the worn marks of the shoe sole and leather uppers whether the shoe is the right size and style for the user [...] With options to replace different components—the shoes' uppers, footbeds, and treads can be replaced—as well as re-sizing for children's shoes, there is an opportunity to observe and respond to the parts of the shoe that are the most

and least durable, designing the repair around these and gifting both the shoe and wearer with more time."[40]

Climate change and hotter Australian summers also mean that Birkenstock has recently developed a heat warning that accompanies their shoes, requesting that consumers do not leave their Birkenstocks in the car on really hot days, or exposed to direct sunlight, as the ethylene vinyl acetate (EVA) soles can shrink. This warning is the same for the range of 100 percent EVA products that Birkenstock developed in 2015 for use at the pool and the beach.

BIRKENSTOCK's popularity in Australia in the 2010s and 2020s, however, is not just explained by the shoe's qualities, its adaptation to local conditions, and Australians' embrace of global fashion trends. Rather, wearers of Birkenstocks must also be prepared to break in the shoes, because the footbed, the heart of the minimalist design, can feel unusually hard and unyielding at first.[41]

There are, therefore, intimate, spatial, "physical processes that occur [when wearing in a Birkenstock] that are separate from, however much they are infused with, the social realm" of the shoes.[42] The result of these physical processes is that the individual wearer forms a deeper relationship, a kind of "connection," with the Birkenstocks. The spatial and temporal connectedness resulting from the process of breaking in a pair of Birkenstocks contributes to the wearer's "dependence" on the shoe to enable physical comfort, a sense of self, and opportunities for socialization with like-minded others.[43] This spatial and temporal connectedness is then expanded via the Birkenstock repair processes, which, by prolonging the "life" of the shoe, entangles the wearer even further. "Things become possessed by us, but we have also become possessed by them, by their colour, beauty, memory, associations, etc. The processes [of recognising possession] involve paying attention to, becoming associated with, becoming linked in terms of history and memory."[44] Over the last thirty years in Australia, as the original "die-hard" Birkenstock wearers have clung to their old shoes and committed to wearing in new pairs, new converts have steadily committed to the practice of wearing Birkenstocks, thereby contributing to the shoes' ubiquity, building on the social ideas and symbols associated with the shoes, and developing new "ways of looking" at Birkenstocks and their wearers. No longer does mainstream Australia consider the Birkenstock completely "ugly" and the exclusive shoe of lesbian feminists, grunge kids, or "daggy" German backpackers.

Conclusion

This is the first study to chart how the Birkenstock navigated the Australian social and cultural terrain from the margins of society in the 90s to its fashionable center in the 2020s. With the first models, such as the *Madrid*, the *Zürich* or the *Arizona*, Karl Birkenstock created design-icons of the 20th century. The popularity of the *Arizona* as a queer shoe in the 90s was grounded in its androgyny, its comfort, and its encapsulation of the features of good German design and manufacture: authenticity, practicality, high craftsmanship, and superior quality. Yet it was a gradual path for mainstream Australians to understand and embrace the Birkenstock, because the visual unity of wearer and object did not conform to culturally determined expressions of gender that were perceived as natural. As Australian social movements and subcultures in Sydney from LGBTQIA+ rights to grunge and raves traversed from the margins to the mainstream, both the Birkenstock and I traveled parallel paths through these new social territories; whether a discriminatory practice remains socially acceptable, or whether an object is considered ugly can change vastly over time.

Since 1978, when the 78ers held the first Mardi Gras rally, queer communities have fought to shift Australian popular perceptions of lesbianism from being unnatural and ugly to a lesbian couple becoming the first same-sex married couple in Australia in December 2017, a week after same-sex marriage became legal in Australia.[45] Birkenstocks have similarly moved from being considered ugly "lesbian" shoes to receiving the recognition they deserve as an example of iconic design. In addition to Generation Z's love of the daggy "visual unity," authenticity, and practicality of Birkenstocks, the shoe's pared-down, simple silhouette also appeals to contemporary design practitioners who are interested in environmental and sustainable designs that aim to minimize and reduce the materials used in production, resulting in sleek, streamlined objects. It is likely, therefore, that the key to the Birkenstock's enduring and growing popularity in Australia is that its good design, lack of marketing, cosmetic modifications and repairs to adapt to the environment and to fashion, and not least the wearer's commitment to the shoe, allow for different "ways of looking" and different ways of being and self-expression for each individual and each new generation.

What is a Birkenstock?

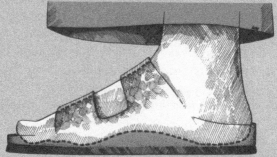

Lightweight, flexible cork footbed forms to your foot.

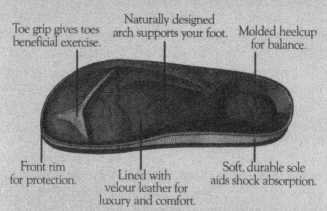

Toe grip gives toes beneficial exercise.

Naturally designed arch supports your foot.

Molded heelcup for balance.

Front rim for protection.

Lined with velour leather for luxury and comfort.

Soft, durable sole aids shock absorption.

Two footbed widths. Adjustable tops to fit your foot properly.

Let your feet make a place for themselves.

BIRKENSTOCK MODELS SINCE 1963

Fig. 69: Poster, Birkenstock (90s).

MADRID
(until 1979 *Original Birkenstock-Footbed Sandal*)
1963

ZÜRICH
(until 1979 *Closed Model*)
1964

ROMA
(until 1979 *Strap Sandal*)
1965

CLOSED – HONNEFER MODEL
1965

EXQUISIT
(variant of *Strap Sandal*)
1966

ATHEN
(until 1979 *Boot*)
1969–70

OSLO
(until 1979 *Loafer*)
1969–70

NOPPY
1970–71

ARIZONA
(until 1974 *Closed Model*, then *Pater Model*, early in 1979 *London*, then *Arizona*)
1973

BOSTON
(until 1979 *Cork Clog*)
1976

MILANO
(until 1979 *Strap Sandal*)
1976

MODEL NO. 024
1977

Birkenstock Models since 1963

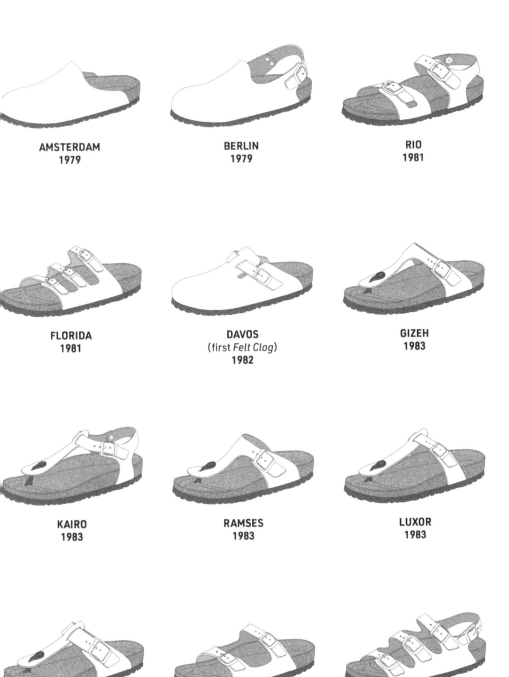

Birkenstock Models since 1963   369

BONN
1983

CAPRI
(PU variant of *Arizona*)
1983

HAWAII
(PU variant of *Florida*)
1983

BREMEN
1983

NEVADA
1983

BRASIL
1983

DELHI
1983

KORSIKA
1985

IBIZA
1985

NOPPY-FLEX
1985

SUPER-NOPPY
1985

NOPPY-FIT
1986

370　Birkenstock Models since 1963

SPORT-NOPPY
1986

LONDON
1986

PARIS
1986

NOVATO
1987

PALMA
1987

MONACO
1987

SPARTA
1987

TOKIO
1987

NOPPY-TRIM
1987

BIRKI
1988

PALERMO
1989

TORONTO
1989

Birkenstock Models since 1963   371

**MIAMI
1989**

**MONTREAL
1989**

**BALI
1990**

**SUPER-BIRKI
1990**

**NEW YORK
1992**

**OXFORD
1992**

**YORK
1992**

**MONTANA
1993**

**PASADENA
1993**

**ALEXANDRIA
1995**

**LUCCA
1995**

**PISA
1995**

PROFI-BIRKI
1995

BIRKI AIR
1995

VERONA
1996

MAYARI
2009

KAY
2014

A 630
2014

YAO
2016

MADRID BIG BUCKLE
2017

SIENA
2018

ARIZONA BIG BUCKLE
2018

STALON
2018

ROTTERDAM
2018

**TULUM
2019**

**ARIZONA CT
2019**

**ZERMATT
2019**

**BRYSON
2020**

**FRANCA
2020**

**KYOTO
2020**

**ANDERMATT
2020**

**NAGOYA
2020**

**BEND MID
2020**

**BEND LOW
2020**

**GIZEH BIG BUCKLE
2021**

**UPPSALA
2021**

Birkenstock Models since 1963

Birkenstock Models since 1963   375

APPENDICES

Fig. 70: Poster, Birkenstock USA (70s).

Notes

Introduction

1 Corporate Archive Birkenstock [hereinafter CA Birkenstock], BS 108, 05.pdf, Carl Birkenstock, manuscript, Probleme um Fuss und Schuh (July 8, 1961), 250.

2 Jennifer Wiebking, Zehn Jahre – zehn Trends, in: FAZ-Magazin, February 2023, 68.

3 The advantage of being able to dress without regard for convention when working from home during the Covid pandemic gave this trend an additional boost.

4 See: Michael Breitenacher, *Leder- und Schuhindustrie: Strukturelle Probleme und Wachstumschancen*, Berlin/Munich 1967.

5 Rainer Karlsch/Christian Kleinschmidt/Jörg Lesczenski/Anne Sudrow, *Unternehmen Sport: Die Geschichte von adidas*, Munich 2018.

6 Anne Sudrow, *Der Schuh im Nationalsozialismus: Eine Produktgeschichte im deutsch-britisch-amerikanischen Vergleich*, Göttingen 2010.

7 Roman Köster, *Seidensticker: Eine Unternehmensgeschichte 1919–2019*, Essen, 2019. The study by Mark Spoerer, *C&A: Ein Familienunternehmen in Deutschland, den Niederlanden und Großbritannien*, Munich 2016, describes the companies' rise to become what has long been the largest textile group in Europe.

8 See, for example: Carsten Burhop/Michael Kießener/Hermann Schöfer/Joachim Scholtyseck, *Merck, 1668–2018: Von der Apotheke zum Weltkonzern*, Munich 2018.

9 Gine Elsner, *Die "aufrechte" Haltung: Orthopädie im Nationalsozialismus*, Hamburg 2019.

10 See, for example: Frida Giannini, *GUCCI: The Making Of*, Rizzoli 2011; Jerome Gautier, *Chanel: Ein Name – ein Stil*, Munich 2015.

11 See, for example: Christoph Spöcker, *Karl Lagerfeld: Kleine Anekdoten aus dem Leben eines Großen*, Munich 2016.

12 See: Pierre-Yves Donzé/Véronique Pouillard/Joanne Roberts, *The Oxford Handbook of Luxury Business*, Oxford 2022.

13 See Alexander von den Benken's essay in this volume.

14 CA Birkenstock, BBG 2.001-19+20, Konrad Birkenstock license agreements (BS 2), Carl Birkenstock patents for the Ideal-Schuh (BS 73) and Birkenstock Post, editions of the *Original Birkenstock-Footbed Sandal*.

15 See Roman Köster's, Jörg Lesczenski's, and Alexander von den Benken's essays and Kai Balazs-Bartesch/Andrea H. Schneider-Braunberger's early history of the entrepreneurial family in this volume.

16 The texts in this volume covering various special topics were authored by Johanna Steinfeld.

17 See Andrea H. Schneider-Braunberger's essay in this volume, "The *System Birkenstock*."

18 See Emily Brayshaw's essay on Birkenstock in film in this volume.

19 See the essays in this volume by Taylor Brydges (North America), Emanuale Scarpellini (Italy), Liz Tregenza (UK), Pierre-Yves Donzé (Japan), and Emily Brayshaw (Australia).

20 Paloma Fernandez/Andrea Colli, *The Endurance of Family Businesses: A Global Overview*, Cambridge 2013.

21 For example, when the shoemaker Johann-Adam Birkenstock died, he left behind his son Johannes, who was just a few months old; Johannes's grandson (Konrad) was later orphaned at the age of 15.

22 See Roman Köster's and Alexander von den Benken's essays in this volume.

23 See CA Birkenstock, BS 04, excerpts from the commercial register.

24 See the essays in this volume by Roman Köster.

25 Cf. Roman Köster, *Hugo Boss 1924–1945. Eine Kleiderfabrik zwischen Weimarer Republik und „Drittem Reich"*, München 2011; Manfred Grieger, *Sartorius im Nationalsozialismus, Generationswechsel im Familienunternehmen zwischen Weltwirtschaftskrise und Entnazifizierung*, Göttingen 2019.

26 Cf. Andrea H. Schneider-Braunberger, *Das Bankhaus Metzler im Nationalsozialismus, Frankfurter Netzwerke in schwierigen Zeiten*, München 2022; id., *Miele & Cie. im Nationalsozialismus. Weg und Rolle eines Familienunternehmens in der Rüstungs- und Kriegswirtschaft*, München 2023.

27 Andrea H. Schneider-Braunberger, *Die Unternehmerfamilie – Risiko für das Familienunternehmen?*, in: Equa-Foundation (ed.), Unternehmerfamilien: Eigentum verpflichtet, Munich 2021, 299–313.

28 The dispute between Carl Birkenstock and his sister-in-law because of an alleged complaint and subsequent denunciation was a heavy family burden (see Jörg Lesczenski's essay in this volume).

29 See Alexander von den Benken's essay in this volume.

30 Konrad Birkenstock was forced to license his inventions twice; Heinrich and Konrad Birkenstock Jr. had to leave the KABI company established in Vienna because of their poor management; Heinrich had to leave Gebr. Birkenstock GmbH in 1931 for a similar reason, etc.

31 See also Roman Köster's essay in this volume.

32 Likewise, during World War II, because rubber was not available, he developed the "Elastigang" insole with a substitute material.

33 Konrad and Carl Birkenstock published a number of articles in professional journals and books. These include: Konrad Birkenstock, *Fußbett: Ein Wunder im Schuh*, Friedberg, n. d.; Carl Birkenstock, *Der Fuß und seine Behandlung*, Steinhude am Meer 1930; Carl Birkenstock, *Mit dem Arzt gegen Fußkrankheiten und Irrlehren*, Steinhude am Meer 1935; Carl Birkenstock, 40 Jahre für die vernünftige Fußbekleidung, Steinhude am Meer 1941 (unpublished); Carl Birkenstock, *Fußorthopädie: Das System Carl Birkenstock*, Düsseldorf 1945/48; [Konrad or Carl Birkenstock], *Die Fußkrankheit und ihre Behandlung*, Friedberg 1956; Carl Birkenstock, *60 Jahre für die vernünftige Fußbekleidung*, Bad Honnef 1961 (unpublished).

34 CA Birkenstock, BS 108, Carl Birkenstock Memoir, June 8, 1961.

35 Nike Breyer, in: Rethinking Footwear, Redefining Aesthetics, part 3 of Ugly for a Reason, in: Birkenstock (Nov. 18, 2022), www.birkenstock.com/us/ugly-for-a-reason/?utm_source=nytimes&utm_medium=referral&utm_campaign=ufar&cpeu=ed_al_sh_al_al_UFAR (accessed May 15, 2023). The episode appeared as a paid post in: The New York Times, www.nytimes.com/paidpost/birkenstock/how-feet-made-us-human.html (accessed May 15, 2023).

36 Christina Blahnik, in ibid.; see also Alice Janssens's essay in this volume.

37 Colin Mayer, *Prosperity, Better Business Makes the Greater Good*, Oxford 2018; id., *Putting Purpose into Practice: The Economics of Mutuality*, Oxford 2021.

38 The success of the healthy footbeds enabled Carl Birkenstock to attempt to have his *Ideal-Schuh* mass-produced in the years of the economic miracle. For years, countless journeys, discussions, lasts, insoles, and prototypes were devoted to this.

39 See Kai Balazs-Bartesch's and Andrea H. Schneider-Braunberger's essays in this volume.

40 CA Birkenstock, BS 6, correspondence.

41 See Alexander von den Benken's essay in this volume.

42 CA Birkenstock, Bestand Carl Birkenstock, various correspondence.

43 Konrad Birkenstock had met him in the Friedrichsheim clinic (see Roman Köster's essay in this volume).

44 See Alexander von den Benken's, Taylor Brydges's, and Emanuela Scarpellini's essays in this volume.

45 See Emanuela Scarpellini's, Hayley Edwards-Dujardin's and Liz Tregenza's essays in this volume.

46 See Pierre-Yves Donzé's essay in this volume.

47 For this reason, marketing at BIRKENSTOCK has not yet been carried out by means of a separate department. The special features are described in Christian Kleinschmidt and Andrea H. Schneider-Braunberger's essays on the "Birkenstock Brand" in this volume.

48 Incidentally, Birkenstock already pointed out in the 60s the great importance of foot health for children. See: Birkenstock Post (1964), in: CA Birkenstock, BBG 2.001-20.

49 Issues of the Birkenstock Post from 1963 to 1974, in: CA Birkenstock, BBG 2.001-18-41, Bestand Birkenstock-Kataloge; see also Christian Kleinschmidt and Andrea H. Schneider-Braunberger's essay in this volume.

50 At that time, only rudimentary ideas regarding gender-neutral fashion existed in the USA, but they disappeared again in the 70s.

51 Jo. B. Paoletti, *Sex and Unisex: Fashion, Feminism, and the Sexual Revolution*, Bloomington, IN, 2015.

52 See Emily Brayshaw's, Alice Janssens's, and Taylor Brydges's essays in this volume.

53 See Emily Brayshaw's essay in this volume.

54 See Mary Yeager's essay in this volume.

55 See Emanuela Scarpellini's essay in this volume.

56 The picture circulating in the media showing Kate Moss in *Arizona* is a photo montage of unknown origin. In fact, she wore the two mentioned here.

57 See Liz Tregenza's essay in this volume.

58 See Pierre-Yves Donzé's essay in this volume.

59 This is probably why Birkenstock sandals have recently become popular in Italy, based on their comfort for hiking in, their durability, and their suitability as travel shoes. See Emanuela Scarpellini's essay in this volume.

60 See Alice Janssens's essay in this volume.

61 See Emily Brayshaw's essay on film in this volume.

62 Gala wrote that the shoes were "without question more than inappropriate." "Diese Looks müssen Sie gesehen haben," in: Gala Digital (Feb. 25, 2019), https://www.gala.de/beauty-fashion/fashion/oscars-2019--diese-looks-muessen-sie-gesehen-haben--22013284.html (accessed May 5, 2023).

63 Ann-Kathrin Riedl, Warum an den Dresscode halten? Frances McDormand kam in Birkenstocks auf die Bühne der Oscars, in: Vogue Germany (Feb. 25, 2019), https://www.vogue.de/mode/artikel/oscars-frances-mcdormand-birkenstock (accessed May 15, 2023).

1774–1895
The Beginnings: The Birth of a Shoemaking Dynasty

1 For more on the changes in the shoemaking trade, see the articles in this volume by Johanna Steinfeld: "From the Traditional Craft of Shoemaking to the Modern Shoe Factory" and "Shoemakers around 1774."

2 In the early 18th century, the village was still called Bergheim. Since the Hessian local government reform in 1970, Langenbergheim has belonged to the municipality of Hammersbach in the Main-Kinzig district.

3 Gemeindevorstand der Gemeinde Hammersbach (ed.), *925 Jahre Langenbergheim*, Hammersbach 1982, 9, 12 ff.

4 See Norbert Ohler, *Reisen im Mittelalter*, Darmstadt 2004, 56 ff.

5 Willi Stubenvoll (ed.), *Die Straße: Geschichte und Gegenwart eines Handelsweges; 750 Jahre Messen in Frankfurt*, Frankfurt am Main 1990, 56 ff.

6 Andreas Grießinger, *Schuhmacher*, in: Reinhold Reith (ed.), *Das alte Handwerk: Von Bader bis Zinngießer*, Munich 1991, 217–222, here: 219.

7 Ludwig Brake, *Die ersten Eisenbahnen in Hessen: Eisenbahnpolitik und Eisenbahnbau in Frankfurt, Hessen-Darmstadt, Kurhessen und Nassau bis 1866*, Wiesbaden 1991, 280 f.

Notes 381

8 Gemeindevorstand der Gemeinde Hammersbach (ed.), *925 Jahre Langenbergheim*, 60; the exact date when the Birkenstock family settled in Langenbergheim cannot be determined with any certainty, because the church registries for the 17th and early 18th centuries do not provide clear information about the family relationships of individual persons.

9 This makes it difficult to determine family relationships, since there are sometimes people with the same first and last names, which means that entries are similar or duplicated.

10 Baptismal certificate of Johann Georg Birkenstock, 1688, in: Hessen-Nassau: Central Archive of the Evangelical Church, Church District of Büdingen, Eckartshausen, Baptismal Registry 1673–1714, Marriage Registry 1673–1714, Burial Registry 1673–1714, Confirmation Registry 1673–1714, www.archion.de (accessed Sept. 8, 2022), image 24; death certificate of Johann Georg Birkenstock, 1748, in: Hessen-Nassau: Central Archive of the Evangelical Church, Church District of Büdingen, Eckartshausen Parish, Baptismal Registry 1757–1799, Marriage Registry 1757–1799, www.archion.de (accessed Sept. 6, 2022), image 484.

11 Regarding the history and historiography of the guilds, see Arnd Kluge, *Die Zünfte*, Stuttgart 2007.

12 Hans Werner Hahn, *Wirtschaft und Verkehr*, in: Winfried Speitkamp (ed.), Handbuch der hessischen Geschichte: Bevölkerung, Wirtschaft und Staat in Hessen 1806–1945, vol. 1, Marburg 2010, 73–251, here: 90 ff.

13 The baptismal certificate of Johann Peter Ditzel's son, who was adopted by Johannes Birkenstock. Baptismal sponsorship of Johannes Birkenstock for the son of a Joh. Peter Ditzel in 1774, in: Hessen-Nassau: Central Archive of the Evangelical Church, Church District of Büdingen, Eckartshausen Parish, Baptismal Registry 1757–1799, Marriage Registry 1757–1799, www. archion.de (accessed Sept. 6, 2022), image 127.

14 See: the baptismal certificate of Johannes Birkenstock, 1749, in: Hessen-Nassau: Central Archive of the Evangelical Church, Church District of Büdingen, Eckartshausen Parish, Baptismal Registry 1702–1756, Marriage Registry 1707–1756, Burial Registry 1703–1756, viewed online at www.archion.de [last accessed: September 6th, 2022], image 149.

15 Georg Emig, *Die Berufserziehung bei den Handwerkerzünften in der Landgrafschaft Hessen-Darmstadt und im Großherzogtum Hessen vom Beginn des 18. Jahrhunderts bis zur Einführung der Gewerbefreiheit 1866*, Frankfurt am Main 1969, 175 f.

16 In the baptismal certificate of one of his children, which bears the name of his uncle and godfather Johann Adam, dated February 5, 1781, it is clear that he was already a master shoemaker at that time; see baptismal certificate of Johann Adam Birkenstock, 1781, in: Hessen-Nassau : Central Archive of the Evangelical Church, Church District of Büdingen, Eckartshausen Parish, Baptismal Registry 1757–1799, Marriage Registry 1757–1799, www.archion.de (accessed Sept. 6, 2022), image 206.

17 Baptismal certificate of Johannes Birkenstock, 1790, in: Hessen-Nassau: Central Archive of the Evangelical Church, Church District of Büdingen, Eckartshausen Parish, Baptismal Registry 1757–1799, Marriage Registry 1757–1799, www.archion.de (accessed Sept. 6, 2022), image 303. There was also a second person in Langenbergheim who was almost the same age as Johannes Birkenstock and bore the same name—his birth is documented in the year 1752. However, it can be assumed that the Johannes Birkenstock in these documents is the brother of Johann Adam and the son of Johann Heinrich Birkenstock, since both brothers take on the sponsorship of each other's children and the documents indicate that in each case the entry refers to the other's brother.

18 Baptismal certificate Heinrich Birkenstock, 1710, in: Hessen-Nassau: Central Archive of the Evangelical Church, Church District of Büdingen, Eckartshausen Parish, Baptismal Registry 1702–1756, Marriage Registry 1707–1756, Burial Registry 1703–1756, viewed online at www. archion.de (accessed Sept. 6, 2022), image 27.

19 Marriage certificate of Johann Adam Birkenstock, 1783, in: Hessen-Nassau: Central Archive of the Evangelical Church, Church District of Büdingen, Eckartshausen Parish, Baptismal Registry 1757–1799, Marriage Registry 1757–1799, www.archion.de (accessed Sept. 6, 2022), image 484. For both brothers, some entries in the church documents were subsequently corrected, since the pastor had put them under the rubric of dates of death, although they involved marriage or baptism. In both cases, the master's title was dropped when they were corrected, but given the guild regulations that were common at the time, it is entirely plausible that they received the master's title immediately after completing their apprenticeship.

20 Birth Certificate of Johannes Birkenstock, 1790, in: Hessen-Nassau: Central Archive of the Evangelical Church, Church District of Büdingen, Eckartshausen Parish, Baptismal Registry 1757–1799, Marriage Registry 1757–1799, www.archion.de (accessed Sept. 6, 2022), image 303; Death Certificate of Johann Adam Birkenstock, 1790 in: Hessen-Nassau: Central Archive of the Evangelical Church, Church District of Büdingen, Eckartshausen Parish, Burial Registry 1757–1799, www.archion.de (accessed Sept. 6, 2022), image 144.

21 Information about this derives from a series of sources from Langenbergheim that have been preserved in the State Archives in Darmstadt.

22 Court files, in: Hessisches Staatsarchiv Darmstadt (hereafter: HStA Darmstadt), G 28 A, 1432 1–8. The multiple references to Johannes Birkenstock in different written formats also verify the two lines of the Birkenstock family in these files.

23 Ibid.

24 HStA Darmstadt, E 13, 1703.

25 The first documented mention of Johannes Birkenstock in Mittel-Gründau is the birth of a child on July 14, 1782, who died shortly after birth and is not named in the church registry; see entry on the birth of an unnamed child in 1782, in: Landeskirchliches Archiv Kassel (Archive of the Evangelical Church of Kurhessen-Waldeck, Gelnhausen, Gründau, church registry 1780–1800), www.archion.de (accessed: Sept. 6, 2022), image 691.

26 A part of Mittel-Gündau's district even belonged to the Electorate of Hesse at this time.

27 There are lists of the number of trades and master craftsmen in the former Hessian district of Gelnhausen; see: Hessian State Archive Marburg [hereafter: HStA Marburg], 180 Gelnhausen, 3470.

28 Alfred Pletsch, *Bevölkerungsentwicklung und Urbanisierung*, in: Winfried Speitkamp (ed.), Handbuch der hessischen Geschichte. Bevölkerung, Wirtschaft und Staat in Hessen 1806–1945, vol. 1, Marburg 2010, 1–73, here: 5–6; baptismal certificate of Johannes Matthäus, 1817, in: Hessen-Nassau: Central Archive of the Evangelical Church, Church District of Büdingen, Eckartshausen Parish, Baptismal Registry 1800–1817, www.archion.de (accessed Sept. 6, 2022), image 286; marriage certificate of Johannes Matthäus, 1845, in: Hessen-Nassau: Central Archive of the Evangelical Church, Church District of Büdingen, Eckartshausen Parish, Marriage Registry 1800–1817, www.archion.de (accessed Sept. 6, 2022), image 252; baptismal certificate of Johann Georg Matthäus, 1863, in: Hessen-Nassau: Central Archive of the Evangelical Church, Church District of Büdingen, Eckartshausen Parish, Baptismal Registry 1800–1817, www.archion.de (accessed Sept. 6, 2022), image 35.

29 Hahn, *Wirtschaft und Verkehr*, 102 f.

30 HStA Marburg, 180 Gelnhausen, 178, 1 ff.

31 Ibid.

32 Emig, *Die Berufserziehung bei den Handwerkerzünften*, 91 ff.

33 Niedergründau (ed.), *750 Jahre Niedergründau: 7., 8., 9., 10. Juni 1968*, Niedergründau 1968, 102 f.

34 Bruno Hildebrand, *Die Nationalökonomie der Gegenwart und Zukunft*, vol. 1 (1848), 178, quoted in Hahn, *Wirtschaft und Verkehr*, 90 ff.

35 It is not possible to reconstruct when Johannes completed his apprenticeship and acquired the master's title, but he is repeatedly referred to as a master shoemaker in the birth certificates of his six children as well as in his death certificate, so he can be considered to have attained this status by 1815 at the latest; presumably he had already completed his apprenticeship a few years prior to this. In this connection, see the baptismal certificates of his children: baptismal certificate of Margaretha Birkenstock, 1815, in: Kurhessen-Waldeck: State Church Archive of Kassel, Gelnhausen, municipality of Mittel-Gründau (Auf dem Berg), baptisms 1812–1835, www.archion.de (accessed Sept. 6, 2022), image 1977; baptismal certificate of Johann Conrad Birkenstock, 1819, in: ibid., image 1991; baptismal certificate of Johannes Birkenstock, 1821, in: ibid., image 2016; baptismal certificate of Johann Georg Birkenstock, 1825, in: ibid., image 2042; baptismal certificate of Katharina Margaretha Birkenstock, 1828, in: ibid., image 2070; baptismal certificate of Elisabetha Birkenstock, 1830, in: ibid., image 2093; death certificate

of Johannes Birkenstock, 1866, in: Kurhessen-Waldeck: State Church Archive of Kassel, Geln-hausen, municipality of Mittel-Gründau (Auf dem Berg), burials 1853–1932, www.archion.de (accessed Sept. 6, 2022), image 1997.

36 Baptismal certificate of Johann Conrad Birkenstock, 1819, in: Kurhessen-Waldeck: State Church Archive of Kassel, Gelnhausen, municipality of Mittel-Gründau (Auf dem Berg), baptisms 1812–1835, viewed online at www.archion.de ([last accessed: September 6, 2022)], image 1991.

37 Emig, *Die Berufserziehung bei den Handwerkerzünften*, 338 f.

38 In 1838, she gave birth to a daughter named Katharina Margaretha; no further records of the family exist.

39 Eckhart G. Franz et al., *Großherzogtum Hessen (1800) 1806–1918*, in: Walter Heinemeyer (ed.), Handbuch der hessischen Geschichte: Hessen im deutschen Bund und im neuen Deutschen Reich (1806) 1815 bis 1945, vol. 4, part 2, delivery 3, Marburg 2010, 718 f.

40 Hahn, *Wirtschaft und Verkehr*, 106 f.

41 More on this topic in the chapter "From the Traditional Craft of Shoemaking to the Modern Shoe Factory".

42 Friedrich Lenger, *Sozialgeschichte des deutschen Handwerks seit 1800*, Frankfurt am Main 1988, 55 f.

43 Hahn, *Wirtschaft und Verkehr*, 152.

44 Sabine Johann, *Schuhherstellung: Von der handwerklichen zur maschinellen Fertigung*, in: Willi Schächter/Michael Wagner (eds.), Vom Zunfthandwerk zum modernen Industriebetrieb: Schuhe und Schuhherstellung in Deutschland seit dem 18. Jahrhundert, Museum für Schuhproduktion und Industriegeschichte Hauenstein, Hauenstein 1998, 45–56, here: 54. The McKay machine automated the process of "pinching," i. e., stapling the shoe upper to the insole with the help of small nails. This sped up the production of shoes considerably.

45 Hartmut Berghoff/Philipp Heldmann, *Vom Massenhandwerk zur Modeindustrie*, in: Schächter/Wagner (eds.), Vom Zunfthandwerk zum modernen Industriebetrieb: Schuhe und Schuh-herstellung in Deutschland seit dem 18. Jahrhundert, Museum für Schuhproduktion und Industriegeschichte Hauenstein, Hauenstein, 1998, pp. 56–78, here: 69.

46 Grießinger, *Schuhmacher*, 219 ff.

47 Ibid.

48 Ibid., 222.

49 Death certificate of Johannes Birkenstock, 1866, in: Kurhessen-Waldeck: State Church Archive of Kassel, Gelnhausen, municipality of Mittel-Gründau (Auf dem Berg), burials 1853–1932, www.archion.de (accessed Sept. 6, 2022), image 1997.

50 Dirk Georges, *1810/11–1993: Handwerk und Interessenpolitik*, Frankfurt am Main 1993, 38 ff.

51 Baptismal certificate of Johannes Birkenstock, 1821, in: Kurhessen-Waldeck: State Church Archive of Kassel, Gelnhausen, municipality of Mittel-Gründau (Auf dem Berg), burials 1853–1932, www.archion.de (accessed Sept. 6, 2022), image 2016; baptismal certificate of Johann Georg Birkenstock, 1825, in: ibid., image 2042; baptismal certificate of Katharina Margaretha Birkenstock, 1828, in: ibid., image 2070; baptismal certificate of Elisabetha Birkenstock, 1830, in: ibid., image 2093.

52 In the 1850s, even then the population of the Grand Duchy as a whole declined slightly. See Hahn, *Wirtschaft und Verkehr*, 90, 134.

53 Mittel-Gründau resolution of April 19, 1849, in: Bundesarchiv Berlin (hereafter: BArch Berlin) DB 51/442, sheet 46, and list of signatures of Mittel-Gründau citizens from April 1849, includ-ing the signatures of Johannes and Conrad Birkenstock at positions 37 and 74, in: BArch Berlin DB 51/442, sheets 188 f.

54 Although the horse census lists only show healthy animals that could be used for military pur-poses, sick animals that were no longer able to work were not of great benefit to their owners and were replaced if necessary.

55 See Walter Uffelmann, *Pferdemusterungen in Mittel-Gründau*, in: Geschichtsverein Gründau e. V. (ed.), Grindaha: 800 Jahre Mittel-Gründau, special issue 7, Gründau 2019, 65–77, here: 66.

56 Baptismal certificate of Johannes Birkenstock, 1856, in: Kurhessen-Waldeck: State Church Archive of Kassel, Gelnhausen, municipality of Mittel-Gründau (Auf dem Berg), baptisms 1836–1865, www.archion.de (accessed Sept. 6, 2022), image 132; death certificate of Johannes Birkenstock, 1856, in: State Church Archive of Kassel, Gelnhausen, municipality of Mittel-Gründau (Auf dem Berg), burials 1853–1932, www.archion.de (accessed 6 Sept. 2022), image 1928; baptismal certificate of Johannes Wilhelm Birkenstock, 1866, with reference to his death in 1867, in: Kurhessen-Waldeck: State Church Archive of Kassel, Gelnhausen, municipality of Mittel-Gründau (Auf dem Berg), baptisms 1866–1895, www.archion.de (accessed Sept. 6, 2022), image 281; death certificate of Johannes Birkenstock, in: Kurhessen-Waldeck: State Church Archive of Kassel, Gelnhausen, municipality of Mittel-Gründau (Auf dem Berg), burials 1853–1932, www.archion.de (accessed Sept. 6, 2022), image 1912.

57 Baptismal certificate of Friedrich Heinrich Birkenstock, in: Kurhessen-Waldeck: State Church Archive of Kassel, Gelnhausen, municipality of Mittel-Gründau (Auf dem Berg), baptisms 1836–1865, www.archion.de (accessed Sept. 6, 2022), image 143; Baptismal certificate of Christian Birkenstock, in: ibid., image 196; Baptismal certificate of Wilhelmine Birkenstock, in: Kurhessen-Waldeck: State Church Archive of Kassel, Gelnhausen, municipality of Mittel-Gründau (Auf dem Berg), baptisms 1866–1895, www.archion.de (accessed Sept. 6, 2022), image 363.

58 Axel Arbinger, *Auf Sohlen aus Metall geht heute keiner mehr: Die Geschichte der Firma Birkenstock – Im "Indianer-Viertel" den Grundstein zum Weltruf gelegt*, in: Friedberg-Magazin (April 1995), in: Stadtarchiv Friedberg (Municipal Archive). The company's commercial register entry still exists in the Darmstadt State Archives: HStA Darmstadt, H 14 Büdingen, R 19.

59 Marriage certificate of Johann Matthäus and Wilhelmine Birkenstock, 1894, in: Hessisches Hauptstaatsarchiv Wiesbaden (henceforth HHStA Wiesbaden), 924, 423.

60 Johann's father, a certain Johannes Matthäus (*1817) had already been a shoemaker and had succeeded the Birkenstock shoemakers who had emigrated.

61 Marriage certificate of Johann Matthäus and Wilhelmine Birkenstock, 1894, in: HHStA Wiesbaden, 924, 423.

62 Frankfurt address books 1896, 1899, 1903, 1905; presumably today's Oeder Weg in Frankfurt's Nordend is meant.

63 Frankfurt address books 1912, 1915.

Shoemakers around 1774

1 See Wilfried Reininghaus, *Gewerbe in der frühen Neuzeit*, Berlin 1990, 35.
2 See ibid., 34.
3 See Bruno Herberger, *Die Organisation des Schuhmacherhandwerks zu Frankfurt a. M. bis zum Ende des 18. Jahrhunderts*, PhD thesis, Frankfurt am Main 1931, 29, 123 f.
4 See Cornelia Rührig, *Stadt und Natur: Frankfurt um 1780:, das Buch der gleichnamigen Ausstellung des Historischen Museums November 1982– Juni 1983*, Frankfurt am Main 1983, 3.
5 See Paul Weber, *Der Schuhmacher: Ein Beruf im Wandel der Zeit*, Aarau 1988, 23, 46.
6 See Weber, *Der Schuhmacher*, 35.
7 See Anke Sczesny, *Zünfte*, Jan. 18, 2012, in: Historisches Lexikon Bayerns, www.historisches-lexikon-bayerns.de/Lexikon/Zünfte (accessed Feb. 25, 2022).
8 François Alexandre Pierre de Garsault, *Der Schuster: Von dem Herren von Garsault*, Leipzig 1990 (first published: Leipzig, 1769), 22 f.
9 See Peter Camper, *Abhandlung von der besten Form der Schuhe*, Hamburg 1781, 5.
10 CA Birkenstock, BS 107, Carl Birkenstock, manuscript "Fuß und Spur in Trittspur", 1961.

From the Traditional Craft of Shoemaking to the Modern Shoe Factory

1 See Karl Rumpf, *Die Schuhmacherei im Grossherzogtum Hessen*, PhD thesis, Giessen 1907, 34.
2 Moritz Schoene, *Die moderne Entwickelung des Schuhmachergewerbes in historischer, statistischer und technischer Hinsicht: Ein Beitrag zur Kenntnis unseres Gewerbewesens*, Jena 1888, 51.
3 See Gustav Schmoller, *Zur Geschichte der deutschen Kleingewerbe im 19. Jahrhundert*, Halle 1870, 626.
4 See Hartmut Berghoff/Philipp Heldmann, *Vom Massenhandwerk zur Modeindustrie*, in: Willi Schächter/Michael Wagner (eds.), Vom Zunfthandwerk zum modernen Industriebetrieb:

Notes **385**

Schuhe und Schuhherstellung in Deutschland seit dem 18. Jahrhundert, Hauenstein 1998, 57-78, here: 62.

5 See Michael Wagner, *Die Entstehung der südwestdeutschen Industrieregion um Pirmasens (1790-1918)*, in: Schächter/Wagner (eds.), Vom Zunfthandwerk, 23-44, here: 26f.

6 See Sabine Johann, *Schuhherstellung: Von der handwerklichen zur maschinellen Fertigung*, in: Schächter/Wagner (eds.), Vom Zunfthandwerk, 45-56, here: 55.

7 See Berghoff/Heldmann, *Massenhandwerk*, 62.

8 See Rumpf, *Schuhmacherei*, 8.

9 See Wagner, *Entstehung*, 32.

10 See Berghoff/Heldmann, *Massenhandwerk*, 66.

11 See ibid., 62.

12 See ibid., 63.

13 See Wagner, *Entstehung*, 34.

14 Schmoller, *Geschichte*, 630.

1896-1945
From a Shoemaker's Workshop to a Manufacturing Company

1 Corporate Archive Birkenstock [hereafter CA Birkenstock], BS 51, Obituary for Mr. Birkenstock Sr., 1950.

2 CA Birkenstock, BS 111, reference book of Carl Birkenstock, 1963.

3 Axel Arbinger, *Auf Sohlen aus Metall geht heute keiner mehr: Die Geschichte der Firma Birkenstock; Im "Indianer-Viertel" den Grundstein zum Weltruf gelegt*, in: Friedberg-Magazin (Apr. 1995), in: Friedberg City Archive.

4 Institute for the History of Frankfurt am Main [hereafter ISG Frankfurt], Frankfurt Address Book, 28th edition (1896).

5 ISG Frankfurt, Birkenstock index.

6 See Johanna Steinfeld's essay in this volume, "The Truly Ethical Man Does Not Cripple Himself."

7 ISG Frankfurt, Birkenstock index.

8 Carl Birkenstock, *50 Jahre System Birkenstock 1897-1947*, Bad Honnef 1947, 3.

9 CA Birkenstock, BS 9, Memorandum of Association of Shoe Orthopedists, around 1936.

10 CA Birkenstock, BS 114, Carl Birkenstock, "40 Jahre Einsatz für vernünftige Fußbekleidung," 1941.

11 Corona Hepp, *Avantgarde: Moderne Kunst, Kulturkritik und Reformbewegung nach der Jahrhundertwende*, Munich 1987; Stefan Bollmann, *Monte Verità 1900: Der Traum vom alternativen Leben beginnt*, Munich 2017.

12 Ibid.

13 CA Birkenstock, BS 114, Carl Birkenstock, "40 Jahre Einsatz für vernünftige Fußbekleidung," 1941, 3f.

14 Arbinger, *Auf Sohlen aus Metall geht heute keiner mehr.*

15 CA Birkenstock, BS 114, Carl Birkenstock, "40 Jahre Einsatz für vernünftige Fußbekleidung," 1941, 3.

16 CA Birkenstock, BS 2, circular letter from Konrad Birkenstock to shoe retailers, Sept. 9, 1909.

17 CA Birkenstock, BS 2, letter from Konrad Birkenstock to master shoemaker, 1912.

18 CA Birkenstock, BS 2, sales brochure, Konrad Birkenstock, 1920.

19 See, for example, Arbinger, *Auf Sohlen aus Metall geht heute keiner mehr.*

20 CA Birkenstock, BS 16, letter from patent attorney Gail to the Reich Patent Office, auditing office for category 71a, Nov. 13, 1935.

21 CA Birkenstock, BS 1, Birkenstock accounting books, 1906.

22 CA Birkenstock, BS 1, letter from the shoe store Carl Stiller to Konrad Birkenstock, Aug. 1, 1908.

23 Deutsches Reichs-Patentamt, no. 343209, entry from Nov. 11, 1925.

24 CA Birkenstock, BS 2, license agreement, Patent-Centrale GmbH, Frankfurt am Main, and Konrad Birkenstock, July 4, 1910; CA Birkenstock, BS 14, decision of the Reich Patent Office on the application from the company Georg Hartmann dated Feb. 8, 1936, Oct. 20, 1936.

25 Carl Birkenstock, *50 Jahre System Birkenstock 1897–1947*, 3.
26 CA Birkenstock, BS 114, Carl Birkenstock, "40 Jahre Einsatz für vernünftige Fußbekleidung," 1941, 4.
27 Ibid., 5 f.
28 CA Birkenstock, BS 2, license agreement, Patent-Centrale GmbH, Frankfurt am Main, and Konrad Birkenstock, Apr. 26, 1910. The patent center acquired a series of the *"Footbed"* (*Fußbett*) insoles.
29 CA Birkenstock, BS 2, license agreement, Patent-Centrale GmbH, Frankfurt am Main, and Konrad Birkenstock, July 4, 1910, and July 8, 1910.
30 CA Birkenstock, BS 2, letter from Patent-Centrale GmbH, Frankfurt am Main, to customers, n. d. [ca. 1910].
31 CA Birkenstock, BS 108, memorandum by Carl Birkenstock, June 8, 1961.
32 CA Birkenstock, BS 114, Carl Birkenstock, "40 Jahre Einsatz für vernünftige Fußbekleidung," 1941.
33 Ibid., 6.
34 Arbinger, *Auf Sohlen aus Metall geht heute keiner mehr.*
35 CA Birkenstock, BS 2, sales brochures, K. Birkenstock, 1920.
36 See CA Birkenstock, BS 108, memorandum of Carl Birkenstock, June 8, 1961, 23 (ms) / 43 (PDF).
37 Manuel Dichtl, *Der Orthopäde Prof. Dr. Franz Schede (1882–1976): Leben und Werk*, PhD diss., Regensburg 2012.
38 Gine Elsner, *Die "aufrechte" Haltung: Orthopädie im Nationalsozialismus*, Hamburg 2019, 110–30.
39 See, for example, CA Birkenstock, BS 20, letter from Wilhelm Thomsen to Carl Birkenstock, Nov. 26, 1945.
40 Udo Benzendörfer, *Die Universitätsmedizin in Frankfurt am Main von 1914 bis 2014*, Münster 2014, 69 ff.
41 As early as 1816, the first orthopedic specialist clinic was opened in Würzburg in the former St. Stephen's Monastery by Johann Georg Heine (1771–1838), who is regarded as the founder of orthopedics in Germany.
42 Georg Hohmann, *Ein Arzt erlebt seine Zeit: Ansprachen, Lebensbilder, Begegnungen*, Munich 1954, 79 f.
43 ISG Frankfurt, magistrate's files, no. 8968, from the history of Friedrichsheim.
44 ISG Frankfurt, municipal files, no. 8968, entry 47/69.
45 CA Birkenstock, BS 108, memorandum of Carl Birkenstock, June 8, 1961.
46 CA Birkenstock, BS 114, Carl Birkenstock, "40 Jahre Einsatz für vernünftige Fußbekleidung," 1941, 10; CA Birkenstock, BS 29, letter from the German Patent Office to Carl Birkenstock, May 29, 1953.
47 CA Birkenstock, BS 108, memorandum of Carl Birkenstock, June 8, 1961.
48 Ibid.
49 Ibid.
50 Ibid.
51 Ibid., 24 (ms) / 44 (pdf).
52 Ibid.
53 See Andrea H. Schneider-Braunberger's essay on podiatry in this volume.
54 CA Birkenstock, BS 1, letter from Kabi-Vertriebsgesellschaft K. and H. Birkenstock to Carl Birkenstock, June 25, 1924.
55 CA Birkenstock BS 1, letter from Kabi-Vertriebsgesellschaft K. and H. Birkenstock to Carl Birkenstock, Aug. 13, 1924.
56 Arbinger, *Auf Sohlen aus Metall geht heute keiner mehr.*
57 Conflicts in this regard are indicated by: CA Birkenstock, BS 1, letter from Konrad Birkenstock to Carl Birkenstock, Oct. 2, 1924.
58 CA Birkenstock, BS 114, Carl Birkenstock, "40 Jahre Einsatz für vernünftige Fußbekleidung," 1941, 12.
59 Lower Saxony State Archive, Dept. Bückeburg [hereafter NLA BU], business card index, L 121b, Acc. 2001, 025, no. 197.

Notes 387

60 CA Birkenstock, BS 4, excerpt from the commercial register B of the district court of Stadthagen regarding the company Gebrüder Birkenstock, limited liability company in Steinhude, Apr. 3, 1937.

61 CA Birkenstock, BS 4, district court Friedberg to the company Gebrüder Birkenstock, certified copy from the commercial register, Sept. 20, 1939; BS 11, People's State of Hesse, trade license from Birkenstock GmbH, Apr. 1, 1933. It is unclear to what extent the registration of a new GmbH in Friedberg has to do with the difficulties encountered by Konrad Birkenstock Sr. in entering his GmbH in the commercial register in Friedberg because he was unable to pay the stamp duties during the global economic crisis. CA Birkenstock, BS 4, letter from Konrad Birkenstock to the Justice Minister of the State of Hesse, Nov. 17, 1931.

62 CA Birkenstock, BS 28, letter from Carl Birkenstock to Konrad Birkenstock Jr., Dec. 7, 1948.

63 Hessian Main State Archives Wiesbaden [hereafter HHStA Wiesbaden], 2001 173, letter from the Hesse Main Supply Office to the Wiesbaden Chamber of Crafts, Jan. 23, 1930.

64 CA Birkenstock, BS 9, *Was Gebrüder Birkenstock sagen, geht jeden modernen Schuhhändler an,* in: Schuh und Leder 79, Oct. 20, 1936.

65 HHStA Wiesbaden, 2001 173, letter from the Association of Orthopedic Master Shoemakers in Germany to the Wiesbaden Chamber of Crafts, Mar. 28, 1922.

66 CA Birkenstock, BS 114, Carl Birkenstock, "40 Jahre Einsatz für vernünftige Fußbekleidung," 1941, 8.

67 William H. Honan, *William Scholl, 81, Designer of a Sandal that Sets a Trend,* in: The New York Times, Mar. 23, 2002. Although this firm disappeared from the German market—probably on account of World War II—it adopted the idea of the sandal from Germany in the 50s and is still today an important manufacturer, whose company history shows some amazing similarities to that of Birkenstock. CA Birkenstock, BS 20, report on the company Carl Birkenstock Steinhude am Meer. Factory for orthopedic specialties, Sept. 18, 1945.

68 CA Birkenstock, BS 114, Carl Birkenstock, "40 Jahre Einsatz für vernünftige Fußbekleidung," 1941, 14.

69 This can, however, only be deduced from the statements of contemporary witnesses, since business figures are not available for the period before 1933.

70 Carl Birkenstock later wrote that his company had so little to do in 1932 that he had to use his employees to build his house in Steinhude. CA Birkenstock, BS 54, statement by Carl Birkenstock to his old followers in the presence of the trade union leader Mr. Otto Jahr, May 2, 1946.

71 CA Birkenstock, BS 2, Birkenstock company brochure: "Ohne Fußbett im Schuh hat der Fuß keine Ruh," 1926.

72 Carl Birkenstock, *Mit dem Arzt gegen Fußkrankheiten und Irrlehren,* Bremen 1935, 9.

73 CA Birkenstock, BS 99, Memoir of Carl Birkenstock, "Mut zur Wahrheit."

74 Elsner, *Die "aufrechte" Haltung,* 117 f.

75 Georg Hohmann, *Fuß und Bein: Ihre Erkrankung und deren Behandlung,* Munich 1939, 102–115. The passage quoted makes it clear that physicians had sovereignty over this aspect of medical discourse. For example, in the contribution of an orthopedic mechanic named Hachtmann, Hohmann explicitly mentioned that this man was a "non-doctor."

76 Birkenstock, *Mit dem Arzt gegen Fußkrankheiten und Irrlehren,* 69.

77 CA Birkenstock, BS 9, author unknown, *Fertigeinlage oder Metalleinlage?,* in: Medizinische Technik, 8/9 (1947).

78 Incidentally, Konrad Birkenstock Sr. was also active as a journalist in the 30s but only published rather small brochures. Konrad Birkenstock, *Fußbett: Ein Wunder im Schuh,* Friedberg n. d. [1930s]; the authorship of the brochure *Die Fußkrankheiten und ihre Behandlung,* self-published in 1956, is not entirely clear. It could possibly also be a brochure from the estate of Konrad Sr.

79 CA Birkenstock BS 33, letter from Carl Birkenstock to Wilhelm Thomsen, 1942.

80 Carl Birkenstock, *Fußorthopädie "System Carl Birkenstock,"* Düsseldorf 1948, 14.

81 Ibid., 60–64

82 Ibid., 65–71.

83 Birkenstock, *Mit dem Arzt gegen Fußkrankheiten und Irrlehren,* 47.

84 Birkenstock, *Fußorthopädie,* 72 f.

85 CA Birkenstock, BS 99, memoir: *Das große Ziel: Richtige Beschuhung; Wie es Carl Birkenstock, Steinhude, sieht*, 1941.

86 CA Birkenstock, BS 99, memorandum of Carl Birkenstock: *Fußdienst – Die große Chance*, 1951.

87 CA Birkenstock, BS 103, manuscript textbook of Carl Birkenstock, untitled, 1950s.

88 CA Birkenstock, BS 109, Carl Birkenstock, draft letter, 1957.

89 CA Birkenstock, BS 108, "Der Weg aus dem orthopädischen Chaos," in: Schuh und Leder, Oct. 20, 1936.

90 Birkenstock, *Mit dem Arzt gegen Fußkrankheiten und Irrlehren*, book cover inside flap.

91 CA Birkenstock, BS 9, letter from the president of the Advertising Council of German Business to Carl Birkenstock, Sept. 23, 1936.

92 For an overview, see Fritz Müller, *Populäre Anatomie und Physiologie des menschlichen Körpers in ihrer Beziehung zur orthopädischen Mechanik: Ein Lehrbuch zum Gebrauch an den einschlägigen Fachschulen und zum Selbstunterricht für Orthopädiemechaniker und Bandagisten*, Munich ²1937.

93 CA Birkenstock, BS 114, Carl Birkenstock, "40 Jahre Einsatz für vernünftige Fußbekleidung," 1941.

94 Birkenstock, *50 Jahre System Birkenstock 1897–1947.*

95 Ibid.

96 Ibid.

97 CA Birkenstock, BS 49, performance report on the Carl Birkenstock company, Steinhude am Meer, Apr. 12, 1942.

98 CA Birkenstock, BS 9, letter from the Hamburg State Education Authority to Carl Birkenstock, Jan. 18, 1935.

99 CA Birkenstock; BS 9, letter from Carl Birkenstock to the state education authority, Feb. 18, 1935.

100 CA Birkenstock, BS 17, letter from Gustav Steinrück to Carl Birkenstock, 1941.

101 CA Birkenstock, BS 23, letter from the Hillig/Greuner law firm to Carl Birkenstock, Mar. 9, 1938.

102 CA Birkenstock, BS 23, letter from the Birkenstock brothers to Greuner, Feb. 4, 1938.

103 CA Birkenstock, BS 99, memoir of Carl Birkenstock: "Unhaltbare Zustände! Wie konnte es soweit kommen?," ca. 1941.

104 Müller, *Populäre Anatomie und Physiologie des menschlichen Körpers*, 120.

105 CA Birkenstock, BS 13, Franz Schede report on the Birkenstock brochure, 1937.

106 CA Birkenstock, BS 13, letter from the Reich working group to combat crippling diseases (Eckhardt) to the Reich Health Office in Berlin, Sept. 3, 1934.

107 CA Birkenstock, BS 8, Alfred Bredthauer, *Die häufigsten Fußkrankheiten und ihre Behandlung*, in: Schuhhändler-Zeitung, Jan. 8, 1935; see also CA Birkenstock, BS 9, letter from the German Association for Crippled Persons' Welfare to Alfred Bredthauer, 1935: "It is surprising when a doctor, without considering the very careful and extensive specialist literature concerning just the foot, prints almost verbatim in the daily press that which the owner of a patent for an insole claims is the sole truth." Birkenstock would later describe Bredthauer as a convinced Nazi who hanged himself at the end of the war. He was also one of his "main tormentors" in Steinhude. CA Birkenstock, BS 54, letter from Carl Birkenstock to Jakob Mölbert, May 24, 1946.

108 Anne Sudrow, *Der Schuh im Nationalsozialismus: Eine Produktgeschichte im deutsch-britisch-amerikanischen Vergleich*, Göttingen 2010, 365–368.

109 CA Birkenstock, BS 108, memorandum of Carl Birkenstock, June 8, 1961.

110 Wilhelm Thomsen, *Kampf der Fußschwäche! Ursachen, Mechanismus, Mittel und Wege zu ihrer Bekämpfung*, Munich ²1942.

111 CA Birkenstock, BS 108, memorandum of Carl Birkenstock, June 8, 1961.

112 Sudrow, *Der Schuh im Nationalsozialismus*, 441 f.

113 See Roman Köster, *Die Wissenschaft der Außenseiter: Die Krise der Nationalökonomie in der Weimarer Republik*, Göttingen 2011, 118.

114 CA Birkenstock, BS 8, author unknown, "25 Jahre Carl Birkenstock," offprint from: Der Schuhmarkt 1, 1941.

115 CA Birkenstock, BS 20, report on the company Carl Birkenstock Steinhude am Meer. Factory for orthopedic specialties, Sept. 18, 1945. However, in a letter from 1942, Carl Birkenstock also

Notes **389**

put the company's current number of customers at 9,500, which makes us somewhat suspicious as to the truthfulness of this statement. NLA BU, L 121, Carl Birkenstock performance report, Mar. 12, 1942.

116 CA Birkenstock, BS 99, memorandum of Carl Birkenstock: "Unhaltbare Zustände! Wie konnte es soweit kommen?," ca. 1941.

117 CA Birkenstock, BS 103, manuscript textbook of Carl Birkenstock, untitled, 1950s.

118 CA Birkenstock, BS 33, letter from Carl Birkenstock to Wilhelm Thomsen, n.d. [1942], 5.

119 CA Birkenstock, BS 108, memorandum, manuscript, "Problems with feet and shoes," July 8 1961; here is the handwritten note, 217 (ms) / 267 (PDF): "Walter Cohen was a Jew, by the way."

120 CA Birkenstock, BCB 4.002, Carl Birkenstock, *60 Jahre für vernünftige Schuhbekleidung*, PDF, 59–65.

121 Ibid.

122 CA Birkenstock, BS 103, manuscript textbook of Carl Birkenstock, untitled, 1950s; see also another perspective in: CA Birkenstock, BS 9, letter from the Reichsgemeinschaft zur Bekämpfung des Krüppeltums (Reich working group to combat crippling diseases) to Carl Birkenstock, May 13, 1938.

123 Reich Group Industry (ed.), *Gliederung der Reichsgruppe Industrie*, Leipzig 1936; Daniela Kahn, *Die Steuerung der Wirtschaft durch Recht im nationalsozialistischen Deutschland: Das Beispiel der Reichsgruppe Industrie*, Frankfurt am Main 2006.

124 CA Birkenstock, BS 103, manuscript textbook of Carl Birkenstock, untitled, 1950s.

125 CA Birkenstock, BS 9, announcement of District President Arnsberg, Dec. 19, 1935.

126 Ibid.

127 CA Birkenstock, BS 9, letter from Carl Birkenstock to Walter Falk, May 5, 1939.

128 Stadtarchiv Friedberg [hereafter StA Friedberg], registration index card Birkenstock.

129 CA Birkenstock, BS 14, letter from Carl Birkenstock to Kaiser/Salzer, Apr. 6, 1937; CA Birkenstock, BS 22, letter from the district court of Berlin to Konrad Birkenstock, Apr. 16, 1937.

130 CA Birkenstock, BS 28, letter from lawyer Schweer to the firm of Konrad Birkenstock, May 24, 1943.

131 Ibid.

132 See, for example, CA Birkenstock, BS 14, letter from Carl Birkenstock to Kaiser/Salzer, Sept. 18, 1937.

133 CA Birkenstock, BS 28, letter from lawyer Schweer to Konrad Birkenstock, May 24, 1943.

134 CA Birkenstock, BS 4, district court Friedberg to the company Gebrüder Birkenstock, certified copy from the commercial register, Sept. 20, 1939; CA Birkenstock, BS 17, Friedberg district court, Birkenstock limited liability company, Apr. 12, 1939.

135 StA Friedberg, Birkenstock registration file.

136 HHStA Wiesbaden, 507238, production permit 26/3622. Heinrich Birkenstock GmbH, June 14, 1947.

137 CA Birkenstock, BS 28, letter from lawyer Schweer to Konrad Birkenstock, Sept. 5, 1941.

138 CA Birkenstock, BS 28, letter from Konrad Birkenstock to Carl Birkenstock, May 19, 1943.

139 For example, see: CA Birkenstock, BS 1, letter from Konrad Birkenstock to Carl Birkenstock, Oct. 2, 1924.

140 CA Birkenstock, BS 28, letter from Heinrich Birkenstock to Carl Birkenstock, Oct. 8, 1948.

141 CA Birkenstock, BS 9, letter from Schweer to Carl Birkenstock, Dec. 3, 1941.

142 For example: CA Birkenstock, BS 28, letter from Carl Birkenstock to Konrad Birkenstock Jr., May 9, 1940; CA Birkenstock, BS 9, letter from lawyer Schweer to Carl Birkenstock, Dec. 3, 1941.

143 CA Birkenstock, BS 21, Reich Statistical Office, production survey questionnaire in the commercial economy for the calendar year 1936, Mar. 15, 1937; CA Birkenstock, BS 10, supplementary survey for industrial reporting November 1944, Dec. 11, 1944.

144 Arbinger, *Auf Sohlen aus Metall geht heute keiner mehr.*

145 CA Birkenstock, BS 49, performance report on the Carl Birkenstock company, Steinhude am Meer, Mar. 12, 1942.

146 See Jörg Lesczenski's essay in this volume, "On the Path to 'Walking as Nature Intended.'"

147 CA Birkenstock, BS 54, statement by Carl Birkenstock to his old followers in the presence of the union leader Mr. Otto Jahr, May 2, 1946.

148 CA Birkenstock, BS 10, sales at Carl Birkenstock Steinhude.

149 CA Birkenstock, BS 54, Questionnaire, Military Government of Germany, Nov. 26, 1945.

150 CA Birkenstock, BS 49, letter from Carl Birkenstock to the Governor of the Province of Westphalia, Dec. 14, 1945; CA Birkenstock, BS 10, overview of production and workforce, 1938–1942, PDF, 52.

151 Roman Köster, *Hugo Boss 1924–1945: Eine Kleiderfabrik zwischen Weimarer Republik und "Drittem Reich,"* Munich 2011, 51 f.

152 CA Birkenstock, BS 17, Memorandum of Carl Birkenstock, "Die Wehrmacht ist nicht mit den bestmöglichen Fußbehelfen ausgerüstet" Nov. 16, 1942.

153 CA Birkenstock, BS 10, overview of production and workforce, 1938–1942.

154 CA Birkenstock, BS 49, letter from Carl Birkenstock to the district court of Schaumburg-Lippe, Feb. 15, 1944; CA Birkenstock, BS 49, letter from Carl Birkenstock to lawyer Schweer, Mar. 20, 1944; CA Birkenstock, BS 54, Questionnaire, Military Government of Germany, Nov. 26, 1945.

155 The dedication was later (1961) crossed out by hand, see CA Birkenstock, BS 114.

156 In the 50s and 60s, he was to have the doctor Erich Druschky take over this task. In the 60s, he pointed out that, in his opinion, Hans Sachs, Jacob Böhme, and the legendary figure Hans von Sagan were to be regarded as the forefathers of the shoemaking trade. CA Birkenstock, BS 111, reference book of Carl Birkenstock, 1963.

157 CA Birkenstock, BS 33, open letter from Heinz Neu to the Reich Guild Association of the Shoemaker Trade, Dec. 31, 1938.

158 In Paracelsus's alleged struggle as an outsider against the "medical caste, who tried to hide the poverty and emptiness of their inner being with incomprehensible Latin, purple robes, gold, and decorative pendants," Neu must have evidently recognized himself. CA Birkenstock, BS 33, manuscript of Heinz Neu, "Paracelsus: Der Kämpfer gegen seine Zeit und seine Sendung für Kulturrevolution und Arzttum unserer Tage," 1941. In 1942, Neu was in the process of writing a "biological novel of life" with the telling title "The Heretic." However, as with his work on Paracelsus, there is no record of its publication anywhere.

159 CA Birkenstock, BS 33, letter from Carl Birkenstock to Wilhelm Thomsen, n. d. [1942].

160 See, for example, Roman Köster, *Seidensticker: Geschichte eines Familienunternehmens 1919–2019*, Essen 2019, 74.

161 CA Birkenstock, BCB 5.002, proof of ancestry and excerpt from paternal proof of ancestry of the municipality of Steinhude (n. d.), registry office document Oct. 17, 1905.

162 CA Birkenstock, BS 49, Carl Birkenstock, report on the Nazi Party Christmas celebration on Dec. 21, 1943. According to his statement, he was referred to at the celebration as a "Jewish half-breed." The ensuing battle of words led to Birkenstock being beaten by auxiliary police officer Beckedorf.

163 See the correspondence in CA Birkenstock, BS 49.

164 CA Birkenstock, BS 49, Alfred Bredthauer, medical certificate of Mr. Karl Birkenstock, Steinhude, Jan. 23, 1944.

165 CA Birkenstock, BS 49, letter from attorney Schweer to Ms. Endres, Jan. 24, 1945. See a detailed description of the conflict from Carl Birkenstock's point of view, in: CA Birkenstock, BS 49, letter from Carl Birkenstock to the Steinhude police station, Oct. 7, 1944. Since 1930, Heinrich Birkenstock had been married to Hertha Maass, who came from Neumünster, while Konrad Jr. was in Berlin at that time. In this respect, they were probably relatives of Carl Birkenstock's wife Emmi. Information from StA Friedberg, microfiche registration file of the city of Friedberg 1928–1977.

166 CA Birkenstock, BS 49, letter from lawyer Schweer to Hobein, Dec. 18, 1945.

"The Truly Ethical Man Does Not Cripple Himself":
Shoe Designs by the *Lebensreform* Movement

1 Paul Schultze-Naumburg, *Die Kultur des weiblichen Körpers als Grundlage der Frauenkleidung*, Jena 1901, 134.

2 See Klaus Wolbert, *Körper zwischen animalischer Leiblichkeit und ästhetisierender Verklärung der Physis*, in: Kai Buchholz et al. (eds.), Die Lebensreform: Entwürfe zur Neugestaltung von Leben und Kunst um 1900, vol. 2, Darmstadt 2001, 339–340, here: 339.

3 The Meyer line was eventually abandoned in the following decades of research on the foot-appropriate shoe; see Anja Helmers, *Der kindliche Fuß*, Berlin 2019, 127.

4 See Nike U. Breyer, *Linientreu: Schuhkonzepte der Lebensreform und ihr Weg durch das 20. Jahrhundert*, in: Kai Buchholz et al. (eds.), Die Lebensreform: Entwürfe zur Neugestaltung von Leben und Kunst um 1900, vol. I, Darmstadt 2001, 597–602, here: 597.

5 See Markwart Michler, *Hoffa, Albert*, in: Neue Deutsche Biographie 9 (1972), 387–388, www. deutsche-biographie.de/pnd118774670.html#ndbcontent (accessed May 5, 2022); Albert Hoffa, *Der menschliche Fuss und seine Bekleidung*, Würzburg 1899, 6.

6 Hoffa, *Menschliche Fuss*, 16.

7 Ibid., 7.

8 See CA Birkenstock, BS 66, Carl Birkenstock advertising circular, n. d.

9 See Nike U. Breyer, *Rationelle Schuhe: Hauptsache, die große Zehe hat die richtige Lage!*, in: Wolfgang Antweiler (ed.), Schritt für Schritt: Die Geburt des modernen Schuhs, Hilden 2013, 53, and Nike U. Breyer, *Asymmetrische Schuhe. Rationelle Formen werden "salonfähig,"* in: ibid., 72.

10 See Anne Sudrow, *Der Schuh im Nationalsozialismus: Eine Produktgeschichte im deutsch-britisch-amerikanischen Vergleich*, Göttingen 2010, 73.

11 See Breyer, *Rationelle Schuhe*, 53; see Breyer, *Asymmetrische Schuhe*, 76.

12 See Nike U. Breyer, *Mannesmann-Zehenkammerschuhe*, in: Wolfgang Antweiler (ed.), Schritt für Schritt: Die Geburt des modernen Schuhs, Hilden 2013, 82.

13 Schultze-Naumburg, *Die Kultur des weiblichen Körpers*, 12.

14 See Breyer, *Linientreu*, 598.

15 See Christian Schneehagen, *Die Freideutsche Jugend und die neue Kleidung*, in: Lotte Frucht/ Christian Schneehagen (eds.), Unsere Kleidung: Anregungen zur neuen Männer- und Frauentracht, Hamburg 1914, 6.

16 Hermann Pfeiffer, *Fußbekleidung*, in: Frucht/Schneehagen (eds.), *Unsere Kleidung. Anregungen zur neuen Männer- und Frauentracht*, Hamburg, 1914, 27–32, here: 28 f.

17 Nike U. Breyer, *"Es gibt keinen gesunden Menschenfuß, der vorn in einer Spitze ausläuft" (Knud Ahlborn): Wandervögel, Jugendbewegung und Schuhreform*, in: Medizin, Gesellschaft und Geschichte. Jahrbuch des Instituts für Geschichte der Medizin, vol. 30 (2011), 85–110, here: 100.

Fish Leather and Wooden Sandals: Leather Shortage during World War II

1 Anna-Brigitte Schlittler, *Bally-Schuhe sind tonangebende Modeschöpfungen. Schuh-Design im Zweiten Weltkrieg*, in: Anna-Brigitte Schlittler/Katharina Tietze (eds.), Über Schuhe: Zur Geschichte und Theorie der Fußbekleidung, Bielefeld 2016, 73–92, here: 74.

2 See ibid.

3 See ibid., 73.

4 See Birgit Haase, *Walking in Crocodile*, in: Anna-Brigitte Schlittler/ Katharina Tietze (eds.), Über Schuhe. Zur Geschichte und Theorie der Fußbekleidung, Bielefeld 2016, 21–34, here: 24.

5 See Dietmar Petzina, *Autarkiepolitik im Dritten Reich: Der nationalsozialistische Vierteljahresplan*, Stuttgart 1968, 57–9, 114 f.

6 See Anne Sudrow, *Vom Leder zum Kunststoff: Werkstoff-Forschung auf der "Schuhprüfstrecke" im Konzentrationslager Sachsenhausen 1940 bis 1945*, in: Helmut Maier (ed.), Rüstungsforschung im Nationalsozialismus: Organisation, Mobilisierung und Entgrenzung der Technikwissenschaften, Göttingen 2002, 214–249, here: 220.

7 The Dassler company became Adidas and Puma after World War II.

8 See Joseph Borkin, *Die unheilige Allianz der I. G. Farben: Eine Interessengemeinschaft im Dritten Reich*, Frankfurt am Main 1981.

9 See Haase, *Walking in Crocodile*, 23.

10 See Anne Sudrow, *Der Schuh im Nationalsozialismus: Eine Produktgeschichte im deutsch-britisch-amerikanischen Vergleich*, Göttingen 2010, 295.

11 *Nützliches zum Schenken*, in: Blatt der Hausfrau 58 (1943), 14.

12 See Sudrow, *Der Schuh im Nationalsozialismus*, 447.

13 See Isabella Belting, *Ready to go! Schuhe bewegen*, Berlin 2019, 176.

14 See Sudrow, *Der Schuh im Nationalsozialismus*, 759.

15 See ibid., 197.

16 See ibid., 200.

17 See also Johanna Steinfeld's essay in this volume, "'If the Shoe Fits ...': Comfortable Shoes on the Rise."

The *System Birkenstock*: The Footprint for Walking as Nature Intended

1 Corporate Archive Birkenstock [hereafter CA Birkenstock], BS 2, license agreements Patent-Centrale GmbH and sales agreements.

2 Flexible insole does not mean that it was flexible in the shoe but that it could bend. It was recommended that the insole be fastened in the shoe with small nails.

3 CA Birkenstock, BS 2, letter from K. Birkenstock, Frankfurt a. M.-South, to the Imperial Police Headquarters, Nov. 24, 1911.

4 CA Birkenstock, BS 2, sales brochures, K. Birkenstock, 1920.

5 CA Birkenstock, BS 2, Birkenstock company brochure: "Ohne Fußbett im Schuh hat der Fuß keine Ruh" (Without a footbed in the shoe, the foot has no rest), 1926.

6 The word *Fußbett* was used earlier in medicine, but in a completely different context: when a leg was broken, it was stretched into a *Fußbett* to keep it in a fixed position while it healed. See German dictionary by Jacob and Wilhelm Grimm, 16 vols., in 32 sub-volumes, Leipzig 1854–1971, Jacobsson 1, 810b–811b. Konrad Birkenstock, however, must not have had this image in mind, since everything that was rigid was repugnant to him. The first advertising graphics, which show a foot and a bed, also point in a different direction.

7 See Roman Köster's essay in this volume.

8 CA Birkenstock, BS 61, footbed advertisement with the ring. D. R. P. stands for Deutsches Reichs-Patentamt (Patent Office of the German Reich).

9 The footbed later retroactively described as *"Blue Footbed"* never had this product name, it was merely a paraphrase.

10 CA Birkenstock, BS 13, Franz Schede report on the Birkenstock brochure, 1937.

11 Carl Birkenstock, *Arzt – Fußkrankheiten – Kampf gegen Irrlehren: Mit dem Arzt gegen Fußkrankheiten und Irrlehren,* Steinhude am Meer 1935.

12 CA Birkenstock, inventory CB, BS 8, Gerichtlicher Vergleich (court settlement). The process ended in a settlement. Small editorial corrections were made in nine passages, which somewhat retracted the statements made by Carl Birkenstock, which were directed against others—e. g., "never" was replaced by "in my view, not," "evidence" with "opinion," and "the expert" with "one."

13 Carl Birkenstock, *Fußorthopädie: Das System Birkenstock,* Bad Honnef 1948.

14 For more detail, see Roman Köster's essay in this volume.

15 Birkenstock, *Fußorthopädie,* 14.

16 Ibid., 2.

17 Ibid., 18.

18 Ibid., 7. He divided his analysis into the following chapters: 1. Anatomy of the foot, 2. Walking as nature intended (footprint system), 3. Shoe defects, 4. Civilization-conditioned walking (3-point system), 5. C. B. Orthopedics, 6. Foot problems.

19 Birkenstock, *Fußorthopädie,* 9.

20 Ibid, 19.

21 Ibid.

22 Ibid., 25.

23 Ibid., 26.

24 Ibid., 22–23.

25 Ibid.

26 Ibid., 98.

27 Ibid, 10.

28 Ibid., 101.

29 See Jörg Lesczenski's essay in this volume.

30 He had already registered the patent rights for various countries. See CA Birkenstock, BS 36–85, Patents.

31 See CA Birkenstock, BS 86, 93, 94, Carl Birkenstock's correspondence with shoe manufacturers.

32 Birkenstock, *Fußorthopädie*, 101.

33 Ibid., 38.

34 Pure materials made of leather, felt, cork, etc., were not suitable for foot support because they changed their shape under the weight of the body and did not return to their original form. Birkenstock, *Fußorthopädie*, 73.

35 Birkenstock, *Fußorthopädie*, 41.

36 Ibid.

37 Ibid., 42.

38 CA Birkenstock, inventory Birkenstock, BS 49 Birkenstock order; BS 2 license certificates and license agreements.

39 See Birkenstock, *Fußorthopädie*, and Roman Köster's essay in this volume, "Misjudged Innovations."

40 Birkenstock, *Fußorthopädie*, 80.

41 Ibid., 88.

42 Anne Sudrow, *Der Schuh im Nationalsozialismus: Eine Produktgeschichte im deutsch-britisch-amerikanischen Vergleich*, Göttingen 2010, 365–368.

43 CA Birkenstock, B2, letter of acknowledgment, Frankfurt am Main, Nov. 18, 1906.

1945–1963
Beginning of the Industrial Era

1 Corporate Archive Birkenstock [henceforth CA Birkenstock], folder/looseleaf portfolio, no title, letter from Staff Doctor Prof. Dr. med. W. Thomsen, Specialist Medical Certification, to Carl Birkenstock, Bad Homburg, Sept. 30, 1945

2 CA Birkenstock, BS 49, letter Coltzau, Carl Birkenstock, Steinhude am Meer, to Firma Carl Birkenstock, Honnef/Rhine, Steinhude am Meer, Oct. 30, 1946.

3 In what was later the State of Lower Saxony, it was the UNRRA, the United Nations Relief and Rehabilitation Administration, that with the help of Jewish support associations primarily managed the total of 14 "DP Camps," the camps for displaced persons. Marlies Buchholz/ Hans-Dieter Schmid, *Juden in Niedersachsen: Eine ethnisch-religiöse Minderheit zwischen Assimilation, Vertreibung und Vernichtung*, in: Gerd Steinwascher (ed.), Geschichte Niedersachsens, vol. 5, Von der Weimarer Republik bis zur Wiedervereinigung, Hanover 2010, 1165–1219, here: 1209.

4 CA Birkenstock, BS 49, letter from Carl Birkenstock to Military Administration, Capt. Renvick, Stadthagen, Nov. 21, 1945.

5 CA Birkenstock, BS 49, Carl Birkenstock, Steinhude am Meer, [list] war damages, Steinhude am Meer, July 10, 1945.

6 CA Birkenstock, BS 49, letter from Carl Birkenstock to attorney Schweer, Stadthagen, no address given [Steinhude am Meer], Oct. 19, 1945; letter from Dr. jur. Ernst Riesel to attorney Schweer, Stadthagen, Steinhude am Meer, Oct. 20, 1945.

7 CA Birkenstock, BS 20, letter from Hako Hammer Kommandit Gesellschaft, Frankfurt/Main, to the Military Administration Wiesbaden, Frankfurt am Main, Sept. 21, 1945.

8 Lower Saxony State Archive, Bückeburg section [henceforth: NLA BU], Dep. 46 A, no. 988. Carl Birkenstock, Steinhude am Meer: Report on the company Carl Birkenstock, Steinhude am Meer, factory for specialist orthopedic articles, [Steinhude am Meer], Oct. 2, 1945.

9 CA Birkenstock, BS 20, letter from Maison Resimont, manufacturer of specialist articles, Liège, Belgium, to Carl Birkenstock, Liège, July 21, 1946.

10 NLA BU Dep. 46 A, no. 988, Carl Birkenstock, Steinhude am Meer: Report on the company Carl Birkenstock, Steinhude am Meer, factory for specialist orthopedic articles, [Steinhude am Meer], Oct. 2, 1945.

11 On the individual phases of denazification in the four occupation zones, see: Clemens Vollnhals, *Das gescheiterte Experiment*, in: id. (ed.), Entnazifizierung: Politische Säuberung und Rehabilitierung in den vier Besatzungszonen 1945–1949, Munich 1991, 7–64.

12 CA Birkenstock, BS 20, letter from Dr. Bless, medical practitioner, to Carl Birkenstock, Bad Honnef, Aug. 15, 1949.

13 Andreas Wiedemann, *Politik und Alltag in den Landkreisen Friedberg und Büdingen 1945–1949*, Friedberg 1994, 15–21.

14 Hessian Main State Archive Wiesbaden [henceforth: HHStA Wiesbaden], 507, no. 238, The President of the State Economic Office for Hessen: Production Permit no. 36/3622, Wiesbaden, July 14, 1947, as well as other documents.

15 Wiedemann, *Politik und Alltag*, 24.

16 CA Birkenstock, BS 20, loose-leaf collection, no title [Documents from the postwar period], letter from Konrad Jr. to Carl Birkenstock, no address [Friedberg], Sept. 19, 1945.

17 HHStA Wiesbaden, 507, no. 238., The President of the State Economic Office for Hessen: Production Permit no. 36/967, Wiesbaden, July 14, 1947, and other documents.

18 The brothers' denazification files have to date not been found.

19 See: Friedberg Municipal Archive, commercial register.

20 CA Birkenstock, BS 54, declaration by Mr. Birkenstock to his old employees in the presence of trade union shop steward Mr. Otto Jahr, May 2, 1946.

21 CA Birkenstock BS 49, Carl Birkenstock, notes, untitled, Dec. 6, 1945. His sister-in-law swore an affidavit, however, repeating the accusation that she had been denounced.

22 CA Birkenstock BS 49, letter from Carl Birkenstock to attorney Schweer, Oct. 19, 1945.

23 CA Birkenstock, BS 49, letter from Carl Birkenstock to the Military Administration, Capt. Renvick, Nov. 21, 1945.

24 CA Birkenstock, BS 49: memo for Mr. Coltzau for his discussion with the English commanding officer of Steinhude am Meer, Oct. 22, 1945.

25 CA Birkenstock, BS 55, letter from Carl Birkenstock to the Lord Mayor, Baden-Baden, Nov. 29, 1945.

26 CA Birkenstock, BS 55, letter from Carl Birkenstock to the Lord Mayor, Dept. of Trade and Commerce, Baden-Baden, Feb. 1, 1946.

27 CA Birkenstock, BS 49, letter from Carl Birkenstock to the Military Administration, Capt. Renvick, Stadthagen, Nov. 21, 1945; memo [Mr.] Coltzau, Dec. 3, 1945.

28 CA Birkenstock, BS 49, Carl Birkenstock, notes, untitled, Dec. 6, 1945.

29 CA Birkenstock, BS 20, letter from attorney Schweer to the mayor in Steinhude, Dec. 18, 1945.

30 See also the family history of the Dasslers: Christian Kleinschmidt et al., *Sport Enterprise: The History of Adidas*, Munich 2018, 55–70; and, more generally: Andrea Schneider, *The Entrepreneurial Family: Risk for the Family Business?*, in: Equa-Foundation (ed.), Entrepreneurial Families: Property Obliges, Munich 2021, 299–313.

31 CA Birkenstock, BS 20, letter from Carl Birkenstock to attorney Schweer, Stadthagen, Feb. 5, 1946.

32 North-Rhine Westphalian State Archive Duisburg [henceforth: LAV NRW], NW 110, no. 428, letter from the State Government of Schaumburg-Lippe, [Mr.] Böve to State President Drake in Detmold, Feb. 4, 1946.

33 LAV NRW, NW 110, Nr. 428, Letter from Carl Birkenstock to the Chief President of the Province of Westphalia, Münster, Feb. 28, 1946.

34 Quoted in: CA Birkenstock, BS 54, letter from Carl Birkenstock to Municipal Director, Bad Honnef, June 11, 1946.

35 CA Birkenstock, BS 54, statement by Carl Birkenstock to his old followers in the presence of the trade union leader Mr. Otto Jahr, May 2, 1946.

36 Ibid.

37 CA Birkenstock, BS 20, 808 (L/R) Mil. Gov. Det. Administrative District of Cologne, Application for Permission to Reopen Industrial Plants in the Area of the Chambers of Commerce and Trades, Mar. 29, 1946, as well as letter from the Headquarters Military Government L/K Siegburg, Subject: Reopening of firm to the company Carl Birkenstock in Honnef/Rhine, n. d.

38 CA Birkenstock, file/folder "Collection of materials on production permit Carl Birkenstock GmbH, 1936–1947," letter from Carl Birkenstock to the District Housing Authority Stadthagen, Mar. 29, 1946, as well as letter from Carl Birkenstock to the District Housing Authority Siegburg, Mar. 29, 1946.

39 CA Birkenstock, BS 20, Military Government of Germany, Province Hanover: Production Permit Industrial Plants; To: Carl Birkenstock, Fabrik für orthopädische Spezialitäten, Steinhude am Meer, Nov. 1946.

40 CA Birkenstock, BS 20, The Economics Minister of the State of North Rhine Westphalia, Provisional Production Permit, Company: Carl Birkenstock, Fabrik für orthopädische Spezialitäten, Honnef, March 24, 1947.

41 CA Birkenstock, BS 20, letter from Konrad Birkenstock to Carl Birkenstock Sept. 19, 1945.

42 On this see: CA Birkenstock, BS 61, note/minutes Carl Birkenstock to Heinrich, Konrad Jr., and Konrad Sr. Birkenstock as well as to Alfred Weber, Oct. 5, 1947.

43 CA Birkenstock, BS 61, letter from Carl Birkenstock to Konrad Birkenstock Sr., Konrad Birkenstock Jr., Heinrich Birkenstock, and Alfred Weber, Mar. 15, 1948; letter from Carl Birkenstock to Konrad Birkenstock Jr., July 7, 1948; letter from Carl Birkenstock to Konrad Birkenstock Jr., July 22, 1948.

44 CA Birkenstock, BS 61, letter from Carl Birkenstock to Konrad Birkenstock Jr., July 22, 1948.

45 CA Birkenstock, BS 61, letter from Konrad Birkenstock Jr. to Carl Birkenstock, no address [Friedberg], July 16, 1948.

46 CA Birkenstock, BS 61, letter from Heinrich Birkenstock to Carl Birkenstock, Oct. 8, 1949.

47 Ibid.

48 Ibid.

49 Ibid.

50 On this, see the wad of letters and notes in: CA Birkenstock, BS 61.

51 CA Birkenstock, BS 61, letter from Carl Birkenstock to Konrad Birkenstock Sr., Konrad Birkenstock Jr., Heinrich Birkenstock, and Alfred Weber, Mar. 15, 1948.

52 See, among other things: CA Birkenstock, BS 61, letter from Carl Birkenstock to the company Konrad Birkenstock, Fabrik für Orthopädie, Re: Terms and conditions – surcharge, Mar. 19, 1951.

53 CA Birkenstock, BS 61, O. A.: minutes/notes, Mar. 9, 1951.

54 CA Birkenstock, BS 61, Articles of Association, Friedberg/Hessen, Apr. 1951.

55 CA Birkenstock, BS 61, letter from Carl Birkenstock to the company Konrad Birkenstock, Fabrik für Orthopädie, June 21, 1951; letter from Konrad Birkenstock Jr. to C. B. Birkenstock, Carl Birkenstock, July 10, 1951.

56 CA Birkenstock, BS 61, letter from Carl Birkenstock, Fabrik für orthopädische Spezialitäten, Bad Honnef/Rhine – Steinhude, to the company Konrad Birkenstock, Fabrik für Orthopädie, Friedberg, July 13, 1951.

57 Hessian State Archive Darmstadt, H 14 Büdingen, R 35, commercial register file on Heinrich Birkenstock, Büdingen; Axel Arbinger, *Auf Sohlen aus Metall geht heute keiner mehr: Die Geschichte der Firma Birkenstock; Im "Indianer-Viertel" den Grundstein zum Weltruf gelegt*, in: Friedberg-Magazin (Apr. 1995), in: Friedberg Municipal Archive.

58 Carl Birkenstock, *Fußorthopädie: System Carl Birkenstock*, Düsseldorf 1948, 7 f.

59 So went his decidedly accurate self-description. See: ibid., 8.

60 CA Birkenstock, BS 57, letter from Carl Birkenstock to Hugo Stortz, Mar. 3, 1947.

61 CA Birkenstock, BS 57, letter from Carl Birkenstock to the Hugo Stortz company, Nov. 18, 1948.

62 CA Birkenstock, BS 57, letter from Hugo Stortz, Managing Director of the Consortium, to the Carl Birkenstock company, Nov. 22, 1948.

63 CA Birkenstock, BS 57, Carl Birkenstock, Fabriken für orthopädische Spezialitäten, Management, agreement, Bad Honnef, July 1, 1949.

64 CA Birkenstock, BS 57, letter from Hugo Stortz, Chairman of the Consortium, to the Carl Birkenstock company, July 20, 1949.

65 See, for example: CA Birkenstock, BS 57, letter from Hugo Stortz, Chairman of the Consortium, to the Carl Birkenstock company, Aug. 16, 1949.

66 CA Birkenstock, BS 57, letter from Carl Birkenstock to the Central Guild Association of the Orthopedics and Bandaging Trades, attn. Mr. Stortz, Sept. 3, 1953.

67 CA Birkenstock, BS 57, letter from Hugo Stortz, Chairman of the Central Guild Association, to the company C.B.-Orthopädie-GmbH, Cologne, Nov. 10, 1953.

68 CA Birkenstock, BS 57, letter from Hugo Stortz, Chairman of the Consortium, to the Carl Birkenstock company, July 28, 1949.

69 Erich Druschky, *Aufgabe, Sinn und Zweck der Kosmetikschule Neckarbischofsheim, der Ausbildungsstätte für Arztfrauen*, in: Journal für medizinische Kosmetik 53, no. 6 (June 20, 1953), in: CA Birkenstock, BS 81.

70 CA Birkenstock, BS 81, letter from Carl Birkenstock to Dr. med. E. Druschky and Dr. med. Ditsch, Aug. 3, 1957.

71 CA Birkenstock, BS 83, Carl Birkenstock: *Fuß-Orthopädie in Verwirrung und Verirrung: Rückschau und Ausschau zum 60jährigen Firmen-Jubiläum*, Bad Honnef/Rhine, n.d. [1957], 1f.

72 CA Birkenstock, BS 57, Guild for the Orthopedics, Surgical, Mechanical, and Bandaging Trades Cologne, Sternengasse Office, Circular no. 1/50, Cologne, Feb. 19, 1950.

73 Peter Pitzen, *Die Geschichte der Deutschen Orthopädischen Gesellschaft: Von der Königsberger Tagung 1936 bis zum 50. Kongress in München 1962*, Stuttgart 1963, 262; on the debates among the podiatric experts, see: ibid., 245–283.

74 See: Franz Schede, *Rückblick und Ausblick. Erlebnisse und Betrachtungen eines Arztes*, Stuttgart 1960.

75 Karl Teppe, *Trümmergesellschaft im Wiederaufbau*, in: Aus Politik und Zeitgeschichte 18–19 (1995), 22–33.

76 Michael Wildt, *Vom kleinen Wohlstand: Eine Konsumgeschichte der fünfziger Jahre*, Frankfurt am Main 1996.

77 On the economic upturn that began in the early 50s, see: Werner Abelshauser, *Deutsche Wirtschaftsgeschichte seit 1945*, Bonn 2005, 200ff., 282ff.; Philipp Heldmann, *Das "Wirtschaftswunder" in Westdeutschland: Überlegungen zur Periodisierung und Ursachen*, in: Archiv für Sozialgeschichte 36 (1996), 323–344; Ludger Lindlar, *Das missverstandene Wirtschaftswunder: Westdeutschland und die westeuropäische Nachkriegsprosperität*, Tübingen 1997.

78 Christoph Kleßmann, *Zwei Staaten, eine Nation: Deutsche Geschichte 1955–1970*, Bonn 1988, 37.

79 Michael Breitenacher, *Leder- und Schuhindustrie: Strukturelle Probleme und Wachstumschancen*, Berlin 1967, 17.

80 Hansjörg Kramer, *Die Vertriebsformen eines Großunternehmens der deutschen Schuhindustrie*, Freiburg im Breisgau 1955, 19f.

81 Ibid., 21.

82 See, for example: CA Birkenstock, BS 66, Carl Birkenstock, Offener Brief: Gedanken zur Fußgesundheitswoche, in: Schuhwirtschaft 29 (July 16, 1953).

83 For details of the characteristics of the individual articles, see: CA Birkenstock, BS 66, Information, no. 10, "Für unsere Herren vom Außendienst!," June 9, 1960.

84 CA Birkenstock, BS 98, Gustav Wulf: "Ein neues Patent! Einlegesohlen 'Zehenfrei,'" Hamburg, Oct. 18, 1956.

85 CA Birkenstock, BS 66, Birkenstock-Orthopäde GmbH, *Das können sie auch! Zehenfrei – Verkaufserfolge im Fachgeschäft einer Mittelstadt.*

86 CA Birkenstock, BS 66, Dr. med. Sigg: "Vieles ginge besser – wenn man mehr ging," joint lecture at the Orthopedics Congress in Baden-Baden, May 1, 1962.

87 CA Birkenstock, BS 83, Carl Birkenstock, *Fuß-Orthopädie in Verwirrung und Verirrung: Rückschau und Ausschau zum 60jährigen Firmen-Jubiläum*, Bad Honnef/Rhine, n.d. [1957], 1f.

88 CA Birkenstock, BS 66, Information, no. IX/61, Report on our May convention in Unkel, 1961.

89 CA Birkenstock, BS 66, Information, "Achtung!!! 1961 sind Riesenumsätze mit 'Zehenfrei' zu erwarten," n.d. [1960–61].

90 Ibid.

91 CA Birkenstock, BS 66, on the individual ad media, see: Information I/61, "Die Saison beginnt!"

92 See, by way of example: CA Birkenstock, BS 66, Information, no. 10, "Für unsere Herren vom Außendienst!," June 9, 1960.

93 As already stated, in the 20s and 30s as well as in the postwar period, exports of the insoles to other European countries was a crucial pillar of company activities. The history of Birkenstock's expansion outside Germany in the years of the economic upturn cannot be reconstructed with great accuracy from the existing records, which at best allow us to make only a few remarks.

94 CA Birkenstock, BS 93, letter from Carl Birkenstock to the Emil Neuffer company, "Goldmark," Re: Foreign Partners, Jan. 27, 1955.

95 Ibid.; CA Birkenstock, BS 61, letter from Carl Birkenstock, C. B. Orthopädie to the Konrad Birkenstock company, July 13, 1951.

96 See Emanuela Scarpellini's essay in this volume.

97 CA Birkenstock, BS 80, Agreement between Carl Birkenstock, Vasilijs Kils, Ray Neil Bryson, and James C. Shorter, May 1952.

98 CA Birkenstock, BS 80, Agreement between C. B. Orthopädie GmbH, Carl Birkenstock, James C. Shorter, Vasilijs Kils, and Serge Knyshynski, Jan. 22, 1954.

99 CA Birkenstock, BS 93, letter from Carl Birkenstock to the Emil Neuffer company, "Goldmark," Re: Foreign Partners, Jan. 27, 1955.

100 Data according to: CA Birkenstock, BS 130-BS 154, opening and annual balance sheets, annual financial statements Carl Birkenstock GmbH Bad Honnef/Rhine. The median return on sales for the period 1953 to 1963 was 1.06 percent. It is hard to assess the returns on sales appropriately as there are no comparative figures for individual companies from the same sector of a comparable size. Moreover, to this day, the return on sales differs greatly from one sector to the next. In 1961, for example, the return on sales for manufacturing as a whole (excl. iron and metalworking companies) came to 2.82 percent, while in the textiles and clothing industry it ran at 1.75 percent. See *Statistisches Jahrbuch der Bundesrepublik Deutschland 1965*, vol. 1964, Stuttgart 1965, 226 f.

101 CA Birkenstock, BS 28, letter from Carl Birkenstock to his three sons, Oct. 15, 1947.

102 CA Birkenstock, BS 93, letter from Emil Neuffer KG to C. B. Orthopädie GmbH, Oct. 13, 1954.

103 The two parties did not argue over the fact that the "Neuffer-Birkenstock-Schuhe" destined for sales regions within West Germany would be exclusively made by Emil Neuffer KG (or, later, potentially by a Neuffer-Birkenstock distribution company); CA Birkenstock, BS 93, [Emil Neuffer KG], memo, Nov. 13, 1954.

104 CA Birkenstock, BS 93, letter from Carl Birkenstock to Emil Neuffer company, "Goldmark-Schuhfabrik," Nov. 23, 1954.

105 CA Birkenstock, BS 93, letter from Emil Neuffer KG to C. B. Orthopädie GmbH, Dec. 3, 1954, and Preliminary Agreement between Emil Neuffer KG, Pirmasens and C. B. Birkenstock GmbH, Dec. 7, 1954.

106 CA Birkenstock, BS 93, C. B. Orthopädie GmbH, specimen letter, Re: Your first order of "Idealschuhe," Dec. 7, 1954.

107 CA Birkenstock, BS 93, Emil Neuffer KG, recitals [and] agreement between the Emil Neuffer KG company, shoe factory, and the C. Birkenstock company, Orthopädie GmbH, Carl Birkenstock, Jan. 18, 1955.

108 CA Birkenstock, BS 93, letter from Emil Neuffer KG to C. B. Orthopädie GmbH, Feb. 3, 1955.

109 CA Birkenstock, BS 93, letter from Emil Neuffer KG to C. B. Orthopädie GmbH, Apr. 27, 1955.

110 CA Birkenstock, BS 93, letter from Emil Neuffer KG, Sales Dept., to C. B. Orthopädie GmbH, Feb. 3, 1955, and letter from [Hr.] Friedrichs, C. B. Orthopädie GmbH, to Emil Neuffer KG, June 1, 1955.

111 See, by way of example: CA Birkenstock, BS 93, letter from Hermann von der Heyde, Textilhaus, to the Carl Birkenstock company, June 11, 1955, as well as letter from Erich Brambsch [?] to Carl Birkenstock, Aug. 5, 1955.

112 CA Birkenstock, BS 93, letter from Emil Neuffer KG to C. B. Orthopädie GmbH, June 23, 1955.

113 CA Birkenstock, BS 93, letter from C. B. Orthopedics of Canada to Emil Neuffer KG, July 8, 1955; letter from Emil Neuffer KG to C. B. Orthopädie GmbH, Jan. 19, 1956; as well as letter from Emil Neuffer KG to Mr. Hans Wilhelm, April 2, 1958.

114 CA Birkenstock, BS 86, Agreement between the Georg Mayer company, shoe factory, Götzis/Voralberg (Austria), and the company C. B. Orthopädie GmbH, Carl Birkenstock, Bad-Honnef/Rhine (Germany), Jan. 30, 1954.

115 CA Birkenstock, BS 86, letter from Georg Mayer to Carl Birkenstock, Sept. 28, 1954; letter from Carl Birkenstock to the Georg Mayer company, shoe factory, Registered mail! For Herr Mayer confidentially, Sept. 27, 1954.

116 Subsequently, the focus was on the interpretation of the contractual details, open receivables, and claims for damages (next to nothing is known about the actual results of the litigation). See: CA Birkenstock, BS 86, letter from Dr. Walter Fulterer, lawyer in Dornbirn to Dr. Walter Derganz, lawyer in Bregenz, June 10, 1955.

117 Data from: Breitenacher, *Leder- und Schuhindustrie*, 37.

118 Ibid., 38.

119 Axel Schildt, *Sozialgeschichte der Bundesrepublik Deutschland bis 1989/90*, Munich 2007, 25.

120 Axel Schildt, *Moderne Zeiten: Freizeit, Massenmedien und "Zeitgeist" in der Bundesrepublik der 50er-Jahre*, Hamburg 1995, 110–121.

121 Breitenacher, *Leder- und Schuhindustrie*, 38.

122 Helge Sternke, *Alles über Herrenschuhe*, Berlin 2006.

123 Letter from Carl Birkenstock to Schuhfabrik Jakob Rumpf & Sohn, Butzbach, dated Jan. 20, 1961.

124 CA Birkenstock BS 94, letter from Chasalla-Schuhfabrik GmbH & Co. KG to Carl Birkenstock, Kassel, Sept. 26, 1961.

125 CA Birkenstock, BS 94, letter from C. B. Orthopädie-GmbH to the management of Chasalla-Schuhfabrik GmbH, Bad Honnef, Aug. 1, 1960; letter from Chasalla-Schuhfabrik GmbH to Carl Birkenstock, C. B. Orthopädie-GmbH, Kassel, Sept. 20, 1960.

126 He made contact with the shoe factory Pioneer GmbH in Emmendigen im Breisgau, the company Ganter in Waldkirch, the Bisi shoe factory in Bad Dürrheim, and Heinrich Schäffert GmbH in Endingen, none of whom were interested in joint projects for different reasons. There were also talks with Metzeler Gummiwerke in Munich, but there are no sources to indicate the outcome. See the relevant correspondence in CA Birkenstock BS 98.

127 The J. Bogenschütz factory did not accept the business principles proposed by Birkenstock and withdrew from the project. FA Birkenstock BS 98, letter from J. Bogenschütz, shoe factory, to Mr. Helmut Wegerth, Steinen/Baden, May 5, 1962.

128 CA Birkenstock, BS 94, letter from Carl Birkenstock to Heinrich, Konrad, and Konrad Jr. Birkenstock and Alfred Weber, Oct. 15, 1942.

129 CA Birkenstock, BS 61, C. B. Orthopädie GmbH to Konrad Birkenstock, Jan. 23, 1963.

130 See Nike U. Breyer, Interview, in: New York Times, *Ugly for a Reason*, 3 episodes, here episode 3, in: www.nytimes.com/paidpost/birkenstock/how-feet-made-us-human.html; www.birkenstock.com/us/ugly-for-a-reason/ utm_source=nytimes&utm_medium=referral&utm_campaign=ufar&cpeu=ed_al_sh_al_al_UFAR (accessed May 15, 2023).

131 The exhibition was curated and shown in 2021 at the Vitra Design Museum, Weil am Rhein, then moved to the Staatliche Kunstsammlungen Dresden, Kunstgewerbemuseum, Dresden, in 2023 to the Tsinghua University Art Museum, Beijing, and from September 2023 to the Möbelmuseum Wien, Vienna.

132 See also the introduction and Andrea H. Schneider-Braunberger's and Alice Janssen's essays in this volume. Karl Birkenstock's creative skills can be found not only in the designs of the sandals but also in the editions of the Birkenstock Post, which acquired a clear and distinct style of their own after he joined the company. See: CA Birkenstock, Sammlung Birkenstock Post.

133 CA Birkenstock, BS 51, Fachkunde, Mar. 19 [1963]; LAV NRW, NW 110, No. 6, letter from CB. Orthopädie GmbH to the Minister for Economy, Small and Medium-Sized Businesses and Transport, Re: Production and distribution of the *Original Birkenstock-Footbed Sandal*, Oct. 21, 1963.

134 CA Birkenstock, BS 51, in: Schuhwirtschaft 17 (Apr. 25, 1963), as well as in: Fachkunde (Mar. 19, 1963).

135 *"Von 'Baumstämmen' zum Bestseller*, Interview mit Karl Birkenstock," in: Schuhmarkt 1 (2000), 2.

136 Ibid.

137 LAV NRW, NW 110, no. 6 [State of North-Rhine Westphalia Ministry of Economics, Small Businesses, and Transport to the Monopolies Commission], [Mr.] Schwefer, memo, Ref.: Phone call Birkenstock on Oct. 18, 1963, Düsseldorf, Oct. 18, 1963.

138 Ibid.

139 Ibid.

140 LAV NRW, NW 110, no. 6, letter from C. B.-Orthopädie GmbH, Carl Birkenstock to the Federal Monopolies Commission, Re: Production and distribution of the *Original Birkenstock-Footbed Sandals*, Ref.: Our phone call, n. d.

141 LAV NRW NW 110, no. 6 letter from Federal Monopolies Commission to C. B.-Orthopädie GmbH, Carl Birkenstock, Re.: Production and distribution of the *Original Birkenstock-Footbed Sandals*, Feb. 20, 1964.

142 Company Archive Continental AG: Akte 6603, Zg. 1/85, A2: [author not legible]: Board presentation on the occasion of the ALSA Group plan meeting, Nov. 6, 1975, Hanover, Nov. 4, 1975.

143 "*Von 'Baumstämmen' zum Bestseller*, Interview mit Karl Birkenstock," in: Schuhmarkt 1 (2000), 3.

144 See CA Birkenstock, Product Catalogues.

145 CA Birkenstock, BS 66, "Muß das sein?," brochure, 1965.

146 CA Birkenstock, BS 66, "Birkenstock: Zu Hause und im Beruf" brochure, 1968. It is unclear whether the chart in the brochure, which gives no actual figures, only reflects domestic sales or also those outside Germany; CA Birkenstock, BS 66., *Honnefer Rundblick*, Nov. 30, 1968.

147 CA Birkenstock, BS 66, Birkenstock prices, valid from Jan. 1, 1960; Stefan Schmitz, "'Gott wird mich nicht fragen, wieviel Schuhe ich verkauft habe': Heinrich Deichmann-Schuhe GmbH & Co. KG," in: Thomas Osterkorn et al. (eds.), *Gründergeschichten: Vom Abenteuer, ein Unternehmen aufzubauen,* Frankfurt am Main 2007, 164.

148 CA Birkenstock BS 130 – BS 154, Sales revenues, net profits (net income/loss for the year) and return on sales in percent, Carl Birkenstock GmbH, Bad Honnef/Rhine, 1949–1970.

149 Ibid.; CA Birkenstock, BS 150–154, annual financial statements 1967 to 1970 of Birkenstock Orthopädie GmbH.

150 CA Birkenstock, BS 66, *Honnefer Rundblick*, Nov. 30, 1968.

151 Frankfurter Rundschau, June 17, 1996; Süddeutsche Zeitung, Aug. 12, 1996.

The Desire for Fashion: From the Jedermann Program to Mass Consumption

1 See Axel Schildt, *Die Sozialgeschichte der Bundesrepublik Deutschland bis 1989/90*, Munich 2007, 8 f.

2 See ibid., 9.

3 See Michael Wildt, *"Wohlstand für alle": Das Spannungsfeld von Konsum und Politik in der Bundesrepublik*, in: Heinz-Gerhard Haupt/Claudius Torp (eds.), Die Konsumgesellschaft in Deutschland 1890–1990: Ein Handbuch, Frankfurt am Main 2009, 305–318, here: 306.

4 See Irmgard Zündorf, *Der Preis der Marktwirtschaft: Staatliche Preispolitik und Lebensstandard in Westdeutschland 1948 bis 1963*, Stuttgart 2006, 69.

5 Ludwig Erhard, *Die neue Marktwirtschaft*, speech (Dec. 16, 1948), in: Der Übersee-Club e. V., www.ueberseeclub.de/index.php/de/datenbank (accessed July 1, 2022).

6 Knut Borchardt/Christoph Buchheim, *Die Wirkung der Marshallplan-Hilfe in Schlüsselbranchen der deutschen Wirtschaft*, in: Hans-Jürgen Schröder (ed.), Marshallplan und westdeutscher Wiederaufstieg: Positionen – Kontroversen, Stuttgart 1990, 119–149, here: 127.

7 The Bizone was the name given to the combination of the American and British occupation zones to form the United Economic Area on January 1, 1947.

8 See Zündorf, *Preis der Marktwirtschaft*, 71.

9 See ibid., 72 f.

10 *Der Schuhbedarf*, in: Frankfurter Allgemeine Zeitung (Dec. 5, 1949), 8.

11 *Schuhwirtschaft muß sich umstellen*, in: Frankfurter Allgemeine Zeitung (Dec. 30, 1949), 7; cf. Karlheinz Reidenbach, *Produktionsgestaltung und Marktwandlungen der pfälzischen Schuhindustrie nach dem 2. Weltkrieg (1945–1954)*, PhD diss., Mainz, 1956, 58.

12 See Anne Sudrow, *Der Schuh im Nationalsozialismus: Eine Produktgeschichte im deutsch-britisch-amerikanischen Vergleich*, Göttingen 2010, 174.

13 Axel Schildt, *Amerikanische Einflüsse auf die westdeutsche Konsumentwicklung nach dem Zweiten Weltkrieg*, in: Heinz-Gerhard Haupt/Claudius Torp (eds.), Die Konsumgesellschaft in Deutschland 1890–1990. Ein Handbuch, Frankfurt/M. 2009, 435–447, here: 437.

14 On the "defensive measures" of the shoe industry, see Reidenbach, *Produktionsgestaltung*, 64–66.

15 See Michael Breitenacher, *Leder- und Schuhindustrie*, Munich 1967, 77.

16 See ibid., 75, and Reidenbach, *Produktionsgestaltung*, 62.

From a Silver Leg to Healthy Shoes: The History of Podiatry and Orthopedic Footwear Technology

1 See *Orthopädie*, in: Wolfgang Pfeifer et al. (eds.), Etymologisches Wörterbuch des Deutschen (1993), digitized and revised by Wolfgang Pfeifer in: *Digitales Wörterbuch der deutschen Sprache*, www.dwds.de/wb/etymwb/Orthopädie (accessed Nov. 3, 2022).

2 See Gundolf Keil, *Geleitwort*, in: August Rütt (ed.), Die Geschichte der Orthopädie im deutschen Sprachraum, Stuttgart 1993, unpaginated.

3 See August Rütt, *Die Geschichte der Orthopädie im deutschen Sprachraum*, in: ibid., 1–79, here: 1.

4 See Keil, *Geleitwort*.

5 See Paul Heller, *Von der Landeskrüppelanstalt zur Orthopädischen Universitätsklinik: Das "Elisabethheim" in Rostock*, Münster 2009, 35.

6 See Michael A. Rauschmann/Klaus-Dieter Thomann, *200 Jahre Orthopädie: Bilder aus der Vergangenheit*, in: Orthopäde 29 (2000), 1008–1017, here: 1009.

7 See ibid., 1008, 1011.

8 See ibid., 1012.

9 See Rütt, *Geschichte der Orthopädie*, 36.

10 See Doris Schwarzmann-Schafhauser, *Orthopädie im Wandel: Die Herausbildung von Disziplin und Berufsstand in Bund Kaiserreich (1815–1914)*, Stuttgart 2004, 251, fig. 14: Deutsche Gesellschaft für orthopädische Chirurgie membership figures (1902–1935).

11 See Manuel Dichtl, *Der Orthopäde Prof. Dr. Franz Schede (1882–1976): Leben und Werk*, PhD Regensburg (2012), 112.

12 See Barbara Oberst, *100 Jahre Orthopädieschuhtechniker. Orthopädieschuhtechniker mit hervorragenden Prognosen, Interview mit ZVOS-Hauptgeschäftsführer Oliver Dieckmann*, Apr. 20, 2017, www.deutsche-handwerks-zeitung.de/orthopaedieschuhtechniker-mit-hervorragenden-prognosen-92318 (accessed Oct. 20, 2022).

13 See Anne Sudrow, *Der Schuh im Nationalsozialismus: Eine Produktgeschichte im deutsch-britisch-amerikanischen Vergleich*, Göttingen 2010, 357.

14 See ibid., 359 f.

15 See Ludwig Schwering, *Die etwas andere Geschichte der Orthopädie*, in: 100 Jahre Orthopädieschuhtechnik: Innovationen, Versorgungskonzepte, Perspektiven, special issue, Orthopädieschuhtechnik (2017), 24–30, here: 30.

16 See Dichtl, *Der Orthopäde*, 137.

17 *Glücklicher Leben*, in: Constanze 6 (1960), quoted in Isabella Belting, Ready to go! Schuhe bewegen, Berlin 2019, 144.

18 See Nike U. Breyer, *Dialog von Fuß und Schuh*, in: taz am Wochenende (July 30, 2005).

19 See Wolfgang Best, *Die Zukunft vor 20 Jahren*, in: 100 Jahre Orthopädieschuhtechnik, 94–96, here: 94.

The Names of the *Original Birkenstock-Footbed Sandals*

1 See detailed information on the business partnership with Margot Fraser in the article by Alexander von den Benken and on Margot Fraser in the article by Mary Yeager in this volume.

1963–2024
Rise to a Global Brand

1 Based on Stephanie Tilly, *"Die guten Zeiten sind … vorbei": Zum Verhältnis von Automobilindustrie, Politik und Automobilverband in den 1970er Jahren*, in: Morten Reitmayer/Ruth Rosenberger (eds.), Unternehmen am Ende des "golden age": Die 1970er Jahre in unternehmens- und wirtschaftshistorischer Perspektive, Essen 2008, 209–232. For criticism of this perception of crisis, see Niall Ferguson, *Crisis, What Crisis?*, in: Niall Ferguson et al. (eds.), The Shock of the Global: The 70s in Perspective, Cambridge, MA, 2010, 1–21. In economic history, the catchphrase "after the boom" was established at the latest with the widely acclaimed study by Anselm Doering-Manteuffel/Lutz Raphael, *Nach dem Boom: Perspektiven auf die Zeitgeschichte seit 1970*, Göttingen ²2010.

2 See information in article *Die Schuhindustrie kommt aus der Talsohle*, in: Frankfurter Allgemeine Zeitung (Mar. 9, 1978), 17.

3 The number of shoe companies fell in 1972 from 485 in the previous year to 450; see: *Die Preise für Lederschuhe steigen weiter*, in: Frankfurter Allgemeine Zeitung (Dec. 19, 1972), 11.

4 See *Nur noch Feuerwehr*, in: Der Spiegel 7 (Feb. 6, 1972).

5 See: *In der deutschen Schuhindustrie spitzt sich die Krise zu*, in: Frankfurter Allgemeine Zeitung (Sept. 25, 1973), 15.

6 See: *Schuhbranche: Noch kein Grund zum Jubel*, in: Frankfurter Allgemeine Zeitung (Nov. 8, 1974), 14.

7 See: *Nur noch Feuerwehr*, in: Der Spiegel 7 (Feb. 6, 1972).

8 See: *Lederschuhe bald nur noch Luxusartikel*, in: Frankfurter Allgemeine Zeitung (Sept. 15, 1976), 11.

9 CA Birkenstock, BBG 1.C. 002, BS Jahresabschlüsse, 1968 annual financial statements of C. B. Orthopädie GmbH Carl Birkenstock, Bad Honnef/Rhine, Nov. 26, 1969, 4.

10 See Jörg Lesczenski's essay in this volume.

11 On the negative attitude of shoe retailers, see: Stiftung Rheinisch-Westfälisches Wirtschaftsarchiv zu Köln [hereafter RWWA] 299, Harald Schuhmacher, *Beklemmende Idylle*, in: Wirtschaftswoche 3 (2003), 62–64, here: 63. On sales, see: CA Birkenstock, BBG 1.C. 002, Jahresabschlüsse, 1972 annual financial statements of Birkenstock Orthopädie GmbH, Bad Honnef/Rhine, Mar. 29, 1974, 5.

12 The trend towards homemade sandals encouraged the rudimentary sale of sandals from the house of Birkenstock, which Margot Fraser started in the early 70s, according to the notes in: CA Birkenstock, Privatarchiv Margot Fraser, BMF 1.A. 001-1, Dokumente, Besprechungen, Birkenstock Internal Analysis dated August 25, 1987, History of Birkenstock Footprint Sandals, Incorporated, 2.

13 Quote from RWWA, 299, Nike Breyer, *Wie man ein Fußbett wach küsst*, in: Kölner Rundschau (June 18, 2000); CA Birkenstock, BBG 4. 053, Dokumente, German, Presse, *Von Baumstämmen zum Bestseller*, interview with Karl Birkenstock, in: Schuhmarkt 1 (2000). The hippie movement was certainly included in the contemporary diagnosis of the change in values—for example, in: Ronald Inglehart, *The Silent Revolution in Europe: Intergenerational Change in Post-Industrial Societies*, in: The American Political Science Review 65 (1971), 991–1017.

14 CA Birkenstock, Privatarchiv Margot Fraser, BMF 1.B. 004-6, Dokumente, Besprechungen, Memorandum by Margot Fraser, "The Birkenstock Story," n.d., 1.

15 CA Birkenstock, Privatarchiv Margot Fraser, BMF 2. 001-4, Schriftgut Werbung Marketing, Advertisements and designs Birkenstock USA 1980s and 1990s, press release "Birkenstock Founder and President Margot Fraser Wins 1997 Regional Entrepreneur of the Year Award," June 1997.

16 See: Reiner Karlsch et al., *Unternehmen Sport: Die Geschichte von adidas*, Munich 2018, 114.

17 See video recording of Margot Fraser's speech at the Renaissance Marin Grand Opening, Sept. 25, 2012, https://www.youtube.com/watch?v=jSdYQFvz3Xg (accessed July 12, 2022).

18 CA Birkenstock, Privatarchiv Margot Fraser, BMF 1.A. 001-1, Dokumente, Besprechungen Birkenstock Internal Analysis vom 25. 8. 1987, History of Birkenstock Footprint Sandals, Incorporated, 2.

19 On the formalization of decision-making regimes in companies, see: Werner Plumpe, *Wie entscheiden Unternehmen?*, in: Zeitschrift für Unternehmensgeschichte 2 (2016), 141–159, here 147, and Toni Pierenkemper, *Moderne Unternehmensgeschichte: Grundzüge der Modernen Wirtschaftsgeschichte*, vol. 1, Stuttgart 2000, 84.

20 References to the original contents of the contract, which are not available here, can be found in a letter from attorney Richard Idell to Margot Fraser, which he wrote in the course of the redesign of the sales organization in the United States in 2000; see: CA Birkenstock, Privatarchiv

Margot Fraser, BMF 1.B. 002, Dokumente, Besprechungen, Litigation Matters, Richard Idell to Margot Fraser, Re: Birkenstock Footprint Sandals, Inc.: Litigation Matters, Feb. 11, 2000, 1; see also: CA Birkenstock, Privatarchiv Margot Fraser, BMF 1.B. 002-9, Schriftgut, Distribution agreement between Birkenstock Orthopädie GmbH & Co. KG and Birkenstock Footprint Sandals, Inc., Vettelschoß, Aug. 15, 2000, 1.

21 CA Birkenstock, Privatarchiv Margot Fraser, BMF 1.B. 002-15, Handakte Margot Fraser, Birkenstock East – Shakti Corporation 1974–1975, Margot Fraser to Guruprem Kaur, Ahimsa Ashram of Kundalini Yoga, Sept. 6, 1974. 3HO is an abbreviation for "Healthy, Happy, Holy Organization," which represents the basic principles of "Kundalini Yoga" or "White Tantra Yoga." Thorsten Laue, *Tantra im Westen: Eine religionswissenschaftliche Studie über "Weißes Tantra Yoga", "Kundalini Yoga" und "Sikh Dharma,"* in Yogi Bhajans "Healthy, Happy, Holy Organization" (3HO) unter besonderer Berücksichtigung der "3H Organisation Deutschland e. V.", Münster 2012, as well as PhD diss., Tübingen 2011.

22 CA Birkenstock, Privatarchiv Margot Fraser, BMF 1.B. 002-15, Handakte Margot Fraser, Birkenstock East – Shakti Corporation 1974–1975, Guruprem Kaur to Birkenstock Footprint Sandals, Inc., Aug. 30, 1974. Background information on the group of companies of the religious leader and entrepreneur Yogi Bhajan, who holds a doctorate, is also provided by Laue, *Tantra im Westen*, 36 ff.

23 There was already research on the economic background of the religious group in the 80s that shed light on the profit orientation of the organization; see: Kirpal Singh Khalsa, *New Religious Movements Turn to Worldly Success*, in: Journal for the Scientific Study of Religion 2 (1986), 233–247, here: 239.

24 CA Birkenstock, Privatarchiv Margot Fraser, BMF 1.B. 002-15, Handakte Margot Fraser, Birkenstock East – Shakti Corporation 1974–1975, Gurujot Singh Taylor to Margot Fraser, Oct. 14, 1974.

25 Ibid., Guruprem Kaur on Birkenstock Footprint Sandals, Inc. Aug. 30, 1974.

26 Ibid., Karl Birkenstock to Gurujot Singh Taylor, 3HO Foundation, Nov. 8, 1974.

27 CA Birkenstock, Privatarchiv Margot Fraser, BMF 1.B. 002-3, Schriftgut, Vertriebsvereinbarung Birkenstock Footprints und Birkenstock East, Distributorship Agreement between Birkenstock Footprint Sandals, Inc. and Birkenstock East, Nov. 29, 1974., Art. 2, Sect. 2.01.

28 CA Birkenstock, Privatarchiv Margot Fraser, BMF 1.A. 001-1, Dokumente, Besprechungen, Birkenstock Internal Analysis, Aug. 25, 1987, History of Birkenstock Footprint Sandals, Incorporated, 2.

29 See: Hartmut Berghoff, *Transaktionskosten: Generalschlüssel zum Verständnis langfristiger Unternehmensentwicklung? Zum Verhältnis von Neuer Institutionenökonomie und moderner Unternehmensgeschichte*, in: Jahrbuch für Wirtschaftsgeschichte 2 (1999), 159–176, here: 162.

30 Proof of ownership of Birkenstock Advertising Inc. can be found in: CA Birkenstock, Privatarchiv Margot Fraser, BMF 1.B. 003-18, Dokumente, Besprechungen, Litigation Matters, Notice of Issuance of Securities Pursuant to Subdivision (h) of Section 25102 of the California Corporations Code, Mar. 23, 1977, 1–3, here: 1; ibid., Birko Advertising, Inc., Memorandum of Exemption from Qualification Under Section 25102 (h) of the California Corporate Securities Act of 1968, Mar. 23, 1977, 1–2, here: 1.

31 For a basic understanding of the marketing mix, see: Jerome E. McCarthy, *Basic Marketing: A Managerial Approach*, Homewood, IL, 1960.

32 CA Birkenstock, Privatarchiv Margot Fraser, BMF 1.B. 003-18, Dokumente, Besprechungen, Litigation Matters, George Ogihara, Department of Treasury – Internal Revenue Service, Information Document Request to Birkenstock Footprint Sandals, Inc., Subject: Contracts, Submitted to: Margot Fraser, Feb. 7, 1986, attached: Explanation of Items, Form 886 A.

33 See the table listing the sales figures and dealers supplied between the financial years 1972 and 1980, in: CA Birkenstock, Privatarchiv Margot Fraser, BMF 1.A. 001-1, Dokumente, Besprechungen.

34 See the few details that the official homepage of the revived "Kalsø" brand presents on its website about the brand and company history, https://www.kalso.com (accessed July 19, 2022).

35 See Rebecca Mead, *Sole Cycle. The homeley Birkenstock gets a fashion makeover*, in: The New Yorker, Mar. 23, 2015, https://www.newyorker.com/magazine/2015 / 03 / 23/sole-cycle-rebecca-mead (accessed June 12, 2023).

36 See: Bruce Lambert, *Raymond Jacobs, 69, Co-Founder of Earth Shoe Company in 1970's,* in: The New York Times (Mar. 20, 1993), 10. See also: Margot Fraser's handwritten notes in the document "Thoughts on US Marketing," n. d. (1995), in: CA Birkenstock, Privatarchiv Margot Fraser, BMF 1.B. 001-6, Schriftgut, Korrespondenz mit Familie Birkenstock 1993–2005.

37 See the chronological entry "1986," https://www.kalso.com (accessed July 19, 2022).

38 CA Birkenstock, BBG 1.C. 003, Jahresabschlüsse, 1974 annual financial statements of Birkenstock Orthopädie GmbH, Bad Honnef/Rhine, Mar. 14, 1975, 4.

39 Ibid., BBG 1.C. 004, 1980 annual financial statements of Birkenstock Orthopädie GmbH, Bad Honnef, June 26, 1981, 3.

40 A list of liabilities can be found in: CA Birkenstock, Jahresabschlüsse, 1980 annual financial statements of Birkenstock Orthopädie GmbH, Bad Honnef, June 26, 1981, 12.

41 A list of the credit line amounts of Commerzbank Bad Honnef, Dresdner Bank Bad Honnef, Deutsche Bank Bad Honnef, Landesbank Rheinland-Pfalz, Stadtsparkasse Bad Honnef, and Volksbank Bad Honnef can be found in: CA Birkenstock, Jahresabschlüsse, 1980 annual financial statements of Birkenstock Orthopädie GmbH, Bad Honnef, June 26, 1981, 13.

42 For a comparison of the employee figures, see: CA Birkenstock, Jahresabschlüsse, 1970 annual financial statements of Birkenstock Orthopädie GmbH, Bad Honnef/Rhine, Mar. 15, 1971; and CA Birkenstock, Jahresabschlüsse, 1980 annual financial statements of Birkenstock Orthopädie GmbH, Bad Honnef, June 26, 1981, 10.

43 The sales volume development from 1976 to 1980 is published in: CA Birkenstock, Jahresabschlüsse, 1980 annual accounts of Birkenstock Orthopädie GmbH, Bad Honnef, June 26, 1981, 10. Due to the high sales, a profit distribution of DM 1 million was made in 1980, which was transferred to the reserves and invested as interest-free loans from the shareholders, see ibid., 6.

44 The annual report for the 1980 fiscal year shows a shortfall of DM 441,000, which was caused by an increase in fixed assets, inventories, and the repayment of long-term liabilities. See CA Birkenstock, Jahresabschlüsse, 1980 annual accounts of Birkenstock Orthopädie GmbH, Bad Honnef, June 26, 1981, 13 f. The calculation of the gross return on sales was made in accordance with Gabler's business lexicon. See Stephan Schöning, *Umsatzrentabilität,* in: Gabler Wirtschaftslexikon, online edition, https://wirtschaftslexikon.gabler.de/definition/verkaufs-rentabilitaet-48066/version-376619 (accessed July 28, 2022).

45 See *Die Schuhindustrie kommt aus der Talsohle,* in: Frankfurter Allgemeine Zeitung, Mar. 9, 1978, 17 and *Es wird wieder mehr Geld für Schuhe ausgegeben,* in: Frankfurter Allgemeine Zeitung (June 22, 1978), 20.

46 See *Über neue Leisten schlagen,* in: Frankfurter Allgemeine Zeitung (Nov. 12, 1966), 52, and *Erfolg mit Kinderschuhen,* in: Frankfurter Allgemeine Zeitung (Apr. 12, 1973), 21.

47 Andreas Wirsching, *Abschied vom Provisorium 1982–1990,* in: Geschichte der Bundesrepublik Deutschland, vol. 6, Munich 2006, 223.

48 See: *Streik in der Schuhindustrie,* in: Frankfurter Allgemeine Zeitung (Nov. 26, 1980), 14; and *6,54 Prozent in der Schuhindustrie,* in: Frankfurter Allgemeine Zeitung (Dec. 4, 1980), 13.

49 On the revolution in Iran, the second oil price crisis, and its epochal character, see: Frank Bösch, *Zeitenwende 1979: Als die Welt von heute begann,* Munich 2019.

50 CA Birkenstock, BBG 1.C. 004, Jahresabschlüsse, 1981 annual financial statements of Birkenstock Orthopädie GmbH, Bad Honnef, May 27, 1982, 10, 14.

51 CA Birkenstock, BBG 1.C. 004, Jahresabschlüsse, 1982 annual financial statements of the company Birkenstock Orthopädie GmbH, Bad Honnef, May 26, 1983, 11.

52 The proportion of materials used in the total expenditure fell from 47.8 percent (1980) to 32.8 percent (1981). See: CA Birkenstock, Jahresabschlüsse, 1981 annual financial statements of Birkenstock Orthopädie GmbH, Bad Honnef, May 27, 1982, 14.

53 See: *Das Gesundheitsbewußtsein steigt,* in: Frankfurter Allgemeine Zeitung (Mar. 23, 1982), 17.

54 Ibid.

55 Compared to the 1979 financial year, sales figures fell from 225,490 to 214,490—however, sales rose from US$ 4.2 million to almost 5 million, suggesting a price increase for the Birkenstock range. See: CA Birkenstock, Privatarchiv Margot Fraser, BMF 1.C. 001-1-15, Bilanzen Birkenstock Footprint Sandals, Inc. 1973 bis 1993, Gesellschafterversammlung Employee Buy-Out 2002, Birkenstock Internal Analysis, Aug. 25, 1987, 2 f.

56 Ibid., 3. The term "preppy" was commonly used in the USA in the 80s to describe the style of dress of students in elite preparatory schools and should not be confused with the term "prepper." See: Lisa Birnbach, *The Official Preppy Handbook*, New York 1980.

57 CA Birkenstock, Privatarchiv Margot Fraser, BMF 1.C. 001-1-15, Bilanzen Birkenstock Footprint Sandals, Inc. 1973 bis 1993, Gesellschafterversammlung Employee Buy-Out 2002, Minutes of Special (Annual) Meeting of Board of Directors of Birko Advertising, Inc., Apr. 16, 1982, p. 1.

58 Fraser changed the unnamed agencies almost every year because she was not convinced of the success of the various advertising campaigns. See CA Birkenstock, Privatarchiv Margot Fraser, BMF 1.C. 001-1-15, Bilanzen Birkenstock Footprint Sandals, Inc. 1973 bis 1993, Gesellschafterversammlung Employee Buy-Out 2002, Birkenstock Internal Analysis, Aug. 25, 1987, 3 f.

59 Ibid., Minutes of Special (Annual) Meeting of Board of Directors of Birko Advertising, Inc., Apr. 16, 1982, 1 f.

60 CA Birkenstock, Privatarchiv Margot Fraser, BMF 1.B. 002-4, Schriftgut, contract "Birkenstock Footprint Limited – A California Limited Partnership – Agreement of Limited Partnership." On Fraser's request for more color choices in upper leather materials, see: Mead, *Sole Cycle*.

61 CA Birkenstock, Privatarchiv Margot Fraser, BMF 1.C. 001-1-15, Bilanzen Birkenstock Footprint Sandals, Inc. 1973 bis 1993, Gesellschafterversammlung Employee Buy-Out 2002, Minutes of Special (Annual) Meeting of Board of Directors of Birko Advertising, Inc., Apr. 16, 1982.

62 CA Birkenstock, Privatarchiv Margot Fraser, BMF 1.C. 001-1-15, Bilanzen Birkenstock Footprint Sandals, Inc. 1973 bis 1993, Gesellschafterversammlung Employee Buy-Out 2002, Minutes of Special (Annual) Meeting of Board of Directors of Birko Advertising, Inc., Feb. 14, 1984.

63 See: *Das Gesundheitsbewußtsein steigt.*

64 Kai-Werner Brand, *Umweltbewegung*, in: Roland Roth/Dieter Rucht (eds.), Die sozialen Bewegungen in Deutschland seit 1945: Ein Handbuch, Frankfurt am Main 2008, 227.

65 Nike Breyer, *Man trug sowas nicht!, interview with Karl Birkenstock,* in: taz am Wochenende (Apr. 15, 2000), 1 f.; *Rosenkrieg bei Birkenstocks,* in: Frankfurter Allgemeine Zeitung (Jan. 23, 2005), 43.

66 See the explanations of the corporate objectives ("Gegenstand des Unternehmens") in: CA Birkenstock, BBG 1.C. 005, Jahresabschlüsse, 1984 annual financial statements of Birkenstock Orthopädie GmbH, Bad Honnef, May 7, 1985, 5; 1985 annual financial statements of Birkenstock Orthopädie GmbH, Bad Honnef, May 26, 1986, 5.

67 For a more detailed account, see: Alfred DuPont Chandler, *Strategy and Structure: Chapters in the History of the Industrial Enterprise,* Mansfield Center, CT, 2013, 29 ff.

68 CA Birkenstock, BBG 1.C. 005, Jahresabschlüsse, Report on the preparation of the 1986 annual financial statements of the Birkenstock Orthopädie Gesellschaft mit beschränkter Haftung, Bad Honnef, July 21, 1987.

69 Ibid., BBG 1.C. 006, Report on the audit of the 1990 annual financial statements of the company Birkenstock Orthopädie Gesellschaft mit beschränkter Haftung, Bad Honnef, July 22, 1991, 9 f.

70 See the information in ibid., Report on the audit of the 1990 annual financial statements of Birkenstock Orthopädie Gesellschaft mit beschränkter Haftung, Bad Honnef, July 22, 1991, 10.

71 CA Birkenstock, BDF 4.B. 003, Transkription des Zeitzeugeninterviews mit Karl-Heinrich Herber, (ehem.) Mitglied der Geschäftsführung der Alsa GmbH bzw. Birkenstock Production Systems, May 19, 2014, 00:07:38:00–00:09:07:00. Since the 70s, Continental AG had concentrated on the core business of tire manufacturing as part of the restructuring strategy and in 1987 even took over one of the five largest tire manufacturers in the United States, General Tire. See: Paul Erker/Nils Fehlhaber, *150 Years of Continental: The Skill of Transformation,* Berlin/Boston 2021, 24. See: *Conti will die Sieben-Tage-Woche einführen,* in: Frankfurter Allgemeine Zeitung (Nov. 15, 1985), 15.

72 Birkenstock is listed in Company Archive Continental, 6603, Zg. 1/85, A 2, Alsa Schuhbedarf GmbH, Planning 1978/79/80, Uerrzell, Sept. 28, 1977, in the Alsa customer file as a company with "satisfactory" to "good" business development.

73 CA Birkenstock, BDF 4.B. 003, Transkription des Zeitzeugeninterviews mit Karl-Heinrich Herber, (ehem.) Mitglied der Geschäftsführung der Alsa GmbH bzw. Birkenstock Production Systems, May 19, 2014, 00:36:30:00–00:42:30:00. The "Adilettes" were an important part of the new Adidas division in sports and leisure clothing, which Adidas had been systematically expanding alongside the established shoe business since the 70s. See: Karlsch et al., *Unternehmen Sport*, 125 ff. See also: Company Archive Continental, 6603, Zg. 1/85, A 2, Alsa Schuhbedarf GmbH, Planning 1978/79/80, Ürzell, Sept. 28, 1977, in which reference is made to a "positive situation" in the cooperation with Adidas.

74 See: Archiv der sozialen Demokratie, Bestand Gewerkschaft Holz und Kunststoff HV, 5/ GHKA000273 (A) 1993–1995 [hereafter AdsD, 5/GHKA000273 (A)], Copy of the notarial certification of the takeover of "Continental-Alsa Schuhbedarf GmbH" by Karl Birkenstock, negotiated in Königswinter on Jan. 4, 1989, issued on Jan. 5, 1989.

75 CA Birkenstock, BDF 4.B. 003, Transkription des Zeitzeugeninterviews mit Karl-Heinrich Herber, (ehem.) Mitglied der Geschäftsführung der Alsa GmbH bzw. Geschäftsführer Birkenstock Productions Hessen GmbH, May 7, 2019, 00:21:53:00–00:23:49:00.

76 In a framework agreement dated Apr. 27, 1989, Birkenstock Orthopädie GmbH made a commitment to Alsa to purchase new production facilities in order to be able to meet the increased demand for footbeds. See: CA Birkenstock, BBG 1.C. 006, Jahresabschlüsse, Report on the audit of the 1990 annual financial statements of the company Birkenstock Orthopädie Gesellschaft mit beschränkter Haftung, Bad Honnef, July 22, 1991, 10. See also: CA Birkenstock, BDF 4.B. 004, Transkription des Zeitzeugeninterviews mit Klaus Noll, Director Technic Birkenstock Productions Rheinland-Pfalz GmbH, Feb. 28, 2019, 00:10:35:16–00:11:31:05.

77 *Säureregen: "Da liegt was in der Luft!,"* in: Der Spiegel 47 (Nov. 15, 1981).

78 *Polarstern wird Ozonschicht in der Arktis messen,* in: Frankfurter Allgemeine Zeitung (May 8, 1987), 10; *Ein Ozonloch über der Antarktis,* in: Frankfurter Allgemeine Zeitung (Oct. 27, 1986), 10. Even before the intention was in place for a subsequent international agreement, the United States actually considered an import ban on CFC-containing products at the beginning of 1987; see: *Mehr Schutz für Ozonschicht: Washington droht mit Importstopp,* in: Frankfurter Allgemeine Zeitung (Feb. 13, 1987), 7.

79 In the mid-70s, there had already been discussions about whether CFCs could, in theory, be held responsible for the depletion of the ozone layer. See: Willy Lützenkirchen, *Abbau der Ozonschicht durch Fluorkohlenwasserstoffe?,* in: Frankfurter Allgemeine Zeitung (Jan. 2, 1975), 2; see also: *Klima für Dinosaurier,* in: Der Spiegel 35 (Aug. 21, 1977); see also: *Stärkerer Ozonabbau durch Fluorkohlenwasserstoffe?,* in: Frankfurter Allgemeine Zeitung (Nov. 28, 1979), 31. In 1977, an international research project to measure the ozone content in the earth's atmosphere was carried out for the first time. See: *Der Ozonschleier offenbar stabiler als gedacht,* in: Frankfurter Allgemeine Zeitung (Oct. 10, 1978), 9.

80 See the law on protection against harmful environmental effects from air pollution, noise, vibrations, and similar processes (Federal Immission Control Act BImSchG), version of May 22, 1990, in: Federal Law Gazette Part I, Bonn 1990, 881 ff. Under pressure from the US Environmental Protection Agency (EPA), a decision was made by over 40 nations to enshrine a CFC reduction in law in their respective countries. See: Marc Landy et al., *The Environmental Protection Agency: Asking the Wrong Questions; From Nixon to Clinton,* New York/Oxford 1994, 257.

81 "PVC" is an abbreviation for polyvinyl chloride.

82 At the end of the 80s, a full 93.3 percent of all shoes sold in West Germany came from abroad; see: *Viele Schuhproduzenten müssen schließen,* in: Frankfurter Allgemeine Zeitung (Sept. 16, 1989), 14; in 1989, Klöckner Ferromatic Desma GmbH was still building with the Soviet "Serja" shoe production group, a German-Soviet joint venture near Moscow to manufacture machines and tool parts for the Soviet shoe industry; see: *Klöckner verstärkt Geschäft mit Sowjetunion,* in: Frankfurter Allgemeine Zeitung (Dec. 12, 1989), 20.

83 CA Birkenstock, Privatarchiv Margot Fraser, BMF 1.B. 004-6, Betriebsinformationen Birkenstock USA, Brochure "Natur beachten – Natur verstehen – Natur schützen," July 24, 1990.

84 Ibid., 2

85 Ibid., 9.

406 **Appendices**

86 CA Birkenstock, BMF 1.B. 004-6, Transkription des Zeitzeugeninterviews mit Karl-Heinrich Herber, (ehem.) Mitglied der Geschäftsführung der Alsa GmbH bzw. Geschäftsführer Birkenstock Productions Hessen GmbH, May 7, 2019, 00:36:30:00–00:42:30:00.

87 CA Birkenstock, Privatarchiv Margot Fraser, BMF 1.B. 004-6, Betriebsinformationen Birkenstock USA, "Natur beachten – Natur verstehen – Natur schützen," brochure, July 24, 1990, 12.

88 The term "plastic world" is used, for example, in the history of the Adidas company in Karlsch et al., *Unternehmen Sport*, 124.

89 CA Birkenstock, BDF 4.B. 004, Transkription des Zeitzeugeninterviews mit Klaus Noll, Director Technic Birkenstock Productions Rheinland-Pfalz GmbH, Feb. 28, 2019, 00:16:38:03–00:17:28:06.

90 Ibid., 01:10:11:00–01:13:17:00.

91 Ibid., 00:08:29:00–00:09:08:16 and 00:16:38:03–00:17:06:04.

92 See table with information on sales development in the first half of the 80s in CA Birkenstock, BBG 1.C. 005-006, Jahresabschlüsse, 1984 annual financial statements of Birkenstock Orthopädie GmbH, Bad Honnef, May 7, 1985, 11, as well as the information on the second half of the 80s up to and including 1990 in the report on the audit of the 1990 annual financial statements of Birkenstock Orthopädie GmbH, Bad Honnef, July 22, 1991, 16.

93 Wolfgang Stiller, *Die Wirtschaftswunderdoktoren*, in: Capital 11 (1990), 12–14; and *Wer kennt einen, der paßt?*, in: Der Spiegel 3 (Jan. 13, 1991).

94 CA Birkenstock, BDF 4.B. 003, Transkription des Zeitzeugeninterviews mit Karl-Heinrich Herber, (ehem.) Mitglied der Geschäftsführung der Alsa GmbH bzw. Geschäftsführer Birkenstock Productions Hessen GmbH, May 7, 2019, 00:59:37:00–01:03:39:00.

95 Ibid., 00:58:18:00–00:59:05:00.

96 Quotations from: Marcus Böick, *Die Treuhand: Idee – Praxis – Erfahrung 1990–1994*, Göttingen 2018, 567. The information on Karl Birkenstock's travels comes from CA Birkenstock, BDF 4.B. 004, Transkription des Zeitzeugeninterviews mit Klaus Noll, Direktor Technik, Birkenstock Productions Rheinland-Pfalz GmbH, Feb. 28, 2019, 01:16:15:23–01:16:54:15.

97 See *VEB Trumpf Schuhfabrik Seifhennersdorf*, https://www.industrie-kultur-ost.de/datenbanken/online-ruinen-datenbank/veb-schuhfabrik-trumpf-seifhennersdorf/ (accessed Aug. 8, 2023).

98 CA Birkenstock, BBG 1.D. 002, Betriebsrat Birko Schuhtechnik Juli 1993 bis Dezember 1994, press release "Weiterhin ungewöhnlich positive Firmenentwicklung: Drei neue Firmen in der Birkenstock-Gruppe," n.d.

99 CA Birkenstock, BDF 4.B. 003, Transkription des Zeitzeugeninterviews mit Karl-Heinrich Herber, (ehem.) Mitglied der Geschäftsführung der Alsa GmbH bzw. Geschäftsführer Birkenstock Productions Hessen GmbH, 00:59:37:00–01:03:39:00.

100 Birkenstock had originally given the press an investment commitment of DM 10 million and promised to take on 90 jobs. See: Katrin Prenzel, *Birkenstock setzte im Kreis Löbau "Zeichen des Aufschwungs"*, in: Löbauer Zeitung (Apr. 6 1993), 11. On the failure of the takeover negotiations, see Bundesarchiv Koblenz [hereafter BArch], B 136/35974, Federal Chancellery, finance, asset, and debt management of the federal government, restructuring in the new federal states, correspondence between the Treuhandanstalt and Birkenstock Orthopädie GmbH. Birkenstock itself always blamed the Trust administration and the unions for the failure of the takeover negotiations. See: CA Birkenstock, BBG 1.D. 002, Betriebsrat Birko Schuhtechnik Juli 1993 bis Dezember 1994, press release "Weiterhin ungewöhnlich positive Firmenentwicklung: Drei neue Firmen in der Birkenstock-Gruppe," n.d. See also: CA Birkenstock, BBG 2. 005-4, Betriebsrat-Streit, *400 neue Arbeitsplätze in Sachsen*, in: Birkenstock-Information 2 (1995), 1–15; Alsa manager Herber provides information on Birkenstock's supplier in the new federal states in CA Birkenstock, BDF 4.B. 003, Transkription des Zeitzeugeninterviews mit Karl-Heinrich Herber, (ehem.) Mitglied der Geschäftsführung der Alsa GmbH bzw. Geschäftsführer Birkenstock Productions Hessen GmbH, 00:48:48:00–00:53:00:00. For the renegotiations with Birkenstock in 1995, see Anon: *Noch ist der letzte Funke Hoffnung nicht verloren*, in: Sächsische Zeitung (May 12, 1995). Ilja Mieck, *Kleine Wirtschaftsgeschichte der Neue Bundesländer*, Stuttgart 2009, 195 ff. gives a general overview of failed takeover negotiations.

101 CA Birkenstock, BDF 4.B. 004, Transkription des Zeitzeugeninterviews mit Klaus Noll, Director Technic Birkenstock Productions Rheinland-Pfalz GmbH, Feb. 28, 2019, 01:15:22:09–01:15:53:02.

102 Rolf Hill, *Untergegangene Textil-Industrie*, in: Sächsische Zeitung (Oct. 23, 2016), https:// www.saechsische.de/untergehene-textil-industrie-3523163.html (accessed Aug. 21, 2022); *80.000 Euro für Sanierung des Lautex-Stammhauses in Neugersdorf – Förderung aus Sonderprogramm noch möglich*, https://www.kreis-goerlitz.de/Aktuelles/Archiv-der-Meldungen.htm/Bekannt-machen/80-000-Euro-for-renovation-of-the-Lautex-headquarters-in-Neugersdorf-funding-from-the-special-program-still-possible.html?keyword=2180,2306,2182&eps=25 (accessed Aug. 21, 2022). Documents on the Schönbach location can be found under BArch, DC 14/881, Investitionsvorhaben VEB Lautex Neugersdorf, Standort Schönbach zum 30. Jahrestag der DDR, 1979.

103 CA Birkenstock, BDF 4.B. 003, Transkription des Zeitzeugeninterviews mit Karl-Heinrich Herber, (ehem.) Mitglied der Geschäftsführung der Alsa GmbH bzw. Geschäftsführer Birkenstock Productions Hessen GmbH, May 7, 2019, 01:03:52:00–01:05:16:00.

104 On the low productivity of the GDR economy, see: André Steiner, *Von Plan zu Plan: Eine Wirtschaftsgeschichte der DDR*, Berlin 2007, 252 ff.; see also Ilja Mieck's description of how the falsified economic and company statistics produced when the GDR planned economy was integrated into the market economy of the Federal Republic often led to serious problems with takeovers: Ilja Mieck, *Kleine Wirtschaftsgeschichte der Neue Bundesländer*, Stuttgart 2009, 195 f.

105 CA Birkenstock, BDF 4.B. 003, Transkription des Zeitzeugeninterviews mit Karl-Heinrich Herber, (ehem.) Mitglied der Geschäftsführung der Alsa GmbH bzw. Geschäftsführer Birkenstock Productions Hessen GmbH, May 7, 2019, 01:05:28:00–01:07:35:00.

106 On the relocation of the Schönbach plant to Görlitz, see Herber's further comments in: ibid., Birkenstock, BDF 4.B. 003, 01:20:16:00–01:25:00:00.

107 On Alex and Stephan's admission to management, see Audit of the 1994 annual financial statements of Birkenstock Orthopädie GmbH, Bad Honnef, Dec. 12, 1995, 6. Karl Birkenstock's youngest son, Christian, was not admitted to the management until 1996; see: CA Birkenstock, BBG 1.C. 007, BS annual report, Report on the audit of the 1996 annual financial statements of Birkenstock Orthopädie GmbH Bad Honnef, Bad Honnef, n. d., 5.

108 CA Birkenstock, BBG 1.C. 006, Jahresabschlüsse, Report on the audit of the 1990 annual financial statements of Birkenstock Orthopädie GmbH, Bad Honnef, July 22, 1991, 8.

109 Hartmut Berghoff/Ingo Köhler, *Verdienst und Vermächtnis: Familienunternehmen in Deutschland und den USA seit 1800*, Frankfurt am Main/New York 2020, 12. According to the annual financial statements for 1990, these family members were Karl and Gisela as well as Stephan and Alex Birkenstock. See CA Birkenstock, BBG 1.C. 006, Jahresabschlüsse, Report on the audit of the 1994 annual financial statements of Birkenstock Orthopädie GmbH, Bad Honnef, Dec. 12, 1995, 7.

110 These Birkenstock startups also initiated the transition in the family business from a functional unitary form to a multidivisional corporate structure; see: Hartmut Berghoff, *Moderne Unternehmensgeschichte: Eine themen- und theorieorientierte Einführung*, Berlin/Boston ²2016, 61–71.

111 CA Birkenstock, BBG 1.D. 002, Betriebsrat Birko Schuhtechnik Juli 1993 bis Dezember 1994, press release "Weiterhin ungewöhnlich positive Firmenentwicklung: Drei neue Firmen in der Birkenstock-Gruppe," n. d.

112 CA Birkenstock, Privatarchiv Margot Fraser, BMF 1.B. 002-1, Schriftgut, Korrespondenz mit Familie Birkenstock, Letter from Fraser to Birkenstock, June 21, 1993; CA Birkenstock, Privatarchiv Margot Fraser, 1.B. 003-2/19, strategy paper "Birkenstock Organizational Development Project," ca. 1992, 1.

113 See ibid., 2. In the German business press, in particular, translated articles from the United States that gave popular scientific advice on optimizing management processes were often used on the market. See Bernhard Dietz, *Aufstieg der Manager: Wertewandel in den Führungsetagen der westdeutschen Wirtschaft, 1949–1989*, Wertewandel im 20. Jahrhundert, vol. 7, Berlin/Boston 2020, 396.

114 CA Birkenstock, BBG 1.C. 006, Jahresabschlüsse, Audit of the 1994 annual financial statements of Birkenstock Orthopädie GmbH, Bad Honnef, Dec. 12, 1995, 13.

115 Wolfgang Michael, *Karls Krieg: Wie ein Familienbetrieb zum Kampfplatz wurde*, in: Geo 12 (1996), 105–120, here: p. 106. The company tariff was recognized by the unions but found to be in need of improvement, according to AdsD, 5/GHKA000273 (A), Letter from Werner Rieß to Norbert Mikulski, Oct. 31, 1990.

116 On the social partnership concept of the works family, which was particularly influential in German family companies since the imperial era, see: Berghoff/Köhler, *Verdienst und Vermächtnis*, 238f.

117 The prestige Birkenstock also enjoyed among the trade unions became apparent when the two unions literally fought over who was allowed to set up employee representation at Birkenstock over the next three years. AdsD, 5/GHKA000273 (A), Letter from Norbert Mikulski, Leather Union, to Werner Rieß, GHK, Gießen office, Nov. 29, 1990.

118 Michael, *Karls Krieg*, 107.

119 AdsD, 5/GHKA000273 (A), Letter from Werner Riess to Norbert Mikulski, Oct. 31, 1990.

120 In the 70s, despite resistance from the employers' associations, the social-liberal governments of Willy Brandt and Helmut Schmidt pushed through legislation stipulating that employee representatives should have a voice not only in on-site production management but also in business management. See: Dietz, *Aufstieg der Manager*, 287.

121 See Lutz Bellmann/Peter Ellguth, *Verbreitung von Betriebsräten und ihr Einfluss auf die betriebliche Weiterbildung*, in: Jahrbücher für Nationalökonomie und Statistik 5 (2006), 487–504, here: 492.

122 The wording of BetrVG § 1 [Betriebsverfassungsgesetz = Works Constitution Act], "In the companies, works councils are formed in accordance with this law," gives the impression that there was an obligation to form works councils. However, the employer was not legally obliged to initiate the formation of a works council. See: Works Constitution Act of Oct. 11, 1952, Part One: General Provisions, in: Federal Law Gazette Part I, Bonn, Oct. 14, 1952, 691.

123 It should be mentioned that over 90 percent of all companies with more than 500 employees have a works council. See: IAB Establishment Panel 2017, Beschäftigte in Betrieben mit Betriebsrat 1993–2017, https://www.iab-forum.de/die-betriebliche-mitdetermination-lost-an-bottom/ (accessed Aug. 21, 2022). See Bellmann/Ellguth, *Verbreitung von Betriebsräten*, 490f.

124 AdsD, 5/GHKA000273 (A), File memo from Frank Schmidt to the executive board, regarding organizational disputes with the leather trade union at Birkenstock Schuhtechnik GmbH, GST Andernach, May 19, 1993.

125 AdsD, 5/GHKA000273 (A), Letter from Helga Nielebock (GHK legal department) to members of the GHV, FAO Frank Schmidt, Jan. 14, 1993.

126 Ibid., File memo from Frank Schmidt to the Executive Board, regarding organizational disputes with the leather trade union at Birkenstock Schuhtechnik GmbH, GST Andernach, May 19, 1993, 2.

127 Ibid., Memo from Frank Schmidt GHK HV-HA II to Horst Morich HV-HA I, Aug. 30, 1993.

128 The leather union insisted that, according to the statutes, they were responsible for the entire shoe industry and thus also for Birkenstock as a member of the Main Association of the German Shoe Industry. See ibid., letter from Werner Dick 1. VS leather union to GHK HV, Chairman, Aug. 26, 1993, and letter from Werner Dick to Gisbert Schlemmer, GHK-HV, Nov. 18, 1993; see: Michael, *Karls Krieg*, 107.

129 In addition to the works council leader Gereon Frank and Karl Birkenstock, the chairman of the timber and plastics union, Gisbert Schlemmer, was also to have his say and address the topic of labor and co-determination rights as well as collective bargaining for pay. In agenda item 5, "Debate," the invitation to the works meeting points to the need for discussion and clarification on the part of the employee representatives. See: CA Birkenstock, Betriebsrat, Invitation from the works council of Birko Schuhtechnik GmbH to the management for the 1st regular works meeting on Dec. 21, 1993, at 10: 30 am in the canteen at Plant 4, St. Katharinen, Dec. 8, 1993. A copy can also be found in Archiv der sozialen Demokratie; see: AdsD, 5/GHKA000273 (A), Letter from Gereon Frank, works council chairman Birko-Schuhtechnik St. Katharinen to Gisbert Schlemmer GHK HV HA I, Düsseldorf, St. Katharinen, Dec. 1, 1993.

130 Michael, *Karls Krieg*, 109.

131 See: AdsD, 5/GHKA000273 (A), Letter from Wolfgang Conrad GHK, Andernach office, to Peter Berg GHK-HV HA I, Düsseldorf, Jan. 11, 1994, 1; see also: Michael, *Karls Krieg*, 108.

132 More than a dozen works council proposals can be viewed in: CA Birkenstock, Betriebsrat Birko Schuhtechnik GmbH Juli 1993 bis Dezember 1994.

133 Ibid., Letter from Karl Birkenstock to the Chairman of the Works Council, Gereon Frank, Sept. 17, 1993.

134 Ibid., Letter from the Birko Schuhtechnik works council to the management, regarding the WA meeting, Oct. 22, 1993.

135 AdsD, 5/GHKA000273 (A), Letter from Wolfgang Conrad GHK, Andernach office, to Peter Berg GHK-HV HA I, Düsseldorf, Jan. 11, 1994, 1.

136 In a hastily drafted statement, they asked Birkenstock to excuse them "for our unhelpful behavior and lack of support during the works meeting" and assured him they would "in no way represent the opinion of the works council." CA Birkenstock, BBG 1.D. 002, Betriebsrat Birko Schuhtechnik GmbH Juli 1993 bis Dezember 1994, Letter from Birko team leader to Karl Birkenstock, Dec. 22, 1993.

137 On the difficulties of delimiting and attempts to define "senior employees" as "employees with employer responsibilities," see: Dietz, *Aufstieg der Manager*, 39 f.

138 AdsD, 5/GHKA000273 (A), Letter from Wolfgang Conrad GHK, Andernach office, to Peter Berg GHK-HV HA I, Düsseldorf, Jan. 11, 1994.

139 See: CA Birkenstock, BBG 1.D. 002, Betriebsrat Birko Schuhtechnik GmbH Juli 1993 bis Dezember 1994, Employee survey of Jan. 3, 1994.

140 In the article *Klima wie in der Ex-DDR*, which appeared in Koblenz's Rhein-Zeitung in mid-January 1994, the public was informed for the first time about the pre-Christmas quarrels in the Birkenstock factory in St. Katharinen. In this, the Andernach timber union functionary Wolfgang Conrad was quoted as saying that the working atmosphere was "comparable to the terror regime in the former GDR" and made extremely serious accusations against the company management. See: *Klima wie in der Ex-DDR*, in: Rhein-Zeitung (Jan. 18, 1994), 17.

141 See: *Hiobsbotschaft: Birko reduziert*, in: Rhein-Zeitung (Feb. 24, 1994), 19; *200 Mitarbeitern droht Entlassung*, in: General Anzeiger (Feb. 25, 1994), 6; see also: *Betriebsrat fühlt sich bedroht*, in: Rhein-Zeitung (Feb. 26, 1994).

142 "A good relationship with the works council is the best guarantee of keeping the unions out," was Schmalz's final recommendation to the offended company patriarch Birkenstock. See Michael, *Karls Krieg*, 110.

143 See: *Bei Birkenstock drückt der Schuh gewaltig*, in: Rhein-Zeitung (Mar. 7, 1994).

144 CA Birkenstock, BBG 1.D. 002, Betriebsrat Birko Schuhtechnik GmbH Juli 1993 bis Dezember 1994, Walter Voigt, 1st authorized representative of IG Metall, Neuwied administrative office to Birko Schuhtechnik GmbH & Co KG, Jan. 24, 1994.

145 Attempts were made, for example, to limit the influence of the timber union by banning it from the premises, which was only moderately successful. See: CA Birkenstock, BBG 1.D. 002, Betriebsrat Birko Schuhtechnik GmbH Juli 1993 bis Dezember 1994, Birko Schuhtechnik GmbH management to Wolfgang Conrad, January 28, 1994.

146 For example, the leather union held information events in St. Katharinen to recruit new members or to motivate timber union members to change unions. See: CA Birkenstock, BBG 1.D. 002, Betriebsrat Birko Schuhtechnik GmbH Juli 1993 bis Dezember 1994, Letter to the employees of Birko Schuhtechnik GmbH, Feb. 25, 1994. This action was met with sharp protest from the head office of the timber union, in: AdsD, 5/GHKA000273 (A), Letter from Gisbert Schlemmer to Werner Dick, Feb. 21, 1994.

147 CA Birkenstock, BBG 1.D. 002, Betriebsrat Birko Schuhtechnik GmbH Juli 1993 bis Dezember 1994, Notice, "936,531 pairs of unfinished shoes," June 23, 1994.

148 See the development of turnover in the report on the audit of the 1996 annual financial statements of Birkenstock Orthopädie GmbH, Bad Honnef, n.d, 10, in: CA Birkenstock, BBG 1.C. 007, Jahresabschlüsse.

149 Contrary to what was rumored in the press, it was still possible to install a general works council in split-up companies; see: Works Constitution Act under § 47 BetrVG from the

Works Constitution Act of January 15, 1972, Part Two: Works council, works meeting, central works council, and combine works council (§§ 7–59a), Division Five: Central works council (§§ 47–53), in: Federal Law Gazette Part I, published in Bonn, Jan. 18, 1972, 47 ff.

150 The contracts can be found at CA Birkenstock, BBG 1.C. 007, German, Altverträge Gudrun Wittlich, Verträge Birkenstock, including the framework contract between Birkenstock Orthopädie GmbH and Albero-Schuhtechnik GmbH dated Oct. 25, 1994; trademark agreement with Betula Schuh GmbH dated Mar. 25, 1994; brand agreement with Birko Schuh GmbH dated Mar. 22, 1994; framework agreement with Happy Schuh GmbH shoe production dated June 29, 1994; and the trademark agreement with Tatami Schuh GmbH dated Mar. 22, 1994.

151 A list of the numerous, contractually linked sub-companies can be found in: CA Birkenstock, Jahresabschlüsse, Report on the audit of the 1995 annual financial statements of Birkenstock Orthopädie GmbH, Bad Honnef, n. d., 7 f.

152 Information from *Beschimpfungen und Proteste bei Birkenstock*, in: Frankfurter Allgemeine Zeitung (Mar. 27, 1995), 24.

153 CA Birkenstock, BBG 1.D. 004, Betriebsrat-Streit, Letter from Norbert Blüm to Karl Birkenstock, June 26, 1995; see also *Haftbefehl gegen Birkenstock senior beantragt*, in: Rhein-Zeitung (Sept. 27, 1995), 12.

154 It was only through various press agency reports on the pending court cases in Linz and Koblenz that the nationwide daily press first became aware of the events in St. Katharinen. See: *Beschimpfungen und Proteste bei Birkenstock*, in: Frankfurter Allgemeine Zeitung (Mar. 27, 1995), 24; *Skurriler Streit*, in: Handelsblatt (Mar. 27, 1995), 24; *Behinderung des Betriebsrates*, in: Frankfurter Allgemeine Zeitung (Mar. 31, 1995), 22; *Birkenstock bleibt in Neuwied*, in: Frankfurter Allgemeine Zeitung (Apr. 10, 1995), 18; see: *Strafbefehl beantragt*, in: Frankfurter Allgemeine Zeitung (July 6, 1995), 19.

155 Michael, *Karls Krieg*, 105–120; *Das Imperium schlägt zurück*, in: Stern 34 (1994), 186–187; *Krieg im Werk*, in: Die Zeit (May 17, 1996); *Psychoterror bei Birkenstock*, in: taz (Mar. 5, 1996), 7.

156 For an example of reporting at a national level, see: Isabelle Sender, *Birkenstock USA Confirms German Labor Disputes*, in: Footwear News (Mar. 10, 1994), 1 and 23; Karen Lowry Miller, *No Lovefest at Birkenstock*, in: Business Week (Mar. 25, 1996), 26.

157 CA Birkenstock, BBG 1.D. 003, Betriebsrat, Betriebsrat 1993 bis 1996, Resolution of Bündnis 90/Die Grünen "Solidarität mit den Beschäftigten der DeP in St. Katharinen," June 13, 1996.

158 CA Birkenstock, Privatarchiv Margot Fraser, BMF 1.B. 002-1, Korrespondenz mit Familie Birkenstock 1993–2005, Letter from Margot Fraser to Theo Sommer, Die Zeit (May 31, 1996).

159 Sven Hansen, *Der Konflikt ist endlich ausgelatscht*, in: taz (Feb. 5, 1997), 7.

160 CA Birkenstock, BBG 1.C. 007, Jahresabschlüsse, Report on the audit of the 1997 annual financial statements of Birkenstock Orthopädie GmbH, Bad Honnef, n. d., 10.

161 See CA Birkenstock, Privatarchiv Margot Fraser, BMF 1.B. 005-2, Schriftgut Werbung Marketing, Award certificate of the Order of Merit of the Federal Republic of Germany (with ribbon), Margot Fraser, Sept. 16, 1986.

162 Ibid., BMF 1.A. 002-1, Vorträge in Deutschland 1984 bis 1999, Lecture, February 1999.

163 Ibid., BMF 1.A. 002-3, Speech manuscript, Margot Fraser "What is my vision for [the] company?," ca. 1996.

164 CA Birkenstock, Privatarchiv Margot Fraser, BMF 1.B. 002-1, Schriftverkehr, Korrespondenz mit Familie Birkenstock 1993 bis 2005, Margot Fraser to Alex Birkenstock, Feb. 19, 1995.

165 CA Birkenstock, Privatarchiv Margot Fraser, Schriftverkehr, Korrespondenz mit Familie Birkenstock 1993 bis 2005, Letter from Margot Fraser to Karl Birkenstock, June 21, 1993.

166 CA Birkenstock, Privatarchiv Margot Fraser, Schriftverkehr, Korrespondenz mit Familie Birkenstock 1993 bis 2005, Letter from Karl Birkenstock (p. p. Stephan Birkenstock) to Margot Fraser, Oct. 5, 1998.

167 CA Birkenstock, Privatarchiv Margot Fraser, Schriftverkehr, Korrespondenz mit Familie Birkenstock 1993 bis 2005, Letter from Margot Fraser to Karl Birkenstock, Aug. 17, 2000.

168 CA Birkenstock, Privatarchiv Margot Fraser, Schriftverkehr, Korrespondenz mit Familie Birkenstock 1993 bis 2005, Letter from Margot Fraser to Karl Birkenstock, Aug. 5, 2000.

169 See in addition, inheritance tax and gift tax law (ErbStG) § 13a, recognition of business assets, of businesses in agriculture and forestry and of shares in corporations, new version of February

27, 1997, in: Federal Law Gazette Part I, Bonn, Mar. 6, 1997, 385 f. For the calculation of the effective tax burden, see the Family Business Foundation (ed.), *Die steuerliche Belastung von Familienunternehmen beim Generationswechsel: Daten und Fakten zur Rolle des Betriebsvermögens*, Munich 2014, 18 f.

170 CA Birkenstock, Privatarchiv Margot Fraser, BMF 1.B. 002-1, Schriftverkehr, Korrespondenz mit Familie Birkenstock 1993 bis 2005, Letter from Karl Birkenstock to Margot Fraser, Aug. 21, 2000.

171 CA Birkenstock, Privatarchiv Margot Fraser, BMF 1.B. 001-2, ME, Margot Fraser circular, Mar. 16, 2001.

172 CA Birkenstock, Privatarchiv Margot Fraser, BMF 1.B. 001-4, ME, Gene Kunde, Germany Trip Recap, Dec. 3–11, 2002.

173 Ibid., Gene Kunde, Trip Overview, Aug. 17, 2003.

174 CA Birkenstock, Privatarchiv Margot Fraser, BMF 1.B. 004-7, Schriftgut, Agreement with Christian Birkenstock on BFS 2005, Stephan/Alex Birkenstock to Margot Fraser/Board of Directors, Birkenstock Footprint Sandals, Inc., n.d.

175 Ibid., Stephan/Alex Birkenstock to Margot Fraser/Board of Directors/Board of Trustees, Mar. 23, 2005.

176 CA Birkenstock, Privatarchiv Margot Margot Fraser, BMF 1.B. 004-7, Schriftgut, Agreement with Christian Birkenstock on BFS 2005, Declaration of intent, "Acquisition of 75.1 % of the shares by Mr. Christian Birkenstock," n.d.; press release "Christian Birkenstock plans entry into Birkenstock Footprint Sandals," Apr. 18, 2005.

177 See: ibid., Birkenstock Board and Trustees Meeting, Apr. 16, 2005, Pivotal Points and Margot Fraser/Gene Kunde to Christian Birkenstock, Apr. 15, 2005; Stephan/Alex Birkenstock to Margot Fraser/Board of Directors, Birkenstock Footprint Sandals, Inc., n.d.

178 Ibid., Distributor agreement dated Oct. 1, 1974. Notice of termination, May 6, 2005.

179 CA Birkenstock, Privatarchiv Margot Margot Fraser, BMF 1.B. 004-7, Schriftgut, Distribution agreement between Birkenstock Orthopädie GmbH & Co. KG and Birkenstock Footprint Sandals, Inc., or the subsidiary to be founded: Birkenstock Distribution USA Inc., Aug. 15, 2005.

180 Ibid., BMF 1.A. 001-13, "Sales Contracts" with Birkenstock Sales USA LLC and Papillio Schuh GmbH, Birko Orthopädie GmbH, Footprints Schuh GmbH and Birkenstock Orthopädie GmbH & Co. KG.

181 Simon Hage, *Birkenstock – Die Rettung der Ökoschuhe*, in: manager magazin (Dec. 6, 2015), www.manager-magazin.de/magazin/artikel/birkenstock-so-wurde-aus-dem-oeko-treter-eine-welt-marke-a-1064525.html (accessed June 12, 2023). Christian Birkenstock, for example, even developed "high heels" because he wanted to grow the brand more toward fashion and lifestyle. Photos of the prototypes can be found in: CA Birkenstock, Privatarchiv Margot Fraser, BMF 1.B. 004-7, Schriftgut, Korrespondenz mit Familie Birkenstock 1993–2005.

182 Elisabeth Schönert, *Richter soll kommende Woche Sandalenkrieg beenden*, in: Welt am Sonntag (Feb. 6, 2005), 33.

183 *Rosenkrieg bei Birkenstocks beendet*, in: Frankfurter Allgemeine Zeitung (Feb. 10, 2005), www.faz.net/aktuell/wirtschaft/einigung-rosenkrieg-bei-birkenstocks-beendet-1210032.html (accessed June 12, 2023); *Ende eines Sandalenkriegs*, in: Frankfurter Allgemeine Zeitung (Feb. 13, 2005), 42; *Der tiefe Fall der Susanne Birkenstock*, in: manager magazin (Aug. 7, 2006), www.manager-magazin.de/unternehmen/karriere/a-430455.html (accessed June 12, 2023).

184 Claudia Cornelsen/Wolfgang Hirn, *Falsche Schuh-Größe*, in: manager magazin (Sept. 22, 2005).

185 Jana Ulbrich, *Neue Birkenstock-Halle wächst*, in: Sächsische Zeitung (Dec. 16, 2006), 15; Frank Seibel, *Birkenstock zieht nach Görlitz*, in: Sächsische Zeitung (Mar. 20, 2008), 23.

186 Silke Wichert, *Lass laufen*, in: Süddeutsche Zeitung (Dec. 31, 2019/Jan. 1, 2020), 9.

187 Friedemann Karig, *Auf lauten Sohlen*, in: Die Zeit (Sept. 24, 2015), 36.

188 Hage, *Birkenstock – Die Rettung*.

189 Statista, *Umsatz von Birkenstock weltweit in den Jahren von 2007 bis 2020 (in Millionen Euro)*, https://de.statista.com/statistik/daten/studie/276058/umfrage/umsatz-von-birkenstock-welt-weit/ (accessed Apr. 11, 2023).

190 *Duo ringt um Birkenstock*, in: Frankfurter Allgemeine Zeitung (Feb. 2, 2021), 19; *Birkenstock kurz vor Verkauf*, in: Frankfurter Allgemeine Zeitung (Feb. 26, 2021), 20; Nolan Giles, *Notes on a Sandal*, in: Monocle 148 (2021), 172–175.

Outsourcing and the Division of Labor: The Global Shoe

1 See Eva-Maria Knoll et al., *Globalisierung*, in: Eva-Maria Knoll (ed.), Lexikon der Globalisierung, Bielefeld 2011, 126–129, here: 126.
2 See Gerold Ambrosius, *Globalisierung: Geschichte der internationalen Wirtschaftsbeziehungen*, Wiesbaden 2018, 400.
3 Anne Sudrow, *Der Schuh im Nationalsozialismus: Eine Produktgeschichte im deutsch-britisch-amerikanischen Vergleich*, Göttingen 2010, 801, Table 37: Beschäftigte in der Lederschuhindustrie, Deutsches Reich, Großbritannien und USA, 1925–1950.
4 See Eike W. Schamp, *Decline of the District, Renewal of Firms: An Evolutionary Approach to Footwear Production in the Pirmasens Area, Germany*, in: Environment and Planning 37 (2005), 617–634, here: 622.
5 See Michael Wagner, *Hauenstein und die deutsche Schuhindustrie: Ein historischer Überblick*, Hauenstein 1997, 31.
6 See Eike W. Schamp, *Fashion Industries on the Move: Spatial Restructuring of the Footwear Sector in the Enlarged European Union*, in: Zeitschrift für Wirtschaftsgeographie 60 (2016), 155–170, here: 157.
7 See Schamp, *Decline*, 622. On this, see Johanna Steinfeld's essay in this volume, "The Desire for Fashion."
8 See Christopher Herb, *Restrukturierung von Wertschöpfungsketten in der Digitalisierung: Eine Analyse der deutschen Schuhbranche vom Hersteller bis zum Konsumenten*, Würzburg 2022, 64 f.
9 See Schamp, *Fashion Industries*, 159.
10 See Wagner, *Hauenstein*, 32.
11 See Jürgen Dispan/Sylvia Stieler, *Leder- und Schuhindustrie: Branchentrends und Herausforderungen*, Informationsdienst des IMU Instituts 3, Stuttgart 2015, 35, 57, www.boeckler.de/pdf_fof/91013.pdf (accessed Sept. 1, 2022).
12 See ibid., 34, 41.
13 See Jürgen Dispan/Laura Mendler, *Branchenanalyse Leder- und Schuhindustrie: Entwicklungstrends und Herausforderungen*, Düsseldorf 2021, 14, www.boeckler.de/fpdf/HBS-008057/p_fofoe_WP_210_2021.pdf (accessed Sept. 3, 2022).
14 See Ute Engelen et al., *Geschichte der Schuhindustrie in der Südwestpfalz*, www.wirtschaftsgeschichte-rlp.de/aufsaetze/schuhindustrie-suedwestpfalz.html (accessed Sept. 5, 2022).
15 See Herb, *Restrukturierung*, 68.
16 See Dispan/Stieler, *Leder- und Schuhindustrie*, 42 f.
17 See ibid., 43.
18 See Herb, *Restrukturierung*, 66.
19 See Dispan/Mendler, *Branchenanalyse*, 97.
20 See Dispan/Stieler, *Leder- und Schuhindustrie*, 49.
21 See, among others, Tim Dörpmund, *"Kooperation mit Chamatex, Salomon investiert in französische Schuhfertigung*, in: Textilwirtschaft (Sept. 23, 2020), https://www.textilwirtschaft.de/business/sports/franzoesische-outdoormarke-investiert-in-heimische-fertigung-salomon-will-in-frankreich-schuhe-produzieren-227421 (accessed Sept. 14, 2022).
22 See Matthias Becker, *Globalisierung im Rückwärtsgang, Warum Unternehmen nach Deutschland zurückkehren*, in: Deutschlandfunk Kultur (Aug. 1, 2022), https://www.deutschlandfunkkultur.de/globalisierung-im-rueckwaertsgang-100.html (accessed Sept. 5, 2022); Dispan/Stieler, *Leder- und Schuhindustrie*, 38.

Health Loafers and Eco-footwear: The Sandals of the Protest Movements

1 See Ingrid Gilcher-Holtey, *Die 68er Bewegung: Deutschland, Westeuropa, USA*, Munich 2005, 11–17.
2 See Jens Gmeiner, *Mythos Minirock: Eine Modeikone der 1960er Jahre zwischen Emanzipation, Jugend und Massenkonsum*, in: Robert Lorenz/Franz Walter (eds.), 1964: Das Jahr, mit dem "68" begann, Bielefeld 2014, 97–110.
3 See Joachim Scharloth, *1968: Eine Kommunikationsgeschichte*, Munich 2011, 334.

4 See Anna-Brigitte Schlittler, *Queere Schuhe?*, in: Gertrud Lehnert/Maria Weilandt (eds.), Ist Mode queer? Neue Perspektiven der Modeforschung, Bielefeld 2016, 59–72, here: 65 f.

5 See ibid., 63.

6 See Anneliese Durst/Lerke Gravenhorst, *Frauenschuhe: Spannungen, Paradoxien, Entwicklungen in der Inszenierung von Weiblichkeit*, in: Michael Andritzky (ed.), Z.B. Schuhe: Vom blossen Fuss zum Stöckelschuh, eine Kulturgeschichte der Fussbekleidung, Giessen 1988, 202–207, here: 204 f.

7 See Taylor Brydges's essay in this volume, "From Hippie to High Fashion."

8 Peter Paul Polte, *Die Ästhetik der Armut*, in: TextilWirtschaft (Apr. 25, 1996), 52.

9 Harald Schumacher, *Beklemmende Idylle: Wie Karl Birkenstock auf gesunden Sandalen die Welt eroberte*, in: Wirtschaftswoche (Jan. 10, 2002), 62.

10 *Kohl in Leinen, oder was?*, in: TextilWirtschaft (June 16, 1994), 54.

11 See, for example, Thomas Hoffmann, *Talfahrt bei Öko- und Umweltmagazinen*, in: Horizont (Oct. 8, 1993), 54; Hans Ludwig, *Innovationen: Gummi mit Grips*, in: Wirtschaftswoche (Jan. 29, 1998), 74.

12 Holger Howind, *Raus aus der Nische!*, in: food service (Dec. 1, 1994), 36.

BIRKENSTOCK: A Purpose Brand

1 See Anna Sophie Kühne, *Der beharrliche Herr Birkenstock*, in: FAZ (May 21, 2023).

2 See Roman Köster's and Jörg Lesczenski's essays in this volume.

3 Letters of Acknowledgment, in: Company Archive Birkenstock [hereafter CA Birkenstock], BS 2 License Certificates and License Agreements.

4 CA Birkenstock, BS 2 license documents and license agreements; BS 14 Correspondence Litigation.

5 See editions of the Birkenstock Post and Information, in: CA Birkenstock.

6 In line with the early writings by Konrad and Karl Birkenstock, which were aimed at a specialist readership, these books and brochures were now also aimed at retail customers. See "Buch der Fußgesundheit" (ca. 1970) and "Fuß-Fibel" (1983).

7 Although the various BIRKENSTOCK catalogs were each aimed at specific target groups—i.e., the young generation, the family, or professionals—they also included people "at home and at work." All in all, the brand appealed to ALL segments of the population.

8 Christian Kleinschmidt, *Der produktive Blick: Wahrnehmung amerikanischer und japanischer management- und Produktionsmethoden durch deutsche Unternehmer 1950-1985*, Berlin 2002, 221–259.

9 Werner Faulstich (ed.), *Die Kultur der 60er Jahre*, Munich 2003; Axel Schildt/Detlef Siegfried, *Deutsche Kulturgeschichte: Die Bundesrepublik von 1945 bis zur Gegenwart*, Munich 2009, 179–244, 245.

10 CA Birkenstock Privatarchiv Margot Fraser, BMF 1.B.007, Folder_Nancy_Margot_Fraser_Biography. *Margot Fraser Birkenstock: Forty Years of Peace, Love, and Clunky Sandals* (June 2009), magazine article, p. 16.

11 Success in the USA was based on Fraser's increasingly professional advertising and marketing activities, the opening of "concept stores" in the 70s, the introduction of new products such as "soft clogs" and the "Laguna and Rio models," the use of synthetic materials for shoe manufacturing, the use of computers in the company, and finally, in the early 80s, the opening of a larger headquarters in Novato, California.

12 "For the first ten years, I had trouble getting them to put color into the product," CA Birkenstock, private archive Margot Fraser, BMF 1.A., documents, reviews, 696 f.; ibid., Margot Fraser/ Documents/International/Birkenstock US/MargotFrazer/Biographie_Folder_Nancy_Margot_Fazer_Biography, 12.

13 This health and protective function for the feet is also reflected in the Birkenstock logo, which is emblazoned on almost all the advertising material, showing an upside-down foot on a blue background next to a cross with a halo, reminiscent of medical aid or first aid organizations.

14 On the other hand, this was also a concession to the zeitgeist, because plastic seemed to be the material of the future, especially in the consumer goods sector. Since the 50s, plastics and

414 **Appendices**

fibers had established themselves in the clothing sector as well as in toys, in packaging, and in the leisure sector. Around 1970, the "plastics age" reached its peak, shortly before the discussion about the limits of growth began a few years later, and the oil price crisis increasingly called this into question. See Christian Kleinschmidt, *"Marmor, Stein und Eisen bricht ...": Westdeutschlands Aufbruch ins Kunststoffzeitalter*, in: Technikgeschichte 68, no. 4 (2001), 355–372.

15 Ibid.

16 In the 2000s, the entire product range comprised 100 pages; the catalog of work shoes for medicine, kitchen, and catering ("Birkenstock Professional") had grown to 60 pages. CA Birkenstock, BBG 2. 010-5, Birkenstock_2013_Birkenstock_Katalog_Das_Original_2013_A2b.

17 CA Birkenstock, BBG 2. 001-41, 74_Birkenstock_Orthopaedics_healthy_feet_beautiful_legs_1974_A2b.

18 The product presentation now resembled the catalog of the German department store chain Quelle—colorful and relaxed, with children playing and people in work clothes presenting the variety of Birkenstock products. CA Birkenstock, 74_Birkenstock_Fußgesundheit_1974_A2b.

19 Schildt/Siegfried, *Deutsche Kulturgeschichte*, 403–553.

20 CA Birkenstock, Privatarchiv Margot Fraser, BMF 1.A. 001-1, documents, reviews, Birkenstock Internal Analysis, 8/25/1987, p. 697.

21 Schildt/Siegfried, *Deutsche Kulturgeschichte*, 425–440.

22 CA Birkenstock, BBG 2. 004-1, 90_Birkenstock_Information_1_1990_A2b, Birkenstock Information, 1.1990.

23 See Alice Janssens's essay in this volume.

24 CA Birkenstock, BBG 2. 006-4, Birkenstock_98_Birkenstock_Händler_Information_July_1998_A2b.

25 CA Birkenstock, BBG 2. 007-7, Birkenstock_01_Birkenstock_Händlerinformation_March_2002_A2b.

26 According to a "Brigitte communication analysis", in: CA Birkenstock, BBG 2.007-13/15.

27 CA Birkenstock, BBG 2. 007-13, Birkenstock_04_Birkenstock_Händlerinformation_December_204_A2b; CA Birkenstock, BBG 2. 008-14, Birkenstock_09_Birkenstock_Rock_Star_Baby_Collection_A2b.

28 www.youtube.com/watch?v=hml3NnUm_24&t=1s (accessed May 20, 2023].

29 CA Birkenstock, BBG 2. 007-2, Birkenstock_00_Birkenstock_Shop_Concept_2000_A2b.

30 CA Birkenstock, BBG 2. 012-1, Birkenstock_15_Birkenstock_Shop_in_Shop_System_DACH_Version_2015_DE_A2b, pp. 1, 7.

31 Michael Stephan/Martin J. Schneider, *Marken- und Produktpiraterie: Fälscherstrategien, Schutzinstrumente, Bekämpfungsmanagement*, Düsseldorf 2011, 20.

32 CA Birkenstock, BBG 2. 001-25, 66_Birkenstock_Post_16_A2b, 22.

33 CA Birkenstock, BBG 1.B.017, Birkenstock trademark law, completed proceedings 2013/1, printout mail C. Mennebröcker, June 25, 2013; printout mail A. Wichmann to B. Hillen, Sept. 9, 2011.

34 CA Birkenstock, BBG 2. 015-1, *Birkenstock News*, July 2017, Birkenstock declares war on brand and product pirates, 29.

35 See the contribution by Alexander von den Benken in this volume.

"If the Shoe Fits ...": Comfortable Shoes on the Rise

1 Peter Camper, *Abhandlung von der besten Form der Schuhe*, Hamburg 1781, 97.

2 *Bequem*, in: Deutsches Wörterbuch von Jacob Grimm und Wilhelm Grimm / Neubearbeitung (A–F), digitized version in: Wörterbuchnetz, Trier Center for Digital Humanities, version 01/21, www.woerterbuchnetz.de/DWB2?lemid=B02209 (accessed Sept. 15, 2022).

3 Hermann Meyer, *Procrustes ante portas! Ein kulturgeschichtliches Zerrbild*, in: Monatsschrift des wissenschaftlichen Vereins in Zürich 2 (1857), 62–72, here: 64.

4 See *Der Schuh nach Maß*, in: Das Handwerk: Zeitschrift für das deutsche Handwerk 1 (1947), 19.

5 See Isabella Belting, *Ready to go! Schuhe bewegen*, Berlin 2019, 144.

6 See Karl Sigg/Felix Oesch, *Schuhmode und Gesundheit*, Berlin 1958, 5. As exemplified in the "Basler Nachrichten" at the end of the 50s; see some excerpts in: ibid., 34 ff.

7 Ibid., 41.

8   See Nike U. Breyer, *Orthopädische Schwester-Schuhe*, in: Wolfgang Antweiler (ed.), Schritt für Schritt: Die Geburt des modernen Schuhs, Hilden 2013, 120.

9   See Belting, *Ready to go*, 144.

10 See ibid., 185.

11 See Alison Gill, *Limousines for Feet: The Rhetoric of Sneakers*, in: Giorgio Riello/Peter McNeil (eds.), Shoes: A History from Sandals to Sneakers, New York 2006, 372–385, here: 377.

12 See ibid., 377, 382.

13 Susan L. Sokolowski, *Sneakers*, in: Valerie Steele (ed.), The Berg Companion to Fashion, Oxford 2009, 640–644, here: 641.

14 Inga Clausen, *Alles läuft auf leichten Sohlen*, in: TextilWirtschaft (Dec. 10, 1998), "Das Jahr" supplement.

15 See the essays by Alice Janssens and Christian Kleinschmidt in this volume.

16 See *Businessschuh: Eleganz und Tragekomfort vereint*, in: Creditreform: Das Unternehmermagazin (Jan. 4, 2013), 22.

Birkenstock Identities

1   The foot was dragged into debates about racial/religious differences in 19th-century Germany along with the shoe. The more the feet of Jewish men were singled out as flat-footed and ill-formed, the more attention was paid to shoes as a cover-up for difference. The shoe is also a social product, subject to consumer criticism. See Sander Gilman, *The Jew's Body*, New York 1991, esp. 39, 44, 51. Also Rebecca Mead, *Sole Cycle: The Homely Birkenstock Gets a Fashion Makeover*, in: The New Yorker (Mar. 23, 2015), 5, https://www.newyorker.com/magazine/2015/03/23/sole-cycle-rebecca-mead (accessed July 7, 2023). Paraphrasing Sander Gilman, Mead writes, "In anti-Semitic German-language literature of the fin de siècle, a flat, malformed foot was no less a caricature of the Jew than was a hooked nose."

2   Amartya Sen, *The Fog of Identity*, in: Politics, Philosophy & Economics 8, no. 3 (2009), 285–288, and *Identity and Violence: The Illusion of Destiny*, New York/London 2006.

3   Reiteration of Amartya Sen.

4   See Margot Fraser/Lisa Lorimer, *Dealing with the Tough Stuff: Practical Wisdom for Running a Values-Driven Business*, San Francisco 2009, 69. Margot mentions a first husband, (Gordon F. Fraser, whose name she does not divulge) and a divorce in 1970. She describes him as an importer of modern furniture and implements for the home, the owner of a retail store who moved into wholesale before he sold the business. He urged her to become a wholesaler and suggested that she market her first Birkenstocks in health-food stores. Although he may have had a finger or two in her early Birkenstock business, customers complained that he had not managed things well. Her second marriage was to practicing psychiatrist Stephen Schoen (1924–2018), whom she acknowledges in her introduction, along with a stepson (Jeffrey Schoen 1956–2006, unnamed). Of Karl's trips to America to understand the market, Fraser writes that he "sometimes brought his family along. So I knew his three sons from the time they were babies. On our travels we formed very close relationships with all of our retailers ... It was very important to have those connections ..."

5   The literature on sex/women/gender is vast; that on masculinities has developed more slowly but is now well established, more outside the domain of business than within it. On debates about gender identities involving women in business, see Angel Kwolek-Folland, *Engendering Business: Men and Women in the Corporate Office, 1870–1930*, Baltimore, MD, 1994; *Incorporating Women: A History of Women and Business in the United States*, New York, 1998; Wendy Gamber, *The Female Economy: The Millinery and Dressmaking Trades, 1860–1930*, Urbana/Chicago, IL, 1997; Melissa Fisher, *Wall Street Women*, Durham, NC, 2012; Mary A. Yeager, *Women in Business*, 3 vols., Cheltenham/North Hampton, MA, 1999, especially the introduction, x–xcii, and the entry, "Will There Ever Be a Feminist Business History," 3–43; Mary A. Yeager, *Gender, Race and Entrepreneurship*, in: The Routledge Companion to the Makers of Global Business, Abingdon 2019, 69–92.

6 Jeffrey Fear, *Mining the Past: Historicizing Organizational Learning and Change*, in: Organizations in Time: History, Theory and Methods, Oxford 2014, 179.

7 See the essay by Roman Köster in this volume.

8 Corporate Archive Birkenstock [hereinafter CA Birkenstock], BS 74, Memoire Descriptif, deposé a l'appui d'une demande de BREVET D'INVENTION formée par Monsieur Carl BIRK-ENSTOCK et Madame Emmi Birkenstock pour: Chaussure. B.18.088 J.V. 71395/51. 507288. PatentBelgium.

9 Margot's nearly 40-year tenure at Footprint Sandals, Inc. represents a narrow but critical slice of a much longer Birkenstock history. What she chooses to reveal and to hide offers a fascinating portrait of gender and business identities at work. She describes how she saw herself and the kinds of choices she made before, during, and after her retirement as CEO in 2002, the same year that Karl Birkenstock also retired. She allows her emotions to run, especially when discussing her reactions to the sale of the company to her employees Kyla Stevens, HAPPY FEET SHOE NEWS, The History of Birkenstock: A Timeline of the Birkenstock Era. https:///www.happyfeet.com/blog/history-of-birkenstock/. Since 2021, the company, renamed Birkenstock Group, B.V. & Co. KG, runs 16 operational sites in Germany, and sales offices in at least 16 other nations, employing over 5,500 employees world wide. It is majority owned by L Catterton, the world's largest growth investor in the consumer goods industry, and Financiere Agache, a holding company controlled by Agache, the holding company of the Arnault family. Curiously, published obituaries are hard to find. The Birkenstock obituary was short, one paragraph long. "Birkenstock Mourns the Loss of Margot Fraser," 2/5, https:///. birkenstock-group.com/de/en/detail-press/birkenstock-mourns-the-loss-of-margot-fraser. I found no obits for her in any of the major US newspapers, including The New York Times, Los Angeles Time, or Wall Street Journal.

10 Margot was born June 15, 1931 or March 27, 1929 as Henriette Immoor. She died in 2017. There are links in Ancestry.com to her father Johann Heinrich Immor (1905–1992—spelled Jmmoor in Ancestry). There is little information on her mother, although Margot's middle name offers some clues. Fraser's middle name is Henriette, the female form of Heinrich, which is a German and Jewish (Ashkenazic) name, most common in Germany.

11 Margot co-edited the book *Dealing with the Tough Stuff*, in which she describes her version of the difficult decisions she made in building her Birkenstock distribution and business.

12 Margot Fraser and Lisa Lorimer, *Dealing with the Tough Stuff: Practical Wisdom for Running a Values-Driven Business*, (San Francisco: Berrett-Koehler Publishers, Inc.). The book is not an autobiography. Fraser's contribution is one of several narratives about the tough choices faced by business people in different industries. The book's strength is its practicality and illumination of the choices that business people make in the process of doing business. Fraser offers very little information about her family or ancestry.

13 Louisa Schaefer, quoting Wolf Bittner, a former activist and lawyer, in *1968 Lives On*, in: DW (Apr. 11, 2008), https://amp.dw.com/en/68-movement-brought-lasting-changes-to-german-society/a-3257581 (accessed July 7, 2023).

14 John Robert Stark, *The Overlooked Majority: German Women in the Four Zones of Occupied Germany, 1945–1949: A Comparative Study*, PhD diss., Ohio State University, 2003.

15 Karl Birkenstock Jr., 1960: "An individually correctable shoe that does justice to the user's foot." See the essay by Roman Köster in this volume.

16 Duncan Channon, *Birkenstock for President*, in: DC (Aug. 24, 2008), https://www.duncanchannon.com/services/advertising/print-and-outdoor/birkenstock-for-president (accessed July 7, 2023).

17 Birkenstock Archives, Folder: Gender Inequality.

18 Ibid.

19 Douglas L. Fugate/Joanna Phillips, *Product Gender Perceptions and Antecedents of Product Gender Congruence*, in: Journal of Consumer Marketing 27, no. 3 (2010), 251–261.

20 Kurt Soller, *Birkenstocks Are Still Ugly—but at Least Now They're Cool*, in: Bloomberg (June 26, 2014), https://www.bloomberg.com/news/articles/2014-06-26/birkenstocks-are-fashionable-as-sales-rise-celebrities-wear-them#xj4y7vzkg (accessed July 7, 2023).

21 See the essay of Jörg Lesczenski in this volume.

Notes   **417**

22 Veit Bachmann, *From Jackboots to Birkenstocks: The Civilianisation of German Geopolitics in the Twentieth Century*, School of Geography, University of Plymouth, 2010: https://doi.org/10.1111/j.1467-9663.2009.00542.x (accessed July 7, 2023); Barbara Schneider-Levy, *Birkenstock Is Voted Most Animal-Friendly Shoe Company by PETA's Youth Group*, in: FN (Feb. 14, 2018). In 2016, PETA Deutschland presented Birkenstock with the Vegan Fashion Award for a vegan model of its iconic Madrid sandal. Birkenstock CEO Oliver Reichert expressed his thanks: "Especially among younger customers, there is a growing percentage who choose the vegan way of life. We offer many vegan products for these customers."

23 Dan Herman, *Outsmart the MBA Clones: The Alternative Guide to Competitive Strategy*, Rochester, NY, 2015.

24 See the essay of Roman Köster in this volume.

25 Ibid. See also Olivia King et al., *Sociology of the Professions: What It Means for Podiatry*, in: Journal of Foot and Ankle Research 1 (2018), https://doi.org/10.1186/s13047-018-0275-0, which offers an overview of theories of professionalization and suggests that podiatry and the foot sciences had a hard time achieving legitimacy, in contrast to the authority and professional respect accorded to dentistry.

26 Fraser/Lorimer, *Dealing with the Tough Stuff*, 133. Fraser writes that in 1968 she translated his [Carl Birkenstock's] German catalog into English, bought one hundred thousand copies, and had them shipped to the United States.

27 Stark, *The Overlooked Majority*, 292–293.

28 See the essay of Jörg Lesczenski in this volume.

29 Fraser/Lorimer, *Dealing with the Tough Stuff*, 60, 79.

30 Cf. Fraser/Lorimer, *Dealing with the Tough Stuff*, 12–15.

31 For a much fuller discussion of the context, one that zeroes in on sex/gender debates and the role of American and German women in postwar Germany under Allied occupation, see Stark, *The Overlooked Majority*, esp. 276–360. Businesswomen, alas, were generally overlooked by Allied occupiers, and by this historian, perhaps because of inattention to women like Margot who were interested in business.

32 A classic study is Gamber, *The Female Economy*.

33 The observation is that of Michael Lewis, *The Irresponsible Investor*, in: The New York Times (June 6, 2004).

34 Recounted by Cathy Horyn, *The Dwarf, the Prince, and the Diamond in the Mountain*, in: The Cut, https://www.thecut.com/2018/08/cathy-horyn-on-birkenstocks-unlikely-rise.html (accessed July 7, 2023), and in Mead, *Sole Cycle*.

35 Birkenstock archives, Folders: Advertising USA; Catalogue Covers.

36 Fraser/Lorimer, *Dealing with the Tough Stuff*, 176.

37 Richard H. Thaler/Cass R. Sunstein, *Nudge: The Final Edition*, London 2021. The details in the text above are developed more thoroughly in the essays of Christian Kleinschmidt/Andrea H. Schneider-Braunberger and Alexander von den Benken in this volume.

38 Geoffrey Jones, *Deeply Responsible Business: A Global History of Values-Driven Leadership*, Cambridge, MA, 2023, includes Anita Roddick of Body Shop but, alas, not Margot Fraser.

39 Quoting Birkenstock's head of public relations, Jochen Gutzy, in Horyn, *The Dwarf, the Prince, and the Diamond in the Mountain*.

40 Mary Pischke, Human Resources manager, Novato, interviewed by Brenda Sunoo, *Birkenstock Braces to Fight the Competition*, Personnel Journal, vol. 73, no. 8 (August 1994), 6875.

41 Fraser/Lorimer, *Dealing with the Tough Stuff*, various pages; the descriptors are experience- and time-specific but not explicitly dated in the book.

42 Ibid., Kindle version, 80, quoting a male Dutch distributor at Berrett-Koehler Publishers.

43 Fraser/Lorimer, Dealing with the *Tough Stuff*, Kindle version, 81.

44 Fariba Karimi et al., *Inferring Gender from Names on the Web: A Comparative Evaluation of Gender Detection Methods*, Proceedings of the 25th International Conference Companion on World Wide Web (2016), https://doi.org/10.48550/arXiv.1603.04322; Steven Saxonberg, *From Defamilialization to Degenderization: Toward a New Welfare Typology Social Policy & Administration*, in: Social Policy Administration 1 (2013), 26–49.

Different Sides to Shoes: Protection, Status Symbol, Emblem

1 See Günter Gall, *Kunsthandwerk, Volkskunde, Völkerkunde, Fachtechnik*, Offenbach am Main 1956, 104.
2 See *Schuh*, in: Wolfgang Pfeifer et al., Etymologisches Wörterbuch des Deutschen (1993), www.dwds.de/wb/etymwb/Schuh (accessed July 5, 2022).
3 See Anne Sudrow, *Der Schuh im Nationalsozialismus: Eine Produktgeschichte im deutsch-britisch-amerikanischen Vergleich*, Göttingen 2010, 70.
4 See Klaus Schreiner, *Rituale, Zeichen, Bilder: Formen und Funktionen symbolischer Kommunikation im Mittelalter*, Cologne 2011, 203.
5 See Giorgio Riello/Peter McNeil, *Introduction. A Long Walk: Shoes, People and Places*, in: Giorgio Riello/Peter McNeil (eds.), *Shoes: A History from Sandals to Sneakers*, New York 2006, 2–29, here: 3.
6 See Jonathan Walford, *Der verführerische Schuh: Modetrends aus vier Jahrhunderten*, Heidelberg 2007, 11.
7 See Sue Blundell, *Beneath Their Shining Feet: Shoes and Sandals in Classical Greece*, in: Riello/McNeil (eds.), *Shoes, A History from Sandals to Sneakers*, (New York, 2006), 30–49, here: 46 f.
8 See Sylvia Heudecker, *Schuh*, in: Günter Butzer/Joachim Jacob (eds.), *Metzler Lexikon literarischer Symbole*, 334–335, here: 334; Claus Korte, *Literarische Schuh-Symbole*, in: Michael Andritzky et al. (eds.), *Z. B. Schuhe: Vom bloßen Fuß zum Stöckelschuh; Eine Kulturgeschichte der Fußbekleidung*, Giessen 1988, 30–41, here: 36.
9 See Isabella Belting, *Ready to go! Schuhe bewegen*, Berlin 2019, 80.
10 See Isabel Cardigos, *Schuh*, in: Rolf Wilhelm Brednich et al. (eds.), Enzyklopädie des Märchens Online, vol. 12, 2016, www.degruyter.com/database/EMO/entry/emo.12.048/html. [last accessed Aug. 15, 2022]
11 Ibid.
12 See Sudrow, *Schuh im Nationalsozialismus*, 85, 96; Heudecker, *Schuh*, 335.
13 See Heudecker, *Schuh*, 334.
14 Ibid.

International Fashion and Luxury in Birkenstocks

1 Jane's Addiction, *Live & Insane,* https://janesaddiction.org/bootography/janes-addiction/cd/live-and-insane/ (accessed 10.5.2022); Listen to Sassy, *February 1989 Fashion Etc.: Flips, Clogs & Baths*, episode 50, https://listentosassy.com/episode/050/ (accessed May 10, 2022).
2 This chapter, which looks at the success story of Birkenstock against the background of the structures of the fashion and luxury industry, draws on information from Birkenstock's corporate archives, international media reports, and semi-structured interviews with Birkenstock employees and partners.
3 Oxford English Dictionary, *Fashion*, https://en.oxforddictionaries.com/definition/fashion (accessed May 10, 2022).
4 Fashion Theory, *Aims and scope*, https://www.tandfonline.com/action/journalInformation?-show=aimsScope&journalCode=rfft20 (accessed May 10, 2022).
5 Christopher Breward, *Fashioning London*, Oxford 2004, 11.
6 Yuniya Kawamura, *Fashion-ology*, London 2018, 42.
7 Christopher Breward, *Fashioning London*, Oxford 2003.
8 Ibid.
9 Mariangela Lavanga, *The Role of The Pitti Uomo Trade Fair in the Menswear Fashion Industry*, in: Blaszczyk et al. (eds.); The Fashion Forecasters: A Hidden History of Color and Trend Prediction, London 2018, 191–209, here 193; Regina Lee Blaszczyk, *Imagining Consumers: Design and Innovation from Wedgwood to Corning*, Baltimore 2002; Elizabeth Block, *Dressing Up: The Women Who Influenced French Fashion*, Cambridge MA 2021, 40; Agnès Rocamora, *Fashioning the City: Paris, Fashion and the Media*, London 2009; Justine De Young, *Fashion and the Press*, in: Gloria Groom (ed.), Impressionism, New Haven 2012, 232–243; Kawamura, *Fashion-ology*, 30; Jennifer Smith Maguire/Julian Matthews (eds.), *The Cultural Intermediaries Reader*, London 2014.

Notes **419**

10 Renate Stauss, *What Fashion Is Not (Only)*, in: On Capital, Vestoj 9 (2019), 55–76; C.M. Belfanti, *Was Fashion a European Invention?*, in: Journal of Global History 3 (2008) 419–443.

11 Breward, *Fashion*; Agnès Rocamora, *Mediatization and Digital Media in the Field of Fashion*, in Fashion Theory 21(5) (2016), 1–18.

12 Kawamura, *Fashion-ology*.

13 Giovanni Luigi Fontana, *Style through Design: Form and Function*, in: Giorgio Riello/Peter McNeil (eds.), Shoes: A History from Sandals to Sneakers, London 2011, 326–352, here 327–329; Cheryl Buckely/Hazel Clark, *Fashion and Everyday Life: London and New York*, London 2017.

14 Fontana, *Style through Design*; Kawamura, *Fashion-ology*; Breward, *Fashion*, 21.

15 Jon Cope/Dennis Maloney, *Fashion Promotion in Practice*, London 2019, 79.

16 Breward, *Fashion;* Buckley/Clark, *Fashion and Everyday Life*.

17 Colin McDowell, *Shoes: Fashion and Fantasy*, New York 1989, 200.

18 Jonathan Walford, *The Seductive Shoe: Four Centuries of Fashion Footwear*, London 2007, 185, 214; Scholl, *100 Years of Experience*, https://www.scholl.com.sg/why-scholl/100-years-of-experience/ (accessed June 1, 2022); Imogen Fox, *Why Do Certain "Ugly" Shoes Become Fashionable?*, in: The Guardian (July 22, 2010), https://www.theguardian.com/lifeandstyle/2010/jul/22/worishofer-ugly-shoe-fashionable-crocs (accessed Mar. 6, 2022).

19 Scholl, *100 Years of Experience*; Walford, *The Seductive Shoe*.

20 Company Archive Birkenstock [hereafter CA Birkenstock], BCB 4. 005, BS_Fussorthopaedie_Buch_EN. (1).pdf, 1948; CA Birkenstock, Privatarchiv Margot Fraser, BMF 1.B. 003-7, Publicity. pdf, "Birkenstock: A History and Tradition", n.d.

21 CA Birkenstock, Privatarchiv Margot Fraser, BMF 1.B. 003-7 Publicity.pdf, "Birkenstock: A History and Tradition", n.d.

22 CA Birkenstock, BCB 4. 005, BS_Fussorthopaedie_Buch_EN. (1).pdf, 1948; CA Birkenstock, Privatarchiv Margot Fraser, BMF 1.B. 003-7 Publicity.pdf, "Birkenstock: A Brief History," n.d.; CA Birkenstock, BCB 4. 005, Carl Birkenstock, *Mit dem Arzt gegen Fußkrankheiten und Irrlehren*, Bremen, 1935; CA Birkenstock, BCB 4. 002, Carl Birkenstock, *60 Jahre für die vernünftige Fußbekleidung*, 1961, 19–21; CA Birkenstock, BS 16, BS_16_komplett.pdf; CA Birkenstock, BS 86, BS_86_komplett.pdf; CA Birkenstock, BS 93, BS_93_komplett.pdf.

23 CA Birkenstock, Privatarchiv Margot Fraser, 1.A. 001-4, Publicity.pdf, Birkenstock Footprint Sandals, Inc. Promotional Material, "An In-Depth Look at Birkenstock Sandals," n.d.

24 Nike U. Breyer, *Man trug so was nicht!*, in: Die Tageszeitung am Wochenende (Apr. 15, 2000), 1–2.

25 CA Birkenstock, BBG 2. 001-22, 65_Birkenstock_Post_14_1965_A2b.pdf, "Birkenstock Post August 1965," Aug. 1965, 14; CA Birkenstock, BBG 2. 001-25, 66_Birkenstock_Post_16_1966_A2b.pdf, "Birkenstock Post August 1966," Aug. 1965, 19–21.; CA Birkenstock, BBG 2. 001-30, 68_Birkenstock_Anschreiben_Fachkurs_1968_A2b.pdf, "Birkenstock-Preise," Oct. 1, 1968; Tamsin McLaren/Fiona Armstrong-Gibbs, *Marketing Fashion Footwear: The Business of Shoes*, London 2017, 34.

26 CA Birkenstock, BBG 2. 001-25, 66_Birkenstock_Post_16_1966_A2b.pdf, "Chic im Beruf, Chic zu Hause, Chic in der Freizeit," 1966, 26.

27 CA Birkenstock, Privatarchiv Margot Fraser, BMF 2. 001-1, Historical Ads, Photos.pdf, Birkenstock Footprints Sandals Inc. Promotional Material, "Why Birkenstocks Feel So Good," 1975.

28 CA Birkenstock, BBG 2. 018-1, 19_Birkenstock_NEWS_Magazin_Ausgabe_1_2019_PL.pdf, Birkenstock News Magazine Poland 1, "OD BOLZANO, PRZEZ WŁOCHY, NA CAŁY ŚWIAT", 2019, 97–99.

29 NaturalLook, *Plenty of Ideas, Application and Foresight*, https://www.naturallook.it/en/blog/ideas-application-and-foresight/ (accessed June 1, 2022).

30 CA Birkenstock, Privatarchiv Margot Fraser, BMF 1.B. 003-7, Publicity.pdf, "Margot Fraser Biographical Information," n.d.; CA Birkenstock, Privatarchiv Margot Fraser, BMF 1.B. 003-7, Publicity.pdf, "Birkenstock: A Brief History," n.d.

31 CA Birkenstock, Privatarchiv Margot Fraser, BMF 2. 001-1, Historical Ads, Photos.pdf, Birkenstock Footprints Sandals Inc. Promotional Material, "Why Birkenstocks Feel So Good," 1975; CA Birkenstock, Privatarchiv Margot Fraser, BMF 1.B. 003-5, Articles Feet.pdf, Betty Franklin, "The Crimes We Commit against Our Feet," n.d.

32 CA Birkenstock, Privatarchiv Margot Fraser, BMF 1.B. 001-2, ME.pdf, "Birkenstock Executive Bios," 1999; "CA Birkenstock, Privatarchiv Margot Fraser, BMF 1.B. 003-7, Publicity.pdf, "Birkenstock: A Brief History," n.d.

33 Leigh Buchanan, *How I Did It: Margot Fraser*, in: Inc Magazine (June 1, 2009), https://www.inc.com/magazine/20090601/how-i-did-it-margot-fraser.html (accessed Feb. 1, 2022).

34 Buchanan, *How I Did It.*

35 CA Birkenstock, BDF 4.B. 005, Zeitzeugen_Robert_Lusk_Transkription.docx, Interview with Retailer Robert Lusk, n.d., 6, 11–12; McLaren and Armstrong-Gibbs, *Marketing Fashion Footwear*, 34.

36 CA Birkenstock, BDF 4.B. 005, Interview with Retailer Robert Lusk, 29.

37 Ibid., Interview with Retailer Robert Lusk, 9.

38 McLaren/Armstrong-Gibbs, *Marketing Fashion Footwear*, 34; CA Birkenstock, BDF 4.B. 005, Interview with Retailer Robert Lusk, 42.

39 CA Birkenstock, BDF 4.B. 006, 181026_Zeitzeugen_ITV_Yasuyuki_Umino_Clean_Version_V2.mp4, Interview with Yasuyuki Umino, Oct. 26, 2018.

40 CA Birkenstock, BBG 2. 001-45, 75_Birkenstock_Erzeugnisse_Orthopädie_Was_der_Arzt_1975_A2b, "Birkenstock Erzeugnisse für Orthopädie," 1975, 3.; CA Birkenstock, BBG 10. 002, 1980S_InternalAdvertising_PressAdvertising_Snobs.tif, "Snobs," n.d.; CA Birkenstock, BBG 10. 002, 1980s_InternalAdvertising_PressAdvertising_FunnyLookingBirkenstockSandals.tif, "Funny-Looking Birkenstock Sandals", n.d.

41 Display Ad 564, New York Times (Oct. 27, 1985), L123, in: ProQuest History Newspaper Archive [hereafter PQHNA].

42 *Shoo Away All of Those Fashion-Mad Footwreckers,* Irish Independent (Jan. 30, 1986), 11, in: British Newspaper Archive [hereafter BNA].

43 Ibid.

44 James Laver, *Costume and Fashion: A Concise History*, London 2002.

45 Giorgio Riello, *A Foot in the Past: Footwear in the Long Eighteenth Century*, Oxford 2006, 1.

46 Yuniya Kawamura, *The Japanese Revolution in Paris Fashion*, London 2004.

47 Kim Knott, *Jap*, in: Elle UK (Nov. 1, 1985), 120–123.

48 Kawamura, *The Japanese Revolution.*

49 Jane Pratt, *What Next: These Shoes Are Made for Walking*, in: Sassy Magazine (Feb. 1, 1989), 15.

50 Pratt, *What Next.*

51 Jane Pratt, *Inside Out: What's This?*, in: Sassy Magazine (Feb. 1, 1989), 87.

52 CA Birkenstock, Privatarchiv Margot Fraser, BBG 1.B. 003-8, Birkenstock Testimonials.pdf, "Famous, Well-Known Persons & Celebrities Who Wear Birkenstock Footwear," n.d.

53 Felix Petty, *Andre Walker Still Believes in Elegance*, in: i-D (14.9.2022), https://i-d.vice.com/en/article/z34ye3/andre-walker-still-believes-in-elegance (accessed Oct. 15, 2022).

54 Brenda Paik Sunoo, *Birkenstock Braces to Fight the Competition*, Personnel Journal 73, no. 8 (Aug. 1994), 68–75, here 70; Margo DeMello, *Feet and Footwear: A Cultural Encyclopedia*, Santa Barbara 2009, 39.

55 Leslie Brokaw, *Feet Don't Fail Me Now*, in: Inc Magazine (May 1, 1994), https://www.inc.com/magazine/19940501/2912.html (accessed Mar. 1, 2022).

56 Richard Stengel, *Be It Ever So Birkenstock*, in: The New York Times (Aug. 30, 1992), 8.

57 Woody Hochswender, *Is the Killer Jacket Losing Its Grip?*, in: The New York Times (Aug. 8, 1990), C1.

58 Hochswender, *Is the Killer Jacket Losing Its Grip?*; Hans-Christoph Blumenberg, *Die Rache des Montgomery*, in: Die Zeit (Sept. 14, 1990), https://www.zeit.de/1990/38/die-rache-des-montgomery (accessed Mar. 13, 2022), translated by the author.

59 Vogue Runway, *Perry Ellis Spring 1993 Ready-to-Wear*, in: Vogue US (Sept. 19, 1992), https://www.vogue.com/article/naomi-campbell-marc-jacobs-perry-ellis-grunge-collection (accessed Mar. 1, 2022).

60 Christian Allaire, *Naomi Campbell Just Re-Wore Her Look From Marc Jacobs's 1993 Grunge Show*, in: Vogue.com (Sept. 9, 2018), https://www.vogue.com/article/naomi-campbell-marc-jacobs-perry-ellis-grunge-collection (accessed Mar. 1, 2022); Suzy Menkes, *The Conundrum of See-Through*, in: The New York Times (May 16, 1993), v8.

61 Bridget Foley, *Grunge Again*, in: Women's Wear Daily (Nov. 7, 2018), 24.

62 Alexandra Jacobs, *Call It the Birkenstock Summer*, in: The New York Times (Aug. 21, 2014), E7.

63 CA Birkenstock, BBG 3. 004-32, message from margot 2.pdf, "Birkenstock Featured in Perry Ellis Show," Footprint Forum 80 (Sept. 1992), 2.

64 Peter Davis, *Talking Fashion: Once a Symbol of a True Bohemian, Birkenstocks Are Stepping Out Again*, in: Vogue 182 (Nov. 1, 1992), 350.

65 Kathleen Boyes, *Balancing Acts*, in: Chicago Tribune (Aug. 5, 1992), https://www.chicagotribune.com/news/ct-xpm-1992-08-05-9203100252-story.html (accessed Mar. 7, 2022); Brokaw, *Feet Don't Fail Me Now*; Stengel, *Be it Ever So Birkenstock*; Harper's Bazaar Deutschland, *Men-Things: Sandals for TrendWalker*, in: Harper's Bazaar Deutschland 3 (1992).

66 Amy Spindler, *Innocence Is the Winner*, in: PQHNA, The New York Times (Oct. 15, 1993) B9; Sabine Spieler, *Back to Birkenstock*, in: TextilWirtschaft 6 (Feb. 10, 1994), 150.

67 The Face Archive, *The 3rd Summer of Love*, in: The Face (Apr. 17, 2019), https://theface.com/archive/kate-moss-summer-of-love (accessed, Oct. 10, 2021); Linda Watson, *Corinne Day*, in: The Independent Historical Archive [hereafter IHA], The Independent (Sept. 6, 2010), 9.

68 CA Birkenstock, BDF 4.B. 005, Interview with Retailer Robert Lusk, 23.

69 *Eye: Earth Girls*, in: Women's Wear Daily 160 (Sept. 6, 1990), 28.

70 Anne-Marie Schiro, *By Design: Sensible Shoes*, in: The New York Times (Aug. 18, 1992), B18; *Cover*, in: Time: The Weekly News Magazine 140 (Sept. 21, 1992).

71 Vogue, *Fashion: Travelling Light*, in: Vogue Archive [hereafter VA], Vogue USA, 183 (Apr. 1, 1993), 358–373; Vogue, *Fashion: Eastern Light*, in: VA, Vogue USA, 183, 12 (Dec. 1, 1993), 234–255.

72 Spieler, *Back to Birkenstock*, 150, translated by the author.

73 CA Birkenstock, BBG 1.D. 002-1, Betriebsrat Birko-Schuhtechnik GmbH Juli 1993 bis Dezember 1994.pdf, Press Release, "Weiterhin ungewöhnlich positive Firmenentwicklung: Drei neue Firmen in der Birkenstock-Gruppe", n. d.

74 CA Birkenstock, Zeitzeugen_Nick_Wang_Transkription.docx, Interview with Nick Wang, n. d., 16; Melanie Rickey, *Buy Me*, in: IHA, Independent (May 14, 1996), 15; CA Birkenstock, BDF 4.B. 007, Zeitzeugen_Nick_Wang_Transkription.docx, 16.; Rickey, *Buy Me*; Birkenstock, *History of Birkenstock*.

75 CA Birkenstock, BDF 4.B. 008, Zeitzeugen_Koji Tanemoto_Transkription.docx, 3, 16.

76 CA Birkenstock, BDF 4.B. 006, 181026_ZEITZEUGEN_ITV_YASUYUKI_UMINO_CLEAN-VERSION_V2.mp4, Birkenstock Contemporary Witness Filmed Interview with Yasuyuki Umino, Oct. 26, 2018.

77 CA Birkenstock, BDF 4.B. 009, 180724_ZEITZEUGEN_ITV_SYNC_YUKIKO TEKAWA.mp4., Birkenstock Contemporary Witness Filmed Interview with Yukiko Tekawa, July 24, 2018.

78 CA Birkenstock, BDF 4.B. 005, Interview with Retailer Robert Lusk, 18.

79 CA Birkenstock, BDF 4.B. 010, ZZ_TRANSKRIPTION_Goerke.docx, Interview with Marcel Goerke Transcript, Oct. 2, 2019, 15.

80 CA Birkenstock, BDF 4.B. 010, Interview with Marcel Goerke Transcript, 15–16.

81 Katherine Betts, *Fashion: The Best & Worst Looks of the '90s*, in: VA, Vogue USA 186 (Jan. 1, 1996), 125–126.

82 *Fashion: Techno Color*, in: VA, Vogue USA 187 (Dec. 1, 1997), 310–319; *Fashion: Celtic Chic*, in: VA, Vogue USA 188 (Sept. 1, 1998), 536–553; Andre Leon Talley, *Fashion: Period Drama*, in: VA, Vogue USA 189 (Sept. 1, 1999), 606.

83 Melanie Rickey, *Off the Peg*, in: IHA, Independent Magazine (Sept. 5, 1998), 32; Susannah Conway, *The Golden Fleece*, in: IHA, Independent on Sunday (Sept. 6, 1998), 9.

84 Rickey, *Off the Peg*; Conway, *The Golden Fleece*.

85 Trish Donnally, *Don't Smirk at Birks: Birkenstocks Trendy, and Not Just among the Granola Set*, in: SF Gate (Aug. 20, 1998), https://www.sfgate.com/entertainment/article/DON-T-SMIRK-AT-BIRKS-Birkenstocks-trendy-and-2996044.php (accessed May 3, 2022); firstVIEW, *Paco Rabanne – Ready-to-Wear – Runway Collection – Women* (Spring/Summer 1999), https://www.firstview.com/collection_images.php?id=775#.Yt0nzuxBwWq (accessed May 2, 2022); CA Birkenstock, BBG 4.B. 055, FootwearNews_SuitingDown_1999.pdf, "Suiting Down," Footwear News 55 (Feb. 22, 1999), front cover.

86 CA Birkenstock, BBG 13. 001, PostInterviewEmailBirkenstockInternalSourceOne.pdf, Email from Birkenstock Internal Source One, June 4, 2022.

422 **Appendices**

87 CA Birkenstock, BBG 13. 001, Birkenstock Internal Source One Birkenstock 250 Project Interview 1 Transcript.doc, 1.4.2022; CA Birkenstock, BBG 13. 001, Birkenstock Internal Source One Birkenstock 250 Project Interview 2 Transcript.doc, May 25, 2022.

88 *Fashion: Easy Street*, in: VA, Vogue USA, 191 (Dec. 1, 2001), 264–275; Plum Sykes/Eviana Hartman, *Summer in the City*, in: VA, Vogue USA, 192 (May 1, 2002), 213–233; *Give the Gift of Yourself*, in: VA, Vogue USA, 192 (Dec. 1, 2002), 163–169; *Fashion: Power Games: Winning Streak*, in: VA, Vogue USA, 194 (Mar. 1, 2004), 562–569.

89 *Bald Men Go Back into Hiding*, in: Dublin Evening Herald (Jan. 15, 2000), 13.

90 Elisa Anniss. *Totterers Out of Step*, in: The Financial Times (Jan. 15, 2005), 9, in: Financial Times Historical Archive [hereafter FTHA].

91 Libby Brooks, *Succès de sandal*, in: The Guardian (June 30, 2003), https://www.theguardian.com/lifeandstyle/2003/jun/30/fashion.beauty (accessed Feb. 1, 2022).

92 CA Birkenstock, BDF 4.B. 005, Interview with Retailer Robert Lusk, 21.

93 Ibid., Interview with Retailer Robert Lusk, 22.

94 Julie Bosman, *Hippie Shoes Reveal Their Inner Heidis*, in: PQHNA, New York Times (June 18, 2006), 8.

95 *Denim Dish: Denim Made for Walking*, in: Women's Wear Daily 180 (Nov. 2, 2000), 11, in: Women's Wear Daily Archive [hereafter WWDA].

96 Guy Trebay, *Noticed: Even Macho Toes Like to Breathe*, in: PQHNA, New York Times (June 10, 2010), E8.

97 *Hello Operator*, in: VA, Vogue USA, 193 (May 1, 2003), 266.

98 CA Birkenstock, BBG 4. 009, Birkenstock styled by Heidi Klum – Schriftverkehr 2002.pdf, "Projekt Heidi Klum Manuskript 'Making of,'" 2002, 1–3.

99 CA Birkenstock, BBG 4. 009, Birkenstock styled by Heidi Klum – Schriftverkehr 2002.pdf, Press Release, "Press Release: Exclusive Collection in 2003, Heidi Klum visits Birkenstock," 2002; CA Birkenstock, BBG 4. 009, Birkenstock styled by Heidi Klum – Schriftverkehr 2006.pdf, Letter from Günther Klum to Alex Birkenstock and Bernd Hillen, June 8, 2006.

100 CA Birkenstock, BBG 10. 005, 2003_Article_Vegas_HeidiKlumTheUbermodelThatRoars.jpg, Vegas Magazine "Heidi Klum: The Übermodel That Roars," 2003.

101 Niamh O'Rourke, *Spending It: Mac Back*, in: BNA, Irish Independent (June 27, 2003), 21; CA Birkenstock, BBG 4. 010, Birkenstock styled by Heidi Klum – Entwürfe Heidi Klum – Reichnungen Fotos Materialien.pdf file, n. d.

102 CA Birkenstock, BBG 4. 009, Birkenstock styled by Heidi Klum – Schriftverkehr 2002.pdf, "Kunden für Heidi-Klum-Präsentation am 1. Februar 2003," 2002; CA Birkenstock, BBG 4. 009, Birkenstock styled by Heidi Klum – Schriftverkehr 2003.pdf, "Einladungskarte," 2003.

103 CA Birkenstock, BBG 4. 009, Birkenstock styled by Heidi Klum – correspondence 2004.pdf, letter from Oliver Weibel to Heidi Klum and Günther Klum, Mar. 26, 2004.

104 CA Birkenstock, BBG 4. 009, Birkenstock styled by Heidi Klum – Schriftverkehr 2006.pdf, letter from Bernd Hillen to Gene Kunde, June 9, 2006.

105 Yves Béhar, *Birkenstock Footprints: The Architect Collection Green from the Inside Out*, in: Innovation: Industrial Design Excellence Yearbook 23 (2004), 142–145, here 142.

106 Kristi Cameron, *Peep Shoe*, in: Metropolis Magazine (June 1, 2003), https://metropolismag.com/programs/peep-shoe/ (accessed Mar. 1, 2022).

107 CA Birkenstock, BDF 4.B. 008, Birkenstock Internal Source One Birkenstock 250 Project Interview 1 Transcript.doc, 18.

108 CA Birkenstock, BDF 4.B. 008, Zeitzeugen_Koji Tanemoto_Transkription.docx, 6, 7, 13; CA Birkenstock, 181026_Zeitzeugen_ITV_Yasuyuki_Umino_Clean_Version_V2.mp4, Oct. 26, 2018.

109 CA Birkenstock, BDF 4.B. 009, Zeitzeugen_Koji Tanemoto_Transkription.docx, 6–9, 10–11; CA Birkenstock, BBG 4.B. 055, 2005_Editorial_NonNo_Fashion.tiff, 2005, "Fashion"; CA Birkenstock, BBG 4.B. 055, 2007_Editorial_Boon_TatamiXABathingApe.tiff, "Collaborative Select Shop Birkenstock, '07 Spring/Summer," 2007.

110 CA Birkenstock, BDF 4.B. 006, 180724_Zeitzeugen_ITV_Sync_Yukiko Tekawa.mp4, July 24, 2018.

111 Ibid.

112 CA Birkenstock, BDF 4.B. 006, 181026_Zeitzeugen_ITV_Yasuyuki_Umino_Clean_Version_ V2.mp4.

113 CA Birkenstock, BBG 3.002-3-11, 02_Birkenstock_Spring_summer_collection_2001_JP_A2b. pdf, Birkenstock Japan Catalogue, 2001; CA Birkenstock, 04_Birkenstock_Reluxing_life-Spring_Summer_2004_JP_Ab2.pdf, Birkenstock Japan Catalogue, "reluxing life Spring and Summer 2004," 2004; CA Birkenstock, 04_Birkenstock_Autumn_Winter_collection_2004_ JP_A2b.pdf, Birkenstock Japan Catalogue, "Natural mode 04 Autumn & Winter Collection," 2004; CA Birkenstock, 06_07_Birkenstock_The_living_tradition_Autumn_winter_collection_2006_2007_JP_A2b.pdf, Birkenstock Japan Catalogue, "The Living Tradition Autumn & Winter 06–07 Collection," 2006; CA Birkenstock, 07_Birkenstock_Life_knowledge_007_ JP_A2b.pdf, Birkenstock Japan Catalogue, 2007; CA Birkenstock, 08_09_Birkenstock_Class_ and_chic_Autumn_winter_collection_2008_2009_JP_A2b.pdf, Birkenstock Japan Catalogue, "Class & Chic 2008–09 Autumn & Winter Collection," 2008.

114 CA Birkenstock, BBG 3.002-7, 05_Birkenstock_Style_book_dazed_confused_2005_JP_A2b. pdf, Birkenstock Japan Catalogue, "Birkenstock Style Book," 2005.

115 Emilie Marsh et al., *Buyers Note Color, Wearability at Milan Shows*, in: WWDA, WWD, 199 (June 23, 2010), 4–6.

116 Harriet Walker, *Designed for Bunion Sufferers, Adopted by Fashion Followers*, in: IHA, Independent (June 21, 2010), 20.

117 Elisa Anniss, *You Automatically Feel Like Slowing Down and Kicking Back*, in: FTHA, The Financial Times (Apr. 3, 2010), 7.

118 Cathy Horyn, *Céline Keeps the Paris Winners Coming*, in: PQHNA, New York Times (Oct. 1, 2012), C8; Marsh et al., *Buyers Note Color*, 4–6.

119 Misty White Sidell, *Are Birkenstocks Cool Again? Céline, Giambattista Valli & More (PHOTOS)*, in: The Daily Beast (Nov. 12, 2012), https://www.thedailybeast.com/are-birkenstocks-cool-again-celine-giambattista-valli-and-more-photos (accessed Mar. 15, 2022).

120 Rebecca Mead, *Sole Cycle*, in: The New Yorker (Mar. 16, 2015), https://www.newyorker.com/magazine/2015/03/23/sole-cycle-rebecca-mead (accessed Feb. 15, 2022); Vogue Runway, *Burberry: Spring 2013 Menswear*, in: Vogue Runway, https://www.vogue.com/fashion-shows/spring-2013-menswear/burberry-prorsum/slideshow/collection#28 (accessed Feb. 15, 2022).

121 Rachel Strugatz, *Accessories: Social Media's Impact on Spring*, in: WWDA, WWD 204 (Nov. 12, 2012), 8.

122 Simon Chilvers, *It's the Year of the Birkenstock*, in: The Guardian (Feb. 5, 2013), https://www.theguardian.com/fashion/shortcuts/2013/feb/05/its-year-of-the-birkenstock (accessed Feb. 15, 2022).

123 Chioma Nnadi, *Pretty Ugly: Why Vogue Girls Have Fallen for the Birkenstock*, in: Vogue (June 29, 2013), https://www.vogue.com/article/pretty-ugly-why-vogue-girls-have-fallen-for-the-birkenstock (accessed Feb. 15, 2022).

124 Cathy Horyn, *The Dwarf, the Prince and the Diamond in the Mountain: An Unlikely Fable, in Which Birkenstocks Become Cool and Double Sales Overnight*, in: The Cut (Aug. 20, 2018), https://www.thecut.com/2018/08/cathy-horyn-on-birkenstocks-unlikely-rise.html (accessed Feb. 15, 2022).

125 CA Birkenstock, BBG 13. 001, Birkenstock Internal Source One Birkenstock 250 Project Interview 1 Transcript.doc, 10–13.

126 Ibid., 14–15.

127 Ibid., 15.

128 CA Birkenstock, BDF 4.B. 008, Zeitzeugen_Koji Tanemoto_Transkription.docx.

129 Ibid., 11; CA Birkenstock, BDF 4.B. 006, 181026_Zeitzeugen_ITV_Yasuyuki_Umino_Clean_ Version_V2.mp4.

130 CA Birkenstock, BDF 4.B. 008, Zeitzeugen_Koji Tanemoto_Transkription.docx, 11, 14.

131 Hypebeast, *TATAMI 2013 Capsule Collection*, https://hypebeast.com/2013/8/tatami-2013-capsule-collection (accessed Jan. 10, 2022).

132 Amanda Kaiser, *Chitose Abe: The Enigma*, in: WWD (Apr. 29, 2015), https://wwd.com/fashion-news/designer-luxury/chitose-abe-the-enigma-designer-wwd6-10117900/ (accessed Feb. 10, 2022); CA Birkenstock, BDF 4.B. 008, Zeitzeugen_Koji Tanemoto_Transkription.docx, 9; CA Birkenstock, 2013_PublicCommunications_PressRelease_TatamiXPendleton.tiff, "Tatami

x Pendleton," 2013; CA Birkenstock, BBG. 4. 055, 2013_PublicCommunicatons_PressRelease_TatamiXPeopleTree.tiff, "Tatami x People Tree," 2013; Hypebeast, *Letting the Dogs Out: A Look at the Return of Sandals in Fashion*, https://hypebeast.com/2013/7/letting-the-dogs-out-a-look-at-the-return-of-sandals-in-fashion (accessed Feb. 15, 2022).

133 CA Birkenstock, BBG 13. 001, Klaus Baumann Interview Transcript.doc, "Klaus Baumann Interview Birkenstock 250 Project," Apr. 1, 2022, 8.

134 Mead, *Sole Cycle.*

135 Horyn, *The Dwarf, the Prince and the Diamond in the Mountain*; Emily Sutherland, *Beyond the Comfort Zone*, in: Drapers (Aug. 16, 2019), 22.

136 Katya Foreman, *Birkenstock Opens Global Paris Office*, in: WWD (Jan. 10, 2019), 6; Silke Wichert, *Lass laufen*, in: Süddeutsche Zeitung (Dec. 31, 2019), 9.

137 Mead, *Sole Cycle.*

138 Ibid., 19.

139 Friedmann Karig, *Auf Lauten Sohlen,* in: Die Zeit (Sept. 24, 2015).

140 Mead, *Sole Cycle.*

141 CA Birkenstock, BBG 13. 001, Klaus Baumann Interview Transcript.doc, 4, 7.

142 Ibid., 13.

143 CA Birkenstock, BBG 13. 001, Melissa Drier Interview Transcript.doc, 4–5.

144 CA Birkenstock, BBG 13. 001, Birkenstock Internal Source One Birkenstock 250 Project Interview 1 Transcript.doc, 15, 5.

145 Ibid., 7, 8.

146 Jean-Noël Kapferer, *Kapferer on Luxury: How Luxury Brands Can Grow Yet Remain Rare,* London 2015, 1.

147 Danielle Alleres, *Spécificités et strategies marketing des differents univers du luxe*, in: Revue Français du Marketing 132 (1991), 71–95.

148 Yann Truong et al., *New Luxury Brand Positioning and the Emergence of Masstige Brands*, in: Brand Management 16 (2009), 375–382, 376; Michael Silverstein et al., *Trading Up: Why Consumers Want New Luxury Goods—and How Companies Create Them*, London 2008.

149 Pierre-Yves Donzé, *A Business History of the Swatch Watch Group: The Rebirth of Swiss Watchmaking and the Globalization of the Luxury Industry*, Basingstoke 2014, 8–9.

150 Lea Chernikoff, *The Top 20 Designer Collaborations: A Timeline*, in: Fashionista (Apr. 9, 2014). https://fashionista.com/2012/06/the-top-20-designer-collaborations-a-timeline (accessed Nov. 16, 2022); David Livingstone, *MEN'S FASHION: J.Crew's Frank Muytens is moving menswear into the future with his cool understanding of the past*, in: Fashion (Apr. 21, 2012), https://fashion-magazine.com/style/mens-fashion-jcrew-frank-muytjens/ (accessed Nov. 16, 2022).

151 CA Birkenstock, BBG 13. 001, Birkenstock Internal Source One Birkenstock 250 Project Interview 2 Transcript.doc, 13.

152 CA Birkenstock, BBG 13. 001, Post Interview Email Birkenstock Internal Source One June 4 2022 J.Crew Mens Launch Email.pdf, "J.Crew Men's Launch," June 4, 2022.

153 CA Birkenstock, BBG 13. 001, Post Interview Email Birkenstock Internal Source One June 4 2022 J.Crew Mens Launch Email.pdf; Gina Marinelli, *Even Jenna Lyons Is Surprised That Birkenstocks Are Back*, in: Refinery29 (June 14, 2014), https://www.refinery29.com/en-us/2014/06/69554/jenna-lyons-jcrew-birkenstocks (accessed Mar. 15. 2022).

154 White Sidell, *Are Birkenstocks Cool Again?*

155 Vanessa Patrick/Alokparna (Sonia) Basu Monga, *Building and Growing Luxury Brands: Strategies for Pursuing Growth While Maintaining Brand Coherence*, in: Felicitas Morhart et al., Research Handbook on Luxury Branding, Cheltenham 2020, 117–138.

156 CA Birkenstock, BBG 13. 001, Birkenstock Internal Source One Birkenstock 250 Project Interview 1 Transcript.doc.

157 CA Birkenstock, BBG 13. 001, Jérôme LaMaar Birkenstock 250 Project Interview Transcript April 25 2022.doc, "Jérôme LaMaar Birkenstock 250 Project Interview Transcript," Apr. 25, 2022, 7, 8, 16; CA Birkenstock, Screen Shot 2022-05-06 at 10.22.02 AM.png, n. d.

158 CA Birkenstock, BBG 13. 001, Jérôme LaMaar Birkenstock 250 Project Interview Transcript April 25 2022.doc, 12.

Notes 425

159 Fawnia Soo Hoo, *Birkenstock Not Surprised by Its Runway Domination*, in: Fashionista (Sept. 10, 2013), https://fashionista.com/2013/09/birkenstocks-rep-on-the-brands-runway-domination-we-did-see-it-coming (accessed Apr. 3, 2022).

160 Hayley Phelan, *Uhly Is in for Summer Footwear*, in: Fashionista (July 5, 2013), https://fashionista.com/2013/07/ugly-is-in-when-it-comes-to-footwear (accessed Apr. 3, 2022).

161 Alexandra Jacobs, *Call It the Birkenstock Summer*, in: New York Times (Aug. 21, 2014) E7, in: PQHNA; Vogue Runway, *Calvin Klein Collection Pre-Fall 2014*, in: Vogue (Dec. 4, 2013), https://www.vogue.com/fashion-shows/pre-fall-2014/calvin-klein-collection (accessed Mar. 17, 2022); Jo Ellison, *Chanel's Fly Buy*, in: The Financial Times (Aug. 7, 2015), 10, in: FTHA.

162 CA Birkenstock, BBG 13. 001, Humberto Leon Birkenstock 250 Project Interview Transcript April 26, 2022, "Humberto Leon Birkenstock 250 Project Interview Transcript," 7; Daisy Sitch, *Opening Ceremony's Birkenstocks: Are These the Ugliest Shoes of All Time?* In: Huffington Post (Aug. 14, 2014), https://www.huffingtonpost.co.uk/2014/08/14/opening-ceremony-s-birkenstocks-are-these-the-ugliest-shoes-of-all-time_n_7333456.html (accessed Mar. 17, 2022).

163 CA Birkenstock, BBG 13. 001, Humberto Leon Birkenstock 250 Project Interview Transcript April 26, 2022, 5.

164 Steff Yotka, *Opening Ceremony Spring 2018 Ready-to-Wear*, in: Vogue (Mar. 8, 2018), https://www.vogue.com/fashion-shows/spring-2018-ready-to-wear/opening-ceremony (accessed Mar. 17, 2022); CA Birkenstock, BBG 13. 001, Humberto Leon Birkenstock 250 Project Interview Transcript April 26, 2022, 9–10.

165 CA Birkenstock, BBG 13. 001, Humberto Leon Birkenstock 250 Project Interview Transcript April 26, 2022, 9–10.

166 Hypebeast, *Aaron De La Cruz for 55DSL & Birkenstock, Curated by Arkitip Official Launch* (Feb. 8, 2014), https://hypebeast.com/2014/2/the-55dsl-x-arkitip-x-aaron-de-la-cruz-x-birkenstock-launches (accessed Mar. 18, 2022).

167 CA Birkenstock, BBG 13. 001, Birkenstock Internal Source One Birkenstock 250 Project Interview 2 Transcript.doc, 11.

168 Drier, *CEO Talks*, 19–20.

169 Melissa Drier, *Birkenstock Taps Dan Tobin Smith for New Campaign*, in: WWD (Jan. 31, 2017), https://wwd.com/business-news/marketing-promotion/birkenstock-taps-dan-tobin-smith-for-new-campaign-10770480/ (accessed Mar. 19, 2022); Birkenstock, *Behind the Scenes: 2017 Spring/Summer Photo Shoot*. https://www.birkenstock.com/nl-en/magazine/dan-tobin-smith/ (accessed Mar. 19, 2022).

170 Birkenstock, *Die Birkenstock Personality Kampagne*, n. d., https://www.birkenstock.com/ch/magazine/personality-campaign/#:~:text=Die%20Personality%20Kampagne%20ist%20als,pers%C3%B6nlichen%20Umfeld%20in%20Szene%20setzt. (accessed Mar. 14, 2022); Birkenstock, *Die Birkenstock Personality Kampagne Erzählt von Vielfalt und Charakter* (Aug. 14, 2018), https://www.birkenstock-group.com/de/de/detail/die-birkenstock-personality-kampagne-erzaehlt-von-vielfalt-und-charakter/ (accessed Mar. 14, 2022); Samantha Conti, *Manolo & Kristina Blahnik Star in Birkenstock's Latest Campaign*, in: Footwear News (Jan. 30, 2020), https://footwearnews.com/2020/business/marketing/kristina-manolo-blahnik-birkenstock-personality-campaign-1202912734/ (accessed Mar. 14, 2022).

171 CA Birkenstock, BBG 13. 001, Birkenstock Internal Source Two Birkenstock 250 Project Interview Transcript.doc, 10.

172 CA Birkenstock, BBG 13. 001, Birkenstock Internal Source One Birkenstock 250 Project Interview 1 Transcript.doc, 11.

173 Kathy Foreman, *Birkenstock Opens Global Paris Office*, in: WWDA, WWD (Jan. 10, 2019), 6; Conti, *Manolo & Kristina Blahnik Star in Birkenstock's Latest Campaign.*; Lisa Lockwood, *Proenza Schouler Partners with Birkenstock*, in: WWD (Sept. 6, 2019), 4, in: WWDA.

174 CA Birkenstock, BBG 2. 018-1, 19_Birkenstock_NEWS_Magazin_Ausgabe_1_2019_DE.pdf, "Global Press Factory Event" in: Birkenstock News (2019) 75–82, 77, Translation by the author.

175 Ibid.

176 Horyn, *The Dwarf, the Prince and the Diamond in the Mountain.*

177 CA Birkenstock, 18_Birkenstock_NEWS_Special_Messe&Event_2018_EN.pdf, "Birkenstock News Trade Fair and Event Special," 2018, 9.

178 Lavanga, *The Role of The Pitti Uomo Trade Fair in the Menswear Fashion Industry.*

179 Luke Leitch, *BirkenShock! After 242 Years, Birkenstock Premieres at Paris Fashion Week*, in: Vogue (June 25, 2017), https://www.vogue.com/article/paris-fashion-week-birkenstock (accessed Apr. 3, 2022); CA Birkenstock, GSC_WELCOME.docx, "Birkenstock Spring/ Summer 2018 Presentation," 2017.

180 CA Birkenstock, BBG 13. 001, KCDbriefing (2).pdf, "Marketing A.W Production Review," 2017; CA Birkenstock, Birkenstock_GSC_Paris.pdf, "Birkenstock Orangerie Éphémere Des Tuileries Paris," 2017; CA Birkenstock, BBG. 4. 055, Birkenstock_Paris_Invite_21 × 261_010617.pdf, "Invitation," 2017; CA Birkenstock, BBG. 4. 055, Ersparnisse Paris_final.pdf, "Overall Budget inkl. Beds and Cosmetics," 2017; CA Birkenstock, BBG. 4. 055, Birkenstock Internal Source Two Birkenstock 250 Project Interview Transcript.doc, 2.

181 Drier, *CEO Talks*, 20.

182 Birkenstock, *Birkenstock Makes its Pitti Uomo 93 Appearance in Florence* (Jan. 10, 2018), https://www.birkenstock-group.com/de/en/detail/birkenstock-makes-its-pitti-uomo-93-appearance-in-florence/ (accessed Mar. 17, 2022).

183 Ibid.; CA Birkenstock, BBG 2. 017-1, 18_Birkenstock_NEWS_Special_Messe&Event_2018_EN.pdf, 5.

184 Katya Foreman et al., *Retailers Praise Pitti Uomo's Good Vibrations*, in: WWDA, WWD (June 15, 2018), 22; Sandra Salibian, *Florence to Bloom during Pitti Uomo*, in: WWDA, WWD (May 17, 2018), 8.

185 CA Birkenstock, BBG 13. 001, Birkenstock Internal Source Two Birkenstock 250 Project Interview Transcript.doc, 7; CA Birkenstock, BBG. 4. 055, Birkenstock Event Images.pdf, 2018.

186 CA Birkenstock, BBG 13. 001, Birkenstock Internal Source Two Birkenstock 250 Project Interview Transcript.doc, 9.

187 CA Birkenstock, BBG 13. 001, Birkenstock Internal Source One Birkenstock 250 Project Interview 2 Transcript.doc, 4.

188 CA Birkenstock, BBG 13. 001, Birkenstock Internal Source One Birkenstock 250 Project Interview 2 Transcript.doc, 4; CA Birkenstock, Klaus Baumann Interview Transcript.doc, 17.

189 Patrick/Basu Monga, *Building and Growing Luxury Brands*, 117.

190 CA Birkenstock, BBG 13. 001, Birkenstock Internal Source Two Birkenstock 250 Project Interview Transcript.doc, 5.

191 Ibid., 12.

192 CA Birkenstock, BBG 13. 001, Klaus Baumann Interview Transcript.doc, 16.

193 Ibid., 19.

194 Birkenstock, *Birkenstockbox.com/* (2017), https://www.birkenstock.com/nl-en/box-murkudis/ (accessed Oct. 10, 2021).

195 CA Birkenstock, BBG 13. 001, Birkenstock Internal Source Two Birkenstock 250 Project Interview Transcript.doc, 1.; CA Birkenstock, BBG 13. 001, Gonzalez Haase AAG, Judith Haase and Pierre Jorge Gonzalez Interview Transcript Birkenstock 250 Project.doc, "Gonzalez Haase AAG, Judith Haase and Pierre Jorge Gonzalez Interview Birkenstock 250 Project," Mar. 10, 2022, 1–5.

196 CA Birkenstock, BBG 13. 001, Birkenstock Internal Source Two Birkenstock 250 Project Interview Transcript.doc, 1.

197 CA Birkenstock, BBG 13. 001, Gonzalez Haase AAG, Judith Haase and Pierre Jorge Gonzalez Interview Transcript Birkenstock 250 Project.doc, 3.

198 Ibid., 2–3.

199 Birkenstock, *His Limited Edition* (2017) https://www.birkenstockbox.com/berlin/his-limited-edition (accessed Oct. 3, 2022); Birkenstock, *Birkenstock Box Opens At Its First Location At Andreas Murkudis Berlin* (2017) https://www.birkenstock.com/nl-en/magazine/events/murkudis/ (accessed Oct. 3, 2021); Birkenstock, *Gonzalez/Haase in Conversation With Andreas Murkudis* (2017), https://www.birkenstockbox.com/berlin/text-messages/view (accessed Oct. 3, 2021); CA Birkenstock, BBG 13. 001, Birkenstock Internal Source Two Birkenstock 250 Project Interview Transcript.doc, 1–2.

200 CA Birkenstock, BBG 13. 001, Birkenstock Internal Source One Birkenstock 250 Project Interview 2 Transcript.doc, 15–16.

201 Birkenstock, *Birkenstock Box #2: Birkenstock Box opens in Manhattan in collaboration with BARNEYS NEW YORK* (2017), https://www.birkenstock.com/nl/box-barneys/ (accessed Oct. 3, 2021); Whitney, *Art Party 2017* (2017), https://whitney.org/art-party2017 (accessed Oct. 3, 2021); Birkenstock, *The Whitney Museum of American Art in New York City hosted its annual Art Party with BIRKENSTOCK* (2017), https://www.birkenstock.com/nl-en/magazine/events/whitney-art-party-2017/ (accessed Oct. 3, 2021).

202 Birkenstock, *Birkenstock Box #3: 10 Corso Como Mailand* (2017), https://www.birkenstock.com/nl-en/10-corso-como/ (accessed Oct. 3, 2021); Anja Probe, *Birkenstock Box macht Halt bei 10 Corso Como*, in: TextilWirtschaft (Sept. 22, 2017), https://www.textilwirtschaft.de/business/news/retail-konzept-birkenstock-box-macht-halt-bei-10-corso-como-206601 (accessed Oct. 14, 2021); CA Birkenstock, BBG. 4. 055, 01_EN 10CC_ BIRKENSTOCK BOX.Press Release 07092017.pdf, "Birkenstock Box, The Brand's Mobile Retail Concept Continues Its Journey to Milan in Partnership with 10 Corso Como and Renowned Artist Kris Ruhs," 2017; 10 Corso Como, *10 Corso Como x Birkenstock Evening* (Sept. 22, 2017), https://www.10corsocomo.com/events-archive/10-corso-como-x-birkenstock-evening/ (accessed Oct. 14, 2021).

203 Dominique Muret, *Carla Sozzani (10 Corso Como): "È la Moda che si è ispirata a Birkenstock, e non il contrario!"*, in: Fashion Network (Sept. 25, 2017), https://it.fashionnetwork.com/news/carla-sozzani e la moda che si e ispirata a birkenstock-e-non-il-contrario-,872569.html (accessed Oct. 14, 2021), translation by the author.

204 Marcy Medina, *Fashion Scoops: In the Box*, in: WWD (Apr. 18, 2018), 22, in: WWDA; Julia Russo, *Michèle Lamy and Stefano Tonchi Kick Off the Global Launch of Birkenstock Box x Rick Owens in Los Angeles*, in: Vogue (Apr. 18, 2018), https://www.vogue.com/article/birkenstock-box-rick-owens-launch-party-los-angeles-2018 (accessed Oct. 18, 2021); CA Birkenstock, BBG. 4. 055, 11.4. 2018 – BIRKENSTOCK BOX L. A. RICK OWENS (DE), Press Release, 2018.

205 CA Birkenstock, BBG 13. 001, Birkenstock Internal Source Two Birkenstock 250 Project Interview Transcript.doc, 2.

206 Nicole Phelps, *Rick Owens: Spring 2019 Ready-to-Wear*, in: Vogue (Sept. 27, 2018), https://www.vogue.com/fashion-shows/spring-2019-ready-to-wear/rick-owens (accessed Oct. 18, 2021); Luke Leitch, *Rick Owens: Spring 2019 Menswear*, in: Vogue (June 21, 2018), https://www.vogue.com/fashion-shows/spring-2019-menswear/rick-owens (accessed Oct. 18, 2021); CA Birkenstock, BBG 13. 001, Birkenstock Internal Source Two Birkenstock 250 Project Interview Transcript.doc, 2; CA Birkenstock, BBG 13. 001, Rick Owens X Birkenstock @ I. T.pdf, n. d.

207 CA Birkenstock, BBG 13. 001, Marie-Louise Sció Interview Birkenstock 250 Project 21 March 2022 Transcript.doc, "Marie-Louise Sció Interview Transcript Birkenstock 250 Project," 2.

208 Birkenstock, *Birkenstock and the Hotel Il Pellicano Launch the Il Dolce Far Niente Collection for SS 2019* (May 15, 2019), https://www.birkenstock-group.com/de/en/detail/birkenstock-and-the-hotel-il-pellicano-launch-the-il-dolce-far-niente-collection-for-ss19/ (accessed Feb. 5, 2022); 8.

209 CA Birkenstock, BBG 13. 001, 1774_BIRKENSTOCK_X_Il_Pellicano_Breakfast_Event_Report_March_3_Paris.pdf, "1774 Birkenstock and Hotel Il Pellicano," 2019; CA Birkenstock, BBG 13. 001, Marie-Louise Sció Interview Birkenstock 250 Project 21 March 2022 Transcript. doc, 10–12; CA Birkenstock, BBG 13. 001, Birkenstock Internal Source Two Birkenstock 250 Project Interview Transcript.doc, 4–6; CA Birkenstock, BIRKENSTOCK_IL_Pellicano_Press_launch_Event_Facebook2 low.pdf, "Facebook: Birkenstock Il Pellicano Il Dolce Far Niente Press Launch Event April 2019," 2019; CA Birkenstock, BBG 13. 001, BIRKENSTOCK-GLCE_PopUp_Event_Images.pdf, "Galeries Lafayette Champs Élysées Collection Pop Up," 2019.

210 CA Birkenstock, BBG 13. 001, Alistair O'Neill, Central Saint Martins Interview Transcript.doc, "Alistair O'Neill, Central Saint Martins Birkenstock 250 Interview Transcript," Mar. 25, 2022, 5, 7, 12, 15–24; CA Birkenstock, BBG 13. 001, BIRKENSTOCK MA Fashion Project Fashion Design and Theory CSM.pdf, "MA Fashion Project| Birkenstock 1774: Fashion Design, History and Theory," n. d.

211 Laura Hawkins, *Birkenstock Sandals Redesigned by Central Saint Martins Students*, in: Wallpaper (Mar. 1, 2021), https://www.wallpaper.com/fashion/birkenstock-sandal-redesigned-central-saint-martins-students (accessed Mar. 12, 2022); Birkenstock 1774, *Alecsander Rothschild*, 2021, https://www.birkenstock.com/nl/1774/csm/rothschild/ (accessed Mar. 12, 2022); Birkenstock 1774, *Dingyun Zhang*, 2021, https://www.birkenstock.com/nl/1774/csm/zhang/

(accessed Mar. 12, 2022); Birkenstock 1774, Alex Wolfe, 2021 https://www.birkenstock.com/nl/1774/csm/wolfe/ (accessed Mar. 12, 2022); Birkenstock 1774, *Saskia Lenaerts*, 2021, https://www.birkenstock.com/nl/1774/csm/lenaerts/ (accessed Mar. 12, 2022).

212 Hypebeast, *Central Saint Martin's MA Fashion Students Rework Your Favourite WFH Birkenstocks,* 2021, https://hypebeast.com/2021/3/birkenstock-central-saint-martins-alex-wolfe-alecsander-rothschild-saskia-lenaerts-dingyun-zhang (accessed Mar. 12, 2022).

213 CA Birkenstock, BBG 13. 001, Alistair O'Neill, Central Saint Martins Interview Transcript.doc, 26.

214 Katya Foreman, *Birkenstock Opens Global Paris Office*, in: WWDA, WWD (Jan. 10, 2019), 6.

215 CA Birkenstock, BBG 13. 001, Birkenstock Internal Source Two Birkenstock 250 Project Interview Transcript.doc, 3.

216 Jonathan Heaf, *Birkenstock: Inside a $ 5 bn Brand*, in: The Financial Times (Mar. 7, 2022), https://www.ft.com/content/64c71db0-dd59-450d-94c6-5dea111dc752 (accessed Apr. 8, 2022).

217 CA Birkenstock, BBG 13. 001, Birkenstock Internal Source Two Birkenstock 250 Project Interview Transcript.doc, 21.

218 CA Birkenstock, BBG 13. 001, Klaus Baumann Interview Transcript.doc, 10, 24.

219 Heaf, *Birkenstock*.

220 CA Birkenstock, BBG 13. 001, Robert Younger Birkenstock 250 Interview Transcript.doc, "Robert Younger Birkenstock 250 Project Interview Recording Transcript," Apr. 14, 2022, 4–5, 17–18.

221 CA Birkenstock, BDF 4.B. 006, 181026_Zeitzeugen_ITV_Yasuyuki_Umino_Clean_Version_V2.mp4; Kelly Wetherille, *Neighbourhood Watch: Growth in Ginza*, in: WWD 211 (May 18, 2016), 42.

222 CA Birkenstock, BBG 4. 055, Market Launch Japan_Birkenstock_English.pdf, "Press Release: Market Launch Japan," November 2017.

223 CA Birkenstock, BBG 4. 055, Market Launch Japan_Birkenstock_English.pdf.

224 CA Birkenstock, BBG 4. 055, BIRKENSTOCK Group – UK Market Entry Press Release, "Press Release: Global footwear brand Birkenstock takes over direct distribution in the UK," 2017; CA Birkenstock, BBG 4. 055, London_Store-PressRelease_DRAFT_6-101117, "Press Release: Birkenstock Opens First Official Brand Store in the UK," Nov. 10, 2017.

225 CA Birkenstock, BBG 4. 055, Direct Distribution UK – Additional Information.docx, "Direct Distribution UK," n.d., 1.

226 Birkenstock, *Birkenstock Opens First Brand Store in Denmark,* May 30, 2018, https://www.birkenstock-group.com/de/en/detail-press/birkenstock-opens-first-brand-store-in-denmark/ (accessed Apr. 3, 2022); Birkenstock, *Birkenstock Online Now Available in Japan*, July 17, 2017, https://www.birkenstock-group.com/de/en/detail-press/birkenstock-online-store-now-available-in-japan/ (accessed Apr. 3, 2022).

227 Barbara Schneider-Levy, *Birkenstock Opens Second US Store, This Time in California's Hip Venice Beach*, in: Footwear News (Aug. 1, 2019), https://footwearnews.com/2019/business/retail/birkenstock-store-venice-beach-abott-kinney-los-angeles-1202810713/ (accessed Apr. 3, 2022); Jan Schroder, *Birkenstock expandiert in London*, in: Fashion United (Aug. 19, 2019), https://fashionunited.de/nachrichten/einzelhandel/birkenstock-expandiert-in-london/2019081932814 (accessed Apr. 3, 2022); Alicia Mares, *Birkenstock desembarca en Puebla con su tienda number 12 a nivel nacional,*in: Fashion Network (July 31, 2019), https://mx.fashionnetwork.com/news/Birkenstock-desembarca-en-puebla-con-su-tienda-numero-12-a-nivel-nacional,1125594.html (accessed Apr. 3, 2022)

228 Isabel Leonhardt, *Birkenstock übernimmt Vertrieb in der Schweiz in Eigenregie*, in: Fashion Network.de (Nov. 5, 2019), https://de.fashionnetwork.com/news/Birkenstock-ubernimmt-vertrieb-in-der-schweiz-in-eigenregie,1154433.html (accessed Apr. 3, 2022).

229 Heaf, *Birkenstock*.

230 Ibid.

231 Alexandra Pastore, *Business Insight: Consumers Are Trading in Summer Vacation Plans for the Great Outdoors*, in: WWD (June 9, 2020), https://wwd.com/business-news/business-features/coronavirus-trends-consumers-are-trading-in-summer-vacation-plans-for-the-great-outdoors-1203646550/ (accessed May 6, 2022).

232 Tianwei Zhang, *Lyst: North Face Nuptse Jacket Is the Hottest Item Online,* in: WWD (Jan. 6, 2021), 5, in: WWDA.

233 CA Birkenstock, BBG 13. 001, Birkenstock Internal Source Two Birkenstock 250 Project Interview Transcript.doc, 3.

234 Jennie Bell, *How Birkenstock Won 2020 & Became FN's Brand of the Year,* in: Footwear News (Dec. 6, 2020), https://footwearnews.com/2020/business/awards/birkenstock-fnaa-2020-brand-year-1203080978/ (accessed Apr. 14, 2022).

235 Heaf, *Birkenstock.*

236 Ibid.

237 Ibid.

238 CA Birkenstock, BBG 4. 055, LCatterton_2021 CA Birkenstock.docx, "Strategische Partnerschaft mit L Catterton und Bernard Arnault," Feb. 26, 2021.

239 Evan Clark, *Birkenstock and L Catterton Talks Get Exclusive,* in: WWD (Feb. 8, 2021), https://wwd.com/business-news/financial/birkenstock-l-catterton-lvmh-bernard-arnault-sandals-1234725626/ (accessed Apr. 14, 2022); Sarah Butler, *German Sandal Maker Birkenstock in €4bn Takeover Battle,* in: The Guardian (Feb. 9, 2021), https://www.theguardian.com/business/2021/feb/09/german-sandal-maker-birkenstock-in-4bn-takeover-battle (accessed Apr. 14, 2022).

240 CA Birkenstock, BBG 4. 055, LCatterton_2021 CA Birkenstock.docx.

241 Nolan Giles, *Notes on a Sandal.* In: Monocle (Nov. 2021), 172.

242 CA Birkenstock, BBG 4. 055, LCatterton_2021 CA Birkenstock.docx.

243 Miles Socha, *Fashion Scoop: Down to Earth,* in: WWDA, WWD (Sept. 14, 2020) 29; Hypebeast, *Rick Owens Renuintes with Birkenstock for an All-Black Collection,* https://hypebeast.com/2021/6/rick-owens-birkenstock-boston-arizona-rotterdam-release-details (accessed Apr. 15, 2022); Hypebeast, *Birkenstock and Proenza Schouler Serve Up Polished Unisex Capsule,* https://hypebeast.com/2021/8/birkenstock-proenza-schouler-collaboration-release-info (accessed Apr. 15, 2022); Hypebeast, *KITH Introduces Bold Patterns and Collaborations in Wide-Ranging Spring 2021 Collection,* https://hypebeast.com/2021/2/kith-spring-2021-lookbook-collaborations-details (accessed Apr. 15, 2022); Hypebeast, *The Revival of the Air Jordan 4 'Lightening' Strikes Hard in This Week's Best Footwear Drops,* https://hypebeast.com/2021/8/best-sneaker-releases-august-week-4-air-jordan-4-lightning-sacai-fragment-design-nike-ldwaffle-blackened-blue-wtaps-new-balance-990v2 (accessed Apr. 16, 2022); Hypebeast, *Jil Sander+ and Birkenstock Update Signature Silhouettes for Lifestyle Outdoors,* https://hypebeast.com/2021/6/jil-sander-birkenstock-collaboration-luke-lucie-meier-release-details (accessed Apr. 16, 2022); Hypebeast, *Toogood's Birkenstock Collaboration Includes Luxe Sandals, Apparel and Even a Bed,* https://hypebeast.com/2021/4/toogood-birkenstock-forager-mudlark-beachcomber-sandals-bed-apparel-collaboration (accessed Apr. 16, 2022).

244 Alexandre Marin, *Dior collabore avec Birkenstock!,* in: Vogue (Jan. 21, 2022), https://www.vogue.fr/vogue-hommes/article/dior-birkenstock-automne-hiver-2022-2023 (accessed Jan. 22, 2022).

245 Alice Newbold, *Manolo Blahnik Crystalizes Birkenstocks for His Most Memorable Collab to Date,* in: Vogue (Mar. 14, 2022), https://www.vogue.com/article/manolo-blahnik-birkenstock-collaboration (accessed Mar. 14, 2022).

Bare Toes under Straps: The History of the Sandal

1 See Kate Ravilious, *Ältester Lederschuh der Welt ist überraschend modern,* in: National Geographic (Jan. 15, 2020), www.nationalgeographic.de/geschichte-und-kultur/2020/01/aeltester-lederschuh-der-welt-ist-ueberraschend-modern (accessed July 22, 2022); Thomas J. Connolly, *Fort Rock Sandals,* in: Oregon Encyclopedia, www.oregonencyclopedia.org/articles/fort_rock_sandals/#.YwL-BvHP3Ko (accessed July 5, 2022).

2 See Tamara Spitzing, *Auf Schusters Rappen durch die Geschichte,* in: Michael Andritzky et al. (eds.), Z. B. Schuhe: Vom bloßen Fuß zum Stöckelschuh; Eine Kulturgeschichte der Fußbekleidung, Giessen 1988, 47–57, here: 47.

3 See Klaus Heyer, *Von Homer bis Caligula,* in: Michael Andritzky et al. (eds.), *Z. B. Schuhe, Vom bloßen Fuß zum Stöckelschuh. Eine Kulturgeschichte der Fußbekleidung,* (Giessen, 1988), 42–46, here: 45.

4 See Angelika Starbatty, *Aussehen ist Ansichtssache: Kleidung in der Kommunikation der römischen Antike*, Munich 2010, 157; Spitzing, *Auf Schusters Rappen*, 47.

5 See Peter Knötzele, *Römische Schuhe: Luxus an den Füssen*, Stuttgart 2007, 55.

6 See *Sandale*, in: Digitales Wörterbuch der deutschen Sprache, www.dwds.de/wb/Sandale (accessed Aug. 22, 2022); Rolf Hurschmann, *Sandale*, in: Hubert Cancik/Helmuth Schneider (eds.), Der Neue Pauly (Antike), dx.doi.org/10.1163/1574-9347_dnp_e1100700 (accessed July 24, 2023).

7 See Ruth Maria Hirschberg, *Schuhwerk im ländlichen Bereich*, (2003), 6, www.brandenburg1260. de/schuhwerk.pdf (accessed June 15, 2022).

8 See Gabriele Praschl-Bichler, *Affenhaube, Schellentracht und Wendeschuh. Kleidung und Mode im Mittelalter*, Munich 2011, 166.

9 See Jonathan Walford, *The Seductive Shoe: Four Centuries of Fashion Footwear*, London 2007.

10 See Gerhard Schulz, *Die deutsche Literatur zwischen Französischer Revolution und Restauration*, part 1, *1789–1806*, Munich 22000, 63.

11 See Sabine Huschka, *Merce Cunningham und der Moderne Tanz: Körperkonzepte, Choreographie und Tanzästhetik*, Würzburg 2000, 60.

12 See Anne Sudrow, *Der Schuh im Nationalsozialismus: Eine Produktgeschichte im deutsch-britisch-amerikanischen Vergleich*, Göttingen 2010, 61.

13 Ibid., 63f.

14 See Ulrich Linse, *Procrustes ante Portas! Oder: Wo dem Bürgertum der Schuh drückt*, in: Michael Andritzky et al. (eds.), *Z. B. Schuhe. Vom bloßen Fuß zum Stöckelschuh. Eine Kulturgeschichte der Fußbekleidung*, Giessen 1988, 72–80, here: 74.

15 Diamant Schuhfabrik, *Firmenchronik*, https://www.diamant.net/unternehmen/firmenchronik (accessed Aug. 14, 2022).

16 See Berkemann, *Geschichte des Unternehmens Berkemann*, www.berkemann.com/unternehmen/geschichte/ (accessed Sept. 10, 2022); see also the essay by Jörg Lesczenski in this volume.

17 See Nike U. Breyer, *Gymnastiksandale nach Prof. Thomsen*, in: Wolfgang Antweiler (ed.), Schritt für Schritt: Die Geburt des modernen Schuhs, Hilden 2013, 126.

18 Gerhard Neckermann/Hans Wessels, *Struktur und Wettbewerbsfähigkeit der Schuhindustrie in der Bundesrepublik Deutschland*, Berlin 1988, 30.

19 See *Salonfähige Sandale*, in: TextilWirtschaft (June 26, 1997), 122.

Brands without Borders: Collaborations in the Fashion Segment

1 See Ellen Burney, *Design für alle? Die Geschichte der H&M-Designer-Kooperationen*, in: Vogue (Oct. 18, 2018), www.vogue.de/mode/artikel/geschichte-der-hm-designer-kooperationen (accessed July 10, 2022); *Wie viel sind die H&M-Klamotten von Lagerfeld jetzt noch wert?*, in: Focus (Sept. 5, 2019), www.focus.de/finanzen/news/unternehmen/karl-lagerfeld-fuer-h-m-wie-viel-sind-die-klamotten-jetzt-noch-wert_id_10347732.html (accessed July 1, 2022).

2 See Ellie Pithers, *Kenzo: Are We Bored of High-Low Fashion Collaborations?*, in: Vogue (Nov. 3, 2016), www.vogue.co.uk/article/are-we-bored-of-high-low-fashion-collaborations (accessed July 10, 2022).

3 See Pierre-Yves Donzé, *Luxury as an Industry*, in: Pierre-Yves Donzé et al. (eds.), The Oxford Handbook of Luxury Business, Oxford 2022, 59–78, here: 67.

4 See ibid., 60.

5 See Silvia Ihring, *Kooperationen von Modemarken. Jetzt geht Zalando mit Marni*, in: NZZ Bellevue (Oct. 24, 2016), bellevue.nzz.ch/mode-beauty/bringen-es-die-alljaehrlichen-mode-kooperationen-heute-noch-jetzt-geht-zalando-mit-marni-ld.123477 (accessed June 20, 2022).

6 See Paula Soito, *Why Art Is the Cornerstone of Luxury Brands*, in: Art Market Magazine, artmarketmag.com/why-art-is-the-cornerstone-of-luxury-brands (accessed June 21, 2022).

7 See Kasia Hastings, *Mode trifft Kunst: Die legendärsten Kooperationen aller Zeiten*, in: Vogue (July 24, 2019), www.vogue.de/mode/artikel/die-besten-mode-kunst-kooperationen-aller-zeiten (accessed June 25, 2022).

8 See Hastings, *Mode*; Annamma Joy/Russell W. Belk, *Why Luxury Brands Partner with Artists*, in: Pierre-Yves Donzé et al. (eds.), The Oxford Handbook of Luxury Business, Oxford 2022, 309–330, here: 316.

9 Uniqlo, *UNIQLO & KUNST,* in: Uniqlo Today (Feb. 1, 2021), www.uniqlo.com/de/de/news/top-ics/2021020101/ (accessed June 12, 2022).

10 Anna Steiner, *Reich werden mit Turnschuhen,* in: FAZ (Apr. 8, 2018), www.faz.net/aktuell/finanzen/meine-finanzen/sparen-und-geld-anlegen/sneaker-als-geldanlage-das-grosse-geschaeft-mit-raren-sportschuhen-15531092.html (accessed June 13, 2022).

11 See Osman Ahmed, *Stronger Together: Why Designer Collaborations Are Good Business,* in: Vogue (June 12, 2019), www.vogue.fr/fashion/article/stronger-together-why-designer-collaborations-are-good-business (accessed June 13, 2022); Joy/Belk, *Why Luxury Brands,* 309.

12 See Maria Ratzinger, *Skims x Fendi: Kim Kardashian ist ein Ritterschlag in der Modebranche gelungen,* in: L'Officiel (Oct. 26, 2021), www.lofficiel.at/fashion/skims-x-fendi-kim-kardashian-ist-ein-ritterschlag-in-der-modebranche-gelungen (accessed June 20, 2022).

13 See Eduardo Limón, *Nike Air Force 1: Kennen Sie die bedeutendsten Kollaborationen des Kult-Sneakers?,* in: GQ (July 11, 2022), www.gq-magazin.de/mode/artikel/nike-air-force-1-bedeutendsten-kollaborationen (accessed Sept. 27, 2022).

14 See Triana Alonso, *Bershka präsentiert umweltfreundliche Kollaboration mit National Geographic,* in: Fashion Network (Nov. 7, 2019), https://de.fashionnetwork.com/news/Bershka-prasentiert-umweltfreundliche-kollaboration-mit-national-geographic,1155823.html (accessed June 18, 2022).

15 See Tobias Bayer, *Zweiter Teil der Collab Tommy X Timberland. Wie können wir das besser machen?,* in: Textilwirtschaft (Nov. 9, 2021), www.textilwirtschaft.de/fashion/news/zweiter-teil-der-collab-tommy-x-timberland-wie-koennen-wir-das-besser-machen-233232 (accessed June 12, 2022).

From Hilarious Hippies to Hair-Raising Horror and High Fashion: 30 Years of Birkenstocks in Film

1 Jennifer Kaytin Robinson, dir., *Do Revenge,* Netflix 2022.

2 Amy Heckerling, dir., *Clueless,* Paramount Pictures 1995; Michael Lehmann, dir., *Heathers,* New World Pictures 1989.

3 See Ashley Spencer, *"Do Revenge": Paying Homage to Teen Classics by Way of Hitchcock,* in: The New York Times, Sept. 14, 2022, https://www.nytimes.com/2022/09/14/movies/do-revenge-netflix.html (accessed May 2, 2023).

4 Drake Stutesman, *Cooking: Studying Film Costume Design,* in: Sofia Pantouvaki/Peter McNeil (eds.), Performance Costume: New Perspectives and Methods, London 2021, 28.

5 Sheila Whiteley, *Counterculture: The Classical View,* in: James D. Wright (ed.), The International Encyclopedia of the Social and Behavioural Sciences vol. 5, Amsterdam 2015, 80.

6 Britton Stiles Rhuart, *Hippie Films, Hippiesploitation, and the Emerging Counterculture, 1955–1970,* PhD diss., Bowling Green State University 2020, 72.

7 Barry Miles, *Hippie,* New York 2004, 91.

8 Donatella Barbieri, *Costume in Performance: Materiality, Culture, and the Body,* London 2017, 116.

9 Laura Van Waardhuizen, *Birkenstocks,* in: Annette Lynch/Mitchell D. Strauss (eds.), Ethnic Dress in the United States: A Cultural Encyclopedia, Lanham 2014, 32.

10 *New Birkenstocks in Store Now!,* in: Whole Earth Provision Co., Mar. 18, 2022, https://www.wholeearthprovision.com/blog/new-birkenstocks-in-store-now (accessed May 2, 2023).

11 Ribiero, cited in Lou Taylor, *The Study of Dress History,* Manchester 2002, 145.

12 Rina R. Bousalis, *The Counterculture Generation: Idolized, Appropriated, and Misunderstood,* in: The Councilor: A Journal of the Social Studies 82 (2021), 4.

13 Robert Horvitz, *R. Crumb Interview,* in: Whole Earth Collection, July 3, 2018, https://ia903102.us.archive.org/11/items/InterviewWithR.Crumb/RCrumb-interview.html (accessed May 2, 2023).

14 Van Waardhuizen, *Birkenstocks,* 32.

15 Barbieri, *Costume in Performance,* 25.

16 James Melkonian, dir., *The Stoned Age,* Trimark Pictures 1994.

17 Samantha Eddy, *Groped and Gutted: Hollywood's Hegemonic Reimagining of Counterculture,* in: Screen Bodies 5 (2020), 33.

18 Danielle Sepulveres, *25 Years Later, I Now Realise That Travis Birkenstock Is the Real Hero of* Clueless, in: Esquire, July 19, 2020, https://www.esquire.com/entertainment/movies/a33349827/clueless-25-year-anniversary-travis-birkenstock-breckin-meyer-essay/ (accessed May 2, 2023).

19 Christopher Guest, dir., *A Mighty Wind*, Warner Bros. Pictures 2003.

20 Jason Kaufman/Matthew E. Kaliner, *The Re-accomplishment of Place in Twentieth-Century Vermont and New Hampshire: History Repeats Itself, Until It Doesn't*, in: The Journal of Theory and Society 40 (2011), 124.

21 Jason Reitman, dir., *Thank You for Smoking*, Fox Searchlight Pictures 2006.

22 Barbieri, *Costume in Performance*, 114–115.

23 Coeli Carr, *Thank You for Insulting Our Sandals*, in: The New York Times, Mar. 3, 2006, https://www.nytimes.com/2006/03/12/fashion/sundaystyles/thank-you-for-insulting-our-sandals.html (accessed May 2, 2023).

24 Ibid.

25 Ibid.

26 Kaufman/Kaliner, *The Re-accomplishment of Place*, 132.

27 Marc Lawrence, dir., *Two Weeks Notice*, Warner Bros. Pictures 2002.

28 Ibid.

29 Roger Michell, dir., *Notting Hill*, Universal Pictures 1999.

30 Peter Billingsley, dir., *Couples Retreat*, Universal Pictures 2009.

31 *Jason Bateman Couples Interview*, in: Female.com.au, https://www.female.com.au/jason-bateman-couples-retreat-interview.htm (accessed Feb. 20, 2023).

32 David Wain, dir., *Wanderlust*, Universal Pictures 2012.

33 Dennis Dugan, dir., *Grown Ups*, Sony Pictures Releasing 2010.

34 Joshua Michael Stern, dir., *Jobs*, Open Road Films 2013.

35 Dani Anguiano, *Steve Jobs' Old Birkenstocks Sell for Nearly $ 220,000*, in: The Guardian, Nov. 16, 2022, https://www.theguardian.com/technology/2022/nov/15/steve-jobs-old-birkenstocks-sold-auction-sandals (accessed May 2, 2023).

36 Stutesman, *Cooking*, 26.

37 Robert Zemeckis, dir., *What Lies Beneath*, DreamWorks Distribution/20th Century Fox 2000.

38 Stutesman, *Cooking*, 31.

39 Zal Batmanglij, dir., *The East*, Fox Searchlight Pictures 2013.

40 The Freegan movement has the goal of reduced participation in capitalism and recovers waste goods and foods. The movement shares elements with the Diggers, an anarchist street theatre group based in Haight-Ashbury in San Francisco in the 60s who organized free housing and clinics and gave away salvaged food. Warren James Belasco, *Appetite for Change: How the Counterculture Took on the Food Industry*, Ithaca 2007.

41 Josh Anderson, dir., *Oil on Canvas*, [short film] 2023. The tight costume budget meant that we could not afford real Birkenstocks for the costume, but the fake Birkenstocks, or 'Fakenstocks' looked genuine on film.

42 Allan Lloyd Smith, *Postmodernism/Gothicism*, in: Victor Sage/Allan Lloyd Smith (eds.), Modern Gothic: A Reader, Manchester 1996, 11.

43 Smith, *Postmodernism/Gothicism*, 14.

44 Danny Boyle, dir., *The Beach*, 20th Century Fox 2000; Greg McLean, dir., *Wolf Creek*, Roadshow Entertainment 2005.

45 Nancy Meyers, dir., *Something's Gotta Give*, Sony Pictures Releasing/Warner Bros. Pictures 2003.

46 Adam Geczy/Vicki Karaminas, *Queer Style*, London 2013.

47 Ben Falcone, dir., *Tammy*, Warner Bros. Pictures 2014.

48 See Taylor Brydges's essay in this volume, "From Hippie to High Fashion."

49 Jesse Peretz, dir., *Our Idiot Brother*, The Weinstein Company 2011.

50 Michael Mayer, dir., *Single All the Way*, Netflix 2021.

51 Greta Gerwig, dir., *Barbie*, Warner Bros. Pictures 2023.

52 Ilana Kaplan, *Meet Alana Morshead, the Costume Designer behind* Do Revenge's *Most Iconic Looks*, in: Alternative Press, Oct. 6, 2022, https://www.altpress.com/alana-morshead-do-revenge-interview/#:~:text=Meet%20Alana%20Morshead%2C%20the%20costume%20designer%20behind%20Do%20Revenge (accessed May 2, 2023).

53 Greta Gerwig, dir., *Barbie*, Warner Bros. Pictures 2023.

54 CA Birkenstock, BBG 4. 054, Email 9.8.2023, Comms Birkenstock.

55 Shane Black, dir., *Iron Man 3*, Walt Disney Studios Motion Pictures 2013; Sam Warner, *Iron Man 3 Star Reveals This Weird Detail about His Big Fight Scene*, in: Digital Spy, Mar. 20, 2020, https://www.digitalspy.com/movies/a31804940/iron-man-3-guy-pearce-birkenstocks-marvel/ (accessed May 2, 2023).

56 Footwear News, *Jason Momoa Breaks Down His Birkenstock Love Story*, YouTube, Dec. 9, 2020, https://www.youtube.com/watch?v=n-0wdpx15mw (accessed May 2, 2023).

57 Brooke Marine, *Frances McDormand Has Always Taken Risks on the Red Carpet*, in: W Magazine, Apr. 28, 2021, https://www.wmagazine.com/fashion/frances-mcdormand-style-evolution (accessed May 2, 2023).

58 Tomas Alfredson, dir., *Let the Right One In*, Sandrew Metronome 2008.

59 Phoebe Waller-Bridge, exec. prod., *Fleabag*, BBC Three/BBC One 2016–2019; Tom Kapinos, exec. prod., *Lucifer*, Fox/Netflix 2016–2021.

60 Christopher Storer, exec. prod., *The Bear*, Hulu 2022–present; Danny Parisi, *How* The Bear *Created the Best Fictional Menswear Icon in a Decade*, in: Glossy, Aug. 15, 2022, https://www.glossy.co/fashion/how-the-bear-created-the-best-fictional-menswear-icon-in-a-decade/ (accessed May 2, 2023); Cam Wolf, *Actually,* The Bear *is a Menswear Show*, in: GQ, July 27, 2022, https://www.gq.com/story/the-bear-is-a-menswear-show (accessed May 2, 2023).

61 Michael Patrick King, exec. prod., *And Just Like That*, HBO Max 2021–present.

1963 – 2023
The Development of Birkenstock in the Early Key Markets

From Hippie to High Fashion: The Evolution of Birkenstock in North America

1 CA Birkenstock, Privatarchiv Margot Fraser, BMF 2. 001-4, Werbeanzeigen und Entwürfe Birkenstock USA1980er und 1990er.pdf, "Nordstrom Bay Area Region Welcome from Your Support Team," Jan. 30, 2004.

2 CA Birkenstock, BS 64 Patent Shoe Insole Canada 1960–1953, Birkenstock Patent, Jan. 16, 1953.

3 See Jörg Lesczenski's essay in this volume.

4 Cathy Horyn, *The Dwarf, the Prince, and the Diamond in the Mountain*, in: The Cut, https://www.thecut.com/2018/08/cathy-horyn-on-birkenstocks-unlikely-rise.html (accessed June 13, 2023).

5 Barbara Schneider-Levy, *Margot Fraser, Entrepreneur Who Introduced Birkenstock to the U. S., Dies*, in: Footwear News (Apr. 24, 2017), https://footwearnews.com/2017/business/uncategorized/birkenstock-margot-fraser-dies-342412/ (accessed June 13, 2023).

6 Robert Klara, *The Reputation of the Birkenstock*, in: Adweek, https://www.adweek.com/brand-marketing/how-birkenstocks-morphed-from-geeky-to-trendy/ (accessed June 13, 2023).

7 Horyn, *The Dwarf, the Prince, and the Diamond in the Mountain*.

8 Helen Jennings, *The Secret of Birkenstock's Enduring Success*, in: CNN Style (Aug. 14, 2020), https://www.cnn.com/style/article/birkenstocks-history-comfortable-shoes-sandals/index.html (accessed June 13, 2023).

9 CA Birkenstock, Privatarchiv Margot Fraser, BMF 2. 001-4, Werbeanzeigen und Entwürfe Birkenstock USA1980er und 1990er.pdf, "Nordstrom Bay Area Region Welcome from Your Support Team," Jan. 30, 2004.

10 The Official Crumb Site, *Robert Crumb Biography* (Nov. 22, 2022), https://www.crumbproducts.com/Robert-Crumb-Biography_b_12.html (accessed June 13, 2023).

11 Lambiek Comiclopedia, *Gilbert Shelton*, https://www.lambiek.net/artists/s/shelton.htm (updated Oct. 4, 2022).

12 Lambiek Comiclopedia, Underground Comix and the Underground Press, https://www.lambiek.net/comics/underground.htm (accessed June 13, 2023).

13 Museum of Pop Culture, *Woodstock at 50: The Festival That Almost Wasn't* (Aug. 19, 2019), https://www.mopop.org/about-mopop/the-mopop-blog/posts/2019/august/woodstock-at-50-the-festival-that-almost-wasnt/ (accessed June 13, 2023); Stewart Brand, *Whole Earth Catalog*, Fall 1968, https://monoskop.org/images/0/09/Brand_Stewart_Whole_Earth_Catalog_Fall_1968.pdf (accessed June 13, 2023).

14 Peter Braunstein/Michael William Doyle, *Imagine Nation: The American Counterculture of the 1960's and 70's*, Routledge 2013.

15 John Ortved, *How Much Would You Pay for Steve Jobs's Birkenstocks?*, in: The New York Times (Dec. 5, 2022), https://www.nytimes.com/2022/12/05/style/birkenstocks.html (accessed June 13, 2023).

16 Kristopher Fraser, *Steve Jobs' Well-Used Birkenstock Sandals Sell for Nearly $ 220,000 at Auction*, in: Women's Wear Daily (Nov. 16, 2022), https://wwd.com/fashion-news/fashion-scoops/steve-jobs-sandals-auction-birkenstock-arizona-1235421821/ (accessed June 13, 2023).

17 Dani Anguiano, *Steve Jobs' Old Birkenstocks Sell for Nearly $ 220,000*, in: The Guardian (Nov. 15, 2022), https://www.theguardian.com/technology/2022/nov/15/steve-jobs-old-birkenstocks-sold-auction-sandals (accessed June 13, 2023).

18 Ibid.; Fraser, *Steve Jobs' Well-Used Birkenstock Sandals*.

19 Coeli Carr, *Thank You for Insulting Our Sandals*, in: The New York Times (Mar. 12, 2006), https://www.nytimes.com/2006/03/12/fashion/sundaystyles/thank-you-for-insulting-our-sandals.html (accessed June 13, 2023).

20 Birkenstock, *Our Commitment* https://www.birkenstock.com/ca/education/our-commitment/ (accessed June 13, 2023).

21 CA Birkenstock, Privatarchiv Margot Fraser, BMF 2. 001-4, Werbeanzeigen und Entwürfe Birkenstock USA1980er und 1990er.pdf, "Nordstrom Bay Area Region Welcome from Your Support Team," Jan. 30, 2004, in: The Guardian.

22 Ibid.

23 Ibid.

24 Steph Eckardt, *"And Just Like That ..." Fashion Recap Episode 5: Carrie Ditches Heels?!*, in: W Magazine (Dec. 31, 2021), https://www.wmagazine.com/culture/just-like-that-episode-5-recap (accessed June 13, 2023).

25 Jennings, *The Secret of Birkenstock's Enduring Success*.

26 Ibid.

27 Melanie Ward, *The 3rd Summer of Love*, in: The Face (Apr. 17, 2019), https://theface.com/archive/kate-moss-summer-of-love (accessed June 13, 2023) (photo: Corinne Day).

28 Jennings, *The Secret of Birkenstock's Enduring Success*.

29 Ibid.

30 Horyn, *The Dwarf, the Prince, and the Diamond in the Mountain*.

31 Rebecca Mead, *Sole Cycle*, in: The New Yorker (Mar. 16, 2015), https://www.newyorker.com/magazine/2015/03/23/sole-cycle-rebecca-mead (accessed June 13, 2023).

32 Julia Marzovilla, *38 Fashion Trends from the '00s That Play on Slow Loop in Your Nightmares, 2022*, in: Marie Claire (Mar. 11, 2022), https://www.marieclaire.com/fashion/g26907530/2000s-fashion-trends/ (accessed June 13, 2023).

33 Donovan Barnett, *From "Seinfeld" to Steve Jobs: What Was Normcore and What Is It Now?*, in: High Snobiety, https://www.highsnobiety.com/p/what-is-normcore/ (accessed June 13, 2023).

34 Adrian Nuñez, *Birkenstocks Aren't Normcore Says Birkenstocks SVP*, in: Esquire (Apr. 2, 2015), https://www.esquire.com/style/mens-fashion/news/a34093/birkenstock-denies-normcore-ties/ (accessed June 13, 2023).

35 Alex Williams, *The New Normal*, in: The New York Times (Apr. 2, 2014), https://www.nytimes.com/2014/04/03/fashion/normcore-fashion-movement-or-massive-in-joke.html (accessed June 13, 2023).

36 Horyn, *The Dwarf, the Prince, and the Diamond in the Mountain*.

37 Ibid.

38 Jennings, *The Secret of Birkenstock's Enduring Success*; Alice Newbold, *Dior Bets Big on a Birkenstock Collab for Everyone*, in: Vogue (Jan. 21, 2022), https://www.vogue.com/article/dior-birkenstock-collaboration (accessed June 13, 2023); Jessica Iredale, *See Birkenstock's New Collection*

Notes   **435**

with Manolo Blahnik, in: Wall Street Journal Magazine (Mar. 11, 2022), https://www.wsj.com/articles/birkenstocks-manolo-blahnik-collab-11646946678 (accessed June 13, 2023).

39 Patrick Witschi/Aparna Bharadwaj/Jean-Manuel Izaret/Lauren Taylor, *Understanding the Global Price-Sensitive Consumer*, in: Boston Consulting Group (July 14, 2021), https://www.bcg.com/publications/2021/consumer-price-sensitivity (accessed June 13, 2023).

40 Justin Krajeski, *Why We Love Birkenstock Arizona EVA Sandals*, in: The New York Times (Oct. 18, 2021), https://www.nytimes.com/wirecutter/reviews/birkenstock-arizona-eva-sandals-review/ (accessed June 13, 2023).

41 Ella Chochrek, *The Best Birkenstock Sandals, According to Enthusiastic Customer Reviews*, 2021. Footwear News. https://footwearnews.com/feature/best-birkenstock-sandals-customer-reviews-1202958493/ (accessed June 13, 2023).

42 Jake Silbert, *Birkenstock Arizona: Why All Luxury Brands Are Copying the Design*, 2021, Highsnobiety. https://www.highsnobiety.com/p/birkenstock-arizona-dupes/ (accessed June 13, 2023).

43 Ari Shapiro, *Nearly 250-Year-Old Shoe Company Sees a Spike in Popularity amid the Pandemic*, in: National Public Radio (Aug. 4, 2020), https://www.npr.org/2020/08/04/899060826/nearly-250-year-old-shoe-company-sees-a-spike-in-popularity-amid-the-pandemic (accessed June 13, 2023).

44 Jennie Bell, *How Birkenstock Managed to Make 2020 One of Its Best Years Yet*, in: Footwear News (Sept. 22, 2020), https://footwearnews.com/2020/business/power-players/birkenstock-ceo-oliver-reichert-interview-1203056382/ (accessed June 13, 2023).

45 Lyst Insights, *The Lyst Index 02 2020*, https://www.lyst.com/data/the-lyst-index/q220/, (accessed June 13, 2023).

46 Bell, *How Birkenstock Managed*.

47 Sheena Butler-Young, *Birkenstock Isn't Having a Moment, It's Building the Nike of the Comfort Market*, Footwear News (Jan. 21, 2021), https://footwearnews.com/2021/business/mergers-acquisitions/birkenstock-valuation-billions-nike-1203097281/ (accessed June 13, 2023).

48 Silbert, *Birkenstock Arizona*.

Birkenstock in Italy: A Creative Adventure

1 Corporate Archive Birkenstock [hereafter CA Birkenstock], BBG 7. 001, Carl Birkenstock – Orthopädie to Karl Fill, Bad Honnef-Rhein, Dec. 13, 1957 (BI Schreiben 1957).

2 Interview with Ewald Pitschl, Founder of NaturalLook, Bolzano, Oct. 11, 2018, in: CA Birkenstock, BDF 4.B.002.

3 Emanuela Scarpellini, *Italian Fashion since 1945: A Cultural History*, Cham 2019, 149–156, 233–236.

4 Alessandra Ceriani/Filippo Caserio, *Vigevano nel boom. Scarpe, benzolo e altre storie. Gli anni Sessanta tra luci e ombre*, Vigevano 2021.

5 Scarpellini, *Italian Fashion*, 138–166.

6 Interview of Ewald Pitschl; Interview of Gerhard Pitschl, CEO of NaturalLook, Bolzano, May 10, 2018, in: CA Birkenstock, BDF 4.B.002.

7 Giorgio Riello/Peter McNeil, *Shoes: A History from Sandals to Sneakers*, London 2011; Elisabeth Semmelhack, *Shoes: The Meaning of Style*, Chicago 2017.

8 Albertoni/Pitro, *La sfida Birkenstock*, 15–17.

9 Ibid., 21–22.

10 Salvatore Rossi, *La politica economica italiana*, Roma-Bari 2008; Ignazio Visco, *Politica monetaria e inflazione in Italia, 1994–96*, in: N. Acocella et. al. (eds.), Saggi di politica economica in onore di Federico Caffè, Rome 1999.

11 Albertoni/Pitro, *La sfida Birkenstock*, 27.

12 Albertoni/Pitro, *La sfida Birkenstock*, 29; Chamber of Commerce, Industry, Crafts and Agriculture of Bolzano, Company Register Archive, Company historical file: NaturalLook S.r.l., Jan. 25, 2023.

13 CA Birkenstock, BBG 7. 008, Italien, correspondence, letter by Ewald Pitschl to Birkenstock, Bolzano, Aug. 10, 1999; Response letter by Bernd Hillen and Hans-Peter Wohleb to Ewald Pitsch, Vettelschloß, Aug. 20, 1999.

14 Albertoni/Pitro, *La sfida Birkenstock*, 47.
15 Albertoni/Pitro, *La sfida Birkenstock*, 53.
16 Interview of Gerhard Pitschl.
17 The interviews were carried out by the author in the period February-September 2022, in person or online. In this article, the most interesting ones have been included.
18 Interview of Angelo R., June 20, 2022.
19 Interviews of Elena P. and Angela F., Milano, Mar. 14, 2022.
20 Interview of Mauro L., Robbiate (LC), Sept. 23, 2022.
21 Interview of Elena F., online, July 21, 2022.

Birkenstock in Britain

1 Francesca Luard, *Buzzwords*, Daily Mail, Aug. 1, 1991, 20.
2 Jill Geoghegan, *The Natural Shoe Store Ceases Trading*, in: Drapers, Oct. 19, 2018. Available online: https://www.drapersonline.com/news/the-natural-shoe-store-ceases-trading (accessed July 1, 2022).
3 Ann Galloway, *Shopping in Covent Garden*, in: Harpers and Queen, July 1979, 52 and 58.
4 Corporate Archive Birkenstock [hereafter CA Birkenstock], Interview with Robert Lusk, Feb. 21, 2019.
5 Ibid.
6 Melanie Ward, *The 3rd Summer of Love*, in: The Face, Apr 17, 2019. https://theface.com/archive/kate-moss-summer-of-love (accessed July 5, 2022) (photo: Corinne Day).
7 Ibid.
8 Interview with Julian Vogel, 2022; https://www.theworldsbest.events/blog/julian-vogel (accessed Aug. 27, 2022).
9 Claudia Levy, *Just What the Doctor Ordered*, in: Daily Mail, July 28, 1994, 41.
10 Libby Brooks, *Success de Sandal*, in: The Guardian, June 30, 2003. https://www.theguardian.com/lifeandstyle/2003/jun/30/fashion.beauty (accessed July 10, 2022).
11 CA Birkenstock, Interview with Robert Lusk, 2019.
12 Letter from Ted Polhemus to Linda Lloyd Jones, Jan. 16, 1989, in: Victoria & Albert Museum Registry Street Style Exhibition files, MA/28/502 [hereafter V&A Registry].
13 V&A Registry, MA/28/502, Information sheet, Nov. 1992.
14 Lou Taylor, *Establishing Dress History*, Manchester 2004, 123.
15 V&A Registry, MA/28/502, Information sheet, Nov. 1992.
16 Taylor, *Establishing Dress History*, 123.
17 V&A Registry, MA/28/502, Information sheet, Nov.1992.
18 V&A Registry, MA/28/502, End of exhibition visitor analysis, n.d. c 1995.
19 CA Birkenstock, Interview with Robert Lusk, 2019.
20 V&A Registry, Registry File no: 95/1591.
21 V&A Registry, MA/28/502, V&A streetstyle design brief (first draft), n.d. c 1993.
22 Brooks, *Success de Sandal*, June 30, 2003.
23 Alison Gill/Abby Mellick Lopes, *On Wearing: A Critical Framework for Valuing Design's Already Made*, in: Design and Culture, 3:3 (2011), 320.
24 V&A Registry, MA/28/502, Letters from Amy de la Haye to Nicola Boyd (Marketing manager, the Boot Tree ltd), Mar. 30, 1994 and June 8, 1994.
25 Emily Chan, *Katharine Hamnett on Sustainability in Fashion*, June 11, 2019; https://www.vogue.co.uk/article/katharine-hamnett-on-sustainability-in-fashion (accessed 1 August 2022).
26 Alison Gwilt, *A Practical Guide to Sustainable Fashion*, London 2020, 26.
27 Isabella Tree, *Cornish Pasties- Made in Germany*, in: The Times, June 8, 1996, 8.
28 V&A Registry, Street Style Exhibition files: MA/28 / 502, Future Street Style garments, 1994.

Birkenstock in France: Uber Fashionable?

1 Interview of Marianne Deparis led by author. June 13,2023.
2 Interview of Jean-Michel Gross led by author, June 13,2023.

Notes 437

3 Ibid.

4 Corporate Archive Birkenstock [hereafter CA Birkenstock], BBG 2. 001-16, Export Catalogue. pdf, Birkenstock Post. Revue-Export, 1961.

5 Hoki Archive, Catalogue, *Birkenstock pour la détente et le travail*, 3. Translated by author. All translations are by the author.

6 Elizabeth Semmelhack, *Shoes. The meaning of style*, Reaktion Books, London, 64.

7 Denis Bruna, *Marche et démarche. Une histoire de la chaussure*, MAD, Paris, 2019, 63.

8 Fashion Channel, *Martine Sitbon Spring Summer 1994 Paris*, YouTube, https://www.youtube. com/watch?v=uizqXHshAo8 (accessed Mar. 14, 2023).

9 Interview of Pierre Fournier led by author. June 1,2023.

10 *Georgianna la frimeuse*, in: Elle, Mar. 3, 1997, 83.

11 Laurence Benaim, *Un raz de marée de gris déferle sur Milan*, in: Le Monde, Mar. 7, 1998, https://www.lemonde.fr/archives/article/1998/03/07/un-raz-de-maree-gris-deferle-sur-milan_3659376_1819218.html (accessed Mar. 15, 2023).

12 Anne-Laure Quilleriet, *Le retour des claquettes*, in: Le Monde, June 13, 1998, https://www. lemonde.fr/archives/article/1998/06/13/le-retour-des-claquettes_3677630_1819218.html. (accessed Mar. 15, 2023).

13 *Enroulez-vous dans un chèche!*, in: Elle, July 13, 1998, 63.

14 *Campagne anti-froid*, in: Elle, Nov. 23, 1998, 153.

15 *En avant les sabots*, in: Elle, Oct. 26, 1998, 70.

16 *Périscope spécial*, in: Vogue Paris, Sept. 1998, 141.

17 *Agenda Perso*, in: Vogue Paris, June 1998, 83.

18 *Jupes longues et talons plats*, in: Elle, Nov. 9, 1998, 140.

19 Alexia Charlot, *Carambolage de siècles*, in: Le Monde, Oct. 16,1998, https://www.lemonde.fr/ archives/article/1998/10/16/carambolage-de-siecles_3694351_1819218.html (accessed Mar. 27, 2023).

20 Anne Boulay, *Tendances hype. Prémices mode. Mme de Fontanges a incarné la hype au XVIIe siècle. Le camouflage y est entré en 1995. Le Rubik's Cube revivra-t-il son heure d'avant mode?*, in: Libération, Sep. 26, 1999, https://www.liberation.fr/culture/1999/09/25/tendances-hype-premices-mode-mme-de-fontanges-a-incarne-la-hype-au-xviie-siecle-le-camouflage-y-est-_284483/ (accessed Mar. 18, 2023).

21 "Birkenbeauf" is a contraction of Birkenstocks and the French word *beauf* that could be translated as "tacky," coined by the French journalist Marie-Hélène Martin.

22 Marie-Hélène Martin, *L'homme mue des pieds*, in: Libération, June, 24, 2000, https://www. liberation.fr/guide/2000/06/24/l-homme-mue-des-pieds_328411/ (accessed Mar. 21, 2023)

23 Interview of Marianne Deparis led by author. June 13,2023.

24 Interview of Jean-Michel Gross led by author. June 13,2023.

25 Clément Ghys, *"Normcore", la banalité en étendard*, in: Libération, Mar. 7, 2014, https://www. liberation.fr/mode/2014/03/07/normcore-la-banalite-en-etendard_985365/ (accessed Mar. 21, 2023).

26 Vogue Runway, Celine Spring 2013 Ready-to-Wear, in: Vogue US, Sept. 29, 2012, https://www. vogue.com/fashion-shows/spring-2013-ready-to-wear/celine (accessed Mar. 12, 2023)

27 Elizabeth Semmelhack, *Shoes. The meaning of style*, Reaktion Books, London 2019, 297.

28 On the subject of "ugly fashion", see Alice Pfeiffer, *Le gout du moche*, Flammarion, Paris, 2021.

29 Emmanuèle Peyret and Elisabeth Franck-Dumas, *Grolles de drame*, in: Libération, Jan. 10, 2014, https://www.liberation.fr/mode/2014/01/10/grolles-de-drame_972001/ (accessed Mar, 18. 2023).

30 Alice Pfeiffer, *Le gout du moche*, Flammarion, Paris, 2021, 180.

31 Melody Thomas, *Le mauvais gout-existe-t-il encore?*, in: L'Officiel, May 18, 2018, https://www. lofficiel.com/pop-culture/le-mauvais-gout-existe-t-il-encore (accessed Mar. 28, 2023)

32 Interviews led by author.

33 Interview of Pierre Fournier led by author. June 1, 2023.

34 Interview of Marianne Deparis led by author. June 13,2023.

35 Laurianne Melierre, *Après des années à vivre en paria, les Birkenstock prennent leur revanche*, in: Le Parisien, 23.08.2017, https://www.leparisien.fr/laparisienne/mode/apres-des-annees-a-vivre-en-paria-les-birkenstock-prennent-leur-revanche-21-08-2017-7204827.php (accessed Mar. 30, 2023).

36 Finn Blythe, *Solemates. The likes of Ryan McGinley and Luna Picoli-Truffaut show us their beloved Birkenstocks*, in: Hero Magazine, 15.08.2018, https://hero-magazine.com/article/130674/the-likes-of-ryan-mcginley-and-luna-picoli-truffaut-show-us-their-beloved-birkenstocks (accessed Mar. 27, 2023).

37 *Birkenstock Opens Global Paris Office*, in: WWD, Jan. 10, 2019, 6.

38 *Showroom Birkenstock 1774*, in: Milk Decoration, Aug. 26, 2019, https://www.milkdecoration.com/showroom-birkenstock-1774/ (accessed Mar. 25, 2023).

39 Frédéric Therin, *Birkenstock: c'est moche mais ça marche!*, in: Capital, Sept. 6, 2019, https://www.capital.fr/entreprises-marches/birkenstock-cest-moche-mais-ca-marche-1349408 (accessed Mar. 25, 2023).

40 Interview of Jean-Michel Gross led by author, June 13,2023.

41 Marnie Fogg, *Pourquoi est-ce un chef d'œuvre*, 2014, Eyrolles, Paris, 72.

42 Interview of Marianne Deparis led by author. June 13,2023.

43 Cécile Boutelet, *Bernard Arnault rachète les sandales Birkenstock*, in: Le Monde, Feb. 26, 2021, https://www.lemonde.fr/economie/article/2021/02/26/bernard-arnault-rachete-les-san-dales-birkenstock_6071333_3234.html (accessed Mar. 26, 2023).

44 Sophie Fontanel, *Vêtements modèles*, 2020, Mucem, Marseille, 16.

45 Alexandre Marain, *Dior collabore avec Birkenstock!*, in: Vogue Paris, Jan. 21, .2022, https://www.vogue.fr/vogue-hommes/article/dior-birkenstock-automne-hiver-2022-2023 (accessed Mar. 20, 2023).

46 *Dior by Birkenstock*, Birkenstock website, https://www.birkenstock.com/fr/1774/dior/ (accessed Mar. 20, 2023).

Birkenstock in Japan

1 Pierre-Yves Donzé, *Luxury business in Japan*, in: Donzé et al. (eds.), *Oxford Handbook of Luxury Business*, Oxford University Press, 2021, 182.

2 Corporate history of Sanyei Corporation, website of the firm, https://www.sanyeicorp.com/company/history.html (accessed June 6, 2022).

3 Nihon keizai shimbun, Nov. 6, 1997.

4 Corporate Archive Birkenstock [hereafter CA Birkenstock], filmed interview with Teruo Sugi-hara, former employee of Sanyei, undated.

5 Nihon sangyo shimbun, Mar. 18, 2003.

6 Sayako Miura, *The developmental history of the insole market in Japan: Rising health consciousness and an unintended shift toward fashion (1984–2010)*, in: Japanese Research in Business History, 38, 2021, 43–61.

7 Shoichi Shimizu, *Arukukoto, ashi soshite kutsu* [Walking, feet, and shoes]. Futoh-sha, 1995.

8 Nihon ryutsu shimbun, June 15, 1989.

9 Interview with Masayuki Ozawa, writer and specialist in the history of shoes in Japan, Oct. 18, 2022 (online).

10 Yoko Isozaki/Pierre-Yves Donzé, *Dominance versus collaboration models: French and Italian luxury fashion brands in Japan*, in: Journal of Global Fashion Marketing, forthcoming.

11 Nihon keizai shimbun, Sept. 19, 1994.

12 Interview with Toshiki Ebe, editor and writer at the fashion magazine OCEANS, Jan. 19, 2022 (online) and interview with Ozawa, op, cit.

13 W. David Marx, *Ametora: How Japan saved American style*, New York 2015.

14 Interview with Toshiki Ebe, op. cit., and website of Labrador Retriever, https://labrador.buy-shop.jp/about (accessed June 8, 2022).

15 Interview with Tomonori Shibasaki, employee of the fashion retailer Beams, Sept. 8, 2022.

16 Nihon keizai shimbun, Nov. 6, 1997.

17 CA Birkenstock, filmed interview with Kohji Tanemoto, head of Seed Co, undated.

18 Nihon sangyo shimbun, Mar. 18, 2003.

19 Nihon keizai shimbun, Oct. 31, 1998.

20 Interview with Yasuyuki Umino, CEO of Benexy, Jan. 18, 2022 (online).
21 https://jp.mercari.com/ (accessed June 10, 2022).
22 Nihon keizai shimbun, Jan. 9, 1999.
23 Interview with Ozawa, op. cit.
24 Nihon keizai shimbun, Aug. 27, 1998; Nihon sangyo shimbun, Dec. 2, 1998.
25 Nihon kinyu shimbun, Mar. 15, 2002 and www.benexy.com/about/ (accessed June 10, 2022).
26 Nihon kinyu shimbun, Mar. 15, 2002.
27 Nihon keizai shimbun, Mar. 19, 1998.
28 Nihon ryutsu shimbun, July 23, 1998.
29 Asahi shimbun, May 25, 1999.
30 CA Birkenstock, interview with Tanemoto, op. cit.
31 Interview with Shibasaki, op. cit.
32 Ibid.
33 Website of Benexy (formerly Birkenstock Japan), https://www.benexy.com/about/ (accessed June 17, 2022).
34 Interview with Yasuyuki Umino, CEO of Benexy, Jan. 18, 2022 (online).
35 Ibid.
36 For example, *Birukenshutokku no miryoku* [The charm of Birkenstock], special issue of Fudge, November 2005; *Birkenstock Style*, Dazed & Confused Japan, 2005; Birkenstock Japan (ed.), *Life Knowledge*, INFAS, 2007.
37 Nihon sangyo shimbun, Nov. 26, 2008.
38 CA Birkenstock, filmed interview with Yukiko Tekawa, employee of Benexy, undated.
39 Interview with Yasuyuki Umino, CEO of Benexy, Jan. 18, 2022 (online).
40 Nikkei MJ, May 9, 2012.
41 Nihon sangyo shimbun, Aug. 19, 2009.
42 CA Birkenstock, filmed interview with Tekawa, op. cit.
43 Nikkei MJ, Mar. 7, 2008.
44 Nikkei MJ, Oct. 6, 2014 and Nov. 26, 2014.
45 Website of Benexy, https://www.benexy.com/about/ (accessed June 17, 2022).

Birkenstock in Australia 1992 – 2022: A Stable Shoe for Shifting Terrains

1 *Put on your daggiest duds you dag!*, in: Macquarie Dictionary https://www.macquariedictionary.com.au/blog/article/620/ (accessed Sep. 20, 2023).
2 Giorgio Riello/Peter McNeil, *Introduction: A Long Walk. Shoes, People and Places*, in: Giorgio Riello and Peter McNeil (eds.), Shoes: A History from Sandals to Sneakers, New York 2011, 2–29, here 3.
3 *Lesbian, German, Christian or a Bit Outdoorsy*, in: Star Observer, Apr. 20, 2008, https://www.starobserver.com.au/news/national-news/new-south-wales-news/lesbian-german-christian-or-a-bit-outdoorsy/7476 (accessed Sep. 20, 2023).
4 Marcel Goerke, interview with author, Aug. 28, 2022.
5 Rebecca Sullivan, *How I Learned to Love Birkenstocks*, in: news.com.au, June 19, 2015, https://www.news.com.au/lifestyle/fashion/fashion-trends/how-i-learned-to-love-birkenstocks/news-story/b41b72ec0feb35e1ab30cb3b8f779ea3 (accessed Sep. 20, 2023).
6 Kjetil Fallan/Grace Lees-Maffei, *Designing Worlds: National Design Histories in an Age of Globalization*, New York 2016.
7 Susannah Guthrie, *What the Australian New Car Market Looked Like in 1991*, in: Drive.com.au, Sep. 4, 2020, https://www.drive.com.au/caradvice/australian-car-sales-1991/ (accessed Sep. 20, 2023).
8 Emily Brayshaw, *Oskar Schlemmer's Kitsch (1922): A Contextualisation and Translation*, in: Journal of Aesthetics and Culture 13 (2021), https://doi.org/10.1080/20004214.2021.1945239, here 2, (accessed Sep. 20, 2023).
9 Max Bill, *Die gute Form*, in: Das Werk: Architektur und Kunst = L'oeuvre: architecture et art 4 (1957), 138–140, here 140.
10 Fallan/Lees-Maffei, *Designing Worlds*, 3.

11 Marcel Goerke, interview with author, Aug. 28, 2022.
12 Joanne Entwistle, *The Fashioned Body: Fashion, Dress and Social Theory*, Malden 2015, 265.
13 Christopher Breward, *The Suit: Form, Function and Style*, London 2016.
14 Rebecca Arnold, *Fashion, Desire and Anxiety: Image and Morality in the 20th Century*, London 2001, 118.
15 Riello/McNeil, *Introduction*, 5.
16 Sara L. Crawley, *Are Butch and Fem Working-Class and Anti-Feminist?*, in: Gender and Society 15 (2001), 175–196; Adam Geczy/Vicki Karaminas, *The Body*, in: Alexandra Palmer (ed.), A Cultural History of Dress and Fashion in the Modern Age, London 2021, 63–84; Adam Geczy/Vicki Karaminas, *Queer Style*, London 2013; Katrina Rolley, *Love, Desire and the Pursuit of the Whole: Dress and the Lesbian Couple*, in: Juliet Ash/Elizabeth Wilson (eds.), Chic Thrills: A Fashion Reader, London 1992, 30–39; Lisa M. Walker, *How to Recognize a Lesbian: The Cultural Politics of Looking Like What You Are*, in: Signs 18 (1993), 866–890.
17 Geczy/Karaminas, *Queer Style*, 35.
18 Geczy/Karaminas, *Queer Style*, 23.
19 Clare Lomas et al., *Beyond the Rainbow: Queer Shoes*, in: Giorgio Riello/Peter McNeil (eds.), Shoes: A History from Sandals to Sneakers, New York 2011, 290–305, here 291.
20 Lomas et al., *Beyond the Rainbow*, 291.
21 *History of Sydney Mardi Gras*, in: Sydney Gay and Lesbian Mardi Gras, 2022, https://www.mardigras.org.au/history-of-sydney-mardi-gras/ (accessed Sep. 20, 2023).
22 Ibid.
23 *Timeline: 22 Years between First and Last Australian States Decriminalising Male Homosexuality*, in: ABC News, Aug. 24, 2015, https://www.abc.net.au/news/2015-08-24/timeline:-australian-states-decriminalise-male-homosexuality/6719702?nw=0&r=HtmlFragment (accessed Sep. 20, 2023).
24 Lomas et al., *Beyond the Rainbow*, 290.
25 A 78er is a member of the group of people who were at the 1978 events. *Who are the 78ers?*, in: First Mardi Gras, accessed Sept 17, 2022, https://www.78ers.org.au/the-78ers (accessed Sep. 20, 2023).
26 Jochen Strähle/Noemi Jahne-Warrior, *Case Study: Grunge Music and Grunge Style*, in: Jochen Strähle (ed.), Fashion and Music, Reutlingen 2018, 51–70.
27 Lomas et al., *Beyond the Rainbow*, 302–303.
28 The British magazine The Face featured in 1990 an image of the supermodel Kate Moss aged 16 wearing Birkenstocks.
29 *Reclaim the Night – Sydney*, in: PSA, 2022, https://psa.asn.au/women/reclaim-the-night-sydney/#:~:text=Reclaim%20the%20night%20is%20a,the%20lives%20of%20women%20globally (accessed Sep. 20, 2023).
30 Marcel Goerke, interview with author, Aug. 28, 2022.
31 Ibid.
32 Ibid.
33 *About Us*, in: Birkenstock Soul, 2022, http://www.birkenstocksoul.com.au/about-us/ (accessed Sep. 20, 2023).
34 Simon Chilvers, *It's the Year of the Birkenstock!*, in: The Guardian Feb. 6, 2013, https://www.theguardian.com/fashion/shortcuts/2013/feb/05/its-year-of-the-birkenstock (accessed Sep. 20, 2023).
35 Lauren Sams, *It's the Summer of the Ugly Sandal (and Your Feet Were Never Happier)*, in: Australian Financial Review Magazine, Jan. 25, 2021, https://www.afr.com/life-and-luxury/fashion-and-style/it-s-the-summer-of-the-ugly-sandal-and-feet-have-never-been-happier-20201125-p56hxj (accessed Sep. 20, 2023).
36 Evangeline Poluymeneas, *Who is the TikTok "weird girl" and why are we all dressing like her?*, in: Vogue, Aug. 14, 2022, https://www.vogue.com.au/shopping/weird-girl-aesthetic/image-gallery/c08e93b5679569f7baddf779b5e44c03 (accessed Sep. 20, 2023).
37 Alice Cicolini, *Historism and Historical Revival*, in: Valerie Steele (ed.), The Berg Companion to Fashion, Oxford 2010, 419–421, here 420.
38 Marcel Goerke, interview with author, Aug. 28, 2022.
39 Ibid.

40 Alison Gill/Abby Mellick Lopes, *On Wearing: A Critical Framework for Valuing Designs Already Made*, in: Design and Culture 3 (2011), 303–327, here 321.

41 Gill/Mellick Lopes, *On Wearing*, 321.

42 Ian Hodder, *Entangled: An Archaeology of the Relationships Between Humans and Things*, Chichester 2012, 95.

43 Hodder, *Entangled*, 18, 22.

44 Hodder, *Entangled*, 24.

45 Patrick Williams, *The First Same-Sex Couple to Wed in Australia Were Only Married for 48 Days before Death Parted Them*, in: ABC News, Mar. 7, 2018, https://www.abc.net.au/news/2018-03-07/heartbreaking-story-behind-australias-first-same-sex-marriage/9523098 (accessed Sep. 20, 2023).

Literature and Archives

Literature

Werner Abelshauser, *Deutsche Wirtschaftsgeschichte seit 1945*, Bonn 2005.
Alessandra Albertoni/Susanne Pitro, *La sfida Birkenstock: Cronaca di un successo*, Bolzano 2008.
Gerold Ambrosius, *Globalisierung: Geschichte der internationalen Wirtschaftsbeziehungen*, Wiesbaden 2018.
Axel Arbinger, *Auf Sohlen aus Metall läuft heute keiner mehr*, in: Friedberg-Magazin (April 1995).
Rebecca Arnold, *Fashion, Desire and Anxiety: Image and Morality in the 20th Century*, London 2001.

Veit Bachmann, *From Jackboots To Birkenstocks: The Civilianisation of German Geopolitics in the Twentieth Century*, in: Journal of Economic and Human Geography 3 (2010), 320–332.
Donatella Barbieri, *Costume in Performance: Materiality, Culture, and the Body*, London 2017.
Warren James Belasco, *Appetite for Change: How the Counterculture Took on the Food Industry*, Ithaca 2007.
Carlo Marco Belfanti, *Was Fashion a European invention?*, in: Journal of Global History 3 (2008), 419–443.
Lutz Bellmann/Peter Ellguth, *Verbreitung von Betriebsräten und ihr Einfluss auf die betriebliche Weiterbildung*, in: Jahrbücher für Nationalökonomie und Statistik, 5 (2016), 487–504.
Isabella Belting, *Ready to go! Schuhe bewegen*, Berlin 2019.
Udo Benzendörfer, *Die Universitätsmedizin in Frankfurt am Main von 1914 bis 2014*, Münster 2014.
Hartmut Berghoff/Philipp Heldmann, *Vom Massenhandwerk zur Modeindustrie*, in: Willi Schächter/Michael Wagner (eds.), Vom Zunfthandwerk zum modernen Industriebetrieb: Schuhe und Schuhherstellung in Deutschland seit dem 18. Jahrhundert, Hauenstein 1998, 57–79.
Hartmut Berghoff, *Transaktionskosten: Generalschlüssel zum Verständnis langfristiger Unternehmensentwicklung? Zum Verhältnis von Neuer Institutionenökonomie und moderner Unternehmensgeschichte*, in: Jahrbuch für Wirtschaftsgeschichte 2 (1999), 159–176.
Hartmut Berghoff, *Moderne Unternehmensgeschichte: Eine themen- und theorieorientierte Einführung*, Berlin 2016.
Hartmut Berghoff/Ingo Köhler, *Verdienst und Vermächtnis: Familienunternehmen in Deutschland und den USA seit 1800*, Frankfurt 2020.
Wolfgang Best, *Die Zukunft vor 20 Jahren*, in: 100 Jahre Orthopädieschuhtechnik: Innovationen, Versorgungskonzepte, Perspektiven, special issue, Orthopädieschuhtechnik (2017), 94–96.
Max Bill, *Die gute Form*, in: Das Werk: Architektur und Kunst = L'oeuvre: architecture et art 4 (1957), 138–140.
Carl Birkenstock, *Der Fuß und seine Behandlung*, 1930.
Carl Birkenstock, *Mit dem Arzt gegen Fußkrankheiten und Irrlehren*, Bremen 1935.
Carl Birkenstock, *40 Jahre für die vernünftige Fußbekleidung*, 1941 (unpublished).
Carl Birkenstock, *50 Jahre System Birkenstock 1897–1947*, Bad Honnef 1947.
Carl Birkenstock, *Fußorthopädie "System Carl Birkenstock,"* Düsseldorf 1948.
Konrad Birkenstock, *Fußbett: Ein Wunder im Schuh*, Friedberg n.d.

Regina Lee Blaszczyk, *Imagining Consumers: Design and Innovation from Wedgwood to Corning*, Baltimore 2002.

Elizabeth Block, *Dressing Up: The Women Who Influenced French Fashion*, Cambridge, MA, 2021.

Sue Blundell, *Beneath Their Shining Feet. Shoes and Sandals in Classical Greece*, in: Giorgio Riello/Peter Mcneil (Ed.), Shoes: A History from Sandals to Sneakers, New York 2006, 30–49.

Stefan Bollmann, *Monte Verità 1900: Der Traum vom alternativen Leben beginnt*, Munich 2017.

Knut Borchardt/Christoph Buchheim, *Die Wirkung der Marshallplan-Hilfe in Schlüsselbranchen der deutschen Wirtschaft*, in: Hans-Jürgen Schröder (ed.), Marshallplan und westdeutscher Wiederaufstieg: Positionen – Kontroversen, Stuttgart 1990, 119–149.

Joseph Borkin, *Die unheilige Allianz der I. G. Farben: Eine Interessengemeinschaft im Dritten Reich*, Frankfurt 1981.

Marcus Böick, *Die Treuhand: Idee – Praxis – Erfahrung 1990–1994*, Göttingen 2018.

Frank Bösch, *Zeitenwende 1979: Als die Welt von heute begann*, Munich 1991.

Rina R. Bousalis, *The Counterculture Generation: Idolized, Appropriated, and Misunderstood*, in: The Councilor: A Journal of the Social Studies 82 (2021), 4.

Ludwig Brake, *Die ersten Eisenbahnen in Hessen: Eisenbahnpolitik und Eisenbahnbau in Frankfurt, Hessen-Darmstadt, Kurhessen und Nassau bis 1866*, Wiesbaden 1991.

Kai-Werner Brand, *Umweltbewegung*, in: Roland Roth/Dieter Rucht (eds.), Die sozialen Bewegungen in Deutschland seit 1945: Ein Handbuch, Frankfurt 2008, 227.

Peter Braunstein/Michael William Doyle, *Imagine Nation: The American Counterculture of the 1960's and 70's*, Routledge 2013.

Emily Brayshaw, *Oskar Schlemmer's Kitsch (1922): A Contextualisation and Translation*, in: Journal of Aesthetics and Culture 13 (2021).

Michael Breitenacher, *Leder- und Schuhindustrie: Strukturelle Probleme und Wachstumschancen*, Berlin/ Munich 1967.

Christopher Breward, *Fashioning London*, Oxford 2004.

Christopher Breward, *The Suit: Form, Function and Style*, London 2016.

Nike U. Breyer, *Linientreu: Schuhkonzepte der Lebensreform und ihr Weg durch das 20. Jahrhundert*, in: Kai Buchholz et. al. (eds.), Die Lebensreform: Entwürfe zur Neugestaltung von Leben und Kunst um 1900, vol. 1, Darmstadt 2001, 597–602.

Nike U. Breyer, *"Es gibt keinen gesunden Menschenfuß, der vorn in einer Spitze ausläuft" (Knud Ahlborn): Wandervögel, Jugendbewegung und Schuhreform*, in: Medizin, Gesellschaft und Geschichte: Jahrbuch des Instituts für Geschichte der Medizin 30 (2011), 85–110.

Nike U. Breyer, *Gymnastiksandale nach Prof. Thomsen*, in: Wolfgang Antweiler (ed.), Schritt für Schritt: Die Geburt des modernen Schuhs, Hilden 2013, 126.

Nike U. Breyer, *Orthopädische Schwester-Schuhe*, in: Wolfgang Antweiler (ed.), Schritt für Schritt: Die Geburt des modernen Schuhs, Hilden 2013, 120.

Nike U. Breyer, *Rationelle Schuhe: Hauptsache, die große Zehe hat die richtige Lage!*, in: Wolfgang Antweiler (ed.), Schritt für Schritt: Die Geburt des modernen Schuhs, Hilden 2013, 53.

Nike U. Breyer, *Mannesmann-Zehenkammerschuhe*, in: Wolfgang Antweiler (ed.), Schritt für Schritt: Die Geburt des modernen Schuhs, Hilden 2013.

Marlies Buchholz/Hans-Dieter Schmid, *Juden in Niedersachsen: Eine ethnisch-religiöse Minderheit zwischen Assimilation, Vertreibung und Vernichtung*, in: Gerd Steinwascher (ed.), Geschichte Niedersachsens, vol. 5: Von der Weimarer Republik bis zur Wiedervereinigung, Hanover 2010, 1165–1219.

Cheryl Buckley/Hazel Clark, *Fashion and Everyday Life: London and New York*, London 2017.

Carsten Burhop et al., *Merck, 1668–2018: Von der Apotheke zum Weltkonzern*, Munich 2018.

Peter Camper, *Abhandlung von der besten Form der Schuhe*, Hamburg 1781.

Alessandra Ceriani/Filippo Caserio, *Vigevano nel boom: Scarpe, benzolo e altre storie; Gli anni Sessanta tra luci e ombre*, Vigevano 2021.

Alice Cicolini, *Historicism and Historical Revival*, in: Valerie Steele (ed.), The Berg Companion to Fashion, Oxford 2010, 419–421.

Jon Cope/Dennis Maloney, *Fashion Promotion in Practice*, London 2019.

Sara L. Crawley, *Are Butch and Fem Working-Class and Anti-Feminist?*, in: Gender and Society 15 (2001), 175–196.

Manuel Dichtl, *Der Orthopäde Prof. Dr. Franz Schede (1882–1976): Leben und Werk*, diss., Regensburg 2012.

Bernhard Dietz, *Aufstieg der Manager: Wertewandel in den Führungsetagen der westdeutschen Wirtschaft, 1949–1989*, Berlin 2020.

Jürgen Dispan/Sylvia Stieler, *Leder- und Schuhindustrie: Branchentrends und Herausforderungen*, Informationsdienst des IMU Instituts 2015.

Jürgen Dispan/Laura Mendler, *Branchenanalyse Leder- und Schuhindustrie: Entwicklungstrends und Herausforderungen*, Düsseldorf 2021.

Pierre-Yves Donzé, *A Business History of the Swatch Watch Group: The Rebirth of Swiss Watchmaking and the Globalization of the Luxury Industry*, Basingstoke 2014.

Pierre-Yves Donzé et al., *The Oxford Handbook of Luxury Business*, Oxford 2022.

Pierre-Yves Donzé, *Luxury as an Industry*, in: Pierre-Yves Donzé et al. (eds.), The Oxford Handbook of Luxury Business, Oxford 2022, 59–78.

Anselm Doering-Manteuffel/Lutz Raphael, *Nach dem Boom: Perspektiven auf die Zeitgeschichte seit 1970*, Göttingen 2010.

Erich Druschky, *Aufgabe, Sinn und Zweck der Kosmetikschule Neckarbischofsheim, der Ausbildungsstätte für Arztfrauen*, in: Journal für medizinische Kosmetik 53, no. 6 (June 20, 1953).

Alfred DuPont Chandler, *Strategy and Structure: Chapters in the History of the Industrial Enterprise*, Mansfield Centre, CT, 2013.

Anneliese Durst/Lerke Gravenhorst, *Frauenschuhe: Spannungen, Paradoxien, Entwicklungen in der Inszenierung von Weiblichkeit*, in: Michael Andritzky et al. (eds.), Z. B. Schuhe: Vom blossen Fuss zum Stöckelschuh; Eine Kulturgeschichte der Fussbekleidung, Giessen 1988, 202–207.

Samantha Eddy, *Groped and Gutted: Hollywood's Hegemonic Reimagining of Counterculture*, in: Screen Bodies 5 (2020), 33.

Gine Elsner, *Die "aufrechte" Haltung: Orthopädie im Nationalsozialismus*, Hamburg 2019.

Georg Emig, *Die Berufserziehung bei den Handwerkerzünften in der Landgrafschaft Hessen-Darmstadt und im Großherzogtum Hessen: Vom Beginn des 18. Jahrhunderts bis zur Einführung der Gewerbefreiheit 1866*, Frankfurt 1969.

Joanne Entwistle, *The Fashioned Body: Fashion, Dress and Social Theory*, Malden 2015.

Paul Erker/Nils Fehlhaber, *150 Jahre Continental: The Skill of Transformation*, Berlin/Boston 2021.

Kjetil Fallan/Grace Lees-Maffei, *Designing Worlds: National Design Histories in an Age of Globalization*, New York 2016.

Werner Faulstich (ed.), *Die Kultur der 60er Jahre*, Munich 2003.

Jeffrey Fear, *Mining the Past: Historicizing Organizational Learning and Change*, in: Marcelo Bucheli/R. Daniel Wadhwani (eds.), Organizations in Time: History, Theory and Methods, Oxford 2014, 169–191.

Niall Ferguson et. al. (eds.), *The Shock of the Global: The 1970s in Perspective*, Cambridge, MA, 2010.

Paloma Fernandez/Andrea Colli, *The Endurance of Family Businesses: A Global Overview*, Cambridge 2013.

Melissa Fisher, *Wall Street Women*, Durham, NC, 2012.

Inez Florschütz (ed.), *Step by Step: Schuh; Design im Wandel*, Offenbach 2019.

Giovanni Luigi Fontana, *Style through Design: Form and Function*, in: Giorgio Riello/Peter McNeil (eds.), Shoes: A History from Sandals to Sneakers, London 2011, 326–352.

Eckhart G. Franz et. al., *Großherzogtum Hessen (1800) 1806–1918*, in: Winfried Speitkamp (ed.), Handbuch der hessischen Geschichte: Hessen im deutschen Bund und im neuen Deutschen Reich (1806) 1815 bis 1945, Marburg 2010.

Douglas L. Fugate/Joanna Phillips Melancon, *Product Gender Perceptions and Antecedents of Product Gender Congruence*, in: Journal of Consumer Marketing 3(2010), 251–261.

Günter Gall, *Kunsthandwerk, Volkskunde, Völkerkunde, Fachtechnik*, Offenbach am Main 1956.

Wendy Gamber, *The Female Economy: The Millinery and Dressmaking Trades 1860–1930*, Chicago 1997.

François Alexandre Pierre de Garsault, *Der Schuster: Von dem Herren von Garsault*, Leipzig 1990 (first published Leipzig 1769).

Jérôme Gautier, *Chanel: Ein Name – ein Stil*, Munich 2015.

Adam Geczy/Vicki Karaminas, *Queer Style*, London 2013.

Adam Geczy/Vicki Karaminas, *The Body*, in: Alexandra Palmer (ed.), A Cultural History of Dress and Fashion in the Modern Age, London 2021, 63–84.

Gemeindevorstand der Gemeinde Hammersbach (ed.), *925 Jahre Langenbergheim*, Hammersbach 1982.

Dirk Georges, *1810/11 – 1993: Handwerk und Interessenpolitik*, Frankfurt 1993.

Frida Giannini, *GUCCI: The Making Of*, Rizzoli 2011.

Ingrid Gilcher-Holtey, *Die 68er Bewegung: Deutschland, Westeuropa, USA*, Munich 2005.

Sander Gilman, *The Jew's Body*, New York 1991.

Alison Gill, *Limousines for Feet: The Rhetoric of Sneakers*, in: Giorgio Riello/Peter Mcneil (eds.), Shoes: A History from Sandals to Sneakers, New York 2006, 372–385.

Alison Gill/Abby Mellick Lopes, *On Wearing: A Critical Framework for Valuing Design's Already Made*, in: Design and Culture, 3 (2011), 307–327.

Jens Gmeiner, *Mythos Minirock: Eine Modeikone der 1960er Jahre zwischen Emanzipation, Jugend und Massenkonsum*, in: Robert Lorenz/Franz Walter (eds.), 1964: Das Jahr, mit dem "68" begann, Bielefeld 2014, 97–110.

Andreas Grießinger, *Schuhmacher*, in: Reinhold Reith (ed.), Das alte Handwerk: Von Bader bis Zinngießer, Munich 1991, 217–223.

Alison Gwilt, *A Practical Guide to Sustainable Fashion*, London 2020.

Birgit Haase, *"Walking in Crocodile,"* in: Anna-Brigitte Schlittler/Katharina Tietze (eds.), Über Schuhe: Zur Geschichte und Theorie der Fußbekleidung, Bielefeld 2016, 21–34.

Hans Werner Hahn, *Wirtschaft und Verkehr*, in: Winfried Speitkamp (ed.), Handbuch der hessischen Geschichte: Bevölkerung, Wirtschaft und Staat in Hessen 1806 – 1945, vol. 1, Marburg 2010, 73–251.

Philipp Heldmann, *Das "Wirtschaftswunder" in Westdeutschland: Überlegungen zur Periodisierung und Ursachen*, in: Archiv für Sozialgeschichte 36 (1996), 323–344.

Paul Heller, *Von der Landeskrüppelanstalt zur Orthopädischen Universitätsklinik: Das "Elisabethheim" in Rostock*, Münster 2009.

Anja Helmers, *Der kindliche Fuß*, Berlin 2019.

Corona Hepp, *Avantgarde: Moderne Kunst, Kulturkritik und Reformbewegung nach der Jahrhundertwende*, Munich 1987.

Christopher Herb, *Restrukturierung von Wertschöpfungsketten in der Digitalisierung: Eine Analyse der deutschen Schuhbranche vom Hersteller bis zum Konsumenten*, Würzburg 2022.

Bruno Herberger, *Die Organisation des Schuhmacherhandwerks zu Frankfurt a. M. bis zum Ende des 18. Jahrhunderts*, diss., Frankfurt 1931.

Dan Herman, *Outsmart the MBA Clones: The Alternative Guide to Competitive Strategy*, Rochester, IL, 2015.

Sylvia Heudecker, *"Schuh,"* in: Günter Butzer/Joachim Jacob (eds.), Metzler Lexikon literarischer Symbole, 334–335.

Klaus Heyer, *Von Homer bis Caligula*, in: Michael Andritzky et al. (eds.), Z. B. Schuhe: Vom bloßen Fuß zum Stöckelschuh; Eine Kulturgeschichte der Fußbekleidung, Giessen 1988, 42–46.

Ian Hodder, *Entangled: An Archaeology of the Relationships Between Humans and Things*, Chichester 2012.

Georg Hohmann, *Fuß und Bein: Ihre Erkrankung und deren Behandlung*, Munich 1939.

Georg Hohmann, *Ein Arzt erlebt seine Zeit: Ansprachen, Lebensbilder, Begegnungen*, Munich 1954.

Sabine Huschka, *Merce Cunningham und der Moderne Tanz: Körperkonzepte, Choreographie und Tanzästhetik*, Würzburg 2000.

Ronald Inglehart, The Silent Revolution in Europe: Intergenerational Change in Post-Industrial Societies, in: The American Political Science Review 65 (1971), 991–1017.

Yoko Isozaki/Pierre-Yves Donzé, *Dominance versus collaboration models: French and Italian luxury fashion brands in Japan*, in: Journal of Global Fashion Marketing 13 (2022), 294–408.

Sabine Johann, *Schuhherstellung: Von der handwerklichen zur maschinellen Fertigung*, in: Willi Schächter/Michael Wagner (eds.), Vom Zunfthandwerk zum modernen Industriebetrieb: Schuhe und Schuhherstellung in Deutschland seit dem 18. Jahrhundert, Hauenstein 1998, 45–56.

Geoffrey Jones, *Deeply Responsible Business: A Global History of Value-Driven Leadership*, Cambridge 2023.

Annamma Joy/Russell W. Belk, *Why Luxury Brands Partner with Artists*, in: Pierre-Yves Donzé et al. (eds.), The Oxford Handbook of Luxury Business, Oxford 2022, 309–330.

Daniela Kahn, *Die Steuerung der Wirtschaft durch Recht im nationalsozialistischen Deutschland: Das Beispiel der Reichsgruppe Industrie*, Frankfurt 2006.

Jean-Noël Kapferer, *Kapferer on Luxury: How Luxury Brands Can Grow Yet Remain Rare*, London 2015.

Fariba Karimi et al., *Inferring Gender from Names on the Web: A Comparative Evaluation of Gender Detection Methods*, in: Computers and Society Sciences (Mar. 14, 2016).

Rainer Karlsch et al., *Unternehmen Sport: Die Geschichte von adidas*, Munich 2018.

Jason Kaufman/Matthew E. Kaliner, *The Re-accomplishment of Place in Twentieth-Century Vermont and New Hampshire: History Repeats Itself, Until It Doesn't*, in: The Journal of Theory and Society 40 (2011), 124.

Yuniya Kawamura, *The Japanese Revolution in Paris Fashion*, London 2004.

Yuniya Kawamura, *Fashion-ology*, London 2018.

Gundolf Keil, *Geleitwort*, in: August Rütt (ed.), *Die Geschichte der Orthopädie im deutschen Sprachraum*, Stuttgart 1993.

Olivia King et. al., *Sociology of the Professions: What It Means for Podiatry*, in: Journal of Foot and Ankle Research 30 (2018), online publication.

Christian Kleinschmidt, *"Marmor, Stein und Eisen bricht ..." – Westdeutschlands Aufbruch ins Kunststoffzeitalter*, in: Technikgeschichte 68, no. 4 (2001), 355–372.

Christian Kleinschmidt, *Der produktive Blick: Wahrnehmung amerikanischer und japanischer management- und Produktionsmethoden durch deutsche Unternehmer 1950–1985*, Berlin 2002.

Christoph Kleßmann, *Zwei Staaten, eine Nation: Deutsche Geschichte 1955–1970*, Bonn 1988.

Arnd Kluge, *Die Zünfte*, Stuttgart 2007.

Eva-Maria Knoll et al., *"Globalisierung,"* in: Eva-Maria Knoll et al. (eds.), Lexikon der Globalisierung, Bielefeld 2011, 126-129.

Peter Knötzele, *Römische Schuhe: Luxus an den Füßen*, Stuttgart 2007.

Jörg Koch, *Marketing: Einführung in die marktorientierte Unternehmensführung*, Munich 1999.

Roman Köster, *Die Wissenschaft der Außenseiter: Die Krise der Nationalökonomie in der Weimarer Republik*, Göttingen 2011.

Roman Köster, *Hugo Boss 1924–1945: Eine Kleiderfabrik zwischen Weimarer Republik und "Drittem Reich,"* Munich 2011.

Roman Köster, *Seidensticker: Geschichte eines Familienunternehmens 1919–2019*, Essen 2019.

Hansjörg Kramer, *Die Vertriebsformen eines Großunternehmens der deutschen Schuhindustrie*, Freiburg i. Br. 1955.

Angel Kwolek-Folland, *Engendering Business: Men and Women in the Corporate Office 1870–1930*, Baltimore 1994.

Angel Kwolek-Folland, *Incorporating Women: A History of Women and Business in the United States*, New York 1998.

Marc Landy et al., *The Environmental Protection Agency: Asking the Wrong Questions; From Nixon to Clinton*, New York/Oxford 1994.

Thorsten Laue, *Tantra im Westen. Eine religionswissenschaftliche Studie über "Weißes Tantra Yoga", "Kundalini Yoga" und "Sikh Dharma,"* in: Yogi Bhajans, Healthy, Happy, Holy Organization (3HO) unter besonderer Berücksichtigung der 3H Organisation Deutschland e. V., Münster 2012, diss., Tübingen 2011.

Mariangela Lavanga, *The Role of The Pitti Uomo Trade Fair in the Menswear Fashion Industry,* in: Regina Lee Blaszczyk/Ben Wubs (eds.), The Fashion Forecasters: A Hidden History of Color and Trend Prediction, London 2018, 191–209.

James Laver, *Costume and Fashion: A Concise History*, London 2002.

Friedrich Lenger, *Sozialgeschichte des deutschen Handwerks seit 1800*, Frankfurt 1988.

Ludger Lindlar, *Das missverstandene Wirtschaftswunder: Westdeutschland und die westeuropäische Nachkriegsprosperität*, Tübingen 1997.

Ulrich Linse, *Procrustes ante Portas! Oder: Wo dem Bürgertum der Schuh drückt*, in: Michael Andritzky et al. (eds.), Z. B. Schuhe: Vom bloßen Fuß zum Stöckelschuh; Eine Kulturgeschichte der Fußbekleidung, Giessen 1988, 72-80.

Clare Lomas et al., *Beyond the Rainbow: Queer Shoes*, in: Giorgio Riello/Peter McNeil (eds.), Shoes: A History from Sandals to Sneakers, New York 2011, 290-305.

Hans van der Loo/Willem van Reijen, *Modernisierung: Projekt und Paradox*, Munich 1997.

Ingrid Loschek, *Wann ist Mode? Strukturen, Strategien und Innovationen*, Berlin 2007.

W. David Marx, *Ametora: How Japan saved American style*, New York 2015.

Colin Mayer, *Prosperity: Better Business Makes the Greater Good*, Oxford 2018.

Colin Mayer, *Putting Purpose into Practice: The Economics of Mutuality*, Oxford 2021.

Jerome E. McCarthy, *Basic Marketing: A Managerial Approach*, Homewood, IL, 1960.

Colin McDowell, *Shoes: Fashion and Fantasy*, New York 1989.

Tamsin McLaren/Fiona Armstrong-Gibbs, *Marketing Fashion Footwear: The Business of Shoes*, London 2017.

Rebecca Mead, *Sole Cycle: The Homely Birkenstock Gets a Fashion Makeover*, in: The New Yorker Magazine (Mar, 23, 2015), 5.

Heribert Meffert et al., *Marketing: Grundlagen marktorientierter Unternehmensführung*, Wiesbaden 2012.

Hermann Meyer, *Procrustes ante portas! Ein kulturgeschichtliches Zerrbild*, in: Monatsschrift des wissenschaftlichen Vereins in Zürich 2 (1857), 62-72.

Ilya Mieck, *Kleine Wirtschaftsgeschichte der neuen Bundesländer*, Stuttgart 2009.

Barry Miles, *Hippie*, New York 2004.

Sayako Miura, *The Developmental History of the Insole Market in Japan: Rising Health Consciousness and an Unintended Shift toward Fashion (1984-2010)*, in: Japanese Research in Business History 38 (2021), 43-61.

Fritz Müller, *Populäre Anatomie und Physiologie des menschlichen Körpers in ihrer Beziehung zur orthopädischen Mechanik: Ein Lehrbuch zum Gebrauch an den einschlägigen Fachschulen und zum Selbstunterricht für Orthopädiemechaniker und Bandagisten*, Munich 1937.

Gerhard Neckermann/Hans Wessels, *Struktur und Wettbewerbsfähigkeit der Schuhindustrie in der Bundesrepublik Deutschland*, Berlin 1988.

Niedergründau (ed.), *750 Jahre Niedergründau: 7., 8., 9., 10. Juni 1968*, Niedergründau 1968.

Norbert Ohler, *Reisen im Mittelalter*, Darmstadt 2004.

Thomas Osterkorn (ed.), *Gründergeschichten: Vom Abenteuer, ein Unternehmen aufzubauen*, Frankfurt 2007.

Jo B. Paoletti, *Sex and Unisex: Fashion, Feminism, and the Sexual Revolution*, Bloomington, IN, 2015.

Vanessa Patrick/Alokparna (Sonia) Basu Monga, *Building and Growing Luxury Brands: Strategies for Pursuing Growth While Maintaining Brand Coherence*, in: Felicitas Morhart et al., Research Handbook on Luxury Branding, Cheltenham 2020, 138-150.

Dietmar Petzina, *Autarkiepolitik im Dritten Reich: Der nationalsozialistische Vierteljahresplan*, Stuttgart 1968.

Hermann Pfeiffer, *Fußbekleidung*, in: Lotte Frucht/Christian Schneehagen (eds.), Unsere Kleidung: Anregungen zur neuen Männer- und Frauentracht, Hamburg 1914, 27-32.

Toni Pierenkemper, *Moderne Unternehmensgeschichte* (Grundzüge der Modernen Wirtschaftsgeschichte 1), Stuttgart 2000.

Peter Pitzen, *Die Geschichte der Deutschen Orthopädischen Gesellschaft: Von der Königsberger Tagung 1936 bis zum 50. Kongress in München 1962*, Stuttgart 1963.

Alfred Pletsch, *Bevölkerungsentwicklung und Urbanisierung*, in: Winfried Speitkamp (ed.), Handbuch der hessischen Geschichte: Bevölkerung, Wirtschaft und Staat in Hessen 1806-1945, vol. 1, Marburg 2010.

Werner Plumpe, *Wie entscheiden Unternehmen?*, in: Zeitschrift für Unternehmensgeschichte 61 (2016), 149-159.

Gabriele Praschl-Bichler, *Affenhaube, Schellentracht und Wendeschuh: Kleidung und Mode im Mittelalter*, Munich 2011.

Michael A. Rauschmann/Klaus-Dieter Thomann, *200 Jahre Orthopädie: Bilder aus der Vergangenheit*, in: Orthopäde 29 (2000), 1008–1017.

Reichsgruppe Industrie (ed.), *Gliederung der Reichsgruppe Industrie*, Leipzig 1936.

Karlheinz Reidenbach, *Produktionsgestaltung und Marktwandlungen der pfälzischen Schuhindustrie nach dem 2. Weltkrieg (1945–1954)*, diss., Mainz 1956.

Wilfried Reininghaus, *Gewerbe in der frühen Neuzeit*, Berlin 1990.

Giorgio Riello, *A Foot in the Past: Footwear in the Long Eighteenth Century*, Oxford 2006.

Giorgio Riello/Peter McNeil, *Shoes: A History from Sandals to Sneakers*, London 2011.

Giorgio Riello/Peter McNeil, *Introduction: A Long Walk; Shoes, People and Places*, in: Giorgio Riello/ Peter McNeil (eds.), Shoes. A History from Sandals to Sneakers, New York 2006, 2–29.

Agnès Rocamora, *Fashioning the City: Paris, Fashion and the Media*, London 2009.

Agnès Rocamora, *Mediatization and Digital Media in the Field of Fashion*, in: Fashion Theory 21 (2016), 1–18.

Katrina Rolley, *Love, Desire and the Pursuit of the Whole: Dress and the Lesbian Couple*, in: Juliet Ash/ Elizabeth Wilson (eds.), Chic Thrills: A Fashion Reader, London 1992, 30–39.

Salvatore Rossi, *La politica economica italiana*, Rome 2008.

Cornelia Rührig, *Stadt und Natur: Frankfurt um 1780*, Frankfurt 1983.

Karl Rumpf, *Die Schuhmacherei im Grossherzogtum Hessen*, diss., Giessen 1907. August Rütt, *Die Geschichte der Orthopädie im deutschen Sprachraum*, in: August Rütt (ed.), Geschichte der Orthopädie im deutschen Sprachraum, Stuttgart 1993, 1–79.

Steven Saxonberg, *From Defamilialization to Degenderization: Toward a New Welfare Typology Social Policy & Administration*, in: Social Policy Administration 1 (2013), 26–49.

Emanuela Scarpellini, *Italian Fashion since 1945: A Cultural History*, Cham 2019.

Eike W. Schamp, *Decline of the District, Renewal of Firms: An Evolutionary Approach to Footwear Production in the Pirmasens Area, Germany*, in: Environment and Planning 37 (2005), 617–634.

Eike W. Schamp, *Fashion Industries on the Move: Spatial Restructuring of the Footwear Sector in the Enlarged European Union*, in: Zeitschrift für Wirtschaftsgeographie 60 (2016), 155–170.

Joachim Scharloth, *1968: Eine Kommunikationsgeschichte*, Munich 2011.

Franz Schede, *Rückblick und Ausblick: Erlebnisse und Betrachtungen eines Arztes*, Stuttgart 1960.

Axel Schildt, *Moderne Zeiten: Freizeit, Massenmedien und "Zeitgeist" in der Bundesrepublik der 50er-Jahre*, Hamburg 1995.

Axel Schildt, *Sozialgeschichte der Bundesrepublik Deutschland bis 1989/90*, Munich 2007.

Axel Schildt, *Amerikanische Einflüsse auf die westdeutsche Konsumentwicklung nach dem Zweiten Weltkrieg*, in: Heinz-Gerhard Haupt/Claudius Torp (eds.), Die Konsumgesellschaft in Deutschland 1890–1990: Ein Handbuch, Frankfurt 2009, 435–447.

Axel Schildt/Detlef Siegfried, *Deutsche Kulturgeschichte: Die Bundesrepublik von 1945 bis zur Gegenwart*, Munich 2009.

Anna-Brigitte Schlittler, *"Bally-Schuhe sind tonangebende Modeschöpfungen": Schuh-Design im Zweiten Weltkrieg*, in: Anna-Brigitte Schlittler/Katharina Tietze (eds.), Über Schuhe: Zur Geschichte und Theorie der Fußbekleidung, Bielefeld 2016, 73–92.

Anna-Brigitte Schlittler, *Queere Schuhe?*, in: Gertrud Lehnert/Maria Weilandt (eds.), Ist Mode queer? Neue Perspektiven der Modeforschung, Bielefeld 2016, 59–72.

Gustav Schmoller, *Zur Geschichte der deutschen Kleingewerbe im 19. Jahrhundert*, Halle 1870.

Christian Schneehagen, *Die Freideutsche Jugend und die neue Kleidung*, in: Lotte Frucht/Christian Schneehagen (eds.), Unsere Kleidung: Anregungen zur neuen Männer- und Frauentracht, Hamburg 1914.

Andrea Schneider-Braunberger, *Die Unternehmerfamilie – Risiko für das Familienunternehmen?*, in: Equa-Stiftung (ed.), Unternehmerfamilien: Eigentum verpflichtet, Munich 2021, 299–313.

Moritz Schoene, *Die moderne Entwickelung des Schuhmachergewerbes in historischer, statistischer und technischer Hinsicht, ein Beitrag zur Kenntnis unseres Gewerbewesens*, Jena 1888.

Klaus Schreiner, *Rituale, Zeichen, Bilder: Formen und Funktionen symbolischer Kommunikation im Mittelalter*, Cologne 2011.

Gerhard Schulz, *Die deutsche Literatur zwischen Französischer Revolution und Restauration*, part 1: *1789–1806*, Munich 2000.

Paul Schultze-Naumburg, *Die Kultur des weiblichen Körpers als Grundlage der Frauenkleidung*, Jena 1901.

Doris Schwarzmann-Schafhauser, *Orthopädie im Wandel: Die Herausbildung von Disziplin und Berufsstand in Bund Kaiserreich (1815–1914)*, Stuttgart 2004.

Ludwig Schwering, *Die etwas andere Geschichte der Orthopädie*, in: 100 Jahre Orthopädieschuhtechnik: Innovationen, Versorgungskonzepte, Perspektiven, special issue, Orthopädieschuhtechnik (2017), 24–30.

Elisabeth Semmelhack, *Shoes: The Meaning of Style*, Chicago 2017.

Amartya Sen, *Identity and Violence: The Illusion of Destiny*, New York 2006.

Amartya Sen, *The Fog of Identity*, in: Politics, Philosophy & Economics 3 (2009), 285–288.

Shoichi Shimizu, *Arukukoto, ashi soshite kutsu* [Walking, Feet, and Shoes], Tokyo 1995.

Karl Sigg/Felix Oesch, *Schuhmode und Gesundheit*, Berlin 1958.

Michael Silverstein et al., *Trading Up: Why Consumers Want New Luxury Goods—and How Companies Create Them*, London 2008.

Allan Lloyd Smith, *Postmodernism/Gothicism*, in: Victor Sage/Allan Lloyd Smith (eds.), Modern Gothic: A Reader, Manchester 1996, 11.

Jennifer Smith Maguire/Julian Matthews (eds.), *The Cultural Intermediaries Reader*, London 2014.

Susan L. Sokolowski, *Sneakers*, in: Valerie Steele (ed.) The Berg Companion to Fashion, Oxford 2009, 640–644.

Tamara Spitzing, *Auf Schusters Rappen durch die Geschichte*, in: Michael Andritzky et al. (eds.), Z. B. Schuhe: Vom bloßen Fuß zum Stöckelschuh; Eine Kulturgeschichte der Fußbekleidung, Giessen 1988, 47–57.

Mark Spoerer, *C&A: Ein Familienunternehmen in Deutschland, den Niederlanden und Großbritannien*, Munich 2016.

Christoph Spöcker, *Karl Lagerfeld: Kleine Anekdoten aus dem Leben eins Großen*, Munich 2016.

Angelika Starbatty, *Aussehen ist Ansichtssache: Kleidung in der Kommunikation der römischen Antike*, Munich 2010.

John Robert Stark, *The Overlooked Majority: German Women in the Four Zones of Occupied Germany, 1945–1949; A Comparative Study*, diss., Ohio State University, 2003.

Renate Stauss, *What Fashion Is Not (Only)*, in: On Capital, Vestoj 9 (2019), 55–76.

Michael Stephan/Martin J. Schneider *Marken- und Produktpiraterie: Fälscherstrategien, Schutzinstrumente, Bekämpfungsmanagement*, Düsseldorf 2011.

Helge Sternke, *Alles über Herrenschuhe*, Berlin 2006.

Stiftung Familienunternehmen (ed.), *Die steuerliche Belastung von Familienunternehmen beim Generationswechsel: Daten und Fakten zur Rolle des Betriebsvermögens*, Munich 2014.

Britton Stiles Rhuart, *Hippie Films, Hippiesploitation, and the Emerging Counterculture, 1955–1970*, diss., Bowling Green State University, 2020.

Jochen Strähle/Noemi Jahne-Warrior, *Case Study: Grunge Music and Grunge Style*, in: Jochen Strähle (ed.), Fashion and Music, Reutlingen 2018, 51–70.

Willi Stubenvoll, *Die Straße: Geschichte und Gegenwart eines Handelsweges; 750 Jahre Messen in Frankfurt*, Frankfurt 1990.

Drake Stutesman, *Cooking: Studying Film Costume Design*, in: Sofia Pantouvaki/Peter McNeil (eds.), Performance Costume: New Perspectives and Methods, London 2021.

Anne Sudrow, *Vom Leder zum Kunststoff. Werkstoff-Forschung auf der "Schuhprüfstrecke" im Konzentrationslager Sachsenhausen 1940 bis 1945*, in: Helmut Maier (ed.), Rüstungsforschung im Nationalsozialismus: Organisation, Mobilisierung und Entgrenzung der Technikwissenschaften, Göttingen 2002, 214–249.

Anne Sudrow, *Der Schuh im Nationalsozialismus: Eine Produktgeschichte im deutsch-britisch-amerikanischen Vergleich*, Göttingen 2010.

Brenda Sunoo, *Birkenstock Braces to Fight the Competition*, in: Personnel Journal 8 (1994), 68–75.

Arnold Sywottek, *Wege in die 50er Jahre*, in: Axel Schildt/Arnold Sywottek (eds.), Modernisierung im Wiederaufbau: Die westdeutsche Gesellschaft der 50er Jahre, Bonn 1998.

Lou Taylor, *Establishing Dress History*, Manchester 2004.

Karl Teppe, *Trümmergesellschaft im Wiederaufbau*, in: Aus Politik und Zeitgeschichte, B 18–19 (1995), 22–33.

Richard H. Thaler/Cass R. Sunstein, *Nudge: The Final Edition*, New York 2008.

Wilhelm Thomsen, *Kampf der Fußschwäche! Ursachen, Mechanismus, Mittel und Wege zu ihrer Bekämpfung*, Munich 1942.

Stephanie Tilly, *"Die guten Zeiten sind ... vorbei": Zum Verhältnis von Automobilindustrie, Politik und Automobilverband in den 1970er Jahren*, in: Morten Reitmayer/Ruth Rosenberger (eds.), Unternehmen am Ende des "goldenen Zeitalters": Die 1970er Jahre in unternehmens- und wirtschaftshistorischer Perspektive, Essen 2008, 209–232.

Walter Uffelmann, *Pferdemusterungen in Mittel-Gründau*, in: Geschichtsverein Gründau e. V. (ed.), Grindaha: 800 Jahre Mittel-Gründau, special issue 7, Gründau 2019.

Ignazio Visco, *Politica monetaria e inflazione in Italia, 1994–96*, in: N. Acocella et al. (eds.), Saggi di politica economica in onore di Federico Caffè, Rome 1999.

Clemens Vollnhals, *Das gescheiterte Experiment*, in: Clemens Vollnhals (ed.), Entnazifizierung: Politische Säuberung und Rehabilitierung in den vier Besatzungszonen 1945–1949, Munich 1991.

Laura Van Waardhuizen, *Birkenstocks*, in: Annette Lynch/Mitchell D. Strauss (eds.), Ethnic Dress in the United States: A Cultural Encyclopedia, Lanham 2014.

Michael Wagner, *Hauenstein und die deutsche Schuhindustrie: Ein historischer Überblick*, Hauenstein 1997.

Michael Wagner, *Die Entstehung der südwestdeutschen Industrieregion um Pirmasens (1790–1918)*, in: Willi Schächter/Michael Wagner (eds.), Vom Zunfthandwerk zum modernen Industriebetrieb: Schuhe und Schuhherstellung in Deutschland seit dem 18. Jahrhundert, Hauenstein 1998, 23–44.

Jonathan Walford, *The Seductive Shoe: Four Centuries of Fashion Footwear*, London 2007.

Lisa M. Walker, *How to Recognize a Lesbian: The Cultural Politics of Looking Like What You Are*, in: Signs 18 (1993), 866–890.

Paul Weber, *Der Schuhmacher: Ein Beruf im Wandel der Zeit*, Aarau 1988.

Sheila Whiteley, *Counterculture: The Classical View*, in: James D. Wright (ed.), The International Encyclopedia of the Social and Behavioural Sciences, vol. 5, Amsterdam 2015.

Andreas Wiedemann, *Politik und Alltag in den Landkreisen Friedberg und Büdingen 1945–1949*, Friedberg 1994.

Michael Wildt, *Vom kleinen Wohlstand: Eine Konsumgeschichte der fünfziger Jahre*, Frankfurt 1996.

Michael Wildt, *"Wohlstand für alle": Das Spannungsfeld von Konsum und Politik in der Bundesrepublik*, in: Heinz-Gerhard Haupt/Claudius Torp (eds.), Die Konsumgesellschaft in Deutschland 1890–1990: Ein Handbuch, Frankfurt 2009, 305–318.

Andreas Wirsching, *Abschied vom Provisorium 198–1990* (Geschichte der Bundesrepublik Deutschland, vol. 6), Munich 2006.

Klaus Wolbert, *Körper zwischen animalischer Leiblichkeit und ästhetisierender Verklärung der Physis*, in: Kai Buchholz et al. (eds.), Die Lebensreform: Entwürfe zur Neugestaltung von Leben und Kunst um 1900, vol. 2, Darmstadt 2001, 339–340.

Mary A. Yeager, *Women in Business*, Northampton, MA, 1999.

Mary A. Yeager, *Gender, Race and Entrepreneurship*, in: Teresa da Silva Lopes et al. (eds.) Routledge Companion to the Makers of Global Business, Abingdon 2019, 69–92.

Justine De Young, *Fashion and the Press*, in: Gloria Groom (ed.), Impressionism, New Haven, CT, 2012, 232–243.

Irmgard Zündorf, *Der Preis der Marktwirtschaft: Staatliche Preispolitik und Lebensstandard in Westdeutschland 1948 bis 1963*, Stuttgart 2006.

Archives

Archiv der sozialen Demokratie
British Newspaper Archive
Bundesarchiv Koblenz
Firmenarchiv Birkenstock
Hessisches Hauptstaatsarchiv Wiesbaden
Hessisches Staatsarchiv Darmstadt
Hessisches Staatsarchiv Marburg
Landeskirchliches Archiv Kassel, Archiv der evangelischen Kirche von Kurhessen-Waldeck
Niedersächsisches Landesarchiv, Abt. Bückeburg
Nordrhein-Westfälisches Landesarchiv Duisburg
ProQuest History Newspaper Archive
City of Sydney Archives
Stadtarchiv Friedberg
Stiftung Rheinisch-Westfälisches Wirtschaftsarchiv zu Köln
Unternehmensarchiv der Continental AG
Zentralarchiv der Evangelischen Kirche Hessen-Nassau

Film and Television

Tomas Alfredson Director), "Let the Right One In," Sandrew Metronome 2008.
Josh Anderson (Director), "Oil on Canvas," [short film] forthcoming.
Zal Batmanglij (Director), "The East," Fox Searchlight Pictures 2013.
Peter Billingsley (Director), "Couples Retreat," Universal Pictures 2009.
Shane Black (Director), "Iron Man 3," Walt Disney Studios Motion Pictures 2013.
Danny Boyle (Director), "The Beach," 20th Century Fox 2000.
Dennis Dugan (Director), "Grown Ups," Sony Pictures Releasing 2010.
Ben Falcone (Director), "Tammy," Warner Bros. Pictures 2014.
Greta Gerwig (Director), "Barbie," Warner Bros. Pictures 2023.
Christopher Guest (Director), "A Mighty Wind," Warner Bros. Pictures 2003.
Amy Heckerling (Director), "Clueless," Paramount Pictures 1995.
Tom Kapinos (Executive Producer), "Lucifer," Fox/Netflix 2016–2021.
Michael Patrick King (Executive Producer), "And Just Like That," HBO Max 2021–present.
Marc Lawrence (Director), "Two Weeks Notice," Warner Bros. Pictures 2002.
Michael Lehmann (Director), "Heathers," New World Pictures 1990.
Michael Mayer (Director), "Single All the Way," Netflix 2021.
Greg McLean (Director), "Wolf Creek," Roadshow Entertainment 2005.
James Melkonian (Director), "The Stoned Age," Trimark Pictures 1994.
Nancy Meyers (Director), "Something's Gotta Give," Sony Pictures Releasing/Warner Bros. Pictures 2003.
Roger Michell (Director), "Notting Hill," Universal Pictures 1999.
Jesse Peretz (Director), "Our Idiot Brother," The Weinstein Company 2011.
Jason Reitman (Director), "Thank You for Smoking," Fox Searchlight Pictures 2006.
Jennifer Kaytin Robinson (Director), "Do Revenge," Netflix 2022.
Joshua Michael Stern (Director), "Jobs," Open Road Films 2013.
Christopher Storer (Executive Producer), "The Bear," Hulu 2022–present.
David Wain (Director), "Wanderlust," Universal Pictures 2012.
Phoebe Waller-Bridge (Executive Producer), "Fleabag," BBC Three/BBC One 2016–2019.
Robert Zemeckis (Director), "What Lies Beneath," DreamWorks Distribution/20th Century Fox 2000.

The Authors

Kai Balazs-Bartesch
Kai Balazs-Bartesch studied history, political science, and American studies at the Goethe University Frankfurt until 2019 with a focus on 19th-century history. During his studies, he worked as a student assistant on the project "The Hanseatic League and Its Law" and in general administration. Since the end of 2019, he has been a research assistant and archive team leader at the Gesellschaft für Unternehmensgeschichte.

Alexander von den Benken
Alexander von den Benken is a research assistant at the Institute for Historical Studies at the Rhenish Friedrich Wilhelm University in Bonn. His research and teaching focus on consumer, mobility, and business history. He is currently doing his doctorate on a family business in the automotive industry of the 70s.

Emily Brayshaw
Emily Brayshaw is an honorary research fellow in the Faculty of Design, Architecture, and Building at the University of Technology Sydney with a focus on costume, fashion, and design history. Emily also works as a costume designer, appears as a fashion expert on Australian radio, and is a member of the Footwear Research Network.

Taylor Brydges
Taylor Brydges is a research principal at the Institute for Sustainable Futures, University of Technology Sydney. Her focus is on sustainability and the transition to a circular economy in the fashion industry. Dr. Brydges earned a BA (Hons) in urban studies, an MA in human geography from the University of Toronto, and a PhD in human geography from Uppsala University, Sweden.

Pierre-Yves Donzé
Pierre-Yves Donzé is a professor of business history at Osaka University, Japan, and a visiting professor at the University of Fribourg, Switzerland, and at EM Normandie Business School, France. His research focuses mainly on the dynamics of global competition in creative industries (fashion, luxury, and watches).

Hayley Edwards-Dujardin
Hayley Edwards-Dujardin is a freelance art and fashion historian and curator. She received her MA in art history from L'École du Louvre, Paris, and her MA in fashion curation from the London College of Fashion. She teaches fashion history, visual culture, and fashion sociology in Paris. Her research interests and publications cover the decolonization of fashion theory, the relationship between art and fashion, modern and contemporary fashion theory, fashion and the self, decorative arts, and fashion photography.

Alice Janssens
Alice Janssens is a freelance business historian, fashion economist, and project manager working between academia and industry. She is an associate lecturer at the British School of Fashion at Glasgow Caledonian University (UK) and a PhD candidate at Erasmus University Rotterdam (Netherlands) undertaking research on the Berlin fashion industry during the 20s and 30s.

Christian Kleinschmidt
Christian Kleinschmidt has been head of the Institute for Economic and Social History at Philipps University of Marburg since 2009. He has numerous publications to his name, including "Konsum im 19. und 20. Jahrhundert" (2021) and "Wirtschaftsgeschichte der Neuzeit: die Weltwirtschaft 1500–1850" (2017).

Roman Köster
Roman Köster is a researcher at the Bavarian Academy of Science in Munich. His main research areas are the history of economic crises and the history of waste management. In addition, he has many years of experience in business history and has authored books on "Hugo Boss" (2011) and "Seidensticker" (2019). He has recently published a book on the global history of waste.

Jörg Lesczenski
Jörg Lesczenski studied history and sociology at the Ruhr University in Bochum and is a research assistant at the Gesellschaft für Unternehmensgeschichte mbH. He has numerous publications on economic history, including "100 percent Messer: The Return of the Family Business" (2019) and "Unternehmen Sport: Die Geschichte von adidas" (2018).

Emanuela Scarpellini
Emanuela Scarpellini is full professor of modern history at the University of Milan. She has been a visiting professor at both Stanford and Georgetown universities and is the founder and director of the research center MIC (Fashion Image and Consumer Culture). Her publications include "Italian Fashion since 1945: A Cultural History" (2019).

Andrea H. Schneider-Braunberger
Andrea H. Schneider-Braunberger received her doctorate from the Goethe University Frankfurt in 1996 and has been managing director of the Gesellschaft für Unternehmensgeschichte since then. She was president of the European Business History Association (EBHA), is a member of the Board of Governors of the Long Run Initiative (LRI), and is on the boards of various journals. Her research focuses on family businesses and banks in the first half of the 20th century. Her most recent publication is "Metzler im Nationalsozialismus" (2022).

Johanna Steinfeld
Johanna Steinfeld has researched and taught on issues of economic and business history at the Goethe University in Frankfurt and at the University of Konstanz. She wrote her dissertation on the corporate organization of the foundation company Optische Werkstätte Zeiss Jena.

Liz Tregenza
Liz Tregenza is a fashion and business historian. She works as a lecturer at London College of Fashion and runs her own vintage business. She has previously worked as a curator and researcher for various museums including the Victoria and Albert Museum. Liz was awarded her PhD on the fashion designer Frederick Starke in 2018. She is the author of "Wholesale Couture: London and Beyond, 1930–1970" (2023) and editor of "Everyday Fashion: Interpreting British Clothing since 1600" (2023).

Mary A. Yeager
Mary A. Yeager is a professor emerita of business and economic history at University of California, Los Angeles. She is well known for her numerous publications on gender and feminism in the field of business history, which include the three-volume edited collection "Women in Business" (1999).

Index of Persons and Companies

3HO Foundation (USA) **178**
55DSL (clothing company) **273**

A

A Bathing Ape (clothing company)
  267, 270
ABC Mart **352**
Abe, Chitose **270**
Abloh, Virgil **265**
Aboud, Joseph **260**
Adenauer, Konrad **144**
Adickes, Franz **71**
Adidas **20, 189, 224, 229, 265, 348, 392, 406**
Albero Schuh GmbH **203**
Albertoni, Alessandra **318**
Alexander McQueen **274**
Alsa Schuhbedarf GmbH **164, 189, 190,
  192, 193, 194, 195, 196**
Alto, Alvar **279**
Anatomica **338, 340**
Andry, Nicolas **149**
Angulus-Patos Schuhfabrik **254**
Apple **274**
Arbus, Amy **256, 257**
Arnault, Bernard **283, 284, 342**
Arola Schuh AG **99**
August Wessels Schuhfabrik **78**

B

Bally (shoe manufacturer) **99**
Barneys New York **278, 279**
Bateman, Jason **293**
Baumann, Klaus **270, 271, 278**
Beams **346, 348, 351**
Beauvoir, Simone de **235**
Bed 'n Back **251**
Béhar, Yves **267**
Bell, Kristen **293**

Benaïm, Laurence **338**
Benexy **281, 282, 351, 352**
Benjamin, Walter **362**
Bensberg, Markus **215, 270**
Berkemann (shoe manufacturer) **138,
  159, 171, 254, 338**
Berliner Verkehrsbetriebe (BVG) **265**
Bershka **265**
Betula Schuh GmbH **203, 209, 210, 211,
  213, 260, 267, 270**
Bhajan, Yogi **178**
Biesalski, Konrad **70**
Birckenstock, Johannes Georg **38**
Birkenstock, Alex **196, 198, 204, 209,
  211, 212, 214, 215, 260, 266, 270, 283,
  342, 347**
Birkenstock, Anna Maria, née Blumen
  40
Birkenstock (Berlin) **91, 92, 125**
Birkenstock, Carl **8, 12, 14, 20, 21, 22,
  23, 24, 25, 26, 27, 28, 29, 45, 62, 64, 66,
  67, 68, 69, 70, 71, 72, 73, 74, 75, 80, 81,
  83, 84, 85, 86, 87, 88, 89, 90, 91, 92, 93,
  94, 95, 96, 97, 98, 105, 106, 107, 108,
  109, 110, 111, 113, 114, 115, 116, 117,
  120, 121, 122, 123, 125, 126, 127, 128,
  129, 130, 131, 132, 133, 134, 135, 136,
  137, 138, 139, 140, 145, 146, 147, 148,
  153, 155, 156, 157, 158, 159, 167, 168,
  175, 177, 196, 218, 220, 223, 234, 237,
  238, 240, 242, 249, 305**
Birkenstock, Catharina, mar. Weber
  24, 62, 74, 91, 125, 133, 234
Birkenstock, Christian (son of Johann
  Conrad B.) **53**
Birkenstock, Christian (son of Karl B.)
  **196, 209, 211, 213, 214, 215, 260, 266,
  270, 283, 342**
Birkenstock Distribution USA Inc. **213**
Birkenstock East, Inc. (USA) **178**
Birkenstock, Elisabetha **48**

Birkenstock, Elisabeth, née Fleischhauer 53, 62, 91, 234
Birkenstock, Emmi, née Dietrich 91, 97, 234, 240
Birkenstock Fachgeschäft GmbH & Co KG 189
Birkenstock Footprint Sandals, Inc. (USA) 177, 178, 179, , 198, 210, 212, 213, 214, 234, 239, 258, 258, 417
Birkenstock, Friedrich Heinrich 53
Birkenstock, Gisela, née Merkelbach 175, 193, 363
Birkenstock, Heinrich 23, 24, 41, 62, 73, 74, 90, 91, 92, 124, 125, 129, 130, 131, 132, 133, 136, 234, 380
Birkenstock, Jakob 41
Birkenstock Japan 268, 340, 348, 349, 351, 352
Birkenstock, Johann Adam 8, 23, 36, 40, 41, 46, 54
Birkenstock, Johann Conrad 28, 47, 48, 51, 52, 54, 62
Birkenstock, Johannes Jr. 23, 28, 40, 46, 47, 48, 49, 51, 52, 54, 383
Birkenstock, Johannes Sr. 8, 23, 34, 36, 40, 46, 47
Birkenstock, Johannes (son of Johann Conrad B.) 52
Birkenstock, Johannes (son of Johannes B. Jr.) 48
Birkenstock, Johannes Wilhelm 52
Birkenstock, Johann Georg (son of Johannes B. Jr.) 48
Birkenstock, Johann Heinrich 40
Birkenstock, Karl 8, 14, 19, 21, 22, 24, 25, 27, 28, 29, 30, 31, 32, 33, 93, 109, 116, 145, 147, 158, 159, 160, 161, 162, 164, 165, 166, 167, 168, 169, 171, 175, 176, 177, 178, 179, 180, 187, 188, 189, 190, 192, 193, 194, 195, 196, 199, 201, 202, 203, 204, 209, 210, 211, 214, 216, 220, 222, 223, 233, 234, 237, 238, 239, 240, 242, 249, 260, 305, 306, 318, 357, 363, 365, 381, 389, 390
Birkenstock, Katharina Margaretha 48
Birkenstock, Konrad 14, 21, 22, 23, 24, 25, 26, 27, 28, 29, 32, 36, 40, 42, 51, 53, 62, 63, 64, 65, 66, 67, 68, 69, 70, 71, 72, 73, 74, 75, 77, 80, 87, 88, 90, 91, 92, 93, 94, 96, 97, 98, 104, 105, 106, 108, 113, 114, 116, 155, 177, 218, 223, 224, 233, 234, 237
Birkenstock, Konrad Jr. 24, 62, 73, 74, 90, 91, 92, 124, 125, 130, 131, 132, 133, 155, 234

Birkenstock, Margaretha, mar. Meininger 48
Birkenstock Schuhproduktion GmbH (Saxony) 203
Birkenstock, Stephan 196, 209, 210, 211, 212, 214, 215, 260, 266, 270
Birkenstock, Susanne 214
Birkenstock USA 16, 21, 269, 271, 272, 273, 274
Birkenstock, Valentin 23, 41
Birkenstock, Wilhelmine, née Euler 52, 62
Birkenstock, Wilhelmine, mar. Matthäus 53
Birki Schuh GmbH 198, 209, 270
Birko Advertising, Inc. (USA)/since 1984 Birko Orthopaedic, Inc. 179, 187, 200
Birko Orthopädie GmbH 203
Birko Schuhtechnik GmbH & Co KG 188, 200, 201, 203, 410
Blahnik, Kristina 275
Blüm, Norbert 204
Blumen, Anna Maria, mar. Birkenstock see B., Anna Maria
Blundstones (shoe manufacturer) 357, 358
BMW 356
Borelli, Alfonso 44
Bottega Veneta 268
Brand, Stewart 288
Bredthauer, Alfred 87, 389
Brennan, Chrisann 294
Breward, Christopher 247
Brooks, Libby 328
Bryson, Ray N. 153
Buccini, Beth 269
Burberry 268
Bürckenstock, Hans 38

C

C&A 20
Calvin Klein 260, 273
Campbell, Naomi 258
Camper, Peter 43, 44, 45, 150, 227
Carl Birkenstock, Fabrik für orthopädische Spezialitäten (Bad Honnef)/ since 1950 C. B. Orthopädie – Carl Birkenstock – Fabrik für orthopädische Spezialitäten/since 1952 C. B. Orthopädie GmbH/since 1970 Birkenstock Orthopädie GmbH 23, 113, 114, 129, 135, 140, 145, 153, 154, 160, 162, 162, 164, 166, 170, 175, 188, 189, 190, 200, 213, 239

Carl Birkenstock GmbH **74**
Carl Stiller (shoe store) **67**
Castelbajac, Jean-Charles de **264**
C. B. Orthopedics of Canada Ltd. **153, 157**
Céline (clothing company) **268, 269, 310, 340, 362**
Central Trade Ltd. **325**
Chambers, Lucinda **256**
Chasalla Schuhfabrik GmbH **159**
Christian Dior **32, 246, 284, 310, 335, 342**
Christians, Alice **346**
Cicero, Marcus Tullius **252**
Clarks (shoe manufacturer) **322**
Claudie Pierlot (clothing company) **338**
Coddington, Grace **275**
Cohen, Walter **89**
Colette (concept store) **339, 341**
Conrad, Wolfgang **204**
Continental AG **164, 189**
Converse Rubber Shoe Company (shoe manufacturer) **229, 258, 348**
Corrigan, Andrew **259**
Cron, Peter **286**
Crumb, Robert **288, 289, 290, 298, 306**
Cyrus, Miley **268**

D

Dalí, Salvador **264**
Davidson, Jack **275**
Day, Corinne **260, 327**
De La Cruz, Aaron **273**
Deichmann **166**
Delerue Roppel (studio) **274**
Deparis, Marianne **335, 340, 341, 342**
Derfeltsche Seifenfabrik (Friedberg) **73**
Deutsche Orthopädie-Werke **74**
DiCaprio, Leonardo **266**
Dietrich, Emmi, mar. Birkenstock see B., Emmi
DiGeronimo, Stephen **261**
Dingwall, Cathie **329**
Disney **267, 350**
Distenfeld, Claire **269**
Ditschler, Philipp **53, 62**
Dolce & Gabbana **297**
Donna Karan New York (DKNY) **254**
Dr. Martens (clothing company) **258, 312**
Dr. Scholl (shoe manufacturer) **75, 249, 338**
Drier, Melissa **271, 274**

Druschky, Dr. Erich **136, 138**
Duke, Randolph **260**

E

Eckhardt, Hellmut **86**
Embury, Howard **177**
Embury, June **177**
Emil Neuffer Schuhfabriken KG **155, 156, 157, 158, 169**
Endres, Familie **127**
Endres, Frau (sister-in-law of Carl B.) **127, 128**
Endriss, Matt **212**
Enzensberger, Ulrich **205**
Euler, Wilhelmine, mar. Birkenstock see B., Wilhelmine

F

Fabrik für Orthopädie, Heinrich Birkenstock (Büdingen) **124, 125, 133**
Farrell, Perry **246**
Ferragamo, Salvatore **102, 258**
Fill, Carolina **249, 315**
Fill, Karl **249, 315**
Financière Agache **246, 283, 342, 417**
Fleischhauer, Elisabeth, mar. Birkenstock see B., Elisabeth
Fogg, Marnie **342**
Footprints Schuh GmbH **203, 209**
Ford, Harrison **259**
Fournier, Pierre **338, 340, 341**
Franck, Norbert **208**
Frank, Sean **275**
Fraser, Margot **16, 21, 30, 31, 169, 176, 177, 178, 179, 186, 187, 195, 198, 204, 209, 210, 211, 212, 213, 214, 215, 216, 222, 233, 234, 235, 238, 240, 242, 250, 306, 307, 309, 402, 405, 414, 416, 417**
Friedan, Betty **235**
Friedrich II, Landgrave of Hessen-Homburg **149**
Friedrichsheimer Klinik (Frankfurt) **69, 70, 71, 80, 87, 104**
Fujiwara, Hiroshi **349**
Fußbett Schuhproduktion GmbH **203**

G

Galeries Lafayette **280**
Galloway, Ann **326**
Ganter (shoe manufacturer) see Aug. Ganter

Garsault, François Alexandre Pierre de **44**
Gebr. Birkenstock GmbH für orthopädische Spezialitäten / Gebr. Birkenstock GmbH (Steinhude) **23, 73, 74, 75, 88, 90, 91, 92, 93, 95, 124, 129, 131, 132, 380**
Gebr. Birkenstock OHG (Friedberg) **74, 91, 127, 133**
Georg Mayer (shoe manufacturer) **158**
Gerwig, Greta **298**
Gianfranco Ferré (clothing company) **316**
Gianni Versace **256, 264, 316, 347**
Giorgio Armani **256, 260, 316, 355**
Glasgow, Shelly **266, 272**
Goerke, Marcel **261, 355, 356, 357, 360, 361, 363**
Goldberg, Whoopi **260**
Gonzalez Haase AAS (architecture and design studio) **278**
Goodyear, Charles **229**
Gottfried "Götz" von Berlichingen **149**
Gross, Jean-Michel **336, 340, 341, 342**
Groß von Ellwangen, Dr. **64**
Gucci **254, 261**
Gustav Krause (insole manufacturer) **81**
Gwilt, Alison **331**
Gygax, Fritz **135**

H

H&M **262**
Hadid, Gigi **311**
Hako Hammer KG **121**
Halston (designer) **262**
Hamnett, Katharine **331**
Happy Schuh GmbH **203**
Hardy, C.Moore **359**
Haye, Amy de la **329**
Heaf, Jonathan **282**
Heckerling, Amy **290**
Heinrich IV, King **37**
Hémisphères **338**
Herber, Karl-Heinrich **189, 192, 194**
Hermès **279, 341**
Hildebrand, Bruno **47**
Hippokrates **149**
Hobein, mayor **126, 127**
Hoesch AG **194**
Hoffa, Albert **76, 77**
Hohmann, Georg **29, 69, 80, 89**
Hoki **336**
Horyn, Cathy **269, 275**

Hugo Boss **95**
Humboldt, Wilhelm von **12**
Hype DC **361**

I

I. G. Farbenindustrie **100**
Il Pellicano **280, 341**

J

Jacobs, Eleanor **180**
Jacobs, Raymond **179**
JCPenney **262**
Jenner, Kendall **312**
Jennings, Helen **308**
Jil Sander **229, 284**
Jobs, Steve **30, 31, 256, 293, 306**
Joneck, Walter **174**
Jones, Kim **284, 342**
Jönsson, Edwin **153**

K

K. Birkenstock GmbH, Fabrik für Platt- und Hohlfußeinlagen / K. Birkenstock GmbH (Friedberg) **69, 73, 75, 91, 92, 104**
Kabi-Vertriebsgesellschaft **72, 73, 105**
Kahan, David **224, 271, 309**
Kalsø, Anne **179**
Kapferer, Jean-Noël **271**
Kardashian, Familie **265**
Karl Birkenstock, Import und Export von Schuhindustriebedarf (St. Katharinen) **189**
Kawakubo, Rei **256, 337**
Kawasaki, Yukari **350**
Kennedy, John. F. **242**
Khalsa International Industries and Trading (USA) **178**
Kils, Vasilijs **153**
Kimura, Takuya **348**
Kith (clothing company) **284**
Klotz (insole manufacturer) **81**
Klum, Heidi **263, 267**
Kneipp, Sebastian **77**
Knyshynski, Serge **153**
Koller, Suzanne **281**
Konrad Birkenstock GmbH (Frankfurt) **21, 63, 138**
Kunde, Eugene **212**
Kunzelmann, Dieter **205**
Kwiatkowski, Jerry **261**

Index of Persons and Companies **459**

L

L Catterton 25, 216, 246, 283, 342
L. Schmitt, C. B. Orthopedics Rio de
  Janeiro 153
La Botte Chantilly 335
Lagerfeld, Karl 262
LaMaar, Jérôme 272, 273
Lamy, Michèle 279
Land Rover 348
Langhans, Rainer 205
Lavanga, Mariangela 276
Le Bon Marché 279
Lenaerts, Saskia 280
Leon, Humberto 273
Levi's 267, 350
Levy, Claudia 328
Louboutin, Christian 266
Louis Vuitton 264, 268, 274, 350
Luard, Francesca 325
Ludloff, Karl 69
Ludwig XVI 12
Lusk, Robert 250, 256, 260, 261, 266, 325,
  326, 327, 328, 330
LVMH Moët Hennessy Louis Vuitton
  283, 284, 342

M

Macy's 258
Madonna 260
Maison Resimont 122
Mannesmann, Max 78
Manolo Blahnik 32, 246, 275, 284, 310
Marc Jacobs 258, 259, 308, 337
Margiela, Martin 337
Martin, Marie-Hélène 339
Matthäus, Johann Georg 39, 53
Matthäus, shoemaker's family 46, 53
Matthäus, Wilhelmine, née Birkenstock
  see B., Wilhelmine
Mazzucca, Matthew 279
McDormand, Frances 33, 299, 300
McNeil, Peter 355
Meindl 321
Meininger, Margaretha, née Birkenstock
  see B., Margaretha
Meininger, Wilhelm 39, 48
Meisel, Steven 261
Merkelbach, Gisela, mar. Birkenstock see
  B., Gisela
Meyer, Gene 261
Meyer, Hermann Georg 76, 150, 227
Michael Kors 273
Miyaki, Issey 256

Miyashita, Takahiro 268
Modrow, Hans 194
Momoa, Jason 300
Montbell 348
Morrison, Jasper 279
Morshead, Alana 286, 298
Moss, Kate 31, 258, 260, 308, 327
Muff, Patrik 277
Murakami, Takashi 264
Murkudis, Andreas 278
Murkudis, Kostas 278
Mutombo, Rachel 297

N

Narimiya, Hiroki 268
Natural Shoe Store 251, 256, 260, 326,
  327, 330
Netflix 286
Neu, Heinz 96, 97, 138
Niemeier, Polizeibeamter 128
Nike 265, 274, 312
Nnadi, Chioma 269
Noll, Klaus 193
Nordstrom 258, 283

O

O'Neill, Alistair 280
Oesch, Felix 229
Old Navy 305
Owens, Rick 277, 279, 284, 310, 341

P

Pajdak, Romany 275
Paltrow, Gwyneth 261
Papillio Schuh GmbH 198, 209, 260, 268
Paracelsus 96
Patagonia 348
Patent-Centrale GmbH Frankfurt/M.
  68
Pearce, Guy 300
Pendleton 270
People Tree 270
Perry Ellis 258, 259, 261, 208, 337
Perugia, André 102
Pfeiffer, Alice 340
Pfeiffer, Hermann 78
Philip Lim (clothing company) 267
Philo, Phoebe 32, 237, 268, 269, 310,
  340, 362
Picoli-Truffaut, Luna 275, 341
Pierce, Susie 288, 289
Pierre Cardin 30, 221

Pitro, Susanne 318
Pitschl, Ewald 153, 249, 250, 315, 317, 318
Pitschl, Frowin 315, 318
Pitschl, Gerhard 250, 315, 319
Platypus Shoe Co. 361
Polder, Hella Jongherius 279
Polhemus, Ted 328, 329
Powers, Tacey 283
Prada 229, 348
Pratt, Jane 256
Puma 224

R

Rabanne, Paco 261, 339
Ralph Lauren 254, 256
Ratty, Sarah 331
Reagan, Ronald 187, 250
Reebok 229
Reeves, Keanu 259
Reichert, Oliver 16, 25, 215, 270, 271,
    274, 276, 279, 280, 281, 283, 284,
    285, 311
Reitman, Jason 292
Riello Giorgio 256, 355
RM Williams (shoe manufacturer) 357
Robbie, Margot 297
Robinson, Jennifer Kaytin 286
Rodriguez, Eddie 261
Rodriguez, Narciso 261, 338, 339
Rohwedder, Detlev Carsten 194
Röntgen, Wilhelm Conrad 150
Rothschild, Alecsander 280
Ruhs, Kris 279
Ruston, Sarah 268

S

Sacai 270
Sager, Craig 265
Sahm, Max 87
Saks Fifth Avenue 267
Salamander (shoe manufacturer) 57,
    195, 224
Sanyei Corporation 250, 261, 267, 281,
    345, 346, 347, 348, 351
Saum, Alfons 164, 189
SB International 215
Schede, Franz 86, 105, 139
Scher, John 261
Schiaparelli, Elsa 264
Schlageter, Leo 96
Schmalz, Ulrich 202
Schmoller, Gustav 58
Schneehagen, Christian 78

Schouler, Proenza 284, 310
Schultze-Naumburg, Paul 78
Schulz, Werner 206
Sciò, Marie-Louise 280
Seed Co. 260, 267, 270, 282, 347, 349, 350
Seidensticker 20
Sensi (shoe manufacturer) 338
Shamask, Ronaldus 258
Shelton, Gilbert 288, 306
Shepherd, Cybill 260
Shorter, James C. 153
Shrimpton, Jean 249
Sigg, Karl 229
Silbert, Jake 311
Sitbon, Martine 260, 337
Smith & Hawken 289
Smith, Dan Tobin 274, 277, 341
Sony 265
Sozzani, Carla 279
Steinhauser, Werner 315, 317
Stengel, Richard 258
Stiller, Carl 67
Stortz, Hugo 29, 134, 135, 136
Stüssy (clothing company) 284
Stutesman, Drake 286, 294
Südhof, Thomas 275
Sullivan, Rebecca 355
Swarovski 272, 273

T

Tabio (clothing company) 350
Takahashi, Jun 347
Talley, André Leon 260
Tanemoto, Koji 260, 267, 347, 350
Tatami Schuh GmbH 198, 209, 210, 260,
    267, 270, 347, 349, 350
Tatsuno, Koji 260
Taylor, Lou 329
Teller, Jürgen 275
Testino, Mario 261
Thomsen, Wilhelm 70, 87, 89, 94, 97,
    116, 136, 138, 159, 254
Thurner, Maria 317
Timberland 265
Tip Top Shoes 259
Tommy Hilfiger 265
Toogood (clothing company) 284
Trippen (shoe manufacturer) 349
Truffaut, François 341
Turk, Edun 273
Turk, Trina 273
Turlington, Christy 258
Tutankhamun, pharaoh 252
Twiggy 249

Index of Persons and Companies 461

U

Umbreen, Shaherazad **230**
United Arrows **348, 351**
Usher **279**

V

Valentino Garavani **32, 300, 316, 319**
Valli, Giambattista **269**
Vans **312**
VEB Oberlausitzer Textilbetriebe Lautex **195**
VEB Trumpf Schuhfabrik Seifhennersdorf **195**
Venel, Jean André **149**
Verres, Gaius **252**
Victoria and Albert Museum **325, 328, 329, 331**
Vivienne Westwood **337**
Vogel, Julian **327, 328, 330**
Vogt, Wiebke **16**
Volkswagen **222**

W

Walker, Andre **256**
Waller-Bridge, Phoebe **300**
Ward, Melanie **327**
Warhol, Andy **264**
Wasserman, Danny **259**
Weber, Alfred **73, 91, 92, 125, 130, 131, 133**
Weber, Catharina, née Birkenstock see B., Catharina
Weber, Erich **92, 133**
Wegerth, Helmut **159**
Whitney Museum of American Art **279, 295**
Wilke-Rodriguez **261**
Wittstock, M. W. **99**
Wolfe, Alex **280**
Wortmann, Raoul **384**

Y

Yamamoto, Yohji **256, 337, 350**
Yasuyuki, Umino **282**
Ysenburg, House of **37, 38, 46, 48**
Yves Saint Laurent **205, 264**

Z

Zhang, Ding Yun **280**

Picture Credits

1983 Amy Arbus:
Fig. 52, p. 257

Alamy Stock Foto:
Fig. 37 (Ron Giling), p. 183
Fig. 40 (David Reed Archive), p. 207

Archive of Bally Schuhfabrik AG, Schönenwerd, Schweiz:
Fig. 11, p. 57

Birkenstock Archive:
Fig. 1 (CA BBG 2.021), p. 10
Fig. 4 (CA BBG 2.001-18/57), p. 19
Fig. 6 (Birkenstock Shop Website), p. 32
Fig. 12 (CA BCB 5.001), p. 60
Fig. 14 (CA BCB 5.002-1), p. 65
Fig. 15 (CA BDF 3.002), p. 66
Fig. 16 (CA BDF 3.A.001), p. 68
Fig. 19 (CA BDF 1.G.001), p. 85
Fig. 20 (CA BDF 1.A.007), p. 91
Fig. 21 (CA BS 73), p. 94
Fig. 23 (CA BBG 4.013), p. 107
Fig. 24 (CA BBG 4.013), p. 110
Fig. 25 (CA BBG 4.013), p. 112
Fig. 26 (CA BDF 3.002), p. 118
Fig. 27 (CA BS 12), p. 124
Fig. 28 (CA BS 8), p. 134
Fig. 29 (CA BDF 3.A.001), p. 137
Fig. 31 (CA 2.001-25/57), p. 151
Fig. 32 (CA BBG 2.001-22/57), p. 163
Fig. 33 (CA BDF 3.003), p. 165
Fig. 34 (CA BDF 1.E.001), p. 170
Fig. 35 (CA BDF 1.E.002), p. 172
Fig. 36 (CA BDF 1.A.002), p. 177
Fig. 38 (Birkenstock Bildbestand), p. 191
Fig. 41 (Birkenstock Bildbestand), p. 213

Fig. 42 (Birkenstock Bildbestand), p. 215
Fig. 43 (CA BBG 2.001-20/57), p. 219
Fig. 44 (CA BBG 2.029), p. 221
Fig. 45 (CA BDF 3.002), p. 225
Fig. 46 (CA BBG 4.013), p. 228
Fig. 47 (CA BBG 2.001-14/57), p. 232
Fig. 48 (CA BBG 2.001-22/57), p. 236
Fig. 49 (CA BDF 1.E.001), p. 241
Fig. 54 (CA BDF 1.H.001), p. 263
Fig. 57 (CA BCB 5.001), p. 303
Fig. 58 (CA BDF 1.B.017), p. 307
Fig. 59 (CA BBG 10.001), p. 309
Fig. 60 (CA BBG 3.004-4), p. 311
Fig. 61 (CA BBG 3.027-1), p. 314
Fig. 62 (CA BDF 1.E.001), p. 324
Fig. 64 (CA BBG 3.002-8/12), p. 344
Fig. 65 (CA BBG 3.009-2), p. 354
Fig. 66 (CA BDF 1.011), p. 356
Fig. 68 (CA BDF 1.011), p. 363
Fig. 69 (CA BBG 10.001), p. 366
Fig. 70 (CA BBG 11.019), p. 376

BPK Picture Agency (BPK Bildagentur):
Fig. 22 (Bpk/photographer NN, 50140179), p. 101
Fig. 30 (Bpk/Erich Andres, 30034366), p. 143

Matteo Carcelli, photographer:
Fig. 63, p. 334

City of Sydney Archives:
Fig. 67 (photographer C.Moore Hardy), p. 360

Max Farago, photographer:
Fig. 55, p. 281

Federal Archive (Bundesarchiv):
Fig. 50 (Bild 183-88532-0003 / photographer: Christa Hochneder), p. 245

Robert Foothorap Jr., photographer:
Fig. 5, p. 31

Footprint Forum:
Fig. 53, p. 259

German Leather Museum (Deutsches Ledermuseum):
Fig. 10 (Nr. 6388), p. 51

Getty Images:
Fig. 56 (Kevin Winter), p. 299

golden sun society GmbH:
Fig. 8, p. 39

House of Art, Zurich (Kunsthaus Zürich):
Fig. 18 (Bibliothek, Nachlass Suzanne Perrottet, photographer: Johann Adam Meisenbach), p. 77

Institute for City History, (Institut für Stadtgeschichte) Frankfurt am Main:
Fig. 13 (ISG Ffm , S7A Nr. 1998-15722, Urheber NN), p. 63
Fig. 17 (ISG Ffm, S7Vö Nr. 2324, Urheber Gottfried Vömel), p. 70

Church Archive Eckartshausen:
Fig. 7 (Kirchenbuch Taufregister 1757–1799, Trauregister 1757–1799, p. 246.), p. 34

Oregon History Society Research Library:
Fig. 51, bb006673, photographer: Luther Cressman, p. 253

Reprint Verlag Leipzig:
Fig. 9 (Der Schuster. Von dem Herrn von Garsault. von Francois de Garsault, p. 105), p. 43

Ritter Production:
Fig. 2, p. 13
Fig. 3, p. 15

Thomas Zehnder, photographer:
Fig. 39, p. 197